THE ALLYN AND BACON GUIDE TO WRITING CENTER THEORY AND PRACTICE

Robert W. Barnett
University of Michigan–Flint

Jacob S. Blumner
Univeristy of Michigan–Flint

Allyn and Bacon
Boston • London • Toronto • Sydney • Tokyo • Singapore

Vice President: Eben W. Ludlow
Editorial Assistant: Grace Trudo
Executive Marketing Manager: Lisa Kimball
Editorial-Production Service: Chestnut Hill Enterprises, Inc.
Manufacturing Buyer: Suzanne Lareau
Cover Administrator: Kristina Mose-Libon
Electronic Composition: Omegatype Typography, Inc.

Internet: www.abacon.com

Between the time Website information is gathered and then published, it is not unusual for some sites to have closed. Also, the transcription of URLs can result in typographical errors. The publisher would appreciate notification where these occur so that they may be corrected in subsequent editions.

Library of Congress Cataloging-in-Publication Data

Barnett, Robert W.
    The Allyn & Bacon guide to Writing Center : theory and practice / Robert W. Barnett, Jacob S. Blummer.
    p. cm.
    Includes bibliographical references and index.
    ISBN 0-205-32186-0
    1. English language—Rhetoric—Study and teaching.   2. Report writing—Study and teaching (Higher)   3. Tutors and tutoring.   4. Writing centers.
I. Title: Allyn and Bacon guide to Writing Center.   II. Blummer, Jacob S.
III. Title.

PE1404 .B29 2000
808'.042'071—dc21
                                                                                00-062067

Printed in the United States of America
10 9 8 7 6 5 4 3 2 1   05 04 03 02 01 00

CONTENTS

CHAPTER 5   WELCOMING DIVERSITY: MULTIPLE CULTURES IN THE WRITING CENTER   333

CHAPTER 6   WRITING CENTERS AND WRITING ACROSS THE CURRICULUM: A SYMBIOTIC RELATIONSHIP?   401

CHAPTER 7   BEYOND THE PHYSICAL SPACE: TECHNOLOGY IN THE WRITING CENTER   473

PREFACE

Online, in conference presentations, and in the literature, we have become adept at exploring the various influences that theory and practice have had on each other. Whether the issue is technology, tutoring philosophy, training, or administration, the forces of theory and practice always emerge to help shape our discussions. And as the literature indicates, widespread agreement does not always exist when it comes to asking the question, "What should the relationship between theory and practice be?"

However, the many answers borne out of this question have invited us—often challenged us—to engage in self-reflection and self-examination in order to more thoroughly understand the complex nature of writing center work. The answers have also lead to more focused questions that provide direction for examining new possibilities: How much does theory and practice affect what we do? How much have our theories and practices changed in the last twenty years? Is practice informed by theory? Is practice corrupted by theory? Have we created theory/practice dichotomies? Should theory and practice feed each other, inspire each other? Should we consider one best theory, or should we consider multiple theories? Is what we do better than what we say we do?

Of course, these questions offer only starting points for further discussion. In organizing *The Allyn and Bacon Guide to Writing Center Theory and Practice*, we have attempted to create sections and include articles that will act as road maps for exploring some of the questions posed above, for asking new questions, and for gaining new knowledge about the past, present, and future of our field. Whether we talk overtly about issues of theory and practice, or whether we see them in light of other issues important to writing centers, the seven sections that make up this collection bring together some of the most important, controversial and influential ideas that have helped shape and reshape how we define ourselves and how we fit into the larger educational picture.

One of the primary goals of this book has been to create a rich, progressive discussion by selecting articles that "speak" to each other in some way. We believe the organization of the literature should spark conversation that not only informs the reader but also invites the reader to become an active participant. Adding our own voices to a preexisting chorus of voices is one of the most productive means of breaking new ground and discovering new possibilities from which we can all benefit in the continuous rethinking and redefining that sustains the life of our field.

For students just beginning their writing center experience, this approach seems ideal. Jeff Brooks's article on minimalist tutoring and Irene Clark and Dave Healy's article on directive versus nondirective tutoring both appear in the section "The Process of Tutoring: Connecting Theory and Practice" and act as a good example of the debates that take place in the field. Students reading these two articles will become privy to two very different ideas about the best approach to tutoring. The readings in a sense create the framework within which students may formulate and test their own ideas, thereby adding their voices to the conversation. By bringing their own views together with those of the authors, students are likely to come away with a broader awareness of the issues as well as a sense that they too are a part of our community,

We hope that students will, over time, begin learning to ask the same kinds of questions that inform the work done by graduate students, new writing center personnel, and seasoned practitioners and researchers. This book, after all, is intended to assist all members of our field in some way. Ours is the first writing center anthology to bring together so many articles (nearly fifty) that have helped shape where we have been, where we are today, and where we might be in the future. We have carefully chosen articles that will benefit instructors at the undergraduate as well as the graduate level; anyone engaged in research will find this collection to be useful as well as time-saving; and, perhaps best of all, this collection can be used as a companion to *The Allyn and Bacon Guide to Peer Tutoring*, edited by Paula Gillespie and Neal Lerner, for use in both undergraduate and graduate courses.

The book is divided into seven sections. Although the articles in each section cannot directly address every issue important to writing center personnel, we hope that the ordering of our sections will offer insightful dialogue that *will* allow us to advance our discussions and address all of the issues. A quick look at the contents will begin to reveal our motives in choosing and sequencing the sections and the articles as we did. The opening section, "A History of Writing Centers: Looking in the Rear-view Mirror," is intended to offer a reflection on our past, to revisit our successes, and to act as a foundation for many of the articles in the rest of the book.

"The Idea of a Writing Center: Building a Theoretical Foundation," seemed an obvious choice to follow the history section because, as the history chapter reveals, our theory is intimately connected to our past, but theory also has the power to help define our present and our future. Not everyone has the same "idea" about what a writing center should be and do, and our theories certainly illustrate the point. The third section, "Defining the Writing Center's Place: Administrative and Institutional Issues," demonstrates some of the ways in which we apply our knowledge of writing center history and theory. Defining ourselves vis-à-vis our institutions (and for ourselves) is an important way for us to help establish writing center personnel as valid, respected participants in the education of our students. This section offers many perspectives in order to assist those opening new writing centers as well as those who find need to develop a more productive relationship with their institutions. It also shows students what administrators do to make a writing center successful.

The fourth section, "The Process of Tutoring: Connecting Theory and Practice," is not only the biggest section of the book, but it is placed exactly where we believe it should be placed—at the very center. While all of the other issues raised in this book are of varying importance to our field, none is more crucial than the practice of tutoring. And as this section suggests, our practices have become as diverse as our individual centers. By providing multiple perspectives on many of the topics covered here, we hope to empower readers to make more informed choices about the practices in which they become engaged on a day-to-day basis.

"Welcoming Diversity: Multiple Cultures in the Writing Center" addresses issues of collaboration, culture, and diversity that drive or inform so much of our practice and theory. By themselves, the articles in this section offer poignant viewpoints on how cultures are defined, shaped, and altered within the writing center space. Read together, however, and read with articles from other sections, they begin to help transform our thinking about the significance of culture and diversity as a part of what we do.

The sixth section, "Writing Centers and Writing Across the Curriculum: A Symbiotic Relationship?" examines—and reexamines—the varied relationships created by writing centers and writing across the curriculum programs. Although not all writing centers are WAC-based, and not all enjoy a mutually beneficial partnership with WAC, the possibilities and pitfalls of writing center/WAC collaboration are explored at length in these articles.

We conclude this anthology with "Beyond the Physical Space: Technology in the Writing Center." As the lead article in this section by Eric Hobson reveals, we have come a long way in our relationship with technology, and the possibilities before us seem limitless. As Hobson and others point out, however, we still have many questions to ask as technology quickly becomes a part of our history, our theory, and our practice.

Where we go from here—with technology as well as with our theory and practice—depends on how we answer those questions. We do not pretend to provide the answers in this book, but we do hope the articles we have compiled will invite all readers to continue the important discussions that will in the end lead us to those answers.

We want to thank reviewers James C. McDonald, University of Louisiana at Lafayette, and Albert C. DeCiccio, Wheelock College, for their helpful suggestions.

FOREWORD

The Allyn and Bacon Guide to Writing Center Theory and Practice introduces the reader to the rich tapestry of writing center history, theory, and practice by placing the writing center in the context of the most significant ideological movements of the twentieth century. *The Allyn and Bacon Guide to Writing Center Theory and Practice* offers a compendium of significant essays on writing centers. A substantial number of these essays are award winners, and all of the essays have played an important role in defining modern and postmodern views of the writing center. The focus on history and theory in these essays underscores the writing center's institutional role—both in terms of instructional goals and objectives and in terms of administrative definitions and functions. How the writing center has found its place and purpose within the academy has been a central concern of theorists, practitioners, and administrators, and this volume does an excellent job in showing the various permutations that have occurred as the writing center has moved from the periphery to the center of academic instruction. Central to this concern is the question of the writing center's relationship to writing across the curriculum (WAC) programs and to curricular initiatives involving distance education and other modes of virtual instruction. Introducing readers to these important structural shifts in the writing center's role and making readers aware of the impact of social change upon the whole of educational theory are important contributions this volume makes toward an understanding of contemporary educational initiatives and practices.

The audiences for *The Allyn and Bacon Guide to Writing Center Theory and Practice* are as varied as the multiple emphases in this excellent and timely collection. Scholars in many fields will appreciate the depth and interrelationship of the essays in this volume as they explore the major emphases of writing center work and accomplishments. Further, they will appreciate the multidisciplinary focus of this volume, which explores writing center theory and practice from the perspectives of cognitive science, linguistics, composition studies, cultural studies, feminism, educational technology, collaborative writing, social constructionism, literacy education, online instruction, and a host of other viewpoints. Those interested in tutoring and in tutor training will find in this volume an extensive exploration of what it means to be a tutor and of how best to carry out that charge. This collection is adept at revealing the complexities and multiple perspectives that underlie the work of the tutor, and it is equally adept at placing these complex issues within explanatory contexts that invite engagement, discussion, and personal explorations of the issues that are raised. The volume does not simplify complex issues but illuminates them so that readers can connect with the personal narratives, program descriptions, case studies, and tutorial conferences that are presented within these pages. In addition to providing the most current and far-ranging essays on tutoring, this volume also offers a unique section on multicultural tutoring that explores and celebrates differences and helps attune tutors to the conferencing strategies and interpersonal skills that define the best and most productive tutoring sessions. For those who direct or administer writing centers, *The Allyn and Bacon Guide to Writing Center Theory and Practice* provides the most extensive and up-to-date critiques of the writing center's role within academics—from the earliest views of the "writing clinic" to the most contemporary views of writing centers online (OWLs) that are integrated into multiple aspects of distance education and of virtual technology. Quite simply put, there is no aspect of writing centers that *The Allyn and Bacon Guide to Writing Center Theory and Practice* fails to explore or to invite the reader to examine and investigate. In this extensive range, *The Allyn and Bacon Guide to Writing Center Theory and Practice* is unique in providing, in one volume, the most thorough and most up-to-date exploration of the writing center field that has ever been offered to scholars, tutors, and administrators.

One thing is certain about *The Allyn and Bacon Guide to Writing Center Theory and Practice*. For all the information it provides and for all the questions it explores, it will invariably invite new questions and explorations on the reader's part. The essays on history invite speculation on what the future of writing centers will be. They also urge readers to think in transformative ways in order to imagine the potential for constructive change that writing centers continue to represent. The personal narratives of frustration, success, accomplishment, and innovation will resonate with all who participate in the educational enterprise and will offer valid perspectives to those responsible for establishing and administering writing centers in a range of academic and professional settings. The essays on the theoretical bases for writing center work will reveal the remarkable shifts in focus and definition writing centers have experienced over the last century. The enormous insights offered by these essays emphasize anew how thoroughly writing center theory is grounded in practice and how fully our practice has always accounted for appreciation of the individual and his or her special differences and experiences. The student-centered focus of the writing center comes through clearly in these essays, as does the full consideration of modes of tutoring that have been shaped by the traditions of expressivism, social constructionism, and liberatory pedagogy. The essays on the administrative and institutional issues that surround writing center work invite readers to consider the writing center's role and whether marginalization, centralization, de-centralization, counter-hegemony, or extra-institutional autonomy will define the writing center's relationship to central administration and to academics as a whole. In a similar vein, essays on writing centers and WAC programs raise questions about the nature of this curricular, instructional, and administrative relationship and whether it has benefitted or has harmed the writing center's search for institutional respect and identity. This last emphasis becomes increasingly important in the virtual worlds of the 21st century where the traditional boundaries of the academy are replaced by global space and global initiatives that will require a creative rethinking of what the future may hold for the purpose of education. Online writing centers represent but one segment within the full spectrum of the amazing possibilities that virtuality offers writing center personnel—from tutors, to administrators, to theorists, to those engaged in community outreach and in corporate alliances. The value of *The Allyn and Bacon Guide to Writing Center Theory and Practice* is that it will aid those interested in the writing center field to understand the impulses for these changes and to participate in shaping the dialogues that will determine future directions and initiatives.

Not to be overlooked is the enormous value of *The Allyn and Bacon Guide to Writing Center Theory and Practice* as a document of writing center culture. No other text, to date, has offered such an extensive record of writing centers in all their varied manifestations and in relation to all the historical, ideological, and social influences that have shaped their goals and achievements. In this regard, *The Allyn and Bacon Guide to Writing Center Theory and Practice* is the most valuable resource writing center theorists and practitioners can have to guide them in their work. The essays in this volume complement tutor training manuals—most especially *The Allyn and Bacon Guide to Peer Tutoring* by Paula Gillespie and Neal Lerner—in filling in the background and in providing the contexts for understanding the tutor's role within this complex matrix of ideas and purposes. The essays, too, reveal the paths of writing center scholarship that have defined the past and the present, and they suggest future paths that writing center scholars will need to explore. For breadth and depth of writing center scholarship, *The Allyn and Bacon Guide to Writing Center Theory and Practice* is unparalleled, and the editors, Robert W. Barnett and Jacob S. Blumner, are to be commended for providing this most important resource that will aid both students and professionals in understanding why writing centers have had such a significant impact in shaping educational debates and practices for over a century. *The Allyn and Bacon Guide to Writing Center Theory and Practice* sets a new standard for what scholarship on writing centers should be in enabling students and professionals alike to experience the culture of the writing center and its legacy of educational innovation.

Christina Murphy
The William Paterson University of New Jersey

1

A HISTORY OF WRITING CENTERS: LOOKING IN THE REAR-VIEW MIRROR

Writing center personnel can learn a lot from knowing writing center history, and they should make decisions with a firm knowledge of what has come before. Contrary to common perception, writing centers own a long history, with roots stemming back nearly as far as first-year composition itself. Writing centers and writing center scholars built the history that has influenced their progeny and writing instruction in general. But building that history is not enough. We, as writing center tutors, administrators, and researchers, must study our past to trace themes and trends so we can duplicate successes and avoid mistakes. It is from our history that we can learn what came before and where we can begin to decide the future of writing centers.

In a sense, this entire book is a history. Writers have contributed to the academic conversation about writing centers, and their texts are collected here. But this first section of the book is historiography. We are fortunate in writing centers to have authors, like some of those represented here, who have searched through professional and personal journals to find writing center research and synthesized it into article form.

This introductory section begins with a piece of history rather than a piece of historiography, "The Writing Clinic and the Writing Laboratory," by Robert H. Moore. In the article first published in 1950, Moore reported from a University of Illinois survey of colleges that had writing clinics or labs. In addition to informing the field of the number of schools that had—or were interested in adding—clinics or labs, Moore defined what he saw as the differences between clinic and lab work. His definitions and concerns still reverberate in our field today. Peter Carino acknowledges this in his article and, through extensive research, he examines the primary issues surrounding centers, including such issues as place, clientele, and staffing. He argues that we should embrace our history so we can shape our future. Judith Summerfield battled and then embraced her own history in the CUNY writing center. Reflecting on her retirement from the center, Summerfield shares the "context" she fought for in her university and encourages readers to see the potential for change that writing centers possess, not just changes in writing instruction but in the way education takes place.

Joyce Kinkead offers a personal history of the National Writing Centers Association. In her article, she outlines how the association came about and what it was meant to accomplish. At the 1999 NWCA conference, the issues Kinkead raises of advocacy, legitimacy, and social possibility were still discussed. Elizabeth H. Boquet closes the section with a view of writing centers pre- and post-open admissions. Published in 1999, her article explores issues raised in all the other articles in this section, and questions the role of the writing center, particularly whether writing center administrators limit writing center potential.

This section gives an overview of what writing centers have been as well as a small glimpse of what their future can be. Moore and Carino work well together by giving a broad survey of what writing centers have and haven't been. Summerfield and Kinkead and Boquet all provide more personal views of their writing centers while pointing to broad theoretical concerns that affect most other centers. All of these articles introduce issues that begin creating a context for the voices that follow in each of the other sections. The works here cannot cover the disparate history of writing centers, but they can reveal some of the pedagogical and advocacy issues that help shape the discussions throughout this book.

The Writing Clinic
and the Writing Laboratory   1950

Robert H. Moore[1]

Writing clinics and writing laboratories are becoming increasingly popular among American universities and colleges as remedial agencies for removing students' deficiencies in composition. A recent survey of one hundred and twenty leading universities and colleges throughout the country was made at the time that a clinic was established at the University of Illinois, to determine the incidence, methods, and effectiveness of such agencies. It procured fifty-five replies, forty-nine of them indicating in some detail the nature of the remedial measures being pursued. Of these forty-nine institutions, twenty-four now make use of writing clinics or laboratories of one sort or another, and eleven others are contemplating their establishment. In other words, 70 per cent of the colleges indicating the nature of their remedial work either now use or are considering using the clinic or laboratory in the solving of students' writing difficulties. And, even if it be assumed that none of the other seventy-five institutions are interested in the device, there remain at least 20 per cent of the colleges selected for the survey which are using the method, and an additional 10 per cent considering its adoption.

The survey was primarily concerned with the clinic and the laboratory rather than with remedial measures in general, so that it is not always possible to determine from the data assembled how much of the remedial burden in a given college is shared with such other devices as the precollege-level course, the segregating of poorly prepared freshmen into special sections of the regular elementary composition course, the upper-class remedial course, the specialized course in technical writing, the graduation proficiency examination, or individual tutoring.[2] The University of Illinois, for

---

[1]University of Illinois
[2]Remedial reading, a related problem, is most often handled by a separate agency, frequently under the guidance of trained psychologists rather than of English teachers.

example, uses the clinic to supplement all the above devices except the segregation of freshmen into special sections of the regular course. Yet it can be said that the two devices are sufficiently successful to enable thirteen universities to depend on the clinic or the laboratory for all remedial work; and at least one, the University of Miami, uses the laboratory method exclusively in its elementary composition program.

The techniques of the clinic and of the laboratory are, of course, far more widespread than are formally established agencies. The clinic is primarily concerned with the diagnosis of the individual student's writing difficulties and the suggestion of remedial measures that might profitably be pursued. Such diagnosis and prescription are an early concern, as well, of the class instructor in conference, the counselor in a university tutoring bureau, the individually procured tutor, and the instructor in the laboratory. The laboratory, in turn, is primarily concerned with the direct and continuing supervision of the remedial efforts of the individual student, and such supervision, in greater or less degree, must also be given by the class instructor, the tutor, and the clinician. The advantages of the formally established agency, then, lies less in its possession of esoteric methods than in its ready accessibility, its concentration on the removal of specific deficiencies, and its development of instructors particularly skilled in remedial procedures.

As the methods of the clinic and the laboratory overlap, so does the terminology. As the names imply, the clinic is chiefly concerned with suggesting measures for self-help, the laboratory with work done directly under the guidance of an instructor; but in practice the terms are almost interchangeable, "laboratory" being the more common and the laboratory approach being more often used, particularly in those schools depending on such agencies for the bulk of their remedial efforts. For convenience in discussing operating procedures, however, I shall draw theoretical distinctions between the two, with the final reminder that only the initial emphasis on one approach or the other serves, in the last analysis, to distinguish the relationship between the individual student and the clinic or the laboratory to which he turns for help.

The writing clinic customarily supplements other remedial devices, such as the compulsory upper-class remedial course for students whose writing proficiency is deemed inadequate to meet standards prescribed for graduation. Consultation with the clinic, consequently, is likely to be voluntary and to spring from a student's own realization—often reinforced by a dean's or an instructor's comments—that his writing skill is less satisfactory than it should be and is handicapping him in the writing examinations, term papers, and reports. Occasionally, compulsion is involved, most frequently through the device of withholding credit for a course in which writing deficiencies have been noted; but usually the clinic is an agency to which the student himself as an individual applies for help in removing a deficiency of which he is personally aware.

As a result, the problem of diagnosis is often not difficult. A preliminary interview may in itself disclose the basic weakness, particularly with upper-classmen or graduate students who have had a good deal of experience with college writing problems. If the problem is one of spelling or punctuation, for example, the student himself can easily identify it. More frequent, however, and more baffling to the student are weaknesses in the organization and development of papers or examination answers or the tendency to write vague, telescoped, or garbled sentences rather than concise and specific ones. The student with such deficiencies usually knows only that his writing somehow does not say what he thinks it does. But, even with these more complex problems, the experience of the clinician can often enable him to uncover the basic difficulty through an interview alone.

If the preliminary interview does not expose the difficulty, various other means may be employed. If the student has suddenly been impelled to seek assistance because a returned examination or term paper was less successful than he had anticipated, he is likely to have brought the paper with him, particularly if his impulse has been reinforced by tart comments from his instructor. If he has not brought it with him at first, he usually has it at home, perhaps with several others like it, and can produce it for analysis. The most successful diagnosis, probably, is that which results from an analysis, with the student, of specimens of the writing that he has actually done in his classes. And, incidentally, the student can be made aware of the direct connection between writing deficiency and unsatisfactory grades and so takes the first remedial step in the midst of the process of diagnosis itself.

If specimens of his classroom writing are not available—if his consultation, for example, has sprung from a recommendation by a dean concerned with his general academic record—at least two other diagnostic measures may be used, neither wholly satisfactory. One is the analysis of a paper written for the purpose, the other is the interpretation of a diagnostic test or tests. The disadvantages of the first are threefold: it is difficult to find subjects not too remote from the classroom subjects, it is impossible to reproduce the classroom conditions, and (a point to which I shall return) it is impossible for the student to write *as he usually writes when he is not thinking primarily of the quality of his English;* the writing which he produces to order for analysis, consequently, is not his normal writing, whether for better or for worse. The disadvantage of the diagnostic test lies in its basic artificiality: no test of which I am aware is more than indicative of probable deficiencies, so that reasonably certain diagnosis must still await analysis of actual writing, preferably that produced for a classroom situation.

Diagnosis having been made, by one or several of these means, the remedial measures to be followed must be outlined. The more intelligent and eager the student, of course, the easier it is to discover the difficulty in the first place and to determine means to enable him to remove it. The clinic is

[handwritten annotation: deemphasizing role of tutor - most likely to meet institutional concerns]

not, as a rule, concerned with the direct supervision of remedial efforts, with providing extensive tutoring; it is therefore most satisfactory as a supplement to a wider remedial program, since only the intelligent and eager student can be wholly successful in applying even the best self-help measures. Here, as elsewhere, the more resourceful the clinician is in suggesting new approaches to old problems, the more quickly does self-help become effective help. A student who is deficient in many ways may be urged, and in some institutions required, to enroll in remedial classes or to seek private tutoring. Where the clinic is a supplementary agency in a balanced remedial program, the students with numerous and glaring deficiencies will usually have been caught elsewhere in the remedial net. The students who consult the clinic are, as a result, troubled by specific and limited weaknesses, and remedial efforts can be concentrated on those.

Students exhibiting weaknesses in the handling of purely mechanical problems can be referred to specialized study groups, if they are provided, or can be urged to secure private tutoring directed toward removing the specific deficiencies involved, or can be made aware of the existence of numerous specialized remedial texts dealing particularly with their problems. In the last connection it might be remarked that a single publisher provides a convenient, inexpensive, and, on the whole, admirable series of remedial pamphlets, of whose existence most students are completely unaware. In the handling of spelling problems, for example, the appropriate pamphlet in that series offers the best presentation with which I am familiar of the very complex procedures necessary for the removal of spelling difficulty. Spelling classes following the same procedures, however, are superior, since it requires intense ambition on the part of the student to persist in the work on his own. Frequently, of course, the clinician can himself supplement these formal aids with teaching devices suggested by his own experience and the circumstances arising during specific interviews and, wherever possible, will do so. Conscientious work by the student with such materials and periodic visits to the clinic for assistance and for checks on progress will usually result in the removal of the mechanical difficulty. It depends on how willing the student is to make the effort.

Problems in the organization and development of material are more complex but, with intelligent students, are more quickly removed. Frequently, little more is necessary than a demonstration of the technique of phrasing a thesis and constructing a scratch outline which permits winnowing and rearranging ideas. Practice at such preliminary planning of subject matter, with clinical analysis of the resulting writing (writing, preferably, which is directly related to his college courses) can do wonders for the student who somehow—usually because of youthful indifference—never realized that the same techniques, when they were presented in his elementary composition courses, would someday be of personal use to him.

[handwritten annotation: it's that easy??]

Similar writing practice, with emphasis on specific diction, concise phrasing and the necessity for revisional rereading of *what was actually written*, not what was merely intended, can be of nearly equal assistance to the student who, in the haste of writing examinations or belated papers, produces vague, telescoped, or garbled sentences. It must, however, be pointed out that such writing often accompanies garbled information or habitually confused thinking. Psychological clinics can sometimes be called on for assistance in the latter event. The same psychological clinics are frequently equipped to assist in removing writing difficulties which stem from reading deficiencies[3] or from complex personality disorders. They lie, properly, outside the province of the writing clinic.

The writing clinic works with the individual student. The writing laboratory on the other hand, is far more likely to work with the individual as a member of a group, usually a group with varying problems. It is more economical than the clinic, in that one instructor in a given hour can work with ten or twenty students where the clinician can scarcely work with more than four at most. Further, the laboratory can more successfully be used as the sole remedial agency, if the institution is willing to provide only one. It is less likely, however, to uncover individual difficulties as rapidly as the clinic does or to avoid wasting the student's time on material that he does not need. And it adds the actual tutoring of students to the costs of the remedial program. Only by considering the remedial needs of a particular student body can a final choice be made between the two types of agency on grounds of economy.

Customarily, many or all of the students coming to the writing laboratory attend—often willingly, of course—under compulsion, as the result of failure in proficiency examinations or of faculty referral, the latter being frequently accompanied by the withholding of course credit pending the removal of deficiencies. Most laboratories, however, are also open to students voluntarily seeking assistance. With the laboratory, as with the clinic and all other remedial devices, satisfactory results are most readily secured when the student, whatever the means of his coming, is personally convinced of the desirability of improving his writing skill.

Initial diagnosis in the laboratory is more likely than in the clinic to depend upon available tests or on the student's own analysis of his weaknesses. However, some laboratories do also use analysis by the instructor of specimens of the student's writing—of term papers, examinations, or "themes" produced for the purpose. The most successful laboratories, like the clinics, attempt to individualize the work throughout, which, of course, increases the cost and the complexity of the program as it increases its effectiveness.

---

[3]Only a few English clinics deal to any great extent with remedial reading problems.

The remedial treatment used in the laboratory varies widely. Frequently, an entire group is put through the same review course, with roving instructors constantly available to answer questions, advise on organizational problems, and check on progress. Less often, particularly in laboratories to which students may come at any time and leave at will, personal files are kept to record the difficulties and progress of each student, and the instructor turns from each problem to the next as it arises. Least often of all, students with similar problems are segregated in small groups, or students may even be handled individually, particularly in the early stages. Both the last two types of treatment can readily concentrate instruction on specifically defined needs.

Following diagnosis of the student's needs—and those needs are usually fairly clear cut and limited in kind—remedial measures are prescribed. Workbooks or handbooks are often used for preliminary review,[4] the work with them being done in the laboratory, with the instructor available for consultation or, if the entire group is struggling with the same problem, for group explanation and discussion. As soon as the student convinces the instructor that the basic principles are clear, he is put to practicing the kind of writing with which he has trouble, whether he writes "themes" to assigned or self-suggested topics, expositions of subject matter drawn from his other courses, sample answers to examination questions, or the actual papers assigned in his other courses. During all this work the laboratory instructor and the laboratory dictionaries, handbooks, and other reference books are there for the student to consult when his own resources are unable to carry him further. As problems arise, the instructor makes use of all the teaching devices at his command to clarify the basic principles involved and to stimulate the student to apply them in his own practice. The laboratory is a highly successful remedial device for those students who are willing to make intelligent use of the assistance provided.

Most institutions employing the laboratory method send at least some of the students to it under compulsion. The machinery for releasing them from that compulsion is usually of one of two kinds: either a formal proficiency examination, set by the laboratory instructors in the laboratory or by a separate testing agency, must be passed, or the instructors must certify from the work the student has done that he has demonstrated that he has become capable of writing satisfactorily. (Only rarely, it might be remarked parenthetically, is the examination, if there is one, purely of the objective type.) Students who come to the laboratory voluntarily are, as a rule, allowed to stop coming whenever they themselves feel that they have attained a satisfactory degree of skill.

---

[4]Those who use workbooks, it might be remarked, are at least balanced by those who object to them violently.

Except for students working in the laboratory as a regular, assigned part of their composition courses, credit is customarily not given for either laboratory or clinical work.

A very few universities charge the students fees—ranging from five dollars for two quarters to two dollars and a half an hour—for the service. Most of them offer the service without charge, accepting the handling of remedial composition problems as a necessary, if deplorable, part of the task of American colleges and universities. The expense of the agency is usually borne by the English department, perhaps on the ground that it will be blamed anyway—surely unjustly—for all student lapses in English in other courses throughout the university and that it might better protect itself by being able to point to the remedial agencies which it provides. Occasionally the expense is borne by the university itself, as an administrative rather than a teaching expense.

yikes!

Clinic and laboratory staffs are likely to be self-made. Customarily they are experienced members of the English department who are particularly interested in remedial composition, though much of the direct tutoring in the laboratories is provided by graduate assistants, who are, of course, often themselves experienced instructors. Only rarely do members of the staff devote full time to the work, though the equivalent of several full-time instructors is provided for the larger laboratories.

As with all remedial measures, much of the enduring success of the work of the clinic or the laboratory depends on members of faculties outside the English department. The complaint is nationwide that members of other departments carp bitterly to their colleagues in English about the quality of student writing but can only with difficulty be persuaded to point out to the students themselves that clear and effective writing is important. Three universities report having tried the clinic or the laboratory and then having abandoned it because too few students came or were sent to it.[5] The students' indifference to the quality of their writing springs inevitably from faculty indifference to it, even though that faculty indifference may be more apparent than real. In his writing, as in much else, the student will do no more than he has to. I remarked earlier on the difference that often exists between the quality of the writing which a student can produce when he is aware that his writing skill is to be considered and that of his habitual writing. If instructors in non-English courses would insist on the best writing of which the student is capable, they would find—amid much student grumbling—that the English departments have built better than is often supposed.

---

[5] A fourth institution abandoned its clinic when the director moved from the English department to the school of education.

*wc's have no simple evolutionary history

1995

Early Writing Centers: Toward a History

Peter Carino

Since the inception of the *Writing Lab Newsletter* in 1977 and *The Writing Center Journal* three years later, documenting writing center history is not difficult. Articles in these journals enable writing center scholars to construct a reasonably detailed history back into the early 1970s, when open admissions initiatives precipitated the growth of writing centers. While this rich data certainly helps centers of today to locate themselves in relation to the past twenty years, little has been said about writing centers before that time. Though not nearly as numerous as today, centers (usually established under the name lab or clinic) did exist before 1970, and references to them dot historical texts in composition. Writing center discourse, however, has largely ignored early centers or has monolithically represented them as deficient. When they have been mentioned, they have been constructed as poor cousins of English departments, stereotypical "remedial fix-it shops" where an unenlightened staff administers current-traditional pedagogy to underprepared and poorly regarded students.

Witness Ray Wallace's delineation of the features of the writing "lab":

- funded by a single department, English in most cases
- where freshman come to get help
- where the focus is on error
- which is badly staffed
- which is not held in high esteem in the academy
- where "bad" people are sent (even remanded) (83)

From these elements, Wallace constructs a model of the past in an essay which champions the present and future need for building cross-curricular centers. Though some centers may have fit Wallace's model, his rendering

Carino, Peter. "Early Writing Centers: Toward a History." *The Writing Center Journal* 15.2 (1995): 103–15. Reprinted by permission of *The Writing Center Journal*.

of the past, rather than an informed attempt at history, becomes a straw man against which he can set his agenda for current writing centers—a rhetorical strategy that enables his essay to present a vision of progress.

Like Wallace, Andrea Lundsford uses a progressive model to account for writing center history, constructing centers in her now well-known schema of "storehouses" based in current-traditional pedagogy, "garrets" subscribing to a student-centered expressionism, or "Burkean parlors" where tutorials are seen as instances of the social construction of meaning. Here the early center is portrayed as a "storehouse" of grammar drills lacking the theoretical sophistication of the "Burkean parlor" Lunsford advocates.

Similarly, Christina Murphy, in tracing a progressive movement of writing centers toward "current educational theory" (part of her essay's title), posits a deficient past in relation to her picture of a more enlightened model of present centers: "In the 1940s and 50s, writing centers were established to address the instructional problems of weaker students by strengthening their writing and critical thinking skills…" (276). To be fair to Murphy, she also recognizes a liberal mission in early centers—"developing students' potentials and facilitating their intellectual growth"—but implies that this agenda was subsumed by the conservative demand for "the highest number of measurable results for the largest number of students in the shortest time frame" (277).

These constructions, all by notable commentators on writing centers, reflect an evolutionary history of centers often accepted uncritically by the writing center community. I do not mean to say that centers have not "progressed." Nor do I claim for centers of the past the theoretical sophistication that commentators such as Wallace, Lunsford, and Murphy find lacking. Rather, I believe that although we can, to some degree, trace an evolutionary history of writing centers, this history is not a neat march of progress from current-traditional gradgrindianism to theoretically sophisticated nurture. Early centers, as we can reconstruct them from historical texts, were a much more variegated and complex phenomenon than has been represented in writing center discourse. Thus, in this essay I will attempt co trace the evolution of writing centers to demonstrate how early centers conducted practice in ways which both deviate from and foreshadow writing center practice and theory today. I will begin with a diachronic look at centers as an evolving phenomenon before closing with a synchronic perspective comparing centers of the past and present on three issues: clientele, staffing, and institutional identity.

EVOLUTION: CONNECTIONS AND GAPS

Finding the first writing center, in some form that we would recognize in terms of centers today, is like any quest for origins: the further back we go, the more we suspect antecedents beyond those we have discovered. Using documents published in early issues of *English Journal* and other places, however, we can gain some sense of how centers began to evolve early in this century, though we may not discover the first impulse engendering them.

Classroom Origins: The Laboratory Method

As Thomas Hemmeter and David Healy have demonstrated, writing centers today often like to define themselves as an alternative or even an opposition to the classroom. Nevertheless, it is likely that centers evolved from a classroom format known as the laboratory method. This format enabled intervention in the student's writing process through individual help from the instructor and peer editing groups, two methods shared by writing centers and classrooms today.

As early as 1904, Philo Buck, a St. Louis high school teacher, described such a classroom. Long before the birth of Kenneth Bruffee and decades prior to the Dartmouth Conference, Buck's students wrote together on topics of their own choosing while he himself spent time with each individually before having them read and critique one another's papers. Buck may have even coined the term "laboratory method," for the opening of his essay justifies the method by drawing analogies with already established laboratory work in the sciences, a move that subsequent commentators in the early part of the century imitated. Though Buck's method used class time, evidently he was aware of the value of one-to-one instruction and peer critique, techniques at the heart of writing center methodology today.

By the 1910s, it is evident that others were subscribing to the laboratory method. Defending composition instruction against those who were calling for its abolition, an editorial in the first issue of *English Journal* cites the efficacy of the laboratory method. The method continued to flourish, as is evident in Francis Ingold Walker's 1917 article describing a classroom at New Trier High School similar to Buck's but with two days a week set aside for laboratory work. A similar article by Frank W. Cady of Middlebury College two years earlier indicates that the laboratory method had been adopted in post-secondary instruction as well. It is difficult to tell how widespread the method was in either college or high schools, but evidently it was common enough by the end of the 1920s to become the subject of an empirical study for a Master's thesis by West Virginia high school teacher Warren Horner. Horner found that students in the experimental group made small gains in rhetorical and grammatical proficiency but did so in half the instruction time dedicated to a control group of students taught in a recitational format.

A Place of Its Own

By name and method we can see connections between the laboratory classroom and the writing laboratory, but according to the literature surveyed, the writing lab was not more than a classroom approach until the 1930s, when the University of Minnesota and the State University of Iowa (now the University of Iowa) established separate facilities for laboratory instruction in 1934. Adah Grandy relates that the Minnesota lab was housed in the College of Science, Literature, and the Arts and consisted of a large well-lit room with writing tables and reference books, as well as a smaller anteroom where student and tutor could conduct individual consultations (372–3). Grandy also notes in passing that the General College at Minnesota had opened a writing lab a year or two before, but this lab is never described except in a passing remark that "the work carried on in that College is very different from that done in the College of Science, Literature, and the Arts" (372).

Grandy's comment here raises the possibility that the lab in the General College was seen as remedial while his facility served a broader clientele. This distancing of the College Lab from that of the General College is one symptom of larger forces at work in higher education in the 1930s—forces that may have contributed to the development of labs. By the 1930s, colleges and universities were beginning mass education initiatives. Although the masses, despite much egalitarian rhetoric, were still largely defined as white males, children of immigrants and first-generation students began attending state institutions in large numbers. As a result, public institutions in 1933–34 equaled private schools in enrollment for the first time and surpassed them by the end of the decade (Levine 191). In addition, because many of these students were considered underprepared, more schools began initiatives similar to Minnesota's General College. Couple this changing population with the influence of John Dewey's emphasis on pragmatic education designed for the individual student (highly influential by the 1930s), and the time was right for writing labs.

More locally, Grandy's posture of superiority likely stems from the Minnesota lab's ties to the classroom. Classes met in the lab one hour per week in lieu of an hour in the classroom, much like a science laboratory, thus instructing all students rather than only those who chose to come or who were sent for remediation. During this hour, the instructor, assisted by two or three graduate students, would work with students as they planned and wrote papers for the class, sometimes working in groups and sometimes in individual conferences in the anteroom. In contrast to Minnesota's course-bound lab, the lab at Iowa, as reported by Carrie Stanley, offered small-group and one-to-one instruction, on both a referral and voluntary basis, for remedial students and "very good students [who] might drop in to try to straighten out minor difficulties" (424). Stanley depicts an entity that we would recognize as a writing lab by most of today's standards.

It is important to note that the Iowa lab started as a one-to-one facility independent of the classroom (L. Kelly 4–5). Thus, it provided a competing format that eventually became the norm. For instance, the Minnesota lab began to disconnect itself from the classroom at least five years after its inception, as is indicated in an article by Dorothy Kelly about a high-school lab in Elkhart, Indiana. Citing Minnesota's lab as her model, Kelly portrays hers as a place not only used by classes but also open all day for various students.

Armed Forces English and The Communications Emphasis

By the 1940s, free-standing writing labs were a recognizable part of higher education, though it is difficult to know how widespread they were. However, it can be documented that the number of labs increased with the advent of Armed Forces English, on-campus programs for preparing officers for World War II. After the war, these programs developed a communications emphasis, a pedagogy integrating writing, speaking, reading, and listening skills (also the pedagogy that accounts for the word communication in the CCC organization and journal).

Three articles in *College English* in 1944 and 1945 describe the Armed Forces' ambitious program to provide young officers with the equivalent of two years of training in English in just two semesters. As George Wycoff of Purdue noted, the Army's demands placed a strain on English Departments to create an elaborate program for a large number (40 per class) of students of diverse abilities in a short period of time. In addition, the Army insisted that students would learn at their own pace, mastering the material they could cover rather than taking a course covering a prescribed amount of material. Such an approach was natural for the laboratory, both as a classroom technique and in a tutorial setting. With the techniques of the military program tested, it was not surprising, as Grant Redford of the University of Montana predicted, that many of them were adopted for peacetime education.

Growing out of the Armed Forces programs, the communications emphasis, as James Berlin has noted, enjoyed much influence in the late 1940s and persisted in some form well into the next decade. Writing labs or clinics were integral to this emphasis. While the Armed Forces programs were concerned with rapid individual mastery for the pragmatic purposes of the military, communications programs shifted the emphasis to social development and the affective domain. At the University of Denver, graduate-student clinicians, as they were called, worked individually with students, using the techniques of "Rogerian nondirective counseling" (Davidson and Sorenson 84). In addition, clinicians were expected to help students improve grades to promote self-esteem, assemble biographical data about the students to help them overcome their fears, and help those who were "poor in English largely through accident of environment or education" (Davidson and Sorenson 85). This description differs little from what might be a component of the mission statement of many writing centers today. However, with so much emphasis on the affective domain, the Denver lab was criticized for engaging in amateur psychology. Samuel Middlebrook dubbed the program "English I in Cellophane" (140). Even Frederick Sorenson, one of the lab's founders, admitted retrospectively that "informed people could not possibly permit uninformed 'clinicians' to tamper with student lives, and, as it turned out, there was no program for training clinicians in the methods of teaching grammar and rhetoric, let alone how to analyze students" (325).

While the Denver lab, despite its overzealous attempts at counseling, looked somewhat like a writing center today, the communications rubric covered a variety of approaches. At Stephens College, the writing "clinic' was set up for "[t]he student who finds it very difficult to spell correctly or who makes gross errors in English usage. Here causes are determined, exercises under supervision are given, and practical applications to everyday writing are made" (Wikesell 145). This evidently current-traditional effort at Stephens points to the kind of unenlightened model often assumed of all early centers by current commentators. On the other hand, the Denver lab indicates that drill-and-skill pedagogy was not the sole method of the times.

Labs or Clinics? The CCCC Workshop Reports of the 1950s

By 1950, although their identities were not clear, writing centers were beginning to establish themselves as part of writing programs. Robert Moore reports in 1950 that of the 55 of 120 institutions replying to a University of Illinois survey, 24 had writing labs or clinics, and 11 others were planning them. The shape they would take concerned the CCCC workshops on writing centers throughout the first half of the 1950s.

From the inception of CCCC in 1950, four of the first six years of the organization's journal contain conference workshop reports on writing lab workshops. These reports begin to identify and debate issues identical and similar to those that have concerned centers in the last twenty-five years. What kind of place should the lab be? Whom should it serve? Who should work there? What kind of services should be provided? What form should tutorials take? As is the case today, these issues remained unresolved.

Curiously, after 1955 there is little discussion of writing labs and centers in professional journals. One would think that the post-Sputnik emphasis on American education would have spawned more in the late 1950s and early 1960s. However, it may be that with linguistics promising to be the salvation of writing instruction at this time, writing centers were overshadowed as both a method and a subject for professional discourse. Nevertheless, in some form they must have persisted and developed, for eleven years after the last CCCC report, a 1966 article by Dorothy Whitted reports on a remediation effort at Ohio Wesleyan based on tutorials. Despite the focus on a remedial population, Whitted's attitudes toward students begin to foreshadow those of writing centers today. The student is "not someone who fails to meet a mythical arbitrary standard of excellence, but is a non-member of an 'in' group with respect to communication in an academic context" (40).

Whitted's article brings us to the late 1960s, when open admissions initiatives began to proliferate and writing labs and centers along with them. This period is one we know, thanks to Mina Shaughnessy's *Errors and Expectations* and such writing center-specific articles as Judith Summerfield's "Writing Centers: A Long View" and William Yahner and William Murdick's "The Evolution of a Writing Center: 1972–1990."

DIACHRONIC VERSUS SYNCHRONIC HISTORIES

The diachronic history I have sketched of labs and clinics prior to the late 1960s remains hazy, full of gaps. While I would like to claim that it represents an evolutionary march of progress from Buck's early classroom attempts to the multipurpose centers developing after the 1960s, as Hayden White and other poststructuralist historicists have reminded us, such diachronic histories depend as much on the selection and arrangement of events as on the events themselves. While my brief sketch may enable us to conjecture that the idea of the writing center has origins in the classroom laboratory method, that the Minnesota and Iowa labs began the break from the classroom, that the Armed Forces English programs contributed to the growth of labs, that the GI Bill in the early fifties brought students into the academy who could benefit from labs, a more accurate picture requires a synchronic approach comparing how these early clinics and labs stand in relation to labs and centers today. Thus, I would now like to turn to an examination of three current writing center issues as they surface in texts on the clinics and labs of the past: clientele, staffing, and institutional identity.

Clientele: Who Comes In and What Do We Think of Them?

Today, writing centers proudly advertise themselves as places where all students are welcome and are treated, regardless of ability, as writers with something to say. Texts on early labs and clinics indicate that along with some damning attitudes, a supportive view of even underprepared students was evident as far back as the early part of this century and continued into the 1960s.

In his laboratory classroom of 1904, Buck denounces the stultifying topics of the textbooks, proposes that teachers allow students to write on topics of their own choosing, and argues that a teacher should "[s]peak with authority, but also as one who knows the heart and feelings of those he has in his charge" (507). While in 1917 Francis Ingold Walker in one breath refers to his students as "dependents, defectives, and delinquents," he also recognizes them as individuals, castigating teachers who "wear themselves out in a vain attempt to make all pupils conform to one mold" (448).

Cady's description of the Middlebury College lab classroom in 1913 also focuses upon and shows respect for the individual student: "As all the work is individual we build on individual error, calling the student's attention only to errors which he himself makes" (125). Though the mention of error here may indicate a drill-and-skill approach, Cady also mentions posing rhetorical problems that "call for long-continued and detailed thinking and discussion" (125). Likewise, Grandy's account of the lab sections at Minnesota includes concern for such matters as style, organization, transitions, revision, and sentence variety, as well as grammatical matters. In addition, as a classroom extension, the laboratory approaches before 1940, in targeting all students for lab instruction, did not create stigmatized and privileged groups of those who attended the lab and those who did not. In short, the lab approach was viewed as something that could benefit all students, an attitude much akin to that promoted by writing centers today.

In the 1940s, as labs broke from the classroom, accounts of them continue to show respect for individual student abilities, with scornful rhetoric such as Ingold's comment on detectives and delinquents almost nonexistent. But ironically the break from the classroom also fostered the view of the lab as the venue of the inferior student. In the Armed Forces program, as aspiring officers in an era of patriotism, students, of course, would be respected. At the same time, however, the clinical emphasis in subsequent communications programs such as that at Denver began to create an aura of deficiency in students who needed to visit the clinicians. Samuel Middlebrook condemned the scientism of the Denver program as misguided condescension and psychological tampering through which "the milk of human contentment is produced under the care of watchful men in white" (140). Such comments indicate that though the communications emphasis called its facilities clinics and labs in an attempt at scientific rigor, these designations soon were appropriated by administration and instructors not working with the lab to stigmatize students as lab specimens. Even Stanley's lab at Iowa, which provided an early model of Rogerian non-directive tutoring in 1945, was officially designated by the administration at Iowa as a place "to provide instruction for students whose placement themes did not meet departmental standards" (L. Kelly 5).

By the 1950s the CCCC workshop reports indicate that a remedial stigma increasingly followed students into writing labs. One kind of lab discussed in the 1950 report is designated "as a sub-freshman English arrangement for entering Freshman who make a poor showing of the English placement test" (31). Simultaneously, the workshops concerned themselves with the possibility of labs serving all students and addressed such questions as how students should be referred to the lab: by instructors, by teachers campuswide, or by their own volition. These questions continue to occupy writing centers today but also concerned early proponents of writing centers.

Staffing: Who Works in Writing Centers and What Should They Know?

While there was much concern over who would use the lab, there was also much discussion about the qualifications and attitudes of those who worked there. The earliest attempts of the laboratory method in the classroom, of course, relied solely on the teacher. However, in accounts of such classrooms, the attempt by the teacher to abandon the role of traditional authority figure is evident. Buck in 1904 writes, "Come down to the same plane with your pupils and then you can help them" (307). Walker, despite his unkind rhetoric in describing students, condemns red ink and grading symbols and takes much pleasure when a student tells him, "'You aren't the dignified teacher that I used to think you were. You seem just like one of the boys, and I have learned to like English through the laboratory work'" (445). This sensitivity to individual students' needs and this willingness to abdicate some teacherly authority prefigure much that is valued in writing center tutors today.

Early writing centers, however, did not, according to the literature surveyed, use undergraduate peer tutors. Grandy's presentation of the lab at Minnesota in the 1930s and the discussions of the Denver lab in the 1940s mention the use of graduate students, though these tutors were usually working in concert with a faculty member. Nevertheless, it was not assumed that just any faculty member could work in the lab. Redford in 1944 describes teachers in the Armed Forces program at Montana training themselves "to set about developing a philosophy...and methods of teaching the skills involved in communication" (277). Moore in 1950 cites the need for special training and argues that "the more resourceful the [tutor] is in suggesting new approaches to old problems, the more quickly does self help become effective" (390). And the 1951 CCCC report asserts that no instructor should be assigned to the lab who is not trained and willing to do the work it requires.

In each of these examples, the tutor is defined as someone different from the classroom teacher, as someone with a particular perspective on working with students individually. Although the literature does not indicate how, or even if, tutors were trained, it does point to the need for a distinct set of professional competencies that accord the lab an institutional identity apart from the classroom.

Institutional Identity: What is a Writing Center?

Today institutional identity is a hot topic, as writing centers attempt to situate themselves in relation to the classroom, writing programs, and institutional cultures. For early centers, this concern was not nearly as pressing, but it begins to surface by the 1940s. In the 1930s Grandy's and Stanley's articles on the Minnesota and Iowa labs seem content to present them as part of the larger writing program and, because they served all students, are not concerned with the stigma of being perceived as remedial facilities. Their identity, rather, is vested in the difference between classroom and individual instruction. As Dorothy Kelly noted, the idea of her high school lab, based on the Minnesota model, "is that of a workshop: informal, free, and yet serious" (662).

By 1950, however, Robert Moore begins to make a distinction between clinics, which he deems remedial facilities for diagnoses, and labs, which are there to help all students. This concern continues throughout the CCCC reports of the 1950s and prefigures Ray Wallace's 1991 distinction between labs and centers. In the same year that Moore was differentiating two kinds of facilities, the CCCC report identifies five, ranging from the "remedial laboratory for students who have been unusually neglected in their basic writing skills" to a lab open voluntarily "on a college-wide basis to all students from all levels" (31). Though workshop participants, like the writing center community today, were never able to agree on exactly what a lab should be, they concur in 1951 that it "should be what the classroom often is not—natural, realistic, and friendly" (18).

The concern with rejecting the stigma of remediation and with creating an identity separate from the classroom is a recurring motif throughout the CCCC workshops of the 1950s. With the implementation of the GI bill following World War II and the Korean conflict and increased numbers of underprepared students pursuing higher education, more remediation than ever before was needed, and labs were called upon to provide it. At the same time, labs were struggling for respectability. This scenario foreshadows the results of open admissions two decades later when labs and centers proliferated at the same time they were denigrated as havens for the remedial student. Thus, the identity struggles writing centers face today, though perhaps more complicated, have a long history.

CONCLUSION

There remains much we do not know about early writing centers and much that may be irrecoverable, but what we can recover indicates that early writing labs confronted many of the same issues centers do today. Though writing center discourse, following post-Dartmouth composition history, often constructs a near progression from current-traditional rhetoric, to expressionism, to social construction in lab practice, it is wrong to assume that early writing labs were current-traditional dungeons where students were banished to do grammar drills while hiding in shame from their more able peers. While it is evident that drills were part of the methods of early centers, heuristic and global concerns were equally evident. Like centers today, these ancestors did not see themselves as providing only first-aid to the grammatically halt and lame. Indeed, it is likely that writing centers' struggle against being relegated to this role increased after the post-Dartmouth process movement when many instructors saw the center as a place to handle the grammar instruction while they taught process. Although the rhetoric regarding students in early writing center discourse at times seems misguided, even cruel, these facilities preached and practiced many of the same things current writing centers endorse.

Writing centers are fond of seeing themselves in metaphors of family—cozy homes with soft couches where when students go they must be taken in. If we frame early center history in this same sense of family, we may not be able to claim descent from nobility, but neither will we find that our ancestors need to be forgotten and ignored like some crazy old uncle locked in the attic.

WORKS CITED

Berlin, James. *Rhetoric and Reality: Writing Instruction in American Colleges and Universities.* Carbondale: SIU Press, 1987.

Buck, Philo. "Laboratory Method in English Composition." *National Education Association Journal of Proceedings and Addresses of the 43rd Annual Meeting. St. Louis, June 27–July 1, 1904.* Winona, MN: National Education Association, 1905.

Cady, Frank W. "The Laboratory Method at Middlebury College." *English Journal* 4.2 (1915): 124–125.

Davidson, Levette J., and Frederick Sorenson. "The Basic Communications Course." *College English* 8 (1946): 83–86.

Grandy, Adah G. "A Writing Laboratory." *English Journal* 25.5 (1936): 372–376.

Healy, David. "A Defense of Dualism: The Writing Center and the Classroom." *The Writing Center Journal* 14.1 (1994): 16–29.

Hemmeter, Thomas. "The 'Smack of Difference': The Language of Writing Center Discourse." *The Writing Center Journal* 11.1 (1990): 73–79.

Horner, Warren B. "The Economy Of the Laboratory Method." *English Journal* 18.3 (1929): 214–221.

Kelly, Dorothy. "A High-School Writing Laboratory." *English Journal* 30.8 (1941): 660–663.

Kelly, Lou. "One-On-One, Iowa City Style: Fifty Years of Individualized Writing Instruction." *The Writing Center Journal* 1.1 (1980): 4–19.

Levine, David O. *The American College and the Culture of Aspiration, 1915–40.* Ithaca: Cornell UP, 1986.

Lunsford, Andrea. "Collaboration, Control, and the Idea of a Writing Center." *The Writing Center Journal* 12.1 (1991): 3–10.

Middlebrook, Samuel. "English I in Cellophane." *College English* 9 (1947): 140–143.

Moore, Robert H. "The Writing Clinic and the Writing Laboratory." *College English* 11 (1950): 388–395.

Murphy, Christina. "Writing Centers in Context: Responding to Current Educational Theory." *The Writing Center: New Directions.* Ed. Ray Wallace and Jeanne Simpson. New York: Garland, 1991. 276–288.

"Organization and Use of a Writing Laboratory." The Report of Workshop No. 9. *College Composition and Communication* 2 (1951): 17–19.

"The Organization and Use of the Writing Laboratory." The Report of Workshop No. 9A. *College Composition and Communication* 1 (1950): 31–32.

Redford, Grant H. "The Army Air Force English Program and the Schools of Tomorrow." *College English* 5 (1944): 276–280.

"Shall 'Laboratory Work' In Composition Be Given Up?" *English Journal* 1.1 (1912): 48.

"Skills Laboratories for Any Student." Report No. 11. *College Composition and Communication* 7 (1956): 143.

Sorensen, Frederick. "The Basic Communications Course Reconsidered." *College English* 10 (1949): 324–328.

Stanley, Carrie Ellen. "This Game of Writing: A Study in Remedial English." *College English* 4 (1943): 423–428.

Summerfield, Judith. "Writing Centers: A Long View." *The Writing Center Journal* 8.2 (1988): 3–9.

Walker, Francis Ingold. "The Laboratory System in English." *English Journal* 6.7 (1917): 445–453.

Wallace, Ray. "Sharing the Benefits and the Expense of Expansion: Developing a Cross-Curricular Cash Flow for a Cross-Curricular Writing Center." Wallace and Simpson. 82–101.

Weigle, Frederick H. "Teaching English in an Army Air Force College Training Program." *College English* 5 (1944): 271–275.

Whitted, Dorothy. "A Tutorial Program for Remedial Students." *College Composition and Communication* 18 (1966): 40–43.

Wiksell, Wesley. "The Communications Program at Stephens College." *College English* 9 (1947): 143–145.

"Writing Clinics." The Report of Workshop No. 2. *College Composition and Communication* 6 (1955): 125–126.

"The Writing Laboratory." The Report of Workshop No. 9. *College Composition and Communication* 3 (1952): 23–25.

Wykoff, George S. "Army English Experiences Applicable to Civilian, Postwar English." *College English* 6 (1945): 338–342.

Yahner, William, and William Murdick. "The Evolution of a Writing Center: 1972–1990." *The Writing Center Journal* 11.2 (1991): 13–28.

Writing Centers: A Long View

Judith Summerfield

William James says that we live our lives engaged in two fundamentally distinctive activities: *flights* and *perchings*. When we are in *flight*, we are doing, making, surviving, carrying on the work we need to do to stay alive. In James Britton's terms, we are *participating* in the work of the world. We are participants.

When we *perch*, we step back and look at what we have made, how we have done our work, what in fact worked and what didn't, what we would do over again, what now makes sense, what doesn't. Our primary mental activity now is *evaluating*, making sense of, interpreting, criticizing. We are now *spectators* of our own lives, of our makings and doing.

These two activities characterize my involvement with writing centers. For nearly all of the Seventies, I was a participant: doing, making, creating a writing center, paving new ground at the college, establishing satellite programs at local "feeder" high schools—all that is involved in *doing* a writing center. For the past five years or so, I've had the opportunity to take a long perching, a long view, to think about what writing centers are all about, to be a spectator.

About five years ago, I was asked to retire from the writing center at my college. I suppose I had been too noisy, too demanding, too persistent. I kept repeating myself. Parrot-like, I kept asking *why?* And *why not?* Why isn't there more money? Why can't we hire more tutors? Why can't we set up a course for tutors? Why can't we extend hours? Why can't we pay our tutors more? Why can't we get a larger room? Why can't we paint the walls?

At that time, the paint on the walls had dramatically chipped away—the hospital green looked shabbier and shabbier, and with the prospect of in-

Summerfield, Judith "Writing Centers: A Long View." *The Writing Center Journal* 8.2 (1988): 3–9. Reprinted by permission of *The Writing Center Journal*.

creased budget cuts, our spirits reflected those drab walls. I thought a coat of paint might brighten us, as well as the room—a converted class-room that was bursting at the seams.

The bureaucratic machinery opposed the new paint: every turn we took, we hit a stone wall. No, we could not get the writing center painted. When we decided to paint the room ourselves, we heard that the college regulated against using anything but college paint. Finally, after two years, the walls were painted—a shocking, blinding aqua-blue—the only paint, they told us, that was available at that time. Take it or leave it, we were told. We took it.

In short, I guess, I was a nuisance. I wouldn't take *no* for an answer. At one point, I suggested that the Writing Center break from the particular administrative, bureaucratic position we were in. I had called for civil war, secession, independence. I received a polite letter, saying something about the fact that institutions benefited from "rotation of administrators." I was to be *rotated*.

So it has been five years since I've set foot in the writing center. The message was clear—get out and stay out, and don't give the new directors any ideas. *Behave*. A time of nay-saying had set in.

It had been a time of yea-saying when the writing center had been created in 1972. The Writing Workshop (directed at the outset by Sandra Schor; I, one of her assistants, took over the directorship in 1974) had grown up and out of the great social experiment of Open Admissions at the City University of New York. In those years, we were in the hot-seat of school change. The University made a commitment to the under-classes of New York City: we would open our doors to all who wanted to attend. We would make it possible for them to pursue their own American dreams. We would open *new* doors. In those early experimental, exhilarating years, the writing center, its actual establishment, was seen as integral to these political, social, and pedagogic experiments.

It had been this social context that had induced the work of Mina Shaughnessy, Robert Lyons, Donald McQuade, Marie Ponsot, and Kenneth Bruffee. A new population of students demanded that we look at what we had been doing traditionally, habitually, in the college classroom. The spirit of innovation, of daring, of saying "*Yes*—it's possible"—was everywhere. It was a time when instructors opened the doors of their classrooms. Instructors who were faced with a new population of college student left the privacy, and the virtual isolation, of the classroom and peeked out into the halls and asked for support from their colleagues. "What can I do?" they asked each other, and the pronoun shifted to *we*—"What can *we* do?"—as a spirit of collaboration was born, it seems, almost overnight. One day we were working there alone, and the next day we were all engaged—instructor, student, administrator, tutor—in collaborative doing. Nothing seemed impossible.

We began to school ourselves: the maps had not yet been drawn. The territory was new. There were voices we called upon: Jerome Bruner on learning, James Moffett on the universe of discourse, William Labov on Black English, Noam Chomsky on transformational-generative grammar, but those were the days before ethnography, word-processing, collaborative learning, writing across the disciplines. I suppose that some administrators expected us to do no more than help students write correct sentences. But we weren't satisfied. We read all the grammar books we could find: transformational-generative, structural, Allen's X-word grammar, and traditional grammars. We read social histories, to try to place ourselves. We set up informal seminars for ourselves: one summer some of us decided to read James Britton's *Language and Learning and Writing Abilities*. We read and read, and when we had the time, we talked about what we had read.

Mostly, we *did*. We taught courses and ran tutor-training sessions and tutored students ourselves. We recognized that the tutors were key to the whole enterprise, that we were schooling a generation of teachers, some of whom are still the best teachers in our writing program. We started a weekly newsletter. We printed collections of students' writings. Of tutors' writings. We read each others' works. We put tutors in the classroom. We brought classes to the writing center. It was an extraordinary time of learning for all of us—and for many of us, even though we may not be directly related to writing centers now, the spillover still lasts, for it is in the writing center that many of us cut our teeth on a *kind* of doing that we still do. It is that which I will focus on now—what is it that we still do that is worth doing? What is it that is worth preserving? What is it that came out of these early experiments with writing centers?

The it can be summarized in a clause: that all teaching, tutoring, writing, reading, indeed, all languaging acts, are ineluctably social. The workshop experiment forced that upon us. Taking the long view, we might say that there have been two stages in this process:

1. The first was the focus on the individual, on the individual *process*.
2. The second is a focus on the individual in context, or to use Vygotsky's term: *The Mind in Society*.

Let me reflect on the first stage. What we began to recognize, particularly through the one-to-one encounter in tutoring was that we are all different. There are different ways of composing, of reading, of experiencing the world. Different minds, different experiences. Those of us who came to tutoring from teaching quickly realized that we could no longer construe our students as a homogeneous blob. Our perceptions and experiences of teaching and learning and language had fundamentally changed, not only in degree, but in kind. These shifts we see reflected in just about every textbook in the field: the shift from something called *product* to *process.* The focus on revision, on collaborative-learning, on peer-editing all began to make its way into our jargon under the catch-word *process.*

At its best, researchers began to explore the ways writers compose, revise, construct meaning. We all now take for granted that writing is *recursive,* a move back and forth, a taking in of what has been generated as we consider what is to come next. We know, for example, from Sondra Perl's research that inexperienced writers stop themselves, as they go back over the words they have already written, crossing out, correcting, rewriting the surface features, and not allowing themselves to write long stretches of discourse.

At its worst, the process of *process* has become reified, so that those who have not plumbed the depths of what it means to compose, to construct meaning, make *static* a fluid act. Look to the textbooks now that offer process in *stages:* first pre-write, then draft, then revise. At its worst, process has become institutionalized—one institution I know dictates that all students in all composition courses *must* write a certain number of drafts. The writer who does, in fact, get it all down in a first/final draft is highly suspect. Revision, institutionalized in these ways, is just as suspect as any other description that turns prescriptive.

When I hear a program or a text described as taking a "process-approach," I am immediately suspicious. And what I often find is that the emperor is not wearing any clothes, even though he claims to have a new wardrobe. My bet is that those who talk in these ways have had nothing to do with writing centers (or teaching), that they claim to understand what composing is all about, but their agenda is pre-emptive: it is an agenda. In the same way, I now see textbooks advertised as promoting a *workshop* approach—what precisely that means must be questioned. We must become skeptical, to make certain that the *workshop approach* does not become reified, institutionalized, and therefore, neutered, as *process* has become.

What is truly valuable about the experiment of writing centers/ workshops has to do with the second stage, with the recognition of the social nature of language and learning. A genuine workshop is one that builds a community of writers, readers, listeners, talkers, thinkers, who are encouraged to understand how they write as individuals, but equally important, as members of a community. The process-approach lays on the individual student a method. The true workshop approach inquires into the mind working in society.

In a genuine workshop, writing is an interactive engagement between writer and reader. It is not a one-dimensional focus on what the writer does. Rather, writing is seen in terms of what it does *to* a reader, or better, to *readers.* In this dynamic interaction, the words a writer writes come to life as they are received, reacted to, by a live reader(s) who reads not only out of her own personal preferences, biases, associations, memories, but also, out of what

Stanley Fish calls interpretive communities. We do not write in a social vacuum. Nor do we read in a social vacuum. And the writing center, given its constraints of grades and exams and institutional requirements, allows us to make our own courses—to construct what Robert Scholes calls a "local curriculum" which grows out of the students' needs and interests and the instructor/tutor's awareness of those needs. In the context of schooling in the academy, the workshop offers an extraordinary freedom. The agendas can be ours. We do not need to be cut off from students at the ends of semesters. Our courses can continue. Even for years. And when it works, we find a possibility for growth, for a kind of recycling: students become tutors become teachers. I have seen it happen.

The nature of the writing center, then, is community—and that is precisely why it can become problematic. Institutions don't necessarily *like* little communities within their walls, for there is power in numbers. As students come together, they can ask *why* and *why not*? "Why is my reading of this poem *wrong*?" Why is this phrase *awkward*? What does this grade mean? Why can I revise in this class and not in that one? Why did instructor X give this paper an A and instructor Y give the same paper a C-? How can you write a journal if it's graded? Who am I writing for? How can writing be "free?" Tutors and students question together. They often conclude that teachers in classrooms take particular stands in order to keep control, in order to manage behavior. These conversations challenge the "nature" of authority and expose underlying values, politics, ideology, and epistemology.

For we are talking about nothing less than this—about ways of knowing the world, about ways the dominant culture works (in the schools), about domination and subjugation, in the complex arena of writing and reading texts. If I, teacher Z, say that this is what this text means, then who are you to disagree with me? And if you persist, just remember that it is I who give the grade. (I grow uneasy with the loose usage of the word *power*: if we, as teachers, set assignments, evaluate texts, and *give grades*, then we are the primary holders of power; to deny so is to deny the fundamental "nature" of schooling in the culture.)

As I look back now, from my long perching, I revise the evaluations that I began with when I started this text. For some time, when I stopped to think about my ousting from the writing center, I construed it personally. I had annoyed the authorities. I had asked too many questions, demanded too much. I had been made to feel that I hadn't *behaved* properly. But this is a personal reading. There's more I see now, with my advantage of spectatorship, my advantage of time. I can talk about this personal story within a public context, a history.

The history has to do with what happened to CUNY and its budget crises of the mid- to late-Seventies, with the fact that yea-saying had turned, overnight, into nay-saying. It was money—economics—that changed the environment from positive to negative. But it is not just CUNY that we must talk about; we must take a hard took at what happened to the experiments of the Sixties, with the fact that the doors that had been opened now began to close. You could see it happening. Open Admissions faded into the woodwork. The impetus to interact with colleagues turned sour as jobs were cut. The Sixties had brought Directors of Writing Programs together to form CAWS (the CUNY Association of Writing Supervisors) and had led to WPA (Writing Program Administrators)—these are the direct outgrowths of those times. But the energies that had been poured into collaboration now began to shift. The history of this experiment has not yet been written: perhaps we're still too close. And some of us have not yet given up some of the battle.

But it's clear to me that energies are now being directed to two areas: testing and computers. If you look at each—testing and computers—if you read these "new" movements politically, you'll see that each calls for the individual to confront his situation alone. One, the individual student facing a test chat will determine whether or not she will be allowed to earn a college degree. Each man for himself because that is the nature of the beast. No collaborative activity is admitted when one is *taking* a test. That is the ineluctable fact.

In the same way, while the computer/word-processor may make writing and revision easier, it CAN threaten the community of the writing center. I know that much of the time now spent in the writing center at my school is spent on tutoring students to pass the CUNY Writing Assessment Test: that is the first order of business. I know, as well, that we are fortunate in having a director who is using computers in ways that do not threaten the collaborative community of the writing center. But I know, too, that the temptation must be great to call up a software program and call that tutoring.

I wasn't fighting for blue walls, for new paint, for more money: I was fighting for a *context*. The more I explored it, the richer it became, and the possibilities for an epidemic, an explosion of this kind of learning and languaging, made me dizzy. And the corresponding movements in other fields—of reader-response theories, of semiotics, cultural anthropology, sociolinguistics, of ethnography itself—all seemed to point in a direction that was, indeed, revolutionary. Shirley Brice Heath talks about the same kind of spirit in her seminal work, *Ways With Words,* in which she describes the community spirit and activity that sparked a small Southern town in the late Sixties, early Seventies, where school officials, teachers, parents, businessmen, children, clergymen, were working together on the *possibilities* of integration. Her epilogue, however, tells us that the participants mostly gave up or were pushed out, as money dried up, as government grants ended, as disillusionment set in, as the realization became clear—that the system would need to be dynamited in order for it to change. She had spent ten years there. Now she is a spectator of that past, just as we all are when we took back on the past and try to make sense of it.

Now that I come to the end of this text, I see the past a little more clearly—for the moment. The *no* I kept hearing had to do with the times, with going back, with pulling back, with the Nixons of the time saying: watch out for those who assemble. There is power in numbers. *We* must divide to conquer. *We* must send those noisy schoolteachers back into the recesses of their classrooms and insist that they keep their doors shut. Danger lurks when teachers gather in the halls or when they engage in talk, in something new that seems to be cropping up all over the place—something called a *writing center. Decentralize.*

I have visited some writing centers of late. Some astonish me. They are plush, with luxurious carpets, modern (or post-modern) prints on the walls, secretaries, computer terminals, stocked libraries, spacious surroundings—and *cubicles.* I say watch out for cubicles. Watch out for computer terminals. Watch out for all evidence of attempts to break down the gathering of minds.

The National Writing Centers Association as Mooring: A Personal History of the First Decade[1]

Joyce Kinkead

To begin recounting a history of the National Writing Centers Association, I invoke the words of Eugene O'Neill. About the time the NWCA was forming in 1982, I was acting in a campus production of *A Moon for the Misbegotten*. Still with me are the lines of one of its characters: "There is no present, no future. Only the past. You can't get away from it." Although more pessimistic in tone than is suitable for a celebration of NWCA, these lines suggest that the past is always with us, and, in fact, I would argue that we do not want to get away from our past as an organization, not just because "if we do not remember our past we are doomed to repeat it," but because knowing our past helps us know ourselves.

To that end, I want to address some basic questions: Why is there a national organization for writing centers? What road has led us to plans for a third (Inter)National Writing Centers Conference? Why was CCCC not enough? Why was Writing Program Administration (WPA)—established prior to NWCA—insufficient? What were the conditions that led to the charter of NWCA in 1982? In recounting this chronicle, I stress that this a personal history, gathered from a number of sources, including back issues of *The Writing Center Journal* and *Writing Lab Newsletter*, convention programs and proceedings, nine years of NWCA minutes when I served as executive secretary, miscellaneous correspondence, and a fallible memory. Finally, I was one of several others present at the beginning, and I acknowledge they could tell this story as well—if not better—than I.

Kinkead, Joyce. "The National Writing Centers Association as Mooring: A Personal History of the First Decade." *The Writing Center Journal* 16.2 (Spring 1996): 131–143. Reprinted by permission of *The Writing Center Journal*.

HISTORICAL CONTEXT: 1971–79

To understand the chartering of the NWCA, it is necessary to review briefly the historical context of the previous decade. Before 1973, writing centers did exist, and Peter Carino has done much to document that early history. However, Steward and Croft note that their ERIC search of 1969 "turned up a single article about a then-existing lab." Besides the early University of Iowa Writing Laboratory, going on sixty years of age, early 1970s labs included the University of Michigan-Flint (1971), Berkeley (1973), the Brooklyn College Writing Center (1973), and Purdue (1975). During this time of bell bottoms, the 18-year-old voting movement, and Ken Macrorie's *A Vulnerable Teacher,* the "laboratory approach to writing" meant peer tutoring either in a centralized room or in the classroom itself (Laque and Sherwood 7).

In 1973, the CCCC charged a committee to investigate skills centers and the "degree to which they promote and/or hinder the objectives of English courses" (Conference 4). Two fears rested at the heart of this survey: 1) that teachers would be replaced by mechanized programs, and 2) that skills centers "care only about the mechanical aspects of writing" (16). The resulting report, "Learning Skills Centers," indicates that since skills center sessions began at NCTE and CCCC in 1971, presentations shifted from discussing grammar and sentence structure to writing process pedagogy, and the people involved shifted from being instructors who failed students to lab staff no longer responsible for evaluation who became advocates for writers. Labs initially seduced by programmed instruction increasingly left that material in supply closets (15). In brief, the news was heartening to CCCC.

By 1978, "a College English Association survey of composition programs found several hundred schools listing writing labs as part of their instructional method" (Steward and Croft 2). Hawkins and Brooks describe the increase in the number of writing centers this way: "Today's writing centers were not conceived in the most orderly and organized fashion. It has been a chaotic beginning.... [S]ome would question our future" (vii). While the impetus for these early centers often was remedial instruction, there was a growing feeling that a writing center might serve the entire campus community and even beyond.

At the 1977 CCCC, a group of sixty writing center directors decided they needed more contact than was offered by an annual meeting (Harris, "Growing Pains" 2), so Muriel Harris took out pencil and paper, collected names and addresses, and in April the First issue of the *Writing Lab Newsletter* appeared, produced on a Sears typewriter, cut and pasted—somewhat askew—at Mickey's kitchen table. Its first page included a now-familiar plea for a dollar contribution to "mollify" the departmental "keeper of the budget."

WRITING CENTERS ASSOCIATION BEGINS—1979

A special interest group of writing lab directors was organized by Harris for the 1979 and 1980 CCCC and became an annual event, including a materials exchange table. Topics of these sessions ranged from a "Unified Records System" to "Toward Academic Status for Writing Lab Directors" (1981 CCCC program). A representative handout from the materials table, called a "Sketchbook" from the Writer's Gallery at Lincoln High School (Nebraska), promised students: "When you have completed this sketchbook, you will be able to correctly use the comma before coordinating conjunctions in compound sentences."

Also in 1979—in hindsight, a benchmark year—a group of directors in what is now called the East Central region decided to organize a spring meeting. The Writing Centers Association met for the first time that May; from this group, the NWCA would eventually arise. At the CCCC that had just taken place in Minneapolis, a resolution on the professional status of full-time instructors of composition calling for equality in salary and tenure status had been passed, and Mildred Steele of Central College in Pella, Iowa asked in the December *WLN* if "others feel as I do" that writing lab directors should be "assured the same kind of protection." (A resolution on the status of writing lab professionals was passed at the 1981 CCCC, a topic revisited in 1987 with a second resolution authored by Jay Jacoby.) Also in 1979, the *Journal of Basic Writing* began, and the *WPA Newsletter* became a new refereed journal—*WPA: Writing Program Administration*, edited by Kenneth Bruffee.

Only a year later, the *WLN* had grown from its inaugural issue of two pages to six, charged $3, included cartoons by tutor Bill Demaree on "Great Moments in Writing Lab History," noted rare Ph.D. programs with an emphasis in rhetoric and composition, and reached over 650 subscribers (February 1980 issue). Also in 1980, Lil Brannon and Stephen North began *The Writing Center Journal*, in which they posed the question, "Why another journal in the teaching of writing?" and answered it in two parts: scholarly and political. They wrote optimistically that it is in "these centers that great new discoveries will be, are being, made: ways of teaching composing, intervening in it, changing it. Writing centers provide, in short, opportunities for teaching and research that classrooms simply cannot" (1). Referring to writing centers as being in an "adolescent" stage of growth, they pointed out that pedagogical movements—the writing center being one such movement—are often short-lived, and a journal is an "outward sign of growing professional legitimacy (1)."

By 1981, the *WLN* had over 1,000 subscribers, and several books focusing on writing centers appeared: Hawkins and Brooks' *Improving Writing Skills*, Harris's *Tutoring Writing*, Steward and Croft's *The Writing Laboratory*, plus a peer tutor's journal from the Bay Area Writing Project at Berkeley. During the next two CCCCs, conversations among those attending the Writing Lab Directors Special Interest Sessions turned increasingly toward organizing a national group. Taking the lead, Nancy McCracken (then director of the writing center at Youngstown State University) contacted NCTE to obtain information about forming an Assembly, a status granted in November, 1982. In the December *WLN*, she issued a call to "anyone who is involved in or organizing a regional writing centers association...to discuss membership in the National Writing Centers Association—an NCTE assembly" (6).

The organizers of the Fifth Annual Conference of the Writing Centers Association, held at Purdue in May 1983, may nor have realized how prophetic its theme—"New Directions, New Connections"—turned out to be, for it was at that meeting that nominations for the inaugural NWCA Executive Board were taken from the floor during the business meeting of the WCA, shortly to become the East Central WCA. As president of the WCA, McCracken became acting president of the national organization until a time when a slate of officers could be elected.

THE NATIONAL WRITING CENTERS ASSOCIATION CONVENES—1983

In a September, 1983 *WLN* article, "News from the National WCA Mc-Cracken writes that membership dues are $1 and defines the assembly:

> *Members from all regions of the country elect a National Executive Board, vote on Position Statements of the NWCA, and elect one or more members of the NCTE Board of Directors to represent interests of writing centers.... The Executive Board, to be elected this October, will direct future activities of the NWCA, including: (1) establishing a network among the regions for sharing of research and conference information, and (2) formulating position statements, for membership approval, on matters of professional interest to writing centers—such as academic freedom, assessment and evaluation, professional status, training and development. ("News" 6)*

The ballot for the board resulted in the following charter members, largely located east of the Mississippi: Mary K. Croft, University of Wisconsin-Stevens Point; Diana George, Michigan Technological University; Jeanette Harris, Texas Tech University; Jay Jacoby, University of North Carolina-Charlotte; Harvey Kail, University of Maine; Joyce Kinkead, Utah State University; Nancy McCracken, Youngstown State University, Janice G. Neuleib, Illinois State University; Marcia Silver. Brooklyn College; and Jeanne Simpson, Eastern Illinois University.

The NWCA's first formal appearance occurred at the NCTE Convention in Denver, a one-day workshop filled to its capacity of 170 and "Moving Out from the Center," featuring presentations on research in the writing center, computers, the writing center as hub of WAC programs, teacher education, secondary school writing centers, and a position statement on professional concerns. The first business meeting took place the preceding evening when the newly-elected board members edited and approved a constitution for the National Writing Centers Assembly, elected officers—Nancy McCracken, President; Jeanette Harris, Vice-President; Joyce Kinkead, Executive Secretary; Mary K. Croft, Recording Secretary—and developed committees to oversee professional concerns, publications, and research. Professional concerns included problems such as "loss of lab." Subcommittees on tutors, two-year colleges, and K–12 writing centers were formed. According to the secretary's minutes, the committees agreed to "meet at the 4 Cs...to recruit members, more specifically identify functions, and begin deliberations."

A few months later at the 1985 CCCC meeting in New York—a conference marked by blizzard, trains at a standstill, and Broadway's *Noises Off*—the NWCA had a membership of 310, a treasury of $665, official stationery, and an agreement from the editors of *WLN* and *WCJ* to become official NWCA publications, each retaining strong editorial authority. Also in the works were awards for outstanding research and service, a committee chaired by Diana George.[2] McCracken suggested in a letter to board members following CCCC (10 April 1984) that "NWCA sponsor the Special Interest Session at CCCC," which had been organized informally, the chair being whomever had arranged the materials exchange table the previous year. Not until 1986, when Jeanne Simpson chaired this session, did it move formally to NWCA-affiliated status.

EARLY ISSUES: REPRESENTATION, REGIONS, RELATIONSHIPS

Quickly, the NWCA declared its territory, making claims on the professional landscape of writing centers. For instance, the fledgling organization officially designated at its 1984 board meeting in Detroit at NCTE that a high school representative be added, heading off the possibility of a parallel group being started for elementary and secondary school writing centers. Two-year college representation had been already included. Jeanette Harris and I noted at this meeting that we had been selected as editors of *The Writing Center Journal*. The new editors added an annual "checklist of writing center scholarship" compiled by Jay Jacoby, made it a refereed journal, and called on NWCA members as an editorial board. Some discussion ensued about making the *WLN* a refereed publication, but members noted that the newsletter is like a kaffeeklatsch and "you cannot have a refereed kaffeeklatsch." The revised constitution of the Assembly[3] added regional representatives and made the editors of *WLN* and *WCJ* ex-officio members. A nationwide writing center directory and a position statement on the role of writing center personnel[4] were two projects listed in the 1984 annual report on affiliate activities sent to NCTE.

Obviously, some regionals have had a longer history than the national association, most notably the East Central group (formerly the Writing Centers Association), which suffered some disruption and, possibly, resentment in the move from national to regional status, confounded early on by a muddled collection of membership dues.[5] Other regionals also preceded the national organization. Two years after WCA formed in 1979, the Southeast WCA began meeting, followed by the Midwest WCA in October, 1982; the Texas WCA in March, 1983; and the Rocky Mountain WCA in June, 1983. After the NWCA's first meeting in November, 1983, New England and Mid-Atlantic regionals began organizing at the instigation of Harvey Kail and Marcia Silver. Irene Lurkis Clark convened a Pacific association in 1985.

Regional associations were of some concern because of overlap of states, particularly muddy between the Midwest and East Central. The issue of regional boundaries and map making appears in minutes of NWCA periodically as "the continuing dilemma of regional association boundaries" (11/25/85), and a lengthy discussion resulted in polling the membership (3/22/90) about a draft map, accompanied by a carefully worded statement that the national was seeking information, not imposing boundaries. The causes of the "map problem," as it came to be termed, were two: members inquired "to which regional do I belong," and the NWCA wondered how to insure accurate regional representation on the board. Eventually, the NWCA opted for a decentralized governance approach, leaving it to the regionals to figure out their own appropriate boundaries and representatives, keeping in mind the early tense history between the national and earlier-organized regionals.

Changes in the offices of NWCA included the deletion of a recording secretary in November, 1984 and the addition of a second vice-president in 1988, as well as dividing the duties of planning the NWCA-sponsored sessions at NCTE and CCCC. Initially, membership on the board was restricted to directors of writing centers, but the constitution was amended to those with "demonstrated interest and experience teaching in writing centers" (1984). Because NWCA originally organized at NCTE conventions, its initial constitution specified the November meeting as the official time and place, later changed to CCCC at the board meeting of November 18, 1984. (In actuality, the NWCA Board now meets at all three conferences—CCCC, NCTE, and NWCA—mindful that the secondary school membership is more likely to attend NCTE and the college membership more likely to attend CCCC. The question of where substantive business occurs continues as an issue.)

THE ROLES OF NWCA

In considering my initial question about why a national association for writing centers, several reasons appear. First, CCCC did not entirely meet the needs of this special interest group. I suspect that writing lab directors attending CCCC in the 1970s did not find sufficient sessions on their special interests and also felt that proposals for sessions were viewed by conference organizers as peripheral. In addition, the CCCC leadership was not represented by writing center staff. The WPA, a more specialized group that attempted to be inclusive of writing center directors, focused primarily on directors of composition programs, not writing centers. In this arena, the NWCA provided a legitimate professional organization for writing center directors who wanted to focus exclusively on the concerns of this membership. This political reason, similar to the impetus Brannon and North cite in establishing *WCJ*, had effects in the center as well as beyond. A network of writing center personnel formed, offering dialogue about problems and successes, sharing research, and gaining information about how to best present funding requests.

The NWCA thus saw itself in an advocacy role, offering the authority of a professional organization. Giving awards for outstanding research and service—followed by letters of commendation to the winners and their administrators, plus press releases—was one way to provide that validity. Likewise, grants to graduate students focusing on writing centers in their dissertations were created to reward them and also to provide more writing center entries in DAI. Providing advice via starter kits on setting up a writing center increased the number of writing centers, the NWCA taking on an evangelistic role. NWCA members and nonmembers made frequent requests to the secretary for information, such as the following letter I received in 1984:

> *I have been appointed Director of the Writing Center at the University of Tulsa beginning this fall. Our Writing Center is staffed and directed by graduate students, and we have little faculty assistance, especially regarding new ideas and procedures in the operation of a Writing Center. We are desperate for material, particularly anything to do with ESL.... Any suggestions...would be gratefully received by our bewildered staff. (Sharon A. Winn, 23 May 1984)*

Written requests and telephone calls were common, and occasionally an NWCA member would drop by my office in Logan—perhaps on a summer family camping trip—to ask about setting up a writing center.

In some respects, the NWCA saw itself as something of a labor union, offering professional support to those whose labs or positions were in crisis. I sometimes fantasize about an inspirational poster with Mickey Harris's intense portrait, arm upraised, and the caption, "writing lab directors unite." By coming together, writing centers become more powerful, locally and nationally. The two different NCTE resolutions on the status of writing lab directors are evidence of this NWCA role. Lobbying to get as many writing center proposals as possible accepted to NCTE and CCCC was and continues to be a priority. Quite simply, one goal was to make sure writing centers lasted. Although Hawkins and Brooks pondered that "such extra-classroom efforts and remedial classes have too long a history for us to suggest that the next ten years will bring us the insight and skill to do away with our need for all the help we can get in teaching students to write" (99), there was some feeling in 1981 that the state of writing centers might be perilous.

Yet another mission of NWCA was to champion theory and praxis, ranging from the process movement of the 1970s to the social constructionism of more recent times. Often based in pragmatism, writing centers can be what Michael Spooner calls a "hothouse of knowledge-making" serving a clientele "as diverse as ESL..., WAC..., basic writers, continuing ed writers, as well as run-of-the-mill undergrad writers" and offering "face-to-face tutoring, on-line support, research opportunities, teaching opportunities, faculty workshops" (3) plus a range of other services. The checklist of writing center scholarship, originally published annually in *The Writing Center Journal* was meant to quantify and lend credence to the legitimacy role mentioned earlier, as one way to develop the intellectual capital of the profession.

NWCA also provides a social forum. A term sometimes applied to *WLN*, "kaffeeklatsch," is appropriate to NWCA as well. On the other hand, given the popularity of WCENTER since its instigation by Lady Falls Brown in 1991, perhaps "network" has become a more useful term. Typically somewhat isolated on campuses by the nature of their roles, directors of writing centers find on WCENTER a large community of people in similar circumstances. It might be fair to say that a writing center is constructed at least in part as a result of these electronic conversations as users on the information highway call for advice in asking why student writing center use decreases during spring term, how tutors should deal with essays written on sensitive issues, or what to include in a tutor seminar. Nowhere in the bylaws of the NWCA will these reasons for its existence be made explicit, but they are there, unwritten, evidenced by the actions of the organization.

The last set of minutes that I wrote for NWCA occurred at the NCTE meeting in Atlanta in 1990 and reported a membership of 830 with a healthy treasury. Four years later, the First National Writing Centers Association

Conference was yet another example of the maturity of the organization. In maturity, there is stability, but there is also the danger of becoming mired in tradition, of becoming static. We would do well as an assemblage to remember that NWCA was created because other groups did not satisfactorily meet our needs. To remain dynamic, NWCA must listen to its members, make explicit its goals, communicate well, and plan strategically for the future.

To look into the crystal ball of our future, we have only to analyze similar organizations older than the NWCA. While CCCC has grown tremendously, it, too, began as a comfortable home for a special-interest group—perhaps more cocktail party than kaffeeklatsch—and has diversified into multiple focus groups, losing some of the coziness of its early days. Writing Program Administrators (WPA) has grown as well and continues to rely upon tried and true events such as the summer workshops for new administrators. Both CCCC and WPA sought official sessions at the MLA to extend their sphere of influence. The holding of a national conference focused solely on writing centers is an example of a separatist move. A challenge for writing center specialists will be to continue to support the focused conferences and journals while maintaining a profile in the more mainstream journals such as *CCC, College English,* and even higher education journals such as *College Teaching* and *Change.*

While WCENTER does much to ensure a sense of community among its members, no doubt old-timers of NWCA will begin to talk sentimentally about the "early days" of the organization when "everyone knew everyone else." It is to be expected that splinter groups within the organization will appear, a natural part of growing pains. As a group, we are most likely more cynical than we were at decade ago when we embraced the optimism of North and Brannon's view of "great new discoveries" being within our reach.

While I tend to view writing centers as having moved away from adolescence and into maturity, some of our public personae and statements do not mirror a mature view. This manifests itself at meetings with what I call a "celebration of marginality." Messages that focus on what is being done to us (e.g., limited space and funding), rather than what we do well, place writing centers in a reactive rather than proactive stance. Perhaps Ellis is not surprising in an age when politics pervade academic conversation. I am not suggesting that writing center personnel slather on silly happy faces, spout cheery thoughts, and ignore all negative reports like some kind of Stepford Staff. Rather, I suggest that our image is determined by us, and if the image we project is that of strong, capable, wise, and caring teachers, then that is how we will be perceived. We need to share our success stories with our various publics, to instill confidence in a way of teaching and learning that lies at the heart of writing center practice, and to provide leadership whenever the opportunity arises. It is through such strength and resilience that we can be most effective in our local and national academic communities and can help place our writing centers at the core of academe.

Over ten years ago, a group of individuals created an organization to benefit the profession as a whole, working for common goals. The NWCA functions—as stated modestly in its early membership brochure—"to foster communication among writing centers and to provide a forum for concerns." The heart of our work in writing centers is service—in its largest sense—and leadership. That ethic applies as well to the National Writing Centers Association.

One final metaphor for the National Writing Centers Association appeals to me personally and reinforces O'Neill's notion of the importance of the past. Early in Toni Morrison's *Song of Solomon*, a character reminisces about what it is like to live as an adult in the house where she spent her childhood. One of the characteristics about the house that is most vivid in her memory is the walnut dining room table where fresh flowers sat. Each day the flowers were changed, their aroma filling the air. No longer are flowers on the table. All that is left is a watermark, a ring where the vase sat, yet this watermark is a "mooring" for the character, an image that conjures up the look and the smell of the flowers even though they are no longer there. My professional mooring continues to be the NWCA, the writing center, and those who populace that world. In spite of its relatively young age, the NWCA is a stable mooring, a place to anchor. For that, I am grateful to have been there—as many others were—at its inception, to be part of an exciting and energizing history.

NOTES

[1]This article is a revision of the keynote address delivered at the First National Writing Centers Conference in New Orleans on April 13, 1994.

[2]Awards are listed in *The Writing Center Journal*. Muriel Harris received the first service award in 1984, Stephen North and Thomas J. Reigstad and Donald A. McAndrew the first research awards in 1985, and Evelyn J. Posey the first graduate student award in 1986.

[3]By March 1985, Assembly was replaced by *Association*, and the official title became the "National Writing Centers Association: An NCTE Assembly," a designation that still appears on its publications.

[4]Written by Jeanne Simpson, the statement appeared in the 5.2/6.1 (1985) issue of *The Writing Center Journal*.

[5]A recent NCTE publication by Toni Flynn and Mary King brings together the best presentations from the ECWCA's first ten years.

WORKS CITED

Ballard, Kim, and Richard Anderson. "The Writing Lab Newsletter: A History of Collaboration." *Composition Chronicle* 1.9 (January 1989): 1–2.

Brannon, Lil, and Stephen North. "From the Editors." *The Writing Center Journal* 1.1 (1980): 1–3.

Bruffee, Kenneth A. *A Short Course in Writing*. 2nd ed. Cambridge: Winthrop, 1980.

———. "Staffing and Operating Peer-Tutoring Writing Centers." Kasden and Hoeber. 141–49.

Carino, Peter. "Early Writing Centers: Toward a History." *The Writing Center Journal* 15.2 (1995): 103–115.

Conference on College Composition and Communication. *Learning Skills Centers: A CCCC Report*. Urbana: NCTE, 1976.

Connors, Robert. "Journals in Composition Studies." *College English* 46 (1984): 348–365.

Flynn Tom, and Mary King. *Dynamics of the Writing Conference: Social and Cognitive Interaction*. Urbana, IL: NCTE, 1993.

Goldsby, Jackie. *Peer Tutoring in Basic Writing: A Tutor's Journal*. Classroom Research Study No. 4. University of California, Berkeley: Bay Area Writing Project, 1981.

Haring-Smith, Tori, Nathaniel Hawkins, Elizabeth Morrison, Lisa Stern, and Robin Tatu. *A Guide to Writing Programs: Writing Centers, Peer Tutoring Programs, and Writing-Across-the-Curriculum*. Glenview, IL: Scott, Foresman, 1985.

Harris, Muriel. "Growing Pains: The Coming of Age of Writing Centers." *The Writing Center Journal* 2.1 (1982): 1–8.

———, ed. *Tutoring Writing: A Sourcebook for Writing Labs*. Glenview, IL: Scott, Foresman, 1982.

Harris, Muriel, and Tracey Baker. "New Directions, New Connections." *Proceedings of the Writing Centers Association Fifth Annual Conference*. Purdue University, May 5–6, 1983.

Hartwell, Patrick. "A Writing Laboratory Model." Kasden and Hoeber. 63–73.

Hawkins, Nathaniel. "An Introduction to the History and Theory of Peer Tutoring in Writing." Haring-Smith et al. 7–18.

Hawkins, Thom, and Phyllis Brooks, eds. *Improving Writing Skills*. No. 3, *New Directions for College Learning Assistance*. San Francisco: Jossey-Bass, 1981.

Kasden, Lawrence N., and Daniel R. Hoeber, eds. *Basic Writing: Essays for Teachers, Researchers, and Administrators* Urbana, IL: NCTE, 1980.

Kelly, Lou. "One on One, Iowa City Style: Fifty Years of Individualized Instruction in Writing." *The Writing Center Journal* 1.1 (1980): 4–19.

Kinkead, Joyce A. "Minutes of the National Writing Centers Association, 1983–91."

Kinkead, Joyce A., and Jeanette G. Harris. *Writing Centers in Context: Twelve Case Studies*. Urbana, IL: NCTE, 1993.

Laque, Carol Feiser, and Phyllis A. Sherwood. *A Laboratory Approach to Writing*. Urbana, IL: NCTE, 1977.

McCracken, Nancy. "News from the National WCA" and "News from the Regions." *Writing Lab Newsletter* 8.1 (Sept. 1983): 6–7.

———. "Notice of NWCA." *Writing Lab Newsletter* 7.4 (Dec. 1982): 6.

Morrison, Elizabeth, and Robin Tatu. "From Rags to Riches: Writing Centers Grow Up." Haring-Smith et al. 1–6.

North, Stephen M. "Writing Centers: A Sourcebook." Ph.D. Diss. State University of New York, 1979.

Simpson, Jeanne. "What Lies Ahead for Writing Centers: Position Statement on Professional Concerns." *The Writing Center Journal* 5.2/6.1 (1985): 35–39.

Spooner, Michael. "Circles and Center: Sonic Thoughts on the Writing Center and Academic Book Publishing." *Writing Lab Newsletter* 17.10 (June 1993): 1–3, 10.

Steele, Mildred. "A Proposal for the 1980 CCCC?" *Writing Lab Newsletter* 4.4 (Dec. 1979): 3.

"A Statement Given in Behalf of a Resolution About Writing Lab Professionals." *Writing Lab Newsletter* 5.10 (June 1981): 4.

Steward, Joyce S., and Mary K. Croft. *The Writing Laboratory: Organization, Management, and Methods.* Glenview, IL: Scott, Foresman, 1982.

"Our Little Secret": A History of Writing Centers, Pre- to Post-Open Admissions [1999]

Elizabeth H. Boquet

> *Judy Russell didn't have an appointment but she waited anyway outside the new writing center at Fairfield University...She had never been to the writing center before and had no idea what it would be like.*
>
> *"My history teacher recommended the center to me," she said. "I hope I can get a fresh idea. I just didn't want to do a paper on Louis XIV."*
>
> *"It was terrific," Judy said. "She came up with it in two minutes. It was like her own little secret that she was saving for someone."*
> *(Lomuscio A6)*

Ten minutes later, the article goes on to tell us, Judy beamed with enthusiasm as she walked down the hall. A consultant from the center, English professor Laura Ress, had just given her a unique topic: how the French went to Ireland to help with the Irish Revolution. The photo inset shows a student seated next to Professor Ress, who is apparently talking and, pen in hand, seems poised to write.

I came across this article as I searched the archives of the writing center I now direct, the writing center at Fairfield University. Judging solely from this introduction, James Lomuscio's article, "Students get help at writing center," published in the Fairfield *Fairpress* on March 3, 1982, confirms the suspicions of many faculty and administrators and the worst fears of writing center professionals. At first glance, the student seems the passive recipient of the tutor's expertise and knowledge. Judy walks away with *the tutor's* secret, a slant on the topic that Judy acknowledges *the tutor* "came up with."

The rest of the article, however, consists of interviews with area writing center directors (from Fairfield, Yale, and the University of Connecticut), all of whom express fairly contemporary views on the methods and missions of their writing centers. The directors, for example, attribute the growth of writing centers to a recognition that incoming students have had little experience writing for "diverse audiences and in different subject areas" (A6). For this reason, these directors stress that their writing centers are open to anyone, and they cite examples of students coming to the center to work on graduate school applications and senior theses, as well as first-year composition papers. Dr. Mariann Regan, who developed the writing center at Fairfield University, explains, "The consultant works by questioning the student." Students cannot simply drop off their papers, Regan quips, because "we're not a laundry" (A6). Instead, she emphasizes the importance of students working *with* consultants.

It is difficult to know which of these is the master narrative in this case. Is it the one in which Judy leaves the writing center after ten minutes (!) to write a paper on the topic Professor Ress has "given" her? (Is Judy even capable of writing such a paper?) Or is it the one in which students are questioned, drawn out, in which student input is valued and encouraged? Is the writing center, in other words, primarily a *space*, a "laundry" where work is dropped off and picked up, where students are brushed off and cleaned up? Or is it primarily a *temporality*, an interaction between people over time, in which the nature of the interaction is determined not by site but by method?

When I began this history, I would have been afraid to admit how often the writing centers I've worked in—and now how often the one I direct—resembles the 1982 Fairfield writing center of Mariann Regan and Laura Ress. Too often, I've felt that my life in the writing center is a secret one, as I struggle with the injunction not to reveal too much in a writing center session, as I search for a positive spin on one of the writing center's less-than-successful ventures. My tutors now lead secret lives of their own, sneaking into my office and closing the door behind them so that they might broach a sensitive issue in private. Sometimes such privacy is warranted: when their concerns hint at their discomfort with a professor's pedagogical approach, for instance. Other times, though, their secrecy suggests an insecurity with their own perceived lack of expertise, and I wonder why they feel the question is worthy of such behavior. In fact, *what* they have to say is almost always less troubling than *how* they say it: the submissive posture, the eyes cast downward, the barely audible latching of the door, the thinly-veiled frustration in the voice.

As a graduate student, I turned to the literature on writing centers, I believe, searching for some consistency, so that I might be honest, in some idyllic sense, about what happens here. What I've learned since I began this history five years ago—and they are five years that have seen me move beyond my graduate program and into a permanent position—is to think differently about this secrecy, to view it not as hypocritical or dishonest or even (to be generous) strategic, but instead as endemic to the institutional position of writing centers.

I offer this piece of history of my own center, the writing center at Fairfield University, because it is so typical of the discourse framing writing center theory and practice, a discourse so perfectly at odds with itself. I say perfectly at odds because the at-odds-ness of the discourse so successfully escapes notice, suggesting that the contradiction exists, in the minds of those who use it, in the equilibrium that is characteristic of all apparently natural things. My aim here is in part to expose the existence of this contradiction in order to make possible a more self-conscious appraisal of the identity of writing centers at an especially crucial time in their history. This brief history of writing labs/clinics/centers makes evident the tension between the writing center whose identity rests on method and the writing center whose identity rests on site by offering an analysis of the sequence of discursive maneuvers that collapsed and distinguished and collapsed again the difference between method and site. This prying apart of space and method represents a rare but necessary move in our discussions of pedagogical practices.

In general our field has failed to consider writing centers an appropriate area of inquiry into composition's politics of location, yet writing centers remain one of the most powerful mechanisms whereby institutions can mark the bodies of students as foreign, alien to themselves. Foucault shows us, in the first pages of *Discipline and Punish*, that to extend power is to put it at risk. This has certainly been true of the university's relationship to the writing center, a symbiosis highlighting the degree to which institutional power becomes most vulnerable at the very point at which it becomes most visible. Nowhere in our field has this tension been more apparent than in the writing center, a space where the consolidation of power shifts as the idea of the writing center metamorphoses from being one whose identity rests on method to one whose identity rests on site, and back again.

THE EMERGENCE OF THE WRITING LABORATORY METHOD

Much ink has already been spilled, in this and other forums, on the 19th century "creation" of composition. It is difficult to know, from there, where to begin to trace the germ of an idea for the writing lab (as it was first called).

Is it, as Neal Lerner has suggested in "The Writing Conference as Dominant Practice," in the proliferation of the conference method of the late 1800s? Is it, as Anne Ruggles Gere's work might suggest, in the "extracurriculum" of composition? Before answering this question, I want to look at what is at stake in the potential conclusions we draw. If we accept that contemporary writing centers grew out of early methods, then we have strong support for a reading of writing centers as producing and sustaining hegemonic institutional discourses. Such a reading leads us to theories like that of Grimm's regulatory model, which constructs the writing center as an institutional site concerned with controlling the production of literacy. If, on the other hand, we locate writing center origins in the extracurriculum, we then set the precedent for a counter-hegemonic model of writing center operations, one which attempts to wrest authority out of the hands of the institution and place it in the hands of the students. (See, for example, the work of Marilyn Cooper and John Trimbur.)

Personally, I find Gere's account more appealing, though it is difficult to place the writing lab in Gere's extracurriculum of composition, precisely because the sites described by Gere were designed to foster empowerment and autonomy, ideas for which there is painfully scant support in the early articles on the writing lab method. I find locating the writing lab in Gere's extracurriculum of composition tempting because this configuration highlights the politics of location that have proven so crucial in discussions about the institutional placement of writing centers. As much as I might like to think that the extracurriculum exerted the primary influence over the development of writing labs, ultimately I am inclined to trace the development through the more typical institutional channels. Doing so makes Lerner's conference method theory more probable, particularly when we consider the intimate links between early writing labs and first-year composition instruction. Neither account, however, makes sense of the at-odds-ness noted throughout. The origin of that story of the writing center, the story that writing center staff live on a day-to-day basis, is in the later moment when the lab shifted from method to site and when the liberatory possibilities of the writing center arose, in Foucauldian terms, as an "accident," an ever-present, always possible, though not necessarily intended, outcome ("Nietzsche" 144).

The writing laboratory of the early 20th century was conceived of not as a *place* at all but rather as a *method* of instruction, the key characteristic of which appears to have been that all work was to be done during class time, enabling the instructor "to eliminate errors or other weaknesses at their source and not allow their use at all, thus precluding the possibility of their becoming habitual through thoughtless repetition" (Horner 218).[1] Under the careful gaze of the instructor, students labored, afforded the opportunity first to self-correct errors in drafts and, failing that, to have their papers corrected immediately, line by line, by the instructor himself, thereby encouraging the internalization of discursive norms.

That the laboratory method changed the conditions under which students composed seems true enough. Students went from listening to instructors talk about writing to actually doing the writing themselves. That the method emerged from or resulted in a fundamental reconception of knowledge production and dissemination in the classroom or beyond, however, seems doubtful. Rather, it seems to have simply shifted, slightly but significantly, the *site* of discursive regulation.

AUTONOMOUS WRITING LABS

A slow drift occurred between the 1920s, when the writing lab was most recognizably a method of instruction, and the 1940s, when it became most recognizably a site, and the writing on writing labs begins to show evidence of the tension emerging between the institutional space of the writing center and the individual pedagogies enacted in that space.

Structurally, writing labs remained closely tied to the scene of the classroom and became integral parts of the institutional desire to track students according to ability. At some institutions, students each week attended a writing lecture and a writing lab.[2] Pedagogically, though, instructors began to demonstrate an awareness of the benefits of the writing labs for students, independent of the administrative hierarchies in which they functioned (Stanley; Grandy). These authors framed the work of the writing lab as encouraging dialogue, even dialectic, much as we in writing centers do today.[3] The execution of that work proceeded, however, in a manner that belied consideration of writing lab space in those terms. Instead, individual students— like Judy, whom we met at the beginning of this piece—were portrayed as having been shown the light, for which they were eternally grateful. For example, when Stanley, the first director of the writing lab at the University of Iowa, writes of the benefits of having a student think through what he or she wants to say before writing it, she claims, "In this way is the once baffled one now truly learning to guide his own thinking" (425).

All in all Stanley sees the writing center as "com[ing] very close to meeting the ends of true education" by encouraging students to be independent writers and thinkers (428). She does not, however, elaborate on what such an ideological becoming might entail, and her readers are left to wonder if true education means internalizing organizational patterns and mechanical rules, as the early part of her article suggests, or if it has more to do with the empowerment she writes of at the end of her article, "the tangible evidence of accomplishment, eagerness and industry and pride [which] begin to replace indifference and laziness; [the] fear and antagonism [which] begin to give way to self-confidence and optimism" (428).

Stanley's article, one of the first to tease out the pedagogical significance of the writing lab, is also perhaps the first to hint at the at-odds-ness of the writing lab's existence. Her rhetoric suggests the degree to which the site of the writing lab carries with it the politics of the writing lab, a fact which becomes clear to her readers when they learn years later that, as the writing lab at Stanley's University of Iowa becomes increasingly autonomous, it also becomes increasingly tied to specific students, namely remedial students, and tied to serving a specific curriculum. Stanley's earlier vision of the writing lab as a site for dialectical engagement—though problematic in its execution, as noted earlier—is supplanted by a view of the writing lab as a center for remediation, replaced by what is later termed the lab's "official function: to provide instruction for the students whose placement themes did not meet departmental standards" (Kelly 5).

The call for standards and individuation, like that taking place at the University of Iowa, was part of a larger political agenda driving educational initiatives at this time, as Berlin has discussed at great length elsewhere (see *Rhetoric and Reality*). Two resultant educational initiatives (both an outgrowth of World War II) spurred on the transition from classroom-bound to free-standing labs: (1) the appointment of a Presidential Commission on Higher Education, charged with studying the role of higher education in shaping and maintaining the democratic fabric of the nation and (2) the communications programs appearing on campuses nationwide.[4] Taken together, these initiatives resulted in a curriculum geared to present information in conservative, current-traditional terms, ostensibly, according to Berlin, "in the service of the democratic ideals recently challenged from abroad," ("Writing Instruction" 202) an emphasis resulting in a focus on the individual, practical, skills-centered nature of composing (Berlin, *Rhetoric and Reality* 97). The writing labs they spawned focused primarily on the individual rather than the social nature of composing, and individual improvement was often seen as necessary only for remedial students. Hence the situation at University of Iowa.

Another striking example occurred at the University of North Carolina's Composition Condition Laboratory, a center designed specifically as a grammar fix-it shop. At UNC, if an instructor thought that a student needed to work on his (or possibly her) writing, the instructor would place a "CC" behind the final grade, indicating that the student had, apparently, a "composition condition" and should be tested at the writing lab. Descriptions such as these place increasing responsibility on the student for his or her failure and decreasing responsibility on the educational system, specifically on classroom instructors. The bodies of writers are thus publicly marked for their deficiencies and treated appropriately.

What is lacking in the UNC example is any discussion or characterization of the work done in the "CC" lab. Readers are left to wonder, in other words, about the relationship between site and method in this instance. After all, a "CC" may tell us something about the institutional climate in which the lab was operating, particularly since the UNC composition laboratory apparently served as a deterrent on campus, but it tells us nothing beyond that.[5] I continue to remind myself to work against the temptation of focusing on the shortcomings of much of the early literature, and my own writing center helps to keep me honest in this regard. This morning, for example, a student arrived in my writing center with a previously graded paper which he was trying to revise. Set apart from the instructor's comments, stretching diagonally across the bottom of the page, was one dictate: "Go to the Writing Center!" This directive strikes me as not so different from the "CC" of decades ago, and it is a frequent occurrence in the writing center, one about which I have been able to do very little. Certainly I can talk to my colleague about this problematic demand, explain to him how it makes our job in the writing center that much more difficult. But I probably cannot significantly impact the perspective which led him to pen this, even if on occasion I do succeed in getting him to stop writing it.

Though my colleague still sees the writing center as a disciplinary measure, I would like to think that what students find once they arrive here is something exceeding that. While I resist the formulation of the writing center as a "safe house," as an unthreatening environment where students feel free to explore ideas, I do believe that it offers possibilities not intended or accounted for in the original administrative idea of the writing center. Such accidents exploit the tension set out in this essay. And, as we move through the history, we can begin to see more clearly the emergence of these counter-institutional impulses.

The most significant of these moves occurred when the autonomous writing lab gained legitimacy through its association with psychological principles. The field of composition has long relied on its association with psychology to shore up its claims about language development and acquisition. Beginning in the 1940s, psychology offered educators another means of thinking about the ways of regulating behavior, a model based less on the behaviorist principles alluded to above—with its fear of reinforcement and emphasis on aversion—and more on the cognitivist principles gaining respect in psychotherapeutic circles. Davidson and Sorenson, the two most vocal proponents of this psychotherapeutic approach to writing lab work, advocate an approach they refer to as Rogerian nondirective counseling, a method which has psychotherapists ask questions in order to draw out their patients, leading to knowledge these clients presumably already possess. Rogerian nondirective counseling provided then yet another means for individual students to be held accountable for their own successes as well as for their shortcomings by making students responsible for accessing information which continually eludes them.

More importantly, however, the Rogerian nondirective method succeeds in securing the space of the writing lab as sacrosanct, as distinct from the classroom, a space where students should feel secure in their expression of thoughts and ideas, as they should in a therapist's office. It is through this therapeutic closed-door policy that writing centers begin to engage in some version of counter-hegemonic work, supported by a doctor-patient privilege which ushers in both a model for professionalism and an invitation for tutors to assume a neutral posture (at least as an ideal).

It is also at this time that we begin to see the institutional goals for these labs and clinics, goals clearly linked to remediation, to preparing the un-(der)prepared, conflicting with the goals of individual writing center staff members, who reject the marginalization of either the writing lab or the students who chose (or were sent) to use it. Writing labs begin to be characterized in the literature as places where average students can get help with content and organizational problems, a step forward from the primarily remediation-oriented labs mentioned earlier. They become places where the time lag between writing and response can be addressed and where the importance of immediate feedback on writing is valued and encouraged (Millet and Morton). Students are encouraged to write about what interests them, and models for response are cast in more collaborative, even dialogic, terms (Perrin). It remains unclear whether institutions viewed their writing centers in this manner. In fact, it seems more likely that the literature at this time offers the beginnings of an articulation of professionalism predicated on doctor-patient privilege bordering at times on the collusion of staff and students against administration, a familiar refrain in later writing center work.

Davidson and Sorenson themselves, in their advocacy of the psychotherapeutic approach to tutoring, invoke narratives recognizable to contemporary composition professionals—the problem of writer's block, the teaching of grammar only in context, and the goal of producing independent writers, for example (86). In their writing about the communications course, however, Davidson and Sorenson fall prey to the same kinds of stock characterizations as Stanley, with the clinician poised, *deus ex machina,* to rescue the plot. They write, for example, that the writing clinic benefits all students, but not for the reasons we might expect. They note that exceptional students are often not "adequately adjusted in the field of human relations" and that "students who have received A grades in high school English are often ego-centric introverts" (84).

Because the clinic's strategies blurred the line between composition and therapy in ways that left many professionals uncomfortable and pathologized student behavior (as the above quote suggests), Denver's methods quickly came under fire. Shortly after Frederick Sorenson left the University of Denver, he publicly recanted his earlier methods in *College English*:

> The "Writing Clinic" was a tragic semantic blunder on the part of somebody who figured that if there was a Speech Clinic and a Reading Clinic, there should be a Writing Clinic too. (325)

Of course, he fails to explain why the Speech Clinic and the Reading Clinic were not "tragic semantic blunders" as well.

THE "MYSTERIOUS DISAPPEARANCE" OF THE WRITING LAB

Sorenson's recantation began to seem premonitory as I searched for traces of writing labs and clinics in the literature of the mid- to late 1950s; for, while writing labs seemed to hold great promise in the early part of that decade (see Moore 1950), they effectively disappear shortly thereafter. The disappearance may in part simply be attributed to "a limitation in the documentary record" (Stephen North, personal correspondence, 7 January 1998). The question remains, though: Why, just as writing labs were gaining some legitimacy as an area of academic inquiry, did they suddenly fall out of intellectual favor?

In his 1995 article "Early Writing Centers: Toward a History," Carino considers this disappearance curious, noting, "One would think that the post-Sputnik emphasis on American education would have spawned more [writing labs] in the late 1950s and early 1960s" (108). Here, Carino is partially correct: the Cold War did indeed generate public interest in the adequacy of American students' educational preparedness. That interest manifested itself, however, primarily in the arenas of math and science.[6]

A more plausible theory, also briefly entertained by Carino, involves the resurgence of linguistics (108). Coupled with the cross-disciplinary rise of formalism in the 1950s, linguistics provided a mechanism through which readers could go in search of a stable, independent meaning in each text. The task of writers, then, was simply to produce such a text. (See "Where Did Composition Studies Come From: An Intellectual History," Nystrand, Greene, and Wiemelt.) The rise of linguistics, particularly structural linguistics, in the composition classroom of the 1950s marked a return to the scientific, objectivist thought of earlier eras. It rationalized the study of language, taxonomized the complexities of human discourse. The implications for writing labs become clear when Guyer promises that, through linguistics, these forms and patterns "become manipulable not only intuitively by gifted students but consciously by all students" (310). So, instead of leading us to the lab, as the scientific (lecture-lab) model did in the first few decades of this century, this empirical model lent itself to whole class techniques, patterns which once mastered, *en masse,* enabled any one student theoretically to compose a competent five-paragraph theme. The interdependence of site and method in writing labs had not been so clear since the writing lab method emerged in early twentieth century classrooms. If students did not need to be segregated—if a method were developed, in other words, which offered equal promise to both the strongest and the weakest student—then there would be no need for a separate site, no cause for treatments or cures.

Of course, some writers were in fact left behind in the large-group explanations of phonemes and morphemes and syntax and lexicons—the non-elect, as Harvard called them in the 1870s; the non-trads, as they are often called today—but they were being funneled off university and four-year college campuses in droves in the late 50s and early 60s, shunted off instead to what Shor calls the "budget campuses," community colleges (*Culture Wars* 3).[7] This mass segregation of working class students onto two-year campuses lessened the need for institutional defense mechanisms like writing labs, at least for a while, enabling four-year colleges and universities to get back to the "real business" of teaching. Kitzhaber, for instance, notes "an accelerating decline in the number of remedial courses being offered on college campuses" (qtd. in Berlin, *Rhetoric and Reality* 128). He also notices that "proficiency exams in English for sophomores and juniors were being eliminated because so few students were failing them" (128). A final key observation is the one in which Kitzhaber acknowledges, "As provisions for less able students were decreasing, those for the best students were increasing" (128).

WRITING CENTERS, OPEN ADMISSIONS, AND THE LITERACY CRISIS

Despite the field's insistence that writing centers are institutionally specific (which they are—as is every program on a college campus, to one degree or another), the histories of open-admissions writing centers share some striking similarities. From the beginning, these writing centers were forced to take a defensive stance within their institutions. The theme of crisis intervention is repeated over and over again in the scant histories written about writing centers during the 1970s, as writing centers were created largely to fix problems that university officials had difficulty even naming, things like increasing enrollment, larger minority populations, and declining (according to the public) literacy skills. Exactly how writing centers were to address these problems, however, is never quite clear.[8] Writing centers begin to reappear in the literature at this time, albeit infrequently. Site and method come into more direct conflict as this period progresses, largely because authors move away from mere descriptions of their labs (a tactic which kept the literature fairly focused on site) and toward theoretical justifications of writing lab work. Situating labs within a philosophical framework leads quite naturally to discussions of method, and these conversations make apparent the methodological differences operating in the various lab arrangements. The discussions fall into fairly consistent "camps": (1) those who champion auto-tutorial methods and materials, (2) those who critique these types of programmed instruction, and (3) those who seek alternatives to the traditional forms of instruction heretofore provided by writing labs.

For all its faults, the auto-tutorial model had significant implications for the marriage of site and method in the writing lab. Descriptions of auto-tutorial labs, like those provided in York College's COMP-LAB materials, make obvious as never before the space of the writing lab as a technology. The salient features of these spaces were their headsets, audiotapes, and workbooks, all of which allowed the students to work individually (without a tutor, that is) on grammatical errors (Kirkpatrick 17). Cost was often a key factor in implementing the autotutorial model, since one-time equipment costs are easier to justify administratively than ongoing costs such as staffing. These writing labs were also not without their own pedagogical philosophies, rationales which usually appeal to the participatory nature of the autotutorial, the individual pacing, and the increased sense of student responsibility. One wonders, however, whether students want or even deserve to shoulder that burden. As Lerner ("Drill Pads") notes, these modules conveniently place the blame for students' difficulties on them, rather than acknowledging the responsibilities of their teachers or the educational system or society at large (np).

In a variety of forums, critics of programmed instruction advocate a more careful consideration of work appropriate to student needs and respectful of student intelligence (Almasy; Veit). In his defense of individualized instruction, Veit claims, "Machines take a narrow view of students' needs" (2). While acknowledging the appeal of programmed instruction in notoriously under-staffed, under-funded labs, these critics nevertheless feel committed to what they deem the fundamental principle of the writing lab: one-to-one contact with "a human being who cares" (2). This philosophy, an extension of the Rogerian non-directive/mirroring model of writing lab operations, led these labs to define themselves in opposition to their auto-tutorial counterparts, to characterize the lab spaces as non-threatening (however specious) and to fill them with creature comforts—couches, plants, coffee pots, posters.

Other labs began to fill their spaces for the first time with peer tutors, a move leading to perhaps the greatest long-term implications for the site-method dichotomy in writing labs. Describing his experiences with tutorial assistance in the late 60s and early 70s. Bruffee observed that those students having difficulty with their classes refused to take advantage of the programs designed to assist them

> *because [these programs] seemed to them merely an extension of the work, the expectations, and above all the social structure of traditional classroom learning. And it was traditional classroom learning that seemed to have left these students unprepared in the first place. What they needed...was help of a sort that was not an extension but an alternative to the traditional classroom.* ("Peer Tutoring" 4)

The solution, according to Bruffee, is peer tutoring, an approach which changes not "what people [learn] but, rather, the social context in which they [learn] it" ("Peer Tutoring" 5).

The presence of peer tutors addressed, though imperfectly, both the call for human contact and the very real fiscal constraints faced by labs (since peer tutors are less expensive to employ than faculty). Peer tutors also deepened the writing lab's debt to psychology by relying once again on major figures in that field (specifically, Piaget and Vygotsky) to provide a philosophical rationale for current writing lab operations.

For the first time, the space of the writing center is characterized as active and tutors are portrayed as having as much to learn as they have to teach. Bruffee offers his rationale for the peer tutorial by citing several studies on the importance, and the under-utilization, of peer-group influence on intellectual development. Though he expects that students would "learn and practice judgment collaboratively" ("Brooklyn Plan" 450), he notes what he calls "two not entirely expected results" of this plan: the first, that students need more than help with so-called "skills" development; and second, that the peer tutors themselves actually seem to be benefiting from the program. He writes, "There is nothing in the literature on peer tutoring which would lead us to expect that average and somewhat above-average undergraduates acting as tutors could develop so rapidly through a process of peer influence a capacity so essential to mature thought" ("Brooklyn Plan" 451). By the middle of the article, Bruffee is on to the transformative potential of the writing center: "Peer-groups can influence the means, power, and criteria by which we make discriminations" ("Brooklyn Plan" 453). So, while the original intention of the Brooklyn plan was merely a modified version of the older lab model, with weaker students coming to benefit from the knowledge of stronger students, the plan actually came to embody what would become the focus of Bruffee's work in the field—the benefits of collaborative learning for all participants—while foreshadowing the radical educational thrust of later writing center theorists (Warnock and Warnock, Cooper, Trimbur, Kail and Trimbur).

The presence of peer tutors affected, naturally, the space of the writing lab and the method of writing lab operations, both in terms of the manner of work with students and the preparation of the staff for such work. Upon entering the writing labs, students for the first time saw faces that resembled their own and they saw signs of student investment in that space. Students ceased to simply visit the writing center; they began, with the advent of peer tutoring, to inhabit it, to hang hand-lettered renditions of favorite quotations on the wall, to jot down jokes on the board, to leave their own work on the tables while answering a question. Peer tutors also inhabit student writing in a manner that their faculty counterparts cannot, simply because of their different relationship to the academic system of rewards.

At the same time, peer tutors necessitated the gradual development of a method for training writing lab staff. (Implicit in the rise of this issue is, of course, the assumption that faculty would know how to tutor but students would not.) This training began as, and remains, a hybrid, like the writing center itself, a mix of institutional accountability and critique, of credit-bearing courses and informal discussions over pizza or doughnuts. The tenor of national discussions about the work taking place in these labs changed as well. Beginning in the late 1970s, articles on writing labs in *CCC* and *College English* focus almost exclusively on staff selection and training. Much of the work at this time highlights, as Bruffee's *Liberal Education* article did, the non-authoritarian orientation of the peer tutor's writing lab, contrasting it, in a move that continues to dog writing center staff, with the inherently hierarchical classroom configuration. (See, for example, the February 1980 issue of *CCC*.) In offering specific advice and suggestions for setting up a peer tutoring program, these authors feel compelled, for obvious reasons, to provide a convincing rationale for embarking upon such an undertaking in the first place.

WRITING CENTERS AND POST-OPEN ADMISSIONS

A post-open admissions category is, of course, a slippery slope: How does one know when or whether open admissions became "post?" The concerns of open admissions writing labs were not new, having been factors in the writing lab's existence throughout its history. And the problems of open admissions writing labs have yet to be solved. With that said, I am placing the beginning of the post-open admissions writing center somewhere around 1980, give or take a year or two.[9] By this time, national forums for writing centers have emerged, and influential figures—like Bruffee, Harris, and North—have appeared on the national scene, publicly hashing out, not merely reporting, issues of interest to a growing writing center community. Truth be told, with a few notable exceptions, the most interesting work in writing centers, post-1980, is to be found not in the pages of the major journals in composition or English studies but in the forums designed specifically to house writing center work. The relationship between writing centers and composition studies, as that relationship has been represented in the pages of *CCC* and *College English,* becomes increasingly ambivalent, with writing center scholars continually called on to articulate (as per Grimm's most recent piece) the relevance of writing center work to the field as a whole, as though it were not an area as self-evident as, say, basic writing or computer technology.

Early articles on staff training turn away from a consideration of the writing lab *as* writing lab and turn toward a consideration of the writing lab as a site for work more generally recognizable as contemporary composition studies. In a 1982 *CCC* article, James Collins carefully lays out the rationale for a teacher training program set up to run through his writing lab. North's article in that same issue returns us to a more familiar writing center discussion—tutor training—but his essay too, in contrast to earlier pieces, integrates work emerging on the composing process with the work of tutors in the writing center, positioning the tutor securely *within* the process of writing. While this may be merely a slight shift from earlier work, all of which foregrounds the writing *lab* and backgrounds the writing, it is a significant one and one which sets the stage for North's next piece, the one which has received, in the writing center community at least, the most attention: his 1984 polemic "The Idea of a Writing Center."

Between North's 1982 and 1984 pieces, the only article on writing centers appearing either in the pages of *CCC* or *College English* is Harvey Kail's "Collaborative Learning in Context: The Problem with Peer Tutoring." Kail's article, though it is rarely mentioned, actually prefigures North's "Idea" in both tone and perspective. And, more than either of North's pieces, it suggests the radical/dialogic/liberatory shift which marks much recent writing center work. Kail makes clear that the "problem" of peer tutoring is likely to be the faculty, who are uncomfortable with the shift from a lineal to a nonlineal pedagogy presupposed by a peer tutoring program and who are anxious about the potential such a program has for exposing them and their methods. Kail, therefore, resists the construction of writing center as "other" by downplaying the significance of the site and foregrounding the significance of the method, one which Kail suggests could be equally applicable (if difficult to implement) in classrooms as well as in the writing center. By the end of the article, Kail does not seem at all certain about the continuation of peer tutoring and suggests instead that peer tutoring programs may simply require a greater epistemological shift than our academic institutions can bear (598). Like North, Kail insists that peer tutoring be done "right," in a manner which by design complicates the teacher-student-tutor-director relationship in ways that the lineal model of fix-it shop tutoring did not.

North's "Idea" continues to problematize that relationship; and, as such, it represents the preeminent admission of the at-odds-ness noted throughout this essay. The piece is replete with examples of the ways in which goals of the writing center staff often conflict with institutional goals as those goals are represented by faculty, by administrators, even by the students themselves. North's model is reminiscent of the Rogerian writing center, the sanctified, professional space in which one can engage in counter-hegemonic operations to ultimately sustain institutional goals, often at the expense of the students it purports to serve. That agenda, though, is couched in a decidedly Woolfian interpretation of the value of the writing center, one emphasizing the necessity of room and time and teachable moments.

There is, of course, value in making a case for such luxuries, perks which are too few and far between, particularly for writing center professionals, many of whom still have no job security, heavy teaching loads, and little if any institutional support. "Idea" has been canonized, then, less for what it says about the method of the writing center, philosophies even North himself has admitted are problematic ("Revisiting"), than for what it suggests about the professionalization of the practitioner. "Idea" carved out an institutional space where it was necessary, even preferable, to just *do*, where doing was in fact the height of professionalism, an appealing prospect, in light of composition's recent turn to the theoretical, for those who won't or simply can't sit back and ponder the cause before (or even after) dealing with the effect. But where does this leave us as a scholarly community?

At the 1997 meeting of the National Writing Centers Association, Christina Murphy, one of the association's recent past-presidents, referred to what she perceived as a "bankruptcy of writing center scholarship." Though her comment predictably troubled much of the membership, it did not then and it does not now strike me as wrong. I will admit it, even though I am afraid to: much recent work in writing centers is not interesting to me. While such an admission may sound petulant, it is nevertheless an important criteria for intellectual activity. I say this especially because I am committed to a career in the writing center, because I desperately need to find the space for the kind of sustained intellectual inquiry which led me to choose academia as a profession, and because I know the writing center potentially could be that space. So, while the issues most recent writing center discussions focus on— how to fund, set-up, and publicize an on-line writing lab, for example—are all issues that I too must consider in the administrative execution of my job, they do not get at what is most challenging to me about my work in the writing center: the excessive institutional possibilities that the writing center represents. The way in which the writing center exceeds its space, despite the university's best efforts to contain it; the way in which the writing center exceeds its method, with tutors going off-task, with students (more often than not) setting them back on-track, negotiating academic demands in the midst of an e-mail message from a distant love, a bagel and a smear from the downstairs coffee bar, a brief but meaningful announcement from a comrade in flip-flops and shades that the sun is finally shining and everyone should march outside.

These are moments not accounted for, really, in North's version of the writing center, and the question is, I suppose, why not? It is possible that they didn't even occur, though it seems more likely that they did and that they were just not considered important. They may have even been viewed as drawbacks in a writing center desperately seeking to be taken seriously, to attain some measure of disciplinary status. Patricia Harkin has written that "disciplinary inquiries can be strategies of containment; these strategies achieve coherence by shutting out or repressing the contradictions that have their source in history" (135). Though North's essay does more to expose contradictions than it does to suppress them, it ultimately attempts to contain the interpretation of the writing center, both in terms of site and method. As such it constructs the writing center as a predictably disciplinary entity, complete with spatial boundaries, established protocols and procedures, and reasonably replicable methods.

Yet the writing center is most interesting to me for its post-disciplinary possibilities, for the contradictions it embraces, for its tendency to go off-task. And I would like to argue, as I come to the conclusion of this history, that we would do well to think of the future of writing centers in excessive terms. To do so does *not* mean that writing centers should grow as large as they possibly can or spend as much money as they can get their hands on or stake out claims all over campus in order to ensure their survival. Rather, an excessive theory of writing center operations requires us to seek out the overflow of the expected in all its forms, asks us to create a space for play, as Nancy Welch suggested in a recent keynote address. An excessive writing center rejects the "form-as-reproducible" model (Sirc 10) of low-risk/low-yield tutoring in favor of higher-risk/higher-yield strategies. It does away with the script for the how-to-write-a-research-paper session or the why-the-writing-center-does-not-constitute-plagiarism defense and insists on less predictable but potentially more productive conversations which wander, circle, and return again to the point where they began. This is not a failing; it is instead a part of the process, the nature of scholarly inquiry, and it is what we must engage in ourselves if we hope to model it for our students. Because, for all of our championing of process and collaboration, we have actually constructed writing centers that are all about the singular object, the "thing" that we can point to, and neither the number of computers we install nor the number of students we tutor in a year—evidence, surely, of our fetishization of the finished product—will fundamentally alter that fact. We must, instead, pay more attention to the things that don't always demand our attention, must remember that we only get answers to the questions that we ask and that the asking determines the answers.

Authoring this history has been, for me, a process of de-familiarizing the familiar in order to open up space for new possibilities. Foucault writes that the practice of genealogy invites us "to study the beginning—numberless beginnings whose faint traces and hints of color are readily seen by an historical eye" ("Nietzsche" 145). The history of the writing center is, as I suggested earlier, best told as a history whose intentions are cross-cut by Foucauldian accidents, by unanticipated outcomes. Administrators certainly didn't envision it as a source of radical or liberatory pedagogy, though it is often that. Bruffee didn't initially imagine it as a place where students and tutors alike would profit intellectually, though it is clearly that. Many of us find it difficult to believe that the writing center may be a site of regulation rather than liberation, though it seems certainly that (Grimm, "Rearticulating"). We are left to wonder, then, what we are failing to imagine now for our writing centers. What "faint traces and hints of color" are not present to our eyes? What is being left out of our discussions on teaching writing by our failure to account for the work of the writing center in a critically intellectual manner? And, conversely, what is being left out of our discussions on writing centers by our inability to account, in complex ways, for its relationship to the teaching of writing? By our continued insistence that writing centers give us simply the hard numbers, just the facts?

The Foucauldian accident is, of course, all about perspective, about who gets to author the history being told. Other stories can be brought to light, stories which write the developments of the contemporary writing center in theoretically sophisticated ways, stories which consider the critical capacities of networking, of linking writing centers with WAC programs, of placing peer tutors in classrooms. Stories which draw on the history, and the continued problematic, of the at-odds-ness inherent in the writing center in order to pry apart distinctions which have become fused in our discussions of writing center theory and practice, enabling us to tease them out in a manner consonant with our intimate relationship to the teaching of writing in our institutions. All of these stories can be written. Should be written. Are waiting to be written. Will be written.

Or not.

Acknowledgments: The following people have offered careful readings as well as much-needed support and encouragement throughout the development of this project: Steve North, Nancy Welch, Neal Lerner, Meg Carroll, Peter Gray, Mark Hurlbert and, especially, Geoff Sanborn.

NOTES

1. Horner's article summarizes the findings of his master's thesis, an empirical study which sought to compare the effectiveness of the laboratory method to the

effectiveness of the lecture method. In the end, the results, which are fairly inconclusive, are far less interesting than his point-by-point explanation of the laboratory method.

2. See, for example, Grandy, who describes a writing laboratory in which lecture and lab are combined in one course. On days when the class meets in the lab, students must have some writing completed upon their arrival (thus distinguishing it from Horner's model). Once in the lab, students take their places in assigned seats and begin to write, while "those in charge go around as rapidly as possible to see that no one is off on the wrong track" (374). Grandy acknowledges, "This sometimes happens, and that student has to be put right at once" (374).

3. It is worth noting that the laboratory described by Grandy was administered through the College of Science, Literature, and the Arts solely for students enrolled in Freshman English at the University of Minnesota. This differentiates it from the writing laboratory that was operating at the same time through the General College there. Grandy notes, "[T]he work as carried on in [the General] College is very different" (i.e. remedial) (372).

4. Following the publication of the Commission's report, increasing numbers of schools tied their communications programs to a common core of knowledge emphasizing democratic ideals, in part, it seems likely, to secure a portion of the committee's federal funding recommendations (Berlin, *Rhetoric and Reality* 99).

5. For example, Bailey notes that since students tried to avoid being sent to the lab, they became especially careful about neatness and surface concerns (148).

6. Kitzhaber traces Project English, a program underwritten by the government to update the English education curriculum in America. "Project English," Kitzhaber writes, "was, in the first place, little more than a somewhat delayed reflex action to the stimulus provided by Russian scientific achievements" (135). The primary outcome of Project English, interestingly enough for the purposes of this article, was the development of Curriculum Study Centers, which were touted as "the chief source of hopes for a 'New English' worthy to stand alongside the 'New Math' and 'New Science'" (135).

7. Here, the influence of the Commission's 1947 report, *Higher Education for American Democracy*, seems undeniable. The report offered clear support in its plan for increasing the profile of the community college system; and though the committee cautions against the development of purely vocationally-oriented technical colleges, it appears the warnings went unheeded (69–70).

8. See, for example, the histories of writing centers recounted in Kinkead and Harris' *Writing Centers in Context: Twelve Case Studies.*

9. *The Writing Lab Newsletter*, founded by Muriel Harris, went to press in 1978 and *The Writing Center Journal*, with co-editors Stephen North and Lil Brannon, in 1980.

WORKS CITED

Almasy, Rudolph. "Instructional Materials for the Writing Laboratory." CCC 27 (1976): 400–03.

Bailey, J. O. "Remedial Composition for Advanced Students." *College English* 8 (1946): 145–48.

Berlin, James A. *Rhetoric and Reality: Writing Instruction in American Colleges, 1900–1985.* Carbondale: Southern Illinois UP, 1987.

———. "Writing Instruction in School and College English, 1890–1985." *A Short History of Writing Instruction From Ancient Greece to Twentieth-Century America.* Ed. James J. Murphy. Davis: Hermagoras, 1990. 183–220.

Bruffee, Kenneth A. "The Brooklyn Plan: Attaining Intellectual Growth through Peer-Group Tutoring." *Liberal Education* 64 (1978): 447–68.

———. "Peer Tutoring and the 'Conversation of Mankind'." *Writing Centers: Theory and Administration.* Ed. Gary Olson. Urbana: NCTE, 1984. 3–15.

Carino, Peter. "Early Writing Centers: Toward a History." *Writing Center Journal* 15 (1995): 103–15.

Collins, James L. "Training Teachers of Basic Writing in the Writing Laboratory." *CCC* 33 (1982): 426–33.

Cooper, Marilyn M. "'Really Useful Knowledge': A Cultural Studies Agenda for Writing Centers." *Writing Center Journal* 14 (1994): 97–111.

Davidson, Levette J. and Frederick Sorenson. "The Basic Communication Course." *College English* 8 (1946): 83–86.

Foucault, Michel. *Discipline and Punish:* Trans. Alan Sheridan. 2nd ed. New York: Vintage, 1995.

———. "Nietzsche, Genealogy, History." *Language, Counter-memory, Practice: Selected Essays and Interviews by Michel Foucault.* Ed. Donald F. Bouchard. Ithaca: Cornell UP, 1977. 139–64.

Gere, Anne Ruggles. "The Extracurriculum of Composition." *CCC* 45 (1994): 75–92.

Grandy, Adam G. "A Writing Laboratory." *English Journal* 25 (1936): 372–76.

Grimm, Nancy. "Rearticulating the Work of the Writing Center." *CCC* 47 (1996):523–548.

———. "The Regulatory Role of the Writing Center: Coming to Terms with a Loss of Innocence." *Writing Center Journal* 17 (1996): 5–29.

Guyer, Byron. "Some Uses of Linguistics and Semantics in Freshman English." *College English* 19 (1958): 309–12.

Harkin, Patricia. "The Postdisciplinary Politics of Lore." *Contending with Words: Composition and Rhetoric in a Postmodern Age.* Eds. Patricia Harkin and John Schilb. New York: MLA, 1991. 124–38.

Higher Education for American Democracy, A Report. Vol. 1. Washington: US Government Printing Office, 1945.

Horner, Warren B. "The Economy of the Laboratory Method." *English Journal* 18 (1929): 214–21.

Kail, Harvey. "Collaborative Learning in Context: The Problem with Peer Tutoring." *College English* 45 (1983): 594–99.

Kail, Harvey and John Trimbur. "The Politics of Peer Tutoring." *WPA: Writing Program Administration* 11.1–2 (1987): 5–12.

Kelly, Lou. "One on One, Iowa City Style: Fifty Years of Individualized Instruction in Writing." *Writing Center Journal* 1 (1980): 4–21.

Kinkead, Joyce A. and Jeanette G. Harris, eds. *Writing Centers in Context: Twelve Case Studies.* Urbana: NCTE, 1993.

Kirkpatrick, Carolyn. "The Case for Autotutorial Materials." *New Directions for College Learning Assistance: Improving Writing Skills.* Eds. Thom Hawkins and Phyllis Brooks. San Francisco: Jossey-Bass, 1981. 15–23.

Kitzhaber, Albert. "The Government and English Teaching: A Retrospective View." *CCC* 18 (1967): 135–41.

Lerner, Neal. "Drill Pads, Teaching Machines, and Programmed Texts: Origins of Institutional Technology in Writing Centers." *Wiring the Writing Center.* Ed. Eric H. Hobson. Logan: Utah State UP, 1998. 119–36.

———. "The Writing Conference as Dominant Practice: An Historical View." 12th Annual New England Writing Centers Association Conference. Amherst, MA. 2 March 1996.

Lomuscio, James. "Students Get Help at Writing Center." *Fairfield Fairpress* 3 March 1982: A6.

Millet, Stanton and James L. Morton. "Round Table: The Writing Laboratory at Indiana University." *College English* 18 (1956): 38–39.

Moore, Robert H. "The Writing Clinic and the Writing Laboratory." *College English* 11 (1950): 388–393.

North, Stephen M. "The Idea of a Writing Center." *College English* 46 (1984): 433–446.

———. Personal Correspondence. 7 January 1998.

———. "Revisiting 'The Idea of a Writing Center'." *The Writing Center Journal* 15 (1994): 7–19.

———. "Training Tutors to Talk about Writing." *CCC* 33 (1982): 434–441.

Nystrand, Martin, Stuart Greene, and Jeffrey Wiemelt. "Where Did Composition Studies Come From? An Intellectual History." *Written Communication* 10 (1993): 267–333.

Perrin, Porter G. "Maximum Essentials in Composition." *College English* 8 (1947): 352–360.

Sirc, Geoffrey. "Writing Classroom as A & P Parking Lot." *Pre/Text* 14.1–2 (1993): 27–70. Rpt. at http://jefferson.village.Virginia.EDU:80/~spoons/pretextsirc1. html. 2–34.

Shor, Ira. *Culture Wars: School and Society in the Conservative Restoration, 1969–1984.* Boston: Routledge, 1986.

Sorenson, Frederick. "The Basic Communications Course Reconsidered." *College English* 10 (1949): 324–28.

Stanley, Carrie Ellen. "This Game of Writing: A Study in Remedial English." *College English* 4 (1943): 423–28.

Trimbur, John. "Peer Tutoring: A Contradiction in Terms?" *Writing Center Journal* 7 (1987): 21–28.

Veit, Richard C. "Are Machines the Answer?" *Writing Lab Newsletter* 4.4 (1979): 1–2.

Warnock, Tilly and John Warnock. "Liberatory Writing Centers: Restoring Authority to Writers." *Writing Centers: Theory and Administration.* Ed. Gary Olson. Urbana: NCTE, 1984. 16–23.

Welch, Nancy. "Playing With Reality: Writing Centers After the Mirror Stage." 14th Annual Northeast Writing Centers Association Conference. New London, CT, March 1998.

2

"THE IDEA OF A WRITING CENTER": BUILDING A THEORETICAL FOUNDATION

Writing center theory has evolved quickly in the last half century. The theories we embrace forever challenge us to think and to rethink not only what we do but why we do what we do. The pedagogies that grow out of our theories have, it seems, always struggled to keep up. As the articles in this section illustrate, theory is the backbone of our existence, yet our theories must necessarily consider issues of practice, place, culture, gender, technology, and so forth—issues that help us begin to define, individually and collectively, the writing center self. Most of us would agree that good practice is informed by sound theory, but we must also remember that good theory should produce sound practice as well.

Stephen North opens this section with his mantra, "The Idea of a Writing Center," a now classic writing center article that argues for student-centered rather than text-centered tutoring. By contrasting two models of writing center instruction, North pushes us to consider the implications of the tutor's role in the center. In "Revisiting 'The Idea of a Writing Center'," North suggests that the article he published ten years earlier might not be as useful as it once was. He reflects on the tutor–writer, tutor–teacher, and teacher–institution relationships to illustrate some of the oversimplifications about writing center work that his first essay helped create.

Andrea Lunsford's essay provides a theoretical foundation for writing center tutoring by arguing for a collaborative model of tutoring. One of the pioneers in collaborative learning and the social construction of knowledge, Lunsford illustrates how writing centers shaped by collaborative tutoring have proved superior to writing center models shaped by expressive and current traditional rhetoric. We have chosen Eric Hobson's article to follow

Lunsford's because it attempts to reconcile the primary schools of thought that influence writing center practice. Hobson defines the theoretical premises upon which most writing centers are founded and argues not for a purist approach to theory but for an approach that draws on the best qualities of each.

Christina Murphy presents a comprehensive view of social construction and writing center theory and practice. She cautions us against an uninformed, wholesale acceptance of social constructionist theory. While she acknowledges the value of such an approach, she also addresses its limitations. In a more broad-based discussion of theory and practice in the writing center, Peter Carino addresses the tensions that often arise between the two. Acknowledging that writing centers historically have not been recognized as a discipline, he argues that theory should be seen as a means of establishing credibility and respectability on an institutional level. Creating a theoretical framework, Carino contends, allows writing centers to explain themselves to other departments and units within the academy. (The ideas presented in this article also become useful as a part of the next section of this book.)

We close this section with Terrance Riley's article, "The Unpromising Future of Writing Centers," an article that asks us to reflect on some of the problems created when we achieve professional stability within the mainstream. Riley contends that as our status becomes more respectable, we run the risk of lessening our ability to influence institutional changes. He warns us to avoid the mistakes that other programs and departments have made in the past.

The order in which the articles appear in this section represents somewhat of a theoretical evolution for writing centers. From the general reflections on the importance of sound theories to the specific claims for adopting any one approach over another, these articles create an important dialogue to which we may all add our own voices. The evolution we attempt to present is by no means complete, but it does offer a good starting point for conversations about the theories that inform our practices.

see p. 124
like a political manifesto

issues of professionalization

The Idea of a Writing Center

Stephen M. North

This is an essay that began out of frustration. Despite the reference to writing centers in the title, it is not addressed to a writing center audience but to what is, for my purposes, just the opposite: those not involved with writing centers. Do not exclude yourself from this group just because you know that writing centers (or labs or clinics or places or however you think of them) exist; "involved" here means having directed such a place, having worked there for a minimum of 100 hours, or, at the very least, having talked about writing of your own there for five or more hours. The source of my frustration? Ignorance: the members of my profession, my colleagues, people I might see at MLA or CCCC or read in the pages of *College English*, do not understand what I do. They do not understand what does happen, what can happen, in a writing center.

Let me be clear here. Misunderstanding is something one expects—and almost gets used to—in the writing center business. The new faculty member in our writing-across-the-curriculum program, for example, who sends his students to get their papers "cleaned up" in the Writing Center before they hand them in; the occasional student who tosses her paper on our reception desk, announcing that she'll "pick it up in an hour;" even the well-intentioned administrators who are so happy that we deal with "skills" or "fundamentals" or, to use the word that seems to subsume all others, "grammar" (or usually "GRAMMAR")—these are fairly predictable. But

North, Stephen M. "The Idea of a Writing Center." *College English* 46 (1984): 433–46. Copyright 1984 by the National Council of Teachers of English. Reprinted with permission from people in English departments, people well trained in the complex relationship between writer and text, so painfully aware, if only from the composing of dissertations and theses, how lonely and difficult writing can be, I expect more. And I am generally disappointed.

What makes the situation particularly frustrating is that so many such people will vehemently claim that they do, *really*, understand the idea of a writing center. The non-English faculty, the students, the administrators—they may not understand what a writing center is or does, but they have no investment in their ignorance, and can often be educated. But in English departments this second layer of ignorance, this false sense of knowing, makes it doubly hard to get a message through. Indeed, even as you read now, you may be dismissing my argument as the ritual plaint of a "remedial" teacher begging for respectability, the product of a kind of professional paranoia. But while I might admit that there are elements of such a plaint involved—no one likes not to be understood—there is a good deal more at stake. For in coming to terms with this ignorance, I have discovered that it is only a symptom of a much deeper, more serious problem. As a profession I think we are holding on tightly to attitudes and beliefs about the teaching and learning of writing that we thought we had left behind. In fact, my central contention—in the first half of this essay, anyway—is that the failure or inability of the bulk of the English teaching profession, including even those most ardent spokespersons of the so-called "revolution" in the teaching of writing, to perceive the idea of a writing center suggests that, for all our noise and bother about composition, we have fundamentally changed very little.

Let me begin by citing a couple of typical manifestations of this ignorance from close to home. Our writing center has been open for seven years. During that time we have changed our philosophy a little bit as a result of lessons learned from experience, but for the most part we have always been open to anybody in the university community, worked with writers at any time during the composing of a given piece of writing, and dealt with whole pieces of discourse, and not exercises on what might be construed as "sub-skills" (spelling, punctuation, etc.) outside of the context of the writer's work.

We have delivered the message about what we do to the university generally, and the English department in particular, in a number of ways: letters, flyers, posters, class presentations, information booths, and so on. And, as long as there has been a writing committee, advisory to the director of the writing program, we have sent at least one representative. So it is all the more surprising, and disheartening, that the text for our writing program flyer, composed and approved by that committee, should read as follows:

> *The University houses the Center for Writing, founded in 1978 to sponsor the interdisciplinary study of writing. Among its projects are a series of summer institutes for area teachers of writing, a resource center for writers and teachers of writing,* and a tutorial facility for those with special problems in composition. (*My emphasis*)

I don't know, quite frankly, how that copy got past me. What are these "special problems"? What would constitute a regular problem, and why wouldn't we talk to the owner of one? Is this hint of pathology, in some mysterious way, a good marketing ploy?

But that's only the beginning. Let me cite another, in many ways more common and painful instance. As a member, recently, of a doctoral examination committee, I conducted an oral in composition theory and practice. One of the candidate's areas of concentration was writing centers, so as part of the exam I gave her a piece of student writing and asked her to play tutor to my student. The session went well enough, but afterward, as we evaluated the entire exam, one of my fellow examiners—a longtime colleague and friend—said that, while the candidate handled the tutoring nicely, he was surprised that the student who had written the paper would have bothered with the Writing Center in the first place. He would not recommend a student to the Center, he said, "unless there were something like twenty-five errors per page."

People make similar remarks all the time, stopping me or members of my staff in the halls, or calling us into offices, to discuss—in hushed tones, frequently—their current "impossible" or difficult students. There was a time, I will confess, when I let my frustration get the better of me. I would be more or less combative, confrontational, challenging the instructor's often well-intentioned but not very useful "diagnosis." We no longer bother with such confrontations; they never worked very well, and they risk undermining the genuine compassion our teachers have for the students they single out. Nevertheless, their behavior makes it clear that for them, a writing center is to illiteracy what a cross between Lourdes and a hospice would be to serious illness: one goes there hoping for miracles, but ready to face the inevitable. In their minds, clearly, writers fall into three fairly distinct groups: the talented, the average, and the others; and the Writing Center's only logical *raison d'etre* must be to handle those others—those, as the flyer proclaims, with "special problems."

Mine is not, of course, the only English department in which such misconceptions are rife. One comes away from any large meeting of writing center people laden with similar horror stories. And in at least one case, a member of such a department—Malcolm Hayward of the Indiana University of

Pennsylvania—decided formally to explore and document his faculty's perceptions of the center, and to compare them with the views the center's staff held.[1] His aim, in a two-part survey of both groups, was to determine, first, which goals each group deemed most important in the teaching of writing; and second, what role they thought the writing center ought to play in that teaching, which goals it ought to concern itself with.

Happily, the writing center faculty and the center staff agreed on what the primary goals in teaching writing should be (in the terms offered by Hayward's questionnaire): the development of general patterns of thinking and writing. Unhappily, the two groups disagreed rather sharply about the reasons for referring students to the center. For faculty members the two primary criteria were grammar and punctuation. Tutors, on the other hand, ranked organization "as by far the single most important factor for referral," followed rather distantly by paragraphing, grammar, and style. In short, Hayward's survey reveals the same kind of misunderstanding on his campus that I find so frustrating on my own: the idea that a writing center can only be some sort of skills center, a fix-it shop.

Now if this were just a matter of local misunderstanding, if Hayward and I could straighten it out with a few workshops or lectures, maybe I wouldn't need to write this essay for a public forum. But that is not the case. For whatever reasons writing centers have gotten mostly this kind of press, have been represented—or misrepresented—more often as fix-it shops than in any other way, and in some fairly influential places. Consider, for example, this passage from Barbara E. Fassler Walvoord's *Helping Students Write Well: A Guide for Teachers in All Disciplines* (New York: Modern Language Association, 1981). What makes it particularly odd, at least in terms of my argument, is that Professor Walvoord's book, in many other ways, offers to faculty the kind of perspective on writing (writing as a complex process, writing as a way of learning) that I might offer myself. Yet here she is on writing centers:

> *If you are very short of time, if you think you are not skilled enough to deal with mechanical problems, or if you have a number of students with serious difficulties, you may wish to let the skills center carry the ball for mechanics and spend your time on other kinds of writing and learning problems. (p. 63)*

Don't be misled by Professor Walvoord's use of the "skills center" label; in her index the entry for "Writing centers" reads "See skills centers"—precisely the kind of interchangeable terminology I find so abhorrent. On the other hand, to do Professor Walvoord justice, she does recommend that teachers become "at least generally aware of how your skills center works with students, what its basic philosophy is, and what goals it sets for the students in your class," but it seems to me that she has already restricted the possible scope of such a philosophy pretty severely: "deal with mechanical problems"? "carry the ball for mechanics"?

Still, as puzzling and troubling as it is to see Professor Walvoord publishing misinformation about writing centers, it is even more painful, downright maddening, to read one's own professional obituary; to find, in the pages of a reputable professional journal, that what you do has been judged a failure, written off. Maxine Hairston's "The Winds of Change: Thomas Kuhn and the Revolution in the Teaching of Writing" (*College Composition and Communication*, 33 [1982], 76–88) is an attempt to apply the notion of a "paradigm shift" to the field of composition teaching. In the course of doing so Professor Hairston catalogues, under the subheading "Signs of Change," what she calls "ad hoc" remedies to the writing "crisis":

> *Following the pattern that Kuhn describes in his book, our first response to crisis has been to improvise ad hoc measures to try to patch the cracks and keep the system running. Among the first responses were the writing labs that sprang up about ten years ago to give first aid to students who seemed unable to function within the traditional paradigm. Those labs are still with us, but they're still only giving first aid and treating symptoms. They have not solved the problem. (p. 82)*

What first struck me about this assessment—what probably strikes most people in the writing center business—is the mistaken history, the notion that writing labs "sprang up about ten years ago." The fact is, writing "labs," as Professor Hairston chooses to call them, have been around in one form or another since at least the 1930s when Carrie Stanley was already working with writers at the University of Iowa. Moreover, this limited conception of what such places can do—the fix-it shop image—has been around far longer than ten years, too. Robert Moore, in a 1950 *College English* article, "The Writing Clinic and the Writing Laboratory" (7 [1950], 388–393), writes that "writing clinics and writing laboratories are becoming increasingly popular among American universities and colleges as remedial agencies for removing students' deficiencies in composition" (p. 388).

Still, you might think that I ought to be happier with Professor Hairston's position than with, say, Professor Walvoord's. And to some extent I am: even if she mistakenly assumes that the skill and drill model represents all writing centers equally well, she at least recognizes its essential futility. Nevertheless—and this is what bothers me most about her position—her dismissal fails to lay the blame for these worst versions of writing centers on the right heads. According to her "sprang up" historical sketch, these places simply appeared—like so many mushrooms?—to do battle with illiteracy.

"They" are still with "us," but "they" haven't solved the problem. What is missing here is a doer, an agent, a creator—someone to take responsibility. The implication is that "they" done it—"they" being, apparently, the places themselves.

But that won't wash. "They," to borrow from Walt Kelly, is *us:* members of English departments, teachers of writing. Consider, as evidence, the pattern of writing center origins as revealed in back issues of *The Writing Lab Newsletter:* the castoff, windowless classroom (or in some cases, literally, closet), the battered desks, the old textbooks, a phone (maybe), no budget, and, almost inevitably, a director with limited status—an untenured or non-tenure track faculty member, a teaching assistant, an undergraduate, a "para-professional," etc. Now who do you suppose has determined what is to happen in that center? Not the director, surely; not the staff, if there is one. The mandate is clearly from the sponsoring body, usually an English department. And lest you think that things are better where space and money are not such serious problems, I urge you to visit a center where a good bit of what is usually grant money has been spent in the first year or two of the center's operation. Almost always, the money will have been used on materials: drills, texts, machines, tapes, carrells, headphones—the works. And then the director, hired on "soft" money, without political clout, is locked into an approach because she or he has to justify the expense by using the materials.

Clearly, then, where there is or has been misplaced emphasis on so-called basics or drill, where centers have been prohibited from dealing with the writing that students do for their classes—where, in short, writing centers have been of the kind that Professor Hairston is quite correctly prepared to write off—it is because the agency that created the center in the first place, too often an English department, has made it so. The grammar and drill center, the fix-it shop, the first aid station—these are neither the vestiges of some paradigm left behind nor pedagogical aberrations that have been overlooked in the confusion of the "revolution" in the teaching of writing, but that will soon enough be set on the right path, or done away with. They are, instead, the vital and authentic reflection of a way of thinking about writing and the teaching of writing that is alive and well and living in English departments everywhere.

But if my claims are correct—if this is not what writing centers are or, if it is what they are, it is not what they *should* be—then what are, what should they be? What is the idea of a writing center? By way of answer, let me return briefly to the family of metaphors by which my sources have characterized their idea of a writing center: Robert Moore's "removing students' deficiencies," Hairston's "first aid" and "treating symptoms," my colleague's "twenty-five errors per page," Hayward's punctuation and grammar referrers, and Walvoord's "carrying the ball for mechanics" (where, at least, writing centers are athletic and not surgical). All these imply essentially the same thing: that writing centers define their province in terms of a given curriculum, taking over those portions of it that "regular" teachers are willing to cede or, presumably, unable to handle. Over the past six years or so I have visited more than fifty centers, and read descriptions of hundreds of others, and I can assure you that there are indeed centers of this kind, centers that can trace their conceptual lineage back at least as far as Moore. But the "new" writing center has a somewhat shorter history. It is the result of a documentable resurgence, a renaissance if you will, that began in the early 1970s. In fact, the flurry of activity that caught Professor Hairston's attention, and which she mistook for the beginnings of the "old" center, marked instead the genesis of a center which defined its province in a radically different way. Though I have some serious reservations about Hairston's use of Kuhn's paradigm model to describe what happens in composition teaching, I will for the moment put things in her terms: the new writing center, far from marking the end of an era, is the embodiment, the epitome, of a new one. It represents the marriage of what are arguably the two most powerful contemporary perspectives on teaching writing: first, that writing is most usefully viewed as a process; and second, that writing curricula need to be student-centered. This new writing center, then, defines its province not in terms of some curriculum, but in terms of the writers it serves.

To say that writing centers are based on a view of writing as a process is, original good intentions notwithstanding, not to say very much anymore. The slogan—and I daresay that is what it has become—has been devalued, losing most of its impact and explanatory power. Let me use it, then, to make the one distinction of which it still seems capable: in a writing center the object is to make sure that writers, and not necessarily their texts, are what get changed by instruction. In axiom form it goes like this: our job is to produce better writers, not better writing. Any given project—a class assignment, a law school application letter, an encyclopedia entry, a dissertation proposal—is for the writer the prime, often the exclusive concern. That particular text, its success or failure, is what brings them to talk to us in the first place. In the center, though, we look beyond or through that particular project, that particular text, and see it as an occasion for addressing *our* primary concern, the process by which it is produced.

At this point, however, the writing-as-a-process slogan tends to lose its usefulness. That "process," after all, has been characterized as everything from the reception of divine inspiration to a set of nearly algorithmic rules for producing the five paragraph theme. In between are the more widely accepted and, for the moment, more respectable descriptions derived from composing aloud protocols, interviews, videotaping, and so on. None of those, in any case, represent the composing process we seek in a writing center. The version we want can only be found, in as yet unarticulated form, in the writer we are working with. I think probably the best way to describe a writing center tutor's relationship to composing is to say that a tutor is a holist devoted to a participant-observer methodology. This may seem, at first glance, too passive—or, perhaps, too glamorous, legitimate, or trendy—a role in which to cast tutors. But consider this passage from Paul Diesing's *Patterns of Discovery in the Social Sciences* (Hawthorne, N.Y.: Aldine, 1971):

> *Holism is not, in the participant-observer method, an a priori belief that everything is acted to everything else. It is rather the methodological necessity of pushing on to new aspects and new kinds of evidence in order to make sense of what one has already observed and to test the validity of one's interpretations. A belief in the organic unity of living systems may also be present, but this belief by itself would not be sufficient to force a continual expansion of one's observations. It is rather one's inability to develop an intelligible and validated partial model that drives one on.* (p. 167)

How does this definition relate to tutors and composing? Think of the writer writing as a kind of host setting. What we want to do in a writing center is fit into—observe and participate in—this ordinarily solo ritual of writing. To do this, we need to do what any participant-observer must do: see what happens during this "ritual," try to make sense of it, observe some more, revise our model, and so on indefinitely, all the time behaving in a way the host finds acceptable. For validation and correction of our model, we quite naturally rely on the writer, who is, in turn, a willing collaborator in—and, usually, beneficiary of—the entire process. This process precludes, obviously, a reliance on or a clinging to any predetermined models of "the" composing process, except as crude topographical guides to what the "territory" of composing processes might look like. The only composing process that matters in a writing center is "a" composing process, and it "belongs" to, is acted out by, only one given writer.

It follows quite naturally, then, that any curriculum—any plan of action the tutor follows—is going to be student-centered in the strictest sense of that term. That is, it will not derive from a generalized model of composing, or be based on where the student ought to be because she is a freshman or sophomore, but will begin from where the student is, and move where the student moves—an approach possible only if, as James Moffett suggests in *Teaching the Universe of Discourse* (Boston: Houghton Mifflin, 1968), the teacher (or tutor in this case) "shifts his gaze from the subject to the learner, for the subject is in the learner" (p. 67). The result is what might be called a pedagogy of direct intervention. Whereas in the "old" center instruction tends to take place after or apart from writing, and tends to focus on the correction of textual problems, in the "new" center the teaching takes place as much as possible during writing, during the activity being learned, and tends to focus on the activity itself.

I do not want to push the participant-observer analogy too far. Tutors are not, finally, researchers: they must measure their success not in terms of the constantly changing model they create, but in terms of changes in the writer. Rather than being fearful of disturbing the "ritual" of composing, they observe it and are charged to change it: to interfere, to get in the way, to participate in ways that will leave the "ritual" itself forever altered. The whole enterprise seems to me most natural. Nearly everyone who writes likes—and needs—to talk about his or her writing, preferably to someone who will really listen, who knows how to listen, and knows how to talk about writing too. Maybe in a perfect world, all writers would have their own ready auditor— a teacher, a classmate, a roommate, an editor—who would not only listen but draw them out, ask them questions they would not think to ask themselves. A writing center is an institutional response to this need. Clearly writing centers can never hope to satisfy this need themselves; on my campus alone, the student-to-tutor ratio would be about a thousand to one. Writing centers are simply one manifestation—polished and highly visible—of a dialogue about writing that is central to higher education.

As is clear from my citations in the first half of this essay, however, what seems perfectly natural to me is not so natural for everyone else. One part of the difficulty, it seems to me now, is not theoretical at all, but practical, a question of coordination or division of labor. It usually comes in the form of a question like this: "If I'm doing process-centered teaching in my class, why do I need a writing center? How can I use it?" For a long time I tried to soft-pedal my answers to this question. For instance, in my dissertation ("Writing Centers: A Sourcebook," Diss. SUNY at Albany, 1978) I talked about complementing or intensifying classroom instruction. Or, again, in our center we tried using, early on, what is a fairly common device among writing centers, a referral form; at one point it even had a sort of diagnostic taxonomy, a checklist, by which teachers could communicate to us their concerns about the writers they sent us.

But I have come with experience to take a harder, less conciliatory position. The answer to the question in all cases is that teachers, as teachers, do not need, and cannot use, a writing center: only writers need it, only writers can use it. You cannot parcel out some portion of a given student for us to deal with ("You take care of editing, I'll deal with invention"). Nor should you require that all of your students drop by with an early draft of a research paper to get a reading from a fresh audience. You should not scrawl, at the bottom of a failing paper, "Go to the Writing Center." Even those of you who, out of genuine concern, bring students to a writing center, almost by the hand, to make sure they know that we won't hurt them—even you are essentially out of line. Occasionally we manage to convert such writers from people who have to see us to people who want to, but most often they either come as if for a kind of detention, or they drift away. (It would be nice if in writing, as in so many things, people would do what we tell them because it's good for them, but they don't. If and when *they* are ready, we will be here.)

In short, we are not here to serve, supplement, back up, complement, reinforce, or otherwise be defined by any external curriculum. We are here to talk to writers. If they happen to come from your classes, you might take it as a compliment to your assignments, in that your writers are engaged in them enough to want to talk about their work. On the other hand, we do a fair amount of trade in people working on ambiguous or poorly designed assignments, and far too much work with writers whose writing has received caustic, hostile, or otherwise unconstructive commentary.

I suppose this declaration of independence sounds more like a declaration of war, and that is obviously not what I intend, especially since the primary casualties would be the students and writers we all aim to serve. And I see no reason that writing centers and classroom teachers cannot cooperate as well as coexist. For example, the first rule in our Writing Center is that we are professionals at what we do. While that does, as I have argued, give us the freedom of self-definition, it also carries with it a responsibility to respect our fellow professionals. Hence we never play student-advocates in teacher-student relationships. The guidelines are very clear. In all instances the student must understand that we support the teacher's position completely. (Or, to put it in less loaded terms—for we are not teacher advocates either—the instructor is simply part of the rhetorical context in which the writer is trying to operate. We cannot change that context: all we can do is help the writer learn how to operate in it and other contexts like it.) In practice, this rule means that we never evaluate or second-guess any teacher's syllabus, assignments, comments, or grades. If students are unclear about any of those, we send them back to the teacher to get clear. Even in those instances I mentioned above—where writers come in confused by what seem to be poorly designed assignments, or crushed by what appear to be unwarrantedly hostile comments—we pass no judgment, at least as far as the student is concerned. We simply try, every way we can, to help the writer make constructive sense of the situation.

In return, of course, we expect equal professional courtesy. We need, first of all, instructors' trust that our work with writers-in-progress on academic assignments is not plagiarism, any more than a conference with the teacher would be—that, to put it the way I most often hear it, we will not write students' papers for them. Second, instructors must grant us the same respect we grant them—that is, they must neither evaluate nor second-guess our work with writers. We are, of course, most willing to talk about that work. But we do not take kindly to the perverse kind of thinking represented in remarks like, "Well, I had a student hand in a paper that he took to the writing center, and it was still full of errors." The axiom, if you will recall, is that we aim to make better writers, not necessarily—or immediately—better texts.

Finally, we can always use classroom teachers' cooperation in helping us explain to students what we do. As a first step, of course, I am asking that they revise their thinking about what a writing center can do. Beyond that, in our center we find it best to go directly to the students ourselves. That is, rather than sending out a memo or announcement for the teachers to read in their classes, we simply send our staff, upon invitation, into classes to talk with students or, better yet, to do live tutorials. The standard presentation, a ten-minute affair, gives students a person, a name, and a face to remember the Center by. The live tutorials take longer, but we think they are worth it. We ask the instructor to help us find a writer willing to have a draft (or a set of notes or even just the assignment) reproduced for the whole class. Then the Writing Center person does, with the participation of the entire class, what we do in the Center talk about writing with the writer. In our experience the instructors learn as much about the Center from these sessions as the students.

To argue that writing centers are not here to serve writing class curricula is not to say, however, that they are here to replace them. In our center, anyway, nearly every member of the full-time staff is or has been a classroom teacher of writing, Even our undergraduate tutors work part of their time in an introductory writing course. We all recognize and value the power of classroom teaching, and we take pride in ourselves as professionals in that setting too. But working in both situations makes us acutely aware of crucial differences between talking about writing in the context of a class, and talking about it in the context of the Center. When we hold student conferences in our classes, we are the teacher, in the writers' minds especially, the assigner and evaluator of the writing in question. And for the most part we are pretty busy people, with conference appointments scheduled on the half hour, and a line forming outside the office. For efficiency the papers-in-progress are in some assigned form—an outline, a first draft, a statement of purpose with bibliography and note cards, and while the conference may lead to further composing, there is rarely the time or the atmosphere for composing to happen during the conference itself. Last but not least, the conference is likely to be a command performance, our idea, not the writer's.

When we are writing center tutors all of that changes. First of all, conferences are the writer's idea; he or she seeks us out. While we have an appointment book that offers half hour appointment slots, our typical session is fifty minutes, and we average between three and four per writer; we can afford to give a writer plenty of time. The work-in-progress is in whatever form the writer has managed to put it in, which may make tutoring less efficient, but which clearly makes it more student-centered, allowing us to begin where the writers are, not where we told them to be. This also means that in most cases the writers come prepared, even anxious to get on with their work, to begin or to keep on composing. Whereas going to keep a conference with a teacher is, almost by definition, a kind of goal or deadlines—a stopping place—going to talk in the writing center is a means of getting started, or a way to keep going. And finally—in a way subsuming all the rest—we are not the teacher. We did not assign the writing, and we will not grade it. However little that distinction might mean in our behaviors, it seems to mean plenty to the writers.

What these differences boil down to, in general pedagogical terms, are timing and motivation. The fact is, not everyone's interest in writing, their need or desire to write or learn to write, coincides with the fifteen or thirty weeks they spend in writing courses—especially when, as is currently the case at so many institutions, those weeks are required. When writing does become important, a writing center can be there in a way that our regular classes cannot. Charles Cooper, in an unpublished paper called "What College Writers Need to Know" (1979), puts it this way:

> *The first thing college writers need to know is that they can improve as writers and the second is that they will never reach a point where they cannot improve further. One writing course, two courses, three courses may not be enough. If they're on a campus which takes writing seriously, they will be able to find the courses they need to feel reasonably confident they can fulfill the requests which will be made of them in their academic work.... Throughout their college years they should also be able to find on a drop-in, no-fee basis expert tutorial help with any writing problem they encounter in a paper. (p. 1)*

A writing center's advantage in motivation is a function of the same phenomenon. Writers come looking for us because, more often than not, they are genuinely, deeply engaged with their material, anxious to wrestle it into the best form they can: they are motivated to write. If we agree that the biggest obstacle to overcome in teaching anything, writing included, is getting learners to decide that they want to learn, then what a writing center does is cash in on motivation that the writer provides. This teaching at the conjunction of timing and motivation is most strikingly evident when we work with writers doing "real world" tasks: application essays for law, medical, and graduate schools, newspaper and magazine articles, or poems and stories. Law school application writers are suddenly willing—sometimes overwhelmingly so—to concern themselves with audience, purpose, and persona, and to revise over and over again. But we see the same excitement in writers working on literature or history or philosophy papers, or preparing dissertation proposals, or getting ready to tackle comprehensive exams. Their primary concern is with their material, with some existential context where new ideas must merge with old, and suddenly writing is a vehicle, a means to an end, and not an end in itself. These opportunities to talk with excited writers at the height of their engagement with their work are the lifeblood of a writing center.

The essence of the writing center method, then, is this talking. If we conceive of writing as a relatively rhythmic and repeatable kind of behavior, then for a writer to improve that behavior, that rhythm, has to change—preferably, though not necessarily, under the writer's control. Such changes can be fostered, of course, by work outside of the act of composing itself—hence the success of the classical discipline of imitation, or more recent ones like sentence combining or the tagmemic heuristic, all of which, with practice, "merge" with and affect composing. And, indeed, depending on the writer, none of these tactics would be ruled out in a writing center. By and large, however, we find that the best breaker of old rhythms, the best creator of new ones, is our style of live intervention, our talk in all its forms.

The kind of writing does not substantially change the approach. We always want the writer to tell us about the rhetorical context—what the purpose of the writing is, who its audience is, how the writer hopes to present herself. We want to know about other constraints—deadlines, earlier experiences with the same audience or genre, research completed or not completed, and so on. In other ways, though, the variations on the kind of talk are endless. We can question, praise, cajole, criticize, acknowledge, badger, plead—even cry. We can read: silently, aloud, together, separately. We can play with options. We can both write—as, for example, in response to sample essay exam questions—and compare opening strategies. We can poke around in resources—comparing, perhaps, the manuscript conventions of the Modern Language Association with those of the American Psychological Association. We can ask writers to compose aloud while we listen, or we can compose aloud, and the writer can watch and listen.

In this essay, however, I will say no more about the nature of this talk. One reason is that most of what can be said, for the moment, has been said in print already. There is, for example, my own "Training Tutors to Talk About Writing" (*CCC*, 33, [1982] 434–41), or Muriel Harris' "Modeling: A Process Method of Teaching" (*College English*, 45, [1983], 74–84). And there are several other sources, including a couple of essay collections, that provide some insights into the hows and whys of tutorial talk.[2]

A second reason, though, seems to me more substantive, and symptomatic of the kinds of misunderstanding I have tried to dispel here. We don't know very much, in other than a practitioner's anecdotal way, about the dynamics of the tutorial. The same can be said, of course, with regard to talk about writing in any setting—the classroom, the peer group, the workshop, the teacher–student conference, and so on. But while ignorance of the nature of talk in those settings does not threaten their existence, it may do precisely that in writing centers. That is, given the idea of the writing center I have set forth here, talk is everything. If the writing center is ever to prove its worth in other than quantitative terms—numbers of students seen, for example, or hours of tutorials provided—it will have to do so by describing this talk: what characterizes it, what effects it has, how it can be enhanced.

Unfortunately, the same "proofreading-shop-in-the-basement" mentality that undermines the pedagogical efforts of the writing center hampers research as well. So far most of the people hired to run such places have neither the time, the training, nor the status to undertake any serious research. Moreover, the few of us lucky enough to even consider the possibility of research have found that there are other difficulties. One is that writing center work is often not considered fundable—that is, relevant to a wide enough audience—even though there are about a thousand such facilities in the country, a figure which suggests that there must be at least ten to fifteen thousand tutorials every school day, and even though research into any kind of talk about writing is relevant for the widest possible audience. Second, we have discovered that focusing our scholarly efforts on writing centers may be a professional liability. Even if we can publish our work (and that is by no means easy), there is no guarantee that it will be viewed favorably by tenure and promotion review committees. Composition itself is suspect enough; writing centers, a kind of obscure backwater, seem no place for a scholar.

These conditions may be changing, manuscripts for *The Writing Center Journal*, for example, suggest that writing center folk generally are becoming more research-oriented; there were sessions scheduled at this year's meetings of the MLA and NCTE on research in or relevant to writing centers. In an even more tangible signal of change, the State University of New York has made funds available for our Albany center to develop an appropriate case study methodology for writing center tutorials. Whether this trend continues or not, my point remains the same. Writing centers, like any other portion of a college writing curriculum, need time and space for appropriate research and reflection if they are to more clearly understand what they do, and figure out how to do it better. The great danger is that the very misapprehensions that put them in basements to begin with may conspire to keep them there.

It is possible that I have presented here, at least by implication, too dismal a portrait of the current state of writing centers. One could, as a matter of fact, mount a pretty strong argument that things have never been better. There are, for example, several regional writing center associations that have annual meetings, and the number of such associations increases every year.

Both *The Writing Lab Newsletter* and *The Writing Center Journal*, the two publications in the field, have solid circulations. This year at NCTE, for the first time, writing center people met as a recognized National Assembly, a major step up from their previous Special Interest Session status.

And on individual campuses all over the country, writing centers have begun to expand their institutional roles. So, for instance, some centers have established resource libraries for writing teachers. They sponsor readings or reading series by poets and fiction writers, and annual festivals to celebrate writing of all kinds. They serve as clearinghouses for information on where to publish, on writing programs, competitions, scholarships, and so on; and they sponsor such competitions themselves, even putting out their own publications. They design and conduct workshops for groups with special needs—essay exam takers, for example, or job application writers. They are involved with, or have even taken over entirely, the task of training new teaching assistants. They have played central roles in the creation of writing-across-the-curriculum programs. And centers have extended themselves beyond their own institutions, sending tutors to other schools (often high schools), or helping other institutions set up their own facilities. In some cases, they have made themselves available to the wider community, often opening a "Grammar Hotline" or "Grammaphone"—a service so popular at one institution, in fact, that a major publishing company provided funding to keep it open over the summer.

Finally, writing centers have gotten into the business of offering academic credit. As a starting point they have trained their tutors in formal courses or, in some instances, "paid" their tutors in credits rather than money. They have set up independent study arrangements to sponsor both academic and nonacademic writing experiences. They have offered credit-bearing courses of their own; in our center, for example, we are piloting an introductory writing course that uses Writing Center staff members as small group leaders.

I would very much like to say that all this activity is a sure sign that the idea of a writing center is here to stay, that the widespread misunderstandings I described in this essay, especially those held so strongly in English departments, are dissolving. But in good conscience I cannot. Consider the activities we are talking about. Some of them, of course, are either completely or mostly public relations: a way of making people aware that a writing center exists, and that (grammar hotlines aside) it deals in more than usage and punctuation. Others—like the resource library, the clearinghouse, or the training of new teaching assistants—are more substantive, and may well belong in a writing center, but most of them end up there in the first place because nobody else wants to do them. As for the credit generating, that is simply pragmatic. The bottom line in academic budget making is calculated in student credit hours; when budgets are tight, as they will be for the foreseeable future, facilities that generate no credits are the first to be cut. Writing centers—even really good writing centers—have proved no exception.

None of these efforts to promote writing centers suggest that there is any changed understanding of the idea of a writing center. Indeed it is as though what writing centers do that really matters—talking to writers—were not enough. That being the case, enterprising directors stake out as large a claim as they can in more visible or acceptable territory. All of these efforts—and, I assure you, my center does its share—have about them an air of shrewdness, or desperation, the trace of a survival instinct at work. I am not such a purist as to suggest that these things are all bad. At the very least they can be good for staff morale. Beyond that I think they may eventually help make writing centers the centers of consciousness about writing on campuses, a kind of physical locus for the ideas and ideals of college or university or high school commitment to writing—a status to which they might well aspire and which, judging by results on a few campuses already, they can achieve.

But not this way, not via the back door, not—like some marginal ballplayer—by doing whatever it takes to stay on the team. If writing centers are going to finally be accepted, surely they must be accepted on their own terms, as places whose primary responsibility, whose only reason for being, is to talk to writers. That is their heritage, and it stretches back farther than the late 1960s or the early 1970s, or to Iowa in the 1930s—back, in fact, to Athens, where in a busy marketplace a tutor called Socrates set up the same kind of shop: open to all comers, no fees charged, offering, on whatever subject a visitor might propose, a continuous dialectic that is, finally, its own end.

NOTES

1. "Assessing Attitudes Toward the Writing Center," *The Writing Center Journal*, 3, No. 2 (1983), 1–11.

2. See, for example, *Tutoring Writing: A Sourcebook for Writing Labs*, ed. Muriel Harris (Glenview, Ill.: Scott-Foresman, 1982); and *New Directions for College Learning Assistance: Improving Writing Skills*, ed. Phyllis Brooks and Thom Hawkins (San Francisco: Jossey-Bass, 1981).

Revisiting "The Idea of a Writing Center"[1]

Stephen M. North

I need to begin this essay—somewhat obliquely, I confess—by invoking the 1989 Film *Dead Poets Society*. That movie, as those of you who saw it may recall, tells the story of a group of boys who attend an exclusive private preparatory school called Welton Academy (located in what John Danaher, to whom I am indebted for this line of argument, calls eternally autumnal New England). Set in the early 1960s, the film focuses in particular on how the boys' lives are affected by their English teacher, himself a graduate of Welton: one John Keating (a name chosen, perhaps, for its Romantic resonances), played by Robin Williams.

Keating is the pivotal character in the film. Not the protagonist—in that sense, this really is the boys' story—but clearly the catalyst, the agent for change, the voice of freedom in a one-hundred-year-old boarding school whose four "pillars"—Tradition, Discipline, Honor, Excellence—are represented less as holding the school up than as weighing its students down. Thus, while Mr. Keating is nor featured in all that many scenes, the ones he does appear in take on enormous significance, and none more so than the classroom scenes, three of the most crucial of which I'll sketch here.

The first of these—the students' introduction to Keating on the first day of classes—is set up by what amounts to a highlight film (or, more aptly, a lowlight film) of the other classes the boys attend before they arrive for English at what appears to be the end of the school day. All those classes are taught, as was English until Keating arrived to replace a now–revered retiree, by older men, dour, serious, strict men: the chemistry teacher who not only lays out an intimidating workload for the year, but who announces—with something close to a smirk—that the twenty questions at the end of Chapter One are due tomorrow, the trigonometry teacher who calls for "precision" above all else,

North Stephen M. "Revisiting 'The Idea of a Writing Center.'" *The Writing Center Journal* 15.1 (1994): 7–19. Reprinted by permission of *The Writing Center Journal*.

and warns that every missed homework assignment will cost one point off the final grade ("Let me urge you now not to test me on this point"); the pointer-wielding Scot of a Latin teacher who leads his charges again and again through the declensions of "agricola."

Keating is presented to us in an entirely different way. We see him first peeking at his students from the doorway of his office at the head of the class-room. Then he begins whistling—the *1812 Overture*—and walks, still whis-tling, through the classroom to the hallway door, and on out. There is a pause, a moment of student (and audience) puzzlement, until he sticks his head back in the doorway. "Well, come on!" The boys (and camera) follow him into the school's vestibule where, after urging the "more daring" of them to call him "O captain, my captain" (after Whitman on Lincoln, as he tell them), he turns their attention to the trophy case photos of Welton graduates past. These pic-tured boys-turned-men-turned-moldering-corpses, Keating tells his lads, have a message. "Go on," he tells them, "lean in. Hear it?" And when they are lean-ing in, the camera panning alternately over intent faces and ancient photos, he offers a kind of ventriloqual whisper: "Caaarpe! Caaarpe! Carpe diem! Seize the day, boys! Make your lives extraordinary!"

The second and third of these key classroom scenes serve to further flesh out this image of the English teacher as liberator, as Romantic—or, given the New England setting and the prominence of Thoreau's phrase about "suck-ing the marrow out of life," transcendentalist—revolutionary. In the second, he asks a student to read the textbook's Introduction to Poetry, written by one J. Evans Pritchard, Ph.D. (a name which, it's worth noting, Williams manages to pronounce with considerable derision). It features a formula for computing poetic "greatness" [G = I(mportance) × P(erfection)] that prompts Keating to declare "Excrement!" and to insist that the boys tear the page out and, when they have done that, to keep going, to tear out not only that page, but the entire Introduction: "Rip! Rip it out! We're not laying pipe; we're talking about poetry here." And in the third key classroom scene—after we have seen Keating bring Shakespeare to life with vintage Robin Williams im-pressions of Marlon Brando as Brutus and John Wayne as Macbeth—he climbs atop his desk to dramatize our need to always, always try to see things from a new perspective. Again, he invites the boys to join him, as he invited them to join him in hearing voices and tearing textbooks; and we see in their ready agreement that his teachings are really beginning to take hold.

* * * * *

I don't want to be too hard on this film. In fact, I enjoyed it, in its way, and find it quite moving. Still, as a teacher—and particularly as a teacher of English—I find it annoying, disturbing, irritating. I won't say that no teacher has ever played any version of this John Keating role in a classroom where I was a student; in limited ways, various teachers have, or at least I cast them in it. Nor would I say that I have never assumed such a role—invited, or at least accepted, the kind of teacher-student relationship Keating invites when he urges the "more daring" to call him, not Mr. Keating, but "Oh captain, my captain."

But teaching English, at least for me, is not generally about grand entrances or grand gestures—neither dramatically tearing up textbooks, nor standing on top of desks. Certainly there is, or at least can be, an element of theater, something of the performance, in any teaching. The "scene" of teaching in our culture—our conceptions of knowing, the conversational dynamics of larger groups, and so on—pretty much guarantees that. *Dead Poets Society* sets up, or perhaps plays into, a grandiose, idealized version of that scene that is potentially dangerous for everyone involved—students, teachers, parents, administrators—especially as that idealization is allowed to embody expectations. Film is a wonderful, captivating medium, but it deals in illusion. Classroom life doesn't come scripted or specially lit; there are no second or third takes, no sound track, no score, no editing. In a film like this, the dynamics of teaching are magically compressed; a few minutes of well-chosen footage can evoke a month or more of classroom interaction. In a real classroom, the teacher's John Wayne impression doesn't necessarily last any longer, but the action doesn't end when the cameras stop rolling.

The reason I bring all this up in the context of writing centers, as you may have guessed from my title is that I think my essay "The Idea of a Writing Center" (1984) has performed...well, let us call it an equally ambivalent service for those of us in the writing center business: offered a version of what we do that is, in its own way, very attractive; but one which also, to the extent that it is a romantic idealization, presents its own kind of jeopardy. I don't want to be too hard on this essay, either. Like *Dead Poets Society*, it was directed—explicitly—at a larger public: those, it says, not involved with writing centers; those who have nor directed such a place, worked there a minimum of 100 hours, or talked about their own writing there for 5 hours or more (433). And just as the film no doubt affected (however briefly) the image of English teachers in this country, I think the essay was reasonably effective for its audience: placed prominently in *College English,* it gave lots of essentially ignorant but well-meaning people pause. Tactically speaking, in other words, it worked pretty well.

Nevertheless, its more lasting impact has almost certainly been on us, on writing center people. More to the point here, it has come back—a highly visible version of our mythology, a public idealization—to haunt us in much the same way *Dead Poets Society* comes back to haunt us as English teachers. Indeed, the situation is probably worse with a document like "The Idea of a Writing Center." We can at least partly free ourselves from having to perform in the shadow of Robin Williams' John Keating by pointing out that we were not consulted about the script, and that we would never endorse the film's realism. By contrast, we are bound by "The Idea of a Writing Center" to the extent to which we have endorsed it: asked training tutors to read it, cited it in various writings or talks, used it in arguments with administrators, and so on. And there is plenty of evidence, I think, that we have indeed endorsed it—to good effect, often, and in ways that have provided me with moments of tremendous gratification—but also (therefore) in ways that make it harder for us to disown or renounce what may be its less desirable legacies.

So the primary object of this essay—the point of revisiting "The Idea of a Writing Center"—is to contribute in my own peculiar way to the work of re-imagining of writing centers already well under way in such venues as *The Writing Center Journal* and *Writing Lab Newsletter* (see, e.g., Grimm, Woolbright, Joyner, and many others). To do that, I'm going to go behind the scenes, as it were, to critique and/or amend a selection of the public-directed images the essay offers, relying in particular on my sense of the lived experience of writing centers such images can be said to conceal. Specifically, I'm going to work from four passages, looking in particular at how they characterize three relationships: the tutor and the writer (passages 1 and 2); the tutor and the teacher (passage 2); and the tutor and the institution (passages 3 and 4, and combining, albeit somewhat awkwardly, such entities as the English department an larger administrative units). I'll then conclude by seeing what directions I think such amendments suggest for the future of writing centers.

A. TUTOR AND WRITER

Passage 1:

> *Writers come looking for us because, more often than not, they are genuinely, deeply engaged with their material, anxious to wrestle it in to the best form they can: they are really motivated to write. (443)*

To test the face validity of this claim, I have read it on more than one occasion to a live audience of writing center people, and then paused. The reaction—to the passage, to the pause, to (likely) my raised eyebrows—is telling: people laugh. It isn't, of course, that the writers we see—students, for the most part—*aren't* motivated. They are. But not in the uncomplicated way this passage would suggest. They will, rather, be motivated to (say) finish writing; to be finished with writing; to have their writing be finished. They will be motivated to have the writing they submit for a class win them a good grade, whatever they imagine that will take: for it to be mechanically correct, or thoroughly documented, or to follow the instructor's directions to the letter. [Or, to invoke the most extreme example in my experience, they'll be motivated to satisfy the "sentence" imposed on them by the Student Conduct Committee, which found them "guilty" of Plagiarism, Third Degree (unpremeditated).]

This isn't to be cynical about the possibilities for "genuine" or "deep" engagement. It is, rather, to contextualize such notions, to (re)situate them in the school culture, and indeed the larger culture, that this passage tends to erase. And it is to do so especially, in this case, for the sake of any number of tutors I have talked with—undergraduates, in particular—who, taking this passage pretty much at face value, tend to blame themselves (or, just as problematically, the writers they work with) when their tutorials don't seem to be so unproblematically driven. After all, it does come as a shock when, having been led by your training to expect some deep, unalloyed, genuine engagement—some eager wrestler-of-texts—you meet instead a frightened freshman who seems only to want a super proofreader; a sophomore who seems preoccupied by her fear that the instructor doesn't like her, a senior who seems concerned with doing just enough to pass an S/U course, but not a whit more; or any of the other very complicated, very human creatures who find their way to writing centers. This passage from "The Idea of a Writing Center," whatever its strategic value for other purposes, can lay an unnecessarily heavy burden on such tutors and such writers.

Passage 2:

> Think of the writer writing as a kind of host setting. What we want to do in a writing center is fit into—observe and participate in—this ordinarily solo ritual of writing. To do this, we need to do what any participant-observer: see what happens during this "ritual," try to make sense of it, observe some more, revise our model, and so on indefinitely, all the time behaving in a way that the host finds acceptable. For validation and correction of our model, we quite naturally rely on the writer, who is, in turn, a willing collaborator in—and, usually, beneficiary of—the entire process. (439)

Sure (imagine a brogue here) and it's a charming image, this tutor of enormous restraint, endless curiosity, heightened sensitivities-antennae all atremble—selflessly and unobtrusively joining our unself-conscious freshman as she undertakes (deeply and genuinely engaged) her assignment to…oh, write a paper on some feature of "A Rose for Emily." Okay, so maybe she isn't so entirely unself-conscious; maybe we make her a little nervous. Okay, maybe she isn't entirely a willing collaborator; maybe she came because she got a C or D on an earlier assignment, or because the instructor insisted she come to the Writing Center. Okay, so maybe you were tired or busy or are habitually a little abrupt (I am in confessional mode now) and your greeting was something like "What is it!?!"

Whatever Margaret Mead may have been doing all those years ago (if it is, indeed, the Mead image of anthropology this invokes), and whatever conceptual leverage such an image provides (it was intended, obviously, to emphasize the centrality of the writer and her composing in the tutoring process), it too can offer a curious and troublesome legacy for tutors—especially new ones—who take it at anything like face value. On the one hand, it makes them feel handcuffed (or perhaps gagged): "I better sit here quietly, unobtrusively, not so much a coach or a consultant as a human recorder of some kind, committed above all to my belief in the intrinsic wholeness-as-writers of the people I tutor." On the other, it tends to blind them to, or deny for them, the extent to which they are (always) already enmeshed in a system or systems—educational, political, economic, social, and so on—in ways that render such innocence (and I think that's the right word) impossible. Think of it this way. It isn't only—as might happen with the Mead-image anthropologist—that this low-profile participant-observer might carry into the visited environment a virus which proves dangerous, or even lethal, to the observed. In the (purportedly) analogous writing center situation, the performer-of-the-ritual is enticed (or coerced or whatever) to leave her usual scene of writing, and to perform it instead in…well, the analogy would lead me here to say "hospital," and I'm reluctant to do that. But you see my point. Staging the tutorial in the writing center space—even if it is, as we would no doubt put it, for the writer's good (and nor merely, say, logistically convenient)—constitutes an alteration, not to say invasion, of this "ordinarily solo ritual" that no practiced tutorial (bedside) manner can overcome.

B. TUTOR AND TEACHER

Passage 3:

In all instances the student must understand that we support the teacher's position completely. Or, to put it in less loaded terms—for we are not teacher advocates either—the instructor is simply part of the rhetorical context in which the writer is trying to operate. We cannot change that context: all we can do is help the writer learn how to operate in it and other contexts like it. In practice, this rule means that we never evaluate or second-guess any teacher's syllabus, assignments, comments, or grades. If students are unclear about any of those, we send them back to the teacher to get clear. Even in those instances I mentioned above—where writers come in confused by what seem to be poorly designed assignments, or crushed by what appear to be unwarrantedly hostile comments—we pass no judgment, at least as far as the student is concerned. We simply try, every way we can, to help the writer make constructive sense of the situation. (441)

The language of this passage always makes me want to ask people to raise their right hand and recite it as a pledge: "I promise never ever to evaluate or second-guess any teacher's syllabus, assignments, comments, or grades" and then start a series of big-tent revivals for those who fail to scrupulously live up to such a pledge. I am, moreover, reminded of things I learned working in our writing center over the years: of one colleagues now retired, who used four different colors of ink in responding to student papers, always marked every feature he deemed worth commentary, *and* provided totals ("You have 64 separate errors in this paper, Mr. Johnson."). And then there was another, also now retired, who would not—as a matter of *policy*—talk with her students. Instead, she said, if they wanted to talk about their work, they could bring it to the Writing Center. Every year at Christmas time, though, she would send the Center a two-pound box of chocolates.

The fact is that, from the admittedly peculiar vantage point provided by our centers, we very often get to view our institutions—and especially *teaching* in our institutions—in the way that, say, the police or journalists get to view our larger communities: day in and day out, year in and year out, we see (and participate in) a range of teacher-student interactions very few other members of the institution can match. There are certainly delights and advantages to this, stories we can tell of commitment and learning and kindness and happy endings. But we also see what we at least construe as the seamier side of things—probably, again like the police and journalists, more of the seaminess than most other vantage points would provide. In any case, it adds up and in cumulative form puts a lot of pressure on the sort of tutor-teacher détente proposed by the passage quoted above. And it doesn't help in handling such pressure that, despite the gradual improvement of working conditions for writing center people, they still tend to be viewed as—or at least to *feel* that they are viewed as—lower in institutional pecking orders than the teachers whose practices the passage pledges them to uphold, especially when differentials in paychecks, workload, or job security reinforce such feelings.

C. TUTOR AND INSTITUTION

Passage 4:

I think...writing centers (can be] the centers of consciousness about writing on campuses, a kind of physical locus for the ideas and ideals of college or university or high school commitment to writing—a status to which they might well aspire and which, judging by results on a few campuses already, they can achieve. (446)

Of the four passages I've presented here, this one is likely both the most accurate and, at the same time, the most genuinely laughable. It is the most accurate because what was true when I first wrote those words would appear to be even truer now. Many centers can, in fact, claim such a status, do serve their respective campuses as that institutional node to which primary responsibility for writing is ceded, both functionally and symbolically. They are responsible, then, not only for tutoring the "underprepared" student writers who have so often been understood to be their sole province, but—to offer a sample listing—for any writer, student or otherwise, interested in talking about his or her writing; for the direction and execution of writing- across-the-curriculum programs; for publishing student writing, faculty newsletters, and the like; for training T.A.s; for placement and assessment procedures; for research.

What makes this apparent success, this fulfillment of my essay's prophecy, laughable—and I do apologize for the harshness of that term—are two factors: scale and image. The problems created by scale are, I think, fairly obvious. It may be that on smaller campuses a writing center can establish a tutor-to-student and staff-to-faculty ratio that makes these notions of a physical locus and a center of consciousness loosely plausible. There aren't any magic formulas here, but suppose a campus of 1400 students and 25 full-time faculty has a center with 5 more or less full-time people (i.e., faculty members with part of their load in the center), and 15 undergraduate tutors. That represents 1–70 tutor-student and 1–5 staff-faculty ratios; people could, in fact, talk with and know one another.

As we move up the scale in institutionalize, though, these ratios seem to get swamped pretty quickly. Our center, for example—of which I remain stubbornly proud—nevertheless has something like the staff I just described: six or seven more or less full-time people, and maybe fourteen undergraduate tutors. Unfortunately, our middle-sized research university enrolls some 16,000 students (12,000 undergraduate, 4000 graduate) and has in the neighborhood of 700 faculty (not to mention a raft of T.A.s, lecturers, and people teaching in various part-time capacities). The resulting ratios help explain, I hope, my use of the term laughable: 1–800 for tutor-student, 1–70 staff-faculty. If we are called upon to be this center of consciousness and physical locus—and, indeed, we are—the image that springs to mind comes from all those dinosaur books I read as a child (ignoring, for the moment, their paleontological accuracy): the university as this huge, lumbering stegosaurus, say, with a brain so physically small that it needs a second neural node just to operate its heaquarters; and for which "consciousness," if it can be called that, seems to consist of little more than the awareness of a perpetual hunger, a visceral knowledge that the organism has grown so huge that it must be constantly about the work of eating simply to stay alive. (But imagine the size of the center if we wanted to preserve the ratios I offered above: it would require some 230 tutors, of whom 140 would have to be staff people! Our largest departments rarely reach 50.)

The problems presented by image may be even more acute, not least because they can arise even where problems of scale are not so severe. Michael Pemberton, borrowing from Michel Foucault, has traced in the language of and about writing centers three of the more widely held representations: the center as hospital, prison, and madhouse. I would add to these, on a slightly more metaphysical plane—and as an alternative to the notion of a "center of consciousness"—the center as institutional *conscience,* that small nagging voice that ostensibly reminds the institution of its duties regarding writing. Whichever image one opts for, the point is essentially the same. Regardless of the commitment by a writing center staff to reforming the larger institution, the tendency seems not for the center to become the locus of any larger consciousness. On the contrary, there is a very strong tendency for it to become the place whose existence serves simultaneously to locate a wrongness (in this case, illiteracy, variously conceived) *in* a set of persons (and in that sense to constitute language differences *as* a wrong-ness); to absolve the institution from consideration of such persons, in that they have now been named ("basic," "remedial," "development") and "taken care of"; and, not incidentally, to thereby insulate the institution from any danger to its own configuration the differences such persons are now said to embody might otherwise pose. In short—and to put it in the most sinister terms—this particular romanticization of the writing center's institutional potential may actually mask its complicity in what Elspeth Stuckey has called the violence of literacy.

* * * * *

So where does this critique of "The Idea of a Writing Center" leave me...or take us? In keeping with the less Keating-esque image I have been trying to move toward in this essay, I am obliged to confess (albeit with considerable relief) that institutional arrangements seem to me too idiosyncratic, and writing centers' political visions too varied, for me to tell you where I think "we"—all writing center people—are going. But I *can* say where I'm hoping *our* writing center will head. I have to begin by explaining a bit about where our undergraduate writing program as a whole is heading. Specifically, we are no longer interested in moving each of our 2000 freshmen per year through a composition course or two. I have never had much faith in those courses as they were institutionalized at Albany (and, to be candid, elsewhere), i.e., understood as pre-college, or pre-disciplinary, literally "extracurricular, some sort of literacy inoculation program. It is common enough for people to claim that they want these courses—administrators, parents, faculty, legislators, etc.—but at least in my history with our particular institution (and from what I know of lots of others), *nobody ever wants to to pay for them,* so that they have been and still are nearly always taught by the underpaid, the overworked, the undertrained (see, e.g., Connors, Miller).

So, no more. We don't offer them. In their place, I favor—and we have now formally adopted—what an increasing number of other programs are moving toward (see, e.g., Jenseth): a writing crack through the English major, in this case one called "Writing: Rhetoric and Poetics," which combines what used to be called (and isolated as) "composition," "creative writing," "expository writing," "practical writing," and so on. What we're after is a long-term commitment founded primarily upon the full-time, tenure-track faculty the institution is *in fact* willing to support and a proportionate number of students. Together, this group of teachers and students will teach and learn writing over a four-year cycle of courses.

My amended idea of a writing *center,* then, runs along similar lines. The general ideal, perhaps, can still be said to hold. I believe—want to say that I *know*—that an hour of talk about writing at the right time between the right people can be more valuable than a semester of mandatory class meetings when that timing isn't right. But I no longer believe that our energies are really best applied trying to live up to—*real*-ize—the rather too grand "Idea" proposed in that earlier essay. I'll frame my alternative proposal in terms of the points of critique above:

(1) I want a situation in which writers are, in fact, motivated about engaged in, their writing because they are self-selectively enrolled in a program—a coherent, four-year sequence of study—that values writing. (It is crucial to note, however, that our Writing Sequence imposes no admission requirements. We will provide advisement—much of it in the Writing Center—so that students will, indeed, be able to make informed decisions about whether to enroll. But actual entrance is on a first-come, first-served basis, up to the limits of our resources.)

(2) I want a program in which we've gotten to know the writers and the writers have gotten to know us; a situation, in short, in which talk-about-writing is so common that we can, in fact, carry on such talk, get better at and even fluent in it—not fence, or be forever carrying on those quickie fix-it chats between people who talk twice for a total of an hour...and then never again.

(3) I want a situation in which we are *not* required to sustain some delicate but carefully distanced relationship between classroom teachers and the writing center, not least because the classroom teachers are directly involved with, and therefore invested in the functioning of, chat center. I don't want to substitute another idealization here by suggesting that the center constituted along these lines would achieve perfect harmony. Far from it: bringing center and classroom, teaching and tutoring, into this tighter orbit would surely generate as many new tensions as new opportunities, and I foresee plenty of stormy politics and raised voices. (Indeed, we've had them already, just in planning the program.) But at least these won't be distant and delicate

negotiations; students will play a much greater role in them; and the energy involved—for better and for worse (I'm willing to take my chances)—will return mostly to the center and to the program, and not be dissipated throughout the bureaucratic structures of a large campus, where it has heretofore had little visible or (given the rate of personnel turnover) lasting effect. And if this seems like an attractive model—if other programs, other majors, other departments want to provide such centers for their students—I would urge them to follow the same principles.

(4) I want a situation in which the writing center's mission marches its resources and, to whatever extent possible, its image. Perhaps my favorite portion of the New Testament is the account of the loaves and fishes. So far as I've been able to tell, though, tutorial time does not extend to meet—let alone exceed—the needs of the faithful. Instead, in those all-too-common situations in which workload far exceeds resources, everyone—teachers, tutors, students—just gets weary. Moreover (to pursue the New Testament connection a little further), I do not believe it is finally a good thing for a writing center to be seen as taking upon its shoulders the whole institution's (real or imagined) sins of illiteracy, either: to serve as conscience, savior, or sacrificial victim.

For our purposes, the best way to create this situation is to tie the Center directly to our Writing Sequence through the English major: to make it the center of consciousness, the physical locus—not for the entire, lumbering university—but for the approximately 10 faculty members, the 20 graduate students, and the 250 or so undergraduates that we can actually, sanely, responsibly bring together. They can meet there, and talk about writing.

* * * * *

As I have tried to argue here, images of the kind offered in *Dead Poets Society* and "The Idea of a Writing Center" can be wonderfully inspiring, but they can outlive their usefulness, too, and come back to haunt us: mislead us, delude us or, as seems to be particularly the case in these two instances, lock us into trajectories which—should we persist in following them—are likely to take us places that we don't really want to go. At the end of the Williams film, you may recall, his Keating character has been fired, made the scapegoat for the suicide of a student who, acting on Keating's advice, played Puck in a local production against his father's vehemently expressed opposition. In the final scene—set appropriately in the English classroom, where Keating has been replaced by the repressive headmaster who engineered his dismissal—Keating has come to collect his belongings. As the class carries on (a student is reading aloud the excised Introduction to Poetry by J. Evans Pritchard), Keating walks, visibly dejected, past the rows of desks toward the back of the room. Just as he reaches the doorway, though, his shyest defender finally cries out at the injustice of it all: he is sorry, he declares, and it isn't fair; the students were forced to sign the statement that led to Keating's dismissal. Ordered to silence by the outraged headmaster, the lad instead climbs atop his desk and chants, with all sorts of poignant resonance, "Oh captain, my captain." Soon other boys, one by one, climb atop their desks, too, and pick up the chant. Keating stands in the doorway drinking in this tribute until, visibly heartened, he finally thanks his young men and then, head high, leaves Welton forever.

It's a wonderful cinematic moment, to be sure—nary a dry eye in the house—and not least because it arrives with such tragic and symmetrical inevitability: Keating has been headed unerringly toward it since we first saw him make that same walk, whistling Tchaikovsky, a latter-day Pied Piper. As the finishing touch on the film's image of the English teacher, however, it is rather more problematic. I mean, what's the message? That the inevitable face of the truly talented, truly in-tune, truly committed English teacher— indeed, the litmus rest of that commitment—is a kind of institutional martyrdom? Which means, in turn, that those of us who (like the repressive headmaster) stay on are…what, exactly?

The trajectory plotted by "The Idea of a Writing Center" may be less tragic in a technical sense, in that it does not require that the protagonist be expelled. Nevertheless, it threatens to lead just as surely to an analogous brand of institutional martyrdoms version of what Susan Miller has so aptly termed the "sad women in the basement" (121 ff.) (or, in the case of writing centers, the sub-basement)—and, perhaps more to the point, to create just as powerful a tactical disadvantage: that is, agreeing to serve as the (universal) staff literacy scapegoat gives us no more power to alter what we believe are flawed institutional arrangements than–Keating's departure gives him to affect Welton, and indeed lacks even the short-term power of his grand gesture.

Of course, where we *do* have the advantage over Keating is in still being able to alter that trajectory, to rewrite the script. As I suggested earlier, the amended idea of a writing center I have recommended here will by no means guarantee a happy ending. On the contrary: while this fairly radical restructuring of both writing curriculum and writing center will certainly address some very important problems of writing program life, it will likely also both intensify any number of extant difficulties *and* produce new ones, as-yet unforeseen byproducts of these alternative institutional arrangements. Nevertheless, I believe that it represents a crucial move—albeit a somewhat hard-nosed one—in our long-term campaign to renegotiate the place of writing in postsecondary education.

NOTES

1. My thanks to Deb Kelsh, Anne DiPardo, and John Trimbur for their thoughtful readings of and responses to this essay.

WORKS CITED

Connors, Robert J. "Rhetoric in the Modern University: The Creation of an Under-class." *The Politics of Writing Instruction: Postsecondary*. Ed. Richard Bullock and John Trimbur. Portsmouth NH: Boynton/Cook, 1991. 55–84.

Danaher, John. *Extended Acquaintance with Seemingly Small Matters: A Teacher's Stories.* Diss. SUNY Albany, 1992.

Dead Poets Society. Dir. Peter Weir. With Robin Williams. Buena Vista, 1989.

Grimm, Nancy. "Contesting 'The Idea of a Writing Center': The Politics of Writing Center Research." *Writing Lab Newsletter* 17.1 (1992): 5–6.

Jenseth, Richard. "Surveying the Writing Minor: d Que Es Eso?" Paper presented at CCCC. Boston, 22 March 1991.

Joyner, Michael. "The Writing Center Conference and the Textuality of Power." *The Writing Center Journal* 12.1 (1991): 80–89.

Miller, Susan. *Textual Carnivals: The Politics of Composition*. Carbondale: Southern Illinois UP, 1991.

North, Stephen. "The Idea of a Writing Center." *College English* 46.5 (1984): 433–46.

Pemberton, Michael. "The Prison, the Hospital, and the Madhouse: Redefining Metaphors for the Writing Center." *Writing Lab Newsletter* 17.1 (1992): 11–16.

Stuckey, Elspeth. *The Violence of Literacy*. Portsmouth, NH: Boynton/Cook, 1991.

Woolbright, Meg. "The Politics of Peer Tutoring: Feminism Within the Patriarchy." *The Writing Center Journal* 13.1 (1992): 16–30.

Collaboration, Control, and the Idea of a Writing Center

Andrea Lunsford

The triple focus of my title reflects some problems I've been concentrating on as I thought about and prepared for the opportunity to speak last week at the Midwest Writing Centers Association meeting in St. Cloud, and here at the Pacific Coast/Inland Northwest Writing Centers meeting in Le Grande. I'll try as I go along to illuminate—or at least to complicate—each of these foci, and I'll conclude by sketching in what I see as a particularly compelling idea of a writing center, one informed by collaboration and, I hope, attuned to diversity.

As some of you may know, I've recently written a book on collaboration, in collaboration with my dearest friend and coauthor, Lisa Ede. *Singular Texts/Plural Authors: Perspectives on Collaborative Writing* was six years in the research and writing, so I would naturally gravitate to principles of collaboration in this or any other address.

Yet it's interesting to me to note that when Lisa and I began our research (see "Why Write...Together?"), we didn't even use the term "collaboration"; we identified our subjects as "co- and group-writing." And when we presented our first paper on the subject at the 1985 CCCC meeting, ours was the only such paper at the conference, ours the only presentation with "collaboration" in the title. Now, as you know, the word is everywhere, in every journal, every conference program, on the tip of every scholarly tongue. So—collaboration, yes. But why control? Because as the latest pedagogical bandwagon, collaboration often masquerades as democracy when it in fact practices the

Lunsford, Andrea. "Collaboration, Control, and the Idea of a Writing Center." *The Writing Center Journal* 12.1 (1991): 3–10. Reprinted by permission of *The Writing Center Journal*.

same old authoritarian control. It thus stands open to abuse and can, in fact, lead to poor teaching and poor learning. And it can lead—as many of you know—to disastrous results in the writing center. So amidst the rush to embrace collaboration, I see a need for careful interrogation and some caution.

We might begin by asking where the collaboration bandwagon got rolling. Why has it gathered such steam? Because, I believe, collaboration both in theory and practice reflects a broad-based epistemological shift, a shift in the way we view knowledge. The shift involves a move from viewing knowledge and reality as things exterior to or outside of us, as immediately accessible, individually knowable, measurable, and shareable—to viewing knowledge and reality as mediated by or constructed through language in social use, as socially constructed, contextualized, as, in short, the product of *collaboration.*

I'd like to suggest that collaboration as an embodiment of this theory of knowledge poses a distinct threat to one particular idea of a writing center. This idea of a writing center, what I'll call "The Center as Storehouse," holds [*Traditional*] to the earlier view of knowledge just described—knowledge as exterior to us and as directly accessible. The Center as Storehouse operates as [an] information station or storehouse, prescribing and handing out skills and strategies to individual learners. They often use "modules" or other kinds of individualized learning materials. They tend to view knowledge as individually derived and held, and they are not particularly amenable to collaboration, sometimes actively hostile to it. I visit lots of Storehouse Centers, and in fact I set up such a center myself, shortly after I had finished an M.A. degree and a thesis on William Faulkner.

Since Storehouse Centers do a lot of good work and since I worked very hard to set up one of them, I was loathe to complicate or critique such a center. Even after Lisa and I started studying collaboration in earnest, and in spite of the avalanche of data we gathered in support of the premise that collaboration is the norm in most professions (American Consulting Engineers Council, American Institute of Chemists, American Psychological Institute, Modern Language Association, Professional Services Management Association, International City Management Association, Society for Technical Communication), I was still a very reluctant convert. [*expressionist*]

Why? Because, I believe, collaboration posed another threat to my way of teaching, a way that informs another idea of a writing center, which I'll call "The Center as Garret." Garret Centers are informed by a deep-seated belief in individual "genius," in the Romantic sense of the term. (I need hardly point out that this belief also informs much of the humanities and, in particular, English studies.) These Centers are also informed by a deep-seated attachment to the American brand of individualism, a term coined by

Alexis de Tocqueville as he sought to describe the defining characteristics of this Republic.

Unlike Storehouse Centers, Garret Centers don't view knowledge as exterior, as information to be sought out or passed on mechanically. Rather they see knowledge as interior, as inside the student, and the writing center's job as helping students get in touch with this knowledge, as a way to find their unique voices, their individual and unique powers. This idea has been articulated by many, including Ken Macrorie, Peter Elbow, and Don Murray, and the idea usually gets acted out in Murray-like conferences, those in which the tutor or teacher listens, voices encouragement, and essentially serves as a validation of the students' "I-search." Obviously, collaboration problematizes Garret Centers as well, for they also view knowledge as interiorized, solitary, individually derived, individually held.

As I've indicated, I held on pretty fiercely to this idea as well as to the first one. I was still resistant to collaboration. So I took the natural path for an academic faced with this dilemma: I decided to do more research. I did a *lot* of it. And, to my chagrin, I found more and more evidence to challenge my ideas, to challenge both the idea of Centers as Storehouses or as Garrets. Not incidentally, the data I amassed mirrored what my students had been telling me for years: not the research they carried out, not their dogged writing of essays, not *me* even, but their work in groups, their *collaboration*, was the most important and helpful part of their school experience. Briefly, the data I found all support the following claims:

1. Collaboration aids in problem finding as well as problem solving.
2. Collaboration aids in learning abstractions.
3. Collaboration aids in transfer and assimilation; it fosters interdisciplinary thinking.
4. Collaboration leads not only to sharper, more critical thinking (students must explain, defend, adapt), but to deeper understanding of *others*.
5. Collaboration leads to higher achievement in general. I might mention here the Johnson and Johnson analysis of 122 studies from 1924–1981, which included every North American study that considered achievement or performance data in competitive, cooperative/collaborative, or individualistic classrooms. Some 60% showed that collaboration promoted higher achievement, while only 6% showed the reverse. Among studies comparing the effects of collaboration and independent work, the results are even more strongly in favor of collaboration.

Moreover, the superiority of collaboration held for all subject areas and all age groups. See "How to Succeed Without Even Vying," *Psychology Today,* September 1986.

6. Collaboration promotes excellence. In this regard, I am fond of quoting Hannah Arendt: "For excellence, the presence of others is always required."

7. Collaboration engages the whole student and encourages active learning; it combines reading, talking, writing, thinking; it provides practice in both synthetic and analytic skills.

Given theseu research findings, why am I still urging caution in using collaboration as our key term, in using collaboration as the idea of the kind of writing center I now advocate?

First, because creating a collaborative environment and truly collaborative tasks is damnably difficult. Collaborative environments and tasks must *demand* collaboration. Students, tutors, teachers must really need one another to carry out common goals. As an aside, let me note that studies of collaboration in the workplace identify three kinds of tasks that seem to call consistently for collaboration: high-order problem defining and solving; division of labor tasks, in which the job is simply too big for any one person; and division of expertise tasks. Such tasks are often difficult to come by in writing centers, particularly those based on the Storehouse or Garret models.

A collaborative environment must also be one in which goals are clearly defined and in which the jobs at hand engage everyone fairly equally, from the student clients to work-study students to peer tutors and professional staff. In other words, such an environment rejects traditional hierarchies. In addition, the kind of collaborative environment I want to encourage calls for careful and ongoing monitoring and evaluating of the collaboration or group process, again on the part of all involved. In practice, such monitoring calls on each person involved in the collaboration to build a *theory* of collaboration, a theory of group dynamics.

Building such a collaborative environment is also hard because getting groups of any kind going is hard. The students', tutors', and teachers' prior experiences may work against it (they probably held or still hold to Storehouse or Garret ideas); the school day and term work against it; and the drop-in nature of many centers, including my own, works against it. Against these odds, we have to figure out how to constitute groups in our centers; how to allow for evaluation and monitoring; how to teach, model, and learn about careful listening, leadership, goal setting, and negotiation—all of which are necessary to effective collaboration.

We must also recognize that collaboration is hardly a monolith. Instead, it comes in a dizzying variety of modes about which we know almost nothing. In our books, Lisa and I identify and describe two such modes, the hierarchical and the dialogic, both of which our centers need to be well

*[handwritten margin notes: "seems like the first is more important to WC's"; "delegation of labor would be more like plagiarism *but*"; "the students should need collaboration (that not always self-evident in everyone's writing process)"]*

versed at using. But it stands to reason that these two modes perch only at the tip of the collaborative iceberg.

As I argued earlier, I think we must be cautious in rushing to embrace collaboration because collaboration can also be used to reproduce the status quo; the rigid hierarchy of teacher-centered classrooms is replicated in the tutor-centered writing center in which the tutor is still the seat of all authority but is simply pretending it isn't so. Such a pretense of democracy sends badly mixed messages. It can also lead to the kind of homogeneity that squelches diversity, that waters down ideas to the lowest common denominator, that erases rather than values difference. This tendency is particularly troubling given our growing awareness of the roles gender and ethnicity play in all learning. So regression toward the mean is not a goal I seek in an idea of a writing center based on collaboration.

The issue of control surfaces most powerfully in this concern over a collaborative center. In the writing center ideas I put forward earlier, where is that focus of control? In Storehouse Centers, it seems to me control resides in the tutor or center staff, the possessors of information, the currency of the Academy. Garret Centers, on the other hand, seem to invest power and control in the individual student knower, though I would argue that such control is often appropriated by the tutor/teacher, as I have often seen happen during Murray or Elbow style conferences. Any center based on collaboration will need to address the issue of control explicitly, and doing so will not be easy.

It won't be easy because what I think of as successful collaboration (which I'll call Burkean Parlor Centers), collaboration that is attuned to diversity, goes deeply against the grain of education in America. To illustrate, I need offer only a few representative examples:

1. Mina Shaughnessy, welcoming a supervisor to her classroom in which students were busily collaborating, was told, "Oh...I'll come back when you're teaching."

2. A prominent and very distinguished feminist scholar has been refused an endowed chair because most of her work had been written collaboratively.

3. A prestigious college poetry prize was withdrawn after the winning poem turned out to be written by three student collaborators.

4. A faculty member working in a writing center was threatened with dismissal for "encouraging" group-produced documents.

I have a number of such examples, all of which suggest that—used unreflectively or *un*cautiously—collaboration may harm professionally those who seek to use it and may as a result further reify a model of education as the top-down transfer of information (back to The Storehouse) or a private search for Truth (back to The Garret). As I also hope I've suggested, collaboration can easily degenerate into busy work or what Jim Corder calls "fading into the tribe."

So I am very, very serious about the cautions I've been raising, about our need to examine carefully what we mean by collaboration and to explore how those definitions locate control. And yet I still advocate—with growing and deepening conviction—the move to collaboration in both classrooms and centers. In short, I am advocating a third, alternative idea of a writing center, one I know many of you have already brought into being. In spite of the very real risks involved, we need to embrace the idea of writing centers as Burkean Parlors, as centers for collaboration. Only in doing so can we, I believe, enable a student body and citizenry to meet the demands of the twenty-first century. A recent Labor Department report tells us, for instance, that by the mid-1990s workers will need to read at the 11th grade level for even low-paying jobs; that workers will need to be able not so much to solve prepackaged problems but to identify problems amidst a welter of information or data; that they will need to reason from complex symbol systems rather than from simple observations; most of all that they will need to be able to work with others who are different from them and to learn to negotiate power and control (Heath).

The idea of a center I want to advocate speaks directly to these needs, for its theory of knowledge is based not on positivistic principles (that's The Storehouse again), not on Platonic or absolutist ideals (that's The Garret), but on the notion of knowledge as always contextually bound, as always socially constructed. Such a center might well have as its motto Arendt's statement: "For excellence, the presence of others is always required." Such a center would place control, power, and authority not in the tutor or staff, not in the individual student, but in the negotiating group. It would engage students not only in solving problems set by teachers but in identifying problems for themselves; not only in working as a group—but in monitoring, evaluating, and building a theory of how groups work; not only in understanding and valuing collaboration but in confronting squarely the issues of control that successful collaboration inevitably raises; not only in reaching consensus but in valuing dissensus and diversity.

The idea of a center informed by a theory of knowledge as socially constructed, of power and control as constantly negotiated and shared, and of collaboration as its first principle presents quite a challenge. It challenges our ways of organizing our centers, of training our staff and tutors, of working with teachers. It even challenges our sense of where we "fit" in this idea. More importantly, however, such a center presents a challenge to the institution of higher education, an institution that insists on rigidly controlled individual performance, on evaluation as punishment, on isolation, on the kinds of values that took that poetry prize away from three young people or that accused Mina Shaughnessy of "not teaching."

This alternative, this third idea of a writing center, poses a threat as well as a challenge to the status quo in higher education. This threat is one powerful and largely invisible reason, I would argue, for the way in which many writing centers have been consistently marginalized, consistently silenced. But organizations like this one are gaining a voice, are finding ways to imagine into being centers as Burkean Parlors for collaboration, writing centers, I believe, which can lead the way in changing the face of higher education.

So, as if you didn't already know it, you're a subversive group, and I'm delighted to have been invited to participate in this collaboration. But I've been talking far too long by myself now, so I'd like to close by giving the floor to two of my student collaborators. The first—like I was—was a reluctant convert to the kind of collaboration I've been describing tonight. But here's what she wrote to me some time ago:

> *Dr. Lunsford: I don't know exactly what to say here, but I want to say something. So here goes. When this Writing Center class first began, I didn't know what in the hell you meant by collaboration. I thought—hey! yo!—you're the teacher and you know a lot of stuff. And you better tell it to me. Then I can tell it to the other guys. Now I know that you know even more than I thought. I even found out I know a lot. But that's not important. What's important is knowing that knowing doesn't just happen all by itself, like the cartoons show with a little light bulb going off in a bubble over a character's head. Knowing happens with other people, figuring things out, trying to explain, talking through things. What I know is that we are all making and remaking our knowing and ourselves with each other every day—you just as much as me and the other guys, Dr. Lunsford. We're all—all of us together—collaborative re-creations in process. So— well—just wish me luck.*

And here's a note I received just as I got on the plane, from another student/ collaborator:

> *I had believed that Ohio State had nothing more to offer me in the way of improving my writing. Happily, I was mistaken. I have great expectations for our Writing Center Seminar class. I look forward to every one of our classes and to every session with my 110W students [2 groups of 3 under- graduates he is tutoring]. I sometimes feel that they have more to offer me than I to them. They say the same thing, though, so I guess we're about even, all learning together. (PS. This class and the Center have made me certain I want to attend graduate school.)*

These students embody the kind of center I'm advocating, and I'm honored to join them in conversation about it, conversation we can continue together now.

WORKS CITED

Corder, Jim W. "Hunting for Ethos Where They Say It Can't Be Found." *Rhetoric Review* 7 (1989): 299–316.

Ede, Lisa S., and Andrea A. Lunsford. "Why Write…Together?" *Rhetoric Review* 1 (1983): 150–58

———. *Singular Texts/Plural Authors: Perspectives on Collaborative Writing,* Carbondale: Southern Illinois UP, 1990.

Heath, Shirley Brice. "The Fourth Vision: Literate Language at Work." *The Right to Literacy.* Ed. Andrea A. Lunsford, Helen Moglen, and James Slevin. New York Modern Language Association, 1990.

Khon, Alfie. "How to Succeed without Even Vying" *Psychology Today* Sept. 1986: 22–28.

Maintaining Our Balance: Walking the Tightrope of Competing Epistemologies[1]

Eric H. Hobson

Writing center people prefer to use words like "teaching" instead of "pedagogy"; "tutoring," not "individualized instructional session"; "what works," rather than "effective educative strategies." This simple diction is one feature of our linguistic practice we have celebrated across the writing center community. However, behind this facade of pragmatism, of action over theory, we have been actively involved in debates concerning the epistemologies to which we as a community should pledge our allegiance and on which we should build our instruction. We have been involved because, as James Berlin reminds us in *Rhetoric and Reality*, "every rhetorical system is based on epistemological assumptions about the nature of reality, the nature of the knower, and the rules governing the discovery and communication of the known" (4). While the academy has argued vehemently about ways of knowing, with factions taking stands under such banners as structuralism, post-structuralism, deconstruction, pragmatism, neo-pragmatism, postmodernism, we too have been involved in much the same inquiry.

Unlike the majority of the academic community, however, the writing center community debates questions of epistemology without making a production of it; often, we do so without being too aware of the nature or implications of our theoretical stance. For instance, I was not drawn into this investigation because I have an unfulfilled love for philosophical argument. Rather, this investigation began when I was forced to think through the differences between the tenets on which a writing lab and a writing center are founded. These differences have been a source of a popular argument across the writing center community for at least the past ten years. Much of the discussion of differences in emphasis and founding assumptions between labs and centers refers to shifts in the paradigms on which writing instruction was

Hobson, Eric H. "Maintaining Our Balance: Walking the Tightrope of Competing Epistemologies." *The Writing Center Journal* 13.1 (1992): 65–75. Reprinted by permission of *The Writing Center Journal*.

based—from product to process (to use one trite description); from Current Traditional Rhetoric to the Process Approach (to use another worn moniker).

At the heart of the debate lies a struggle between competing ways of knowing the world, between competing epistemologies. For example, throughout the lab/center debate, positivist assumptions about knowledge as both quantifiable and prescribable—observable in writing labs with remediation in grammar instruction as their primary activity—have been discredited to a large extent by more epistemic assumptions about knowledge as a communal phenomenon of agreement.

As competing epistemologies fight for positions of dominance in writing center theory and practice, I wish to warn of the problems that arise in any theory or practice that tells us it is the TRUE epistemological foundation for writing centers: be it writing center as remediation center; writing center as center for individualized instruction; or, writing center as a model for the social production of knowledge. And, I wish to challenge us to critique those systems of thought that are presented to us in our literature more carefully than we as a community have shown ourselves inclined to. As Berlin reminds us, these issues are important to our work:

> *A particular rhetoric thus instructs students about the nature of genuine knowledge, or truth—sometimes, for example, located in the material world, sometimes in a private perception of a spiritual realm, sometimes in group acquiescence, sometimes in language itself, sometimes in one or another dialectical permutation of these elements. The nature of truth will in turn determine the roles of the interlocutor (the writer or speaker) and the audience in discovering and communicating it. (4)*

The stance(s) we take toward how best to reach writing are determined by our view of where truth is located and how it can be accessed by novice writers.

WE STAND HERE. NO, THERE.

In our writing center work, we have been encouraged to see ourselves as occupying one of three epistemological spaces. By this I mean, in the past twenty years or so, our job description has changed, and we have redefined what are our educative goals. These redescriptions and reconcepcualizations reflect changes in the way we view reality and our function within that view and result from competition between differing political, ideological, and epistemological forces.[2]

The first space we claimed as our home was within an objectivist epistemology. The positivist assumptions about truth—the notion that truth is transcendent and resides "out there" and, as such, can be objectively studied, analyzed, quantified, and eventually prescribed—defined who we were as a community and what we understood our primary educational purpose to be. To fall back once again on worn-out terms, we viewed ourselves as the writing fix-it shop, the place where malfunctioning language users were sent to be reprogrammed. We understood our purpose to be a supplement to writing instruction. Writing in 1975, Betty McFarland typified this attitude by noting,

> *An objective common to each (composition] course is mechanical correctness. Usually time and/or philosophy does not permit the teaching of grammar in each course; further, the variety and irregularity of student errors would not justify doing so. The logical place for such supplemental instruction is in a laboratory. (153)*

I don't think it necessary to rehash all the arguments against the practices and founding philosophies of writing labs in their most positivist-influenced forms. That job has been done repeatedly throughout the past decade or two in the arguments that established expressionist and social constructionist epistemologies as the dominant theoretical positions in post-secondary writing center instruction.

The second epistemological home presented to us has been within the expressionistic or romantic view of knowledge production. Expressionist epistemology conceives of truth/knowledge as being a product of the individual: truth resides "within." The extensive literature produced by the writing center community that tells us to help writers discover their own writing processes, their own voices, and their own truths—attitudes encouraged by the work of such respected teachers as Peter Elbow, Donald Murray, and closer to our home in the writing center, Muriel Harris—is grounded firmly in the belief that truth emanates from within the individual and thus the teacher's/tutor's goal is to assist the student in learning how to tap into that latent repository.

One-to-one instruction in particular reflects the emphasis on the individual location of truth that is at the center of expressionist epistemology, in that it sets two individuals at work with the goal of helping less mature writers access their potential/voice/process. As such, expressionism is the most apparent epistemology at work in the writing center. And I would hazard to guess that most members of the writing center community are romantics to the extent that we maintain, in the words of Steven North, that "our job is to produce better writers, not better writing" (438). We see ourselves as coaches, facilitators, those who help less experienced writers see that they can write successfully. We strive to make these writers see that they do have something to say that is worth hearing. We believe in the worth of the individual.

Then, there is a third epistemological position, epistemic rhetoric/social construction, that has been touted recently as the true home of writing centers. The controlling idea here is that knowledge results from the interaction of individuals and society. The most forward proponent of this epistemological space being the proper home of the writing center is Lisa Ede, who, in a 1989 *Writing Center Journal* article, "Writing as a Social Process: A Theoretical Foundation for Writing Centers," writes, "research on writing as a social process…implicitly argues for the centrality of what we do in our writing centers" (10). Ede wants us to agree with her that writing center instruction implicitly—and I read her to mean explicitly as well, although she does not discuss specific practices in which social constructionist epistemology is evident—works within the epistemic paradigm of a community arriving at agreement about what it will recognize as truth. This is an intellectually compelling and rhetorically effective argument. But I doubt the accuracy of its description of the types of instruction that take place in the writing center, as I doubt the accuracy of either of the two previous descriptions of writing center activity we have discussed.

WHERE IS THAT PERFECT FIT?

Problems exist in the attempt to posit any of these three epistemologies as the one foundation on which writing centers stand. Too often, however, the problems that have been noted by the writing center community with these positions (we have commented on them at times) are not simply theoretical problems, but problems that manifest themselves when we examine the practices we employ generally (and I use "generally" because I am fully aware of the diversity that exists across writing centers at the secondary and post-secondary level).

The problems inherent in taking a positivist epistemology as the foundation for writing center theory and practice are the easiest to locate of the three epistemologies under discussion here. Positivism, and the ways in which its assumptions are made manifest in composition and impact our conceptions of teacher and student roles, has received much attention in the community's literature. But, for our purposes, there exists a more central problem with positivism and the writing center: positivism creates a system of thought that is too rigid to explain adequately all that goes on in the writing center as tutors sit and work with writers. Positivist pedagogy ignores the contextual nature of discourse and the malleability of language. As such it is ill-equipped to deal with the many variations on seemingly endless themes that parade through the writing center on any given day.

For instance, handbooks and grammar workbooks prescribe a standard use of the language that presents writers a reduced range of options to use in their writing. The many contradictions and arcane peculiarities that exist within the rules of standard written English are suppressed within a positivist-influenced philosophy of teaching. Often students are left more bewildered and unsure of their ability to negotiate the terrain of written discourse successfully, and thus are not likely to take any risks in their writing or to trust or value their instinctual understanding of the grammar of their native tongue. More than that, these prescriptive resources deny a valid place in written discourse to grammars and dialects other than those that maintain a position of power and prestige.

Likewise, an exclusively expressionistic epistemology does not provide an adequate description of writing center practice, regardless of how hard we as a community try to present it as sufficient. The primary focus of expressionism is on the individual as the central agent in the process of making meaning. This romantic notion places truth in the domain of the individual, and as such, ignores the extent to which the social group determines what action the individual can take within society. As a result of this very subjective position, expresssionism refuses to acknowledge the extent to which individuals are products of, even inconceivable outside of, the larger social group.

In the writing center, this belief can lead us to ignore or devalue the demands the institution and the academic community place upon writers who wish to join the community of academe. Placing the individual as the locus of truth—as is often the case in Rogerian-influenced one-to-one tutoring—can lend novice writers a false sense of primacy within the communities they wish to join. Foregrounding within the writing center tutorial individuals' beliefs and experiences to the exclusion of the beliefs and experiences of the larger social group suggests an autonomy, an ability for distinct individualism, that may be utopian, unrealizable, and defeating. Such a focus on individuals and their values and interpretations of reality can, in worst case scenarios, allow for the justification of a totally relativistic, all-beliefs-are-equal brand of tutorial interaction; however, such an attitude pointedly ignores/suppresses the fiction of the existence of neutral educational environments.

Equally problematic is the social constructionist position as it has been articulated most often within the context of the writing center by Kenneth Bruffee ("Social Construction"), Lisa Ede, and others. Social constructionist thought looks at discourse production from the perspective of discourse communities and how these communities negotiate and mediate competing statements about reality to arrive at communally acceptable statements of truth. This macroview of discourse production, this investigation of the way the communal group negotiates meaning, minimizes the influence of the individual actor within the social group. With its intellectual tradition grounded in such socially-oriented philosophical positions as Marxism and much postmodern critical thought, social construction observes the group more so than the individual as the locus of the production of meaning. The individual is not considered a primary actor on the stage of discourse production because individuals are conceived most often as pieces of the social system with little possibility of truely autonomous action. The problem I am discussing here arises in social construction's inability to explain chaos in the system, those examples of individual caprice, random and apparently illogical action that individuals in real writing centers seem to deliver from nowhere, and yet that affect the action—the meaning making—that goes on in the center.

Beyond this theoretical problem, social constructionist epistemology also proves problematic when its proponents attempt to demonstrate it in the daily practice of writing centers. The work of Kenneth Bruffee in particular has been heralded as epitomizing the epistemic reality of the writing center. His description of collaborative learning as he forwards it in "Collaborative Learning and the 'Conversation of Mankind'" and "Peer Tutoring and the 'Conversation of Mankind'" supposes that the tutor/tutee relationship is a site upon which knowledge is negotiated and new knowledge is created. While this is a compelling model because it locates the writing center as a locus of knowledge production rather than of knowledge remediation, it is also a limiting model, one that much of the writing center community has accepted uncritically.

A practical problem lies at the heart of Bruffee's description of collaborative learning's inability to explain the many interrelated systems that create the writing center environment. Both Harvey Kail and John Trimbur, for instance, have attempted to demonstrate how impossible it is for Bruffee's idealized conception of peer tutoring to exist within writing centers. Trimbur has demonstrated the many forces of hierarchical social systems that impinge upon the tutoring relationship and that reveal, as his title announces, peer tutoring to be a contradiction in terms. Likewise, Kail has examined the many inherent political problems—institutional and interpersonal—that are ignored most often when members of the writing center community discuss collaborative learning as a process by which knowledge is created.

In a more recent critique, Lisa Ede suggests that Bruffee's vision of collaborative learning is based not on the epistemic model of knowledge production to which it has been linked but on a more romantic idea of the individual as the locus of truth. She points to the fact that "Bruffee at times praises collaborative learning as a means of helping students escape the inevitable solitariness of writing, whose self-imposed isolation is often seen as particularly troubling for beginning writers" (6). Such a point suggests that Bruffee's ideal is to bring individuals through the tutoring process to a point of sophistication that they ultimately can be their own tutor and can then return to the solitary model of reality endorsed by expressionist epistemology.

WHY THIS DESIRE FOR A TRUE HOME?

My point in this essay has been to illustrate that none of the three epistemological locations that historically have been described as the true home of the writing center is able finally to mold the writing center and the work it does to fit that epistemology's specific contours. This inability seems in a large part from the fact that each approach is not able to take into account all of the forces that impact writing center instruction. Too many forces remain outside each of these position's consideration and conceptualization of how diverging views of discourse production act on writing centers. For instance, each epistemology we have considered cannot deal adequately with the many conflicting political agendas and forces that define a writing center from its foundational philosophy to its instructional methods to its physical shape. There are too many departmental forces and agendas, too many larger political forces and agendas, too many instructional forces and agendas that shape every writing center to be adequately explained and integrated by any one version of what is true. This inability is evident even before we bring into play other factors that impinge upon the environment of a writing center such as personal ideologies of the director and staff.

Why then has there been such a clamor in the writing center community for us to locate once and for all the true epistemological home of the writing center? Why have we seemed to be so concerned about whether our work should focus on individual writers or on the way the social group creates knowledge through its discourse? The answers are many, but, I would like to suggest the following as reasons that particularly influence this desire:

1) A maturing understanding of our activities.

As the writing center community's understanding of its role within the educational agenda of most American post-secondary institutions has matured, we have come to realize how limited were some of our original ideas about our activities and how these methods affected the learning we witnessed in our students. We moved beyond purely positivist pedagogies reflected in drill/remediation labs when we recognized they did not adequately explain the varied learning strategies students employ. Likewise, we moved beyond a pure focus on individual writers when we began to recognize how this pedagogy fell short of accounting for the presence of the social group in meaning-making.

Each time we have moved our focus we have had to sacrifice the sense of security achieved in thinking that we knew what we were doing in our centers. Assuredness is a more comfortable position to be in than the flux that results as we attempt to make sense of our activities in light of new perspectives about learning and discourse production. But any sense of certainty may always be a fiction if, according to Wallace and Simpson, "writing centers are dynamic, not static," and "that change and adjustments to new problems come with the territory" (xii). Approaching this situation from a pragmatic angle, my colleague Alan Jackson reminds me that in our attempts to critique writing center theory and practice, we must continually ask ourselves the following question: Have we reached a point of stability that even allows us to get a good look at writing centers?

2) A disciplinary insecurity.

If we can say we do X because we ground our teaching philosophy in Y, we think that we seem more respectable, more normal to the rest of the academic community. After all, we have been led to believe that other members of the academy, especially the sciences, know exactly on what epistemology they base their entire educational project. In other words, the rest of the academy seems to know from where they came intellectually and to where they are headed. The need for a positive sense of self forces us to ignore the many ways in which the theories we forward to explain what we do in the writing center fail to adequately describe the hodgepodge practices we actually employ. A rhetoric of certainty ("Y philosophical stance fully explains X pedagogy") is appealing to—as Louise Wetherbee Phelps describes us— "a young field determined to establish a scholarly ethos" (206); it is seductive. But is such security accurate?

3) A political motivation.

Each time we have claimed a home in a particular epistemology we may have done so not for the ways that version of reality articulates our practice, but for the ways in which it allies us to a powerful political movement within academics. For instance, the process movement and its pedagogical emphasis on the individual, may have been embraced by the writing center community not for the support it lent to such practices as one-to-one instruction, but for the way it fit the writing center and the larger composition community into the powerful social changes ushered in by the challenges leveled at dominant social systems by many sectors of American society in the late sixties and early seventies. Likewise, the current interest in justifying writing center pedagogy by linking it to social constructionist thought can be viewed as an attempt to link the writing center to the intellectually and institutionally powerful forces marshalled under the banners of post-structuralist thought. We have yet to investigate the possibility that our claims to epistemological allegiance are based more on achieving a desired set of political goals than on arriving at an adequate understanding of the writing center environment.

4) A trap of dualist thought.

Amid all the recent calls in the profession for entertaining multiple perspectives about what we do and value, amid the more phenomenological perspective that has attracted many allies within composition studies and the writing center community, I continue to sense the presence of, and quite possibly the hegemonic influence of, positivist systems of thought. What I mean is this: while we have announced that we believe the positivist assumption that one truth exists is a system of thought inadequate to our needs, we still cling to its underlying structure. We have not managed to make the radical break with the dyadic systems of thought that by allegiance to a hermeneutical epistemological position we necessarily need to have made. For the most part, we continue to announce our positions, defend our instructional practices using a dualist rhetoric of yes/no, right/wrong dyads. We have not realized the phenomenologist's perspective (to name one) that "many equally valid descriptions are possible" (Emig 67).

The problem that results most prominently from this dualist trap is that we cannot realize the claims we have made for our allegiance to privileged systems of thought. We cannot find a pristine epistemological home for the writing center because we use a rhetoric that forces us to look for and find credible only those epistemologies that can withstand the withering gaze of a right/wrong questioning. None of the systems I have discussed in this essay are able to do so. Each can only "correctly" describe the writing center within certain parameters; beyond those restrictions they are no longer "right." As we have seen, each of the dominant epistemologies evidenced in writing center theory and practice exists on both sides of the right/wrong dyad. Thus, the desire we express for certainty—for pristine epistemological foundations for the writing center, for a true theory and practice—will, because of our inability to see/use/believe options beyond the limited yes/no choice available through our positivist-influenced ways of thinking, not be realized. We will remain in flux.

THE WRITING CENTER'S EQUILIBRIUM

My title promised some resolution for this discussion. I promised to demonstrate the equilibrium the writing center community has managed to maintain within the battles of competing epistemologies that have raged around us. This equilibrium exists in spite of our best efforts to ignore it or to force it to conform to contours that are not natural to its shape.

I have gained one important insight from my investigation of the epistemologics that affect the writing center: the writing center has the ability to conform to all three epistemologies I explored. This ability reflects the inability I discussed of writing center theory and practice to occupy convincingly only one epistemological space. I believe we have been looking at the writing center and its epistemological influences from the wrong perspective. We have taken a reductionist view of the problem: we have tried to find the one system of thought in which the writing center fits. This is a hopeless effort. I suggest instead that we apply the hermeneutic perspective we as a community have paid lip service to and that we thus acknowledge that each of these three epistemologies is actively present in the theory and practice of the writing center, that together they create a system that is more able to adequately describe the writing center than any of the three can in isolation.

I see the writing center equilibrium resulting from the fact that we, as the people responsible for the continued success of our writing centers, are not actually walking any one of the epistemological tightropes our community has often suggested we are. Rather, I think that each of us, when we honestly examine our theory and practice, will see that we maintain our equilibrium because we are firmly grounded in an epistemological mix: we have one foot planted in both expressivist and social epistemologies, while we keep at least one hand in positivism.

NOTES

1. Without the discussions I have had about these issues with Bob Child, Alan Jackson, Christina Murphy, and Ray Wallace, the ideas presented in this essay would still be nagging me without an apparent outlet. I wish to thank Tom Hemmeter and Alan Jackson, as well, for their willingness to read and respond to numerous drafts of this article.

2. See James Berlin's overview of this subject in *Rhetoric and Reality* (Carbondale: Southern Illinois UP, 1987)

WORKS CITED

Berlin, James A. *Rhetoric and Reality: Writing Instruction in American Colleges, 1900–1985.* Carbondale: Southern Illinois UP, 1987.

Bruffee, Kenneth. "Collaborative Learning and the 'Conversation of Mankind.'" *College English* 46 (1984): 635–52.

———. "Peer Tutoring and the 'Conversation of Mankind.'" *Writing Centers: Theory and Administration.* Ed. Gary A. Olson. Urbana: NCTE, 1984. 3–15.

———. "Social Construction, Language, and the Authority of Knowledge: A Bibliographical Essay." *College English* 48 (1986): 773–90.

Ede, Lisa. "Writing as a Social Process: A Theoretical Foundation for Writing Centers." *The Writing Center Journal* 9 (1989): 3–13.

Emig, Janet. "Inquiry Paradigms and Writing." *College Composition and Communication* 33 (1982): 64–75.

Kail, Harvey. "Collaborative Learning in Context: The Problem with Peer Tutoring." *College English* 45 (1983): 594–99.

McFarland, Betty. "The Non-Credit Writing Lab." *Teaching English in the Two-year College* 1.3 (1975): 153–54.

North, Stephen. "The Idea of the Writing Center." *College English* 46 (1984): 433–46.

Phelps, Louise Wetherbee. *Composition as a Human Science.* New York: Oxford UP, 1988.

Trimbur, John. "Peer Tutoring: A Contradiction in Terms?" *The Writing Center Journal* 7.2 (1987): 21–28.

Wallace, Ray, and Jeanne Simpson, eds. *The Writing Center: New Directions.* New York: Garland, 1991.

The Writing Center and Social Constructionist Theory

Christina Murphy

[handwritten margin note: → thinks social constructivism should be tempered by other theories]

In the research surrounding rhetoric and composition, social constructionist theory has begun to challenge the writing-as-process model as the dominant paradigm defining writing instruction. The emergence of social constructionist theory and its rise to prominence within the last decade have significant implications for writing centers and for the theories of discourse, social interaction, and assessment that define our work.

Certainly the most significant influence of social constructionist theory upon writing centers has been its endorsement of collaborative learning and collaborative writing. With the writing-as-process model, in which writing is largely viewed as a highly personal process and experience to be shaped and guided by a broader understanding of cognitive theory, the influence of the writing center tutor often has been perceived as an unnecessary, perhaps even harmful, intrusion. Lisa Ede has skillfully discussed the influence of the Romantic idea of the writer as solitary individual, concluding that this perspective tends "to view both writing and thinking—the creation of knowledge—as inherently individual activities," thus minimizing the influence of "social and cultural contexts of teaching and learning" (1989, 6). As Ede states. "Think for a moment, for instance, of Flower and Hayes's cognitive-based research—research that has been particularly influential during the past decade. Where in the flow charts depicting task representation, audience analysis, and short-term and long-term memory is the box representing collaboration and conversation?" (7).

Ede argues that "the assumption that writing is inherently a solitary cognitive activity is so deeply ingrained in western culture that it has, until recently, largely gone unexamined" (7) and suggests that this view helps to explain what, for her, has been "a puzzling and frustrating mystery: the fact that those who most resist or misunderstand the kind of collaborative learning that occurs in writing centers are often our own colleagues in departments of English" (9). A corrective to this point of view, Ede suggests, is to broaden—through research and scholarship—our profession's understanding of the writing center's role within collaborative learning (9–11).

Central to this task of broadening an understanding of the writing center's role within the paradigm of collaboration is an assessment of the philosophy of social constructionist theory and its practical implications for writing instruction. Andrea Lunsford addresses the issue in this fashion:

> *We might begin by asking where the collaboration bandwagon got rolling. Why has it gathered such steam? Because, I believe, collaboration both in theory and practice reflects a broad-based epistemological shift, a shift in the way we view knowledge. The shift involves a move from viewing knowledge and reality as things exterior to or outside of us as immediately accessible individually knowable, measurable, and shareable to viewing knowledge and reality as mediated by or constructed through language in social use as socially constructed, contextualized, as in short, the product of* collaboration. *(1991, 4)*

Joseph Petraglia claims that, for the field of rhetoric and composition, social constructionism has come to mean that "knowledge is created, maintained, and altered through an individual's interaction with and within his or her 'discourse community'" and that "knowledge resides in consensus rather than in any transcendent or objective relationship between a knower and that which is to be known" (1991, 38). He suggests that the following premises derived largely from the work of the two best-known advocates of social constructionism in rhetoric and composition, Kenneth Bruffee and James Berlin—form the basis of social constructionism in composition: (1) real entities (reality) include knowledge, beliefs, truths, and selves; (2) all reality is arrived at by consensus; (3) consensus, and thus knowledge, is "discovered" solely through discourse (rhetoric); and (4) reality changes as consensus/knowledge changes (39).

James A. Reither (1986) has suggested that for writing teachers, a social constructionist point of view has meant an emphasis upon discourse communities—communities that share "values, objects of inquiry, research methodologies evidential contexts, persuasion strategies and conventions, forms and formats and conversational forms" (18). As a result of their emphasis upon discourse communities, Petraglia contends that

> [S]*ocial constructionists in composition of all political persuasions have sought to promote access to knowledge—creating communities as a critical first step toward student empowerment. Compared to current traditional and cognitive rhetorics which focus on the individual writer and how he or she can and/or should shape discourse to gain the audience's assent, one*

might say that constructionists focus on the ways' in which the audience (that is, the community) shapes the discourse of its members. (1991. 40)

While many social constructionists in rhetoric and composition—like Bruffee, Berlin, Patricia Bizzell, Lester Faigley, and David Bartholomae—tend to see this process as equitable and empowering, Howard Ryan (1991) argues that the social constructionist paradigm encourages social elitism and accommodation to the existing world order:

> *In the growing composition trends toward collaborative learning and collaborative writing, collaboration normally refers to more than simply having students meet in groups to respond to individual papers; rather, it entails group decision making and group projects. As with other trends, the collaborative literature emphasizes utilitarian ends—that working in groups leads to better ideas, that it teaches the cooperative skills needed for academic and career success. Yet we may also read the literature as implying a particular social vision, and occasionally we find explicit references to larger aspirations. The collaborative better world is one in which people have learned to get along, where we either accept our differences or strive to work them out through cooperative and peaceful means. Oppressive gender, race, or class structures need not lead to divisive political battles in the collaborative better world: cooperative conflict resolution is the key. This vision, which I will call social harmonist, is not limited to advocates of collaborative learning; in fact, we may see it implied in any pedagogy that encourages a strategy of adjustment or accommodation—rather than challenge or confrontation—with the existing world order. (14)*

Ryan is also concerned that a pedagogical emphasis upon collaboration or social harmony stifles dissent and encourages illusory views of peership. As he explains:

> *Social harmonist ideologies are traditional means of elite social control and are used to stifle dissent or to direct dissent into safe channels that leave elite power intact. Members of exploited groups are invited to trust or to accept a false sense of peership with their exploiters.*
>
> *Composition teachers whose work is inspired by visions of a cooperative world must conceive as clearly as possible the terms of that cooperation. Students encouraged to see academe and the workplace beyond as "communities of knowledgeable peers," where "Status equals" engage in agreed-upon discourses (Bruffee 642) may be ill-prepared for their present and future struggles within hierarchical institutions. Perhaps, rather than teach a value of blanket cooperativeness, our classrooms could ask critical questions about collaboration. (14–15)*

While Ryan finds social constructionism problematic on a global or social level, other critics object to the philosophy for its limited understanding of the learning strategies of individual students. Donald C. Stewart argues that the privileging of the group or the community over the individual in social constructionism is "unsound psychologically" since it is not sensitive to different personality types and therefore different learning and writing styles (1988, 75–76). He bases his critique in the Myers-Briggs theory of personality types, which is largely Jungian in emphasis, and argues that collaborative learning privileges extroverts, those who work well in groups, who are intellectually stimulated by talking their ideas out with others before beginning a writing project, and who enjoy making writing sound like talking. Introverts, by contrast, tend to prefer to work alone and feel that they are at their most creative and productive when given time for inner, private reflection. Stewart argues that extroverts, who work well in collaborative learning situations, typically describe those who do not adapt well to these environments as "unmotivated...inflexible," "highly-suspicious," "stubborn," and "infantile" (78–79). Thus, as Paul Heilker contends, "in these judgments we can see clear manifestations of how collaborative learning both privileges the collective side of the collective/individual binary at the expense of the individual side and also imposes constraining forces upon students' thinking and actions" (1991, 7).

Social constructionism has provided an even more fertile ground for dissent within psychology, especially for cognitive and psychoanalytic theorists, many of whom find social constructionism's understanding of the self as a social construct—similar to all other cultural artifacts—to be too restrictive. Joseph H. Smith (1991) contends that to argue that an individual is wholly constructed by his or her social experience and cultural moment is to obviate the very real presence of individual subjective experience—the majority of which is highly symbolic and often not capable of full translation into linguistic codes or sets that are predetermined and defined by one's culture and society. Smith's concern is that much of the early, imagistic, creative thinking involved in personal, reflective efforts to interpret and create meaning will be truncated by a philosophy that favors secondary process thought, or thought that is constructed to take on the contours of the society it addresses. Will the world of each person's innersubjectivity—the source of so much creative thinking and so many creative insights—be lessened and devalued as a result? (17–18).

Further, Alice Brand and Jan Zita Grover express concerns similar to Smith's in arguing that social constructionism valorizes collaboration and cooperation while deemphasizing the emotions. Grover states that "social constructionism has no theory of desire" (1990, 21), while Brand (1991) devotes an entire critique to social constructionism's failure to address the issue of the role the emotions play in an individual's writing processes and claims that "up to now, attempts at social-cognitive theories of writing mask the emotional experience of writing." She concludes that "despite the fact that social cognition provides substantial information about writers, it seems at the same time to give us more ammunition to avoid studying their emotional experience" (396). Richard Gregg endorses the psychoanalytic distinction between individual and social knowledge and asserts that in each individual "there is a constant interaction between individual systems of meanings and a system of socially shared meanings" (1981, 136). Gregg holds that it is our capacity to form idiosyncratic associations and our concomitant ability to generate personal knowledge that define our individuality. Thus, rigid separations between personal and social knowledge are artificial, arbitrary, and, finally, unproductive.

These theorists' comments address a number of the issues surrounding creativity, insight, and self expression. Clearly, all of us who teach writing in a classroom or in a writing center are concerned with these issues; therefore, it is important to consider whether social constructionist theory—with its valorization of collaborative vs. individual learning strategies, its limited understanding of the role the emotions play in the writing process, and its emphasis upon only those aspects of knowledge that can be socially constructed—gives us a broad enough understanding of the meaning-making activities of individual writers to assist us in providing the most effective instruction we can.

Lunsford (1991) believes that social constructionism will have a radical, if not revolutionary, effect upon writing centers, turning them from "Storehouse Centers" and "Garret Centers" into "Burkean Parlor Centers" (4–7). A "Storehouse Center." she explains, is a writing center that holds to an earlier view of knowledge "as exterior to us and as directly accessible."

> *The Center as Storehouse operates as information stations or store-houses, prescribing and handing out skills and strategies to individual learners. They often use "modules" or other kinds of individualized learning materials. They tend to view knowledge as individually derived and held, and they are not particularly amenable to collaboration, sometimes actively hostile to it. (4)*

In contrast, "Garret Centers" are "informed by a deep-seated belief in individual 'genius,' in the Romantic sense of the term" and also by a "deep-seated attachment to the American brand of individualism." Specifically, "Garret Centers"

> *don't view knowledge as exterior, as information to be sought out or passed on mechanically. Rather, they see knowledge as interior, as inside the student, and the writing center job as helping students get in touch with this*

knowledge, as a way to find their unique voices, their individual and unique powers. This idea has been articulated by many, including Ken Macrorie, Peter Elbow, and Don Murray, and the idea usually gets acted out in Murray–like conferences, those in which the tutor or teacher listens voices encouragement, and essentially serves as a validation of the students' "I-search." Obviously collaboration problematizes Garret Centers as well, for they also view knowledge as interiorized, solitary, individually derived, individually held. (5)

For Lunsford, the ideal toward which writing centers should strive under the social constructionist paradigm is the "Burkean Parlor Center." Lunsford then presents her idea of how the "Burkean Parlor Center" would be constituted:

[I]ts theory of knowledge is based not on positivistic principles (that's The Storehouse again), not on Platonic or absolutist ideals (that's The Garret), but on the notion of knowledge as always contextually bound, as always socially constructed. Such a center might well have as its motto [Hannah] Arendt's statement: "For excellence, the presence of others is always required." Such a center would place control, power, and authority not in the tutor or staff, not in the individual student, but in the negotiating group. It would engage students not only in solving problems set by teachers but in identifying problems for themselves; not only in working as a group but in monitoring, evaluating, and building a theory of how groups work; not only in understanding and valuing collaboration but in confronting squarely the issues of control that successful collaboration inevitably raises not only in reaching consensus but in valuing dissensus and diversity. (8–9)

Lunsford's essay is worth quoting at length because it is indicative of many of the concepts and beliefs—both stated and implied—that surround the philosophy of social constructionism. For one, despite all of Lunsford's praise for the transfer of control from teacher/tutor/student to the group, Lunsford, like other theorists, never makes quite clear exactly how this transfer of power is to occur and exactly *how* it will be mediated within the constructs of American education. To say that this process will be difficult and that it *should* occur are far different issues from explaining how it can, or will be, carried out. These theorists never explain, for example, why hegemony of groups—with all the inequities and marginalization hegemony involves—is no less likely to occur than hegemony of individuals. Lunsford, for example, while advocating collaboration, is concerned that it may lead to a type of "homogeneity that squelches diversity, that waters down ideas to the lowest common denominator, that erases rather than values differences" (7). "This tendency is particularly troubling," she states, "given our growing awareness of the roles gender and ethnicity play in all learning" (7). Yet, beyond acknowledging this problem, she provides no sense of how to deal with these issues should they occur. In fact, she does state......as the latest pedagogical bandwagon, collaboration often masquerades as democracy when it in fact practices the same old authoritarian control. It thus stands open to abuse and can, in fact, lead to poor teaching and poor learning" (3–4).

However, while these are valid precautionary points, they do not explain how issues of hegemony and counterhegemony within groups will be dealt with. In some ways they seem, in fact, to echo a principle of the Jeffersonian ideal of democracy that truth will win out if all groups are allowed their say and will reason together toward a consensus. Whether, in actuality, this principle of the Jeffersonian ideal will work in educational settings, social constuctionism has yet to prove to many theorists' satisfaction. Some, like Hugh Tomlinson (1989), do not feel that consensus within a group is necessarily the equivalent of truth, only of agreement. Tomlinson argues that one can agree, in principle, with what is false, harmful, ineffective, and the like. Consensus alone is no guarantee of the merit or validity of one's ideas or beliefs (53–55).

Second, as Stanley Aronowitz and Henry A. Giroux (1985) have argued, philosophies of education generally reflect political philosophies or assumptions, and, with social constructionism the predominant concept of education seems to be preparation of the individual for the workplace. Even Lunsford, for example, buttresses her argument for the "Burkean Parlor Center" with concepts from the workforce. She mentions, for example, that collaboration is the norm for most professions and cites an impressive list to support her case. In emphasizing that "collaborative environments and tasks must *demand* collaboration," she notes that "studies of collaboration in the workplace identify three kinds of tasks that seem to call consistently for collaboration: high-order problem defining and solving division of labor tasks, in which the job is simply too big for any one person; and division of expertise tasks" (6). Are we to assume from this example that educational settings based on collaboration will prepare individuals more adequately for situations they will encounter in the workforce, or are we to assume that what works well in the workforce will also work well in educational settings?

Lunsford is not alone in her emphasis on concepts taken from the workplace and applied to theories of education. Thomas Trzyna and Margaret Batschelet (1990) emphasize how often collaborative writing assignments are "designed to emulate 'real' workplace situations" (23) and note the encroachment of "management techniques" into the structuring of collaborative learning (28). Harvey Wiener (1986) describes the successful teacher as a classroom manager, while Udai Pareek (1981) discusses the relevance of management strategies to effective teaching (168). And Bruffee, in advocating collaboration, states:

In business and industry...and in professions such as medicine, law, engineering, and architecture...collaboration is the norm. All that is new in collaborative learning, it seems, is the systematic application of collaborative principles to that last bastion of hierarchy and individualism, the American college classroom. (1984, 647)

Aronowitz and Giroux call this philosophy "technocratic rationality" (15) and identify it with the conservative view of education in which educational systems are the "mechanism through which the [middle class] reproduces itself culturally" (5). Preparing students to take their place and function well within the workforce has long been an ideal of the conservative philosophy. Perhaps Bruffee is pleased that collaborative learning will remove individualism from the American college classroom, but many theorists find this idea more disturbing than encouraging. Further, Greg Myers (1986) and John McKinley (1980) emphasize that the requirements and aims of collaboration in the classroom are more complex than those of collaboration in the workforce. Collaboration in the workforce, McKinley notes, is "product oriented," while collaboration in the classroom is "inquiry oriented" and "decision oriented" as well.

Identification of social constructionism with methods and ideologies drawn from the workforce creates particular problems for writing center theory. If education is a microcosm of the power relations and oppositional politics that exist in any society and any historical era, embracing the ideas of social constructionism means for writing centers an endorsement of the view that writing centers are effective when they advance a student's mastery of social skills—in this case, skills drawn from the values of consensus, collaboration, group work, and knowledge that is socially constructed. Even Lunsford's choice of the name "Burkean Parlor Centers" suggests an emphasis upon consensus and cooperation, for Kenneth Burke, in A *Rhetoric of Motives*, defines rhetoric as "the use of language as a symbolic means inducing cooperation in beings that by nature respond to symbols" (43).

As Lunsford has indicated, writing centers that endorse this philosophy and become "Burkean Parlor Centers" seek to challenge and supplant "Garret Centers" based upon Romantic notions of individualism, in which knowledge is seen as "interior, as inside the student and the writing center's job as helping students get in touch with this knowledge, as a way to find their unique voices, their individual and unique powers" (5). The difficulty with "Garret Centers," to Lunsford is that they "view knowledge as interiorized, solitary, individually derived, individually held" (5), while the superior approach, one must assume, is to believe that knowledge resides in the power of groups to negotiate and adjudicate what shall and shall not be viewed as knowledge. The implications of this shift are significant: the least effective writing center tutors will be those who operate from a Romantic perspective, while the most effective will be those best adept at inspiring in students a capacity for group work; the mastery of social skills—especially those most adapted to the workforce—will replace a concern for developing the individual's unique voice and unique powers; and consensus will become the greatest measure of truth—even though, as Hugh Tomlinson and Carole Blair point out, consensus is no guarantee of ethics or morality.

Advocates tend to view social constructionism as a liberatory philosophy in emphasizing the decentralization of power within education—moving power away from the control of any one individual—teacher/student/tutor—and giving it to the group. Yet even this particular liberatory view of social constructionism is not sufficient to answer Lunsford's question about "where the collaboration bandwagon got rolling" and "why has it gathered such steam?" (4).

Part of the answer must reside in the fact that social constructionism is a response to the times. The educational community has continued to grow more diverse culturally, and multicultural voices and values have begun to emerge as challenges to monocultural classrooms and writing centers. In addition, major philosophical challenges to conventional education in the postmodern era have made us more aware of a diversity of perspectives. Feminism, for example, has questioned male hegemony in education and the valorization of male ways of knowing that are reflected in our teaching and scholarship. Marxist critics have made us sensitive to "an economic interpretation of the function of schools, including their role as reproducers of prevailing social relations" and have forced us to take seriously Marx's belief that "the ruling ideas of any society, are the ideas of the ruling class" (Aronowitz and Giroux 6). Deconstructionist philosophers like Michel Foucault and Paulo Freire have critiqued the lack of empowerment within education and have proposed viewing education as both a struggle for meaning and a struggle over power relations. In *Power and Knowledge,* for example, Foucault emphasizes how power works on the nature of learning itself by determining what shall be included in mainstream explanations and what shall be excluded. Obviously, social constructionism's belief that knowledge is constructed (and deconstructed) by groups resonates with the challenges to current educational practices expressed by these philosophies.

Within rhetoric and composition, social constructionism reflects an additional trend, one that finds its origins in nineteenth-century discussions of hermeneutics and the nature of language within discourse communities. Many of the issues that define social constructionism reflect the communication-based social theories of Wilhelm Dilthey, Sigmund Freud, Karl Marx, and Friedrich Nietzsche in the nineteenth century, and of Jürgen Habermas, Paul Ricoeur, Jacques Derrida, and Jacques Lacan in the twentieth century. Philosophically, these writers ground their views in an "architectonic view of communication" and emphasize the "complex relationships among thought, discourse, and action." All foreground "communication, not philosophy, in their theories." Their social theories are, in many respects, themselves "responses to perceived flaws in the explanatory scope and heuristic value of philosophy's concerns. They are geared, in other words, toward replacing the issues of being and knowledge with views of communication" (Blair 21–22).

Perhaps the most representative of these philosophers is Habermas (1973), who argues that institutionalized forms of thought are based on what he terms "cognitive interest." The three primary cognitive interests or "knowledge-constitutive" interests, he writes, are the technical, the practical, and the emancipatory. Habermas also envisions a tripartite typology of knowledge with three disciplinary categories each corresponding to one of those cognitive interests. The empirical-analytic disciplines of the natural sciences are underpinned by a technical interest directed toward control over natural phenomena. The historical-hermeneutic disciplines of the social sciences serve to elucidate the conditions that underlie communication and social interaction. Thus, they function to promote intersubjective understanding, those shared cultural meanings that are the prerequisites for social consensus on the practical dimensions of life. The empirical-critical sciences are guided by an emancipatory interest and are distinguished by their capacity to reflect critically upon their own ideological foundations. Empirical-critical sciences represent to Habermas, forms of a depth hermeneutic since they incorporate "in their consciousness an interest which directs knowledge, an interest in emancipation going beyond the technical and practical interest of knowledge" (1973, 9).

Within the choices provided by Habermas, social constructionism is best understood as a historical-hermeneutic philosophy with a "cognitive interest" grounded in cultural critique and an understanding of how language operates for social consensus in daily life. In contrast, the opposite of social constructionism—what Ede and Lunsford have termed the Romantic perspective—is less concerned with social consensus and more focused on the development and enrichment of the individual. In this philosophy, social and cultural contexts are deemphasized in favor of an exploration of the individual's consciousness and innersubjectivity. From this perspective, the Romantic philosophy is best understood as an empirical-critical philosophy with an interest in "emancipation." Lunsford comes close to Habermas's understanding of "emancipation" in her statement that "Garret Centers," representative of the Romantic position, "see knowledge as interior, as inside the student, and the writing center's job as helping students get in touch with this knowledge, as a way to find their unique voices, their individual and unique powers" (5). Specifically, "emancipation" is concerned with exploring "the inner states" of communicants (Rapoport 1954, 199). Given social constructionism's emphasis upon social consensus, it is clear why "emancipation" would tend to be undervalued and collaboration highly valued as a standard for inquiry, evaluation, and action.

The history of rhetoric and composition makes it clear that the oppositions between social constructionism and the Romantic perspective are more than differing viewpoints on how knowledge shall be constructed and evaluated. In the fullest sense, these oppositions represent the history of our discipline and its current struggles in the contemporary era. The discipline of rhetoric and composition has emerged from the humanities and the humanistic traditions—a philosophical perspective that exemplifies Habermas's concept of an empirical-critical tradition of inquiry. Yet, the discipline of rhetoric and composition in the second half of the twentieth century has moved increasingly toward taking on the ethos and methodology of the social sciences. Robert Connors (1983) has documented the desire for scientific status within rhetoric and composition. Social constructionism, with its emphasis upon social consensus and its interpretive frameworks for understanding cultural mediation and societal interaction, thus seems a natural methodological concomitant for an era concerned less with individualism—and all that the term implies—and more with defining the shaping forces of societal structures and giving them a type of quasi-scientific validity and significance.

Louise Wetherbee Phelps (1988) would have us believe that our discipline's progression toward social science status has been tempered by an affiliation with humanistic concerns, thus making the discipline a "human science." Even if the broadest allowances are made to associate the term "human science" with Wilhelm Dilthey's concept of *Geisteswissenschaften,* or the study of human conduct with a focus on "understanding" (*Verstehen*) versus the causal explanation (*Erklaren*) of the social sciences, it is clear that Dilthey's views emerge from the positivism of the nineteenth century and have largely found a more receptive climate and philosophically congruent application in the social sciences, especially psychology, than in the humanities. When composition is looked upon as an art form, in the sense of a creation of a set of symbols, composition as a "human science" becomes tenuous, if not erroneous, for even Phelps admits that "sciences differ [from the humanities, especially philosophy] in the use of measurements, logic, techniques of observation, experiment, narration, and other aspects of method" (24).

Further, Anthony Giddens (1977) points out via a critique of Habermas's *Toward a Rational Society* that a "knowledge-constitutive interest" in the historical-hermeneutic perspective the social sciences embody "has to be seen as complemented by an interest in prediction and control"—both of which are issues much more characteristic of the social sciences than of the humanities or of a humanistic tradition (12–13). Perhaps Louis A. Sass (1988) best articulates the differences in the humanistic versus the social science epistemologies in stating:

> [B]oth humanists and hermeneuticists are heirs to the intellectual tradition
> of Romanticism, itself largely a reaction against the Enlightenment tradi-

tion of objectivism.... Indeed, both these groups can be called humanistic *in a broad sense—if by this we mean committed to developing an approach respectful of the special characteristics of human experience and action, and free of the positivism, mechanism, and reductionism of 19th-century physical sciences and the social sciences modeled on them. (222)*

If W. Ross Winterowd is correct in asserting that "defining literacy is not idle semantic debate or academic hair-splitting but is almost always a consequential political act" (1989, 4), the ongoing debate between the social constructionist and Romantic or humanistic points of view has significant implications for writing center theory and practice. Lunsford has stated that "Burkean Parlor Centers" have revolutionary implications for writing centers and their interactions with the broader academic community. As Lunsford indicates. "This alternative, this third idea of a writing center, poses a threat as well as a challenge to the status quo in higher education" (1991, 9). Part of the status quo in higher education, of course, involves the Romantic or humanistic tradition and its respect for the individual learner. Social constructionism would have us believe that, in the classroom or the writing center, students learn more through collaboration and group work than they do as individual learners. For many theorists, this is a dubious proposition and one that requires further investigation before wholesale acceptance and application within curricula emphasizing critical thinking skills (Mishler 1979, Roderick 1986).

Certainly, the greatest challenge facing rhetoric and composition involves the construction of a maximally inclusive and relevant theory to help those of us teaching in writing classrooms and writing centers be the most effective and beneficial instructors we can be. Social constructionism provides us with a paradigm that explains a number of aspects of writing instruction; however, to argue that it provides all the answers, or even answers sufficient to warrant the devaluing of other theories and philosophies of education—especially the Romantic or humanistic—seems unwise. For one, it is largely still an untested philosophy in educational settings. Even Lunsford describes collaboration as "the latest pedagogical bandwagon" and concedes that the term "collaboration" did not appear in titles for CCCC presentations until 1985 (3). Second, the history of education—and our own experience with students—makes it clear that different students require different pedagogical approaches. While group work and collaboration might be highly beneficial for some, it can also be stifling, intimidating, or silencing for others, and the best teachers and tutors will be aware of this dynamic.

Blair states that social constructionism is the latest in our discipline's searches for a "meta-ideology" (1989, 21). If so, perhaps the greatest value of a "meta-ideology" should reside in its capacity to respect philosophical differences and to find merit in both "Garret Centers" and "Burkean Parlor

Centers." As James Phillips points out, "the consequence of a multiplicity of models is not chaos and capriciousness" but "a dialectical process" in which, no matter what theory we espouse, we must be sure not to use it "to foreclose rather than to continue inquiry" (1991, 377). For tutors in "Garret Centers," "Burkean Parlor Centers," or centers representing a range of philosophical perspectives, Phillips's admonition offers wise and beneficial advice.

REFERENCES

Aronowitz, Stanley, and Henry A. Giroux. 1985. *Education Under Siege: The Conservative, Liberal and Radical Debate over Schooling*. Westport, CT: Bergin & Garvey.

Blair, Carole. 1989. "'Meta-ideology,' Rhetoric and Social Theory: Reenactment of The Wisdom-Eloquence Tension after the Linguistic Turn." *Rhetoric and Ideology: Compositions and Criticisms of Power*. Ed. Charles W. Kneupper. Arlington: Rhetoric Society of America, 21–29.

Brand, Alice. 1991. "Social Cognition. Emotions, and the Psychology of Writing." *Journal of Advanced Composition* 11, 395–407.

Bruffee, Kenneth A. 1984. "Collaborative Learning and the 'Conversation of Mankind.'" *College English* 46, 635–52.

Burke, Kenneth. 1967. A *Rhetoric of Motives*. Berkeley: University of California Press.

Connors, Robert J. 1983. "Composition Studies and Science." *College English* 45, 1–20.

Dilthey, Wilhelm. 1961. *Meaning in History: Wilhelm Dilthey's Thoughts on History and Society*. Ed. H. P. Hickman. London: Allen and Unwin.

Ede, Lisa. 1989. "Writing as a Social Process: A Theoretical Foundation for Writing Centers?" *The Writing Center Journal* 9.2, 3–13.

Foucault, Michel. 1980. *Power/Knowledge: Selected Interviews and Other Writings*. Ed. C. Gordon. New York: Pantheon.

Giddens, Anthony. 1977. *Studies in Social and Political Theory*. New York: Basic Books.

Gregg, Richard B. 1981. "Rhetoric and Knowing: The Search for Perspective." *Central States Speech Journal* 32, 133–44.

Grover, Ian Zita. 1990. "Words to Lust By." *The Women's Review of Books* 8.2, 21–23.

Habermas, Jürgen. 1973. *Theory and Practice*. Boston: Beacon.

Heilker, Paul. 1991. "The Bi-Polar Mind and the Inadequacy of Oppositional Pedagogies (Or the Dead Poets Society Revisited)." *Freshman English News* 19.3, 5–8.

Lawson, Hilary. 1989. "Stories about Stories." *Dismantling Truth: Reality in the Post-Modern World*. Ed. Hilary Lawson and Lisa Appignanesi. New York: St. Martin's, xi–xxviii.

Lunsford, Andrea. 1991. "Collaboration, Control, and the Idea of a Writing Center." *The Writing Center Journal* 12.1, 3–10.

McKinley, John. 1980. *Group Development Through Participation Training*. New York: Paulist.

Mishler, Elliot G. 1979. "Meaning in Context: Is There Any Other Kind?" *Harvard Educational Review* 49.1, 1–19.

Myers, Greg. 1986. "Reality, Consensus, and Reform in the Rhetoric of Composition Teaching." *College English* 48, 154–71.

Pareek, Udai. 1981. "Developing Collaboration in Organizations." *The 1981 Annual Handbook for Group Facilitators.* New York: University Associates, 165–82.

Petraglia, Joseph. 1991. "Interrupting the Conversation: The Constructionist Dialogue in Composition." *Journal of Advanced Composition* 11, 37–55.

Phelps, Louise Wetherbee. 1988. *Composition as a Human Science: Contributions to the Self-Understanding of a Discipline.* New York: Oxford University Press.

Phillips, James. 1991. "Hermeneutics in Psychoanalysis: Review and Reconsideration." *Psychoanalysis and Contemporary Thought* 14, 371–424.

Rapoport, Anatol. 1954. *Operational Philosophy: Integrating Knowledge and Action.* New York: Harper.

Reither, James A. 1986. "Academic Discourse Communities, Invention, and Learning to Write." ERIC, ED 270 815.

Roderick, Rick. 1986. *Habermas and the Foundations of Critical Theory.* New York: St. Martin's.

Ryan, Howard. 1991. "The Whys of Teaching Composition: Social Visions." *Freshman English News* 19.3, 9–17.

Sass, Louis A. 1988. "Humanism, Hermeneutics, and the Concept of the Human Subject." *Hermeneutics and Psychological Theory: Interpretive Perspectives on Personality Psychotherapy, and Psychopathology.* Eds. Stanley B. Messer, Louis A. Sass, and Robert L. Woolfolk. New Brunswick: Rutgers University Press, 222–71.

Smith, Joseph H. 1991. *Arguing with Lacan: Ego Psychology and Language.* New Haven: Yale University Press.

Stewart, Donald C. 1988. "Collaborative Learning and Composition: Boon or Bane?" *Rhetoric Review* 7, 58–83.

Tomlinson, Hugh. 1989. "After Truth: Post-Modernism and the Rhetoric of Science." *Dismantling Truth: Reality in the Post-Modern World.* Eds. Hilary Lawson and Lisa Appignanesi. New York: St. Martin's, 43–57.

Trzyna, Thomas, and Margaret Batschelet. 1990. "The Ethical Complexity of Collaboration." *Writing on the Edge* 2.1, 23–33.

Wiener, Harvey S. 1986. "Collaborative Learning in the Classroom: A Guide to Evaluation." *College English* 48, 52–61.

Winterowd, W. Ross. 1989. *The Culture and Politics of Literacy.* New York: Oxford University Press.

Theorizing the Writing Center: An Uneasy Task

Peter Carino

Writing centers have long comprised a community dedicated to practice. Even the two book-length studies most influential in the community—Muriel Harris's *Teaching One-to-One* and Emily Meyer's and Louise Z. Smith's *The Practical Tutor*—offer more practical methodology than theory. In the past twelve years, however, several attempts have been made to construct a comprehensive theory to define writing centers and explain what they do. The earliest of these efforts attempted to relate tutorial practice to various process paradigms, such as expressionist or cognitive rhetoric, while more recent projects have often turned to social-constructionist and poststructuralist theory with citations to Bakhtin, Derrida, Freire, Eagleton, and the like, if not *de rigueur*, becoming commonplace in center discourse.

For some the move to theory has been suspect. In a letter to the *Writing Lab Newsletter*, Katya Amato expresses concern that the writing center community is merely mimicking the MLA in a bid for status (16). Eric Hobson argues that the rush to theory results from academic insecurity within the community (2). Jeannette Harris argues in a review of *Writing Centers: New Directions* that despite its title, this book tells us "we are primarily pragmatists rather than theorists—in Stephen North's terms practitioners rather than researchers or scholars" (209).

I do not cite these responses to imply that the writing center community can be neatly divided into theorists and practitioners. The practice/theory binary, like most binaries, is largely a false dichotomy. All practice requires some theorizing, even if based on only the trial and error of experience, and all theorizing emerges from reflections on practice. Those who theorize also practice, and vice versa. However, the binary maintains itself politically as theory functions in academic and professional culture. There are courses in

Carino, Peter. Theorizing the Writing Center: An Uneasy Task." *Dialogue: A Journal for Writing Specialists* 2.1 (1995): 23–27. Reprinted with the permission of *Dialogue*.

rhetorical and literary theory, even degree programs in theory. People who "do" theory earn scholarly respect. The previous editors of *The Writing Center Journal*, Ed Lotto, Diana George, and Nancy Grimm encouraged submissions that "view everyday practice through the lens of contemporary theory" (1). Theory thus carries a capital *T* and is empowered as academic currency in a way that practice is not, even though the two cannot be cleanly separated.

This political nature of theory, as a culturally situated phenomenon rather than a means of articulating practice, adds to the writing center community's need to theorize. Because writing center work, historically and presently, is not recognized as a discipline, other than by some who work in centers, theory beckons as a means of establishing disciplinary and institutional respectability. That is, a body of theory, a reasonably stable paradigm, would not only enable writing centers to explain themselves to themselves but to other entities such as the university units funding them and the disciplines to which they are related, particularly composition studies.

As a marginalized arm of composition (itself a discipline often marginalized), the writing center community has faced a difficult theoretical project, an uneasy task. On the one hand, the community has the same objectives as composition studies—teaching writers and examining how people compose. On the other hand, because its practice differs from classroom practice, it sees itself as a separate entity, often opposed to the classroom, as Thomas Hemmeter has noted. Writing center theorists thus must participate in two communities at once, appropriating and accounting for composition theory as it relates to center practice while maintaining the integrity of centers as different from composition. Compounding this difficulty, any theorizing must consider the center's place within the larger context of academe, where centers are not valued for their disciplinary status but for the effect of their practice on such matters as grades, retention, and service. Situated thus, writing center theorists have faced a project fraught with the tensions of trying to juggle two agendas, first elucidating practice through theory, theory's usual role; second, using theory politically to define the center's relationship to composition studies and to establish the center's disciplinary status and place within the institution. My purpose here is to examine these tensions in terms of how they both drive and undermine a representative sampling of past and recent attempts at theorizing the writing center as an institution and a set of practices. In doing so, I hope to map out the theoretical, political, and pedagogical terrain of the past and to locate writing center theory as it is presently situated.

II

Composition historians, most notably James Berlin, have delineated four theoretical paradigms that have driven the teaching of composition: current, traditional, cognitive, expressionist, and social-constructionist rhetoric. Given the influence of these paradigms in composition theory, it is not surprising that they have regularly served to explain writing center practice.[1] It is unnecessary to recount Berlin's paradigms in detail, but a synopses of each is in order to set a context for my remarks. The first, the current-traditional approach, focuses on writing as a product, values grammatical correctness and form, and is grounded in a positivist epistemology that locates knowledge outside the writer. The second, expressionist rhetoric, focuses on writing as a process and locates knowledge inside the writer as something to be drawn out and expressed. The third, cognitive rhetoric drawing heavily on Piaget, Bruner, and Vygotsky, attempts to equate writing proficiencies with stage-models for thinking and views writing as problem solving. The fourth, social construction, sees writing as a process but believes meaning is produced through dialogue, is always open to question, and is a marker of social, ideological, and textual relations rather than an undiscovered entity located either in the individual writer, the text itself, or the world beyond both—a position that shares many of the tenets of post-structuralist literary theory.

III

Although current-traditional rhetoric accounted for much of the "drill-and-skill" emphasis in many centers' responses to the open-admissions initiatives of the late 1960s, writing center practitioners of this persuasion did not see much need for theoretical speculation about their work. As Hobson notes, at many institutions it was assumed that the writing center supplemented classroom instruction by inculcating grammatical rules and product-centered patterns of organization (3). Betty MacFarland's brief 1975 article "The Non-Credit Writing Laboratory" is perhaps the only public pledge of allegiance to current-traditionalism: "Usually time and/or philosophy does not permit the teaching of grammar in each course.... The logical place for such instruction is in a laboratory" (153). Despite a title ambitiously suggesting definition, MacFarland's piece escapes the tensions marking later writing center theory because her position does not threaten the mission of the composition program and supports limited notions of writing proficiency held by many administrators and faculty members not involved in composition. For these same reasons, her thesis undoubtedly would be ignored by the writing center community today and likely was rejected by the many of her contemporaries embracing the largely expressionistic process pedagogy of the time.

   Surprisingly, neither has cognitive rhetoric enjoyed much influence in the writing center community. Given the emphasis of cognitive rhetoricians on constructing models from observable writing behaviors and protocol analyses, the writing center would seem an optimum environment for such inquiry. Although in the 1980s cognitive rhetoricians were conducting what they perceived as empirical research and calling for more, the writing center community ignored the call.[2] This silence can be attributed partly to the institutional and professional politics that marginalized many center directors; struggling to keep their enterprises afloat and often denied full faculty status, few directors had time for the kind of research a cognitive theory of practice would require. Even by the early 1980s, with composition theory beginning to mature and writing centers beginning to appropriate it to explain their work, cognitive theory was largely shunned in favor of expressionism and the beginnings of social construction.

Karen Spear's 1984 essay, "Promoting Cognitive Development in the Writing Center," stands alone as a comprehensive attempt to link writing center practice with the cognitive paradigm. Drawing the models of Piaget, Lawrence Kohlberg, and William Perry, Spear attempts to demonstrate how writing center practices can move students to the highest levels of these respective models, promoting formal operations (Piaget), relativistic thought (Perry), and post-conventional moral development (Kohlberg). Spear offers little new, however, by applying this knowledge to writing center practice. To be fair to Spear, her work predates much of the cognitive theory in composition studies, but it might be said that her central thesis merely reinforces a commonplace: good thinking promotes good writing.

More interesting is her argument that in leading students to Kohlberg's post-conventional stage of moral development, connections between the writing center and cognitive theory not only "bear heavily on the academic purpose of the writing center, but they also suggest that the writing center serves a much larger social purpose" (73). Spear further asserts that in "nurturing [students'] cognitive development, the writing center can benefit society, ensuring that it will be composed of morally principled, responsible members"(74). Thus what begins as an attempt to view practice through cognitive theory perorates to a promise for the writing center that any university as a whole would like to claim as its mission. Few deans or legislators would find it politic to resist supporting any enterprise that could deliver on such a promise. Granted that writing centers, at their best, may contribute to better citizenship, the totality of Spear's promise reveals the institutional and political entanglements that mark most attempts at theorizing the writing center. While her essay offers some provocative conjecture on the relationship between writing center practice and cognitive theory, the claims finally outstrip the evidence. This is not to say that politics should not enter into theory—no theorizing is politically innocent—but that Spear's argument is more compelling for what it implies about the writing center community's political need to overstate its mission than for what it says about writing center practice.

Expressionist and social-constructionist rhetorics have been more ambitious and influential in their attempts to illuminate practice and advance the political causes of writing centers. Four essays contemporary with Spear's illustrate the dynamic interactions of theory, practice, and politics in writing center discourse in the early to middle 1980s: Stephen North's seminal "The Idea of a Writing Center," John and Tilly Warnock's "Liberatory Writing Centers: Restoring Authority to Writers," Lil Brannon and C. H. Knoblauch's "A Philosophical Perspective on Writing Centers and the Teaching of Writing," and Kenneth Bruffee's "Peer Tutoring and the 'Conversation of Mankind.'"

Perhaps the most revered and oft-cited piece of writing center discourse ever written, North's "The Idea of a Writing Center" suggests a theoretical endeavor in its title but delivers more of a political manifesto pugnaciously refuting those who would view centers as remedial handmaidens to the classroom. Without irony or apology, North likens writing centers to Socrates' tutorials in the Athens marketplace: "open to all, no fees charged, offering, on whatever subject a visitor might propose, a continuous dialectic that is, finally, its own end" (466). In taking this high road, however, North is forced to theorize on practice to support his political assertions that the center is an end in itself

Given the dappled nature of composition studies and the newly emerging theoretical outlines available at the time North writes, this is neither an easy nor a comfortable task. Thus his basic move is to return to politics and practice. More honest than theoretically ambitious, North says writing centers simply talk to writers, readily admitting that "[w]e don't know very much, other than in a practitioner's anecdotal way, about the dynamics of the tutorial. The same can be said, of course, with regard to talk about writing in any setting—the classroom, the peer group, the workshop, the teacher student conference and so on" (444). North resists the urge to construct a unifying theory of practice, viewing tutors somewhat like ethnographers, participant-observers, who observe and adjust their methodologies indefinitely, depending on the needs of the writer.

However, North's accounts of practice, his field notes so to speak, imply a pedagogy comprising an amalgam of expressionism and the adumbrations of social construction. Sounding rather like Peter Elbow, he writes, "The only composing process that matters in a writing center is 'a' composing process, and it 'belongs' to, is acted out by, only one given writer" (439). Simultaneously, North is instinctively aware of the social-constructionist perspective not fully articulated until recent years, noting that his tutors are always concerned with "the rhetorical situation—what the purpose of the writing is, who its audience is, how the writer hopes to present herself" (443).

North thus comes to theory by way of politics, driven as much by his need to lay claim to the right of self-definition and the inherent value of practice for its own sake as by any originary desire to theorize. More than a theoretical statement, North's "Idea" is a forthright call for the recognition of practice on its own, albeit vaguely defined, terms. This forthrightness partly accounts for the extensive influence of North's essay, for despite his title, rather than attempting a totalizing or prescriptive theory, North launches a political salvo and presents the practice of tutoring in terms that portray its value as self-evident. These moves make for an essay that articulates the frustrations of the writing center community, its pride in its work, the complexity of its practice, and the difficulty of its theoretical project. Thus, North's essay is finally the statement of a practitioner who, though unable to articulate a theory for center work, nevertheless has faith in practice and no political reservations about saying so.[3]

Reticence toward theory is less evident in the work of the Warnocks and Knoblauch and Brannon, but while they attempt a more comprehensive theory of the writing center, they do so at the cost of oversimplifying the complexities of practice and politics implied in North's Forthrightness. As its title indicates, the Warnocks' "The Liberatory Writing Center" presents the center as a free zone where authority is restored to writers. Against the current-traditional authority of the teacher, the Warnocks offer a primarily expressionist model: "The new role for students in liberatory writing centers allows them to speak what they think...The student can act out familiar life roles that are not permitted in regular classes, where the student is defined as the one who does not know" (20). This position encapsulates the common wisdom and common prejudices of a student-centered practice, yet the Warnocks stop short of pure expressionism with the tracings of a social-constructionist position: "In general, [in the liberatory center] writing is defined as the ability to read a particular situation critically and to decide what kind of symbolic action will work best, given the specific context and motives" (21).

From this position, the Warnocks conclude that in the liberatory center "faculty and textbooks are not the authorities: students are their own authors" (22). While this position may optimize student learning, the Warnocks fail to examine its full implications, placing centers in a politically precarious position: "We are suggesting that the liberatory center remain on the fringes of the academic community, in universities and public schools, to maintain critical consciousness" (22). In opposing the center to both classroom and institution, the Warnocks construct a false binary of inside/outside, suggesting that the practice they endorse can exist only covertly, a self-defeating position that implies writing centers cannot convincingly articulate their missions.

Like the Warnocks, Knoblauch and Brannon attempt to counter the current-traditional model that they suspect governs most classroom instruction. To illustrate the inadequacy of what they call "unexamined tradition," they offer a traditionalist's analysis of a poorly written paragraph in which the student is assigned to write about friendship but finds himself exploring a tense relationship with his sister. Traditionalist teachers, it is argued, would judge this paragraph according to "their private notions of propriety" (40). Knoblauch and Brannon respond with a lengthy protocol analysis of the student composing the paragraph, claiming that the protocol shows "the writer's growing awareness of his own intent: his desire, not merely to complete an assignment, realize some formal absolute, or imitate a teacher's notion of verbal decorum, but to make valuable statements about the meaning of his own experience" (42). The information gleaned from the protocol analysis, they contend, parallels that which the tutor discovers through talk:

> *The center...offers immediate, close, and extensive support to individual writers in a setting where writers and readers can converse directly about the motives for authorial choices and the potential reactions of an audience where more writing can take place on the spot in answer to questions that enable the writer to reconceive ideas or reevaluate strategies. (45)*

Few people associated with writing centers would disagree with this statement. But it is, nevertheless, incomplete because it places writers in an asocial context, a sort of Edenic space where tutor and tutee intellectually cavort beyond the demands of the assignment, not to mention the teacher waiting in the background with her "notions of propriety." Thus, while Knoblauch and Brannon assert themselves theoretically in opposition to current-traditional writing programs that would employ such teachers, like the Warnocks, they do not subject the theory of their practice to political or practical demands beyond the writing center. To do so, I realize, is a tall order, but one might ask how the student and tutor, getting conflicting signals from the teacher and the writing center, would fare in the context Knoblauch and Brannon set forth but fail to negotiate.

Kenneth Bruffee's "Peer Tutoring and the 'Conversation of Mankind'" begins to get at a thicker description of the social dynamics glossed over by the Warnocks and Knoblauch and Brannon. Implicitly rejecting an expressionist model, Bruffee sees the tutorial as a social transaction in which peers work toward the production of what Richard Rorty has called "normal discourse." Normal discourse is that which is written by a peer for a community of knowledgeable peers; thus, it includes academic discourse. Bruffee conceives of normal discourse emerging from a conversation between tutor and tutee:

> *The tutee brings to the conversation knowledge to be written about and knowledge of the assignment. The tutor brings to the conversation knowledge of the conventions of discourse and knowledge of standard written English. If the tutee does not bring to the conversation knowledge of the subject and the assignment, the peer tutor's most important contribution is to begin at the beginning: help the tutee acquire the relevant knowledge of the subject and the assignment.*

> *What peer tutor and tutee do together is not write or edit, or least of all proofread. What they do together is converse. They converse about the subject and the assignment. They converse about, in an academic context, their own relationship and the relationships between student and teacher. Most of all they converse about and* pursuant to *writing. (emphasis original, 10)*

This representation of practice has attracted and influenced many involved with writing centers for good reasons. First, it dissociates tutors from the current-traditional paradigm; they are neither editors nor proofreaders. Second, it exonerates them of suspicions that tutoring borders on the unethical; as peers they work with the student, not for her. Third, it respects the role of the teacher making the assignment, thus recognizing, as the Warnocks and Knoblauch and Brannon do not, pressures outside the tutorial. Fourth, it implies that tutoring gets the business of the university done: academic writing on specified assignments. And finally it aligns tutorials with the larger collaborative paradigm for composition teaching that Bruffee advocates for the classroom.

The influence of Bruffee's work has certainly been evident, and largely deserved, in writing center discourse because it nearly seamlessly integrates writing center practice, classroom practice, composition theory, and institutional concerns regarding academic writing. This seamlessness, however, also produces a totalizing effect that makes writing center people uneasy, for the words *peer* and *collaborative* ascend to the status of what Richard Weaver has called "God terms"; that is, words that become organizing principles and resist critique. Neither the writing center community nor composition theory has let these or any other terms pass uncritically. The community is thoroughly familiar with John Trimbur's critique of the term *peer tutoring* as a contradiction in terms. Perhaps less well known is the work of Greg Myers, who, from a Marxist perspective, has taken Bruffee to task for ignoring the complex ideological structures and personal agendas inscribed in knowledge produced collaboratively. More recently Alice Gillam, though commending Bruffee's challenges to teacher-centered pedagogy, argues that his "theoretical formulations of practice tend to be idealized, unproblematic, and acontextual" ("Collaborative Learning Theory" 39). These theorists have essentially shown that theorizing is more complex than heretofore imagined, and this complexity is borne out further when social constructionists themselves have attempted to theorize the writing center.

IV

Despite a question mark in its title, Lisa Ede's "Writing as Social Process: A Theoretical Foundation for Writing Centers?" calls for "a fully articulated

theory" (5). Linking "professional adulthood" (5) to theory, her essay constitutes one of the more ambitious attempts to wed writing center practice with
social-construction. Evoking a pantheon of social-constructionist notables
such as Bizzell, Bruffee, LeFevre, and Brodkey, as well as literary theorists
Mikhail Bakhtin and Terry Eagleton, Ede exhorts directors "to place their
work in a rich theoretical context" (5) arguing that "we have not…convinced
others in our field of our centrality" (5). Thus along with a foundation for
practice, she promises political clout and prestige.

Ede's essay comprises a fairly comprehensive articulation of the social-
constructionist position, but like previous theorists, she finds it necessary to
construct a drama of heroes and villains as a context for theorizing practice.
Drawing on historical representations of authorship, Ede deconstructs expressionist notions of the author as an individual self. Here the villains are
not the current-traditionalists but literature faculty, "own colleagues in English," whose adherence to the Romantic tradition "has reinforced their often unconscious allegiance to the image of the solitary writer working
silently in a garret" (9). Ironically, to make her case, Ede is not above drawing
upon two figures whom "our own colleagues in English" highly esteem: Eagleton and Bakhtin. The position Ede attributes to English department colleagues—that they misunderstand social-constructionist collaboration—is
even more ironic given the degree to which the discourse of literary theory
has challenged the notion of a unified subject. Literary criticism, by current
convention, is an assemblage of voices, a polyphony with "the critic as host,"
to borrow J. Hillis Miller's words. These voices, of course, are cited and
named, given their due in a way that a writing center tutor cannot be. This
situation, rather than naivete about composing, I would argue, is what
sometimes makes outsiders uneasy when writing center proponents champion collaborative tutorials.

Ede's essay is finally more a political manifesto than an explanation of
practice. In fact, the workings of a social-constructionist tutorial are never
represented. Perhaps this is why Ede sounds uneasy as she pitches her theory to an audience she perceives as largely concerned with practice. On the
one hand, she aligns herself with the writing center community as a practitioner, noting early in the essay that practice has prompted her to theorize
and adopting throughout the communal "we" common to writing center
discourse. At other times, however, she finds it necessary to distance herself
from her readers and address them as "you" who might not understand her
historical digression (9), "you" who might not be "familiar with this research" (10), "you [who] may be surprised to discover the diverse range of
disciplines upon which [social constructionists] draw" (10). Ede continues to
walk this tightrope between speaking as one of the practitioners she imagines as her audience and as missionary theorist bringing gospel to the unenlightened when, near the close of her essay, she again aligns herself with

practitioners, assuring them that while adopting a theoretical perspective "those of us who work in writing centers are just the right folks to help keep theoreticians like Bruffee honest" (11). But rather than investigate how practitioners might do this and why the nature of practice dictates that it be done, Ede's last word is a theoretical call to "*be part of this conversation*" (emphasis original) about writing as social process and a political challenge "to fight [administration] for the time we need to do such thinking and writing" (11).

Ede's sometime co-author, Andrea Lunsford, finds herself in a similar dilemma in her "Collaboration, Control, and the Idea of a Writing Center." With the second half of its title echoing the title of North's seminal essay and having been first delivered as the keynote address at two regional writing center conferences in 1991, Lunsford's essay, like Ede's, implicitly aspires to provide a comprehensive theoretical foundation for practice. Lunsford recasts three models of composition theory as metaphors for writing center practice: a current-traditional storehouse doling out information, an expressionist garret where the individual writer is nurtured to find her true voice, and a Burkean parlor where meaning is "always socially constructed" (9). Dismissing the storehouse as prescriptive and positivist, and the garret as epistemologically naive in its location of meaning in the voice of the writer, Lunsford asserts the primacy of social-construction, calling upon writing centers to become Burkean parlors. Like Ede, however, she does not describe a tutorial that would illustrate social construction *mise en scene*, choosing, rather, to bring her presumed audience of practitioners to the barricades, exhorting them to "lead the way in changing the face of higher education" (9). A challenge, indeed, for facilities often underfunded and run by people with less than full faculty status![4]

While certainly I do not advocate that writing center directors accept marginalization, there is an unintentionally cruel irony in Lunsford's and Ede's calls to arms, for in positions of power they stand like generals safely atop a hill of professional status offering up marginalized writing center practitioners as cannon fodder in an imagined war with budget cutting administrators, Gradgrindian department chairs, and theoretically simple writing program directors. While certainly politics should be addressed in writing center theory, doing so at the expense of addressing practice makes Ede's and Lunsford's essays more clarion calls than anything else. While the writing center community may need such calls from time to time, there is more political savvy in position statements in forums that reach beyond the writing center community: North's "Idea," appearing in *College English*; Diana George's address, "Talking to the Boss," to a conference of English Department chairs; or Valerie Balester's response to the 1991 "Progress Report from the CCCC Committee on Professional Standards." As for local politics, these battles are best fought by individual directors who know the shape of the terrain in the specific cultures of their institutions.

V

While Ede's and Lunsford's essays, like those previously discussed, aim for a comprehensive, generalized theory of the writing center, more recent theorists have set more modest goals, recognizing the complexities of practice and the multiplicity of political pressures on the writing center.

Equally astute politically and theoretically, but more practice-centered than Ede or Lunsford, Alice Gillam, in "Writing Center Ecology: A Bakhtinian Perspective," provides an opportunity not only to imagine how a social-constructionist tutorial might work but to see the extents and limitations of its effectiveness in a particular tutorial situated in a particular institutional context. Though Gillam does not claim to be a social constructionist, in drawing upon Mikhail Bakhtin's notion of dialogical discourse, she falls into this camp. Simply put, the Bakhtinian dialogic Gillam tenders locates knowledge and meaning in a dialogue between what Bakhtin calls the centripetal forces of language—that is, socially validated discourse—and the centrifugal forces of language—that is, the idiosyncrasies of the writer: her dialect, her command of forms, her linguistic representations of her experiences. All texts are thus multivocal. Gillam illustrates the workings of this position as it affects the mission of her center within the political constraints of her university and in a brief case study of a tutorial in which a dialogic perspective might have helped a tutor reconceive a student's difficulties in responding to a particular assignment. Gillam first notes that while her center wishes to encourage the centrifugal forces of the students perspective, it must do so with an eye on the centripetal force of a proficiency test required for junior standing. With her subsequent case study, she illustrates that this seeming dilemma in practice provides "fertile ground for writing and talk about writing" (5).

The case study recounts the struggle of a tutor who can only point out the need to "focus" when confronted with a tutee's rich but rambling narrative about struggling toward literacy while battling alcoholic parents. As a result, the tutor feels she has encouraged the reduction of the essay to "'its skeleton to please her instructor and [herself]'" (5). Gillam conjectures that the tutor's problem here is that she conceives the paper not as an opportunity for a dialogic text but as a battle between the centripetal demands to produce academic discourse and the centrifugal demands of the student's impulse to make sense of painful experience. Framing the down and dirty of this tutorial in her Bakhtinian perspective, Gillam goes on to offer several questions that could be asked to enable the tutee to "puzzle over the off-key shifts in voice as a way of discovering focus.... which need not be univocal nor simple" (7).

The virtue of Gillam's essay resides in her ability to balance theory (the Bakhtnian dialogic) and politics (the pressures of her institution's exit exam and the demands of the tutee's assignment) with practice (the concrete representation of the tutorial). Furthermore, she presents the power of Bakhtinian theory not as a totalizing panacea but as a perspective, to borrow a word from her title, that might help tutors make sense of the raw experience of the difficulties of a particular kind of tutorial. Thus, Gillam's conclusions, unlike those of the work previously discussed (save North's), are much more tentative:

> [W]e who participate in the writing center are responsible for authoring a social discourse that remains perpetually open, continually turning; a social discourse that addresses and answers to many divergent audiences—each other, our own inner audiences, the writers we serve, the faculty, university administrators, and the community at large—and that recognizes the dialogical relationship between centrifugal and centripetal forces. Like our tutors, we who direct writing centers must offer advice, make policies, and act according to our best judgement while at the same time recognizing the absence of fixed answers, predictable outcomes, and determinate meanings. (10)

Gillam's limited claims and call for ongoing revision hark back to North's characterization of tutors as participant-observers meeting the demands of situations as they occur. In a similar vein, Christina Murphy, called for moving theory even closer to the exigencies of practice in a paper presented at the 1993 CCCC. Drawing upon Levi-Strauss's notion of the *bricoleur,* a figure in primitive cultures who makes beautiful things from what is at hand, a sort of artist of the extemporaneous, she likens this figure's activities to writing center practice in which the tutor proceeds from the student's needs and the expedience of the tutorial, rather than from some preconceived theoretical framework. Tutors thus are revising theory constantly in light of practice. Eric Hobson, in a recent essay in *Intersections: Theory-Practice in the Writing Center,* collapses the theory/practice binary even further. Responding to Thom Hawkins' claim that writing centers "must do more than patch together fragments of successful theory," Hobson defends patchwork to argue that the writing center community needs to examine the "lore" of practice as a means of making knowledge and to stop feeling "guilty about being more interested in the practice of writing center work than its theory" (2). Hobson thus calls for theory building that starts in the specific practice of writing centers, rather than appropriating a theory—be it cognition, expressionism, or social construction—and attempting to say it elucidates what writing centers do and validates their place in the institution.

These most recent positions recognize the multiplicity, variety, and idiosyncrasies of tutorial practice. They also indicate that the writing center community is beginning to avoid the same mistake that composition as a whole did when, according to North's narrative in *The Making of Knowledge in Composition,* it devalued practitioner knowledge in favor of theory to seek credibility as a discipline. Certainly theory is necessary, for without it practice defies reflection, but the allure of disciplinary status should not blind the community to its limitations. Totalizing theories may promise stability and prestige, but they also substitute an illusion of "theory hope," to borrow Stanley Fish's words, for the dialogue central to the writing center community's mission. As the writing center community continues to mature, it will need to see theory and practice in a multivocal dialogue, with theory providing a means of investigating practice, practice serving as a check against theoretical reification, and both proceeding with an awareness of the political contexts in which writing centers function collectively as a professional community and individually in institutional contexts. Such a dialogue may be difficult, but it need not be uneasy.

NOTES

1. While writing center theorists have drawn upon other paradigms—for example, Freudian theory (Murphy), femininism (Woolbright), family systems theory (Smith), and Derridean play (Nash)—these attempts have not had the totalizing and often prescriptive agendas of those drawing upon composition theory. Nor have they faced the uneasy task of theorizing the writing center in terms of a larger community of which the center is, on the one hand, a part, but, on the other, an entity itself. In short, no one expects writing centers to explain themselves in term of Freud or feminism (though such efforts have proved valuable), but composition theory offers both a challenge and a tool given that are funded to teach writing,

2. I have in mind here primarily the work of Flower and Hayes and their appropriation of Vygotsky and Piaget to undergird their cognitive model of the writing. Most writing center practitioners are also familiar with Barry Kroll's and Patricia Bizzell's application of William Perry's cognitive model to writing instruction, here used by Spear to explain center practice.

3. In his recent "Revisiting The Idea of a Writing Center," North critiques his position in "Idea" as a Romantic ideal, arguing for a less ambitious mission linked to the composition program "through the English major; to make the [center] the center of consciousness, the physical locus—not for the entire, lumbering university—but for the approximately 10 faculty members, the 20 graduate students, and the 250 or so undergraduates that we can actually, sanely, responsibly bring together"(18). This turning in, I would argue, through less ambitious and inspiring, is a realistic response to the necessities of context, something often missing in theorizing about the center.

4. For a detailed critique of Lunsford's problem in representing the tutorial, see Christina Murphy's "The Writing Center and Social Constructionist Theory."

WORKS CITED

Amato, Katya. "A Reader Comments." *The Writing Lab Newsletter* 16.6 (1992):16.

Balester, Valerie. "Revising the 'Statement' ": On the Work of Writing Centers." "Symposium on the 1991 'Progress Report from the CCCC Committee on Professional Standards.' " *College Composition and Communication* 43.2 (May, 1992):167–171.

Berlin, James. *Rhetoric and Reality. Writing Instruction in American Colleges, 1900–1985.* Carbondale: Southern Illinois UP, 1987.

Brannon, Lil and C. H. Knoblauch. "A Philosophical Perspective on Writing Centers and the Teaching of Writing." Olson 36–47.

Bruffee, Kenneth. "Peer Tutoring and the 'Conversation of Mankind.'" Olson 3–15.

Ede, Lisa. "Writing as Social Process: A Theoretical Foundation for Writing Centers?" *The Writing Center Journal* 9.2 (1989): 3–13.

Gillam, Alice. "Collaborative Learning Theory and Peer Tutoring Practice." Mullin and Wallace 39–53.

———. "Writing Center Ecology: A Bakhtinian Perspective." *The Writing Center Journal* 11.2 (1991):3–11.

George, Diana. "Talking to the Boss: A Preface." *The Writing Center Journal* 9.1 (1988):37–44.

Harris, Jeannette, Rev. of *The Writing Center, New Directions.* Eds. Ray Wallace and Jeanne Simpson. *The Writing Center Journal* 12.2 (1992):205–210.

Harris, Muriel. *Teaching One-to-One: The Writing Conference.* Urbana: NCTE, 1986.

Hemmeter, Thomas. "The 'Smack of Difference': The Language of Writing Center Discourse." *The Writing Center Journal* 11.1 (1990):35–49.

Hobson, Eric, "Writing Center Practice Counters Its Theory. So What?" Mullin and Wallace 1–10.

Lunsford, Andrea. "Collaboration, Control, and the Idea of a Writing Center." *The Writing Center Journal* 12.1 (1991):3–10.

MacFarland, Betty. "The Non-Credit Writing Laboratory." *Teaching English in the Two-Year College* 1.3 (1975):153–54.

Meyer, Emily and Louise Z. Smith. *The Practical Tutor.* New York: Oxford UP, 1987.

Miller, J. Hillis. "The Critic as Host." *Critical Inquiry* 3 (1977):439–47.

Mullin, Joan A., and Ray Wallace, eds. *Intersections: Theory-Practice in the Writing Center.* Urbana: NCTE, 1994.

Murphy, Christina. "Freud in the Writing Center: The Psychoanalysis of Tutoring Well." *The Writing Center Journal* 10.1 (1993):13–18.

———. "The Writing Center and Social Constructionist Theory." Mullin and Wallace 25–38.

———. "Toward a Theory of Knowledge in Writing Center Pedagogy." Paper presented at the 1993 Conference on College Composition and Communication, San Diego, April 2, 1993.

Myers, Greg, "Reality, Consensus, and Reform in the Rhetoric of Composition Teaching." *College English* 48 (1986):154–175.

Nash, Thomas. "Derrida's 'Play' and Prewriting for the Laboratory." Olson 182–196.

North, Stephen. "The Idea of a Writing Center." *College English* 46 (1984):433–446.

———. *The Making of Knowledge in Composition: Portrait of an Emerging Field.* Upper Montclair, NJ: Boynton/Cook, 1987.

———. "Revisiting 'The Idea of a Writing Center.'" *The Writing Center Journal* 15.1 (1994):7–19.

Olson, Gary A., ed. *Writing Center Theory and Administration.* Urbana: NCTE, 1984.

Smith, Louise. "Family Systems Theory and the Form of Conference Dialogue." *The Writing Center Journal* 10.2 (1990):3–14.

Spear, Karen. "Promoting Cognitive Development in the Writing Center." Olson 62–76.

Trimbur, John "Peer Tutoring: A Contradiction in Terms?" *The Writing Center Journal* 7.2 (1987):21–28.

Warnock, Tilly and John. "Liberatory Writing Centers: Restoring Authority to Writers." Olson 16–23.

Weaver, Richard. *The Ethics of Rhetoric*. Chicago: Henry Regnery, 1953.

Woolbright, Meg, "The Politics of Tutoring: Feminism Within the Patriarchy." *The Writing Center Journal* 13.1 (1992):16–30.

The Unpromising Future
of Writing Centers

Terrance Riley

I wish to offer a paradoxical argument here: that the least promising future we can imagine for ourselves and our writing centers is the very one we long for; that our pursuit of success and stability, as conventionally measured, may be our undoing.

I am aware that such an argument must seem insensitive at this point in our history, when many writing center directors are struggling just to keep their rooms open for another semester, and while many more must generate a steady stream of explanations, objectives, and progress reports to counter the skepticism of the university culture. It would seem more appropriate to rejoice in the national recognition of our professional organizations, the appearance of books and dissertations on writing center pedagogy, credit-bearing classes in tutoring in the college catalogues, and tenure for center directors. All these bespeak a level of academic credibility largely unimaginable fifteen years ago, and both those who are struggling and those who have more or less arrived can hope to draw on this credibility to claim an untroubled corner in the university.

In short, the time is wrong for self-criticism. But if I am correct, we may be approaching the last time we are able to make a choice about the sort of future we want to inhabit. We still pride ourselves on our capacity for providing an alternative to mass education: to epistemological conformism within disciplines and courses, to teacher (expert) centrality, to assessment by measurable outcomes, to replicable pedagogics, to the thorough fixation on the isolated mind that above all characterizes the modern philosophy of education. When writing centers work like they're supposed to, they encourage the intellect of the undergraduate writer in ways that either ignore these principles or subvert them: expertise is less important than personal engagement, for instance; cognitive "measurements" are usually abandoned entirely. Because

Riley, Terrance. "The Unpromising Future of Writing Centers." *The Writing Center Journal* 15.1 (1994): 20–34. Reprinted by permission of *The Writing Center Journal*.

our principles are different, the established university culture has difficulty recognizing what writing centers do. Thus we are often regarded with suspicion by alert traditionalists and by administrators who are unable to rethink the notion of "productivity."

But our most visible advances in recent years—the signs of progress noted above—do not serve to strengthen what we pride ourselves on; rather, they simply make our territory look less foreign to academic xenophobes. And as we try to look more familiar, we inevitably move closer to the mass education model.

This claim is liable to strike most of us as simply wrong. Over the last decade, at least, writing centers have set themselves against epistemological conformism and on the side of communities of learning. We are more inclined to understand professionalization as a political move for consolidating the gains of our alternative model and spreading its message, and if we act like the mainstream scholars at times, that is simply a stratagem for accruing the respectability necessary to function as we wish within the university system. Precisely because we believe that some degree of resistance is built into our collective enterprise, we feel capable of playing the hierarchical game *and* maintaining the project of countering the hierarchy. Because we are a new group and a group that considers itself uniquely marginalized, we write a history of ourselves that stresses our outsider status and overlooks our similarity to other, once excluded groups.

But we are hardly the first outsiders to kick at the university doors, nor the first to believe that our fresh ethical perspective could revitalize academic traditions, nor the first to encounter narrow-mindedness, skepticism, and outright rejection. On the contrary, these are the usual conditions of the interest group seeking a place in the university, and the subsequent stages in the evolution of academic respectability follow a predictable pattern as well: high idealism and frustration with institutional inertia result in the attempt to reform and renew the parent discipline from within, an attempt which gradually but surely gives way to a series of compromises in which the original package of revolutionary energy is tapped off into academic business as usual.

I want to recollect the history of three groups now firmly established in the university—American literature, literary theory, and composition studies—whose emergence in the English establishment followed this pattern. The conclusions I hope will materialize are that the power that accompanies a rise in professional status is partly illusory; that both power and status are purchased at great price; and that if those of us devoted to the writing center concept follow the example of other groups, seeking stability in professionalization, we will jeopardize the values that make our work meaningful.

AMERICAN LITERATURE

One hundred and twenty years ago, American literature appeared in the college curriculum only as the occasional special topics course, offered by a senior faculty member with an interest in the area. A regular place in the catalogue was out of the question, for only a handful of professors could imagine what one would do in the classroom. What specialized knowledge was necessary for studying and interpreting works written in our own language by a (nearly) contemporary author? What body of scholarship would the course convey?

That university English departments neglected native writers in favor of the British and the classics was a source of minor scandal in the world of the public intelligentsia, and university professors who advocated a place for American literature in the curriculum were able to draw on the indignation of figures like Horace Scudder, who wrote in 1888 that the study of one's own literature was the "most serviceable means for keeping alive the smouldering coals of patriotism" (47). The professors cited other noble ideals as well: moral growth, and a citizenry possessed of its cultural inheritance. Newton Marshall Hall of Iowa College argued in 1892 that the study of American literature

> should be for every student the coming into an inheritance of truth and beauty, without which his life must be barren and meagre.... It should inspire in some that enthusiasm for letters, that devotion to truth, and pride of patriotism necessary for the wider and more complete development of our national literature. (162)

But neither the nationalistic nor the truth-and-beauty argument carried much weight with English department classicists, to whom American literature still looked hopelessly shallow beside the profundities offered by Indo-European or the Greek polity. Therefore, by and large, the Americanists kept their enthusiasm and their advocacy in the background of their work and sought a foothold in the academy by modeling themselves on the classicists. They wrote histories and biographies; they corrected the well-known texts and discovered new ones; the most devoted among them applied accepted philological and rhetorical analyses to contemporary writers.

Together, they slowly and painstakingly constructed a place for American literature in the university which the journalists could approve and the classicists could at least tolerate. Our culture, the argument went, was no longer European, and our literature was increasingly un-British. But our literature was still rough, intolerant of authority or order; it needed cultivation, or "more complete development," as Hall put it. Scholarly inquiry could serve that end, to refine and organize, and especially to temper the more dangerous tendencies of democracy. Barret Wendell and Chester Greenough's 1904 *History of Literature in America* makes such a case.

> *The spirit of European democracy has been dominated by blind devotion to an enforced equality. In many American utterances you may doubtless find thoughtless assertion of the same dogma. Yet if you will ponder on the course of American history…you must grow to feel that American democracy has a wiser temper, still its own. The national ideal of America has never denied or even repressed the countless variety of human worth and power. It has urged only that men should enjoy liberty within the range of law. (434)*

Clearly there's something for everyone here: a nod at once to the patriot and the philologist, both of whom still spoke the language of national character, but something for the classicists too—a counterforce to enthusiasm and egalitarianism in which the energy of "countless variety" is dissipated "within the range of law."

By 1930, the Americanists could claim a conventional sort of success: a permanent place in the curriculum; acknowledgment of the legitimacy of the Ph.D. in American literature. But with respectability came a pronounced narrowing and limitation, for the scholarship with which the Americanists had purchased credibility was deeply at odds with their populism and their advocacy role. The nationalistic and the truth-and-beauty arguments (themselves at odds, of course) had in common the assumption that literature could serve to provide many Americans with representations of their cultural heritage. But the scholarly justification moved in exactly the opposite direction— toward removing literature from the public, and removing from literature any immediate political or intellectual value. Where a book or poem questioned the dominant ideologies of race or gender or religion, Americanists worked to depoliticize, decanonize, or ignore. The respectable scholarly conception of American literature was, precisely, that it was not popular; it was elite. The advocacy of Scudder, Hall, and others had imagined wide dissemination to a lively audience; but by 1929, the founders of the journal *American Literature* saw fit to add this clarification "To our contributors" in the first issue:

> "American Literature," *as we stated in our preliminary announcement,* "will not…be a pedagogical journal or a journal of contemporary letters; it will be a scholarly publication, not a popular magazine." *Only rarely do we expect to print articles on living authors…. Ordinarily we shall not publish articles bearing directly upon teaching problems. (75)*

So much for living issues and controversies, not to mention living authors. But this was exactly the sort of exclusion that all the other established university disciplines, including English classicism, had grown strong on.

LITERARY THEORY

The same interior tension—a populist orientation irresistibly drawn to the prestige of academic purity—informs the development of literary theory. In part because it was not central to scholarship, but was rather in service to other cultural and pedagogical goals ("ranking" authors, nurturing taste), most academic critical theory at the turn of the twentieth century was exploratory and speculative; though not intended for the general reader, it maintained the unspecialized style found in middle-brow periodicals. And though the early theorists usually had one or another axe to grind—classicist, humanist, aesthetic, impressionist, psychological—they were on the whole remarkably pluralistic. Thus—George Woodberry in 1913 notes that literature can be approached through several intellectual venues because literary works, as part of "the world of phenomena," are

> *subject to the order of time, to current human conditions, to changing judgments intellectual and moral, to varieties of fortune; in short, they are... part of a larger world...and however isolate and absolute may be their aesthetic value, they offer, to say the least, other pertinent phases of interest, when taken as a development in time. (47–8)*

This passage is part of a generous argument which would put some creditable means of criticism into the hands of many, creating a republic of approaches. All that is necessary is some serious attention to one or another of the "Phases of interest" which literature offers. Presumably, then, the sociologist could be as qualified to find something of value in a literary work as the philologist or the rhetorician.

In something like a spirit of fair play, Woodberry makes a full and eloquent case for pluralism. But it is clear that his theoretical sympathies do not lie with inclusiveness when he turns, in the same essay, to represent the alternative. Considering the proliferation of philosophical, psychological, and sociological approaches to literature, he writes:

> *It is plain that in all such labors, ancient or modern, criticism gets ever farther away from the work of art itself; it leaves the matter of life, which art is, for the matter of knowledge; and when we consider the extraordinary variety of the tasks which criticism latterly has set for itself...it certainly seems time to ask whether there be not a more defined sphere, less confounded with all knowledge, for criticism to move in.... (51)*

The critique of pluralism has not changed much since Woodberry's day: extrinsic theories draw the critic "ever farther away" from the text; and as we admit the application of "non-literary" principles, criticism loses its disciplinary character, becoming, as Woodberry says, "confounded with all knowledge."

It was in the passage away from pluralism and toward a "more defined sphere" that theory became an area of contention. Nearly all the critical manifestoes of the early twentieth century—one thinks of Croce, Spingarn, Richards, Eliot—assert one imperial principle or another intended to unify criticism and to distinguish it from other divisions of intellectual work. From the outset, then, one might have predicted the course of American critical theory toward formalism, for only formalism—primarily the New Criticism of the 1930s and '40s—could offer the characteristic of a true discipline: it was unmixed with other genres of knowledge and thus could develop its own terms and traditions, so that ultimately only a trained professional would be able to pursue it; and it held out the promise of a familiar sort of scholarly specialization. Cleanth Brooks and Robert Penn Warren's announced intention in *Understanding Poetry* (1938) to attend to "the poem as a poem" (ix) assumes the superiority of serious, professional reading over the mixed and contradictory reading of amateurs. At nearly the same moment, John Crowe Ransom was taking the next step, calling for the creation of a network of professional critics (albeit with his customary irony; the essay is "Criticism, Inc.") "There are many critics who might tell us" what criticism is, Ransom writes, "but for the most part they are amateurs. So have the critics nearly always been amateurs; including the best ones. They have not been trained to criticism so much as they have simply undertaken a job for which no specific qualifications were required" (327).

In retrospect, it seems clear that establishment of any strict critical orthodoxy would have suppressed the expansion necessary for disciplinary health. What American formalism accomplished was not the lasting preeminence of formalism, but, more broadly, the ascendance of critical monisms over pluralism—that is, the superiority of expert forms of reading over amateur reading. Thus literary theorists today need not trouble themselves overmuch about the substantive positions taken by their theory. Only purity and exclusivity are crucial.

COMPOSITION STUDIES

I will take time only to glance at my final example, since the history of composition studies is well known to most of us. Indeed we are all still writing that history, though we have reached a consensus on much of it. We have agreed, for instance, that we will have no nostalgia for the 1940s and '50s; for while composition teachers, especially those "stuck" there without tenure, were beginning to recognize themselves as an interest group, no prestige and certainly no sense of permanence attached to the role. *College Composition and Communication,* founded in 1950, immediately took up the sorry condition of the basic English teacher as a central theme. But if we look at the journal again we find something else among those writers—an excitement in the newness of the field at least as strong as the malaise of professional nonidentity. A recent *CCC* article describes the early audience of the journal rather ruefully as "literature specialists with a second common concern: student writing" and calls this audience "homogeneous" (Phillips et al. 443). The characterization is surprising if one thinks of the diversity of background and education and pedagogy all those modernists and Miltonists and medievalists brought to their "second concern." Even Brooks and Warren wrote a composition textbook; so did John Crowe Ransom and (famously) Barrett Wendell. One has to imagine a J. Hillis Miller or a Stanley Fish writing a composition textbook today to feel how airtight our subdisciplinary compartments have become—and how professionally homogeneous the readership of *CCC* is now compared to the 1950s.

Its status as a secondary interest in no way limited the scope of composition studies in the 1950s. The May, 1956 issue of *CCC*, for instance, published articles on the use of technology, the conditions of graduate assistants, the provision of audiences for student writing, the role of the "term paper, avoiding superficiality," and high school/college cooperation. Certainly all of these topics are still with us. Gone, though, and perhaps not enough missed, is attention to workaday matters like making and grading assignments, interpreting test scores, teaching grammar (and not just how to, but whether one ought). The many reports of this or that classroom ploy or "successful" assignment in these early issues seem unsophisticated now. But the occasionally quaint enthusiasm with which early compositionists treated classroom practicalities has a vitality almost entirely absent from contemporary theorizing.

Like writing center people today, the composition advocates of the 1950s were tireless in their search for an institutional niche. But setting the boundaries of a newly self-conscious field is an uneasy to-and-fro sort of business. Thus Glenn Leggett in February, 1956: "Freshman English in a large state University ought to be primarily a service course, but nor exclusively so; in a small but very real sense, it is also a 'liberal arts' course" (19). And in a Board Report from the 1955 Conference entitled "Communication Theory and the Study of Communication" (May 1956), the anonymous secretary records a set of themes that appear over and over in the work of the early composition professionals:

> *Why is a theory of communication needed? We agreed that present theory in communication is scattered among many disciplines: linguistics, semantics, social psychology, cybernetics, acoustics, anthropology, philosophy, psychology, etc. We agreed that much of the theory commonly applied to the problem of teaching communication skills is of doubtful, or untested, value and that our understanding of much of this theory is poor.*
>
> *We felt that since communication is an inter-disciplinary discipline a suitable framework is needed to give it form, content, and direction. We felt*

*that this theory cannot be taken whole from other disciplines, but that a new
discipline is needed which will borrow from many others. (133)*

The enthusiasm with which this comprehensive theory is imagined
gleams through the committee-report prose; so does the confusion over
whether composition is to be a plural or a monolithic discipline; and so too
does the confidence with which the monumental project is set out: a "suitable framework" to provide "form, content, and direction:" We may not
lament the passing of articles on Monday-morning practicalities, but we
ought to regret how infrequently it occurs to us to question, in this way, the
foundations of composition as a discipline.

It was at first primarily through calls for "frameworks" and for research
that the discipline took shape through 1975, but as the best research appeared, its reception was tinged with disappointment. Because it was careful, the work of Lloyd-Jones, Emig, Britton, and Shaughnessy sounded no
clarion of professional unity; it remained interdisciplinary, untidy, its borders permeable. Disenchanted by the incidence of research into students and
classrooms, many composition specialists turned away from pragmatics in
the late 1970s and early '80s, and toward theories of composing. The elabo-
ration of conceptual frameworks provided the energy required to drive the
college composition specialists up nearly to the institutional level of the literary and critical specialists. The mundane questions which had invigorated
the dialogues of the 1950s—What do grades mean? Why is one essay better
than another? What should writing students read?—were abandoned.
Teaching writing became composition theory—at great loss, I would argue. In its beginnings, modern composition theory was eclectic, taking whatever materials came to hand and continually returning to classroom
pedagogy; theory served the classroom as, earlier, critical theory had served
literature. And yet, like the other subdisciplines we have recalled, composition studies had from the beginning an understandable yearning for the kind
of permanence and respect which could only be had by way of conventional
scholarships—a scholarship, that is, which would establish a professional in-
group, close the intellectual borders, and develop a rhetoric designed at once
to distinguish and to exclude. The result today is at least that composition
specialists are tenurable. The result is also that only "composition people"
know or care much about what goes on in the first-year class and that composition is very rarely anyone's "secondary interest."

WRITING CENTERS

I have inevitably misrepresented the history of these subdisciplines by reducing them so and by picking and choosing points of emphasis; a few more
comprehensive and perhaps objective accounts are listed below.[1] But anyone

wishing to study the phenomenon of professionalization in all its marvelous complexity need only took to the living example of writing centers in the last few years. For writing centers made the turn toward professionalization some time ago; indeed, we are far along that road, though not so far that we cannot easily see where we were, and not so far that we can call ourselves fully established. If, as is often suggested in the pages of this journal, our most exhilarating successes derive from our intermediate, outside-the-mainstream status vis-a-vis the university, so too do most of our major problems. There is no institutional mechanism for recognition of successes which occur outside the structure; but there *are* powerful and nearly immediate sanctions already in place for academic programs which fail, and for individuals who do not do what they promised or who fail in the promises that were imposed on them. Therefore, like the other interest groups before us, we begin to manage the possibility of failure by redefining the criteria of success. This was the strategy of the three groups considered here: they modeled their activities on disciplines already in the mainstream; they demonstrated that what they were doing was not being done by any other department or discipline; they evolved theories and discourses that highlighted their differences from other areas, and increasingly wrote only for members of the network; they amassed a body of scholarship which looked a good deal like what everyone else was producing; and on these bases they claimed a professional status often and loudly enough that they were listened to. Unfortunately, their cultural and pedagogical ideals did not survive the transition intact.

But let me stress the ethical complexity of these histories. American literature deserves a place in the curriculum. Theories of literature are useful. Composition ought to develop its own pedagogical traditions. All of these goals are worthy now, and they were worthy forty or eighty or one hundred and twenty years ago when they were first proposed—proposed most often by individuals of broad learning and curiosity, and an innovative, boundary-breaking, interdisciplinary frame of mind; individuals so frequently and maliciously stigmatized as amateurs who merited no place or permanence or respect in the academic hierarchy that their goals were inevitably colored by their need for acceptance and security. These they attained eventually not by making a direct case for bringing their fields into the academic mainstream, but by a kind of end run—by a professionalization irrelevant to their ends, and often at odds with their expressed ideals.

The record establishes a consistent formula: professional success is proportional to the degree to which a discipline can overcome its mixed descent and claim a purity of purpose, while creating an environment in which its members can measure themselves according to criteria internal to the discipline.

Writing centers in the 1990s resemble these earlier groups as they moved though their later, yet still uncertain, stages. We are often still called "unscholarly" (what we do seems too easy to some, as American literature once seemed too easy). Like the early literary theory, our work seems too mixed, too heterogeneous to merit the same standing as the work traditional disciplines. Like composition professionals of the 1950s, we carry the presumed stigma of "remedial" and "basic" (and often "temporary"). Therefore the temptations are great to stick to the road that's been walked before, to assert our status by professionalizing. We already identify ourselves as a group with insiders and threatening outsiders. We have begun construction of a history containing our founding theoretical writers and works, and this history will become more elaborate as we grow. We have networks, both new- and old-fangled; we have two national conferences (the National Writing Centers Association and the National Conference on Peer Tutoring in Writing, now in its eleventh year). We have a journal and a newsletter—both remarkably accessible, so far. And we have the two absolutely essential marks of the established English subdiscipline: dissertations, and positions in the MLA Job Information List.

These developments must seem modest to us, especially given the daily trials faced by many writing centers. And, as I noted at the outset, most of us are able to maintain a salutary irony in the game of university power. But we would be politically naive to believe that we can play the game for long without entering into commitments that we will end up regretting.

Ransom's figure of "incorporation" applies literally to departments as they act out their role of guardians of the professions' integrity. A "professional" today is one who can repeat the form and substance of the field, and usually one who promises to do so. But the new professional group has no form or substance. There was, at one time, no academic stuff of American literature; many individuals, collectively and over a period of decades, constructed it. So also in literary theory and composition studies: the subject matters of those professions were forged, not found. As we professionalize, less and less are we able to assert that our philosophy is liberatory and contrarian; we cannot say, "Peer tutoring removes the impediment of the authority structures of the traditional classroom." Removing impediments is not enough; we must do something. And therefore in dissertations and publications, and on the job, we are forced to act as if our "subject matter" had natural, discernible borders, specific research goals and methodologies, and a replicable pedagogy—and where these do not come easily to hand, we have to create them. University administrations and faculty committees, themselves thoroughly incorporated, react favorably to curricular and procedural outlines, and to lists of publications and professional organizations; in fact, they react to little else—certainly not to anything so immaterial as "removing impediments" or "liberating."

It is part of the groundbreaking work of a new discipline to envision positive accomplishments: position statements, educational rationales, bibliographies of supporting material. Without these, no program—traditional or otherwise—can be admitted to the curriculum. A doctoral program, by long-standing tradition, uses the statements and rationales and bibliographies to promise conformity to some already accredited model of instruction. Thus when an institution certifies a Ph.D. candidate and when the young professor takes a job—say, writing center director—the negative sanctions are already in place ensuring that the professor knows what all the other people in the same job know, and that she is capable of doing what they all do; she knows too, by this time, that she violates these implied contracts at her peril.

The same political dynamics tend to impose uniformity as a condition for membership in the new discipline. The founding members of the interest groups recalled above (like those in women's studies and post-colonial literature today) were interdisciplinary thinkers. The early Americanists, for instance, were for the most part trained as classicists of one variety or another—philologists or Latinists or scholars of Anglo-Saxon. The early twentieth-century literary theorists often spent years in the study of philosophy or psychology or sociology. But within two or three generations, their success in reaching mainstream status forced both groups to abandon their interdisciplinarity. Beginning in the 1930s, English department positions in American literature required a Ph.D. in American literature; by the late 1970s, theory positions required theory credentials. (Composition program directors are still something of a mixed group, but certainly no new positions of responsibility are available today for individuals without a dissertation in the area.[2])

Again, the logic of this movement from interdisciplinary to monolithic makes a kind of twisted sense if we consider the current conditions of writing centers. We wish to assert that what we do is worthy of traditional academic rewards, and we can claim that worth only in the terms the university recognizes: advanced study and professional activity. The granting of a Ph.D. in "writing center theory" is in everyone's interest; everyone's status moves up a notch, and the work we do, which we all believe to be of enormous value, is that much more secure.

But the work is changed slightly, with every Ph.D., even with every article like this one. Each conventionally-measured advance in our professional status, every move closer to the mainstream, reduces our variety and our breadth of vision. Consider, for instance, the professionalizing of peer tutor training. The one-semester tutoring course (the preferred approach) ought to attract the best prospective tutors from all across the college, but few devoted physics or history majors will actually risk credits and a grade for a chance to work in the writing center. The course is an attractive option only for English majors, and this tends to keep the writing center in the English department, where most people think it belongs.

On the model of graduate training in rhetoric, the tutoring course covers major theoretical figures; the beginner develops enthusiasm for the larger enterprise. The students contemplate our professional principles: no gainsaying the teacher, no talk about grades, no appropriation of text—in short, no overlapping onto other people's territory. We may even wish to imbue our prospective tutors with something of the glamour of working contrary to the educational mainstream. But all of that goes by the boards at the end of the course, when those with the highest grades take the inside track for next year's tutoring positions. Thus we create a second exclusion: only those who excel in that most conformist art—getting a grade in a conventional class—are worthy of trying the unconventional. But by this time, the writing center is no longer unconventional; it is close to being simply another academic unit, not unlike Composition 1.

Thus generally it will go, I fear. In an attempt to secure something of value, we will end up recreating most of the debilitating hierarchies that we wished to escape. The peer relationship, collaboration, spontaneity, freedom, equality, courage; the excitement of interaction, the energy of student culture—these replaced by constructions of expert and amateur, of protocol, instruction, and tradition. It will be objected (I hope) that this cannot be. We are too involved in the tussle of campus politics and in maintaining our connections to all departments. Negotiating interdisciplinarity is what we do, daily; our very theories centralize struggle. It must seem to us impossible that we could ever lose this edge. But just so it might have seemed to Newton Marshall Hall impossible that the scholar of American literature could ever lose interest in the democratic experiment, or to George Woodberry that "pluralism" would become a term of abuse.

It is not only possible, it is likely that the future of writing centers is exactly in the mainstream of the university—that is, as another academic unit, justifying its existence not by the growth of the students who encounter it, but by publication, professional activity, and course work in the graduate and undergraduate curricula. Every assertion of our professional status renews the promise that we all do the same thing and will continue to deliver the same goods—that writing center people can be trusted to do pretty much the same things in one place as another and to treat all students the same way every time.[3] In this way we will assure the rest of the university that we can be generally trusted, for we are not doing anything outside the mass education model, except that we're doing it one student at a time.

It is beyond what I have intended here to offer a full vision of a more promising future, and I don't think it's necessary. The lessons of history are fairly clear. But they are hard lessons. Fall out of love with permanence; embrace transience. Stake your reputation on service rather than on publication. Acknowledge that directing a writing center does not involve the kind of difficulties for which advanced degree preparation is necessary. Stay impure: welcome mixed descent and cross purposes. Let last year's tutors handle the training. Allow that students may know what they need better than we do.

"Hard" is perhaps understated. But if we want to offer an alternative to mass education, we must reject its mythology of expertise and permanence.

Our energy at present derives from what we have left of happy amateurism, and from our sense of being in transition, our extroversion of purpose, and our interdisciplinarity. If we find a way of publicly rejoicing in our impermanence, we may preserve the energy and the purpose. If nor, we will almost certainly become, like everyone else, introverted and disciplinary. And that will be our success.

NOTES

1. Much important work has been done on the history and professionalization of English, a good deal of it inspired by Arthur Applebee's *Tradition and Reform in the Teaching of English: A History* and especially by Richard Ohmann's *English in America*. Other helpful historical surveys listed below are by Gerald Graff, Graff and Michael Warner, Warner alone, Brian McCrea, and Kermit Vanderbilt.

2. Among Warner's many insights into professionalism in English is that already by 1900 the consequence of the Ph.D. was to shift attention away from what the professional could do (teach or write or explain) and onto the certification. Warner's remarks here on "the critic" extend to all the subdisciplines: "The professional's commodity is himself. He is himself certified and accredited by processes that can be said to have produced him as a critic" (22). In other words, it is his training that the critic "sells," not his ability.

3. In 1990 Irene Lurkis Clark wrote, "I am...a bit wary of the possibility that writing centers will soon take on a 'common form' in the profession, a common form verging on dogma, and it is in response to this idea of a 'common form' that I advocate the maintenance of chaos" (81). My argument differs from Clark's mainly in suggesting that the danger of a "common form" is far greater—deadly, in fact—and more pervasive; but dogmas are indeed part of the problem, and I cheerfully endorse "chaos" as a healthy alternative.

WORKS CITED

Applebee, Arthur. *Tradition and Reform in the Teaching of English: A History*. Urbana: NCTE, 1974.

Brooks, Cleanth and Robert Penn Warren. *Understanding Poetry*. New York: Holt, 1938.

Clark, Irene Lurkis. "Maintaining Chaos in the Writing Center: A Critical Perspective on Writing Center Dogma." *The Writing Center Journal* 11.1 (1990): 81–93.

"Communication Theory and the Study of Communication." Board Report from Conference on College Composition and Communication, 1955. *College Composition and Communication* 7.2 (1956): 133–35.

Graff, Gerald. *Professing Literature: An Institutional History*. Chicago: Univ. of Chicago Press, 1987.

Graff, Gerald and Michael Warner, eds. *The Origins of Literary Studies in America*. New York: Routledge, 1989.

Hall, Newton Marshall. "The Study of American Literature in Colleges." *The Andover Review* 27.104 (August, 1892): 154–62.

Leggett, Glenn H. "The Large State University." *College Composition and Communication* 7.1 (1956): 18–21.

McCrea, Brian. *Addison and Steele Are Dead: The English Department, Its Canon, and the Professionalization of Literary Criticism.* Newark: Univ. of Delaware Press, 1990.

Ohmann, Richard. *English in America: A Radical View of the Profession.* New York: Oxford UP, 1976.

Phillips, Donna Burns, Ruth Greenberg, and Sharon Gibson. "*College Composition and Communication:* Chronicling a Discipline's Genesis." *College Composition and Communication* 44.4 (1993): 443–465.

Ransom, John Crowe. "Criticism, Inc." *The World's Body.* New York: Scribner, 1938. 327–50.

Scudder, Horace E. *Literature in School.* New York: Houghton Mifflin, 1888.

"To Our Contributors." *American Literature* 1.1 (1929): 75.

Warner, Michael. "Professionalization and the Rewards of Literature: 1875–1900." *Criticism* 27.1 (1985): 1–28.

Vanderbilt, Kermit. *American Literature and the Academy: The Roots, Growth, and Maturity of a Profession.* Philadelphia: Univ. of Penn. Press, 1986.

Wendell, Barrett and Chester Noyes Greenough. *History of Literature in America.* New York: Scribner, 1904.

Woodberry, George Edward. "Two Phases of Criticism." Lecture at Kenyon College, 1913. Printed by the Woodberry Society, 1914. Rpt. in *Criticism in America.* New York: Harcourt, 1924.

3

DEFINING THE WRITING CENTER'S PLACE: ADMINISTRATIVE AND INSTITUTIONAL ISSUES

Discussions and debates about how writing centers should define themselves, both individually and collectively, have been a part of our history from the very beginning. Issues such as marginalization, relationships to writing programs, dealing with central administration, and internal versus external identity permeate our ever-growing body of scholarship. A writing center's role within its own institution is rarely, if ever, defined by any one single factor. In fact, writing center directors who consider the many factors that contribute to the center's identity are usually the ones who develop their centers on the most sound theoretical and pedagogical philosophies that in some way speak to the institution's aims as well.

Muriel Harris opens this section by suggesting that we steer away from a set approach to tutoring and administration because both are highly contextualized. Harris works through ten hypothetical dilemmas that illustrate the complex choices writing center administrators must often make. Mark Waldo further attempts to define the writing center's role in his article, which examines the relationship between the writing center and the writing program. He contends that attitudes about the role of the writing program and writing center affect the relationship between the two. He addresses the need for common theoretical and pedagogical philosophies and uses examples to illustrate how problems often occur when directors do not share similar approaches. Karen Rodis extends Waldo's thesis by examining conflicting expectations of tutors and composition teachers about the mission of the writing center. While tutors are trained to work with all aspects of writing, teachers often see writing centers as remedial skills centers. Rodis encourages directors to promote writing centers as nonremedial and to hire professional staff.

The writing center's role within its institution is also defined by its relationship with central administration. Jeanne Simpson acknowledges common perceptions that writing center personnel hold with regard to central administration. As a member of central administration herself, Simpson offers perspective from that point of view and offers insights for writing center personnel to consider when negotiating with central administration. Finally, Bob Barnett takes a holistic approach to defining a writing center's role. He encourages writing center administrators to create a statement of short- and long-term goals and objectives that will work to define the center in relationship to the writing program, the English department, other programs and departments, and with central administration. His contention is that any statement must reflect the writing center mission as well as the mission of the institution.

The articles in this section are ordered in a way that examines the role of the writing center internally and then vis-à-vis other programs, departments, and the like. Read together, the Waldo and Rodis articles create an important conversation about the most involved participants in the writing center's work. Harris and Simpson offer different perspectives on similar issues facing writing centers and directors. And Barnett's article offers a big-picture look at how to define the relationships addressed by the other authors.

Solutions and Trade-Offs in Writing Center Administration

Muriel Harris

Writing center administration, a highly complex task as is, has an added complication in that so many new directors plunge in with an almost total lack of preparation. Undertaking their new responsibilities with the best of intentions but with high levels of anxiety, they normally begin by seeking out the books, journals, and conferences that will help them, and they journey to other writing centers to take notes and ask questions. They inquire about all kinds of specifics on the size of the budget, ways to select staff, methods of evaluation, types of computers and other materials that should be purchased, and so on. All of this is apparently useful as hundreds of thriving writing centers around the country have directors who followed that route. And they have learned from those who traveled the same roads before them.

All of this is comforting. We share our knowledge, our experience, and our handouts with newcomers, but we may also inadvertently be passing along a message we don't intend to distribute—that there is a "right" way to structure a writing center. "Here's how I do it" can too easily be heard as "Here's how it's done." In our rush to help we don't sufficiently warn newcomers that writing centers cannot all function in similar ways or adopt rigid policies and approaches and that writing centers aren't for those who crave absolute answers. Even the guidelines worked out every week by more experienced writing center administrators cannot be removed from a variety

Harris, Muriel. "Solutions and Trade-Offs in Writing Center Administration." *The Writing Center Journal* 12.1 (1991): 63–79. Reprinted by permission of *The Writing Center Journal*.

of contexts and compromises that influence writing center practice. In our quest to find answers for all those matters that keep our heads swirling all day, advice, collaborating in the act of figuring out how to cope with the crisis management that is called "writing lab administration." Thus, in our approaches to administration we incorporate the approaches we advocate in tutoring. As long as we too keep in mind that there are no simple answers, we will remember to file away what we hear as we think about whether it will work for us, in the context of our own centers.

As an exercise in this kind of thinking—and to remind us that there are no right answers or absolute rules in writing center administration—I offer in the following pages a list of situations that come up frequently in writing centers and some solutions that might work, along with some trade-offs for each solution. For part of the lack of simple answers is that every solution has a flip side, a possible disadvantage or limitation that, when recognized, keeps us from leaping to that solution as the only right answer. Instead, we look at different sides, consider the various situation-related issues, and make a more informed decision, just as we expect our tutors to weigh all the factors that are generally relevant and that are operating in any specific setting and come out with a reasonable answer. Thus, it is not likely that any two readers reading through the following lists will come to total agreement about the best solution, and it is also not likely that any reader will even choose the same solution all the time. It is even more probable that different readers will think of other solutions and other trade-offs. But it is the practice in this kind of thinking that helps us maintain our perspective on how we go about writing center administration. I also offer the following situation/solution list as a starter kit for others to use in staff discussions. There is nothing more healthy than sitting around collaboratively and considering how we should handle the various needs, requests, and problems that continually crop up. Like bending and stretching exercises, such discussions limber up our perspectives and keep us from seizing on rigid policies.

SITUATION 1

An instructor from another department with only the vaguest sense of what constitutes good writing is sending her students to the center for help. She has given you a copy of one student paper that she thinks is well written and one on which she has made some very general comments about writing problems and has noted a few grammar errors. She seems intent on having the tutors help the students turn in the kind of paper that she has indicated is acceptable. The students from her class are starting to come to the center, but it is clear that they don't know what kind of help they should ask for. And you and your tutors don't know quite what the instructor wants.

Possible solutions and trade-offs:

• Resign yourself to some lengthy meetings with the instructor (if she'll agree) and help her to see what constitutes effective writing and good assignments. This seems workable, but she may not automatically give up her criteria for yours. She may expect the papers to follow her standards, not yours. She may be working with standards appropriate to her field, but it may also be the case that she is less aware than she should be of what constitutes good writing in her discipline. Another consideration here is whether she will continue to teach this course. You may find yourself making extensive efforts only to have it all discontinued as she moves on to teaching other courses where there is little opportunity to write. But you may or may not have made a friend who sometime in the future will rekindle her interest in her students' writing.

• Rely on your tutors' own sense of what each paper needs. This may result in papers that are even better than the teacher originally expected, or she may feel that her standards are being ignored. If she is suggesting criteria appropriate in her field that are not apparent to the tutors, they may be offering inappropriate assistance. Then again, by seeing papers that embody the principles your tutors are helping their students to learn, the teacher may gain new insight into what good writing is.

• Analyze the papers that the teacher said were good, and try to help students produce similar papers. This may work, but if the criteria are not what normally constitute good writing, the students' writing ability has not improved. In addition, the teacher may persist in her expectations.

SITUATION 2

This week you noticed an increasing number of students coming in with papers due later that day. You know that all that is possible at this stage (and that what the students are asking for) is some quick clean-up proofreading.

Possible solutions and trade-offs:

• Issue a public policy statement that students cannot appear with papers due the same day. This may work, but it may also drive away students who could have been educated to coming in earlier after seeing the problem of coming in at the last minute.

• Explain that your center does not offer proofreading help. This may help students learn what the center is about, but you may be turning away students who could learn a bit about proofreading or students who use the word "proofreading" when they aren't quite sure what kind of help they want.

- Take a step back and see if you are treating the real problem—procrastination or nervousness. When students come in with papers that are due, try to talk with them about causes instead of lecturing them about not proofreading. This may turn some students away who want help with the paper and feel frustrated that no direct, specific assistance was offered. But you may have reached some students in very important ways.
- Show the students some proofreading techniques by looking only at the first page of the paper. Then explain that they can finish the job of proofreading themselves. This is a frequent solution, but some students then continue to think of the writing center as the proofreading place and return with the next paper thirty minutes before that one is to be handed in. (On the other hand, one clever student at our university managed to beat the system by coming in five or six different times in one morning, each time asking the tutor only to look at a particular page or paragraph. As we later figured out, she managed to have the whole paper read through and must have enjoyed listening quietly to each of us explain that we don't proofread whole papers.)
- Adopt a policy of seeing students only if they sign up for several appointments. Some students can quickly spot the way around this bit of bureaucracy by signing up and showing up only for the proofreading session. But, you may also get some conscientious students who thereby learn how valuable on-going tutoring is.

SITUATION 3

One of your peer tutors has alienated a teacher by writing a note which seems to indicate that the tutor and student did some work which the instructor deems counterproductive to the approach he takes in his classroom.

Possible solutions and trade-offs:

- In the future, monitor all notes that the tutors send out by reading them before they are mailed. This may cure the problem, but it announces a lack of trust in the tutors' ability to know what most teachers want. It is also a kind of policing policy that you may not want to have pervade your center.
- Explain to the teacher that the note was somewhat inaccurate and that the tutor and student did follow his approach to writing. This undermines the tutor's authority and doesn't lead to any clearer understanding by the tutor of the differences noticed by the teacher. The tutor may also have merely used an inappropriate or misleading word, and you are thus assuming that the tutor is guilty when in fact she may not be.
- Let it pass. This teacher may be someone who exhibits other symptoms of feeling that peer tutors are not competent to work with his students. This may be the case, but you are losing an opportunity to engage in a dialogue

with the teacher about peer tutors and what they can offer. Also, if there is no response to the teacher, he may become more adamant about his students not coming to the writing center. Then again, if you have a huge teaching staff, you may want to think about how much energy and time you can expend stomping out every brush fire, especially if there is the possibility that the teacher may simply forget about the incident.

• Ask the tutor to talk with the teacher about the situation. This may result in greater understanding between that particular tutor and teacher, but it may also make the rest of the tutoring staff paranoid about those notes they have to write. You'll have to decide whether the teacher will engage in useful conversation with a peer tutor.

SITUATION 4

Your center has hired a non-native student as a tutor, and several students have asked not to work with that tutor. Your assumption as to the cause of the problem is that they think the tutor is not sufficiently competent in English.

Possible solutions and trade-offs:

• Encourage these students to try working with this tutor. You may help to educate them, but you may also cause some to leave and not return because they are indeed having trouble understanding the tutor. (Some students do have more trouble than others in comprehending an accent slightly different from their own.) The tutor may also feel some pressure to be more competent than the other tutors because she perceives herself as being on trial.

• Having noticed how disturbed your non-native tutor is by these rejections, you re-think your policy of hiring non-native tutors in the future. This is, of course, a solution, but you are not confronting students' prejudices and may be losing out on some excellent tutors simply because they were not born into English-speaking families.

• Let it pass. These students can simply work with someone else. This confirms a general policy that students should choose whom they want to work with, not be assigned. But again, this offers no opportunities for the students to learn that they might be wrong. The non-native tutor may also feel relegated to second-class citizen status as she is not being given the opportunity to prove herself.

• Assign this tutor to work primarily with non-native students who come to the center. Again, this announces that the students' perception of the tutor may have some truth to it. Moreover, other non-native students may or may not welcome the opportunity to work with such a tutor because they see the native students as more knowledgeable about English grammar. On the other hand, a non-native tutor is particularly sensitive to the needs of other

ESL students and is often more likely to diagnose writing needs based on his or her own experience. Particularly when cultural conflicts with assignments and/or rhetorical values of English come into play, a non-native tutor is going to be able to spot the difficulty much more quickly than a native speaker who may be oblivious to, for example, an Oriental student's reluctance to criticize American values or a Hispanic student's tendency to transfer to English the Spanish preference for very lengthy sentences.

SITUATION 5

The administration has offered to give your center some funds for computers, but you are not sure that you want to change the emphasis from a collaborative environment of writers working together to a high tech center where each student sits alone in front of his or her own terminal.

Possible solutions and trade-offs:

• Accept the computers but make it clear that the tutors are not going to be replaced by machinery. This may work, but you may also find that the computers soon begin to overwhelm the center. More and more students may be coming in for the computers; you may find that you need consultants to assist with maintenance and student problems with hardware, and teachers may begin to refer students to computer programs on grammar and editing.

• Ask the administrators to define the uses they have in mind for the computers, and consider whether these goals do indeed overlap with the writing center's present responsibilities and goals. Try to bargain for using the computers in ways that are more appropriate for your center. You may then have a more well-defined situation, but you will need to spend time educating students and instructors about how to use those computers in the ways you would like them used.

• Accept the computers only on condition that they are in a room adjacent to yours so that the separation is clear. This may mean that someone else will have to oversee that computer lab which may then develop in ways you may not always be comfortable with.

• Turn down the offer so that you can maintain your emphasis on tutoring. This obviously keeps your collaboratively oriented center on track, but you may be losing the opportunity to work with students who are going elsewhere to seek those computers they want to use. Teachers interested in adding computers to classroom writing will also bypass your center, and you are in danger of being left out of the word-processing revolution. You also are denying the potential benefits of computers to handicapped or writers with learning disabilities who might have come to the center. On the other hand, you don't have to face administration pressures to reduce the number of tutors by turning to self-instruction grammar programs. (Administrators have an uncanny knack of instantly recognizing the savings of one time software purchases over the on-going expenses of tutors' salaries.)

- Accept the computers and move the tutors close to the computers. Help them learn how to set up collaborative sessions while sitting with students while they word process. Talk with tutors about integrating the computers into tutorials, using on-screen methods for planning together, revising, and so on. This can become highly effective, but may take some training, some rethinking about the nature of tutorials, and some analysis of when tutors need to withdraw so that students can write. You'll need to educate any teachers who see this collaboration as the kind of assistance with writing that creates unfair advantages for students whose "tutors helped them write the papers." Other teachers will get suspicious about the use of editing programs that "clean up" the students' prose for them. In short, be prepared to educate your tutors, the students, and the teaching staff about your new approaches.

SITUATION 6

You, as director, are being reviewed for promotion and tenure by people who don't particularly value or understand what writing centers are all about.

Possible solutions and trade-offs:

- Face up to the fact that you will have to do an extensive amount of educating as your only hope is to have these people become better acquainted with what you really do. This will take a great deal of time and emotional energy as you find materials for them to read, meet with them, and engage in endless discussions. You may also need to call on outside sources, evaluators in the field, who can come to campus or write to the people on your campus engaged in the review. There is a very real possibility that you will come out of this feeling drained, unhappy, and unable to regain your sense of dedication. But you may have helped to educate people who need to be enlightened. You may also find that your efforts were unsuccessful, and the consequences of this attempt may be that you have to move on to a position elsewhere. Another very real trade-off is that the process of educating your peers is so time-consuming that you find yourself neglecting your work in your center. As a result, the center may suffer temporarily.

- Ask for a review committee that is more aware of the real nature of your work. This may mean asking for an outside review. The result may be that you can get a more honest review, but you may be seriously alienating people in your department or institution who see their authority and ability to judge as being usurped.

- Delay your review until you have had a year or two to lay the groundwork. Spend time developing a greater awareness of what you do, what your research and scholarly concerns are, and what the theoretical bases of your center's reaching are. You may find people more open to thinking about all of this when they are not being pressured into conducting a review. On the other hand, they might be less inclined to listen as they see no immediate need to concern themselves with you or your work.

- Conduct a campaign that calls in support of your colleagues from other institutions. People in writing centers are inordinately helpful with this, writing letters of review and lending moral support to your work. Again, this might help to educate people, but it is also likely to alienate others who resist outside pressure or who are not likely to value any assessment by people in our field anyway.

- Accept the fact that you will not truly educate people and that it might be better to negotiate for a position that is non-tenured and not subject to faculty review. You may be freer to operate outside some constraints this way, and you may even find yourself in an administrative setting where money flows more freely, budgets are more realistic, and your services are better integrated with other student services on campus. You do, however, remove yourself from voicing your position and views in faculty meetings and have to work against any kind of second-class status for yourself and your center. You might also find your center more likely to be physically removed from the buildings where composition courses are taught.

- Accept the fact that any scholarship in writing centers is not likely to be viewed favorably. Instead, switch to researching and publishing in areas more likely to be considered truly acceptable academic work. This will help you during the review process but will create a dichotomy in your life as you spend your days in the center concerned with tutorial instruction and your nights at your desk reading and writing about completely different matters. Some people have succeeded in this and find themselves happier with broader interests; others find that the questions they find truly interesting are those that they confront all day in the center. They must therefore sidestep intellectually engaging issues and a source for thinking about and researching them. The field, too, suffers as you are perpetuating the myth that writing center theory and practice is not truly scholarly. If you have graduate students working in the center, you are also missing opportunities to train others in the field in writing center research.

SITUATION 7

A faculty member is sending students to the writing center but won't let them bring any papers along because she thinks the tutors will write the papers for the students.

Possible solutions and trade-offs:

• Talk to the teacher and try to convince her that tutors do not write the students' papers. This may be an opportunity for her to learn what tutorial collaboration can offer, but you might also alienate her if she doesn't listen or want to accept what you say. She might simply stop sending students to the center.

• Advise your tutors of this teacher's policy and suggest ways that tutors can work with these students without actually seeing any written work before it is handed in. Tutors can work on planning, have students talk about how a paper is progressing, or ask for sample paragraphs or past papers that have been graded to see if there are any discernible surface errors in grammar and mechanics to work on.

• Ask the teacher to be sure to fill out referral forms indicating what each student should work on. This will, of course, give the tutors clues as to the general area, but without samples of the students' writing, the tutorial is likely to be too general also. It will be harder to motivate the students since their preference will be to work with papers in progress before they are graded.

• Explain to the teacher the value of working with writing-in-progress. If the teacher cannot accept this, then you may find that this teacher no longer uses the writing center. On one hand, you have managed to maintain the general integrity of the center and have staved off other attempts to have teachers dictate what you can and cannot do. On the other hand, some teachers with rigid rules may be less effective than they could be in other matters of teaching writing. Thus, their students might be the ones most in need of tutorial assistance.

SITUATION 8

The administration wants to cut the lab's budget because of general financial needs, and a good place to start, they think, is a student service like the writing center.

Possible solutions and trade-offs:

• Write reports, gather evidence, garner student support, and in general, make the strongest case you can for the need for the writing center. This can work, but administrators have a way of ignoring evidence that suggests courses of action other than what they have determined they want to do.

• Find out what the administration values and emphasize your service in that area. For example, if retention is a major concern, research the writing center's role in retention; if teacher overload is a troubling problem, show the center's role in assisting teachers in meeting the needs of their students; if being a large, impersonal institution hinders recruitment, stress the center's role in providing personal attention; if maintaining high standards of admission is crucial, note the writing center's emphasis on working with students of all abilities, especially those in honors classes and projects; if community outreach is an institutional goal, highlight your grammar hotline help, add short courses for clerical help or evening classes for the community, and so on. The danger, of course, is that like teaching to the test, you are letting the administration dictate the goals of your center, and you may find that you are shifting the emphasis to areas that are of less concern to your students and the composition faculty.

• Add credit-generating courses to your center; integrate it more with classes so that it is not as easily perceived as a peripheral service; assess fees for community use of the center; note the value of peer tutor training classes to the education majors. These solutions again stress areas that might cause the administration to change its perception of the center, but again, you may be diverting resources and energy in directions that take you further from your announced goals and responsibilities.

• Attempt to educate the faculty and the administration about the need for individualized instruction in writing to accompany classroom instruction and about the need to provide tutorial assistance with writing in other disciplines. This keeps you on track in emphasizing what you may see as the real value of a writing center, but you are in danger of presenting arguments that are either not understood or not accepted. If you stress the teaching function of the center, you will also have to downplay the headcount and visibility arguments which might be seen as diminishing the center's emphasis on being a teaching facility. Large numbers certainly prove the notion of heavy use, but as one administrator was heard to comment, "Our recreational gym is the most heavily used student facility on campus, but that doesn't prove that it is part of our college's mission."

• Find one sympathetic administrator and focus your attention on her. She may become your ally and help present your case to the rest of the administration. One trade-off, however, is that when this administrator moves on (as she might), you are back to ground zero. You may also find that the center is the victim of shifting power lines higher up or that you get caught in power struggles or battles you are not even aware of.

SITUATION 9

You've been asked by some faculty in other departments to offer tutoring help to students in their courses, and you find that you are launching into a mini-writing-across-the-curriculum program without adequate compensation, resources, or planning.

Possible solutions and trade-offs:

- Continue to let these services continue in the hope that as they grow you will be able to make a case for more tutors and other resources. The danger, though, is that you can become overwhelmed by the enormity of this responsibility as you find that word-of-mouth causes you to be invited to more and more faculty meetings, committee meetings, and instructor offices. The more you do, the more people expect of you, and a potential problem is that soon your job is mentally redefined to include all the new responsibilities that you have taken on.

- Be more cautious initially and respond by noting some assistance you will need in return. If the faculty in one department want some workshops in structuring assignments, ask for compensation for your time. If a faculty member asks if all seventy-five of his students can stop in with drafts of their final reports, ask for tutorial pay for extra hours. The advantage is that you have the needed resources as you grow. The trade-off is that you will lose some potential users who don't want to make any investments or engage in any real projects without some trial runs to see if it's all worth it. Some faculty back off because they don't see how they can ask their departments for funds for your center before they too are convinced of the need.

- Set some realistic goals about how much additional writing-across-the-curriculum service you can offer. Don't take on everything that is asked of you, but don't turn everyone away either. You can move more gradually here and begin to develop sound programs of assistance which could grow and become institutionalized. Eventually, you might then find administrators amenable to adding either an assistant director or another person to take charge of this aspect of your services. You might, however, also become enmeshed in territorial conflicts if others see writing across the curriculum as a program they want to see expanded but not as an offshoot of the writing center.

SITUATION 10

The writing center, despite all your memos, posters, and notes to teachers, is perceived as a grammar fix-it place by some teachers. When they refer students to the center, they note only grammar problems as needing attention.

Possible solutions and trade-offs:

- Encourage your tutors to work with all aspects of the paper that need attention and hope that this first-hand experience with tutorial collaboration will first change students' perceptions and then eventually filter back to the teachers. You may, though, initially confuse students who come in anxious for the very real help in grammar and mechanics that they think they need.

The notes back to the teachers may cause the teachers to complain that the center is overriding their requests and make them less sympathetic to your attempts to educate them about better uses of tutorial help.

• Continue to send memos to the teachers who persist in sending students only for Band-Aid kinds of grammar help. This kind of effort may go unnoticed as teachers dump your memos in the circular file or read too quickly to gain any useful information from the memo. A general memo also does not address specific concerns of various teachers. You may find that a better solution is personal conversation, a time-consuming but perhaps more effective means of changing perceptions. You may also meet up with adamant teachers or teachers who nod in agreement and continue to use the center in the previous way.

• Hold workshops on topics such as planning strategies, audience awareness, persuasion, revision, coherence, and so on. This announces publicly what the center can do to help writers, and such workshops also draw students who will come back for tutorials. But such workshops are not going to get all the students whom you would like to bring in, so you are still going to miss a portion of the student population whom you could be serving. Moreover, you will have to make these workshops a permanent part of your services as the need to educate each new group of students continues. Such services, while useful, will necessarily subtract time available for tutoring. You are also shifting to group work with this service and away from an announced emphasis on individualized help.

• Enlist the student newspaper to do in-depth articles about the center. You can use this public forum to discuss tutorial instruction in ways that can be enlightening for teachers as well as students. Unfortunately, no student newspaper reaches everyone, and your job is not complete through this route. You will also have to keep doing this every year and will need the cooperation of the student newspaper which doesn't want to repeat features that they have already done last year.

• Attend to the request for help with grammar and mechanics and then go on to work with the whole paper. You have, thus, initially satisfied the student's request as well as the teacher's while hoping to engage the student in broader conversation about the focus, organization, and so on. This means, however, that the tutorial is in danger of either being too long as you try to cover too much or too disjointed as you switch from one topic to another.

• Write off some teachers. You may find that there are some instructors whom you simply have to give up on in the name of making better use of your time. It may also be that in their classrooms or conferences they are attending to more major writing concerns, even though you think your tutors could help, especially in engaging students in collaborative conversation. The trade-off, of course, is that these students might also be missing out on the advantages of tutorials. Also, when they go on to other writing classes or have other writing projects, they may continue to ignore the writing center as a place for effective assistance.

The list of situations, possible solutions, and trade-offs for each of the solutions can clearly be extended—and needs to be—so that constraints and characteristics of your particular setting are factored in. But the above list should provide some suggestions for you and your staff as you engage in the kind of collaborative discussion which allows you to select options for your writing center. Like a truly effective tutorial dialogue, a staff discussion about solutions includes all voices that are participating in the discussion as each has something to contribute. And like any good tutorial planning session, everyone participating needs to be encouraged to turn off the editors in our brain which cause us to start judging and rejecting options before we give them a chance to be examined. Collaborative, flexible, individualized solutions to our administrative concerns are bound to produce worthwhile results, just as our collaborative, flexible, individualized tutorials with students do.

What Should the Relationship Between the Writing Center and Writing Program Be?

Mark L. Waldo

Recently our English Department search committee was interviewing a candidate for a position in rhetoric and composition. Prefacing his first question, a committee member pointed to me as Writing Center Director and then said to the candidate, "Maybe you can mediate between us. Mark says it's not the Writing Center's responsibility to teach grammar, I say it is; I've got better things to do than take up composition class time teaching it. Who is responsible for teaching grammar, the writing center or writing program?" At issue here is not the inappropriateness of his question given the context. Nor is it the evident ignorance of research suggested by the phrase "teaching grammar." What I want to focus on, instead, is the relationship between center and program implied in his comments and question. He seems to view the writing center as subservient to the writing program—one doing the sentence-level repair, often through drill and practice, and the other doing the teaching. Such attitudes, commonplace in English departments, ill affect a potentially powerful union.

What should the relationship between the writing program and the writing center be? An immediate response might be shaped by the similarities between the two operations. Staffed by people who have in common a concern with improving student writing, the answer is that writing programs and centers should share equal and complementary relationship. They should be linked philosophically, each grounded in a similar theoretical perspective from which their pedagogy stems. If the writing program's approach is principally organic, then so too should the writing center's be; if

Waldo, Mark L. "What Should the Relationship Between the Writing Center and the Writing Program Be?" *The Writing Center Journal* (1993): 73–80. Reprinted by permission of *The Writing Center Journal*.

the program's approach is mechanic, then so too should the center's be. It would not be practical, for example, for the center to draw its tutoring practice from organic principles, emphasizing inquiry and collaboration, prewriting strategies, revision and review of drafts, while the program draws its teaching practice from mechanic principles, featuring lectures and teacher-led discussions, study of models, imitation of patterns, and attention to mechanics (see Hillocks, "Presentational Mode," "What Works in Teaching Composition: A Meta-Analysis of Experimental Treatment Studies"). Attempts to marry the organic with the mechanic will be awkward at best.

Some rhetoricians believe it is not possible to join the two with any kind of success. Knoblauch and Brannon, for whom mechanicism characterizes the ancient rhetoric and organicism the modern, argue that "the shift from an ancient to a modern perspective has not been a matter of gradual and slight conceptual adjustment, modern rhetoric growing naturally, imperceptibly, out of its ancient earlier tradition. Instead, the two traditions are essentially opposed, representing a *disfunction* in intellectual history because they derive from two different and incompatible epistemologies, two irreconcilable views of the nature of knowledge and the functions of discourse" (78). Knoblauch and Brannon assert that the consequence to the composition classroom of mixing the organic and mechanic epistemologies is the development of "pseudoconcepts" (i.e., "an essentially modern regard for the process of writing is compromised by a classical mechanistic view of its supposed 'parts'") (80). Dividing such diverse perspectives between writing program and center, to say the least, undermines the effectiveness of each.

While a common theoretical perspective promotes an equal relationship between the two operations, teaching activities will be different, by their nature falling to one or the other. Teachers may work with entire classes on revision, for example, while tutors work individually with students. But the work itself should be similar, complementary. The composition classroom is not, in other words, a place where one focus of activity occurs, the writing center another. It very much undervalues the program or center to give either the "duty" of teaching mechanics and correctness or the task of preparing students to display "writing competence." In fact, if those are the only, or even primary, duties of either operation, its existence and funding is not justified.

In addition to pedagogic philosophies, the writing center and writing program should share the same or complementary goals. Both want to produce the best independent student writers they can. Both want to advance critical thinking skills and show students how writing shapes learning. Both also want to prepare students to step into the academic and professional writing community. For this last goal the models again may be different. The writing program, for example, may offer a variety of writing assignments to students—problem-solution, dilemma, analysis, persuasion—which will prepare them to write in their courses across the curriculum and beyond. The writing center may provide writing consultants to the faculty in the sciences, business, arts, and letters in order to help them design assignments pertinent to their courses—assignments which, like those required of students through the writing program, improve both writing competence and critical thinking. The center, in addition, will offer tutoring to students from any course at any level. The writing program works with large numbers of students in class; the center works with students and faculty one on one. Though the models may be different, their goals should be complementary.

I see the ideal relationship between writing center and program, then as almost symbiotic. These programs work in close association, each benefitting the other and both forwarding writing as a powerful tool for learning. A purposeful bonding, this type of relationship makes the program and center essential to the academic mission of the university, not peripheral to it.

Relationships are rarely ideal, however. And perhaps you might recognize some of the following characteristics as representative too often of the "real" relationship between centers and programs—characteristics reflected in my colleague's remarks quoted earlier. The writing center becomes a subset of the writing program, a clinic to which freshman English instructors can send their least able writers; or more particularly, the center serves the basic writing component of the writing program, working on the sentence-level problems of underprepared student writers. I have seen writing centers which rely heavily on tear-out work sheets, the kind offering ten to twenty sentences with errors that students are supposed to correct; fragments, run-ons, common splices. In many cases, those worksheets have been replaced with computer-aided instruction, worksheets on screens. But whatever the cover, the activity remains drill and practice. For more than two decades, we have known conclusively that isolating sentence-level work from the writing process, has no effect for good on the quality of the writing. And yet it goes on, too often, in the writing center. Why?

Directors who allow workbook instruction into their centers do so for a variety of reasons: the rules for standard written English have historically been taught this way by English departments, so tradition plays a role. Writing centers are often underfunded, and workbooks or CAI, one-time purchases, tend to be cheaper than tutors. As Muriel Harris remarks in her article "Growing Pains: The Coming of Age of Writing Centers," "In a frenzy to keep costs low by limiting staff, and to hand over some of the responsibility for learning to students, some of us rely on self-instruction books, tapes, video and slide programs, and whatever." Perhaps center directors may not know the research concerning drill and practice or may ignore it, relying on the obvious evidence of "improvement" that objective testing gives to administrators.

Because of the tenuousness of their positions and their operations, center administrators may undertake activities they would not otherwise undertake. They may accept the charge to become the grammar garage for the writing program, to prepare students for competency exams, to drill under-prepared and ESL students in the conventions of standard written English. They may take on these activities in the hope that, through accomplishing them successfully, the center will find its niche, become essential to the writing program, English department, and even to the university. Adopting these roles generates at least two serious problems, however: 1) devoting a center to particular tasks, especially onerous tasks, rather than pursuing a broader, more diversified vision, limits potential and actually increases expendability. It is far easier, certainly, for budget cutters to target centers that deal with freshman writing at the sentence level than it is to target those that deal with writing at all levels throughout the academy. And 2) focusing on these roles trivializes the center's relationship with the writing program in much the same way that writing programs were (and are) trivialized by literature programs within English departments.

There are, in fact, some strikingly negative parallels between centers and writing programs, and writing programs and English departments when the centers are service appendages to the programs. Recall that literature teachers used to look down on composition teachers, believing their work to be drudgery, of little intellectual challenge and abundant toil. E. D. Hirsch describes the relationship this way: "It was...natural that our profession should divide itself into two classes—[an] antiutilarian literary elite and an underpaid coolie class who labored in the fields of composition" (14). The writing program was the service side of the department; as such it could be staffed with temporary faculty who had no power within the departmental structure. Because of their humble status, they could be paid wages significantly lower than tenure tract faculty. This type of relationship with an English Department, perhaps to state the obvious, has led to very low morale among composition teachers.

Now consider the writing center when it is the service appendage of the writing program. If the center becomes the editing arm of the writing program, it may readily be viewed as taking care of problems beneath the concern of classroom composition teachers. The center, with its staff of grammar grunts, cares for the sentence-level disabled. Even to members of the writing program, the work lacks significance, treats symptoms. Note Maxine Hairston's characterization: "The writing labs...sprang up about ten years ago to give first aid to students who seemed unable to function within the traditional paradigm. Those labs are still with us, but they're still only giving first aid and treating symptoms" (82). Or Barbara Walvoord's observation, "If you are very short of time, if you think you are not skilled enough to deal with mechanical problems, or if you have a number of students with serious difficulties, you may wish to let the skills center carry the ball for mechanics and spend your time on other kinds of writing and learning problems" (63). Each of these people is an English teacher who should understand that a far better relationship is possible. But each bases her comments on observable data. The types of writing centers they refer to have existed and do exist. Still, the tone of condescension present in each remark is disturbing to those of us who know how good the relationship can be.

In large part problems with the relationship between center and program stem from the level of faculty hired to direct the center: often a person with a master's degree, perhaps a part-timer or lecturer in the writing program; a person who has no possibility of tenure and no research or service role in the department; a person who has little or no formal training in composition theory; in short a person who hasn't much chance of directing the center as a professional equal to his or her peers. [1] This is not, of course, the person's fault but the fault of a system which has taken decades to recognize the complexities, demands, and importance of teaching writing. Uncertain even about the status of writing teachers, English departments remain largely ambivalent about these labs and their directors. Couldn't anybody with a Master's degree, some teaching experience, and a knowledge of grammar set up one of those places and run it? The problem is that writing teachers are too often the ones asking this question. Thus, amending Hirsch's equation, composition teachers become the elite while center staff become the coolies. Even the situation in which the person hired to direct the center is tenure track but answers to the writing director can potentially cause an imbalance. The question is whose vision for the center will prevail under such conditions?

In large part the problems stem from English departments and writing programs themselves. Stephen North observes,

> *The grammar and drill center, the fix-it shop, the first aid station—these are neither the vestiges of some paradigm left behind nor pedagogical aberations that have been overlooked in the confusion of the "revolution" in the teaching of writing, but that will soon enough be set on the right path or done away with. They are, instead, the vital and authentic reflection of a way of thinking about writing and the teaching of writing that is alive and well and living in English departments everywhere.*

North [SUNY Albany's Writing Center Director] is suggesting that English departments get from centers what they expect and have historically practiced themselves. That is, drilling students in standard written English was, and remains, a common way to "teach writing." Even those who believe it is necessary, however, would largely agree that such teaching; lacks challenge. So what should be done with it?

Many programs do as Barbara Walvoord has recommended and "let the skills center carry the ball." But to do so trivializes the work of those in the "skills center," a term which itself smacks jarringly of remediation, punishment, contempt. And the work itself is not necessary. Since drill in mechanics does not improve writing quality, to what end does a college or university fund a skills center? When the skills center manages the editing "part" of the writing process within the context of the student writing (clearly a more pertinent way to "teach grammar"), it still mixes organicism with mechanicism, presenting a compartmentalized view of writing to students. In any case, the skills center, the fix-it shop, the first aid station can hardly bring about the complementary relationship described earlier. What can be done to bring about such a relationship?

I base my response to this question on seven years' experience as a center director, first a Montana State University and now at the University of Nevada, Reno. In 1983, I left a tenure-track position at Ohio State University to take the position at Montana State. It was a move which shocked my colleagues at OSU, because their view of writing centers was colored by the center they had there; directed by a non-tenurable staff member, in fact a graduate assistant, and devoted to developmental English students. How, they wondered, could a person trained to teach and do research in composition theory take such a job?

The position at MSU had built-in safeguards. It was tenure track in the English Department, half in administration and half in teaching. The status of the directors of writing and the writing center was equal, each answering to the English Department Head. All of the principals—the Head, the Director of Writing, the Academic Vice President, and the Center Director—had a vision that extended beyond the "treatment" stage. Our center's mission, we all agreed, should be twofold: first, to assist students in improving the quality of the academic writing they do for their courses, through tutoring all phases of the composing process; second, to consult with instructors who include (or want to include) writing assignments as part of their course requirements. The Center had to be the compositional heart of the institution; it had to show faculty the need for writing across disciplines, and then it had to meet the need through consultancy and tutoring.

From 1983 through 1988, the Center's statistics tell the tale, at least in part, of its success. In AY 1983, when the Center opened, it recorded 5400 student visits from 100 different courses. In AY 1988, it recorded 9000 student visits from 500 different courses. Center writing consultants had, by AY 1988, worked directly with more than 300 of the 500 FTE faculty. The Policies and Planning Committee, initiated to determine which programs could be cut during MSU's perpetual budget crises, judged the writing Center to be "critically important," the only such judgment of a program out of hundreds it made at MSU. The Writing Center was vitally bound to the Writing Program, itself designed to prepare students for academic writing.

If there was a problem with Center relationships at MSU, it stemmed from the large role the Center had university-wide and its high visibility. It appeared to some within the English Department, by which the Center was funded, that the Writing Center received more attention from the University than the English Department. The Writing Center Director's position at MSU offered a greater variety and possibility for creative action than did the position of the Director of Writing. Therefore, when I left, the Writing Director took my job.

At UNR the set of challenges is different. A strong, tenured staff trained in composition theory, for example, was present at MSU when the Center began its work. Though many fine lecturers teach the composition classes at UNR, none is tenured, and only one has theoretical background in composition. The groundwork for a significant cross-curricular writing project was already laid at MSU by a major two-year FIPSE grant. Several faculty were requiring writing as a result of the training they had received. And they were serving as consultants to their colleagues. No such groundwork exists at UNR. Certainly, many faculty require writing assignments in their classes at UNR, but there has never before been a coordinated cross-curricular effort here. The majority of UNR's faculty holds the predictable reservations about requiring writing in classes; they must be convinced of its value, if the program is to succeed, and then trained to design pertinent assignments and evaluate them quickly and fairly. Further, there is some entrenched classicism within the writing program, characterized by study of professional models, imitation of patterns, and some drill in grammar, which did not exist at MSU. But there also seems to be a healthy climate for change.

UNR's Writing Center has been established with a twofold goal in mind: tutoring students and consulting faculty. Instead of being linked by budget to the English Department, it is an independent unit under the Academic Vice President's office and within the College of Arts and Sciences. I am tenured at the associate level. It is one of the most ambitious writing center projects in the United States with start-up costs exceeding $180,000 and a yearly budget of $100,000.

The Writing Program Director at UNR has fostered the climate for change here and has embraced the programmatic shifts required to bring about a complementary relationship between Center and Program. The expectations are high: that the student population will receive an academic transfusion, becoming through writing more immediately and actively involved with their educations, and the faculty will become more engaged in their teaching. First semester statistics are encouraging: the Center recorded visits by 1660 students from seventy-nine different classes; our writing consultants worked with more than 100 faculty both individually and through workshops during the term. Particularly exciting to me is that much of our contact with students and faculty has been generated by positive word of mouth.

Like those at Montana State, the Center and Program and UNR are working together to advance the critical thinking and writing skills of an entire university student population. A comprehensive project of this scope requires the direct support of upper administrators, who see the marked advantages to students and faculty that its success can bring.

NOTES

1. The following job advertisement in the January 1990, issue of the *Writing Lab Newsletter* illustrates my point: "Writing Center Director, Twelve-Month non-tenure track specialist position, renewable, beginning September 1990. Duties include hiring, training, scheduling, and supervising the tutors in the English Department Writing Center, administering and developing the computer program in the center, designing and supervising mini-classes, practice labs in the areas of reading and writing, and managing the budget. PhD preferred, MS required plus related experience in writing center administration, basic reading and writing instruction, and computer lab management." This description tells us something about the type of center this English Department wants, largely a "basic" one; and the type of person, largely a powerless one. Even so, this may not be a bad job, when reviewed comparatively.

WORKS CITED

Hairston, Maxine, "The Winds of Change: Thomas Kuhn and the Revolution in the Teaching of Writing." *College Composition and Communication* 33 (1982).

Harris, Muriel, "Growing Pains: The Coming of Age of Writing Centers." *The Writing Center Journal* 2.1 (1982).

Hillocks, George, Jr. "What Works in Teaching Composition: A Meta-Analysis of Experimental Treatment Studies." Research report, U of Chicago, 1984.

Hirsch, E. D., Jr. "Remarks on Composition to the Yale English Department." *The Rhetorical Tradition and Modern Writing.* Ed. James J. Murphy. New York: MLA, 1982.

Knoblauch, C. H., and Lil Brannon. *Rhetorical Traditions and the Teaching of Writing.* New Jersey: Boynton Cook, 1984.

North, Stephen M. "The Idea of a Writing Center." *College English* 46.5 (1984).

Walvoord, Barbara, E. Fassler. *Helping Students Write Well: A Guide for Teachers in All Disciplines.* New York: MLA, 1981.

Mending the Damaged Path: How to Avoid Conflict of Expectation When Setting up a Writing Center

Karen Rodis

In an article entitled "Talking to the Boss," which appeared in the Fall/Winter 1988 *Writing Center Journal*, Diana George makes a valiant attempt to "mend the damaged path between the English department and the writing center." George rightly sees this damaged path as the result of poor communication between writing centers and English departments—of misunderstandings held by English Departments as to what goes on in writing centers, how it goes on, and why. Her method of mending the damaged path is to talk: to tell our colleagues in English departments (and perhaps in colleges and universities at large) what we do.

She talks well, isolating two basic inequities that she feels are the cause of the damaged path: inequities of purpose and inequities of staff. To mend the broken path, George implies, is to mend those inequities: first, it is essential that the "writing center's philosophy of composition...should reflect [the department's] philosophy of composition"—in other words, the philosophies of teaching writing held by the department should mirror or equal those of the writing center; second, it is essential that the staff of the writing center be perceived by the department and by the college or university at large as equal partners in the teaching of composition.

Rodis, Karen. "Mending the Damaged Path: How to Avoid Conflict of Expectation When Setting Up a Writing Center." *The Writing Center Journal* 10.2 (1990): 45–57. Reprinted with permission of *The Writing Center Journal*,

Talking with the boss, however, is perhaps not the most effective way to eliminate these inequities. We have been talking for many years now, and misperceptions persist. Moreover, to believe that enlightening the boss will bring an end to these inequities implies that the responsibility for these inequities, as well as the power to correct them, lies primarily with the boss. This implication is dangerous to writing centers in that it renders us powerless: the responsibility and the power lie elsewhere; the best we can do is to convince the powers that be to shine on us. In fact, it is empowering to writing centers and to those who work there to realize that much of the fault for these inequities—and, therefore, much of the power to remedy them—lies with us.

The inequities that George speaks of result from what I call Expectation Conflict—that is, the many conflicting expectations that a tutor at a writing center encounters each and every time she tutors a student. Conflict of expectation usually begins with the English department, whose members are often vague as to what they expect of their writing center. "We want to provide our students with a place where they can get help with their writing" is a common enough expectation, but when pressed as to exactly how it is that students are to be helped, department members will often shrug their shoulders and say something about grammar drills and other remedial aids. The instructors of composition, even when they are not members of the department, will often echo these sentiments: writing centers provide a place to send students who have serious syntactical and grammatical problems with their writing. The students who use the writing center often come because an instructor told them to get help with these remedial issues, and so they often expect that these are the only issues which the tutor ought to address. After all, the tutor may say a lot of fine things about the process of writing, but it is the professor who gives the grade. Finally, there are the expectations of the tutors themselves, who above all seek to assist the student in the very complex process of writing by addressing issues of content, structure, logic, and style.

These conflicting expectations are not simply the fault of our bosses and colleagues. Yes, these people often misperceive what it is we can do at our writing centers. And yes, that misperception is sometimes annoying, if not crippling. However, it is perhaps time to examine our own part in Expectation Conflict, to see precisely how much of the responsibility lies with us. This paper is based on research which indicates that much of the responsibility for Expectation Conflict is in fact our own. The degree and kind of conflict vary from institution to institution but seem to be firmly rooted within the very structure, the very set-up, of many of our writing centers. Changing the structure of our centers could lead to centers that run more effectively, freed from the burdens of Expectation Conflict.

Let's examine the matter more closely.

METHODS

In order to understand Expectation Conflict better, I undertook in the winter of 1988 an informal study of three Cleveland area universities: Cleveland State University (where I served that year as director), Case Western Reserve University, and Baldwin-Wallace College. Other than being geographically near one another, the three schools are very different: Cleveland State is a public university in an urban environment, open to any student who wishes to attend; Case Western Reserve University is a prestigious private university known for its engineering school, its medical school, and its programs in the sciences; Baldwin-Wallace is a small, liberal arts college with strong programs in business, education, and music, as well as the humanities. Accordingly, the writing centers at these institutions differ in the kinds of students served, as well as in the kinds of problems which the centers routinely encounter. The centers also differ in size—that is, the number of students served and the number of tutors serving them. However, the three centers share the important objective of helping students to improve their writing. And, because I had been employed at all three centers at one time or another in my early academic career, I knew that they were all in one way or another sharing the problem of Expectation Conflict. In studying these institutions, then, my objectives were three-fold:

1. To map the course of Expectation Conflict as it develops within the composition system of three universities;
2. To determine how this course varies from institution to institution;
3. To clarify what relationship exists between the structure and organization of a writing center and the particular degree and kind of Expectation Conflict from which it suffers.

My method was to distribute three separate questionnaires. The first went to the instructors of composition at all three schools, including professors, adjunct lecturers, and graduate teaching assistants—in short, anyone who was then teaching composition. This questionnaire asked instructors what they expected of writing centers and how these expectations differed from what they themselves taught in their own composition classrooms. Not all instructors responded to the study, but the number of those who did respond was approximately the same at all three schools: 9 from Cleveland State, 8 from Case Western, and 10 from Baldwin-Wallace. A second questionnaire went to the tutors of the three writing centers, questioning them as to what they had expected from their positions as tutors as well as what they felt was expected from them. Because the writing centers vary in size, the number of tutor responses varied: 8 tutors responded from Cleveland State, 2 from Case Western, and 4 from Baldwin-Wallace. A third questionnaire went to the students who used the writing centers at these universities. Students were asked what they expected from writing centers and what they thought they actually accomplished by going to the writing center. Again, the number of responses varied considerably: 100 students responded from Cleveland State, 20 from Case Western, and 60 from Baldwin-Wallace. The responses might surprise you.

CLEVELAND STATE UNIVERSITY

In order to examine Expectation Conflict at these schools, it was important to consider 1) how each writing center was conceived; 2) who staffs each writing center; and 3) who attends each writing center and why. As I said earlier, Cleveland State University is an urban commuter school with an open admissions enrollment policy. In other words, anyone who wishes to attend Cleveland State University may attend. Accordingly, some students at Cleveland State are less prepared for college-level thinking and writing than are their contemporaries at Case Western Reserve or Baldwin-Wallace. The Writing Center at Cleveland State was set up in order to assist some of these poorly-prepared students: it was, in other words, conceived of as a remedial service to be staffed by graduate assistants and attended almost exclusively by students of freshman composition who are required or strongly urged to come.

When I arrived at Cleveland State in the fall of 1987 as the Director of the Writing Center, the center had been running smoothly for many years. I was impressed with the operation: eight tutors (five "on-call" each quarter) serviced as many as two hundred students per quarter, with each student required to come to the center for six visits. The staff was excellent—so excellent, in fact, that I did not at first perceive that Expectation Conflict existed. However, after a few weeks, the grumblings began to occur. The tutors were finding it hard to fulfill the expectations of the instructors and the students—never mind their own expectations—within the confines of the half hour tutorial. The general gripe was with the instructors: "All they think we can do here is grammar," said one tutor. "The paper is a mess, and I'm supposed to work on commas. What good does it do to put all the commas in place when the sentence is absolutely devoid of sense or significance." What did the instructors *really* expect?

In fact, according to my study, two thirds of the nine instructors of composition at Cleveland State University who responded to my survey expected a writing center to be a place for students to get remedial help for writing problems such as grammar, usage, syntax, or punctuation. Even though most of these instructors pay lip service to the idea of writing centers being a place for students to learn how to write, and even though all of these instructors stated that the most important aspects of good writing were content, development, and structure, two thirds of the instructors who responded said that the proper role for writing centers is remedial. "Quite frankly," reported one instructor, "working through the idea is my domain. It's what I do in class. What I don't have time to do in class, or even in conference, is to go through endless sentence fragment drills and comma splice exercises. They can get that at the Writing Center."

The attitude implicit in this instructor's remarks is that the writing center tutor is not considered a fellow teacher of the writing process; rather, the tutor is regarded as merely an assistant to the instructor, someone who will address the "lesser" issues of grammar, syntax, punctuation. Lest you think this conclusion unfounded, consider the following statistics from the study: six of the nine instructors stated clearly that it was the role of the Writing Center to assist the instructor by addressing remedial issues; two felt that the tutor should function as a kind of cheerleader, helping students become more confident and enthusiastic about their own writing. Only one of the instructors felt that the tutors were partners in the teaching of writing. This perception is made even more striking by the fact that some of the instructors at Cleveland State are themselves graduate students at other institutions and have little more training in composition theory and practice than do the tutors there.

The tutors at Cleveland State felt trapped by the instructors' perceptions. The trap was certainly not one that they expected. My study asked tutors what they expected their roles to be within the total composition system. The questionnaire provided several possible answers, including the expectation that they were assistants to the student whose goal it was to become more confident and skilled in the writing process. Most tutors (six of the eight polled) had expected to be teachers of the writing process; the other two had expected to be assistants to students who sought to understand their writing processes. Not one had expected that he or she would be serving as assistants to the instructors of composition. When asked, however, what they perceived their actual role to be according to the expectations of the department at large, they replied unanimously that they were expected to assist the instructors of composition by taking care of those remedial problems which they did not have the time or the desire to address in class. Still, they continued to teach the writing process, even when it meant putting remedial errors aside in favor of initiating a dialogue about the student's ideas. It was often tough going. The tutors found themselves again and again faced with the dilemma of Expectation Conflict.

When questioned as to why this kind of Expectation Conflict existed, tutors replied that it was a matter of the perceived status of writing centers. Not one tutor at Cleveland State perceived his or her status as equal to that of the instructor of composition. One tutor complained that she was at the "bottom of the food chain" in the composition hierarchy. Another tutor said, "Because this Writing Center was initially set up as a remedial service, professors continue to see us exclusively as a place for comma help. Because we provide that sort of remedial help, we are defined as remedial human beings ourselves. In other words, because we are not trusted with important compositional issues, we must not be able to deal with those issues. And so we aren't trusted with those issues. It's the proverbial vicious circle," Added another tutor, "I think that the fact that we're graduate students has something to do with the expectation problem. Even though several of our teaching staff are actually Ph.D. students at other institutions, the premise is that because they've recently earned an M.A.—and we're still working on ours—they're better teachers of composition. However, my M.A. will be in Composition and Rhetoric; their dissertations are on Milton. Who do you think is more fit to teach composition?"

Such poor job perception can have only negative effects. When tutors were asked which position they would prefer, rank and salary being equal, a tutor at the writing center, an instructor of composition, or a lecturer of British or American literature or film, none of the Cleveland State tutors stated that being a tutor would be their position of choice. Neither did any of the lecturers there.

Of course, these negative perceptions are felt by the Cleveland State students as well. Several students at Cleveland State referred to the Writing Center tutorials as "bonehead English"; more than a few expressed—at least initially—tremendous anger about having to come. What's even more interesting is that their expectations concerning the Writing Center in some ways mirrored those of their instructors. When asked what they expected of the Writing Center, 53 of the 100 students polled said they expected better grades; 37 said they expected help with grammar; only 10 said they expected to become better writers by going to the Writing Center. However, perhaps because the Cleveland State tutors assumed the role of teacher of writing, students' expectations changed. At the quarter's end, all students who came repeatedly to the Writing Center came because they expected Writing Center tutors to teach them to write.

Moreover—and this will perhaps come as a blow to those of us who teach composition—the students said, by an overwhelming margin, that they learned more about writing from the Writing Center tutors than they did from their composition instructors. Specifically, students were asked from whom they learned more about writing—their tutor, their instructor, or their own efforts. At Cleveland State University, 44 said they learned more from their tutors. Only 29 said that they learned more about writing from their instructors; 27 said that their own efforts were more fruitful than anything they learned in class. Clearly these results were not what instructors of composition would have expected. Nonetheless, they indicate what writing centers could and should be if they were places at which real teaching and learning of writing could occur.

CASE WESTERN RESERVE UNIVERSITY

The situation at Case Western Reserve is somewhat different than it is at Cleveland State. Case Western Reserve is a private university; it accepts only those students who have proven themselves to be well prepared for an academic career. However, its Writing Center, like Cleveland State's, is also conceived of as primarily a remedial service: students who receive a "D" in Freshman Composition are required in the next summer semester to take a one- or two-hour tutorial at the Writing Center in order to fulfill their composition requirement. Other students who wish to improve their writing can also enroll for a writing center tutorial; still others simply drop in for occasional help. The Writing Center is staffed and directed by graduate students; most of the composition instructors are also graduate students; though the pay is the same, instructorships are generally thought of as more prestigious and, therefore, more desirable then is the position of tutor in the Writing Center.

Even though the instructors and tutors at Case Western Reserve are more clearly equal in status, the same Expectation Conflict exists as that found at Cleveland State. While all eight of the instructors who responded to the survey felt that the priorities of the composition classroom ought to be content, critical thinking, and structure, six felt that the proper concerns of the Writing Center ought to be syntax, usage, and punctuation. Again, even though their status in terms of degree and salary are equal, seven of the eight instructors who responded—a full 86%—felt that it is the job of the tutors to assist them in the teaching of composition. Even at Cleveland State, where some inequity in status exists, this percentage was only 58%. When questioned on this point, one instructor remarked, "Teaching grammar is dull. Why bring it into the classroom when some kids don't need it, and most kinds don't want to hear about it? The Writing Center can teach it. I'm helped out; the student is helped out. Everybody's happy, aren't they?" Another instructor commented, "Somebody's got to teach grammar. Isn't that what writing centers are for?"

It is perhaps time to mention that those of us who work at writing centers are *not averse to teaching grammar*. Somebody *does* have to do it, and more than not it is the writing center. However, we ask, why not let us do more when we are equipped to do more? Certainly tutors at Case Western, like their peers at Cleveland State, expected to do more. Both of the tutors from Case Western who responded expected to teach students the entire writing process. Like their peers at Cleveland State, when asked what they perceived their actual role to be according to the expectations of the department at large, they replied that they were expected to assist the instructor of composition by taking care of those remedial problems which the instructor did not have the time to address in class. They also declared that they had at one time or another felt hampered in the tutoring session by this conflict in expectation.

What's curious about the tutors at Case Western, however, is that their perception of their job is still very positive, despite these status issues. One of the two, in fact, stated that she prefers her position as tutor to an economically comparable position teaching composition or literature or film. Something certainly must be gratifying about her job. Perhaps it has something to do with the students. In fact, though most students came to Case Western Reserve Writing Center either to fulfill a composition requirement or for help with editing a paper, a full 100% of them declared that they learned more about writing from the tutors at the Writing Center than they'd learned from their instructors or from their own efforts. Therefore, even though tutors report feeling frustrated, Expectation Conflict does not seem to interfere with the effectiveness of the Writing Center. However, it should be noted that in other ways Expectation Conflict keeps this center from reaching its full potential: it services far fewer students than do Cleveland State's or Baldwin-Wallace's writing centers. The Case Western Reserve Writing Center has not overcome its reputation as a remedial service; consequently, the number of students seeking or willing to seek help there is very low.

BALDWIN-WALLACE COLLEGE

We've yet to consider Baldwin-Wallace's Writing Lab. Of course, if the degree and kind of Expectation Conflict at Baldwin-Wallace were similar to that experienced at Cleveland State and Case Western, then perhaps there would be little left to say. However, this is not the case. In fact, Baldwin-Wallace suffers little from Expectation Conflict. A look at its initial set-up may tell us why.

Baldwin-Wallace is a small, private, liberal arts college. Its students have more than an average preparation for their academic careers. It's Writing Lab was founded and is still directed by a full professor, who was very careful to follow three important premises:

1. Instead of opening the lab as a remedial center, stress that the lab can service students campus-wide with all sorts of compositional needs;
2. Staff the lab with primarily professional (i.e., M.A.-degreed) personnel (although peer tutors would be used as well);
3. Insist that attendance at the lab be voluntary.

First of all, by refusing to *conceive* of the lab a remedial service, the director avoided its being *perceived* by the instructors of composition as a remedial service. In fact, when Baldwin-Wallace instructors were surveyed as to the expected and appropriate priorities of writing centers, six of the eight who responded to this question (two instructors for one reason or another did not respond) said that writing centers should chiefly concern themselves with matters of content, organization, and logic—the same priorities with which they themselves were concerned in class. Compare this 77% with 34% at Cleveland State and 25% at Case Western Reserve, and you'll see the enormous difference in regards to Expectation Conflict at Baldwin-Wallace. Moreover, only three of the instructors at Baldwin-Wallace (30% here as opposed to 58% at Cleveland State and 86% at Case Western Reserve) felt that the Writing Lab exists in order to help them by addressing remedial issues; the other seven felt that the Writing Lab's chief task is to teach writing. Period.

This sentiment is echoed by the professional tutors themselves, all of whom feel that they are treated as partners in the teaching of writing. I suspect that this feeling of partnership is due to the fact that these tutors are professionals. They were hired as writing specialists, expecting to teach writing. And teaching writing is clearly what they do. Moreover, the status of the director of the Writing Lab reinforces the lab's reputation as a teaching rather than a remedial service: the director is a full professor—a status not shared by the directors at Case Western Reserve, where the Writing Center is directed by a graduate student, or at Cleveland State, where the Writing Center is directed by a Ph.D. whose position is only part time and carries no vote in the department. The difference in status seems significant. With our equals we share hopes; we coordinate goals. We do not force our equals to meet our agenda, to fulfill our expectations. We allow them to fulfill their own.

Student expectation also seems to be met better at Baldwin-Wallace's Writing Lab. Perhaps this is because the students who use the Writing Lab *come* to the lab with expectations that match our own: an overwhelming 43 out of 60 students come for writing instruction; nine come in hopes of a better grade; six come because professors have recommended it—*not* required it; and two come to have their papers proofread—a hope of which they are quickly disillusioned. These expectations indicate a very different attitude toward the Writing Lab than is typical of Case Western Reserve or Cleveland State.

It seems to me that this difference in attitude can be accounted for by the fact that attendance at the Writing Lab is voluntary. Students come because they want to learn to write, not because they have to fulfill a requirement. Moreover, as one tutor remarked, "Instructors are not permitted to require students to attend, so the instructors' wishes and priorities don't get in the way during the tutoring session as much as they might otherwise." In these ways, voluntary attendance produces tutorials which are more effective, more efficient, and more satisfying for the student and tutor as well.

IMPLICATIONS

One could perhaps argue on the basis of these findings that writing centers simply work better at small liberal arts colleges than they do at public and private universities. But this conclusion would only dismay those who work at university writing centers. I am far more convinced by the argument that the way a writing center is set up can and does determine the kind of Expectation Conflict it will experience. Common sense argues that a writing center initially conceived of and justified as a remedial service will continue to be perceived as a remedial service, even when it can do and be much more. As we all know, writing centers, when expected to do great things, can do great things. They can function as writing-across-the-curriculum centers; they can become English-as-a-second-language centers; they can be centers for graduate school applications, resumes, and cover letters; they can even be centers that professors use to get feedback on their own scholarship. The Baldwin-Wallace Writing Lab was used in these ways primarily because it was conceived of as being used in these ways. And yes, it did offer some remedial help—because it was conceived of as including that, too.

Often, however, those of us who are attempting to set up writing centers find that the only way we can sell our idea to the administration is to call it remedial: after all, instructors do need help teaching these issues, and students need help learning them. Most administrators will admit to remedial needs, even when they won't admit to others. In this way many a writing center was born. However, promoting our writing centers to the administration eventually necessitates promoting them as remedial to faculty and to students as well. As a consequence, the writing center handles issues that are chiefly remedial. The potential benefits of the writing center therefore go unrealized.

Such a view of writing centers is of course anachronistic. The wide success of such places in recent years calls for a readjustment of these narrow attitudes. Most writing center directors, aware of their center's remedial or limited usage, turn to public relations as a way to change department and campus perceptions. In fact, the directors of the three writing centers in this study all make use of newsletters, quarterly reports, flyers, even campus radio and newspaper advertisements. This study makes clear, however, that these public relations efforts are not enough. Changes in perception are slow in coming. It is my opinion that the desired changes can be more swiftly made by restructuring a writing center, specifically with regard to attendance policy and staffing.

Making attendance voluntary makes good common sense in terms of avoiding Expectation Conflict. Often directors insist on mandatory attendance at their writing centers because they are afraid of not attracting clientele. In order to justify the cost of running a writing center, a director must be able to point to significant numbers of students who are making use of the facility. If not, the center is in realistic danger of closing. There are, however, other ways of attracting students—namely, public relations and word of mouth. While newsletters and commercials seems to do very little to change departmental perceptions of writing centers, they are very effective in attracting students. Moreover, testimonials from satisfied customers are perhaps the best form of public relations. If a center is used by students who want to be there, chances are their experience of the center will be good. Students are therefore more likely to recommend the center to their friends. Given time, any good writing center should be able to flourish, even with voluntary attendance, as does Baldwin-Wallace's.

Finally, it also makes sense that a professional staff would be able to diffuse Expectation Conflict. Respect commands trust, and trust seems to lessen conflict of expectation. However, it is not always financially feasible to hire a staff of professionals. After all, schools with graduate students will find it more economical to use graduate student tutors; undergraduate institutions will be able to employ peer tutors at little cost. Still, even a small staff of professional tutors—people who can run workshops, provide faculty educations, etc.—can make an enormous difference to a writing center. Consider once again Baldwin-Wallace's Writing Lab. At Baldwin-Wallace, peer tutors and professionals work side by side. The peer tutors are not alone in their attempt to command the respect and trust of the faculty. Rather, the respect and trust are initially won by the professional staff; the peers' task is then to reinforce this respect and trust through competence. If a center absolutely cannot afford a professional staff, the director should be a tenured professor, someone with at least a vote in the department. If the director is a graduate student or other part-time employee, a tenured professor can function as an advisor to the director. The advisor's job should be to see that the writing center is represented departmentally, that it has the ear and voice of someone whose status commands respect campus-wide. In this way, not only will Expectation Conflict be diffused, but many political problems can be avoided.

CONCLUSION

If anything is to be learned from this study, it is that the perception of the writing center—both the perception of its purpose as well as the perception of its staff—often needs to be changed. Communication within the English department and within the institution at large can help effect such changes. However, one can diffuse the potentially explosive dilemma of Expectation Conflict by carefully considering the way one's writing center is structured. In setting up a writing center, one should not promote it as a remedial center, should make attendance voluntary, and, if at all possible, should hire a least a small professional staff. In restructuring an existing writing center, one should rethink the attendance policy and consider the option of a professional staff. Writing centers can then get *off* the damaged path, put the matter of Expectation Conflict behind them, and move on to the important matters which face us all, teacher and student alike—the matters of teaching and learning good writing.

Relevant Questions and Responses From the Study on Expectation Conflict

Questions for Instructors [Number of Responses]	CSU [9]		CWRU [8]		B-W [10]	
What constitutes good writing:	%	#	%	#	%	#
• Mastery of content, logic, structure	100	[9]	100	[8]	100	[10]
• Mastery of paragraphs, syntax, grammar						
What is the proper compositional domain of the writing center?	%	#	%	#	%	#
• Content Logic Structure	33	[3]	25	[2]	77	[6]
• Paragraph Syntax Grammar	67	[6]	75	[6]	23	[2]
• No Responses						[2]
What is the primary purpose of the writing center?	%	#	%	#	%	#
• To assist instructors in the teaching of composition	67	[6]	86	[7]	30	[3]
• To encourage students to work at & enjoy writing	23	[2]	14	[1]	0	[0]
• To teach composition	10	[1]	0	[0]	70	[7]
Questions for Tutors [Number of Responses]	CSU [8]		CWRU [2]		B-W [4]	
What were your initial expectations as a writing center tutor?	%	#	%	#	%	#
• To teach composition	75	[6]	100	[2]	100	[4]
• To encourage students	25	[2]	0	[0]	0	[0]
• To assist instructors	0	[0]	0	[0]	0	[0]
What do you perceive your role to be in the eyes of the department at large?	%	#	%	#	%	#
• To teach composition	0	[0]	0	[0]	100	[4]
• To encourage students	0	[0]	0	[0]	0	[0]
• To assist instructors	100	[8]	100	[2]	0	[0]
What position would you prefer, rank and salary being equal?	%	#	%	#	%	#
• Lecturer of literature or film	67	[4]	50	[1]	50	[2]
• Instructor of composition	33	[2]	0	[0]	25	[1]
• Writing center tutor	0	[0]	50	[1]	25	[1]
• No preference						
Questions for Students [Number of Responses]	CSU [100]		CWRU [20]		B-W [60]	
With what expectations did you come to the writing center?	%	#	%	#	%	#
• Better grades	53	[53]	45	[9]	15	[9]
• Help with grammar	37	[37]	35	[7]	10	[6]
• Improved writing	10	[10]	15	[3]	72	[43]
• Proofreading	0	[0]	5	[1]	3	[2]

Continued

Relevant Questions and Responses From the Study on Expectation Conflict
Continued

Questions for Students [Number of Responses]	CSU [100]		CWRU [20]		B-W [60]	
What sort of help did you actually receive at the writing center?	%	#	%	#	%	#
• Better grades	0	[0]	0	[0]	0	[0]
• Help with grammar	0	[0]	0	[0]	0	[0]
• Improved writing	100	[100]	100	[20]	100	[60]
• Proofreading	0	[0]	0	[0]	0	[0]
From whom did you learn the most?	%	#	%	#	%	#
• Your tutor	44	[44]	100	[20]	54	[32]
• Your instructor	29	[29]	0	[0]	25	[15]
• Your own efforts	27	[27]	0	[0]	21	[13]

Perceptions, Realities, and Possibilities: Central Administration and Writing Centers

Jeanne Simpson

Based on my interactions with writing center personnel over the past dozen years, and, I emphasize, not based on any empirical research, the following are among the most common perceptions that writing center personnel hold with regard to central administration:

1. Central Administration prefers to keep writing centers powerless and marginalized.

2. Central Administration is where all the power is concentrated.

3. Central Administration's distribution of funding support within an institution is unpredictable at best, capricious at worst.

4. Faculty rank and the situating of a writing center within a department accrue important prestige in the Central Administration.

5. Major curricular decisions are made in the Central Administration.

6. Retention, tenure, and promotion decisions are determined primarily by Central Administration.

Other perceptions also operate, but these are the most common and the ones upon which many writing center decisions about design, mission, staffing, and reporting tend to be made. It is important, therefore, to study these perceptions and to determine their accuracy.

To do that, perhaps the best place to go next is Central Administration and talk about its perceptions of writing centers.

1. Actual information, detailed and precise, that Central Administration has about writing centers tends to be fairly sparse, coming forward almost entirely by means of reports.

Simpson, Jeane. "Perceptions, Realities, and Possibilities: Central Administration and Writing Centers." *Writing Center Perspectives*. Ed. Byron L. Stay, Christina Murphy, and Eric H. Hobson. Emmitsburg, MD: NWCA Press, 1995. 48–52. Reprinted by permission of NWCA Press.

Administrators, by and large, are more burdened with paper pushing and meeting schedules than faculty imagine, so that opportunities to get out and visit campus facilities may be governed by crisis, not by desire to acquire knowledge.

The crisis may be a physical plant breakdown or a personnel difficulty, or it may be a more positive crisis, such as an accreditation site visit. But still a crisis—and thus a way of limiting and focusing what Central Administration will be looking at and therefore what they will see and not see.

Thick and detailed reports are not the solution to this problem. Rather, careful planning of what goes into the required reports and carefully timed invitations to Central Administration would be a more effective solution. The point is that writing centers have more control over what Central Administration knows about them than is perceived.

2. Central Administration is interested in information that addresses the issues that concern it.

These are things like accreditation, accountability (assessment), staffing plans, space allocation, and personnel dollars. Those are the nuts-and-bolts concerns, the daily assignment of administration. It is crucial to understand that.

Thus, a writing center for Central Administration is space, student use, personnel dollars, productivity, and a program that requires assessment and evaluation on the basis of institutional mission and priorities. Notice that the quality of instruction is in there, but not obviously and not at the head of the list. That does not mean that quality is not a concern of Central Administration. But the other issues are why Central Administration exists in the first place.

3. Assessment of instructional quality is the business of departments and the faculty of an institution. Central Administration is the place where "big picture" information about assessment is gathered, where the money and time and reporting lines for assessment are addressed. But not the assessment itself.

4. The concept of "marginalization" would be a surprise to Central Administration. If a program is being funded, space provided, salaries paid, assessment and evaluation being conducted, then the assumption of Central Administration is that it is a part of the institution and that some part of the institution's mission is being addressed.

Now that doesn't mean that funds may not be distributed sparingly, that positions may be temporary. But what looks like marginalization from the writing center point of view will be regarded by Central Administration as keeping flexibility available for shifting funds, reallocating staffing positions, redistributing space. In times of budget shortages (and we can expect them for the foreseeable future), flexibility is not only wise, it is required.

"Marginal" then means what can be cut if a budget revisions occur. And they do occur. These decisions are often based on the available unspent or unencumbered funds. A prime target, for example, would be a summer school, if a revision came late in the fiscal year. On the other hand, support service cuts are risky, for they alienate students and reduce retention rates, which in turn will reduce income further. But Central Administration may need to be reminded of that.

The situation is not changed by this difference in perceptions. It is still unpleasant and limits options and possibilities. But the understanding of how to respond to the situation, the development of realistic and effective responses, depends on a clear understanding of how the check-signers perceive the situation. They do not perceive themselves as oppressors and tend to react defensively against such accusations. Even an intransigent, block-headed Central Administration will react negatively to such accusations.

5. Central Administration considers most evaluation decisions (retention, promotion, tenure) to be primarily made at the department level.

The closest, most accurate, and most comprehensive sense of what is going on in a discipline, of what constitutes appropriate and effective scholarship and teaching methodology, and of what are meaningful professional activities, exists in departments and—in institutions that have them—divisions or colleges.

Central Administration will override recommendations made at lower levels, but infrequently. To be regularly at variance with these recommendations is to court dissention, protest, grievances, and lawsuits, none of which is considered desirable by Central Administration (though we face them daily).

Furthermore, it is in the best interests of good assessment and program review for these determinations to be made by knowledgeable people. Central Administration does have a vested interest in valid and positive assessment outcomes.

6. Departmental affiliation is not seen by Central Administration as a prestige issue but as a mechanical/organizational/logistical issue.

Because it is the most common structure, it is therefore the best understood. It determines how funding will be channeled, reporting lines established, and evaluation conducted. It is conventional, defined, and therefore not problematic: the line of least resistance. If a less conventional structure is to be pursued, these issues will have to be sorted out to the satisfaction of Central Administration, and clarity and efficiency should be among the criteria. A frequent difficulty for writing centers is that they do not easily fit the conventional structure and yet are jammed into it because it is familiar to both Central Administration and writing center staff.

An alternative response, also frequent, is to use temporary staffing and soft funding, as much out of inertia (what to do with this odd duck among the various programs?) as out of a desire for flexibility. When in doubt, stall, and these structures are the manifestations of stalling. Once you establish a tenure line and the related evaluation system, you have made a commitment not to move things around. Tenure-line positions mean that the institution is thinking about something for a very long haul. People are in a hurry to get tenure, and they are reluctant to leave once they have it. A tenure-line position is, when you consider it, an institutional commitment of at least 20 years' duration. That means, literally, thousands and thousands of dollars in salary and benefits. For Central Administration, whose responsibility is the prudent management of those dollars, it only makes sense to take a long, squinty-eyed look at any request for such commitment. It is generally not a desire to oppress or marginalize anybody.

Related to this responsibility is the one of supervising and adjusting the institutional structure so that all the parts fit together coherently and efficiently. Programs are not looked at in isolation, though the persons who are involved with them may have that perception. For Central Administration, a writing center may be a discrete unit, but not a separate one, one that fits into the whole. They must consider not just the content of the writing center's activities, but where it fits in the organizational structure. Where should it go? How will other units be affected? The flow of information? Decision-making authority? Funding? Equipment? Space?

Again, departmental affiliation is, superficially, the easiest answer to these questions. In some institutions, a deeper analysis may yield the same answer. But not always.

7. Finally, caprice is complicated and costly. It is very, very seldom what is behind a Central Administration decision. Rather, funding, in whatever form, is at the bottom of *most* Central Administration decisions. Period. All decisions, including tenure, are ultimately budgetary in their implications. Caprice, on the other hand, leads to lawsuits and other difficulties. It creates unusual and time-consuming problems to be solved, distracting Central Administration from the routine work that must be done.

Of course I don't discount Murphy's Law and the Stupidity Factor from the decision-making process. But in analyzing why a Central Administration decision has been made, I urge the application of Occam's Law: the simplest explanation is the likeliest, and in this case, that means budget.

What then are the implications for writing centers and writing center personnel if we proceed from these observations?

The kind of information that writing center directors will need to gather and distribute will not be as closely related to the philosophy and daily functioning of a writing center as it will be to larger, institutional issues. Directors need to be sophisticated enough in their own administrative activities to balance the two levels of knowledge and expertise—theoretical and managerial, pedagogical and budgetary—effectively.

A problem that I see and that I hope will begin to be addressed by our professional literature and organizations is that the professional preparation of writing center personnel is very effective at covering the theoretical and the pedagogical and virtually silent on the managerial and budgetary. We want to strengthen our programs but have almost no good information or understanding of how to do so effectively.

Our idealism, one of the fuels that propels successful and innovative writing centers, is also a problem for us, leading us to misperceive our institutional situations and, frequently, to exacerbate problems by applying the wrong remedy. I would urge that careful study, a lot of talk and legwork, and, above all, the consistent requirement of looking at the whole institution, will be far and away the most effective way to end this matter of "marginalization" for writing centers. We need to adopt the principle that we use so often in tutoring: abandon our preconceived notions and look at what is actually there.

Redefining Our Existence: An Argument for Short- and Long-Term Goals and Objectives

Robert W. Barnett

In his January, 1995 *Writing Lab Newsletter* column, "Writing Center Ethics: Questioning Our Own Existence," Michael Pemberton warns that it is "time to take a hard look at what we do, why we do it, and how we can justify it to people who might be looking to us as expendable budget items in tough—and getting tougher—economic times" (8). While not all writing centers are facing economic hardships, I agree with Pemberton that the time has come for some serious self-reflection.

The time his also come to move beyond the stories that define our existence within our own writing centers and within the writing center community. Such internal definition is valuable in the evolution of individual writing centers, but the fact remains that we are not all the same. In Darwinian terms, we are all members of the same species, but we don't share the same physical features and we don't all socialize with the outside world in the same manner. Because we all exist in highly specialized environments, I believe we need also to define ourselves vis-à-vis these environments as we formulate and administer our own policies. In the process, we will inevitably create a new era of stories which better clarify our roles within our institutions. As Pemberton notes, "It is important for all people who work in writing centers and think of them as important, effective, and ethical sites for learning to be able to rationalize—for anybody at any time—the benefits of what we do" (8).

One step that many writing centers have already taken in this direction is to create mission statements, which they distribute to faculty and administrators. Several writing center colleagues have shared their statements with me, and one commonality I have noticed is a determination to become more visi-

Barnett, Robert W. "Redefining Our Existence: An Argument for Short- and Long-Term Goals and Objectives. *The Writing Center Journal* 17.2 (1997): 123–133. Reprinted by permission of *The Writing Center Journal.*

ble, to be taken more seriously in the larger academic arena. I don't mean to suggest here that we start a mass exodus toward the writing center promised land, because many in our field would respond with a loud chorus of "Include me out!" Not every writing center administrator shares the ambition to move toward the center of the university curriculum. North, for example, makes it perfectly clear that he does not want to participate in the "romanticization of the writing center's institutional potential, [which] may actually mask its complicity in what Elspeth Stuckey has called the violence of literacy" ("Revisiting" 15). Others less cynical than North see a move toward the center as too much work, or they may simply choose to stay out of the institutional spotlight. I don't agree with North's nonparticipatory stance, but I have come to realize that socialization patterns between writing centers and their institutions are as diverse as the very missions that drive each center. In this light, mission statements are important for broadly defining the philosophy of writing centers. I also believe, though, that a document more comprehensive than the mission statement—outlining writing center philosophies, pedagogies and campus services is vital for those attempting to move into the mainstream of the larger university community. In fact, at the University of Michigan-Flint, our existence as a valued component of students' education depends on it.

In addition to the already-tried approaches to justifying the benefits of our writing center, I have found that creating a statement of short- and long-term goals and objectives not only works to legitimize our curricular positioning in the academy, but also addresses important political, theoretical, and rhetorical questions pertaining to our top priority—helping students become better writers. In sharing my story, I hope to illustrate the rewards, opportunities, challenges, and dangers that have presented themselves in the process, all of which contribute to my belief that a promising future does exist for writing centers. As North, Ede, Riley, and countless others have pointed our, we all have compelling stories. Some are inspirational and offer hope, while others paint a bleaker picture of our existence. The best ones, however, provide clear warning signs that should not be ignored. In "Priorities and Guidelines for the Development of Writing Centers," for example, Bene Scanlon Cox cautions that

> the absence of clear priorities and guidelines for future development is a major problem because the staff of each center must rely largely on its own experience and knowledge to provide the rationale to direct services and even to justify survival. Progress towards solving these problems lies in approaching systematically and collectively the priorities for future functions of writing centers. (77)

In a climate of diminishing budgets, accountability, student retention, and sweeping curricular changes, creating a goals and objectives statement has given our writing center a clear advantage because, in addition to establishing ourselves as a necessary and important component of a university education, we now have a short-term and long-term plan for the center's operation that "systematically and collectively" illustrates our priorities. Such a plan becomes particularly significant when justifying the need for more and better space, a larger operating budget, state-of-the-art computer technology, and so on. If deans and provosts see a clear and positive direction for our writing centers, a direction that benefits students and faculty, then they are more likely to invest time and money in our efforts.

In its present form, the goals and objectives statement for UM-Flint's writing center is a lengthy eight pages. It contains the major goals of the center and a list of more specific objectives for attaining each goal....

STUDENT RETENTION

Two particular commitments included in our goals and objectives have helped convince the administration that our writing center deserves a promising future: 1) student retention, and 2) collaboration with faculty and staff across the curriculum. In the university's academic plan, a formal statement outlining the issues needing wide-spread attention in order to strengthen our institution, these components continually surfaced. After a close reading of the 1995 Academic Plan, I am convinced that our writing center and the administration are mutually dependent; we need each other's support to improve the university's student retention efforts. The following excerpt from the section of the document, titled "Enrollment, Retention, and Graduation of Students," illustrates my point:

> *Faculty and staff need to work together to promote a campus culture in which student learning goes beyond classroom contact hours.... Faculty and staff need to receive support to enable them to assume more responsibility for helping students learn how to learn.... We should also establish formal mechanisms for assisting students likely to encounter academic difficulty. Remedial and tutorial services are critical, and their effectiveness should be regularly assessed. (39)*

Other, more specific recommendations call for "enhanced support services addressing the needs of our students" and "increased mentoring." Admittedly, our motivations are not the same—the administration is preoccupied with keeping students' tuition money coming in, while our aim is to bring about long-term change in students' writing abilities for the purpose of helping them succeed in college and thus remain in college—but our combined efforts can produce positive results. In his 1989 article, "Misconceptions Mar Campus Discussions of Student Retention," Vincent Tinto, then director of the Cultural Foundations of Education Program at Syracuse University, reveals what he sees as the true nature of effective student retention efforts: "Although keeping students in college is a natural byproduct of a successful operation, such programs focus first and foremost on ways to insure that all students, not just some, have an opportunity to learn as much as possible while they are in college, regardless of whether they decide to stay or leave" (B2). What better way to ensure that all students are at least offered the help they need with their writing skills than to rely on the services of the campus writing center? After all, helping students improve themselves as writers and as critical thinkers is essential to their academic success. In "What the Writing Center is—and Isn't," Richard Leahy corroborates what writing center personnel have always said. Defending the integrity of writing centers, he says, "They welcome students who come with just an assignment and no idea where to start, with some scribbled notes or in outlines or with a completed draft. They also want to work with all writers, even the strongest ones" (44).

The writing center at the University of Michigan-Flint is no exception. Our cross-curricular design allows all students in all disciplines at all levels to receive the same tutorial assistance. In addition, all first-semester students take an English placement exam, which determines the freshman composition course they must take. Those who score below Composition I or Composition II on the written exam are placed into English 109, a three-credit developmental writing course that includes four hours of contact with a writing center tutor each week. Since the developmental writing program is primarily administered through the writing center, a program which accommodates several hundred underprepared students each semester, the administration can ill-afford to ignore our importance. And since the writing center works with drop-in students from 30–40 different departments, a large number of writers from across campus rely on us to help them succeed in the academy. Statistics such as these send a clear message to higher administration that students value, in fact depend on, our existence. It is no accident, then, that two of the seven goals in our goals and objectives statement specifically address student retention issues:

> *Assist all students in advancing their writing abilities and critical thinking skills in relation to their university education and in preparation for their respective careers.*

> *Maintain and enhance the quality of the English Department's Developmental Writing program as it pertains to the Writing Center to more effectively facilitate students' learning processes.*

These statements may smack of ambition and dedication to the cause, but alone they are not enough to convince the higher-ups that we are committed to helping retain students through collaborative peer tutoring. It is also necessary to include specific tasks which, when executed, will help accomplish the initial goal(s). For example, our center offers tutoring for writers at any level, including first-year students, advanced writers, and graduate students. We train and staff our tutors to accommodate not just freshman writers, but all writers, which is important to faculty and administrators who traditionally view the writing center as a remedial stopping place for bad writers. Spelling out what we do and who we help has changed the negative stereotypes of our office away from that of a "grammar garage" or "fix-it shop," and it has helped educate those who can contribute, financially and politically, to advancing our cause.

Ours is an urban, commuter campus, and most students work an average of 35 hours per week, which means the traditional 9–5 University schedule does not always give them a chance to take full advantage of their college experience. I announced in our goals statement that the writing center would expand its hours to include evenings and weekends so that students would have more opportunities to seek out help with their writing. This impressed the administration because, as our Dean pointed out to me in a memo, we were structuring our office in a way that would maximize students' chances to succeed. In the end, our budget was expanded to include an extra $1,500 for spring and summer tutoring which, until our goals and objectives statement was circulated, had never even been considered.

COLLABORATION WITH FACULTY

Mark Waldo, in "The Last Best Place for Writing Across the Curriculum: The Writing Center," argues that an institution's commitment to a strong writing across the curriculum program must necessarily include a commitment to the writing center. Waldo proposes "a home for WAC on middle ground, between the open space of dialogue and the cloister of English department control. This home needs a physical location well known to faculty and students, situated in some central, easily accessible part of campus" (20). Waldo's comments are significant because in calling for writing centers to coordinate WAC programs he has helped strengthen the argument for the permanence of writing centers. Steven North, in his 1984 article "The Idea of a Writing Center," pleads with colleagues for understanding and respect, to clarify what writing center directors and staff do. Waldo, convinced that we have to some extent already accomplished North's goal, uses the idea of faculty collaboration to further pressure administrators to increase their commitment to the writing center's role in the university curriculum.

Though I don't fully share Waldo's belief that writing centers alone should "house" WAC, the importance he places on faculty collaboration is fundamental to the success of any writing center. As Vincent Tinto notes, "The more faculty members interact with and become engaged with students, the more likely students are to stay in college" (B2). Linking student learning with student retention, he claims that "students who report rewarding contacts with faculty members are also the ones who make the greatest gains in learning and are the most likely to complete their degrees" (B2).

At the University of Michigan-Flint, the writing center has taken steps to help improve the lines of communication between faculty and students, as the examples below illustrate. The point here, though, is that while Tinto's comments do not factor writing centers into the student learning/faculty contact/student retention equation, writing centers can help strengthen the student/faculty connection. Moreover, faculty outreach has been important to our writing center, contributing to a rapid, short-term increase in student visits. I've learned that clearly defining the writing center vis-à-vis the academy is dependent on our commitment to work closely with colleagues across the disciplines, a commitment expressed in our own goals and objectives statement.

Develop the existing partnership between the writing center and the Writing Across the Curriculum program to encourage faculty involvement.

Continue increasing collaborative work with and accommodate the needs of all faculty.

As co-director of our Writing Across the Curriculum committee, a position I share with our Composition Director, I collaborate with colleagues in a number of capacities. Our discipline-based WAC program empowers individual faculty members to incorporate writing into their classes that fits their specific course agendas. Each discipline has its own purposes for writing and creates its own set of values for its discourse community. Acting as facilitator, my task, then, is to help instructors create writing assignments that reflect the purposes and values of their own disciplines and that allow them to use writing as an important tool for learning. Assuming a rhetorically neutral position, I am able to consult with faculty on assignment design, evaluation, and grading criteria. Along the way, the writing center has developed close relationships with several disciplines such as psychology, philosophy, and math because we provide tutoring for students as writing becomes more prominent in their courses. An increasingly open system of communication has evolved, helping to build an important level of trust between faculty and the writing center, and, we hope, between faculty and students. Cultivating collaborative efforts with the disciplines has elevated the writing center (and its mission of bringing writing to the heart of the university curriculum) to respectable status. Not only are we working to educate the campus about the importance of writing as a way to enhance critical thought and students' abilities to succeed in the academy, but the writing center is becoming disentangled from its stereotypical image of a remedial haven for "bad" writers and redefined as a major player in the politics of education.

The writing center's involvement with faculty, though, runs much deeper at UM-Flint. The relationship between writing center tutors, students, and instructors is often obscured by a lack of communication, especially between tutors and instructors. Students who visit the writing center act as liaisons, interpreting instructors' writing assignments for their tutors, explaining what the instructors want them to accomplish. Sometimes the explanations are clear and accurate, but more often tutors become the end participants in a game of writing assignment "telephone." To establish a more open line of communication, and thus a better system for helping students revise their papers, I initiated a writing center Faculty Assignment Drawer (F.A.D.). At the beginning of each semester I send memos and e-mail messages to all faculty, inviting those who use assignment sheets in their classes to submit them to the writing center. Assignment sheets are organized by department and kept on file as reference material for writing center tutors. So, for example, when a psychology student comes to the center for help on a research paper, her tutor can pull the instructor's assignment sheet from the file and in a matter of minutes know exactly what the student needs to accomplish. If the tutor clearly understands the requirements for the assignment, she can quickly focus on the needs of both student and instructor and maximize the quality and quantity of tutorial help she is able to give. Using the F.A.D. in this manner has helped reassure faculty that tutors working with their students are making every effort to preserve the integrity of their assignments by understanding and reinforcing their specific requirements. And as more faculty take advantage of the WAC program, the relationship between tutors, students, and instructors becomes less obscure. Faculty support continues to grow as a result of this and several other collaborative initiatives, sending a clear message to the rest of the university that good writing needs to be an important part of the curriculum and that the writing center should play a central role in helping students become better writers.

TOWARD DEFINING OUR EXISTENCE:

As many writing centers continue the never-ending struggle to convince their institutions that they are more than marginal facilities catering to marginalized students, we need to take another step back and again reevaluate our own existence. Why do we exist? What exactly do we intend to accomplish? Who in our institutions do we really want to reach, and for what purpose(s)? How much are we actually contributing to the development of student writing? What impact does our existence have on the rest of the campus community? Can we justify our existence to those who control our budgets? The answers to some of these questions may not be much different than they were five or ten years ago. Some are, however, and placing writing center issues squarely under the academic microscope may offer our best hope for finding institutional permanence.

Goals and objectives statements, I believe, can only help that cause. In addition to defining the writing center "self," a well-written goals and objectives statement will also define necessary relationships with the entire university community and with the local community and local schools, and it will define and encourage relationships with other writing centers. Working on all of these fronts is no small task, but my experience has taught me that gradual and well-planned implementation of both short- and long-term goals will produce significant results. History paints a clear picture of the impressive evolution of writing centers, both theocratically and pedagogically. Writing centers today are an important part of that history and must continue making progress toward what I see as our ultimate goal—to bring writing to the center of the university curriculum.

WORKS CITED

Cox, Bene Scanlon. "Priorities and Guidelines for the Development of Writing Centers: A Delphi Study." *Writing Centers. Theory and Administration.* Ed. Gary A. Olson. Urbana: National Council of Teachers of English, 1984. 77–84.

Leahy, Richard. "What the College Writing Center Is—and Isn't." *College Teaching* 38.2 (19): 43–48.

North, Steven M. "The Idea of a Writing Center." *College English* 46.5 (1984): 433–46.

———. "Revisiting 'The Idea of a Writing Center.'" *The Writing Center Journal* 15.1 (1994): 7–19.

Pemberton, Michael. "Writing Center Ethics: Questioning Our Own Existence." *Writing Lab Newsletter* 19.5 (1995): 8–9.

Tinto, Vincent. "Misconceptions Mar Campus Discussion of Student Retention." *Chronicle of Higher Education* 6 Sept. 1989: B2–B4.

University of Michigan-Flint, The Academic Planning Committee. *Academic Plan for The University of Michigan-Flint 1995.* Michigan-Flint: 1995.

Waldo, Mark L. "The Last Best Place for Writing Across the Curriculum: The Writing Center." *WPA: Writing Program Administration* 16.3 (1993): 15–26.

4

THE PROCESS OF TUTORING: CONNECTING THEORY AND PRACTICE

Since the process of tutoring gets to the very heart of what writing centers do, it should come as no surprise that this section contains the most articles and is placed at the "center" of the book. While other sections address issues of outreach and definition, the conversations situated in the following articles all address the multiple roles we play, the multiple tasks we as tutors and directors perform, and most importantly how all of our work affects the students who visit our centers. The process of tutoring, and how we prepare ourselves and our future tutors to approach this process, is what defines us more than any other function we perform. Talking about what we do everyday in our centers and sharing our ideas with each other is what ultimately helps us define the goals, objectives, and larger missions of our writing centers. As the articles in this section clearly illustrate, we rarely agree on one definitive process of tutoring, but collectively we explore and debate the many possibilities available to us, which in the end work to transform our thinking about the very best ways to help the students who come to us.

Kenneth Bruffee's article first appeared in the 1984 anthology *Writing Centers: Theory and Administration* and has become a highly influential piece of writing center scholarship. Bruffee argues that conversation is made up of both thought and language (writing), an idea he uses to construct a model of peer tutoring for writing center instruction as well as classroom instruction.

The next several articles create a lively, if not heated, conversation on one of the most controversial issues involved with the practice of tutoring—

directive-versus-nondirective tutoring, and the generalist-versus-the specialist tutor. Jeff Brooks argues for a minimalist, hands-off approach to tutoring that focuses not on the sentence-level, mechanical concerns, but on issues of organization, reasoning, and style. Influenced by Stephen North's idea that our job is to make better writers, not better papers, Brooks explains the assumptions that inform minimalist tutoring and describes several strategies for achieving the aims of this model. Shamoon and Burns challenge Brooks' idea of nondirective tutoring, or "pure tutoring," while at the same time calling for a reexamination of writing center theory. They point to weaknesses in both the expressive and social constructionist ideas that influence so much of our profession. As an alternative, the authors ask us to take a closer look at the advantages of mentorship and directive tutoring in writing center practice.

Healy and Clark add their voices to the conversation in their article, "Are Writing Centers Ethical?" in which they challenge the idea of noninterventionist tutoring policy, insisting that this pedagogy must be judged "ethically suspect." Ultimately, the authors push us to consider a new ethic that "acknowledges the theoretical, pedagogical, and political facts of life."

Jean Kiedaisch and Sue Dinitz's article questions the value of the generalist tutor who works with students from various disciplines. They believe that tutors' discipline-specific knowledge makes them the highest qualified to tutor students in particular disciplines and that training tutors in all disciplines would be impractical. Rather, they suggest campuswide dialogue on how specific disciplines can teach writing more effectively.

Muriel Harris contends that although both writing center tutorials and in-class peer response groups emphasize collaboration, they often do not have the same goals in mind. Her suggestion is that writing center tutoring helps students address a wide variety of issues associated with composing a text, while group tutoring mostly helps students satisfy the more immediate course requirements.

John Trimbur follows this group of articles with a critique that calls into question the fundamental usefulness of the term "peer tutoring." He examines what he see as the contradiction between "peer" and "tutor." First, Trimbur contends that a person who has been trained to tutor acquires skills that set him or her apart from peers. Then, he suggests that well-executed training seminars can help remove the dichotomy created by the two terms.

The section continues with a series of articles intended to help tutors navigate the sometimes deep and muddy waters of the writing center tutorial. The articles suggest practical ways for addressing both ordinary and not-so-ordinary situations. To help the tutor negotiate the revision and feedback process, Christina Murphy explores the importance and quality of interpersonal relationships that tutors build with their students. She compares student/tutor relationships to that of the psychoanalysts and their clients. This article also provides a good supplement to the conversation in the theory section, because by introducing psychoanalytical principles of "personal empowerment through interaction," it offers tutors a "theoretical bridge between the expressionist and social constructionist schools of thought."

With a more specific agenda in mind, Thomas Newkirk provides strategies for and reflections on tutor's interaction with students in the opening minutes of a writing conference. His contention is that tutorials (or other forms of writing conferences), in the first five minutes, constitute some of the most poignant dramas in the university. Dramas of a different sort unfold in Kristin Walker's essay on difficult clients and tutor dependency. Walker provides several approaches tutors can adopt to help dependent writers become more independent.

We close this, the longest section of the book, with Evelyn Posey's article, "An Ongoing Tutor Training Program." We all know that new tutors don't stop learning about their craft after the training course is complete, and Posey offers ways to continue the training of writing center tutors by involving them in the administration and daily operations of the center. This piece could easily be read along with any or all of the articles in this section to create an individualized ongoing raining program for our tutors.

This section on the practice of tutoring merely opens the door to the conversations we might have with our new tutors and with our experienced staff members. Obviously, other important issues exist in our practice, but we simply are not able to represent them all here. We hope that the following articles will help initiate discussions of the other issues and lead to a larger examination of how practice fits into the writing center culture.

Peer Tutoring and the "Conversation of Mankind"   1984

Kenneth A. Bruffee

The beginnings of peer tutoring lie in practice, not in theory. A decade or so ago, faculty and administrators in a few institutions around the country became aware that, increasingly, students entering college had difficulty doing as well in academic studies as their abilities suggested they should be able to do. Some of these students were in many ways poorly prepared academically. Many more of them, however, had on paper excellent secondary preparation. The common denominator among the poorly prepared and the apparently well prepared seemed to be that, for cultural reasons we may not yet fully understand, all these students had difficulty adapting to the traditional or "normal" conventions of the college classroom.

One symptom of the difficulty was that many of these students refused help when it was offered. Mainly, colleges offered ancillary programs staffed by professionals. Students avoided them in droves. Many solutions to this problem were suggested and tried, from mandated programs to sink-or-swim. One idea that seemed at the time among the most exotic and unlikely (that is, in the jargon of the Sixties, among the most "radical") turned out to work rather well. Some of us had guessed that students were refusing the help we were providing because it seemed to them merely an extension of the work, the expectations, and above all the social structure of traditional

Bruffee, Kenneth A. "Peer Tutoring and the 'Conversation of Mankind.'" *Writing Centers: Theory and Administration.* Urbana, IL: NCTE, 1984. 3–15. Copyright 1984 by the National Council of Teachers of English. Reprinted with permission.

I am indebted for editorial advice in revising this essay to Marjory Pena, Baruch College, CUNY, and for conversation regarding issues raised in the essay to her and other Fellows of the Brooklyn College Institute for Training Peer Tutors. The Institute was supported by a grant from the Fund for the Improvement of Postsecondary Education.

classroom learning. And it was traditional classroom learning that seemed to have left these students unprepared in the first place. What they needed, we had guessed, was help of a sort that was not an extension but an alternative to the traditional classroom.

To provide that alternative, we turned to peer tutoring. Through peer tutoring, we reasoned, teachers could reach students by organizing them to teach each other. Peer tutoring was a type of collaborative learning. It did not seem to change what people learned but, rather, the social context in which they learned it. Peer tutoring made learning a two-way street, since students' work tended to improve when they got help from peer tutors and tutors learned from the students they helped and from the activity of tutoring itself. Peer tutoring harnessed the powerful educative force of peer influence that had been—and largely still is—ignored and hence wasted by traditional forms of education.[1]

These are some of the insights we garnered through the practical experience of organizing peer tutoring to meet student needs. More recently, we have begun to learn that much of this practical experience and the insights it yielded have a conceptual rationale, a theoretical dimension, that had escaped us earlier as we muddled through, trying to solve practical problems in practical ways. The better we understand this conceptual rationale, however, the more it leads us to suspect that peer tutoring (and collaborative learning in general) has the potential to challenge the theory and practice of traditional classroom learning itself.

This essay will sketch what seems to me to be the most persuasive conceptual rationale for peer tutoring and will suggest what appear to be some of the larger implications of that rationale. The essay will begin by discussing the view of thought and knowledge that seems to underlie peer tutoring. Then it will suggest what this view implies about how peer tutoring works. Finally, the essay will suggest what this concept of knowledge may suggest for studying and teaching the humanities.

CONVERSATION AND THE ORIGIN OF THOUGHT

In an important essay on the place of literature in education published some twenty years ago, Michael Oakeshott argues that what distinguishes human beings from other animals is our ability to participate in unending conversation. "As civilized human beings," Oakeshott says,

> *we are the inheritors, neither of an inquiry about ourselves and the world, nor of an accumulating body of information, but of a conversation, begun*

in the primeval forests and extended and made more articulate in the course of centuries. It is a conversation which goes on both in public and within each of ourselves.... Education, properly speaking, is an initiation into the skill and partnership of this conversation in which we learn to recognize the voices, to distinguish the proper occasions of utterance, and in which we acquire the intellectual and moral habits appropriate to conversation. And it is this conversation which, in the end, gives place and character to every human activity and utterance.[2]

Arguing that the human conversation takes place within us as well as among us and that conversation as it takes place within us is what we call reflective thought, Oakeshott makes the assumption that conversation and reflective thought are related in two ways: organically and formally. That is, as the work of Lev Vygotsky and others has shown,[3] reflective thought is public or social conversation internalized. We first experience and learn "the skill and partnership of this conversation" in the external arena of direct social exchange with other people. Only then do we learn to displace that "skill and partnership" by playing silently, in imagination, the parts of all the participants in the conversation ourselves. As Clifford Geertz has put it, "thinking as an overt, public act, involving the purposeful manipulation of objective materials, is probably fundamental to human beings; and thinking as a covert, private act, and without recourse to such materials, a derived, though not unuseful, capability."[4]

Since what we experience as reflective thought is organically related to social conversation, the two are also related functionally. That is, because thought originates in conversation, thought and conversation tend to work largely in the same way. Of course, in thought some of the limitations of conversation are absent. Logistics, for example, are no problem at all; I don't have to go anywhere or make an appointment to get together with myself for a talk. I don't even need to dial the phone, although I do sometimes need a trip to the coffeemaker. And in thought there are no differences among the participants in preparation, interest, native ability, or spoken vernacular. On the other hand, in thought some of the less fortunate limitations of conversation may hang on. Limitations imposed by my ethnocentrism, inexperience, personal anxiety, economic interests, and paradigmatic inflexibility can constrain my thinking just as they can constrain my conversation. If my talk is narrow, superficial, biased, and confined to cliches, my thinking is likely to be so, too. Still, it remains the case that many of the social forms and conventions of conversation, most of its language conventions and rhetorical structures, its impetus and goals, its excitement and drive, its potentially vast range and flexibility, and the issues it addresses are the sources of the forms and conventions, structures, impetus, range and flexibility, and the issues of reflective thought.

The formal and organic relationship I have been drawing here between conversation and thought illuminates, therefore, the source of the quality, depth, terms, character, and issues of thought. The assumptions underlying this argument differ considerably, however, from the assumptions we ordinarily make about the nature of thought. We ordinarily assume that thought is some sort of "essential attribute" of the human mind. The view that conversation and thought are fundamentally related assumes instead that thought is a social artifact. As Stanley Fish has put it, the thoughts we "can think and the mental operations [we] can perform have their source in some or other interpretive community."[5] Reflective thinking is something we learn to do, and we learn to do it from and with other people. We learn to think reflectively as a result of learning to talk, and the ways we can think reflectively as adults depend on the ways we have learned to talk as we grew up. The range, complexity, and subtlety of our thought, its power, the practical and conceptual uses we can put it to, as well as the very issues we can address result in large measure (native aptitude, the gift of our genes, aside) directly from the degree to which we have been initiated into what Oakeshott calls the potential "skill and partnership" of human conversation in its public and social form.

To the extent that thought is internalized conversation, then, any effort to understand how we think requires us to understand the nature of conversation; and any effort to understand conversation requires us to understand the nature of community life that generates and maintains conversation. Furthermore, any effort to understand and cultivate in ourselves a particular kind of thinking requires us to understand and cultivate the community life that generates and maintains the conversation from which a particular kind of thinking originates. The first steps to learning to think better are to learn to converse better and to learn to create and maintain the sort of social contexts, the sorts of community life, that foster the kinds of conversations we value.

These relationships have broad applicability and implications far beyond those that may be immediately apparent. For example, Thomas Kuhn has argued that to understand scientific thought and knowledge, we must understand the nature of scientific communities.[6] Richard Rorty, carrying Kuhn's view and terminology further, argues that to understand any kind of knowledge, we must understand what Rorty calls the social justification of belief; that is, we must understand how knowledge is generated and maintained by communities of knowledgeable peers.[7] Stanley Fish completes the argument by positing that these "interpretive communities" are the source not only of our thought and the "meanings" we produce through the use and manipulation of symbolic structures, chiefly language; interpretive communities may also be in large measure the source of what we regard as our very selves.[8]

CONVERSATION, WRITING, AND PEER TUTORING

The line of argument I have been pursuing has important implications for educators, especially those of us who teach composition. If thought is internalized public and social talk, then writing is internalized talk made public and social again. If thought is internalized conversation, then writing is internalized conversation re-externalized.[9]

Like thought, therefore, writing is temporally and functionally related to conversation. Writing is in fact a technologically displaced form of conversation. When we write, having already internalized the "skill and partnership" of conversation, we displace it once more onto the written page. But because thought is already one step away from conversation, the position of writing relative to conversation is more complex than even that of thought. Writing is at once both two steps away from conversation and a return to conversation. By writing, we re-immerse conversation in its social medium. Writing is two steps removed from conversation because, for example, my ability to write this essay depends on my ability to talk through with myself the issues I address here. And my ability to talk through an issue with myself derives largely from my ability to converse directly with other people in an immediate social situation.

The point is not that every time I write, what I say must necessarily be something I have talked over with other people first, although I may well often do just that. What I say can originate in thought. But since thought is conversation as I have learned to internalize it, the point is that writing always has its roots deep in the acquired ability to carry on the social symbolic exchange we call conversation. The inference writing tutors and teachers should make from this line of reasoning is that our task must involve engaging students in conversation at as many points in the writing process as possible and that we should contrive to ensure that that conversation is similar in as many ways as possible to the way we would like them eventually to write.

Peer Tutoring as Social Context

This practical inference returns us to peer tutoring. If we consider thought as internalized conversation and writing as re-externalized conversation, peer tutoring plays an important role in education for at least two reasons—both resulting from the fact that peer tutoring is a form of collaborative learning. First, peer tutoring provides a social context in which students can experience and practice the kinds of conversation that academics most value. The kind of conversation peer tutors engage in with their tutees can be emotionally involved, intellectually and substantively focused, and personally disinterested. There could be no better source of this than the sort of displaced conversation (i.e., writing) that academics value. Peer tutoring, like collaborative learning in general, makes students—both tutors and tutees—aware that writing is a social artifact, like the thought that produces it. However displaced writing may seem in time and space from the rest of a writer's community of readers and other writers, writing continues to be an act of conversational exchange.

Peer Tutoring as a Context for "Normal Discourse"

The second reason is somewhat more complex. Peer tutoring, again like collaborative learning in general, plays an important role in education because it provides a particular kind of social context for conversation, a particular kind of community: that of status equals, or peers. This means that students learn the "skill and partnership" of re-externalized conversation not only in a community that fosters the kind of conversation academics most value, but also in a community like the one most students must eventually write for in everyday life—in business, government, and the professions.

It is worthwhile digressing a moment to establish this last point. Ordinarily people write to inform and convince other people within the writer's own community, people whose status and assumptions approximate the writer's own.[10] That is, the sort of writing most people do most frequently in their everyday working lives is what Rorty calls "normal discourse." Normal discourse, a term of Rorty's coinage based on Kuhn's term "normal science," applies to conversation within a community of knowledgeable peers. A community of knowledgeable peers is a group of people who accept, and whose work is guided by, the same paradigms and the same code of values and assumptions. In normal discourse, as Rorty puts it, everyone agrees on the "set of conventions about what counts as a relevant contribution, what counts as a question, what counts as having a good argument for that answer or a good criticism of it." The product of normal discourse is "the sort of statement that can be agreed to be true by all participants whom the other participants count as 'rational.'"[11]

The essay I am writing here is an example of normal discourse in this sense. I am writing to members of my own community of knowledgeable peers. My readers and I (I suppose) are guided in our work by the same set of conventions about what counts as a relevant contribution, what counts as a question, what counts as an answer, what counts as a good argument in support of that answer or a good criticism of it. I judge my essay finished when I think it conforms to that set of conventions and values. And it is within that set of conventions and values that my readers will evaluate the essay, both in terms of its quality and in terms of whether or not it makes sense. Normal discourse is pointed, explanatory, and argumentative. Its purpose is to justify belief to the satisfaction of other people within the author's community of knowledgeable peers. Much of what we teach today—or should be teaching—in composition and speech courses is the normal discourse of most academic, professional, and business communities. The "rhetoric" taught in our composition textbooks comprises—or should comprise—the conventions of normal discourse of those communities.[12]

Teaching normal discourse in its written form is thus central to a college curriculum because the one thing college teachers in most fields commonly want students to acquire, and what teachers in most fields consistently reward students for, is the ability to carry on in speech and writing the normal discourse of the field in question. Normal discourse is what William Perry calls the fertile "wedding" of "bull" and "cow," of facts and their relevancies: discourse on the established contexts of knowledge in a field that makes effective reference to facts and ideas as defined within those contexts. In a student who can consummate this wedding, Perry says, "we recognize a colleague."[13] This is so because to be a conversant with the normal discourse in a field of study or endeavor is exactly what we mean by being knowledgeable—that is, knowledge*able*—in that field. Not to have mastered the normal discourse of a discipline, no matter how many "facts" or data one may know, is not to be knowledgeable in that discipline. Mastery of a "knowledge community's" normal discourse is the basic qualification for acceptance into that community.

The kind of writing we hope to teach students in college, therefore, is not only the kind of writing most appropriate to work in fields of business, government, and the professions; it is also writing most appropriate to gaining competence in most academic fields that students study in college. And what both kinds of writing have in common is that they are written within and addressed to a community of status equals: peers. They are both normal discourse.

This point having, I hope, been established, the second reason peer tutoring is important in education becomes clear. As a form of collaborative learning, peer tutoring is important because it provides the kind of social context in which normal discourse occurs: a community of knowledgeable peers. This is the main goal of peer tutoring.

Objections to Peer Tutoring

But to say this only raises another question: How can student peers, not themselves members of the knowledge communities they hope to enter, help other students enter those communities? This question is of course a variation of the question most often raised about all kinds of collaborative learning: Isn't it the blind leading the blind?

One answer to this question is that while neither peer tutors nor their tutees may alone be masters of the normal discourse of a given knowledge community, by working together—pooling their resources—they are very likely to be able to master it if their conversation is structured indirectly by the task or problem that a member of that community (the teacher provides.[14] The conversation between peer tutor and tutee, in composition or for that matter any other subject, is structured by the demands of the assignment and by the formal conventions of academic discourse and of standard written English. The tutee brings to the conversation knowledge of the subject to be written about and knowledge of the assignment. The tutor brings to the conversation knowledge of the conventions of discourse and knowledge of standard written English. If the tutee does not bring to the conversation knowledge of the subject and the assignment, the peer tutor's most important contribution is to begin at the beginning: help the tutee acquire the relevant knowledge of the subject and the assignment.

What peer tutor and tutee do together is not write or edit, or least of all proofread. What they do together is converse. They converse about the subject and about the assignment. They converse about, in an academic context, their own relationship and the relationships between student and teacher. Most of all they converse about and *pursuant to* writing.

PEER TUTORING AND THE HUMANITIES

The place of conversation in learning, especially in the humanities, is the largest context in which we must see peer tutoring. To say that conversation has a place in learning should not of course seem peculiar to those of us who count ourselves humanists, a category that includes many if not most writing teachers. Most of us count "class discussion" one of the most effective ways of teaching. The truth, however, is that we tend to honor discussion more in the breach than in the observance. The person who does most of the "discussing" in most discussion classes is usually the teacher.

Our discussion classes have this fateful tendency to turn into monologues because underlying our enthusiasm for discussion is a fundamental distrust of it. The graduate training most of us have enjoyed—or endured—has taught us that collaboration and community activity is inappropriate and foreign to work in humanistic disciplines. Humanistic study, we have been led to believe, is a solitary life, and the vitality of the humanities lies in the talents and endeavors of each of us as individuals.[15] What we call discussion is more often than not an adversarial activity pitting individual against individual in an effort to assert what one literary critic has called "will to power over the text," if not over each other. If we look at what we do instead of what we say, we discover that we think of knowledge as something we acquire and wield relative to each other, not something we generate and maintain in company with and in dependency upon each other.

Two Models of Knowledge

Only recently have humanists of note, such as Stanley Fish in literary criticism and Richard Rorty in philosophy, begun to take effective steps toward exploring the force and implications of knowledge communities in the humanistic

disciplines and toward redefining the nature of our knowledge as a social artifact. Much of this recent work follows a trail blazed a decade ago by Thomas
Kuhn. The historical irony of this course of events lies in the fact that Kuhn
developed his notion about the nature of scientific knowledge after first examining the way knowledge is generated and maintained in the humanities and
social sciences. For us as humanists to discover in Kuhn and his followers the
conceptual rationale of collaborative learning in general and peer tutoring in
particular is to see our own chickens come home to roost.

Kuhn's position that even in the "hard" sciences knowledge is a social
artifact emerged from his attempt to deal with the increasing indeterminacy
of knowledge of all kinds in the twentieth century.[16] To say that knowledge
is indeterminate is to say that there is no fixed and certain point of reference
against which we can measure truth. If there is no such referent, then knowledge must be a made thing, an artifact. Kuhn argued that to call knowledge
a social artifact is not to say that knowledge is merely relative, that knowledge is what any one of us says it is. Knowledge is generated by communities
of knowledgeable peers. Rorty, following Kuhn, argues that communities of
knowledgeable peers make knowledge by a process of socially justifying belief. Peer tutoring, as one kind of collaborative learning, models this process.

Here then is a second and more general answer to the objection most
frequently raised to collaborative learning of any type: that it is a case of the
blind leading the blind. It is of course exactly the blind leading the blind if
we insist that knowledge is information impressed upon the individual
mind by some outside source. But if we accept the premise that knowledge
is an artifact created by a community of knowledgeable peers and that learning is a social process not an individual one, then learning is not assimilating
information and improving our mental eyesight. Learning is an activity in
which people work collaboratively to create knowledge among themselves
by socially justifying belief. We create knowledge or justify belief collaboratively by cancelling each other's biases and presuppositions; by negotiating
collectively toward new paradigms of perception, thought, feeling, and expression; and by joining larger, more experienced communities of knowledgeable peers through assenting to those communities' interests, values,
language, and paradigm of perception and thought.

The Extension of Peer Tutoring

By accepting this concept of knowledge and learning even tentatively, it is
possible to see peer tutoring as one basic model of the way that even the
most sophisticated scientific knowledge is created and maintained. Knowledge is the product of human beings in a state of continual negotiation or
conversation. Education is not a process of assimilating "the truth" but, as
Rorty has put it, a process of learning to "take a hand in what is going on"

by joining "the conversation of mankind." Peer tutoring is an arena in which students can enter into that conversation.

Because it gives students access to this "conversation of mankind," peer tutoring and especially the principles of collaborative learning that underlie it have an important role to play in studying and teaching the humanities. Peer tutoring is one way of introducing students to the process by which communities of knowledgeable peers create referential connections between symbolic structures and reality, that is, create knowledge, and by doing so maintain community growth and coherence. To study humanistic texts adequately, whether they be student themes or Shakespeare, is to study entire pedagogical attitudes and classroom practices. Such are the implications of integrating our understanding of social symbolic relationships into our teaching—not just into *what* we teach but also into *how* we teach. So long as we think of knowledge as a reflection and synthesis of information about the objective world, teaching *King Lear* seems to involve providing a correct text and rehearsing students in correct interpretations of it. But if we think of knowledge as socially justified belief, teaching *King Lear* involves creating contexts where students undergo a sort of cultural change in which they loosen ties to the knowledge community they currently belong to and join another. These two communities can be seen as having quite different sets of values, mores, and goals, and above all quite different languages. To speak in one of a person asking another to "undo this button" might be merely to tell, a mercantile tale, or a prurient one, while in the other such a request could be both a gesture of profound human dignity and a metaphor of the dissolution of a world.

Similarly, so long as we think of learning as reflecting and synthesizing information about the objective world, teaching expository writing means providing examples, analysis, and exercises in the rhetorical modes—description, narration, comparison-contrast—or in the "basic skills" of writing and rehearsing students in their proper use. But if we think of learning as a social process, the process of socially justifying belief, teaching expository writing is a social symbolic process, not just part of it. Thus, to study and teach the humanities is to study and teach the social origin, nature, reference, and function of symbolic structures.

Humanistic study defined in this way requires, in turn, a reexamination of our promises as humanists and as teachers in light of the view that knowledge is a social artifact. Since to date very little work of this sort has been done, one can only guess what might come of it. But when we bring to mind for a moment a sampling of current theoretical thought in and allied to a single field of the humanities, for example, literary criticism, we are likely to find mostly bipolar forms: text and reader, text and writer, symbol and referent, signifier and signified. On the one hand, a critique of humanistic studies might involve examining how these theories would differ from their currently accepted form if they included the third term missing from most of them. How, for instance, would psychoanalytically oriented study of metaphor differ if it acknowledged that psychotherapy is fundamentally a kind of social relationship based on the mutual creation or recreation of symbolic structures by therapist and patient? How would semiotics differ if it acknowledged that connecting "code" and phenomenon are the complex social symbolic relations among the people who make up a semiotic community? How would rhetorical theory look if we assumed that writer and reader were partners in a common, community-based enterprise, partners rather than adversaries?

And having reexamined humanistic study in this way, we could suppose on the other hand that a critique of humanistic teaching might suggest changes in our demonstrating to students that they know something only when they can explain it in writing to the satisfaction of the community of their knowledgeable peers. To do this, in turn, seems to require us to engage students in collaborative work that does not just reinforce the values and skills they begin with but that promotes a sort of resocialization.[17] Peer tutoring is collaborative work of just this sort.

THE LAST FRONTIER
OF COLLABORATIVE LEARNING

The argument I have been making here assumes, of course, that peer tutors are well trained in a coherent course of study. The effectiveness of peer tutoring requires more than merely selecting "good students" and, giving them little or no guidance, throwing them together with their peers. To do that is to perpetuate, perhaps even aggravate, the many possible negative effects of peer group influence: conformity, anti-intellectualism, intimidation, and the leveling of quality. To avoid these pitfalls and marshal the powerful educational resource of peer group influence requires an effective peer tutor training course based on collaborative learning, one that maintains a demanding academic environment and makes tutoring a genuine part of the tutors' own educational development.

Given this one reservation, it remains to be said only that peer tutoring is not, after all, something new under the sun. However we may explore its conceptual ramifications, the fact is that people have always learned from their peers and doggedly persist in doing so, whether we professional teachers and educators take a hand in it or not. Thomas Wolfe's *Look Homeward, Angel* records how in grammar school Eugene learned to write (in this case, form words on a page) from his "comrade," learning from a peer what "all instruction failed" to teach him. In business and industry, furthermore, and in professions such as medicine, law, engineering, and architecture, where to work is to learn or fail, collaboration is the norm. All that is new in peer tutoring is the systematic application of collaborative principles to that last bastion of hierarchy and individualism, institutionalized education.

NOTES

1. The educative value of peer group influence is discussed in Nevitt Sanford, ed., *The American College* (New York: Wiley, 1962), and Theodore M. Newcomb and Everett K. Wilson, eds., *College Peer Groups* (Chicago: Aldine, 1966).

2. Michael Oakeshott, "The Voice of Poetry in the Conversation of Mankind," in *Rationalism in Politics* (New York: Basic Books, 1962), 199.

3. For example, L. S. Vygotsky, *Mind in Society* (Cambridge, Mass.: Harvard University Press, 1978).

4. Clifford Geertz, "The Growth of Culture and the Evolution of Mind," in *The Interpretation of Cultures* (New York: Basic Books, 1973), 76–77. See also in the same volume "The Impact of the Concept of Culture on the Concept of Man" and "Ideology as a Cultural System," Parts IV and V.

5. Stanley Fish, *Is There a Text in This Class? The Authority of Interpretive Communities* (Cambridge, Mass.: Harvard University Press, 1980), 14. Fish develops his argument fully in Part 2, pages 303–71.

6. Thomas Kuhn, *The Structure of Scientific Revolutions,* 2nd ed., International Encyclopedia of Unified Science, vol. 2, no. 2 (Chicago: University of Chicago Press, 1970).

7. Richard Rorty, *Philosophy and the Mirror of Nature* (Princeton, N.J.: Princeton University Press, 1979). Some of the larger educational implications of Rorty's argument are explored in Kenneth A. Bruffee, "Liberal Education and the Social Justification of Belief," *Liberal Education* (Summer 1982): 8–20.

8. Fish, 14.

9. A case for this position is argued in Kenneth A. Bruffee, "Writing and Reading as Collaborative or Social Acts: The Argument from Kuhn and Vygotsky," in *The Writer's Mind* (Urbana, Ill.: NCTE, 1983).

10. Some writing in business, government, and the professions may of course be like the writing that students do in school for teachers, that is, for the sake of practice and evaluation. Certainly some writing in everyday working life is done purely as performance, for instance, to please superiors in the corporate or department hierarchy. So it may be true that learning to write to someone who is not a member of one's own status and knowledge community, that is, to a teacher, has some practical everyday value; but the value of writing of this type is hardly proportionate to the amount of time students normally spend on it.

11. Rorty, 320.

12. A textbook that acknowledges the normal discourse of academic disciplines and offers ways of learning it in a context of collaborative learning is Elaine Maimon, Gerald L. Belcher, Gail W. Hearn, Barbara F. Nodine, and Finbarr W. O'Connor, *Writing in the Arts and Sciences* (Cambridge, Mass.: Winthrop, 1981; distributed by Little, Brown). Another is Kenneth A. Bruffee, *A Short Course in Writing* (Cambridge, Mass.: Winthrop, 1980; distributed by Little, Brown).

13. William G. Perry, Jr., "Examsmanship and the Liberal Arts," in *Examining in Harvard College: A Collection of Essays by Members of the Harvard Faculty* (Cambridge, Mass.: Harvard University Press, 1963); as reprinted in Bruffee, *Short Course*, 221.

14. For examples and an explanation of this process see Kenneth A. Bruffee, *Short Course*, and "CLTV: Collaborative Learning Television," *Educational Communication and Technology Journal* 30 (Spring 1982): 31ff.

15. The individualistic bias of our current interpretation of the humanistic tradition is discussed further in Kenneth A. Bruffee, "The Structure of Knowledge and the Future of Liberal Education," *Liberal Education* (Fall 1981): 181–85.

16. The history of the growing indeterminacy of knowledge and its relevance to the humanities is traced briefly in Bruffee, "The Structure of Knowledge," 177–81.

17. Some possible curricular implications of the concept of knowledge as socially justified belief are explored in Bruffee, "Liberal Education and the Social Justification of Belief," *Liberal Education* (Summer 1982): 8–20.

Minimalist Tutoring: Making the Student Do All the Work _1991_

Jeff Brooks

A Writing Center worst case scenario: A student comes in with a draft of a paper. It is reasonably well-written and is on a subject in which you have both expertise and interest. You point out the mechanical errors and suggest a number of improvements that could be made in the paper's organization; the student agrees and makes the changes. You supply some factual information that will strengthen the paper, the student incorporates it. You work hard, enjoy yourself, and when the student leaves, the paper is much improved. A week later, the student returns to the writing center to see you: "I got an A! Thanks for all your help!"

This scenario is hard to avoid, because it makes everyone involved feel good: the student goes away happy with a good grade, admiring you; you feel intelligent, useful, helpful—everything a good teacher ought to be. Everything about it seems right. That this is bad points out the central difficulty we confront as tutors: we sit down with imperfect papers, but our job is to improve their writers. _Can't we do a little of both?_

When you "improve" a student's paper, you haven't been a tutor at all; you've been an editor. You may have been an exceedingly good editor, but you've been of little service to your student. I think most writing center tutors agree that we must not become editors for our students and that the goal of each tutoring session is learning, not a perfect paper. But faced with students who want us to "fix" their papers as well as our own desire to create "perfect" documents, we often find it easier and more satisfying to take charge, to muscle in on the student's paper, red pen in hand.

To avoid that trap, we need to make the student the primary agent in the writing center session. The student, not the tutor, should "own" the paper and take full responsibility for it. The tutor should take on a secondary role, serving mainly to keep the student focused on his own writing. A student who comes to the writing center and passively receives knowledge from a tutor will not be any closer to his own paper than he was when he walked in. He may leave with an improved paper, but he will not have learned much.

A writing teacher or tutor cannot and should not expect to make student papers "better"; that is neither our obligation, nor is it a realistic goal. The moment we consider it our duty to improve the paper, we automatically relegate ourselves to the role of editor.

If we can't fix papers, is there anything left for us to do? I would like to suggest that when we refuse to edit, we become more active than ever as educators. In the writing center, we have the luxury of time that the classroom teacher does not have. We can spend that time talking and listening, always focusing on the paper at hand. The primary value of the writing center tutor to the student is as a living human body who is willing to sit patiently and help the student spend time with her paper. This alone is more than most teachers can do, and will likely do as much to improve the paper as a hurried proofreader can. Second, we can talk to the student as an individual about the one paper before us. We can discuss strategies for effective writing and principles of structure, we can draw students' attention to features in their writing, and we can give them support and encouragement (writing papers, we shouldn't forget, is a daunting activity).

ASSUMPTIONS

All of this can be painfully difficult to do. Every instinct we have tells us that we must work for perfection; likewise, students pressure us in the same direction. I have found two assumptions useful in keeping myself from editing student papers:

1. The most common difficulty for student writers is paying attention to their writing. Because of this, student papers seldom reflect their writers' full capabilities. Writing papers is a dull and unrewarding activity for most students, so they do it in noisy surroundings, at the last minute, their minds turning constantly to more pressing concerns. It is little wonder that so much student writing seems haphazard, unfocused, and disorganized. A good many errors are made that the student could easily have avoided. If we can get students to reread a paper even once before handing it in, in most cases we have rendered an improvement. We ought to encourage students to treat their own writings as texts that deserve the same kind of close attention we usually reserve for literary texts.

Our message to students should be: "Your paper has value as a piece of writing. It is worth reading and thinking about like any other piece of writing.'

2. While student writings are texts, they are unlike other texts in one important way: the process is far more important than the product. Most "real-world" writing has a goal beyond the page; anything that can be done to that writing to make it more effective ought to be done. Student writing, on the other hand, has no real goal beyond getting it on the page. In the real world when you need to have something important written "perfectly," you hire a professional writer; when a student hires a professional writer, it is a high crime called plagiarism. *isn't that a little discouraging? why did we give student grades, then*

This fairly obvious difference is something we often forget. We are so used to real-world writing, where perfection is paramount, that we forget that students write to learn, not to make perfect papers. Most writing teachers probably have a vision of a "perfect" freshman paper (it probably looks exactly like the pieces in the readers and wins a Bedford prize); we should probably resign ourselves to the fact that we will seldom see such a creature. Most students simply do not have the skill, experience, or talent to write the perfect paper.

BASIC MINIMALIST TUTORING

Given these assumptions, there are a number of concrete ways we can put theory into practice. Our body language will do more to signal our intentions (both to our students and to ourselves) than anything we say. These four steps should establish a cone that unmistakably shows that the paper belongs to the student and that the tutor is not an editor.

1. Sit beside the student, not across a desk—that is where job interviewers and other authorities sit. This first signal is important for showing the student that you are *not* the person "in charge" of the paper.
2. Try to get the student to be physically closer to her paper than you are. You should be, in a sense, an outsider, looking over her shoulder while she works on her paper.

3. If you are right-handed, sit on the student's right; this will make it more difficult for you to write on the paper. Better yet, don't let yourself have a pencil in your hand. By all means, if you must hold something, don't make it a red pen!

4. Have the student read the paper aloud to you, and suggest that he hold a pencil while doing so. Aside from saving your eyes in the case of bad handwriting, this will accomplish three things. First, it will bypass that awkward first few moments of the session when you are in complete control of the paper and the student is left out of the action while you read his paper. Second, this will actively involve the student in the paper, quite likely for the first time since he wrote it. I find that many students are able to find and correct usage errors, awkward wording, even logic problems without any prompting from me. Third, this will help establish the sometimes slippery principle that good writing should sound good.

[margin handwriting: this can be awk., esp for ESL students]

I am convinced that if you follow these four steps, even if you do nothing else, you will have served the student better than you would if you "edited" his paper.

ADVANCED MINIMALIST TUTORING

Of course, there is quite a bit more you can do for the student in the time you have. You can use your keen intelligence and fine critical sense to help the student without directing the paper. As always, the main goal is to keep the student active and involved in the paper. I have three suggestions:

1. Concentrate on success in the paper, not failure. Make it a practice to find something nice to say about every paper, no matter how hard you have to search. This isn't easy to do; errors are what we usually focus on. But by pointing out to a student when he is doing something right, you reinforce behavior that may have started as a felicitous accident. This also demonstrates to the student that the paper is a "text" to be analyzed, with strengths as well as weaknesses. This is where the tutor can radically depart from the role of editor.

2. Get the student to talk. It's her paper; she is the expert on it. Ask questions—perhaps "leading" questions—as often as possible. When there are sentence-level problems, make the student find and (if possible) correct them. When something is unclear, don't say, "This is unclear"; rather, say, "What do you mean by this?" Instead of saying, "You don't have a thesis," ask the student, "Can you show me your thesis?" "What's your reason for putting Q before N?" is more effective than "N should have come before Q." It is much easier to point out mistakes than it is to point the student toward finding them, but your questions will do much more to establish the student as sole owner of the paper and you as merely an interested outsider.

3. If you have time during your session, give the student a discrete writing task, then go away for a few minutes and let him do it. For instance, having established that the paper has no thesis, tell the student to write the thesis while you step outside for a few minutes. The fact that you will return and see what he has accomplished (or not accomplished) will force him to work on the task you have given him probably with more concentration than he usually gives his writing. For most students, the only deadline pressure for their paper is the teacher's final due date. Any experienced writer knows that a deadline is the ultimate energizer. Creating that energy for a small part of the paper is almost the best favor you can do for a student.

DEFENSIVE MINIMALIST TUTORING

So far, I have been assuming that the student is cooperative or at least open to whatever methods you might use. This, of course, is not a very realistic assumption. There are many students who fight a non-editing tutor all the way. They know you know how to fix their paper, and that is what they came to have done. Some find ingenious ways of forcing you into the role of editor: some withdraw from the paper, leaving it in front of you; some refuse to write anything down until you tell them word for word what to write; others will keep asking you questions ("What should I do here? Is this part okay?"). Don't underestimate the abilities of these students; they will fatigue you into submission if they can.

To fight back, I would suggest we learn some techniques from the experts: the uncooperative students themselves.

1. Borrow student body language. When a student doesn't want to be involved in his paper, he will slump back in his chair, getting as far away from it as possible. If you find a student pushing you too hard into editing his paper, physically move away from it—slump back into your chair or scoot away. If a student is making a productive session impossible with his demands, yawn, look at the clock, rearrange your things. This language will speak clearly to the student: "You cannot make me edit your paper."

2. Be completely honest with the student who is giving you a hard time. if she says, "What should I do here?" you can say in a friendly, non-threatening way, "I can't tell you that—it's your grade, not mine," or, "I don't know—it's *your* paper." I have found this approach doesn't upset students as it

might seem it would; they know what they are doing, and when you show that you know too, they accept that.

All of the suggestions I have made should be just a beginning of the ideas we can use to improve our value to our students. I hope that they lead to other ideas and tutoring techniques.

The less we do *to* the paper, the better. Our primary object in the writing center session is not the paper, but the student. Fixing flawed papers is easy; showing the students how to fix their own papers is complex and difficult. Ideally, the student should be the only active agent in improving the paper. The tutor's activity should focus on the student. If, at the end of the session, a paper is improved, it should be because the student did all the work.

A Critique of Pure Tutoring[1] 1995

Linda K. Shamoon

Deborah H. Burns

In our writing center and probably in yours, graduate teaching assistants and undergraduate peer tutors conduct student-centered, one-on-one tutoring sessions. We train these tutors to make use of process-centered writing pedagogy and top-down, writer-centered responses to papers. During the tutoring sessions, tutors are always careful not to appropriate the students' writing and not to substitute their ideas for those of the students. Thus, tutors let students set the agenda, and they resist word-by-word editing of any text. While this cluster of practices has helped us establish a growing clientele and a good reputation, we have begun to wonder about the orthodoxy of these practices, especially as we reflect upon our personal experiences and upon stories from faculty in writing-across-the-curriculum (WAC) workshops who tell us that they "really" learned to write during one-on-one tutoring sessions which were directive and appropriative. In an effort to understand these experiences more clearly, we have turned to research on expertise, social and cognitive development, and academic literacy. These sources have convinced us that directive tutoring, a methodology completely opposite our current tutoring practices, is sometimes a suitable and effective mode of instruction. As a result, we are currently struggling with radically oppositional practices in tutoring, and we are contemplating the places of these oppositional practices in our writing center.

Shamoon, Linda K., and Deborah H. Burns. "A Critique of Pure Tutoring." *The Writing Center Journal* 15.2 (1995): 134–51. Reprinted by permission of *The Writing Center Journal*.

THE ORTHODOXY OF CURRENT PRACTICE

The prevailing approach to writing center tutoring is excellently explained and contextualized in several texts, among them Irene Clark's *Writing in the Center: Teaching in a Writing Center Setting* and Emily Meyer and Louise Z. Smith's *The Practical Tutor*. From these sources tutors learn to use a process approach, to serve as an audience for student writers, and to familiarize students with the conventions of academic discourse (Clark, *Writing* 7–10; Meyer and Smith 31–32, 47). This approach emphasizes a student-centered, non-directive method which suggests that "in order for students to improve in their writing, they must attribute their success to their own efforts and abilities, not to the skill of the tutor" (Clark, *Writing* 7). To encourage active student participation, tutors learn about "legitimate and illegitimate collaboration" (Clark, *Writing* 21). True collaboration occurs when the participants are "part of the same discourse community and meet as equals" (21). Tutors learn that illegitimate collaboration happens when the tutor takes over a student's writing by providing answers rather than by asking questions. Illegitimate collaboration, says Clark, creates dependency: "[T]utor dominated conferences, instead of producing autonomous student writers, usually produce students who remain totally dependent upon the teacher or tutor, unlikely ever to assume responsibility for their own writing" (41). These ideas and others from books about tutoring, along with related concepts from articles in *The Writing Center Journal* and *Writing Lab Newsletter*, provide the bases for current writing center practices.

Upon reflection, however, we find that sometimes these sources become more than simply the research backdrop to writing center practice; sometimes they form a writing center "bible." This bible contains not only the material evidence to support student-centered, non-directive practices, but also codes of behavior and statements of value that sanction tutors as a certain kind of professional, one who cares about writing, and about students, their authentic voices, and their equal access to the opportunities within sometimes difficult institutions. These codes and appeals seem less the product of research or examined practice and more like articles of faith that serve to validate a tutoring approach which "feels right," in fact so right that it is hard for practitioners to accept possible tutoring alternatives as useful or compelling. For example, Jean Kiedaisch and Sue Dinitz, in "'So What?': The Limitations of the Generalist Tutor," note that while those tutors who know the discipline and can supply special information for students' papers may be effective, such tutors may not always be available. Kiedaisch and Dinitz conclude, "If we can't ensure that students writing for upper level courses can meet with a knowledgeable tutor, should we be alarmed about relying on generalist tutors? We think not" (73). Kiedaisch and Dinitz may be drawn to this conclusion because the alternative model examined in the study—that of a knowledgable tutor supplying "special information"—is simply too far outside orthodox writing center practice to be acceptable.

The power of this orthodoxy permeates writing center discourse, where we sometimes find statements that come more from a range of assumed values rather than from researched findings. For example, we read online a writing center tutor's "confession" that she showed a model essay to a student rather than let the student get frustrated at having no readily available, familiar written format to help tame his chaos of ideas. Well over a hundred entries followed assuring the tutor that models have a place in tutoring, as long as they do not transgress upon the authentic voice of the student ("Imitation/ Modeling"). These assurances could be interpreted as obviating the sin of appropriating the student's paper. In addition, Evelyn Ashton-Jones, in "Asking the Right Questions: A Heuristic for Tutors," argues that to promote cognitive growth of students, tutors must engage in a version of "Socratic dialogue" and not "lapse into a 'directive' mode of tutoring" (31–33). Quoting Thom Hawkins, she labels the directive tutor as "shaman, guru, or mentor," and Socratic tutors as "architects and partners" (31). In our culture who would not rather be an architect than a shaman? Finally, in discussing the need for students to be active learners during a tutoring session, Clark asserts that students should never be "disciples sitting in humility at the feet of a mentor"(*Writing* 7).[2] The language and tone here forbid challenge. The idea that one cannot be extremely appreciative of expertise and also learn actively from an expert is an ideological formation rather than a product of research.

In these instances and others, ideology rather than examined practice ("things that go without saying") seem to drive writing center practice. First, writing is viewed as a process tied to cognitive activities occurring in recursive stages. Although these stages have been labeled in numerous taxonomies, Jack Selzer finds that most enumerations include invention, organization, drafting, and revision (280). As a result, tutoring sessions often follow a ritual that begins by noting where a writer is with a text and proceeds by "walking" through the remaining stages. Second, writing center practice assumes that process strategies are global and transferable (Flower and Hayes 365–87). The extreme nonhierarchical, presumably democratic version of this assumption is that anyone who is familiar with the writing process can be of help to anybody. In practice, tutors from any discipline who seem to be good writers help all students, allowing for peer tutoring across the curriculum (Haring-Smith 175–188). A third assumption is that students possess sole ownership of their texts ("Teaching Composition"; Brannon and Knoblauch; Sommers 149–150). In practice, then, the tutors' mission is to help clarify what is in the text and to facilitate revision without imposing their own ideas or their own knowledge and, in so doing, without taking ownership of the text. Thus, tutors follow a script that is question-based and indirect rather than directive. Fourth and closely related, the prevailing wisdom assumes that one-on-one conferencing, can best help students clarify their writing to themselves (Murray, "Teaching" 144). In practice, then, tutoring is conducted in private. Finally, there is the assumption that all texts are interpretive and that the best writing contains statements of meaning or an authentic voice (Schwegler; Murray, *A Writer*; Elbow). In practice, then, much of the tutors' discussion and indirect questioning aims at getting students to voice and substantiate overall statements of meaning. Once this has been achieved, students are often sent home to revise their texts in light of this understanding. In sum, tutoring orthodoxy is: process-based, Socratic, private, a-disciplinary, and nonhierarchical or democratic.

Many points in this characterization of writing have been challenged by social-constructionist views. Social-constructionists characterize writing as a social act rather than as a process of personal discovery or individual expression. Kenneth Bruffee calls writing displaced conversation, implying that writing occurs not in isolation but in response to ideas found in other texts and other forms of communal conversation (*Short Course* 3). Furthermore, Bruffee cites Oakeshott's belief that education is primarily an "initiation into the skill and partnership of this conversation in which we learn to recognize the voices, to distinguish the proper occasions of utterance, and in which we acquire the intellectual and moral habits appropriate to conversation" (638). Patricia Bizzell sharpens the critique by adding that students

> need composition instruction that exposes and demystifies the institutional structure of knowledge, rather than that which covertly reintroduces discriminatory practices while cloaking the force of convention in concessions to the 'personal.' The cognitive focus of process-oriented composition studies cannot provide the necessary analysis. (112)

In these ways, social-constructionists challenge the private, a-disciplinary nature of writing, but according to Robert J. Connors there is little in the *practice* of teaching or tutoring writing that has chanced because of social constructionist views. Connors maintains that, in the classroom, social constructionists still base teaching and tutoring upon stages in the writing process. Thus, the social constructionist critique has broadened our understanding of the contexts of writing, but it has not formed an alternative set of practices.

THE CHALLENGE FROM EXPERIENCE AND FROM WRITING ACROSS THE CURRICULUM FACULTY

The more serious challenge to current tutoring orthodoxy starts for us with some of our personal experiences as we learned to write in our discipline. When Deborah Burns was completing a thesis for her M.A. in English Literature, she was tutored by her major professor. She reports the following experience.

The most helpful writing tutoring I ever received at the university came from the director of my Master's thesis. I wrote what I thought was a fairly good draft of my thesis, then shared it with my director for comments. I remember, at first, being surprised at the number of problems my director found with my draft. He added transitions when needed, showed me how to eliminate wordiness, and formalized my vocabulary. In addition, he offered specific suggestions for rewriting entire paragraphs, and he always pointed out areas where I had lost focus. The most important thing he did for me was to write sentences that helped locate my work in the field of Dickens studies. For example, Dickens critics had thoroughly examined family relationships in the novels, but few worked on alcoholism and its effects on children, the central idea of my thesis. My director's specific suggestions helped me to foreground my unique way of examining some of Dickens's novels. I learned that I was so immersed in the research and articulation of the new ideas I wanted to explore in my thesis, I had neither the time nor the experience to fully understand how to write an extended piece of scholarly work in the discourse community. At first, I was confused about my perceived inability to write like the scholar I was supposed to be, but I soon realized (especially at my thesis defense) that I was fortunate to have as my director a person who showed me how to revise my draft so that it blended with conventional academic discourse. After I watched my director work with my text, and after I made the necessary changes, my thesis and other academic writing was much less of a mystery to me.

For many years Burns puzzled over the direct intervention made by her director while she composed her Master's thesis. The intervention had been extremely helpful, yet it went against everything she had learned in composition studies. Her director was directive, he substituted his own words for hers, and he stated with disciplinary appropriateness the ideas with which she had been working. Furthermore, Burns observed that other graduate students had the same experience with this director: he took their papers and rewrote them while they watched. They left feeling better able to complete their papers, and they tackled other papers with greater ease and success. Clearly, several features of this graduate director's practice violated current composition orthodoxy. His practices seem authoritative, intrusive, directive, and product-oriented. Yet these practices created major turning points for a variety of writers. For Burns and for others, when the director intervened, a number of thematic, stylistic, and rhetorical issues came together in a way that revealed and made accessible aspects of the discipline which had remained unexplained or out of reach. Instead of appropriation, this event made knowledge and achievement accessible.

This challenge to current tutoring practices has been further extended by conversations with faculty from a variety of disciplines during our WAC workshops. We have held faculty workshops semiannually for the last three years, and it is not unusual for faculty members to remember suddenly that at some point late in college or in graduate school, during a one-on-one conference, a professor they respected took one of their papers and rewrote it, finally showing them "how to write." During our first workshop, a colleague from animal science reported that in graduate school his major professor took his paper and rewrote it while he watched. In the colleague's own words, "He tore it to shreds, but I sure learned a lot." When he made this statement, there were looks of recognition and sympathetic murmuring from others in the room. Just recently, in a WAC faculty writing circle, a colleague from nursing reported that in order to complete her doctoral proposal she has sat through numerous revising sessions with the most accessible member of her doctoral committee—each time learning more about writing, about critical theory, and about how to tie the theory to her research methods. In these examples and others, professors were acting like tutors, working one-on-one with student authors to improve their texts, but their methods were hardly nondirective. Over and over in the informal reports of our colleagues we find that crucial information about a discipline and about writing, is transmitted in ways that are intrusive, directive, and product-oriented, yet these behaviors are not perceived as an appropriation of power or voice but instead as an opening up of those aspects of practice which had remained unspoken and opaque.

While we do not pretend that these informally gathered stories carry the same weight as research data, we are struck by the repeated benefits of a tutoring style that is so opposite current orthodoxy. As we discuss these revelations further with WAC faculty, we find that the benefits of alternative tutoring practices are frequent enough to make us seriously question whether one tutoring approach fits all students and situations. Surely, students at different stages in their education, from beginning to advanced, are developing different skills and accumulating different kinds of information, thus making them receptive to different kinds of instruction and tutoring. In fact, "The Idea of Expertise: An Exploration of Cognitive and Social Dimensions of Writing," Michael Carter sets forth a five-stage continuum of cognitive learning that characterizes the progress from novice to expert. Carter explains that novices and advanced beginners utilize global, process-based learning and problem-solving strategies; that intermediate and advanced students shifted hierarchical and case-dependent strategies; and that experts draw intuitively upon extensive knowledge, pattern recognition, and "holistic similarity recognition"(271–72). If students are exercising different cognitive skills at different stages in their learning, it makes sense that they may be responsive to different kinds of information and tutoring styles at different stages, too. Our personal and WAC experiences suggest that, at the very least, for intermediate and advanced students, and perhaps on occasion for beginners, too, one tutoring approach does not fit all.

AN ALTERNATIVE MODE OF PRACTICE: MASTER CLASSES IN MUSIC

Since we have encountered so many positive alternative representations of the tutoring of writing, we have started to ask ourselves when such practices are helpful and exactly how they can be best characterized. Interestingly, in order to find answers we have had to look outside the discipline. This is not surprising since, according to Michael Agar, most of us sometimes have difficulty seeing alternatives to our own ways of thinking, especially to everyday notions that seem based on common sense.

> *There are two ways of looking at differences.... One way is to figure out that the differences are the tip of the iceberg, the signal that two different systems are at work. Another way is to notice all the things that the other [system] lacks when compared to you[rs], the so-called* deficit theory *approach.... The deficit theory does have its advantages. But it's a prison. It locks you into a closed room in an old building with no windows....* (Agar 23, emphasis in original)

In other words, within a strong system generally held notions and behaviors so permeate our lives that only they seem legitimate or make sense, while all other notions and behaviors seem illegitimate. In order for alternative practices to look sensible, they must be appreciated from within another strong system. One such system that may be found outside of writing instruction is the practice of master classes in music education. Master classes are a form of public tutoring that is standard practice in music education (Winer 29). The circumstances and conduct of master classes are almost totally opposite those seen in nondirective tutoring practices.[3]

During a master class an expert music teacher meets with a group of students studying the same specialty, such as piano, voice, strings, brass, etc. The students vary in their achievement levels, from novice to near-expert. Several students come to the session prepared to be tutored on their performance of a piece or a portion of a piece, while others may come as observers. The tutorial typically begins with one student's performance; then the master teacher works over a section of the piece with the student, suggesting different ways to play a passage, to shape a tone, to breathe, to stand or sit, or even to hold an instrument. On occasion, the master teacher has the student play the passage herself and asks the student to play it with her or immediately after her. Then, as a typical end-of-the-tutorial strategy, the master teacher has the student play the whole passage or the piece again. At this time it is not unusual for those who are observing to respond with a new sense of understanding about the music or the technique.

When a master class is at its best, the emotional tone is compelling. The atmosphere is charged with excitement, with a sense of community, and with successive moments of recognition and appreciation. Excitement comes from the public performances, which are often anxiety provoking for the performer; but there is relaxation, too, for no one expects the perfection of a formal performance. Instead, a sense of community animates the participants, who are willing to have their performances scrutinized in order to improve, and everyone recognizes those moments during the tutorial when increased mastery passes into the hands of the student. Indeed, all the participants have a sense of high expectation, for they have access to someone who has mastery, who wants to share this knowledge with them, and who, by showing them about a limited passage of music, reveals a world of knowledge, attitude, and know-how.

Examples of such master classes can be found in the documentary *From Mao to Mozart: Isaac Stern in China,* a film about violinist Isaac Stern's 1979 visit to China. The film, which won an Academy Award for the best documentary of 1980, includes several excerpts from master classes on the violin offered by Stern to a variety of students in China. In one scene, Stern works with a young, extremely able violinist who is having trouble following his precise suggestions. Suddenly, Stern says he will share a secret with her. He plays a passage from her solo piece and then pulls out an extra shoulder pad hidden under his suit jacket. This extra padding enables him to hold his violin in a position that facilitates his playing. Later, the student replays the passage while Stern pushes up and positions her violin as if she, too, were wearing the secret padding. Her performance suddenly improves so much that the audience recognizes the change and bursts into applause. Throughout this episode, there is a sense of delight, of the sharing of important information, and of appreciation.

What strikes us as important about master classes is that they feature characteristics exactly opposite current tutoring orthodoxy. They are hierarchical: there is an open admission that some individuals have more knowledge and skill than others, and that the knowledge and skills are being "handed down." This handing down is directive and public; during tutoring the expert provides the student with communally and historically tested options for performance and technical improvement. Also, a good deal of effort during tutoring is spent on imitation or, at its best, upon emulation. Rather than assuming that this imitation will prevent authentic self-expression, the tutor and the student assume that imitation will lead to improved technique, which will enable freedom of expression. Finally, there is an important sense of desire and appreciation. The students have sought out the expert because they already have recognized the value of her knowledge and skills, and because she seeks to share this expertise with students, both to preserve and to expand the discipline and its traditions. Mutual appreciation and mutual desire seem to be at the center of this kind of teaching. In music master classes, sitting at the feet of the master is one way of learning.

REFLECTIONS UPON ALTERNATIVE
TUTORIAL PRACTICES

Although the master class model has much to offer writing centers, it is not immune to abuse. History is littered with examples of directive, authoritative "tutoring" gone awry, from sports coaching to religious cults. Nor are all music master classes as successful as those portrayed in the documentary about Isaac Stern. The famous German conductor Wilhelm Furtwangler, for example, was known to belittle and physically abuse his students and orchestra members (Fenelon 116). But such cases represent alternative practices run amok, when authoritative has become authoritarian, when directive has become dictatorial, and when initiative has become repressive. The challenge for writing centers is to know the best features of these alternative pedagogics in order to broaden current practice. We need to know enough about these practices to prevent abusive application and to secure their benefits for students and their tutors.

Music is not the only discipline to use alternative tutoring practices. In art education, the studio seminar is an important and widely practiced form of public tutorial. According to Wendy Holmes, a professor of art history at the University of Rhode Island, studio seminar is the crucial intermediate course for art majors, when they start exploring, locating, and solving artistic problems on their own, whether in sculpture, painting, or other media. During studio time, students work on their own projects, and the instructor "visits" and tutors each student individually, suggesting ideas, options, or techniques for the project; and during seminar time, students display their work to each other and to the instructor for public commentary, analysis, and reflection. Studio seminar is a mix of private and public tutoring that is directive. In pharmacy practice internships, senior pharmacy majors are placed in real-world settings to observe their professors in action, to apply their own newly acquired professional knowledge, and to receive guided practice in a mix of private and public tutoring (Hume). Nursing students take "clinicals," courses which provide the same combination of observation and guided practice as do medical internships and residencies (Godfrey). All these examples include practices that are more similar to the music master class than to nondirective writing tutoring. Emulative learning is conducted in a hierarchical environment to facilitate new information or masterly behavior within a domain. While these examples of alternative practices are most commonly found at intermediate or advanced levels, they are sometimes usefully applied with novices, too (as we explain below).

These instances of public tutoring that are the norm within certain disciplines provide an opportunity to reflect upon the constellation of conditions that make directive tutoring fruitful. Three strands of research are important: research on the development of expertise (including connections to imitation and modeling) helps explain the links between directive tutoring and cognitive development; theoretical explanations of subjectivities help us understand directive tutoring and social development; research on academic literacy helps us understand directive tutoring and disciplinary development.

As we have already noted, research about expertise helps elucidate the connections between cognitive skills development and alternative tutoring practices for all learners, from novice to near-expert. Specifically, Carter explains that experts have extensive "repertoires" for problem solving, repertoires built on domain-specific knowledge and experience. He points out that chess grand masters have about "50,000 meaningful chess configurations in their repertoires" (269). Carter argues that novices in all domains build up such repertoires, gradually shifting their modes of thinking from global, general purpose strategies to the hierarchical, domain-specific strategies used by experts in the field (269). Similarly, in her review of the literature on the cognitive aspects of expertise, Geisler points to students in physics solving "thousands of word problems" as they build up domain-specific problem solving repertoires (60). Geister explains that the changes which characterize the cognitive move from novice to expert include the development of abstract representations of specific cases, the replacing of literal description with abstract discourse, and the rehearsal of extended arguments to support solutions to problems (9–54).

With this research in mind, we turn first to intermediate stages of development, followed by a look at the needs of novices. We find that master classes, studio seminars, clinicals, and other representations of directive tutoring enable committed intermediate and advanced students to observe, practice, and develop widely valued repertoires. When the studio instructor turns the student's attention away from the student's own painting and toward the painting of a master, the student sees how an expert has solved the same problem of light, color, and form. When the studio instructor gives some pigment on the student's canvas and transforms the impact of the picture, the student observes how experts handle the major elements of the discipline. Throughout the studio seminar, the student has time to practice similar solutions and try out others. Thus, directive tutoring provides a particularly efficient transmission of domain-specific repertoires, far more efficient and often less frustrating than expecting students to reinvent these established practices. At its best, directive tutoring, provides a sheltered, protected time and space within the discipline for these intermediate and advanced students to make the shift between general strategies to domain strategies. This cognitive shift seems to depend upon observation and extensive practice—often in emulation of the activities of the tutor-expert—leading to the accumulation of expert repertoires and tacit information.

Novice writers can also benefit from observing and emulating important cognitive operations. In "Modeling: A Process Method of Teaching," Muriel

Harris explains that for novice writers, too, composing skills and writing behaviors may be learned through imitation, and that productive patterns of invention or editing may come to replace less useful ones through observation and "protected" practice. In fact, using some of the same techniques that we are arguing for in this article, Harris reports a case study in which she turned to modeling after observing the nonproductive, composing habits of a novice writer named Mike.

> *Scrambling for a better technique [than free writing], I seized on modeling....*
> *In preparation I explained [to Mike] the strategies we would use for the next*
> *few sessions. We would begin by having him give me a topic to write on for*
> *fifteen to twenty minutes. I would begin by thinking about the rhetorical sit-*
> *uation, the "who," "what," "why," plus a few operators to achieve my goal.*
> *After these few minutes of planning, I would start writing and keep wri-*
> *ting.... When I was done, we would reverse roles, and I would give him a*
> *topic. As much as possible, he would try to copy the behavior he had observed.*
> *All of these instructions were preceded by brief explanations of what he would*
> *observe and the principles he would try to use. My intent was to model a*
> *pattern of behavior for Mike to observe and try out and also to monitor his*
> *attempts by listening to his protocol and observing his actions. (78)*

After three such sessions, Harris reports that "Mike's writing improved noticeably." We note that in these sessions Harris was being directive, telling the student what to observe, what topics to write on, and what behaviors to imitate. We note, too, that the modeling continued for several sessions, with Harris providing a repeated, fixed focus upon specific writing repertoires, and that the student engaged in several learning activities—observing, imitating, and practicing—always guided by Harris' supportive words. We take this to be a version of directive tutoring at its best, with periods of observation and protected practice focused upon important skills development. As Harris says "And what better way is there to convince students that writing is a process that requires effort, thought, time and persistence than to go through all that writing, scratching out, rewriting and revising with *and for* our students?" (81, emphasis ours).

Cognitive development, however, is not the only change students undergo as they engage in formal education. Recent work in cultural criticism suggests that as students strive to attain academic knowledge or a new understanding of a profession or career, they inevitably occupy a new subject position, one that may be well-served by directive tutoring practices. These points are most easily explained with respect to intermediate and advanced students, but the ideas apply to beginners as well. Most intermediate or advanced students are highly motivated, active learners, already working with a significant amount of domain knowledge and with the representations of the field given to them by their instructors. As they master this information, they typically start to see themselves as members of a domain community. For example, Faigley and Hansen notes that students who successfully completed an advanced course in psychology "felt confident that they could write a publishable report, suggesting that they viewed themselves at the end of the course as fledgling members of the field, able to think and write like psychologists" (144). Similarly, Geisler states, "Professional becomes part of personal identity" (92). Bizzell notes that admission to the "academic discourse community is as much social as cognitive, that it is best understood as an initiation" (125). In other words, as intermediate and advanced students get a sense of a domain, they start to occupy a subject position as a *participant* in the domain that is both confirmed by others and assumed by the student. But, as Robert Brooke suggests, this experience of shifting subjectivities and the transformation of identity is *not* necessarily limited to intermediate or advanced students. Brooke found that students in an *introductory* level English class who were encouraged to imitate the drafting processes of their teacher were also receptive to other aspects of being a writer, including the expressions of attitudes, values, and stances towards experiences that lie at the heart of a writer's identity. By the end of the semester several of the students in Brooke's study came to view themselves as writers, and they accepted this identity as new and exciting (32–5). All of these researchers draw attention to the social dimensions of learning and to the important connections between domain processes and social identity.

Directive tutoring supports these connections. Not only does directive tutoring support imitation as a legitimate practice, it allows both student *and* tutor to be the subjects of the tutoring session (while nondirective tutoring allows only the student's work to be the center of the tutoring session). For example, when the master musician rephrases a passage for the intermediate or advanced violin student, the tutor's phrasing, tone, and body language become the subject of the session—her skills *and* her way of being a musician— but the student does not necessarily feel that his musicianship has been appropriated. Instead, the student, too, will have his turn as musician in this master class, and this confirms his musicianship. The interaction with the master teacher establishes that he, too, is a musician. The social nature of directive and emulative tutoring serves to endorse the student's worth as an emerging professional. Similarly, directive tutoring of writing presents more than a demonstration of steps in the writing process. It models a writer's attitudes, stances, and values. In so doing, it unites the processes of writing with the subjectivity of being a writer. As Brooke points out, not all students, particularly not all novices, would choose to assume the subjectivity of their writing tutor or teacher, but when they do, they encase writing processes in the values, attitudes, and acts of interpretation that make writing a socially meaningful experience (37–8). There is much to be gained by unifying the processes of writing with the writer herself. Directive tutoring displays this unity, even for novices.

Finally, in light of research on academic literacy, we speculate that directive tutoring lays bare crucial rhetorical processes that otherwise remain hidden or are delivered as candid knowledge throughout the academy. According to Geisler, academic literacy and achievement of professionalism are tied not only to domain content and personal identity but also to mastery of rhetorical processes (88–92). These processes of reasoning, argumentation, and interpretation support a discipline's socially-constructed knowledge base. Those students who learn to recognize these rhetorical processes seem also to come to understand a discipline. Geisler argues that the current system of education is constructed to keep these rhetorical processes hidden from students, usually until sometime during graduate school, thus creating a "great divide" among those who have mastered such processes and those who have not (89–90). Geisler charges that academicians and professionals are complicit in hiding these crucial rhetorical processes from most students and the public, thus ensuring their own social status and power over others. Her book is an attempt to place before the public the argument that rhetorical processes must be made more prominent in education if we are to give all students access to academic literacy and a share in the wealth of our society. Although Geisler does not present a method for revealing rhetorical processes earlier in education, she does present a fascinating case study in which such processes were made public (214–29). In a philosophy class, students had a chance to hear their instructor build an argument for a comparative reading of several texts, tear down that structure, and then rebuild it. When the teacher honestly shared his rhetorical processes in this matter, Geisler found that the students gained both a wide appreciation of a discipline and also an ability to express themselves within it (226–227).

We argue that directive tutoring, at its best, is similarly empowering. Directive tutoring displays rhetorical processes in action. When a tutor redrafts problematic portions of a text for a student, the changes usually strengthen the disciplinary argument and improve the connection to current conversation in the discipline. These kinds of changes and the accompanying metalanguage or marginalia often reveal how things are argued in the discipline. Thus, directive tutoring provides interpretive options for students when none seem available, and it unmasks the system of argumentation at work within a discipline. In fact, we speculate that when faculty have not developed an appreciation of the connections between the social construction of disciplinary knowledge and related rhetorical processes, they treat knowledge of the discipline as self-evident and absolute rather than as changing and socially negotiated. Directive tutoring is based upon the articulation of rhetorical processes in order to make literate disciplinary practice plain enough to be imitated, practiced, mastered, and questioned.

IMPLICATIONS FOR THE WRITING CENTER

Alternative tutoring practices are provocative for the writing center, especially if it is to develop into the kind of writing community Stephen North calls for in "The Idea of a Writing Center," a place where all writers—novices and experts—receive support for their writing. We need to keep in mind the crucial cognitive, social, and rhetorical chances students undergo as they strive to become proficient writers in the academy. The writing center could better help to facilitate these developments by serving as a site where directive tutoring provides a sheltered and protected time and space for practice that leads to the accumulation of important repertoires, the expression of new social identities, and the articulation of domain-appropriate rhetoric. Furthermore, if the crucial difference between novice and advanced expertise is the development of rhetorical practices, then writing centers could be the site where instructors from a variety of disciplines articulate and demonstrate these practices, so that students may observe, emulate, question, and critique them.

Many writing centers are already providing elements of these practices. For example, Muriel Harris reports that professors from across the curriculum participate in writing centers, talking about the features of domain-specific writing ("Writing Center and Tutoring" 168–69.) Kiedaisch and Dinitz, as well as Leone Scanlon, supply examples of knowledgeable students from a variety of domains tutoring in writing centers. At the University of Rhode Island a writing center tutor is present during a physics laboratory, on hand for conversation and consultation as students gather and record data in their lab notebooks, as they write up their lab reports, and as they revise their drafts in light of the instructor's responses. Finally, Louise Smith describes two writing programs that draw on experts for writing instruction. One program at Queens College pairs faculty members with advanced under-graduates, and another at the University of Massachusetts/Boston fosters collaboration between faculty and tutors to disseminate theory and research about composition.

Although these applications of public and domain-based tutoring are interesting and impressive, they are piecemeal and seem prompted by concerns other than critically broadening orthodox tutoring practices. We probably do not know the best systematic application in the writing center of directive, public, and emulative tutoring; we probably do not yet know the writing center equivalent of master classes. We do know, however, at least some of the features that should be part of this application. The writing center can be a site where ongoing conversation about the rhetoric of a domain occurs *in* the rhetoric of the domain. For example, the writing center can be a site where professors work occasionally and *publicly* on their writing and on others' writing. Also, the writing center can be a site where the proficient (such as graduate students and seniors) and the novice converse about "intersubjective knowledge" (Geisler 182), or that kind of discourse which externalizes and argues for domain-appropriate abstractions, which externalizes and argues for domain-appropriate linkages to case-specific data, and which provides opportunities for reflection and critique. This is exactly the kind of discourse now hidden from novices; the writing center is the place to make it public, directive, and available for imitation, appreciation, and questioning. Finally, the writing center can be a site where experts and novices meet often to externalize tacit information—those values, assumptions, and options that inform all texts within a discipline.

Unless writing center research and methods are enlarged to include these practices, writing centers are in danger of remaining part of the social arrangements which, according to Geisler, encourage the a-rhetorical accumulation of domain knowledge and which keep expert rhetorical processes at a distance from the lay public and the novice:

> *Our current educational sequence provides all students with a naive understanding of the more formal components of expertise but withholds an understanding of [the] tacit rhetorical dimension. In this way...a great divide has been created—not a great divide between orality and literacy as literacy scholars originally suggested, but rather a great divide with experts on one side with a complete if disjoint practice of expertise, and lay persons on the other side. (89–90)*

Current writing center and tutoring practices support this social arrangement by making an orthodoxy of process-based, Socratic, private, a-disciplinary tutoring. This orthodoxy situates tutors of writing at the beginning and global stages of writing instruction, it prevents the use of modeling and imitation as a legitimate tutoring technique, and it holds to a minimum the conduct of critical discourse about rhetorical practices in other fields. If writing center practices are broadened to include *both* directive and non-directive tutoring, the result would be an enrichment of tutoring repertoires, stronger connections between the writing center and writers in other disciplines, and increased attention to the cognitive, social, and rhetorical needs of writers at all stages of development.

NOTES

1. The authors wish to thank Meg Carroll, Rhode Island College, and Teresa Ammirati, Connecticut College, for the use of selected resources from their writing centers.

2. Clark does not universally dismiss imitation, modeling, or other directive techniques. In "Collaboration and Ethics in Writing Center Pedagogy," she suggests

that "Imitation may be viewed as ultimately creative, enabling the imitator to expand previous, perhaps ineffective models into something more effective which ultimately becomes his or her own.... Sometimes a suggestion of a phrase or two can be wonderfully instructive" (8–9).

3. The term "master class" may lead to some confusion about the differences between teaching and tutoring. We are referring to "tutoring" as one-on-one instruction, coaching, and responding; and "teaching" as one-to-whole group instruction, coaching, and responding.

WORKS CITED

Agar, Michael. *Language Shock: Understanding the Culture of Conversation.* New York: Wm. Morrow, 1994.

Ashton-Jones, Evelyn. "Asking the Right Questions: A Heuristic for Tutors." *The Writing Center Journal* 9.1 (1988): 29–36.

Bizzell, Patricia. "College Composition: Initiation Into the Academic Discourse Community." *Academic Discourse and Critical Consciousness.* Pittsburgh: U of Pittsburgh P, 1992.

Brannon, Lil, and C. H. Knoblauch. "On Students' Rights to Their Own Texts: A Model of Teacher Response." *College Composition and Communication* 33 (1982): 157–166.

Brooke, Robert. "Modeling, a Writer's Identity: Reading and Imitation in the Writing Classroom." *College Composition and Communication* 39 (1988): 23–4 1.

Bruffee, Kenneth A. "Collaborative Learning and the 'Conversation of Mankind.'" *College English* 46 (1984): 635–52.

———. *A Short Course In Writing: Practical Rhetorical for Teaching Composition through Collaborative Learning.* 3rd ed. New York: HarperCollins, 1993.

Carter, Michael. "The Idea of Expertise." *College Composition and Communication* 41 (1990): 269–86.

Clark, Irene. "Collaboration and Ethics in Writing Center Pedagogy." *The Writing Center Journal* 9.1 (1988): 3–11.

———. *Writing in the Center.* Dubuque: Kendall/Hunt, 1985.

Connors, Robert. J. Address. URI/Trinity College Second Summer Conference on Writing. Kingston, May 1994.

Elbow, Peter. *Writing Without Teachers.* New York: Oxford UP, 1973.

Faigley, Lester, and Kristine Hansen. "Learning to Write in the Social Sciences." *College Composition and Communication* 36 (1985): 140–49.

Fenelon, Fania. *Playing for Time.* New York: Atheneum, 1977.

Flower, Linda, and John R. Hayes. "A Cognitive Process Theory of Writing." *College Composition and Communication* 32 (1981): 365–87.

Geisler, Cheryl. *Academic Literacy and the Nature of Expertise: Reading, Writing, and Knowing in Academic Philosophy.* Hillsdale, NJ: Erlbaum, 1994.

Godfrey, Deborah. Professor of Nursing. University of Rhode Island. Personal interview. 29 July 1994.

Haring-Smith, Tori. "Changing Students' Attitudes: Writing Fellows Programs." *Writing Across the Curriculum: A Guide to Developing Programs.* Ed. Susan H. McLeod and Margo Soven. Newbury Park, CA: Sage, 1992. 177–88.

Harris, Muriel. "The Writing Center and Tutoring in WAC Programs." McLeod and Soven. 154–74.

———. Modeling: A Process Method of Teaching." *College English* 45 (1983): 74–84.

Holmes, Wendy. Professor of Art History. University of Rhode Island. Personal interview. 15 july 1994.

Hume, Anne. Professor of Pharmacy Practice. University of Rhode Island. Personal interview. 15 July 1993.

"Imitation/Modeling as a Teaching Method." Writing Center Discussion List [Online]. 19–30 May 1994. Available e-mail: WCENTER@UNICORN.ACS.TTU.EDU

Kiedaisch, Jean, and Sue Dinitz. "So What? The Limitations of the Generalist Tutor." *Writing Center Journal* 14.1(1993): 63–74.

Meyer, Emily, and Louise Z. Smith. *The Practical Tutor.* New York: Oxford UP, 1987.

Murray, Donald M. *A Writer Teaches Writing.* Boston: Houghton Mifflin, 1968.

———. "Teaching the Other Self. The Writer's First Reader." *College Composition and Communication* 33 (1982): 140–47.

North, Stephen. "The Idea of A Writing Center." *College English* 46 (1984): 433–46.

Scanlon, Leone. "Recruiting and Training Tutors for Cross-Disciplinary Writing Programs." *The Writing Center Journal* 6 (1986): 37–41.

Schwegler, Robert A. "Meaning and Interpretation." URI/Trinity College 2nd. Summer Conf. on Writing. Kingston, May 1994.

Selzer, Jack. "Exploring Options In Composing. *College Composition and Communication* 35 (1984): 276–84.

Smith, Louise Z. "Independence and Collaboration: Why We Should Decentralize Writing Centers." *The Writing Center Journal* 7.1 (1986): 3–10.

Sommers, Nancy. "Responding to Student Writing." *College Composition and Communication* 33 (1982): 148–66.

Soven, Margot. "Conclusion: Sustaining Writing Across the Curriculum Programs." McLeod and Soven. 189–97.

Stern, Isaac. *From Mao to Mozart: Isaac Stern in China.* Dir. Murray Lerner. Harmony Film Group, 1980.

"Teaching Composition: A Position Statement." *College English* 46 (1984): 612–14.

Winer, Deborah G. "Close Encounters: Pros and Cons of Master Classes." *Opera News* 54 (1989): 28–31.

Are Writing Centers Ethical? 1996

Irene L. Clark

Dave Healy

The ethics of writing center assistance have always been subject to question. Even at the present time, when more writing centers exist than ever before, colleagues from a variety of academic departments continue to express concern that the sort of assistance students receive may be inappropriate, perhaps even verging on plagiarism. "The problem is my dean," someone in the process of establishing a new writing center recently confided. "He worries that tutoring students in a writing center will result in plagiarized papers, so he thinks that we should stick to grammar instruction."

The writing center's response to such suspicions has been to embrace a pedagogy of noninterventionism that precludes both the appropriation of student texts and any challenge to teachers' authority occasioned by questioning their judgment of a writer's work. Writing center personnel are cautioned against writing on clients' texts or suggesting specific wording or performing primarily as proofreaders, and with instructors, the writing center has generally accepted Stephen North's dictum: "[W]e never play student-advocates in teacher-student relationships.... [W]e never evaluate or second-guess any teacher's syllabus, assignments, comments, or grades" ("Idea," 441). Precepts of noninterventionism have thus become what Shamoon and Burns refer to as a writing center "bible," an orthodoxy that has attained the force of an ethical or moral code.

However, although these precepts arose out of ethical concerns, a noninterventionist policy as an absolute must ultimately be judged ethically suspect, increasing the center's marginality, diminishing its influence, and compromising its ability to serve writers. Writing centers thus need a new ethic that acknowledges the theoretical, pedagogical, and political facts of life.

Clark, Irene L., and Dave Healy. "Are Writing Centers Ethical?" *WPA: Writing Program Administration* 20.½ (copyright 1996): 32–38.

ORIGINS OF ESTABLISHED WRITING CENTER POLICIES

Current writing center policies—whether referred to as a "bible" (Shamoon and Burns), "mantras" (Blau), or "dogma" (Clark)—began to be articulated in a public forum in the seventies and early eighties, when open admissions policies precipitated the growth of writing centers as separate university entities and when the *Writing Lab Newsletter* in 1977 and *The Writing Center Journal* in 1980 provided a medium for publication. Before that time, as Peter Carino notes, many writing centers consisted of "labs," located within writing classrooms, that utilized an individualized instructional approach designed to help students master a specific content; frequently that content focused on grammar and surface correctness. Carino's purpose is to redeem the bleak picture of early writing centers as "current-traditional dungeons where students were banished to do grammar drills" (113), and he therefore stresses that not all early centers were the same. In many of them, heuristic and global concerns of writing were recognized as important pedagogical goals. Nevertheless, he also acknowledges that "drills were part of the methods of early centers" (113), certainly more so than they are today, and that whatever instruction actually took place, most writing centers were conceived of within the university as centers of remediation where less proficient students labored to master surface correctness. The writing clinic at Stephens College, for example, was set up for "[t]he student who finds it very difficult to spell correctly or who makes gross errors in English usage. Here causes are determined, exercises under supervision are given, and practical applications to everyday writing are made" (Wiskell 145). This emphasis on remedial education and on the mastery of a specific grammar-based content was a "safe" function for writing centers to assume because it was deemed by the academy an unfortunate but necessary supplement to the more important scholarly instruction that occurred in the classroom. When other departments on campus conceived of a writing lab as a center for remediation, they could easily understand and accept what presumably occurred there—skill and drill did not generate either suspicion or controversy. However, as writing centers developed into autonomous entities, and as interest in composition as a discipline led to a rejection of the current-traditional paradigm in favor of a process/collaborative, student-centered approach, skill and drill in the writing center was supplemented. in many instances, it was replaced by a greater emphasis on helping students figure out what they wanted to say in response to a writing assignment, or on providing assistance with the shape and content of an actual text. Many writing centers took to heart James Moffet's conviction that teachers must shift their gaze "from the subject to the learner, for the subject is the learner"

(67). As a result, instruction in the writing center became what Steve North calls

> a pedagogy of direct intervention. Whereas in the "old" center instruction tends to take place after or apart from writing, and tends to focus on the correction of textual problems, in the "new" center the teaching takes place as much as possible during writing, during the activity being learned, and tends to focus on the activity itself. (North, "Idea" 439)

This shift in approach, however, was not greeted with unqualified enthusiasm by faculty members in other departments on campus, who were concerned about the "ethics" of this type of writing center instruction and alarmed that it represented a form of plagiarism.

[handwritten: itself an ideology — however, the dominant, established ideology]

PLAGIARISM, INTELLECTUAL PROPERTY RIGHTS, AND THE RISE OF WRITING CENTER ORTHODOXY

Writing centers' concern with defending themselves against charges of inadvertent or even deliberate plagiarism reflects western culture's emphasis on intellectual property rights, an emphasis manifested in the number of lawsuits concerned with issues of copyright and authorship. Although postmodern theorists have problematized the conception of authors and authorship, the teaching of literature and composition, as Woodmansee and Jaszi point out, "continues to enforce the Romantic paradigm" (9) of the solitary author whose work is absolutely original. In a presentation concerned with writing centers and ethics given at the Conference of College Composition and Communication several years ago, Karen Hodges discussed the wide diversity in attitudes toward collaborative effort among various disciplines. She concluded that English Departments, in particular, were concerned about the shaping of the text and were thus least likely to favor collaborative writing or writing assistance. Hodges's perspective is supported by Bruffee, Trimbur, and Lunsford and Ede, who trace the concept of the solitary author to the eighteenth-century concept of individualism and a nineteenth-century romantic notion of the solitary creative genius that eventually manifested itself in a twentieth-century emphasis "on writing as an individually creative act, and on 'objective' testing as a means of evaluating the intellectual property of solitary writers" (Lunsford and Ede 418). Departments of literature are particularly concerned with the issue of plagiarism in terms of style and text structure, in contrast to departments of science and social science, who tend to focus primarily on the originality of an idea. One particularly amusing but unfortunately apt portrait of English de-

[handwritten: but, appropriateness of style + text structure highly dependent on specific contexts — no completely directive writing pedagogy can deal with addressing the multiplicity of context-specific rhetorical situations which is the —]

partments' attitude toward plagiarism is depicted in Bernard Malamud's novel *A New Life*, whose hero, an English teacher named Levin, has to deal with a suspected plagiarist, Albert O. Birdless, a "D" student who has turned in an "A" paper. Warned by his colleagues that his duty is to locate the original source in order to trap the culprit, Levin spends many evenings in the library, reading "with murderous intent, to ensnare and expunge Albert O. Birdless" (164). But he never finds the source and is compared unfavorably with another instructor, Avis Fliss, who has earned a reputation for her unfailing ability to detect suspected student plagiarists:

> [Avis] *has a knack of going straight to the* Reader's Guide, *looking over the titles of articles on the cribbed subject for a couple of years past or so, and just about right away putting her finger on the one she needs. Her last incident she had this student nailed dead to rights an hour and a half after she read his theme. We had him suspended by his dean and off the campus before five o'clock of the same day.* (161)

Although this portrait is humorous, a concern with avoiding plagiarism, coupled with the second-class and frequently precarious status of writing centers within the university hierarchy, generated a set of defensive strategies aimed at warding off the suspicions of those in traditional humanities departments, who feared that students were receiving assistance that strained the boundaries of ethics.[1] As a result, precepts associated with non-interventionist tutoring became not only the preferred, but often, in fact, the only writing center approach.

Reflecting what may be viewed as a pedagogy of self-defense, articles appearing in early issues of the *Writing Lab Newsletter* delineated strategies aimed at ensuring that tutors did not provide excessive help, thereby averting suspicion of plagiarism. For example, in 1981, Larry Rochelle warned: "We must keep in mind that some 'enemies' of the Center are overwrought English professors, our own colleagues, who really do not like students or teaching, who are very demanding in their classrooms for all the wrong reasons, and who really think that Writing Centers are helping students too much" (7). A 1984 article by Patrick Sullivan contains the similarly suspicious observation that the close relationships which develop between tutors and students sometimes generate their own "special set of problems. The instructor may not be aware that a student has received help with a writing assignment. In this case, instructors may feel that matters related to the policy on plagiarism obtain" (2). The following year, in a subsequent article for the *Newsletter*, Sullivan discussed the results of a survey asking faculty whether or not they "object to tutor assisting your students," admittedly a loaded question. Although many were pleased, even enthusiastic, about this

real reason complete directive tutoring shouldn't be used
Tutors should help students discover the rhetoric that
suits their needs — a kind of problem solving that would
encourage spontaneity and originality while also addressing
the demands of different discourse communities

sort of assistance, a significant number regarded it with great mistrust. "I don't approve of them editing final drafts," one respondent observed. Another indicated his strong disapproval, particularly for non-native speakers:

> *My Vietnamese student who came in to see you received much too much help with his composition—even suggestions for ideas to be incorporated into the paper. In cases where a student has serious grammatical and organizational problems, I would even prefer he or she not take a draft of the paper to the center at all, but rather get help through the use of verb exercises. (6)*

To forestall suspicion, then, the concept of tutor restraint became a moral imperative, dictating a set of absolute guidelines for writing center instruction. For Suzanne Edwards that means training her staff "not to write any portion of the paper—not even one phrase" nor to "edit the paper for mechanical errors. This includes finding or labeling the spelling, punctuation, or grammar mistakes in a paper or dictating corrections" (8). Evelyn Ashton-Jones argues that tutors must engage in a version of "Socratic dialogue" and not "lapse into a 'directive' mode of tutoring." Quoting Thom Hawkins, she labels the directive tutor as "shaman, guru, or mentor," and Socratic tutors as "architects and partners" (31), labels that leave no doubt as to which group is on the side of the angels. More recently, Jeff Brooks, in arguing for "minimalist tutoring," warns: "When you 'improve' a student's paper, you haven't been a tutor at all; you've been an editor. You may have been an exceedingly good editor, but you've been of little service to your student.... The student, not the tutor, should 'own' the paper and take full responsibility for it" (2). Finally, Thomas Thompson describes how tutors at The Citadel's Writing Center easily work within the constraints of a military honor code:

> *[T]utors try to avoid taking pen in hand when discussing a student paper. They may discuss content, and they may use the Socratic method to lead students to discover their own conclusions, but tutors are instructed not to tell students what a passage means or give students a particular word to complete a particular thought. (13)*

An encapsulation of what eventually developed into the writing center credo is an oft-quoted statement from Stephen North: "[I]n a writing center the object is to make sure that writers, and not necessarily their texts, are what get changed by instruction" (438). In that article, North was reacting against the "fix-it shop" concept of writing centers prevalent at that time, and his intention was to enlighten a non-writing center readership about what writing centers really do—that is, help students become writers, not simply clean up their papers. However, another, perhaps less obvious intention was to assure colleagues in the English department that the help students receive in writing centers does not constitute a form of plagiarism. After all, if it is the writer and not the text that improves as a result of a writing center visit, then surely no textual property has been unfairly appropriated.

THEORETICAL LIMITATIONS OF WRITING CENTER ORTHODOXY: THE COMPLEXITY OF "OWNING" TEXTS

Despite the salutary influence of North's "The Idea of a Writing Center," both inside and outside writing centers, its philosophy of textual noninterventionism has not served writing centers well. As we have noted, such a philosophy perpetuates a limited and limiting understanding of authorship in the academy. By privileging individual responsibility and accountability and by valorizing the individual writer's authentic "voice," the writing center has left unchallenged notions of intellectual property that are suspect at best. Furthermore, as Lisa Ede, Andrea Lunsford, Marilyn Cooper, and others have argued, the idea that writing is fundamentally a solitary activity and that individual writers can and should "own" their texts relegates the writing center to a limited bystander's role, even as it limits writers' understanding of their options and of their relationship to others.

Ede notes that some collaborative learning theorists, such as Bruffee, seem to view collaboration as a compensatory strategy for inexperienced writers. The implication is that accomplished writers won't need to "interrupt" their essentially solitary writing process with dialogue. If writing centers adopt such a view, says Ede, they implicitly limit their clientele and their mission: "[A]s long as thinking and writing are regarded as inherently individual, solitary activities, writing centers can never be viewed as anything more than pedagogical fix-it shops to help those who, for whatever reason, are unable to think and write on their own" (7).

Lunsford labels those writing centers that view knowledge as individual either "storehouses" or "garrets." The former locate knowledge outside the knower, "stored" in texts or other repositories, while garret centers "see knowledge as interior, as inside the student, and the writing center's job as helping students get in touch with this knowledge, as a way to find their unique voices, their individual and unique powers" (5). Storehouse and Garret centers are limited, says Lunsford, by their epistemologies—positivistic, Platonic, and absolutist. To "enable a student body and citizenry to meet the demands of the twenty-first century...we need to embrace the idea of writing centers as Burkean Parlors, as centers for collaboration" (9).

Cooper, too, critiques epistemologies that are based on "a preexisting coherent and rational self," that see writing as "a matter of subduing the text to the self by achieving personal control over it" and "achieving an authentic voice" (101). Writing centers founded on such epistemologies, says Cooper, will tend to focus on helping students "fix" papers rather than concentrating on "what students know and need to know about writing" (99). Writing centers will be more effective and their clients better served by a different view of textual ownership:

> [T]utors can best help students become agents of their own writing by helping them understand how and the extent to which they are not owners of their texts and not responsible for the shape of their texts, by helping them understand, in short, how various institutional forces impinge on how and what they write and how they can negotiate a place for their own goals and needs when faced with these forces. (101)

Ironically, the same fix-it mentality that these theorists see as the legacy of a limiting epistemology prompted Stephen North's apology for writing centers in a recent article that itself helped perpetuate that very epistemology. In fairness to North, it should be observed that in "Revisiting 'The Idea of a Writing Center,'" the passage about not second-guessing teachers is one of four that he singles out to revisit. He acknowledges that in the writing center we see "what we at least construe as the seamier side of things," which "in cumulative form puts a lot of pressure on the sort of tutor-teacher détente proposed by the [original] passage" ("Revisiting," 13). However, North's second article provides no suggestion that writing center personnel should directly challenge the pedagogical status quo. Instead, it argues for a new curricular state of affairs wherein the writing center would work primarily with students enrolled in a "Writing Sequence," a "program—a four-year sequence of study—that values writing" (16). Such a program presumably minimizes conflicts between the writing center and instructors "because the classroom teachers are directly involved with, and therefore invested in the functioning of, that center" (16).

PEDAGOGICAL LIMITATIONS OF WRITING CENTER ORTHODOXY

Textual noninterventionism is suspect not only on theoretical grounds, as we have been arguing; it also overlooks the possibility that for some students, an interventionist, directive, and appropriative pedagogy might be more effective—as well as ethically defensible. Deborah Burns, for example, points out that her thesis director, who supervised the writing of her master's thesis using directive intervention, was the person most helpful to her in her graduate studies. Yet everything he did violated entrenched writing center policy. He "was directive, he substituted his own words for hers, and he stated with disciplinary appropriateness the ideas with which she had been working" (Shamoon and Burns 138). As a compositionist, Burns puzzled over the effectiveness of her director's interventions. Moreover, she observed, he was equally effective with other graduate students:

> [H]e took their papers and rewrote them while they watched. They left feeling better able to complete their papers, and they tackled other papers with greater ease and success.... His practices seem authoritative, intrusive, directive, and product-oriented. Yet these practices created major turning points for a variety of writers. (138)

Shamoon and Burns cite other similar examples from faculty workshops in which professors, acting like tutors, were equally directive:

> Over and over in the informal reports of our colleagues we find that crucial information about a discipline and about writing is transmitted in ways that are intrusive, directive, and product-oriented, yet these behaviors are not perceived as an appropriation of power or voice but instead as an opening up of those aspects of practice which had remained unspoken and opaque. (139)

This type of directive tutoring is consistent with Vygotsky's concept of "the zone of proximal development," which is defined as "the distance between the actual development level as determined by the independent problem solving and the level of potential development as determined through problem solving under adult guidance or in collaboration with more capable peers" (86). In terms of writing center pedagogy, Vygotsky's view of learning suggests that tutors should work on "functions that have not yet matured, but are in the process of maturation, functions that will mature tomorrow, but are currently in an embryonic state" (86). Such functions might require the tutor to assume a more directive role until the student can assume the function alone. As Vygotsky points out, "what children can do with the assistance of others might be in some sense even more indicative of their mental development than what they can do alone" (85). However, inflexible precepts against directive tutoring preclude this sort of assistance and overlook variation in student need and tutorial context. In an essay concerned with tutoring strategies for learning disabled students, for example, Julie Neff points out that orthodox tutoring practices are often not very effective because such students require a great deal more specific and directive assistance. For students from nonwestern cultures as well, nondirective tutoring may be insufficient, particularly since many of them are unfamiliar with the western conceptions of academic discourse and have little understanding of the purpose or components of the essays they are expected to produce. Harris and Silva refer to the "sometimes bewilderingly different rhetorical patterns and conventions of other languages" (525) sometimes manifested in a "seemingly meandering introduction or digressions that appear irrelevant" (526). In dealing with these students, Harris and Silva point out that

> [i]n terms of the tutor's role, there may have to be adjustments in their pedagogical orientation. Tutors who work with ESL students may have to be "tellers" to some extent because they will probably need to provide cultural, rhetorical, and/or linguistic information which native speakers intuitively possess and which ESL students do not have, but need to have to complete their writing assignments effectively. (533)

In terms of fostering the best environment for assisting student writing, then, it is important to recognize the virtues of flexibility since "one tutoring approach does not fit all" (Shamoon and Burns 139).

ILLEGITIMATE COLLABORATION AND IMITATION

Of course, deciding just how much and what kind of assistance to provide is not an easy task, often requiring tutors to walk a fine line between legitimate and illegitimate collaboration. Tutoring is "a balancing act that asks tutors to juggle roles, to shift identity, to know when to act like an expert and when to act like a co-learner" (Trimbur 25), and when we say that writing centers foster the spirit of "collaborative learning," it is sometimes difficult to define exactly what we mean. True collaboration occurs between colleagues who are both members of the same discourse community. True colleagues collaborate without fear of text appropriation, in its ideal form, collaboration between colleagues involves mutual assistance and mutual learning.

Collaboration in writing centers, however, often involves a writer who is not a full-fledged member of the academic discourse community. In fact, the purpose of the tutoring is often to help the author attain that status. Moreover, although practitioners frequently use the term "peer tutor" to refer to undergraduate tutors in the writing center, many tutors are not peers in any sense of the word. Some of them may be graduate students or composition teachers who are considerably older than the students seeking their assistance, and all of them, young or old, even those who are, indeed, undergraduates, were selected to be tutors because they have demonstrated an ability to write. By definition, then, writing center tutoring takes place in a hierarchical context in which there is danger that a tutor might assume an unethically dominant role in creating and developing a text. Hence the rationale for a nondirective pedagogy.

Blind adherence to any absolute principles of tutoring, however, can be counterproductive to student learning because it precludes other instructional possibilities, in particular the role of imitation. In his discussion of the history of plagiarism, St. Onge points out that "in the vast arrays of animal behaviors, mimicry is a fine art. The mocking bird plagiarizes the calls of any one of its peers and has been known to tease human whistlers" (17). Vygotsky similarly implies a key relationship between imitation and learning. Yet, as Anne Gere has pointed out, our culture, in its privileging of original creation, is predisposed to distrust imitation as a learning tool, even though imitation was once considered a method of choice. In her discussion of the development of oratory, Gere cites Isocrates' concept of the teacher who "must in himself set such an example that the students who are molded by him and are able to imitate him will, from the outset, show in their speaking a degree of grace and charm greater than that of others" (8). Gere also refers to Cicero and Quintillian, who recommend "paraphrase because of its challenge to achieve expression independent of the original" (8). *They Say, I Say*

Muriel Harris advocates modeling, even for novice writers, pointing out that imitation can be useful for teaching composing skills and writing behaviors such as invention and editing. Harris cites a case study in which she used modeling to help a student improve his composing process, working through the process herself as the student observed, helping the student decide what topics to choose, what information to gather, and what writing behaviors to engage in. "And what better way is there," Harris asks, "to convince students that writing is a process that requires effort, thought, time, and persistence than to go through all that writing, scratching out, rewriting, and revising with and for our students?" (81).

CONCERN WITH PLAGIARISM

Let us suppose, however, that as a result of Harris's use of imitation and modeling, her student had appropriated a few of her "ideas" or phrases for his own paper. Should Harris's approach then be regarded as unethical? Would the results be considered "plagiarism"? Would the student need to acknowledge Harris in a full citation or else be guilty of a moral offense? Some faculty members would probably answer "yes" to all of these questions. But one might also argue that few of us can know with any certainty how or where we obtained our own ideas in the first place, a view expressed by many writers. Accused of plagiarism at a young age, Helen Keller, for example, characterizes her writing as a mixture of assimilation and imitation: "It is certain that I cannot always distinguish my own thoughts from those I read, because what I read becomes the very substance and text of my mind. Consequently, in nearly all that I write, I produce something which very much resembles the crazy patchwork I used to make when I first learned to sew" (67–68). Similarly, Virginia Woolf writes in her diary that "reading Yeats turns my sentences one way: reading Sterne turns them another" (119). A poststructuralist perspective "does away with origins.... Thus, writing can be nothing more than a tissue of quotations, a pastiche of passages possessing no authorial affiliation and therefore belonging to no one" (De Grazia 301).

Moreover, as Woodmansee and Jaszi point out, "studies of writing practices from the Renaissance to the present suggest that the modern regime of authorship, far from being timeless and universal, is a relatively recent formation" (2–3). In fact, "quotation marks were not used on a regular basis until the end of the eighteenth century" (De Grazia 288). Before this time, they were used for the antithetical purpose of highlighting a commonplace or statement of truth that could be appropriated by all readers, "facilitating the 'lifting' of the passages they marked.... In brief, rather than cordoning off a passage as property of another, quotation marks flagged the passage as property belonging to all—'common places' to be freely appropriated (and not necessarily verbatim and with correct authorial ascription)" (289). Our conception of plagiarism as a reprehensible moral offense, then, is a relatively recent notion.

In the context of writing center pedagogy, however, that notion suggests that because nondirective tutoring has the smallest risk of becoming a form of plagiarism, it is, by definition, the most effective and hence "ethical" approach. Yet, as Barry Kroll suggests, it is not necessarily true that plagiarism is counterproductive to student learning. What would happen, Kroll asks,

> if one comes to suspect that plagiarism (particularly the familiar case of copying a paragraph or so from a source) does not inevitably damage learning—at least, no more seriously than quoting the same passage would damage learning[?] In fact, from the view of consequences to oneself, there would seem to be no morally significant difference between quoting and copying without acknowledgment; neither is more or less likely to lead to creativity, to learning, or to independent thought. And what if one could show that copying a passage from a source sometimes leads to learning or improved writing? (5)

This is not to say, of course, that writing centers should write students' papers for them or relinquish their insistence that students take responsibility for their own work. However, as the Internet becomes an increasingly common means of communication and facilitates easy access to texts of various sorts, it is important that the writing center begin to question the absolutism of its noninterventionist policies in favor of a more flexible "rhetorically situated view of plagiarism, one that acknowledges that all writing is in an important sense collaborative and that 'common knowledge' varies from community to community and is collaboratively shared" (Lunsford and Ede 437).

POLITICAL LIMITATIONS OF WRITING CENTER ORTHODOXY

Writing center practitioners who let ethical concerns drive a noninterventionist, nonappropriative praxis suffer not only pedagogically; they suffer politically as well. An ethics based on defensiveness is ill-suited to challenge the prevailing order. If writing centers limit themselves merely to fixing what comes in the door, they run two risks. First, as Nancy Grimm has observed, in the interest of conforming to a perhaps flawed standard of academic writing, they may end up trying to fix what isn't broken. Second, by accepting what comes in the door as given—including the assignments, pedagogies, assumptions, and epistemologies that lie behind clients' texts—writing centers abandon the ground from which they are in a position to contest the larger political reality of which all of us—teachers, students, and tutors—are a part.

For the fact is that writing centers are well positioned to question the status quo. Writing centers occupy what Harvey Kail and John Trimbur have called "semiautonomous" institutional space located "outside the normal channels of teaching and learning." By providing a place where students can experience some distance from "official strictures," the center can help them "reengage the forms of authority in their lives by demystifying the authority of knowledge and its institutions" (11). Writing centers can be sites of what Nancy Welch calls "critical exile," from where we can encourage students to "reconsider the kinds of conversation we value in academia" and to "resist the pressure of perfection" (7). "Writing centers," argues Marilyn Cooper,

> are in a good position to serve as a site of critique of the institutionalized structure of writing instruction in college, and...as a consequence of this, the role of the tutor should be to create useful knowledge about writing in college and to empower students as writers who also understand what writing involves and who act as agents in their writing. (98)

Too often, though, the writing center's "service ethic" silences its potentially revolutionary voice.

> [B]ecause writing centers are represented in positions of uncritical service, writing center practice often focuses on fixing students who have nothing wrong with them, supporting a literacy curriculum that is often out of sync

> *with the needs of today's students, and talking about assignments with stu-*
> *dents as though these assignments were not implicitly loaded with one cul-*
> *ture's values. Even more troubling is that the close contact writing centers*
> *have with students provides a special kind of knowledge, a knowledge that*
> *challenges the wisdom of mainstream practices, a knowledge that forms the*
> *stories we tell each other. Yet as writing centers are currently theorized, fac-*
> *ulty are protected from this knowledge. (Grimm 11)*

Because of its location in "semiautonomous space," its status as "critical exile," and its access to "a special kind of knowledge," the writing center is
uniquely positioned to challenge business as usual in the academy. Centers
may resist making that challenge for a variety of reasons, including their
sometimes tenuous institutional standing and the typically untenured status
of writing center directors. But political timidity may also result from ethical
naivete, from a conviction that the center's proper role is narrowly responsive rather than initiatory. By being so careful not to infringe on other's
turf—the writer's, the teacher's, the department's, the institution's—the
writing center has been party to its own marginality and silencing.

Another political danger confronting the orthodox writing center is a
kind of classism or elitism. By holding clients to a standard that writing center practitioners and educators in general do not observe, the center may relegate them to an inferior role. In refusing to write on a student's paper or
supply occasional phrasing or suggest specific lines of inquiry, writing center personnel are withholding from clients precisely the kind of directive, appropriative intervention that is routinely offered to publishing academics by
colleagues and editors. The authors of this article frequently show their writing to others who have suggested and sometimes actually made specific, detailed changes in their texts. Do students deserve less than what we expect
for ourselves?

Of course, one must qualify that the kind of mentoring performed by a
thesis advisor or among colleagues is different from what typically goes on in
a writing center. Nevertheless, the difference, we would argue, is one of degree
rather than kind. Writing center consultants—whether they are undergraduates, graduate students, or professional staff—have knowledge and expertise
that many writing center clients lack. A failure to share that knowledge and
expertise inhibits the acquisition of academic literacy by writing center clients.
It is ironic indeed if that failure stems from ethical concerns about the appropriateness of directive, interventionist conferencing strategies.

It would be simplistic to demand that writing center personnel practice
everything they preach and preach only what they practice. Any of us who
teach or tutor writing regularly recommend strategies we ourselves do not
use. Teachers or tutors may suggest that a writer try freewriting or looping

or outlining even if they never employ those techniques themselves, because they realize that everyone writes differently and that others may benefit from practices they personally have not found especially helpful. Similarly, they may choose not to suggest some method they themselves utilize—out of a conviction that a given writer would not benefit from that particular approach. But it is worse than simplistic to require that writing centers withhold helpful information and refrain from helpful practices out of a misguided sense of what is ethical.

A NEW ETHICS FOR THE WRITING CENTER

So what would an ethical writing center look like? Let us suggest three components,

1. The ethical writing center will be proactive. Though writing centers must, by their nature, be responsive to other people's writing, assignments, and goals, centers must not let responsiveness and a misguided sense of ethics give way to knee-jerk acquiescence and accommodation. The people who work in writing centers should be confident of their own expertise and insight and should be willing to use their unique position in the academy to challenge the status quo by critiquing institutional ideology and practice.

2. The ethical writing center will exercise a broad, encompassing vision. The center will look past individual texts and writers to consider the whole range of literate practices in the academy. Writing centers need to move beyond Stephen North's oft-quoted dictum that "[o]ur job is to produce better writers, not better writing" ("Idea" 438). The center's job encompasses not only individual writers, but also the larger discourse communities of which they are a part. The college and university classroom has few windows. Because of its one-to-one work with students, the writing center is a window into the classroom, and it ought to show some concern for that realm, just as it does for the individual writers it serves.

3. The ethical writing center will take full advantage of its hallmark: individualized writing instruction. As Roger Garrison has said, "A group, a class, has no writing problems; there are only individuals who have difficulty saying what they mean" (1). Writing centers need to maximize what they do best by consistently treating writers as individuals. Leveling its clientele through rigid policy statements—e.g., "Refuse to proofread," or "Don't even hold a pencil when you're tutoring"—denies the diversity found in any center and stifles the creativity of writing center consultants. Writing centers need to be creative in opening up the world of discourse to their clients and their clients to that world.

DANGERS OF THE NEW ETHICS

This new conception of writing center ethics is not without its dangers. We conclude by suggesting three ways that writing centers might go awry.

1. Although we believe that unfounded fears of appropriation and uncritical notions of textual ownership have limited the writing center's effectiveness, it's clear that writers can and do misrepresent their work and that unwary tutors could be party to such misrepresentation. Writing centers are not likely to become replicas of "Tailormade," the paper-writing business described in a recent Harper's article (Witherspoon), but they can be drawn into questionable practices. However (to risk a shop-worn bromide), their focus should not be on the products their clients produce but rather on the process they undergo in the center. The question "Is this the writer's work?" should be interpreted as "What work has this writer done to produce this result?" We have suggested that writing centers can relax a bit about the question of ownership, but they should not relax about the question of agency. One obvious way that agency manifests itself is in simple volume. If a writer comes to the writing center with nothing written and a consultant writes something, that something is likely to overshadow or unduly influence anything the client might subsequently produce. Interventionist strategies with existing text, on the other hand, run less risk of appropriating agency.

2. Although social-constructionist and collaborative-learning theories are central to the ethical writing center as we have described it, an uncritical acceptance of those theories could lead, as Christina Murphy has warned regarding social constructivism, to an overvaluation of consensus and to "illusory views of peership" (27) and could blind writing centers to the importance of the individual's emotions in intellectual development. Alice Gillam, in a critique of collaborative learning theory, notes that collaborative learning's critics have suggested that "its emphasis on group process and consensus-building enforces conformity, lowers standards, and denies the importance of the individual mind" (40). Gillam also observes that some versions of collaborative learning theory emphasize social and political goals to the neglect of educational goals. Writing, she suggests, can sometimes get lost in the shuffle.

3. Although we have called for the people who work in writing centers to be less timid in their encounters with writers, teachers, texts, assignments, syllabi, and curricula, they must not let a sense of ethical liberation lead to arrogance or tactlessness. North's maxim of curricular nonintervention cited above ("we never evaluate or second-guess any teacher's syllabus, assignments, comments, or grades") follows a previous observation that writing centers "do a fair amount of trade in people working on ambiguous or poorly designed assignments, and far too much work with writers whose writing has

received caustic, hostile, or otherwise unconstructive commentary" ("Idea," 440). We have argued that writing centers do themselves and the larger institutions of which they are a part a disservice by maintaining a complicity of silence about the academy's shortcomings, but how should they go about addressing the sins North enumerates? His observation about bad assignments and teacher commentary, as long as it is generalized and abstract, will offend no one because teachers will recognize only others, not themselves, in his indictment. But what happens when a specific writer brings to the writing center a specific paper based on a specific instructor's poorly designed assignment and already subject to that specific instructor's obviously unconstructive commentary? The ethical writing center must always be characterized by tact and sensitivity, recognizing that although our writing may be initiated by someone else's assignment (and in school it almost always is), for most of us our writing represents our selves and the words on the page seem to be our own words. Intervening in someone else's writing ought to feel perilous and ought to continue to be approached with humility and care.

The "goodness" or "badness" of current writing center policy cannot be judged as absolutes, but must ultimately be evaluated in terms of specific consequences to or behaviors of the clients and institutions it serves. In its current form, the writing center, out of a misguided sense of ethical responsibility, has catered to ill-founded fears and outdated epistemologies, and consequently has not ethically served its clientele. The ethical writing center can and should be a force for change—in writers and in writing and in the academy at large.

NOTE

1. For a discussion of the writing center's response to faculty suspicions of plagiarism, see Behm.

WORKS CITED

Ashton-Jones, Evelyn. "Asking the Right Questions: A Heuristic for Tutors." *The Writing Center Journal* 9.1 (1988): 29–36.

Behm, Richard. "Ethical Issues in Peer Tutoring: A Defense of Collaborative Learning." *The Writing Center Journal* 10.1 (1989): 3–12.

Blau, Susan. "Issues in Tutoring Writing: Stories from Our Center" *Writing Lab Newsletter* 19.2 (Oct. 1992): 1–4.

Brooks, Jeff. "Minimalist Tutoring: Making the Student Do All the Work." *Writing Lab Newsletter* 15.6 (Feb. 1991): 1–4.

Bruffee, Kenneth. "Collaborative Learning and the Conversation of Mankind." *College English* 46 (1984): 645–52.

Bruner, Jerome. *Toward a Theory of Instruction*. Cambridge: Belknap of Harvard University Press, 1966.

Carino, Peter. "Early Writing Centers: Toward a History." *The Writing Center Journal* 15.2 (1995): 103–115.

Clark, Irene L. "Collaboration and Ethics in Writing Center Pedagogy." *The Writing Center Journal* 9.1 (1988): 3–12.

———. "Leading the Horse: The Writing Center and Required Visits." *The Writing Center Journal* 5.2/6.1 (1985): 31–34.

Cooper, Marilyn. "Really Useful Knowledge: A Cultural Studies Agenda for Writing Centers." *The Writing Center Journal* 14.2 (1994): 97–111.

De Grazia, Margreta. "Sanctioning Voice: Quotation Marks, the Abolition of Torture, and the Fifth Amendment." Woodmansee and Jaszi 281–302.

Ede, Lisa. "Writing as a Social Process: A Theoretical Foundation for Writing Centers?" *The Writing Center Journal* 9.2 (1989): 3–13.

Edwards, Suzanne. "Tutoring Your Tutors: How to Structure a Tutor-Training Workshop." *Writing Lab Newsletter* 7.10 (June 1983): 7–9.

Garrison, Roger. *One-To-One: Making Writing Instruction Effective*. New York: Harper & Row, 1981.

Gere, Ann Ruggles. "On Imitation." Paper given at the Conference on College Composition and Communication. Atlanta, March 1987.

Gillam, Alice M. "Collaborative Learning Theory and Peer Tutoring Practice." Mullin and Wallace 39–53.

Grimm, Nancy Maloney. "Divided Selves: Exploring Writing Center Contradictions." Address. Midwest Writing Centers Association. Kansas City, 7 Oct. 1994.

Harris, Muriel. "Modeling: A Process Method of Teaching." *College English* 45 (1983): 74–84.

Harris, Muriel, and Tony Silva. "Tutoring ESL Students: Issues and Opinions." *College Composition and Communication* 44 (1993): 525–537.

Hodges, Karen. "The Writing of Dissertations: Collaboration and Ethics." Paper given at the Conference on College Composition and Communication. Atlanta, March 1987.

Kail, Harvey, and John Trimbur. "The Politics of Peer Tutoring." *WPA: Writing Program Administration* 11.1 (1987):5–12.

Keller, Helen. *The Story of My Life*. New York: Doubleday, 1903, 1954.

Kroll, Barry. "Why is Plagiarism Wrong?" Paper given at the Conference on College Composition and Communication. Atlanta, March 1987.

Lunsford, Andrea. "Collaboration, Control, and the Idea of a Writing Center." *The Writing Center Journal* 12.1 (1991): 3–10.

Lunsford, Andrea, and Lisa Ede. "Collaborative Authorship and the Teaching of Writing." Woodmansee and Jaszi 417–138.

Malamud, Bernard. *A New Life*. New York: Dell, 1961.

Moffett, James. *Teaching the Universe of Discourse*. Boston: Houghton, 1968.

Mullin, Joan A. and Ray Wallace, eds. *Theory and Practice in the Writing Center*. Urbana: NCTE, 1994.

Murphy, Christina. "The Writing Center and Social Constructionist Theory." *Intersections: Theory and Practice in the Writing Center*. Ed. Joan A. Mullin and Ray Wallace. Urbana: NCTE, 1994. 25–38.

Neff, Julie. "Learning Disabilities and the Writing Center." Mullin and Wallace 81–95.

North, Stephen M. "The Idea of a Writing Center." *College English* 46 (1984): 433–446.

———. "Revisiting 'The Idea of a Writing Center.'" *The Writing Center Journal* 15.1 (1994): 7–19.

Rochelle, Larry. "The ABC's of Writing Centers." *Writing Lab Newsletter* September 1981: 7–9.

Shamoon, Linda K., and Deborah H. Burns. "A Critique of Pure Tutoring." *The Writing Center Journal* 15.2 (1995): 134–151.

St. Onge, K. R. *The Melancholy Anatomy of Plagiarism.* Lanhom, MA: U Press of America, 1988.

Sullivan, Patrick. "The Politics of the Drop-In Writing Center." *Writing Lab Newsletter* 8.9 (May 1984): 1–2.

———. "Do You Object to Tutors Assisting Your Students With Their Writing?" *Writing Lab Newsletter* 10.4 (December 1985): 6–8.

Thompson, Thomas C. "'Yes, Sir!' 'No, Sir!' 'No Excuse, Sir!' Working with an Honor Code in a Military Setting." *Writing Lab Newsletter* 19.5 (Jan. 1995): 13–14.

Trimbur, John. "Peer Tutoring: A Contradiction in Terms." *The Writing Center Journal* 7.2 (1987): 21–28.

Vygotsky, Lev. *Mind in Society: The Development of Higher Psychological Processes.* Cambridge: Harvard University Press, 1978.

Weiner, Bernard. *Achievement Motivation and Attribution Theory.* New Jersey: General Learning Press, 1974.

Welch, Nancy. "From Silence to Noise: The Writing Center as Critical Exile." *The Writing Center Journal* 14.1 (1993): 3–15.

Wicksell, Wesley. "The Communications Program at Stephens College." *College English* 9 (1947): 143–145.

Witherspoon, Abigail. "This Pen for Hire." *Harper's* June 1995: 49–57.

Woodmansee, Martha, and Peter Jaszi, eds. *The Construction of Authorship: Textual Appropriation in Law and Literature.* Durham and London: Duke University Press, 1994.

Woodmansee, Martha, and Peter jaszi. "Introduction." Woodmansee and Jaszi 1–15.

Woolf, Virginia. *The Diary of Virginia Woolf.* Vol 3, 1925–1930. Penguin: New York, 1982.

"Look Back and Say 'So What'": The Limitations of the Generalist Tutor 1993

Jean Kiedaisch

Sue Dinitz

Since 1983, when Toby Fulwiler arrived at the University of Vermont and began promoting faculty interest in writing across the curriculum, our writing center has increasingly worked with students and recruited tutors from across the curriculum. Other writing centers have also moved in this direction. In the mid-1980's several articles appeared in the Writing Lab Newsletter and The Writing Center Journal encouraging writing centers to work with students and recruit tutors from across the disciplines (Haviland, Luce, Scanlon, Smith).

Initially, we were not very concerned about our tutors' ability to help students from various disciplines. We felt pretty confident that if we trained our tutors to be good facilitators, to use questioning to help students clarify their ideas, and to guide students through the writing process, they could help almost any student working on almost any paper. In an article in The Writing Center Journal, Susan Hubbuch goes so far as to suggest that the "ignorant" or generalist tutor can often be of more help than a tutor familiar with the discipline: "The ignorant tutor, by virtue of her ignorance, is just as likely—perhaps even more likely—than the expert to help the student recognize what must be stated in the text" (28).

But a few years ago our own experience teaching intermediate-level writing classes made us question this optimism. We had begun to encourage students to write the sorts of papers they might write within their disciplines. In working with these papers, we ourselves sometimes felt uncertain about what to say to students. For example, a business major wrote a market analysis divided into twenty subsections. When Sue said it seemed choppy and suggested transitions, the student responded that this is how market

Kiedaisch, Jean and Sue Dinitz. "Look Back and Say 'So What': The Limitation of the Generalist Tutor." *The Writing Center Journal* 14.1 (1993): 63–74. Reprinted by permission of *The Writing Center Journal*.

analyses are written. When Jean pointed out to an engineering student that she seemed to have similar information in her results, conclusions, and implications sections, the student responded that this is how lab reports are written. From our experience working with faculty and students in each of these disciplines, we suspected the business student was right and the engineering student was wrong. But how could we expect our peer tutors, less familiar with academic writing, to know when to accept the judgment of the "knowledgeable" student?

Wanting to look more closely at how a tutor's knowledge of the discipline affects a tutoring session, we videotaped twelve sessions over papers written in literature courses designed for majors, assuming that these papers would be expected to follow disciplinary conventions. At the end of each session, we had the tutor and student fill out a questionnaire so that we could determine whether they saw any connection between the quality of their session and the tutor's knowledge of the discipline. They did not. All of the students rated their sessions highly and credited their tutors with a good understanding of how to write literature papers. The tutors also rated their sessions highly, and none of them expressed concern over their level of knowledge of the discipline.

Thinking a teacher in the discipline might assess the help a student got differently from the student or the tutor, we asked three English teachers to view eight of the tapes and fill out a similar questionnaire. They did not find the sessions so uniformly good. All agreed that two of the sessions were excellent, two were good, and four were weak. And they did see a correlation between the tutor's knowledge of the discipline and the quality of the session: the disciplinary knowledge of the tutors in the excellent sessions was rated as high, while that of the tutors in the weak sessions was rated as low.

This preliminary work made us want to identify more precisely how the tutor's knowledge of the discipline affected each session. So we turned to analyzing the transcripts of the videotapes. What we saw led us to conclude that the "ignorant" or generalist tutor sometimes has limitations.

Anna, a senior English major, comes into the writing center with a paper for her Shakespeare course. The tutor on duty is David, a business major who had come to us highly recommended by two writing teachers. Anna's draft begins,

> *Othello is a play that depicts the essense of deception. In the play, each character, except Iago, is deceived and in return they deceive. Iago is the master of deception and seeks out to deceive Othello who will in return eventually deceive his love, Desdemona. Iago is successful in his search for revenge*

upon Othello and he accomplishes his goal and that is to destroy the lives of the newly-married couple, Othello and Desdemona. Iago plants the seed of suspicion and then waits as Othello brings destruction to the life of Desdemona as well as himself.

The rest of the draft falls into three sections, each of which opens with a Roman numeral and heading:

   I. Why does Iago want to deceive Othello?
  II. How does Iago go about deceiving Othello?
 III. Othello deceives Desdemona

The last few sentences of the introduction and the outline both suggest that the draft moves quickly into a retelling of the plot. In a journal entry written for his tutor training class, David shows he recognizes that the paper needs to be more analytical: "She did a lot of plot summary, there is too much. It doesn't analyze the story."

To help Anna make the paper more analytical, David first tries to get her to narrow her focus:

David: What are three things you're trying to tell the reader!

Anna: Show how Iago is obsessed with deceiving Othello.... To show why he deceives Othello. And how he does it. And then show how Othello is deceived. And how Othello in return deceives someone else.

David's journal entry shows he's satisfied with this list: "She needed to cut her focus down to smaller pieces. I got her to list three or four main points she wanted. They overlapped a bit, but at least I got her down to fewer points to be made." David doesn't seem to realize that the new list actually matches the Roman numeral headings that organize Anna's draft.

For the rest of the hour-long session, David and Anna read through the paper paragraph by paragraph. After each few paragraphs, David stops and asks her the point of that section, explaining:

> The best questions to try and answer I've always found are "so what" and "why." When you're trying to make a point after a few paragraphs, look back and say "so what." That will bring out of the summary your voice. That's what you definitely want, those two questions.

Does this general advice help Anna make the paper more analytical? Throughout the session, in response to David's questions, she re-describes that particular section of Othello, adding even more details about the plot and characters, as in the following example:

Anna: It's nor really deception that he's doing at first.... He's getting ready to plant the seed of suspicion, so to get ready to do that you have to make sure that the person you're going to deceive...that they're going to trust you...and that they're going to be manipulated by this game.

David: OK, answer why.

Anna: Why? Because if Iago...doesn't have Othello's trust, it's not going to work, so he has to be sure he has Othello's trust.... One of the ways he knows he can do this is by saying that he's mad at Roderigo for doing this to Brabantio.... [She continues to explain how Iago gains Othello's trust.] He can't really go on with his plan till he knows for a fact that Othello's going to trust him.

David: [pause] Um, can you answer "so what" to that?

Anna: I guess I see it as really important because if I was in Iago's shoes, I would never go about a plan, until I knew I had that person's loyalty and trust....

David: That's the kind of stuff you need in this as opposed to plot summary.

David doesn't seem to realize that in answering his questions Anna just keeps repeating her original point.

There's no evidence in the session that using the "so what" question helps Anna think more analytically. Even though they spend an hour going through the paper, the two never come up with any insights that will make the paper more analytical. Anna leaves the session saying, "So I just need to go through and after each paragraph add in a sentence saying why or so what." David responds, "Yeah, yeah."

This session made us question a generalist tutor's ability to help when a paper is discipline-specific. David seems unable to see that Anna's answers to his general questions about focus and the point of each section remain on the level of plot summary. Or perhaps he does see this but doesn't know what to do. Indeed, he seems uncomfortable during much of the session, stopping often to look at his watch, pausing often to think about what to do next, even asking, in seeming desperation, "Are you going to be seeing your professor before turning this in?" David doesn't seem to know what to do to move Anna beyond plot summary; he can't use her answers to generate even more questions and get a process going which will help Anna make her paper more analytical.

Cory, who is taking the sophomore-level introductory survey required of English majors, comes into the writing center with a paper that goes beyond plot summary to include several insights into Hawthorne's "The Birthmark." He is writing in response to the following assignment:

> *Both the scientists in "The Birthmark" and "Rappaccini's Daughter" could be described as mad or fatally flawed. But critics have also associated these scientists with artists. What do Aylmer, Rappaccini and Raglioni have in common with artists? Could Hawthorne be expressing his anxiety about art as well as science? Discuss how Hawthorne connects art and science in one of these stories and what it means for him to do so.*

This assignment asks the student to come up with two insights: one into how art and science are connected, and another into the meaning of this connection. Cory's paper begins,

> *In Hawthorne's, "The Birthmark," Aylmer tries everything in his earthly power to improve upon a being that is as close to earthly perfection as possible. It is this relentless pursuit of perfection that ultimately leads to the destruction of Georgiana. The tension premising the story is the rivalry between Aylmer's two loves—the love he has for his wife, Georgiana, and the equal, if not superior love he has for science.*

He goes on to offer several insights into the story, as is evident from the lead sentences to the six paragraphs that make up the body of the paper:

1. Like an artist has passion for his art, Aylmer has passionate [sic] for both his love of his wife and his love of science.
2. Nature is a reoccurring theme throughout the story. As an artist wishes to capture Nature, to mimic it, Aylmer wished to go a step further—to exercise "control over Nature."
3. As a poet is inspired by his muse, Aylmer is inspired by Georgiana.
4. Like an artist, Aylmer sought to create something that will live on eternally, something that would bare his mark, something that would prove that he had once inhabited this earth.
5. Perhaps Hawthorne was using science as a metaphor for art.
6. Perhaps, in some way, Aylmer was Hawthorne. Hawthorne may have been venting his frustrations at not being widely published.

These insights do go beyond plot summary. And they seem to match the two parts of the assignment: one through four are insights into how Hawthorne connects art and science and five and six are insights into what it means for him to do so. But there is no controlling insight. The ideas seem to be randomly ordered and taken together don't lead to an answer to the two main questions posed by the assignment.

But this does not seem to concern the tutor. Michelle, a political science major and one of our brightest and most sought-after tutors, comments, "I just think in each of these [paragraphs] it needs to be expanded a little bit." The two then go through the paper paragraph by paragraph discussing the points she thinks need to be expanded, such as what sort of passion Aylmer has for Georgiana, how an artist seeks to live on through his art, and whether Aylmer's failure results from his not being objective. In several paragraphs, she wants more detail about the artist in general, explaining, "I don't think we have a grip of what an artist is, in order to be able to compare a scientist to an artist." Even when Cory offers Michelle an opportunity to comment on more global concerns, she reassures him that he only needs to expand:

Cory: Take into account this is a first draft and all I did was write down ideas.

Michelle: It still is a good paper.... You're a good writer.... Your ideas, they flow and everything, they all make sense. I just think that they can be explained more.

Both David and Michelle failed to address global problems in their students' papers, but both were working with students who lacked knowledge of how to go about writing literature papers. Was a generalist tutor of more help to a knowledgeable student? Carl, another sophomore in the survey course for English majors, was writing in response to the following assignment: "Going beyond what was said in lecture, discuss androgyny in The Sun Also Rises." His paper begins,

> *The Hemingway man, on the whole, has a preoccupation with death. Once one is dead, one is dead. Therefore, the man must enjoy as many sensual pleasures as possible in his fleeting time on earth. It is this preoccupation that causes him to live life to the fullest. The Hemingway man is an avid lover, drinker, and eater. He enjoys and respects sport for the pure thrill, excitement, and for its intricacies; not necessarily because he is good at it. Where the typical Hemingway man is self-reliant and independent, the woman is passive and vulnerable—a pawn to be manipulated by her environment. She is the antithesis of the male. In The Sun Also Rises, Hemingway creates characters whose genders don't necessarily reflect their sex.*
>
> *In TSAR the ideal man is Pedro Romero. Of all the characters, Romero exemplifies what Hemingway sees as the quintessential man—both inside the ring and out.*

The paper goes on to discuss the male and female characteristics of all the main characters, beginning with Pedro Romero, the "quintessential man," followed by Brett and Jake, who exemplify both male and female character-istics, and ending with Robert Cohn, the "least masculine by Hemingway's standards."

Going beyond plot summary, Carl has classified the characters by the degree to which they're androgynous. He does have a controlling insight, which is supported in an organized and coherent essay. So this draft seems further along than Anna's or Cory's. What help can the generalist tutor provide here?

Jill, a psychology major, notices the lack of coherence between the last sentence of the first paragraph, which states that characters' genders don't reflect their sex, and the second paragraph, which discusses a character whose gender does reflect his sex. To solve this problem, Jill suggests reversing the order of the paragraphs so that Carl discusses the most feminine character (who happens to be a man) first. Carl suggests an even simpler solution; inserting the words "a spectrum" to alert the reader to how he's organized the paper. Carl changes the last sentence of the first paragraph to read: "In The Sun Also Rises Hemingway creates a spectrum of characters whose genders don't necessarily reflect their sex."

Jill and Carl continue to work on the paragraph and sentence levels, addressing such concerns as what aspects of Brett's nature are feminine, whether the paper "flows between characters well," what should be in the conclusion, whether more quotations are needed, and what "vague places" need work on the sentence level. But they ignore the possibility of making more global improvements. Carl's paper shows that there is androgyny in the novel, but this is stated in the assignment. We think most English teachers would expect students to go further, connecting descriptions of technique (the use of androgynous characters) to the meaning, effect, or context of the text. Again, a generalist tutor focused on local rather than global concerns.

Indeed the only tutors who worked successfully on the global level were knowledgeable tutors, as illustrated in the following session between Margaret, a sophomore working on the same Hawthorne assignment as Cory, and Tammi, a senior English major. Margaret's paper begins,

During the period of american renassace [sic] the issue of science and art were a constant issue of ethics, still present today. It was a period of change and breaking from the norm. Today we try and use science as a way of altering or "fixing" nature, those who believe that medicine should prolong the lives of those incapable of sustaining their own lives. Hawthorne, as depicted in The Birthmark connects the meaning of art and science, and expresses his anxiety towards these new ideas and his conflict of whether in order for one to succeed the other must fail.

Rather than working with Margaret's draft, Tammi sets the paper aside after reading a few pages and talks with her about the assignment and the story. Over and over, Tammi brings Margaret back to the two key questions in the assignment, as in the following examples:

- So, if you're choosing "The Birthmark," how does he do it, connect issues of art and science, how does he do it?
- Ok, so the question here is "How does Hawthorne connect art and science in one of these stories?"
- Now if I ask you a question like "How does Hawthorne connect art and science in the story?" Ok, then, what does it mean for him to do it that way?
- So what does it mean then for him to have Aylmer as an artist and as a scientist?

In the following excerpt, Tammi uses questioning and repetition to help Margaret talk through her ideas to the point where she sees that one of her original answers can't be supported by the text:

Tammi: So what does it mean then for him to have Aylmer as an artist and as a scientist?

Margaret: That the two in his personality don't work together.

Tammi: How so?

Margaret: Because they conflict each other.

Tammi: How?

Margaret: Because in order for one to succeed.

Tammi: OK, for the scientist to succeed and to make.

Margaret: For him to be a good scientist.

Tammi: To be a good scientist, yes.

Margaret: The art part has to fail and to be bad.

Tammi: Why?

Margaret: Because, because what he created failed, it died.

Tammi: Oh, so for him to create the scientific purity, Georgiana without the birthmark.

Margaret: Right, he created her.

Tammi: He finishes his scientific project, he's made her.

Margaret: Perfect in his eyes.

Tammi: Perfect in his eyes.

Margaret: Then he ends up failing anyway because now he doesn't have her anymore.

Tammi: Ok so now we've discussed his role as scientist. How is that.

Margaret: I guess he doesn't fail as an artist.

By responding to Tammi's questions, Margaret ends up completely changing her answers to the assignment questions. Rather than saying Hawthorne connects art and science through nature, she concludes they're connected in the person of Aylmer. And rather than saying for one (art or science) to succeed, the other must fail, she concludes that Aylmer succeeds as both an artist and as a scientist, but at the cost of life itself.

Tammi, an English major, is able to assess how well Margaret's insights are supported, is confident enough to put Margaret's paper aside and turn to looking at the text with her, and knows what questions to ask to help Margaret reach new insights that can be supported using evidence from the text. Tammi knows not only what the disciplinary conventions are but also what process produces a paper that follows them. This is the process Margaret needs to learn to write other English papers. It makes sense for Tammi and Margaret to work on these higher-level thinking skills before turning to the other problems evident in her introduction, such as word choice and sentence structure.

We found, however, that the tutor's familiarity with the conventions of the discipline doesn't guarantee a good session. When Sandy, who is working on a Yeats paper for the survey class, meets with Joanne, an English major who has taken the same course with the same teachers, it leads to just what Susan Hubbuch is concerned about: the knowledgeable tutor taking an "authoritative stance" (26), thinking of "writing in terms of the final product" (29), and so, in Joanne's case, focusing on correcting the student's paper in order to help her get a better grade. Joanne begins by reading through the paper and making corrections. Within the first few minutes she adds some quotation marks, changes "onto" to "unto," underlines some repeated words, and corrects some spelling errors. She notes a sentence fragment and rewords to correct it. At one point Sandy asks the tutor to please use pencil rather than pen in case she decides not to make the changes.

In addition to editing the paper, Joanne insists on some specific changes in the ideas. As she reads along, she comes to the idea that "Yeats turns to religion and everlasting art." She stops and suggests a different relationship between the two ideas: "Or does he turn to everlasting art as a religion!" Sandy responds, "I thought that but then [I noticed] how he made the reference to God." Joanne continues to defend her interpretation concluding, "I think that the interconnection of art there with religion—sort of that God has to do with the creation of eternal art, that whole idea—I think you can safely connect those.... You can say he turns to everlasting art as a religion."

Is Joanne tempted to do too much because she knows so much? While making her corrections on Sandy's paper, Joanne explains, "I took this course, and I can't overemphasize the importance of a clean copy." We don't believe Joanne typically took an authoritative stance: there were no red flags in her journal, her lognotes, or her mock tutoring sessions to suggest she did.

We know we can't reach conclusions based on this small number of cases, but in the sessions we looked at, the tutor's knowledge of how to think and write in the discipline did seem important. Good tutoring strategies alone were not enough. All of the tutors were trained to address global before local concerns, to use questioning to draw out a student's ideas, to refrain from appropriating the student's paper. All of them had had numerous sessions with students in introductory writing courses in which they had successfully demonstrated these strategies. But David, Michelle, and Jill seem unable to apply them when working with students on assignments that require knowledge of a discipline other than their own. And Joanne, in her eagerness to use her knowledge, seems to forget her general tutoring strategies.

We began this project knowing that conventions differ from discipline to discipline and wondering whether tutors need to know these conventions to tutor effectively. Looking closely at these sessions suggested that tutors who don't know how to go through the process of writing a paper in a discipline may be limited in what they can accomplish, and that tutors who do know this process may be tempted to appropriate the student's paper. If more research supports these conclusions, what would be the implications for writing centers?

The most significant implication would be that students writing papers for upper level course would be best served by carefully trained tutors with knowledge of the discipline. If this is true, should writing centers try to provide such tutors? One method would be to match upper-level students with trained tutors from the discipline. But matching in a drop-in lab seems unwieldy, though it might be possible for special projects involving either classes. Another method would be to turn our generalist tutors into knowledgeable tutors through a series of training sessions on writing across the curriculum, as suggested by Leone Scanlon. But would brief training sessions enable more sessions like Tammi's to occur? Tammi's work with Margaret makes us question this assumption. We could perhaps describe some of the disciplinary conventions in an hour or two but would this enable tutors to help students write papers that follow them? In the case of literature papers, wouldn't students outside the discipline need to go through the process themselves, need to learn how to ask questions, analyze, and interpret a text? Doing this for several disciplines would be impossible in a one-semester course. Still, it remains a possibility when a writing center knows a group of students will be coming from a certain discipline. For example, because we have so many students working on literature papers, we now not only have English professors come talk to the tutors about their expectations for such papers but also have all of the tutors write a critical analysis of a text, so that they go through the process of thinking in the discipline.

If we can't ensure that students writing for upper-level courses can meet with a knowledgeable tutor, should we be alarmed about relying on generalist tutors? We think not. First of all, in many of our sessions the tutors don't need to be more than generalists. About 70 percent of our sessions are over papers for composition classes, papers usually written to a general audience. And some upper-level students are sent to the writing center with papers written for a lay audience, such as an engineer's position paper on an environmental issue.

Second, it's hard to be alarmed when students leave pleased with their experience and enthusiastic about working further on their papers. All of the above students rated their session 5 on a scale of 1 to 5 (1 = not successful, 5 = very successful). all answered "very satisfied" to the question concerning the choices made about what to work on in the session, and all said they left with a clear idea of what to work on next. We feel that if students leave satisfied and motivated, they have benefited. A session that is less than it could be is not by definition a bad session.

Third, it doesn't seem fair to place on our tutors' shoulders the responsibility for showing students how to think and write in the disciplines. It doesn't even seem fair to place learning this on the student writers' shoulders. Isn't this the responsibility of the departments? Indeed, when we see many students lacking knowledge of the process for writing within a discipline (though the students and tutors might not be aware of this lack), perhaps as directors we should go back to the department. In our case, we could share with our English faculty what we've learned about the difficulties some of their students are having, which might lead to a discussion of how writing in the discipline is being taught. Thus we have an opportunity to take up the charge given to writing centers by Nancy Grimm in her talk at the 1992 Conference on College Composition and Communication: to take what we have learned from working with students back to the academy.

WORKS CITED

Grimm, Nancy M. "Contesting 'The Idea of a Writing Center': The Politics of Writing Center Research." Conference on College Composition and Communication, Cincinnati, 21 March 1992.

Haviland, Carol Peterson. "Writing Centers and Writing-Across-the-Curriculum: An Important Connection." The Writing Center Journal 5.2 (1985): 25–30.

Hubbuch, Susan. "A Tutor Needs to Know the Subject Matter to Help a Student with a Paper: ___ Agree ___ Disagree ___ Not Sure." The Writing Center Journal 8.2 (1988): 23–30.

Luce, Henry. "On Selecting Peer Tutors: Let's Hear It For Heterogeneity." Writing Lab Newsletter May 1986: 3–5.

Scanlon, Leone. "Recruiting and Training Tutors for Cross-Disciplinary Writing Programs." The Writing Center Journal 6.2 (1986): 37–41.

Smith, Louise Z. "Independence and Collaboration: Why We Should Decentralize Writing Centers." The Writing Center Journal 7.1 (1986): 3–10.

Collaboration Is Not Collaboration Is Not Collaboration: Writing Center Tutorials vs. Peer-Response Groups 1992

Muriel Harris

Collaboration, a process writers engage in and teachers facilitate, is firmly entrenched in our thinking about the teaching of writing. But the term is also used as a blanket tossed over a variety of activities that are not identical, thereby blurring useful distinctions. "I don't use the Writing Lab," a composition teacher told me recently, "because I have peer-response groups in my classroom." To a degree she is correct in seeing some overlap. Both tutoring and response groups are student-centered approaches that rely on collaboration as a powerful learning tool—to promote interaction between reader and writer, to promote dialogue and negotiation, and to heighten writers' sense of audience. In addition, both move the student from the traditional passive stance of receiving knowledge from an authority to an active involvement which makes talk integral to writing. Yet tutorials and response groups, though collaborative in their approaches, also have different underlying perspectives, assumptions, and goals. Moreover, tutors, unlike peer readers, are trained to use methods that lead to results very different from the outcome of response groups. Clearly, these different forms of collaboration should not be conflated.

My purpose here is to examine the differences and, because I work in a writing center, also to help those outside the center appreciate what tutoring can offer. But first, we need to disentangle these forms of collaborative learning from what is more appropriately termed collaborative writing. Although there has been some confusion in the use of "collaboration" to refer both to collaborative writing and collaborative learning about writing, collaborative

Harris, Muriel. "Collaboration Is Not Collaboration Is Not Collaboration: Writing Center Tutorials vs. Peer-Response Groups." *College Composition and Communication* 43.3 (1992): 369–383. Copyright 1992 by the National Council of Teachers of English. Reprinted with permission.

writing is now identified as writing involving two or more writers working together to produce a joint product. When writing collaboratively, each may take responsibility for a different portion of the final text, and there may be group consensus or some sort of collective responsibility for the final product. When there is shared decision-making power and responsibility for a text, Nancy Allen and her co-authors use the term "shared document collaboration." Lisa Ede and Andrea Lunsford describe their collaborative writing as "co-authorship," a melding process by which they create one text together, discovering and thinking through ideas together, talking through sections together, and writing drafts together.

Collaborative writing thus refers to products of multiple authors while collaboratively learning about writing involves interaction between writer and reader to help the writer improve her own abilities and produce her own text—though, of course, her final product is influenced by the collaboration with others. Instructors who are suspicious of writing-center tutorials because they assume tutors help write the papers fail to see the distinction between multiple authorship collaboration—where there are joint decisions—and collaboration in learning about writing—where one writer claims ownership and makes all final decisions. But more subtle are the differences between collaboration in tutorials and collaboration in response groups. Like oranges and apples, tutorial and peer-group collaboration are the same but different, and we need to know more about what to expect when we group students together in a classroom and when we refer them to the writing center. We also need to see how to prepare for each because without adequate preparation of tutors and response groups, successful collaboration isn't likely to happen spontaneously.

A BRIEF HISTORY OF RESPONSE GROUPS AND WRITING TUTORIALS

Response groups, as Anne Ruggles Gere has noted in her extensive study, *Writing Groups: History, Theory, and Implications*, have existed in various forms for over two hundred years but have recently gained new status. While Gere differentiates various forms of writing groups by the locus and degree of authority from within or outside the group, the collaborative effort of responding to writing can also be viewed as varying from informal to more formally structured or institutionalized ways. From this perspective, perhaps the least studied of the widespread uses of collaboration in writing groups is that informal network of assistance and support that goes on in residence halls, study rooms, coffee shops, libraries, and faculty offices—where peers help each other by reading each other's drafts when asked. Faculty who recognize the value of such assistance from their colleagues tend to offer credit and graceful notes of appreciation in journal articles and books. Students, however, tend to downplay public recognition of informal collaboration, fearing that it somehow diminishes the effort expected of them. Thus, while students value the help they get, they too often overlook the importance of the reader-writer interaction that has occurred. The nature of this informal collaboration among students also varies widely. When interviewing prospective tutors about their peer-group experience, I hear them describe their efforts either as editorial work ("When someone learns that I got A's in comp classes, they drop by my room before a paper is due and ask me to check for grammar and stuff") or as reader response ("My roommate gives me his papers and I tell him what I think is clear and what isn't"). In either case, this collaboration is closer to tutoring, in that there is likely to be an implicit recognition that the reader is either as skilled or more skilled than the writer and that the focus of the collaboration is on the writer.

Tutorial collaboration in writing centers has a more recent history than writing groups, though it too has evolved from earlier conceptions, in this case conceptions of what tutors should and could do. When the literacy-crisis awareness of the 1970s coincided with great waves of open admissions, teachers and administrators sensed the need for tutorial assistance, in the traditional sense of the more knowledgeable helping the less knowledgeable. Emphasis on competency testing and formalist approaches that stressed surface-error correctness in written products reinforced the notion of establishing centers where students could learn how to correct the fragments and comma splices that littered their pages. But despite those limited notions of what writing tutors should do and because composition theory and practice were making the great shift to a process orientation, it quickly became evident that tutors were offering their students a great deal more than a place to review apostrophe rules.

Articles on writing center theory in books and in publications such as the *Writing Center Journal* and the *Writing Lab Newsletter*, training manuals for tutors, and those hundreds of reports writing center directors write every year for administrators all arrest to the widely-accepted view that tutoring in writing is a collaborative effort in which the tutor listens, questions, and sometimes offers informed advice about all aspects of the student's writing in order to help the writer become a better writer, not to fix whatever particular paper the student has brought to the center. Thus, even though a specific paper may be the subject of discussion, the tutor is always cautioned to work more broadly toward strengthening the writer's skills in ways that will carry over to future writing. The tutor's role ranges among a variety of tasks: offering reader response, leading the student toward finding her own answers, suggesting strategies to try, diagnosing possible underlying problems, listening while the student articulates her message, and offering needed support during the composing struggle. To do all this, tutors must be selected and trained and, in the process, become a hybrid creation—neither a teacher nor a peer. The tutor's job is to help writers move beyond requests for someone to "proofread" or "fix" their papers.

DETERMINING THE GOALS

Like tutoring, peer response has well-articulated goals. Anne Ruggles Gere and Robert Abbott, reviewing published statements on peer response, list its effectiveness in improving critical thinking, organization, and appropriateness of writing; improving usage; increasing the amount of revision; and reducing apprehension. Gere and Abbott also note that teachers endorse peer response because it develops a better sense of audience, reduces paper grading, exposes students to a variety of writing styles, motivates them to revise, and develops a sense of community. In addition, Carol Berkenkotter's list of the benefits of peer response includes the experience of writing and revising for less threatening audiences than the teacher, of learning to discriminate between useful and non-useful feedback, and of learning to use awareness of anticipated audience responses as writers revise. Adding to this list, Richard Gebhardt notes the ability of peers to offer each other needed emotional support. And Karen Spear notes that peers offer each other feedback which contributes to the evolution of ideas, that peer response makes the audience real, and that sharing drafts helps to shape and test thought, to extend the invention process. At the very least, says Spear, students should "become responsible for editing, proofreading, and correcting their peers' texts" (5).

The kind of editorial work that Spear mentions can be valuable for students, in that it helps them learn the difficult art of proofreading their own papers, but there is an underlying assumption here that helping someone name or locate an error ("I think you need a comma before that word" or "You ought to have a transition there") is sufficient. Sometimes this is the case, and such peer response alerts writers to more careful proofreading as well as to considerations they need to keep in mind. But we have to leave to the tutorial any instructional assistance in learning why there is an error, how it should be corrected, and what the student needs to know for the future. The goal of a tutorial might be to help the student identify a few of the most commonly recurring problems and to set up some sequence of meetings that would aim at helping the student generalize the concept for future writing.

Peer responders, on the other hand, are not normally asked to move into the questioning and explaining stage as tutors are. Instead, peer readers critique a draft of an assignment that all members of the group are working on. This keeps the discussion focused on specific drafts, though one of the larger goals is still to improve the skill of critical response by this kind of repetition. The assumption is that the more the student reads and responds, the more her critical skills improve. The more the writer hears reader response, the stronger his sense of audience will be. While these kinds of skill building by repetition happen in peer response groups, tutorials do not normally aim at providing the student with practice in critical reading of texts composed by other writers. (Tutors, of course, get a great deal of practice in critical reading of texts of others, though that is not the tutor's purpose for working with the student.) Instead, as Stephen North reminds us, the paper the student brings in to the writing center is only the medium for discussion because, as North explains to his tutors, "our job is to produce better writers, not just better writing" (439). This, notes Jeff Brooks, is the central difficulty tutors must confront, because "we sit down with imperfect papers, but our job is to improve their writers" (2). The struggle, as any tutor can confirm, is that we have to squelch our editorial urge to tinker with that paper and our human urge to help that writer sitting next to us turn in a better product. Instead, the tutor must focus on general writing skills. To do so, tutorial conversation may also deal with the writer's anxiety, poor motivation, cultural confusions, ineffective or dysfunctional composing strategies, lack of knowledge, or inability to follow assignment directions. Tutors can also achieve their goals by touching upon the specific paper very minimally; the peer responder, however, would be remiss if he offered only minimal response to the paper.

Peer response also tends to have a different time frame than tutorials. In one or two sessions, all the members of the response group usually have their turns at hearing the responses of their peers. Then they are done until convened again for the next assignment. Often, tutors also meet with students in a cyclical fashion tied to the completion of specific assignments, but with the student's cooperation or assent (or the teacher's urging), the tutor can propose a sequence of several sessions to tackle a specific topic. Or the tutor and student can meet for weeks to work on mastering one or more higher-level skills. For example, Matthew-Livesey, a peer tutor, describes his work with one student as an ongoing effort to have her learn how to anticipate her readers' questions. While the goal of the tutor and the members of the peer-response group is the same, in that all are working toward more effective writing abilities and heightened awareness of general writing concerns, tutors are free to roam through the seemingly infinite variety of problems that every less-than-perfect writer might have and to choose a specific goal that is different for every writer. Hence, writing tutorials are highly individualized since each student can ask whatever questions are on her mind, talk about whatever possibilities she is considering, or linger over problems she sees; and tutors can explore a variety of sources to tap for solutions and strategies that will help that particular student.

The emphasis on general skills in response groups rather than individualized concerns in tutorials also explains why the collaboration is different in each setting. In the response group, there is back-and-forth conversation intended to offer mutual help as writing groups work together in a give-and-take relationship. Generally, all are expected to benefit both from the responses they receive about their writing and from the practice they get as critical readers of the discourse of other writers. In tutorial collaboration, however, students are asked only to respond to their own texts. That is, a tutor might initially ask questions such as the following: "What did you like most about the paper? What do you think needs revision? What would you like to work on in this paper?" If the student has no suggestions to offer, then the tutor is the primary critical reader of the text. The focus of the effort and attention of both people is solely on the writer. The intense amount of personalizing that takes place in tutorials occurs only because there is an overt recognition that the writer's concerns will dominate the interaction.

SETTING THE AGENDA FOR COLLABORATION

The agenda for tutorial interaction is set differently than in response groups. In Peter Elbow's teacherless classrooms, groups set their own agendas for what will be accomplished. Classrooms with teachers operate a bit differently, for as Harvey Weiner notes, the teacher's role is to structure the setting, assign the task, and then disappear. And the students' responsibility is to help each other and to use whatever they have learned to improve their own papers. While there is variation in the degree to which teachers or groups structure the setting and the specific tasks, response groups generally move forward after achieving consensus about what they will do together. The goals negotiated in the student-tutor session may also be a result of consensus, but more often there are multiple goals reached through several levels of compromise. In a tutorial, tension exists when the writer wants to improve the paper she brought in or successfully complete the assignment she has been given and the tutor wants to improve the writer. Thus, the student may want feedback on all aspects of the paper ("Is the conclusion OK?" or "Are my sentences too choppy?"), while the tutor wants to focus on one or two topics and deal with them until the student is more confident in that area. In such cases, tutors and their students have to negotiate some middle ground in which the discussion can proceed, but tutors too often feel—and strain against—the tug of the student's desire to get this particular paper finished and handed in. Or students come to tutorials with goals that are too limited because they are firmly convinced that the paper will be acceptable if the spelling is checked or the introductory paragraph begins with a snappy sentence or if they can stretch the length by another fifty to one hundred words.

Tutorial negotiation becomes even more complex when the tutor and student also include the teacher's suggestions in the agenda-setting conversation.

Tutors are expected to include the teacher's preferences for the agenda, even when the teacher's list doesn't overlap very much with the tutor's or the student's goals. For example, a student may come to the writing center with the teacher's recommendation that he needs to learn how to define a focus for his essays. But the student has a draft in hand and wants to know if it meets the assignment (not how well it achieves its purpose, but a basic need to know, for instance, if the paper is an expressive essay) or if it "flows"—two very frequent student requests—and the tutor may hear in the initial conversation with the student so much hostility, indifference, or anxiety that the tutor needs to backtrack and deal with that. Because consensus is unlikely to occur in such a situation, the collaborative effort becomes one of either working on several matters simultaneously ("multi-tasking," in the argot of the world of computers), or agreeing to tackle some matters first and delay others, perhaps to later meetings.

By comparison, the agenda of the students in a response group is usually to read and respond to each other's writing—the response taking various forms, as determined by the teacher. One widely-used approach employs structured response sheets, though some teachers oppose such sheets because they inhibit response (Benesch, Grimm). Another approach is to have each reader write down a response to each paper, though Joan Wauters counsels against structured response as too confrontational. Behind such differences, the underlying similarity in peer-group work is an assumption that in the give-and-take of discussing specific drafts, writers can offer each other evaluative responses or suggestions for revision while sharpening their own critical reading skills. While Karen Spear's book on peer-response groups does suggest ways to take groups through generating ideas, much peer-response work focuses on drafts. When Anne Ruggles Gere and Ralph S. Stevens studied peer-response groups to see what they actually do, they found that "students in writing groups tell authors what they think the language [in their drafts] says, they ask questions about the places which confuse them, and they suggest ways for the writing to do its job better" (97).

Writers working with tutors also come in for revision help, but it is equally common for writers to come in at other stages of composing (e.g., searching for a topic, trying to narrow it, doing some verbal planning, attempting to organize wads of notes into longer papers, or finishing a draft by working out an introduction or conclusion). While writing groups usually focus on whole papers, tutors are often asked by students to focus only on specific sections or parts that seem weak or underdeveloped. Despite the seemingly paper-specific tasks that may dominate a tutorial, the tutor's task is still primarily to help the student with the larger abilities involved. Thus a discussion about a weak or non-existent introduction in a specific paper should also be about the broader subject of how to write introductions.

METHODS

Because the tutor is expected to individualize, the tutor needs the time and the appropriate methods to find out what a particular writer's needs and interests are. Here the tutor has an advantage over the teacher who most often works alone at her desk using clues on the page—a product-oriented method—to identify the writer's strengths and weaknesses. The tutor, with the student sitting next to her, can ask questions, engage in conversation, listen, ask more questions, offer support, and ask a few more questions. Tutors can rely on questions as much or more than evidence in the paper. Thus, successful question-asking and listening are skills that are heavily stressed in manuals for writing tutors (Arkin and Shollar; B. Clark; I. Clark; Harris, *Teaching;* Meyer and Smith). I've found one of the tutor's best questions to be "Why did you do that?" because, when students answer, they so often help tutors see what is needed or lacking. For example, when a student says that a particular type of support for an argument is there because that's all she could think of, the tutor hears something useful about the need for work on invention. Another powerful question in the tutorial is "How did you write this paper?" Tutors hear about some of the student's *writing methods and strategies, and this information can help them decide where the conversation should go next.*

Tutors are likely to get both honest answers and honest questions from students (usually preceded by "I know this is a dumb question, but...") because the tutor has the unique advantage of being both a nonjudgmental, nonevaluative helper—a collaborator in whom the writer can confide—and a skilled colleague, one whom the writer trusts as someone reasonably knowledgeable. As such, the tutor can encourage open discussion about a variety of problems that may be affecting the writer's writing. It might take almost a semester to find that a writer is making no progress because she has become defeated by her teacher's responses to her papers (see Weller), or 15 minutes to discover that the writer has only vague ideas about how to tackle an essay on cultural criticism or that she thinks she has to have her topic sentence in mind before writing a draft. I often find the real problem is that the writer just doesn't understand the assignment and is wallowing in confusion. Tutors must also be skilled enough to notice text features that are inappropriate; uncover student assumptions that prevent further learning (Harris, "Contradictory"; Rose); recognize the need to work with different learning styles; deal with the different discourse communities for which students write (e.g., the various academic disciplines); recognize the difficulties of writers coming from cultures with discourse conventions different than the ones they are writing for; and help with attitudinal problems, emotional difficulties, writing anxiety, lack of confidence, and other affective concerns. Tutors trained in a variety of diagnostic procedures can, in addition to questioning and listening,

try methods such as observing writers as they write or taking writing protocols (Harris, "Diagnosing") or using personality preference tests, such as the
Myers-Briggs Type Inventory (Jensen and DiTiberio; Maid et al.).

The methods tutors use for uncovering writing problems or incom-
pletely-articulated questions aren't generally suggested for peer-response
groups because individualizing is not a major goal of peer response. Instead,
peer response is intended to build a generally-heightened awareness of readers and critical reading skills. Teachers who structure response sheets may
vary the sheets somewhat according to the assignment, but generally groups
become more proficient at their tasks by doing them over and over, learning
not only how to respond as they practice response but also how to function
as a group. In one study of what response groups actually do, Anne Ruggles
Gere and Robert Abbott observed that peer response proceeds primarily by
directive comments. The most frequent idea units were expressed in comments about the content of a writing (e.g., "This part doesn't fit in because
there is nothing about it earlier in the story") or about writing processes (e.g.,
"Okay, write one more sentence"). Other studies of what occurs during peer
response are similar in that they report categories of comments. For example,
Marion Crowhurst notes that the responses of the fifth-graders she studied
generally fell into three categories: encouraging comments ("I like the part
where...") comments on content ("Some places don't seem realistic"), and
suggestions for improvement ("Maybe you could add more at the end...")
Francine Davis's analysis of peer-response groups indicated four kinds of
verbal activity: asking questions, proposing suggestions for revision, agreeing or disagreeing with the recommendations of peers, and explaining intentions about stylistic choices.

These categories of response-group comments also help to differentiate
group work from tutorials, in that tutors are discouraged from making such
directive comments. Training manuals consistently emphasize the tutor's
role in helping the writer to find her own answers, in guiding the student by
questioning rather than by telling or explaining. For example, here is the first
instructional guideline in Arkin and Shollar's *The Tutor Book*:

> *Guide your tutee toward doing his or her own work. Get the student as
> actively involved in the learning process as possible. Do not do the work for
> the student (for example, write a paper, solve a problem). (17)*

Similarly, Beverly Lyon Clark cautions that the tutor "should not make corrections but help the tutee to correct and improve herself" (110). Meyer and Smith
also advise tutors about their nondirective role: "You can help a writer elaborate and refine ideas by asking thoughtful, specific questions. This practice is
preferable to supplying answers, offering evaluations, or giving general ad-

vice, because it encourages the writer to do the thinking" (37). The emphasis on helping the writer to do her own work is, says Stephen North, a matter of asking "'How are you going to get from here to there?' instead of 'Here's how you get from here to there'" (439). Unlike peer response then, which emphasizes informing, tutorials emphasize the student's own discovery.

A tutor who frequently tells students what to do is not a particularly effective or appropriate tutor, but a writing group member offering "try this/try that" comments is developing the ability to find revising solutions for a draft in progress at the same time that the writer is developing the ability to weigh possibilities. Response-group work is closer to the joint authorship that goes on in collaborative writing. And, since real-world writing is often collaborative writing, peer-response groups are also closer to what writers may find themselves doing in their jobs.

SOME CAUTIONARY REMINDERS

When considering the potential benefits of peer-response groups and tutoring, we also need to look at the problems that seem to trail along with them. Peer response, having been the subject of numerous studies, has a track record of conflicting results. While Ronnie Carter's study showed no noticeable effects on student writing, there have been reports that peer evaluation is as effective as teacher evaluation (Beaven); that peer response results in a better sense of audience (Glassner; Kantor); that there are measurably better gains in writing proficiency when students work in response groups (Clifford; Karegianes et al.); and that, although students tend to make little use of comments in their revisions in the early stages, they do learn over time how to interact and how to be good critics (Ziv). But Karen Spear also notes the gap between the theory, with its powerful potential for having students share thoughts and drafts, and the practice, in which teachers "often regard group work with anything from mild reservation to outright frustration" (v). Carol Berkenkotter's three case studies remind us that students who write for peer readers as well as teachers "might not necessarily reap the advantages we'd like to imagine" (318); one student in Berkenkotter's study was unable to respond positively to feedback he received and was unable to give constructive suggestions, another student gained no help from her peers, and the third student experienced some loss of confidence because of peer comments before she finally regained control of her writing. Other studies also remind us that students may not be immediately ready to be competent critics. For example, the students in Elizabeth Flynn's study seemed unable to recognize the substantive but less blatant problems in the essays they read, looking instead for surface errors or minor problems. Flynn emphasizes the need for training:

The reading histories of most of our students make it unlikely that they will suddenly and automatically become good readers of their classmates' essays. They must be trained to recognize incoherence, and the training must be rigorous enough to counter their conditioned expectations about the nature of written texts. (127)

Similarly, Diana George observed that her peer-response groups had trouble reading each other's essays helpfully. Moreover, in George's study there was evidence that some groups failed to interact successfully and that much of what was said was lost because writers failed to assimilate suggestions. Some of this failure to interact may result from lack of training in group skills, but peer pressure can cause students to withhold negative comments, a case of what Jane Brown aptly calls the "unwritten code based on mutual protection [which] will inhibit honest, productive evaluation" (48). I hear echoes of these research studies when I talk with students in tutorials or interview applicants for peer tutoring. Some students dismiss peer responses because they question the skills of the person offering the advice, because the group never gets beyond the level of "The paper's OK" or "You misspelled a word," or because they too feel the peer pressure not to embarrass each other. On the other hand, some writers come to our Writing Lab determined to work on the group's suggestions or apply to be tutors because their peer-group work has gotten them excited about talking about writing.

Since it takes time for students' skills in critiquing to mature, no one should expect immediate successes with peer groups. But Thomas Newkirk also raises another problem, for a study of his showed that students and instructors frequently use different criteria for judging student work. "For this reason," Newkirk points out, "the two groups might profitably be viewed as distinct evaluative communities" (309). If students evaluate writing with one set of standards and teachers evaluate with another, as Newkirk's study suggests, then students may likely be reinforcing each others abilities to write discourse for their peers, not for the academy—a sticky problem indeed, especially when teachers suggest that an appropriate audience for a particular paper might be the class itself.

Even stickier is a related problem in tutoring. Tutors are supposed to be trained to be better acquainted with the conventions of academic discourse than students in peer-response groups, but the more skilled tutors are, the further they are from being peers in a collaborative relationship. Students who see the tutor as a knowledgeable insider (i.e., someone who can tell them what to do) want answers from the tutor, and a common problem tutors face is straining against telling students what to do. Students ask questions that seek specific answers (for example, "What should I put here?"—a question every tutor hears frequently), and students can become frustrated, even angry, when their questions are met with more questions, not answers.

The collaborative relationship that the tutor has attempted to establish may easily break down in this situation. Jeff Brooks's answer is to move to what he describes as "minimalist tutoring" in order to shift the responsibility back to the student. Though the tutor may be successful in helping the student find her own answers, a problem that persists in all writing centers is that too many students continue to come in for the wrong reasons, because they recognize that tutors are more than merely peers. "Can someone fix my paper?" is a request that reverberates against the walls of every writing center, every semester, despite constant attempts by writing center directors to educate students in what to expect in the center. It is a conflict writing centers are likely to be forever saddled with: tutors must be skilled to perform their work, and students know that skilled readers can give them the answers they want. After all, that's why they came to the writing center in the first place—to get expert help. Maintaining a stance of collaboration rather than co-authorship in the tutorial is a constant struggle—and it can disappoint the student. On an evaluation form a student filled out after a tutorial session with me, he rated me as "not very effective" because, he explained, "she just sat there while I had to find my own answers."

A different problem is that inadequately trained tutors have a number of counterproductive tendencies. As Mary Dossin describes them, such tutors are prone to tackling the obvious kinds of surface errors instead of more substantive issues (a tendency similarly noted by Flynn in some peer-response groups); they tend to talk too much and overwhelm the writer; and they are likely to "act like detectives assigned to ferret out all the errors they can spot" (11), thereby hindering the writer from taking control of her own writing. So a tutor must be trained to be more than a peer who happens to be sitting in the writing center. But the tutor cannot move too far toward the position of a teacher because, as Mary Broglie vividly illustrates, tutors are not teachers who have shifted their chairs to the writing center. Broglie argues that the tutor, unlike the teacher, is neither the authority in charge who gives directions and determines what will happen nor an evaluator who indicates where a paper met or failed to meet acceptable criteria. A tutor may assess what the writer should work on, but statements such as "You need to organize this paragraph" or "Your conclusion isn't logical" aren't appropriate comments from a tutor. Tutors too far down the road toward "teacherhood" are no longer sympathetic, supportive helpers, sensitive to the needs of fellow students whose world isn't very far removed from that of the tutor. I was vividly reminded of how useful it is for tutors to draw from their own experience as students when I overheard one of our Writing Lab tutors vigorously questioning a student before she returned to the library for more research on a political science paper. Why, I wondered, was the tutor so busily asking the student what headings, key words, and terms the student would use in her search? The tutor later explained that he recognized a tendency he shares—to become so intimidated by all the resources that all one can do is wheel-spin, frantically noting every possible topic and source that might be remotely related to the paper. "I wanted her to have a shopping list so she wouldn't check out everything in the *Readers' Guide*," the tutor explained. Good tutors must be fellow learners as well as fellow writers. Experienced teachers know this, but new tutors anxious to prove their credentials can—unless reminded—try too hard to cast aside their "studentness" and play the all-knowing professional.

The tutor, then, is a hybrid, somewhere between a peer and a teacher, who cannot lean too much one way or the other. Suspended with a foot in each discourse community, tutors perform a valuable service for their students. Since tutors speak with words students recognize and understand, they act as interpreters for those bewildered by the critical vocabulary of teachers. But this sensitivity to what students are unable to understand can become dulled if the tutor, enamored of the jargon of the field, moves too far into the teacher's world. John Trimbur describes new tutors as often "caught in the middle, suspended in a no-man's land between the faculty and the students" (23). Tutoring, continues Trimbur, is a balancing act that asks tutors to juggle roles, to shift identity, and to know when to act like an expert and when to act like a co-learner. Those of us who train peer tutors frequently have to remind over-enthusiastic novices, delighted with their newly expanded vocabulary, that we can talk about "heuristics" and "restrictive clauses" and "cohesion" in our training group but that these are not words to sprinkle into tutorial talk.

A somewhat different problem—one shared by teachers who promote peer response and by those who work in writing centers—is the marginalizing of this kind of pedagogy. The problem in the writing center is explained by Virginia Perdue and Deborah James:

> The teaching in writing centers runs counter to the conventional notion of teaching: students, not teachers, set the agenda; the tutor responds and suggests rather than directs. The student may or may not take the suggestions, and for that matter, may not return for another session. And of course, there are no grades or evaluations. Because the teaching that occurs in writing centers is often informal, collaborative, and egalitarian, it is invisible. And this invisibility makes writing centers vulnerable to uncertain budgets, staffing, and locations, but most importantly, vulnerable to misunderstanding that marginalizes writing centers not just within our home institutions, but even within our departments' writing programs. (7)

This marginalizing also creeps in when writing center directors are reviewed for promotion and tenure. I have yet to convince one of my colleagues that I fulfill part of my teaching obligation to the department when I tutor. Classroom teachers who use peer-response groups are equally prone to being marginalized because their teaching has a similar kind of invisibility. The work of preparing, structuring, and monitoring groups is overlooked by people who see the teacher as someone who puts students in groups and then spends her time staring out the window.

This reminder of shared problems brings us back to the ways in which tutoring and peer response are similar, for we recognize that they share a commitment to the collaborative, interactive talk that helps writers return to their writing with a better sense of where to go next and how to do it. When working well, both forms of collaboration should keep the student active and in control of her own writing, but neither tutoring nor peer response precludes the other. Tutoring offers the student individualized help over a broad spectrum of writing skills and problems, help which includes instruction of a kind often available only in the personalized, collaborative, nonjudgmental environment of a tutorial. And because the tutor is a skilled responder, the response time is spent more productively than is possible in group work until students learn how to respond. But tutors can also create confusion for writers when they intrude with criteria different from the teacher's. An advantage of peer response, therefore, is that it is done in the context of course guidelines. In peer groups, students also read a variety of other responses to an assignment and they get a lot of practice in responding. But to be productive, peer response requires that class time be spent in developing group skills and in learning how to offer and receive responses.

Given the advantages and disadvantages of tutoring and group work, then, there is indeed a solid argument to be made for helping our students experience and reap the benefits of both forms of collaboration.

WORKS CITED

Allen, Nancy, Dianne Atkinson, Meg Morgan, Teresa Moore, and Craig Snow. "What Experienced Collaborators Say About Collaborative Writing." *Journal of Business and Technical Communication* 1.2 (Sept. 1987): 70–90.

Arkin, Marian, and Barbara Shollar. *The Tutor Book.* New York: Longman, 1982.

Beaven, Mary. "Individualized Goal Setting, Self-Evaluation, and Peer Evaluation." *Evaluating Writing, Describing, Measuring, Judging.* Ed. Charles Cooper and Lee Odell. Urbana: NCTE. 1977. 135–56.

Benesch, Sarah. *Improving Peer Response: Collaboration Between Teachers and Students.* ERIC, 1984. ED 243 113.

Berkenkotter, Carol. "Student Writers and Their Sense of Authority over Texts." *College Composition and Communication* 35 (Oct. 1984): 312–19.

Broglie, Mary. "From Teacher to Tutor: Making the Change." *Writing Lab Newsletter* 15.4 (Dec. 1990): 1–3.

Brooks, Jeff. "Minimalist Tutoring: Making the Student Do All the Work." *Writing Lab Newsletter* 15.6 (Feb. 1991): 1–4.

Brown, Jane. "Helping Students Help Themselves: Peer Evaluation of Writing." *Curriculum Review* 23 (Feb. 1984): 47–50.

Carter, Ronnie. *By Itself Peer Group Revision Has No Power.* ERIC, 1982. ED 226 350.

Clark, Beverly Lyon. *Talking about Writing.* Ann Arbor: U of Michigan, P., 1985.

Clark, Irene. *Writing in the Center: Teaching in a Writing Center Setting.* Dubuque: Kendall/Hunt, 1985.

Clifford, John. "Composing in Stages: The Effects of a Collaborative Pedagogy." *Research in the Teaching of English,* 15 (Feb. 1981): 37–53,

Crowhurst, Marion. "The Writing Workshop: An Experiment in Peer Response to Writing." *Language Arts* 56 (Oct. 1979): 752–62.

Davis, Francine. *Weaving the Web of Meaning: Interaction Patterns in Peer Response Groups.* ERIC, 1982. ED 214 202.

Dossin, Mary. "Untrained Tutors." *Writing Lab Newsletter* 15.4 (Dec. 1990): 11.

Ede, Lisa, and Andrea Lunsford. "Why Write...Together?" *Rhetoric Review* 1 (Jan. 1983): 150–57,

Elbow, Peter. *Writing without Teachers.* New York: Oxford. 1973.

Flynn, Elizabeth. "Students as Readers of Their Classmates' Writing: Some Implications for Peer Critiquing." *Writing Instructor* 3 (Spring 1984): 120–28.

Gebhardt, Richard. "Teamwork and Feedback: Broadening the Base of Collaborative Writing." *College English* 42 (Sept. 1980): 69–74.

George, Diana. "Working with Peer Groups in the Composition Classroom." *College Composition and Communication* 35 (Oct. 1984): 320–26.

Gere, Anne Ruggles. *Writing Groups: History, Theory, and Implications.* Carbondale: Southern Illinois UP, 1987.

Gere, Anne Ruggles, and Robert Abbott. "Talking about Writing: The Language of Writing Groups." *Research in the Teaching of English* 19 (Dec. 1985): 362–85.

Gere, Anne Ruggles, and Ralph Stevens. "The Language of Writing Groups: How Oral Response Shapes Revision." *The Acquisition of Written Language: Response and Revision.* Ed. Sarah Warshauer Freedman. Norwood: Ablex, 1985. 85–105.

Glassner, Benjamin. *Discovering Audience/Inventing Purpose: A Case Study of Revision in a Cooperative Writing Workshop.* ERIC, 1983. ED 227 513.

Grimm, Nancy. "Improving Students' Responses to Their Peers' Essays." *College Composition and Communication* 37 (Feb. 1986): 91–94.

Harris, Muriel. "Contradictory Perceptions of Rules of Writing." *College Composition and Communication* 30 (May 1979): 218–20.

———. "Diagnosing Writing-Process Problems: A Pedagogical Application of Speaking-Aloud Protocol Analysis." *When a Writer Can't Write.* Ed. Mike Rose. New York: Guilford, 1985. 166–81.

———. *Teaching One-to-One: The Writing Conference.* Urbana: NCTE, 1986.

Jensen, George, and John DiTiberio. *Personality and the Teaching of Composition.* Norwood: Ablex, 1989.

Kantor, Kenneth. "Classroom Contexts and the Development of Writing Intuitions: An Ethnographic Case Study." *New Directions in Composition Research.* Ed. Richard Beach and Lillian Bridwell. New York: Guilford, 1984. 72–92.

Karegianes, Myra, Ernest Pascarella, and Susanna Pflaum. "The Effects of Peer Editing on the Writing Proficiency of Low-Achieving Tenth Grade Students." *Journal of Educational Research* 73.4 (March/April 1980): 203–07.

Livesey, Matthew. "Ours *Is* to Wonder Why." *Writing Lab Newsletter* 15.2 (Oct. 1990): 9–11.

Maid, Barry, Sally Crisp, and Suzanne Norton. "On Gaining Insight into Ourselves as Writers and as Tutors." *Writing Lab Newsletter* 13.10 (June 1989): 1–5.

Meyer, Emily, and Louise Smith. *The Practical Tutor.* New York. Oxford UP, 1987.

Newkirk, Thomas. "Direction and Misdirection in Peer Response." *College Composition and Communication* 35 (Oct. 1984): 300–11.

North, Stephen. "Training Tutors to Talk about Writing." *College Composition and Communication* 33 (Dec. 1982): 434–41.

Perdue, Virginia, and Deborah James. "Teaching in the Center." *Writing Lab Newsletter* 14.10 (June 1990). 7–8.

Rose, Mike. "Rigid Rules, Inflexible Plans, and the Stifling of Language: A Cognitivist Analysis of Writer's Block." *College Composition and Communication* 31 (Dec. 1980): 389–401.

Spear, Karen. *Sharing Writing: Peer Response Groups in English Classes.* Portsmouth: Boynton/Cook, 1988.

Trimbur, John. "Peer Tutoring: A Contradiction in Terms?" *Writing Center Journal* 7.2 (Spring/Summer 1987): 21–28.

Wauters, Joan. "Non-Confrontational Pairs: An Alternative to Verbal Peer Response Groups." *Writing Instructor* 7 (Spring/Summer 1988): 156–66.

Weiner, Harvey. "Collaborative Learning in the Classroom." *College English* 48 (Jan. 1986): 52–61.

Weller, Rebecca. "Authorizing Voice: Pedagogy, Didacticism, and the Student-Teacher-Tutor Triangle." *Writing Lab Newsletter* 17.2 (Oct. 1992): 9–12.

Ziv, Nina. *Peer Groups in the Composition Classroom: A Case Study.* ERIC, 1983. ED 229 799.

Peer Tutoring: A Contradiction in Terms?

John Trimbur

⟶ I don't think it matters

Over the past several years, I've asked the peer tutors I train and supervise to describe their initial expectations when they started tutoring. This request was at first a matter of personal curiosity, but I've found that their descriptions have given me some important leads in thinking about the aims of peer tutor training. Harvey Kail says that peer tutors teach us how to train them. I think he's right. Let me describe my tutors' expectations and what I think the implications are for tutor training.

The undergraduates who become peer tutors in writing centers begin with a combination of high hope and nagging doubt. For one thing, the tutors want to share their enthusiasm for writing with their tutees, to make their tutees into committed writers. Matt, for example, thought "my major objective would be to fire up my students to want to attack their writing assignments." This enthusiasm, of course, can lead to unrealistic expectations. "My expectations when I started tutoring," Ellen wrote in her tutoring log, "were to turn all the students I tutored into 'A' students." And at times this enthusiasm can take on a positively evangelical quality. Geoff thought his task was "to save the English language from apparently inevitable decline."

Mixed in with these hopes, realistic and otherwise, are the considerable doubts tutors feel about their ability to tutor effectively. They are often insecure about their mastery of rhetoric, style, grammar, and usage. Despite (or maybe because of) their good intentions, tutors aren't always sure they'll be able to help their tutees write better. This combination of enthusiasm and uncertainty is familiar to experienced writing center directors who train peer tutors. We all face the problem of making sure that peer tutors' initial expectations don't backfire on them. I've seen it happen. Tutors are delicate mech-

Trimbur, John. "Peer Tutoring: A Contadiction in Terms?" *The Writing Center Journal* 7.2 (1987): 21–28. Reprinted by permission of *The Writing Center Journal*.

anisms, without the protective coating and resiliency most of us develop as professionals. So there's the risk tutors' initial expectations will be shattered, leading to disappointment or even cynicism. When their hopes are not realized, when tutoring sessions don't go well or when tutees' grades don't go up, tutors may start to blame the students they work with. More often, the tutors blame themselves, and their feelings of inadequacy can turn into a debilitating sense of guilt about not getting the job done.

The problem, however, is not just the tutors' ego-investment. The problem concerns what the tutors have invested their energy doing. Tutors' initial standards for defining the aims and evaluating the results of tutoring are predictably conventional ones, informed by the prevailing reward structure that makes grades the central measure of success in higher education. It certainly helps to explain that peer tutoring is more interested in the long-term development of a tutee's writing ability than in the short-term results of any given writing assignment. As Stephen North put it so well, the job of tutoring is to produce better writers, not just better writings. But the mode of production tutors are most familiar with is the traditional academic mode of reaching and learning, a hierarchical structure in which the teacher passes down knowledge to the students and then measures how much the students received. This traditional model invariably shapes, to one extent or another, tutors' initial expectations—and can lead to considerable confusion about their work as peer tutors.

WHAT IS A PEER, WHAT IS A TUTOR?

There's a certain irony operating here because the tutors' hopes and doubts about their work as peer tutors come in part from their own success as undergraduates. As a rule, tutors are highly skilled academic achievers: they are independent learners, they get good grades, they know how to "psych out" a course, they are accustomed to pleasing their instructors. Since they're used to performing successfully for evaluation, new tutors tend to measure learning by grades and to expect that tutoring will raise their tutees' grades, if not win them "A's."

At the same time, however, the traditional model of teaching and learning tells new tutors that they are not qualified to tutor, to pass down knowledge to their tutees. As any faculty opponent of peer tutoring will tell you, students do not possess the expertise and credentials—the professional standing—to help their peers learn to write. According to prevailing academic standards, faculty traditionalists are correct: peer tutoring doesn't make much sense. If anything, peer tutoring looks like a case of the "blind leading the blind."

Now most of us involved in writing centers have developed good arguments to counter our unreconstructed colleagues. Kenneth A. Bruffee makes a telling point when he argues that peer tutoring replaces the hierarchical model of teachers and students with a collaborative model of co-learners engaged in the shared activity of intellectual work. As writing center directors and peer tutor trainers, we may feel secure about the significance of collaborative learning and the way it redefines learning as an event produced by the social interaction of the learners—and not a body of information passed down from in expert to a novice. But for the undergraduates who become peer tutors, the insecurities linger. Rewarded by the traditional structure of teaching and learning, tutors have often internalized its values and standards and, in many respects, remain dependent on its authority.

In other words, new tutors are already implicated in a system that makes the words "peer" and "tutor" appear to be a contradiction in terms. How, many good tutors want to know, can I be a peer and a tutor simultaneously? If I am qualified to tutor, then I am no longer a peer to those I tutor. On the other hand, if I am a peer to my tutees, how can I be qualified to tutor? To be selected as a peer tutor in the first place seems only to confirm the contradiction in terms by acknowledging differences between the tutors and their tutees. The tutors' success as undergraduates and their strengths as writers single them out and accentuate the differences between them and their tutees—thereby, in effect, undercutting the peer relationship. Appointment to tutor, after all, invests a certain institutional authority in the tutors that their tutees have not earned. For new tutors, the process of selection itself seems to set the terms "peer" and "tutor" at odds. It induces cognitive dissonance by asking new tutors to be two things at once, to play what appear to them to be mutually exclusive roles.

In practice, new tutors often experience cognitive dissonance as a conflict of loyalties. They feel pulled, on one hand, by their loyalty to their fellow students and, on the other hand, by loyalty to the academic system that has rewarded them and whose values they have internalized. On a gut level, new tutors often feel caught in the middle, suspended in a no-man's-land between the faculty and the students.

The tutors' loyalty to their peers results from their shared status as undergraduates. Both tutors and tutees find themselves at the bottom of the academic hierarchy. Tutors and tutees alike confront a faculty who control the curriculum, assign the work, and evaluate the results. This common position in the traditional hierarchy, moreover, tends to create social bonds among students, to unionize them. Undergraduates have always banded together to deal with the emotional and cognitive demands of college, and, in one respect, peer tutoring simply institutionalizes and accords legitimacy to the practices of mutual aid students have always engaged in on their own.

But if peer tutoring programs are efforts by educators to tap the identification of student with student as a potentially powerful source of learning, peer tutoring can also lead to the further identification of peer tutors with the system that has rewarded them, underscoring the tutors' personal stake in the hierarchical values of higher education. New tutors feel not only the pull of loyalty to their peers. They may also feel the pull of competing against their peers and of maintaining the sense of cultural superiority the academic hierarchy has conferred on them. Tutors such as Geoff, whom I quoted earlier, may see themselves as missionaries on a crusade to save their college by bringing literacy to the masses. They may in fact wind up sounding like our most conservative colleagues. Geoff, for example, went so far as to suggest that the way the writing center could improve student writing was to picket the admissions office to raise entrance standards.

Now I don't mean to smirk at one tutor. All writing center directors have encountered peer tutors who are "bossy" and competitive know-it-alls unable to extricate themselves from the authoritarian attitudes and behaviors of the traditional academic hierarchy. Besides, at the other extreme are those peer tutors who use their superior learning, in this case out of loyalty to their peers, to co-author student papers, who cross the boundaries of the writing center and enter the realm of ghost writing and plagiarism. If you're like me, you may find the latter aberration from the norms of peer tutoring—a misguided sense of student solidarity—somewhat easier to correct and perhaps more forgivable. But the point is both instances threaten to subvert the educational promise of peer tutoring.

These aberrations, of course, are extreme, and happily they are rare. The vast majority of the peer tutors I've trained and supervised have handled the conflicting loyalties they experience with considerable grace and common sense. The usefulness of looking at these extreme instances is that they illustrate the social pressures peer tutors are likely to feel. In fact, we might say that to become a peer tutor is to invite these pressures. Peer tutoring invariably precipitates a crisis of loyalty and identity for the undergraduates who join the staff of a writing center. This crisis, I would argue, is a potentially fruitful one for students. And for writing center directors and peer tutor trainers, it is our unique responsibility to help tutors negotiate this crisis and put the terms "peer" and "tutor" together in practical and meaningful ways.

MODELS OF TUTOR TRAINING

Let's take a took now at what peer tutors' initial expectations—the hopes and doubts and conflicting loyalties—suggest for tutor training. There is at present a considerable body of literature and accumulated experience in training peer tutors. As Nathaniel Hawkins points out, this work contains a problem similar to the one I've just outlined. The dilemma for tutor trainers, Hawkins says, is "whether to emphasize the tutor's role [as peer and co-learner] or his knowledge of grammar and theory" (9). We have, on the one hand, a model of tutor training that emphasizes the tutor component of the equation. This model regards the peer tutor as an apprentice and often designs training courses as an introduction to teaching writing. The book list for such a course may well look like ones used in a practicum for graduate teaching assistants—Tate's bibliographical essays, *Research in Composing*, Grave's *Rhetoric and Composition*, and so on. The second model emphasizes the peer component. This model casts peer tutors as co-learners. Bruffee's Brooklyn Plan is no doubt the seminal influence here, with its focus on the dynamics of collaborative learning and on the peer tutors' activity as writers and readers. Its goal is not so much to produce expertise as it is to produce an experiential knowledge of the process of peer critiquing and co-learning to write.

Each of these models, of course, has something to recommend it. We want tutors to know about writing and to be competent in talking to their tutees about the composing process. At the same time, we want them to be capable of collaborating with their peers and of making their own experience in writing and receiving criticism accessible to their tutees. If the tutors are not well trained, they won't be able to help their tutees. But, as Bruffee argues, if they are "too well trained, tutees don't perceive them as peers but as little teachers, and the collaborative effect of working together is lost" (446). Maybe, then, we need what Marvin Garrett calls a "delicate balance"—just the right amount of expertise and theory mixed with just the right amount of peership and collaboration.

If you expect me, at this point, to offer a tutor training program that balances the peer and the tutor components, you're going to be disappointed. Let me explain why. At a recent conference on peer tutoring, a colleague suggested that the apparently contradictory nature of peer tutoring could be resolved by helping tutors develop the judgment to know when to shift roles from that of tutor to that of peer and back again. Tutoring, that is, is a balancing act that asks tutors to juggle roles, to shift identity, to know when to act like an expert and when to act like a co-learner. What seems to me the case, however, is that making role shifts or balancing contrary identities is precisely what peer tutors cannot do. Peer tutors do not possess a strategic ego center outside their experience as peers and tutors from which to maneuver—to make such shifts or to achieve such balances. Rather they are peers and tutors simultaneously. In fact, I would argue that we should think of the terms "peer" and "tutor" not so much as roles to be played but as social pressures that converge on peer tutors, leading to the conflict of loyalty and identity crisis that inhere in peer tutoring. Tutor training, then, is not so much a matter of learning what roles to play as it is a matter of learning how to negotiate the conflicting claims on the tutors' social allegiances.

TRAINING AND TIMING

The two models of tutor training—the apprentice model and the co-learner model—reproduce at the professional level the contradiction of terms "peer" and "tutor" that students experience at a gut level. The tilt of tutor trainers toward either the peer or the tutor component of the equation carries important implications not only for tutor training but also for the design and function of peer tutoring programs in writing centers. To follow the apprentice model and emphasize expertise and theory is to conceive of peer tutoring as an arm of the writing program, a way to deliver state-of-the-art instruction in writing to tutees. To follow the co-learner model and emphasize collaboration and experiential learning is to conceive of peer tutoring as a semi-autonomous activity that contributes to the formation of a student culture that takes writing seriously.

I don't pretend these two models can be easily reconciled. It may be the case, however, that the contradictory nature of the terms "peer" and "tutor" will make more sense if we stop talking about them in spatial terms, as roles to balance, and talk about them instead as a temporal sequence to be played out. I want to suggest a rather messy solution to tutor training that incorporates elements from both models but at different stages. What I have in mind is a sequence of tutor training that treats tutors differently depending on their tutoring experience—in short, that treats tutors developmentally. This developmental sequence would begin with a Bruffeesque approach to the peer tutors as collaborative learners. Given the way the traditional hierarchy influences new tutors' expectations and definitions of their activity as tutors, they initially need concrete and practical experience co-learning. Most peer tutors have had important experiences collaborating in everyday life but rarely in academic contexts. So they need practice if they are going to be effective co-learners. To my mind, this stage is the most significant because it demands that students unlearn some of the values and behaviors—the competitive individualism of traditional academics—that have already rewarded them and shaped their identities as students. They need, in effect, to relinquish some of their dependence on faculty authority and conventional measures of success (the source, we have just seen, of both their hopes and doubts as peer tutors) and to experience instead the authority co-learners invest in each other as they forge a common language to solve the problems writers face.

Tutors need, that is, to develop confidence in their autonomous activity as co-learners, without the sanction of faculty leaning over their shoulder and telling them and their tutees when something is learned and when not. For most new tutors, the terms "peer" and "tutor" come together in meaningful ways as tutors learn to work with their tutees, when together they jointly control their purposes, set the agenda, and evaluate the results of their learning—as autonomous co-learners outside official academic channels. It is this autonomous activity that creates the social space for peer tutoring and makes writing centers an extension of the social solidarity and collaborative practices in student culture.

To return to Kail's remark about how peer tutors teach us how to train them, I must admit that often new tutors want me to teach them how to teach. They expect me to tell them what to do, to tell them what messages to send to their tutees, and to give them the methods to deliver these messages. But these questions are part of the old script, the script new tutors bring with them from their experience in the academic hierarchy of passing down knowledge. The initial stage of tutor training must address these expectations but indirectly, by structuring activities in which new tutors can gain experience co-learning. The point of tutor training at this stage is to resocialize tutors as collaborative learners within student culture. For this reason, I agree with Bruffee that tutor training must avoid producing "little teachers." It's important to see, though, that the problem is not just the half-truth that a little knowledge can be a dangerous thing. The problem is that knowledge is a powerful thing that aligns people with particular communities. To emphasize expertise in the initial stages of tutor training treats tutors as apprentices who are learning to join the community of professional writing teachers. I would argue that expertise in teaching writing is not so much dangerous as it is premature because it takes peer tutors out of student culture, the social medium of co-learning.

For me, tutor training is a matter of timing and community allegiance. The apprentice model of tutor training invokes a kind of knowledge—the theory and practice of teaching writing—that pulls tutors toward the professional community that generates and authorizes such knowledge. Instead of imparting the professional expertise of the community of writing teachers, tutor trainers need to tap and organize the native expertise of co-learning that is latent in the student's own community of undergraduates. What I'm arguing is that we need to resist the temptation to professionalize peer tutors by treating them as apprentices and by designing training courses as introductions to the field of teaching writing. We need to treat peer tutors as students, not as paraprofessionals or preprofessionals, and to recognize that their community is not necessarily ours.

Through their tutoring experience, students may well gravitate toward the community of professional writing teachers, become interested in composition studies, and perhaps go on to graduate school and careers as writing teachers. Most of us involved in peer tutoring programs have seen this happen. In fact, tutors are in general so bright and articulate it is tempting to took at writing centers as recruiting grounds, not just for English or writing majors but for colleagues. My point here is simply that if experienced peer tutors do gravitate toward our profession, this should grow out of their own experience as co-learners in the semi-autonomous territory of writing centers.

Tutor trainers need to nurture the development of experienced tutors as much as that of new tutors, and advanced tutor training courses or practicums can help tutors deepen their awareness of the collaborative process of learning to write. Advanced training courses might well include composition theory and pedagogy, but this study should take place in a developmental sequence of the tutors' interests and purposes—the result of their experience tutoring and not a prerequisite to it. My worry is that the conception of tutoring as an apprenticeship treats students as extensions of our profession and can reinforce their dependence on faculty authority. To emphasize expertise at the expense of an experiential knowledge of co-learning risks short circuiting the dynamics of collaboration in student culture—the communities of readers and writers that are always in the process of formation when peers work together in writing centers.

WORKS CITED

Bruffee, Kenneth A. "Training and Using Peer Tutors." *College English* 40 (1978): 432–49.

Garrett, Marvin. "Toward a Delicate Balance: The Importance of Role-Playing and Peer Criticism in Peer Tutor Training." *Tutoring Writing.* Ed. Muriel Harris. Glenview: Scott, 1981. 94–100.

Hawkins, Nathaniel. "An Introduction to the History and Theory of Peer Tutoring in Writing." *A Guide to Writing Programs: Writing Centers, Peer Tutoring, Writing Across the Curriculum.* Ed. Tori Haring-Smith. Glenview: Scott, 1984. 7–18.

Kail, Harvey. "Collaborative Learning in Context." *College English* 45 (1983): 592–99.

North, Stephen. "Training Tutors to Talk about Writing." *College Composition and Communication* 33 (1982): 434–41.

Freud in the Writing Center: The Psychoanalytics of Tutoring Well

Christina Murphy

"A Writing Teacher Is Like a Psychoanalyst, Only Less Well Paid," Jay Parini declares in a recent essay in *The Chronicle of Higher Education*. One part of Parini's equation is almost self-evident to writing teachers since they know that, of the degreed professionals, college professors are among the least well paid for their efforts. The second half of the equation, the ways in which teaching writing mirrors aspects of the psychoanalytic process, is perhaps less apparent and clear. I would like to suggest that this correlation is most apparent in the interaction between tutors in a writing center and those students who come to seek their services. Unlike students who enroll in courses for a spectrum of reasons from "the course is required" to "it fits into my schedule," students come to a writing center for one reason only—they want help with their writing.

The fact that students come to the writing center wanting help and assuming they will receive it places those students in a different type of relationship with the tutor than with the instructor in a traditional classroom setting. While the teacher's role is primarily informative and focused upon the method of presentation that will best convey instruction to the class as a whole, the tutor's role often is primarily supportive and affective, secondarily instructional, and always directed to each student as an individual in a unique, one-to-one interpersonal relationship.

As in psychoanalysis, the quality of that interpersonal relationship between therapist and client, tutor and student, determines how successful the interaction as a whole will be. L. D. Goodstein, in an essay titled "What Makes Behavior Change Possible," argues that the quality of a therapeutic relationship is "an essential ingredient of behavior change." And what are the qualities of a good relationship of supportive intervention like therapy or tutoring? Carl Rogers states that all good therapists or supportive inter-

Murphy, Christina. "Freud in the Writing Center: The Psychoanalyhtics of Tutoring Well. *The Writing Center Journal* 10.1 (1989): 13–18. Reprinted by permission of *The Writing Center Journal*.

veners manifest a real concern for those in their charge. They direct to these individuals, in Roger's terms, "unconditional positive regard" by demonstrating a basic interest, concern, and desire to help another human being. Empathetic understanding expressed as honesty or a genuine openness of character is the second quality. The more this quality is perceived or felt by clients or students, the more impact it has on them.

Rogers places such a high premium upon the nature of the interpersonal relationship between therapist and client because so many of the people who enter in therapy are "hurt"—they are suffering from negative feelings or emotions, interpersonal problems, and inadequate and unsatisfying behaviors. The same is often true of individuals who come to a writing center. They, too, are "hurt" in that they display insecurities about their abilities as writers or even as academic learners, express fear to the tutor that they will be treated in the same judgemental or abusive way that they have been treated by teachers or fellow students before, or exhibit behavior patterns of anxiety, self-doubt, negative cognition, and procrastination that only intensify an already difficult situation.

> *"I know you're going to tear this paper to shreds,"* they say, *"but here goes anyway."*
>
> *"I've never been able to write. This is hopeless."*
>
> *"I know you can't help me, but I thought I'd try the writing center anyway."*
>
> Or maybe they are defensive: *"This teacher gives dumb assignments. If he'd just give me something I could write about, I know I'd do better."*
>
> Sometimes they are self-deceived; *"I've always made A's in English in high school, so I know I should be making A's in college, too."*
>
> Other times they are self-defeating: *"Can you help me with this paper? It's due at 2:00."*
>
> *"Well, that only gives us thirty minutes."*
>
> *"I know, but maybe you could go over it and help me write an ending."*

By and large, the students who come "hurt" to a writing center are those who suffer from writer's block or a high degree of inhibiting anxiety associated with the process of producing writing that will be evaluated by others. These students demonstrate the principle endorsed by Rogers and other humanistic educators that learning is not simply a cognitive process. These students do not have difficulty writing because of any inherent flaws or limitations in the type of instruction they have received from their teachers or because they necessarily lack abilities as writers. Instead, they represent individuals whose talents as writers and as academic learners can be realized only within a specific set of conditions and circumstances. C. H. Patterson, in

Theories of Counseling and Psychotherapy, indicates that, for these types of individuals with inherent abilities but inhibiting fears, the psychoanalytic concept of information theory may provide the most productive conceptual understanding and approach. This theory "views the individual as actively attending to, selecting, operating on, organizing, and transforming the information provided by the environment and by internal sources. Thus, the individual defines stimuli and events and constructs his or her own world" (668).

For the tutor, "information-processing psychology is concerned with understanding the nature of internal events, and more particularly, processes occurring within the individual as he or she handles and organizes his or her experience" (Wexler and Rice 15–20). Achieving the goals and possibilities of this theory, or of any client-centered theory, requires an empathetic bond between tutor and student in the interventive process. When such a structure is established by the tutor, the relationship that develops is experienced by the student as "safe, secure, free from threat, and supporting but not supportive" (Patterson 498). Rogers describes this process as "one dealing with warm living people who are dealt with by warm living counselors" (Patterson 499).

Some might argue against or minimize the importance of the relationship that develops between tutor and student or claim that, even though this relationship is potent in itself, it really bears little resemblance to the relationships established in a psychoanalytic setting. Truax and Carkhuff, in *Toward Effective Counseling and Psychotherapy*, would contend, however, that fundamental and profound similarities exist amongst all the interventive processes, from therapy, to education, to the managerial interactions of employer and employee. They state "the person (whether a counselor, therapist, or teacher) who is better able to communicate warmth, genuineness, and accurate empathy is more effective in interpersonal relationships no matter what the goal of the interaction" (116–17).

Most of what goes on in a writing center is talking and the range of interpersonal interactions available through words. In coming to a writing center for assistance, students must explain to a tutor what they want and what they hope to achieve. In the course of this type of interaction, the students make themselves vulnerable in opening themselves up to understanding or misunderstanding, judgment or acceptance, approval or disapproval.

Jim W. Corder, in an interesting essay titled "A New Introduction to Psychoanalysis, Taken as a Version of Modern Rhetoric," describes psychoanalysis, from a rhetorical perspective, as "the talking cure." Thomas Szasz calls psychotherapy "iatrology," or "healing words" (29). Psychotherapy, like rhetoric, understands the power of words, especially "healing words." As psychotherapists or tutors, we function like the old medicine man in *Ceremony*, the novel by Leslie Silko, who says, "That was the responsibility that went with being human…the story behind each word must be told so that there could be no mistake in the meaning of what had been said" (35). As psychotherapists or tutors, we share with those in our charge the responsibility that goes with being human. And in our very human roles, we share the powers of language to express emotions, to inspire creative thought, and to change perceptions of the self and others. We share the power of language to transform thought and being.

It is to psychotherapy that we owe the clearest model of the types of transformative interactions and outcomes that can occur in a writing center setting. For psychotherapy to be successful, (1) two persons are in contact; (2) one person, the client, generally is in a state of incongruence, being vulnerable or anxious; (3) the other person, the therapist, is congruent in the relationship, (4) the therapist experiences unconditional positive regard toward the client; (5) the therapist experiences an empathetic understanding of the client's internal frame of reference; and (6) the client perceives, at least to a minimal degree, the therapist's empathetic understanding of the client's internal frame of reference. As a result of the process of psychotherapy, (1) the client is more congruent, more open to his or her experiences, less defensive; (2) as a result, the client is more realistic, objective, extensional in his or her perceptions; (3) the client is consequently more effective in problem-solving; (4) as a result of the increased congruence of self and experience, his or her vulnerability to threat is reduced; (5) as a result of the lowering of his or her vulnerability to threat or defeat, the client has an increased degree of self-regard, and (6) as a result of all of the above factors, the client's behavior is more creative, more uniquely adaptive and more fully expressive of his or her own values (Patterson 486–87).

If we substitute *tutor* and *student* here for *therapist* and *client*, the model holds true for the learning strategies and experiential awarenesses that go on in a writing center environment. A good psychoanalyst and a good tutor both function to awaken individuals to their potentials and to channel their creative energies toward self-enhancing ends. Within the focus of the one-on-one tutorial, the student and tutor work to interpret the cognitive strategies the student has employed to be expressive, insightful, concise, and clear. To work with the student in deciphering and assessing creative processes, in suggesting new ways to interpret data, methods of inquiry, and philosophical perspectives, and in determining a philosophy of personal expression requires from the tutor a sensitivity to the affective and intellectual dimensions of the student's personality. At the core of tutoring and psychotherapy are the interactional dynamics of a search for insight that involves an intimate transference of trust and vulnerability between two individuals intent upon and intimately involved in finding answers.

Jim W. Corder states that "human frailty sets immediate and overpow-ering limits":

> *Every utterance belongs to, exists in, issues from, and reveals a rhetorical universe. Every utterance comes from somewhere (its inventive origin), emerges as a structure, and manifests itself as a style. All of the features of utterance—invention, structure, and style—cycle, reciprocate, and occur simultaneously. Each of us is a gathering place for a host of rhetorical uni-verses. Some of them we share with others, indeed with whole cultures; some of them we inhabit alone, and some of them we occupy without know-ing that we do. Each of us is a busy corner where multiple rhetorical uni-verses intersect. (141)*

Part of the transformative power of a writing center is that it is a setting in which rhetorical universes are shared. In this way, the tutoring process, like the psychotherapeutic process, partakes in the power of language to reshape and empower consciousness. James Hillman in *Re-Visioning Psychol-ogy* calls words "independent carriers of soul between people" (9). Perhaps no better description of the interaction that goes on in tutoring and in ther-apy can be found. If it is true that words transform consciousness, and changes in consciousness transform the self, then language-based processes like therapy and tutoring provide a dynamic for self-awareness and self-actualization. To this extent, they are liberatory philosophies in the manner that Paulo Freire uses that term to describe how the power of words can empower the consciousness of ourselves and others.

Perhaps, when all is said and done, the old medicine man of Leslie Silko's *Ceremony* is a Freudian, believing in the humanness of liberation and in the power of reintegrating consciousness through the language of one's tribe. Per-haps the old medicine man works daily in writing centers across America, re-sponding to the questions of those who come, apprentice fashion, to learn.

"Can you help me with my writing?"
"Yes, I can, but first let us start with your words."

WORKS CITED

Corder, Jim W. "A New Introduction to Psychoanalysis, Taken as a Version of Mod-ern Rhetoric." *Pre/Text* 5.3–4 (1984): 137–69.

Goodstein. L. D. "What Makes Behavior Change Possible?" *Contemporary Psychology* 22 (1977): 578–79.

Hillman, James. *Re-Visioning Psychology.* New York: Harper and Row, 1975.

Parini, Jay. "A Writing Teacher is Like a Psychoanalyst, Only Less Well Paid." *The Chronicle of Higher Education* 2 Nov. 1988. B2.

Patterson, C. H. *Theories of Counseling and Psychotherapy.* 3rd ed. New York: Harper and Row, 1980.

Rogers, Carl R. "The Necessary and Sufficient Conditions of Therapeutic Personality Change." *Journal of Consulting Psychology* 21 (1957): 95–103.

Schor, Ira, and Paolo Freire. *A Pedagogy for Liberation: Dialogues on Transforming Education.* South Hadley: Bergin and Garvey, 1987.

Silko, Leslie Marmon. *Ceremony.* New York: Viking Penguin, 1977.

Szasz, Thomas. *The Myth of Psychotherapy: Mental Healing as Religion, Rhetoric, and Repression.* New York: Anchor Press/Doubleday, 1978.

Truax, C. B., and R. R. Carkhuff. *Toward Effective Training in Counseling and Psychotherapy.* Chicago: Aldine, 1967.

Wexler, D. A., and L. N. Rice, eds. *Innovations in Client-Centered Therapy.* New York, Wiley, 1984.

The First Five Minutes: Setting the Agenda in a Writing Conference

Thomas Newkirk

Freshmen are usually allowed to hide—at least at large universities. Most of their courses meet in large lecture halls where they are taught by professors who don't, who really can't, learn the names of their students. In class, students listen and take notes, but do not speak. Examinations, by necessity, take the form of multiple-choice or short-answer questions, and the results are posted by Social Security number with an accompanying distribution curve to indicate where the student ranks.

The invariable exception to this pattern is freshman composition where, for better or worse, the student cannot hide. The student is called by name and, on an almost weekly basis, receives a response to his or her writing. Hiding is particularly difficult in the composition course where teacher and student meet for regular conferences in which the student must speak, explain, evaluate; where he or she must make what are often the first awkward steps in the direction of analytic conversation, the staple of the academic world. I will contend in this chapter that these meetings, and in particular the first few minutes of these meetings, constitute some of the most poignant dramas in the university.

I don't mean to overemphasize the confrontational nature of the writing conference by echoing Joe Louis's warning to Billy Conn—"You can run, but you can't hide." Most conferences seem casual, supportive; there is regular laughter and, at the end of the course, appreciation for the personal attention received. But the seemingly effortless, conversational quality of conferences belies their complexity, for both teacher and student are filling paradoxical roles. The teacher must balance two opposing mandates: on the one hand to respond to the student, evaluate, to suggest possible revisions and writing strategies; and on the other to encourage the student to take the initiative, to self-evaluate, to make decisions, to take control of the paper. There is no neat way to reconcile these mandates, no formula to prevent missteps—just the endless prospect of gambling, of risking silence at some points and assertiveness at others.

The student meets this dilemma from the other end and fills a role at least as paradoxical. When asked the question, "What did you think of your paper?" or one of its many variants, the student knows that the question is really, "How did you (acting as member of a community that you are not yet a member of) react to this paper?" Furthermore, the person asking the question is a member of that community and very likely has a better answer—at least in the opinion of the student. Yet, despite the awkwardness of the situation, the student recognizes (usually) that the question is a valid one and works to formulate an answer. So if the teacher is a gambler, the student is often the actor, pretending her or his way into a role.

To complicate matters further, both student and teacher need to come to a meeting of minds fairly early in a writing conference; they need to set an agenda, agree to one or two major concerns that will be the focus of the conference. The agenda often deals with a possible revision of the paper, but there are other possibilities: it could deal with the writing process of the student or with a paper that is yet to be written. Unless a commonly-agreed-upon agenda is established, a conference can run on aimlessly and leave both participants with the justifiable feeling that they have wasted time. The efficient setting of an agenda is particularly important in the conferences that will be analyzed in this chapter. Each lasts about fifteen minutes and, in some, part of this time is used for reading the paper. There is little time to meander.

The conferences were held as part of the freshman English course at the University of New Hampshire and occurred in the third week of the course (in most cases they were the second student-teacher conference). In virtually all sections of freshman English, students are not graded until mid-semester and then only on work that both student and instructor feel is the best produced to that point. For that reason, instructors in these early conferences are not under pressure to give or justify grades. Each conference was taped by the instructor, a first-semester teaching assistant, who transcribed the conference and then annotated it, identifying crucial junctures and critical mistakes. The procedure used by Carnicelli (1980) served as a model.

I will present the opening segments, lasting about five minutes, of three conferences that show different ways in which agendas are negotiated or fail to be negotiated. The papers for these conferences are similar; they are first drafts dealing with personal experiences, and, like many early papers in freshman English, they lack focus. An instructor reading these papers away from the student could conceivably write a similar comment for each. But the student is present, and this presence changes the nature of the teaching act.

"IT MIGHT BE KIND OF DUMB..."

The paper for the following conference was entitled "My Favorite Course," five double-spaced pages which began with the student's love for horses as a child (she had a toy palomino). From this beginning she moves on to describe how she was admitted to a horsemanship course, the things she has learned so far in the course, and positive and negative points about her horse. After reading the paper (and before reading the transcript), I expected the conference to deal with the issue of focus. But it didn't, and the reason why should be evident from the opening segment (in this and the following transcriptions, *T* = teacher and *S* = student):

T: All right, now let's talk about your paper. I'm going to spend a few minutes on it now and then we'll talk about it.

S: OK. [Teacher reads paper]

T: OK. Uh, why don't you tell me a little about your paper. What was it like writing it?

S: Oh, I liked it. I really like the class, you know, and I liked writing about it.

T: So you enjoyed it?

S: Yeah. it's a fun class.

T: Was it a fun paper?

S: Yeah. Well, you know, I wanted to write about it. Maybe it's really boring because I really just wrote it for me, but I guess I just wanted to. It, you know, doesn't say much. Just about my class.

T: Well, I enjoyed reading it. It was fun reading it. I could see, I could tell that you liked the class and I liked the way your enthusiasm really shows.

S: Yeah.

T: Was there a part that you really enjoyed writing?

S: Well, I enjoyed writing the whole paper pretty much.

T: Uh huh. Is there a part you liked best, you know, a favorite part?

S: Oh, yeah. I really liked the part about Trigger [the toy horse]. Remembering him. I still have him somewhere at home. It might be kind of dumb though, a plastic horse.

T: Oh no. I really liked that. I had a dog, a stuffed shaggy dog that I remembered while reading it. He's somewhere now. I guess everyone grows up with these animals and then keeps them forever. [Laughter.] But I liked that part, I could really relate to it. Was there a part that you thought needed work still? You know, something you were sort of unhappy with?

S: Well, I wondered if it would be boring. You know, too long. It doesn't really say much.

T: Did you, uh, did you want it to say something? What did you want to tell me?

S: Oh, well. I just wanted to tell you about my riding class.

T: Uh huh.

S: That's all.

T: Uh huh. Um. You know you told me about yourself, too.

S: What?

T: Well, that part about Trigger?

S: Oh yeah. [Laughs.]

T: And you know, about being tested. Your dedication. Not only getting up at the crack of dawn and all, but the work. Like it sounds like you're really working your body, so it's a lot of hard work as well as fun.

This conference stumbles at the beginning over the reference to "it." In the first five exchanges, the teacher uses "it" three times, in each case referring to the paper or the writing of the paper. The student uses "it" three times, each time referring to the horsemanship class and ultimately leading her to misunderstand the teacher's question:

T: So you enjoyed it?

S: Yeah. It's a fun class.

T: Was it a fun paper?

One senses the student's lack of familiarity with the intent of the conference and her lack of awareness that the teacher's primary concern at this point in the conference is with the process of writing. The student doesn't, in fact, quite know what it means to "talk about your paper." This discomfort with the analytic intent of the conference becomes even more evident when the teacher pushes (ever so gently) for a critical evaluation of the paper.

In response to the teacher's request for an analytic judgment, the student consistently gives a global evaluation—of the paper, of the class, and most devastatingly, of herself. When asked to tell about the writing of the paper (an implicit request for analysis), the writer replies with, "Oh, I liked it."

When asked, this time more explicitly, if there was a *"part* that you really enjoyed writing,"* the student replies that she liked "writing the whole paper pretty much." And again later in the segment, when asked about the main point of the paper, she replies globally that she "just wanted to tell you about my riding class." The only tentative move toward an analytic view is the student's admission that she liked the part about the toy horse. For this student, the text seems to exist as a whole that cannot be differentiated into features or parts. And because she brings this frame to her paper, the teacher comes up empty in most of the exchanges.

But not totally empty. For in these replies, the student is making clear her lack of confidence in her own writing ability and her doubts about the validity of her experience as a topic for writing. In these first few minutes the student characterizes her writing as: "boring" (twice), "it doesn't say much," "it might be kind of dumb," and "too long." It is this message that the teacher picks up on and makes the focus of the conference agenda. In her analysis of the conference, the teacher wrote:

> *She told me in a previous conference…[that] she is the first one of her extended family to go to college. Her self-confidence is very shaky), and she considers her acceptance into UNH to be a fluke. She doesn't think she is "college material." She has a pattern of trashing herself, telling me how "dumb" she is compared to all the "real" students around her…. I have an agenda of support for her and, if possible, some sort of positive response against her habit of self-denigration.*

So the teacher gambles. She focuses on supporting the student, allaying the student's fears that she is an inadequate writer and that her experiences are "boring." The gamble is that by ignoring, for a time, various technical problems in the writing and by emphasizing the positive, the writer will, in the near future, gain enough confidence to deal with these technical matters. Another gamble is that this support will not be taken by the student as a definitive evaluation—"I enjoyed reading it" may be translated by the student into "This is an *A* paper." The teacher gambles…and waits.

"…LIKE A MACK TRUCK"

The second conference deals with an untitled paper about the function of pets. It begins in a fairly technical way with the sentence, "I wonder what part domestic animals play in the ecosystem." For most of the paper, however, the writer shifts to a more casual language to describe her own relationship with her dog as they went out in the woods after a snow:

She would suddenly stop, lie on the ground and chew at the ice. Sometimes it was severe enough to cause her paws to bleed leaving red splotches on the snow. I knew it was more painful for her if I attempted to yank out the ice.

At the end of the paper, the writer returns to the more distant vocabulary of the beginning, when she concludes that "Pets are machines for us to lavish affection on or proclaim superiority over."

The paper alone suggests two major issues. The radical shift of tone after the beginning is jolting, and the conclusion comparing pets to machines seems at odds with the affectionate description of the writer's relationship with her own pet. Ironically, both teacher and student in the following excerpt agree on the central problem in the paper, yet the conference misfires badly.

T: Now, what did you think your purpose was in writing the paper?

S: Well, I was just kind of dealing with the fact that people have animals. And are nice to them. And we're not really nice to other organisms besides ourselves. You know, I wonder why people are so uncommonly nice to domesticated animals.

T: Yeah? So—umm—did you come to any conclusion about that?

S: No. (Laughs.]

T: But at the end you say: "I have had a pet as a companion. Pets are machines for us to lavish affection on or to proclaim superiority over." That sounds like you've come to a conclusion.

S: Well, it's more of an observation.

T: Oh. You see, I think it's a false conclusion. I mean I think you still don't know.

S: I don't.

T: And I think it's better that you don't know. I mean you're saying there ought to be some reason for this, but I love my dog.

S: Yeah.

T: And so for me the last paragraph was—I think I said that before—that you have a tendency to be asking questions and think you have to find some answer.

S: Umhumm.

T: And I don't think—I mean whatever answer you find, it's probably going to be a question and it's probably going to be inherent in the whole piece.

S: So I don't really have to…

T: You're saying, "God this is strange, we're funny creatures." And that's the answer. You don't have to what?

S: I don't have to make it so—like I ought to stick on this conclusion—which is unnecessary.

T: And also, when you do that you tend to lapse into this scientific language that really—you sound like you've turned into a computer or something…. Were there any parts of this that you liked better than other parts, that you enjoyed writing?

S: Yeah, I liked describing—like the skiing and walking through the woods and stuff. I enjoy writing like that. 'Cause I enjoy doing it so…

T: And were there any parts that gave you trouble?

S: I don't think so. It's kind of like—I felt that it wasn't—like I—this first part, you know, I was just wondering in general and then I kinda switched into my own experience and that wasn't too smooth, I don't think. Yeah, you know, I just—the part where I was describing what we did.

T: Yeah, well you need the—let's see: "I wonder what part domestic animals play in the ecosystem…. Domesticated animals are personalized diversions for humans." See, you've answered it too soon.

S: But…that's like an observation.

What stands out in this conference is the domination of the teacher. She speaks more than twice as much as the student (351 to 162 words), but a word count alone does not make clear the nature of that domination. The teacher seems to have in mind what Knoblauch and Brannon (1984) call an "ideal text." She has an image of the true version which this paper should ultimately conform to. In this truer state, the paper would illustrate, through the description of the author and her pet, the reasons why we treat pets in special ways. The language of the paper would be "human" and avoid broad assertions that might *answer* the question raised in the paper; rather, the author should indicate no more certainty than to suggest that, "God this is strange, we're funny creatures." Indeed, just after the excerpt I've quoted here, the teacher offers the student language from this ideal text, urging the student to qualify her assertions with "it seems to me…"—whereupon the student reminds the teacher that their textbook tells them to avoid "it seems."

Many changes that the student might make in moving toward this ideal text *would* improve the writing. The conclusion does seem too assured, and it doesn't deal with the complexity of the question raised. The problem is the lack of negotiation in the conference. The teacher identifies a problem and suggests remedies before the student is even convinced that a problem exists. Even at the very end of this first segment, the student repeats her justification of the conclusions as "observations." Paradoxically, when given an opportunity to state her own judgment of the paper, the student identifies the mismatch between the opening and the descriptive parts which, she claimed, she enjoyed writing more than the "scientific" opening. This judgment is not really so far from the agenda the teacher opens with. The conference might have looked a great deal different if the teacher had begun by focusing on the effectiveness of the descriptive passages and then encouraged the student to fit the opening and conclusions to this effective writing.

But because the teacher's agenda is set rather inflexibly early on, she misses this and other opportunities to build on the observations of the student. The student is shut out in two ways: first, she is put on the defensive when the instructor calls her conclusion "false." Then, even when the conclusion/observation issue is momentarily dropped, the teacher doesn't hear the student's contributions. When the student attempts a summary of the teacher's suggestions about the conclusion, the teacher changes the subject:

S: I don't have to make it so—like I ought to stick on this conclusion—which is unnecessary.

T: And also, when you do that you tend—to lapse into this scientific language.

It is not at all clear that the student understands what is to be done with the ending, but the teacher moves on. Similarly, she fails to follow up on the student's comment about enjoying the writing of the descriptive parts. In her analysis of the transcript, the instructor admits that when the student identifies the problem with the shift from scientific to more casual descriptive language, she "stubbornly cling[s] to my diagnosis about questions and answers." This conference illustrates what Freedman and Sperling (1985) call "cross-purpose talk":

> With no match in focal concern, T and S will likely be talking at cross purposes and may not even be attending to what the other is saying.... This cross-purpose talk manifests itself in a T-S conference when S and T each bring up a topic of concern over and over again, no matter what the other wants to focus on, indicating that T and S often have different agendas for what needs to be covered in the conference. (117)

The teacher reviewing the conference put the problem a bit more bluntly: "Mea culpa. I ran over this kid like a Mack truck."

"IT JUST DIDN'T MAKE SENSE"

The final conference excerpt deals with a paper called "Mailaholic," which attempts to explain the writer's addiction to getting letters. It starts out in a lighthearted, almost "cute" way, detailing her love of various kinds of stamps and stationery and the way she and other dorm members place unopened letters on their lunch trays to flaunt the fact that someone has written to them. Then, as in the previous paper, there is a shift in tone, and, in brief paragraphs, the writer explains what letters from mother, boyfriend, and best friend mean. At first reading, this short paper—about 700 words total—seems the least promising of the three (the word superficial comes to mind). But like an expert canoeist, the teacher follows the current of the student's language to a real insight.

T: How do you feel about this paper?

S: I don't like it. I like the topic. I like the title, but I had a hard time…I had a lot of ideas I wanted to put in…and they didn't seem to flow. Like I read the paper that you gave us Thursday…I just liked it. Like everything flowed and went together smoothly. And this, I'm like…it just doesn't say anything. I wanted to say something but I didn't say it the right way,

T: OK. Tell me what you were trying to say…in a few sentences…if you had to tell me what your paper was about.

S: How much getting a letter means to me. But I just…I don't know…I like a lot of times, you know, it just didn't make sense. It was like I didn't know how to say it.

T: Do you think you addressed that anywhere on the page?

S: Yeah. I think where I'm saying about how I go about reading a letter. You know after I…if there's one there…after I've gotten a letter and just sit there and let everyone see it. And then when I get in the privacy of my own room…then I read it, 'cause then I feel I'm with the person rather than having all this noise around me and I can't concentrate.

T: Yes?

S: And then if I don't get a letter…I like sort of envy them and am real jealous. And it's like when they do what I do…it's wrong because they're hurting me. I do the same thing. I put it on my lunch tray and let everyone see the letter.

T: Yes?

S: I like that part of it. Maybe I just don't like the beginning or how I get into it. I don't like the transitions. Sometimes I don't see how I get where I'm going.

T: OK. Then you think that perhaps you were trying to find your topic, found it, and then ran out of it?

S: Yeah.

T: Where do you think you really started to get into it?

S: On the second page.

T: All right…

S: But I don't really dig into the mess. What I understood about it is…I think that's where I actually start talking about what I mean to say about it, you know.

T: Yes?

S: So I suppose if I just cut off the first page and start it out with the rest?

T: Yes?

S: What I should try to do…

T: What other kind of things are you trying to say?

S: Uh…

T: When you think about what getting a letter really means.

S: Well, on the last page…about when I get a letter from my boyfriend, or my best friend, or my mom…what feelings I get when I get it…a letter from them.

By this point the agenda is set. The rest of the conference explores what these feelings are, and as the writer talks, she moves beyond the juvenile tone of the original draft to an insight into her own need for letters:

S: And like I was really close to my mom this summer. So it's like I'm up here and I don't want them to forget me. And so I just want to keep grasping…you know…to make sure that life is still going on. And when I go home…everything isn't going to be the same, but it isn't going to be dramatically different.

While this observation still relies, to a degree, on the commonplace "make sure that *life is still going on*," the writer seems to have found a reason for her need for letters.

She has been able to make these moves toward understanding because the teacher gave her room. The ratio of teacher talk to student talk differs radically from the second conference quoted earlier. Here the teacher speaks only 97 words to the student's 397, and in many of the exchanges she simply prods the student with a "yes." Such a ratio, of course, may not be an "ideal" to work towards; so much student talk could be digressive. But in this case, the student seems to be working from a global and unformed dissatisfaction with her paper to a more analytic evaluation that will guide her revision. The writer's initial evaluative responses were scattered: it doesn't "flow," it has a lot of ideas, it "doesn't say anything," and "I don't think I did it the right way." The teacher's question about the intent of the paper causes the writer to identify her purposes—to explain what letters meant to her. And again, in response to the teacher's question, the student notes that only on the second page does she really deal with her newly stated purpose. The writer is closing in; she admits that although she begins to deal with her focus on the second page, she doesn't "really dig into the mess." The teacher then pushes her in this direction by asking what things she was trying to say about getting letters; the agenda for the rest of the conference is set.

Or almost set. The student does offer up a concern early in the conference—a concern the teacher wisely ignores. In her first evaluation of the paper, the student says, "I don't think I did it the right way." This comment, common in an early writing conference, suggests that the student has been taught some ironclad rules for writing essays, and she wants to see whether these rules still apply. Toward the end of the conference, this concern once again surfaces as the student asks about her conclusion:

S: When you write a conclusion, is it supposed to be restating the beginning of the thing? I had a hard time. I didn't know how to end it.

The teacher responds that the writer must decide for herself and that each paper is different.

Finally, this conference illustrates the role of talk in revision. Revision is often used synonymously with rewriting; we change our writing by writing again and making changes. The student in this conference is revising by talking; she is creating an alternative text, an oral text that can be juxtaposed against the one she has written. The next draft she might write is not simply a nebulous possibility; rather, it is a draft that has, to a degree, been spoken. Near the end of the conference the teacher asks what she might do next, and the student answers, "I think I'll probably cut off the first page and a half and work on...I don't know...giving examples. *Like what I told you a few minutes ago.*"

This emphasis on allowing students to speak these oral texts may seem almost insultingly self-evident. But in reading and annotating these transcripts, teachers were appalled at the opportunities that were missed—when they cut off students, and when they told students to expand a section rather than allowing them to expand orally. Students did not get a chance to hear what they know.

IMPLICATIONS

The lessons to be learned from this kind of self-examination are painfully obvious—but worth remembering because, in our eagerness to teach, we often forget the obvious.

1. We all tend to talk too much. The little lecturettes that pop up in writing conferences usually bring things to a grinding halt.

2. The opening minutes of the conference are critically important in giving the conference direction—they act as a kind of *lead*. The student's contributions in these opening minutes need to be used to give the conference a mutually agreeable and mutually understood direction.

3. These agendas should be limited to one or two major concerns. Conferences seem to break down when a discussion about a "high-level" concern like purpose veers abruptly to a discussion of sentence structure.

4. Potentially, student contributions to the agenda-setting process often are missed if the teacher has *fixed* on a problem early. It is particularly easy for the teacher to fix on the agenda if he or she takes the papers home and marks them up before the conference. Furthermore, a marked-up paper indicates to the student that the agenda has *already* been set.

5. While the teacher must be responsive to the student's contributions in the writing conference, this does not mean that the teacher is nondirective, Students like the one in the first conference, may at first be unfamiliar with the evaluative-analytic language of the writing conference. These students often need to see how the teacher reads so they might get an operative understanding of what a term like "focus" means. The modeling described by Richard Beach (this volume) is vitally important in this type of conference.

Unfortunately, listing conclusions like this implies that the difficulty of conferences can be smoothed out and problems prevented. This is not my position.

I see the writing conference as a dialectic encounter between teacher and student, in which both assume complex roles. The teacher, in particular, cannot escape the difficult choices between praise and support, suggestion and silence, each choice carrying with it a risk. For that reason, I am uncomfortable with some of the metaphors increasingly used to describe this complex relationship, many of which echo private property and contractual law. The writer, we are told, "owns" the text, which should not be "appropriated" by the teacher (Knoblauch and Brannon 1982). Graves (1983) has similarly urged that the student has "ownership" of the text. Knoblauch and Brannon (1984) describe the ideal reading of a student text as follows:

> *It is the rare composition teacher who reads student writing with the assumption that composers legitimately control their own discourses, who accepts the possibility that student intentions matter more than teacher expectations as a starting-point for reading, and who recognizes that the writer's choices are supposed to make sense mainly in terms of those intentions, not in proportion as they gratify a reader's point of view of what should have been said. (120)*

The polarization of terms in this description is striking: student intentions/ teacher expectations, student control/teacher control. And the term "legitimately" introduces, once again, the implication that in defining the role of the teacher we are working within clear, almost legal, boundaries.

But if we push on these metaphors a bit, they wobble. Ownership implies clear property lines guaranteed by legal statutes that are (at least to lawyers) clearly spelled out. For the most part, those who own property can do what they want to with it, so long as the owner is not creating a major inconvenience to others. Those of us who view the property may have opinions about the esthetics of the house built on it, but the owner need not listen, and we need to be very careful about passing on these judgments.

The metaphor of ownership is not slippery enough. To a degree, the student owns his or her paper, but the paper is *intended* for others in the way property isn't; and so, to a degree, the writing is also owned by its readers. No one (I hope) condones the practice condemned by Knoblauch and Brannon in which students must guess at some Platonic text that exists in the teacher's imagination. But by the same token, the expectations of the teacher, the course, and the academy must interact with the intentions of the student. Intention, in other words, cannot be an absolute, a "God-term."

Let's take this paragraph you are now beginning to read. Who owns it— you or I? Does my intention *matter* more than your response? Questions like these divide the writing act in an unhelpful way. The text is neither mine nor yours—no one owns it. Even in writing it, I didn't feel that I was putting *my* meaning into language that would fit *your* needs. Rather, there was a constant interplay between audience and intention so that I can no longer disentangle my meanings from your expectations. I did not feel set against you, my audience; rather, you became part of me in the act of writing. And so it is in a good writing conference, like the third one I quoted, where the teacher becomes an active instrument in the student's search for meaning.

I began this chapter by claiming that few courses at the university push freshmen to assume responsibility for their own learning. I'd like to close with an instance of one that did, a philosophy course, which caused an almost Copernican shift in the writer's view of what it is to be a student. It is, I believe, the same kind of shift that a good writing course can initiate. The paper, written for a freshman English course, is entitled "Philosophy is Messing Up My Life," and it begins with the anxiety the student felt about taking an introductory philosophy course. At first the professor appeared intimidating, with a "strong philosophical nose, and eyes that could eat a question mark right through you." When the roll was called the writer barely managed an audible "here." Once the class started, the student opened his notebook and expected the instructor to begin by writing a definition of philosophy on the board. But he didn't. He asked questions to show the students that philosophy is, in this student's words, a "process of questioning and answering things you don't understand in an attempt to arrive at the 'right' answer, which usually doesn't exist anyway."

This process of questioning has taken hold and started to "mess up his life":

> *I start out by asking myself questions about life. I've come up with some disturbing answers.... The reason I called this paper "Philosophy Is Messing Up My Life" is because most of the answers make me look bad. I don't like that at all. Realizing that I have a philosophy has opened up a whole new world for me that I never knew existed. I'm not sure I'm ready for the truth yet. But I've made truth my responsibility...*

When we push students to speak, to evaluate; when we listen and don't rush in to fill silences, we may be able to transform the rules of studenthood in the way this philosophy professor did. And when we pose this challenge, we will be working at the very epicenter of a liberal education.

ACKNOWLEDGMENTS

I would like to acknowledge the help of graduate students who recorded, transcribed, and annotated the conference excerpts used in this chapter. Thanks also to Elizabeth Chiseri Strater for her help on this project.

REFERENCES

Carnicelli, T. 1980. The Writing Conference: A One-to-One Conversation. In *Eight Approaches to Teaching Composition*, edited by T. Donovan and B. McClelland, 101–32. Urbana, Ill.: National Council of Teachers of English.

Freedman, S., and M. Sperling. 1985. Written Language Acquisition: The Role of Response in the Writing Conference. In *The Acquisition of Written Language: Response and Revision*, edited by S. Freedman, 106–30. Norwood, N.J.: Ablex.

Graves, D. 1983. *Writing: Teachers and Children at Work*. Exeter, N.H.: Heinemann.

Knoblauch, C., and L. Brannon. 1982. On Students' Rights to Their Own Texts: A Model of Teacher Response. *College Composition and Communication* 33:157–66.

Knoblauch, C., and L. Brannon. 1984. *Rhetorical Traditions and Modern Writing*. Upper Montclair, N.J.: Boynton/Cook.

Difficult Clients and Tutor Dependency: Helping Overly Dependent Clients Become More Independent Writers

Kristin Walker

Darren first came to the writing center at Midlands Technical College last spring semester. After sitting down with Darren and asking him what he was working on, I was happy to see that Darren was very open and talkative about the paper he had just gotten back from his English instructor. The last page of the paper was branded with a large, red *F*, and faulty organization, subject/verb disagreement, and comma splices were the culprits. "I have to revise this paper in order to get a better grade," Darren said to me. "I *have got* to do better in this class. I just can't fail it!" I understood Darren's desperation, and I began reading his paper. After I had finished reading the paper, I made a few general comments about ways to improve the paper's organization. Then, I went to help another student, saying to Darren as I left that I would check back with him a little later to see how he was progressing.

As I helped the other student at a nearby desk, I could see Darren out of the corner of my eye writing and erasing, writing and erasing. The second I stood up from helping the other student, Darren summoned me. "I can't think of what to say." He was trying to formulate a thesis. "Why don't you list a few points and then make a sentence that states how you will cover those points?" I suggested. "I tried," he replied, "but Dr. Smith says we can't start sentences with *I* or *there*, and I can't think of any other way to start." I responded by listing some ways to write a thesis without using those words, just to show him that it was possible to write a thesis without *I* or *there*. "What was the second option you mentioned?" Darren asked. He was trying to copy my every word. "Your thesis should be in your own words," I protested. "Well, I just need some help getting started," Darren said. "I've been out of school for a long time, and it's so hard to know how to start."

I became very frustrated with Darren because he wanted me to be with him every step of the way as he was writing his paper. I knew that simply ignoring Darren or refusing to help him would not solve any of his problems; he would have to learn to work on his own writing with limited guidance from me. Darren continued to pressure me by asking me to suggest specific ways he could revise the grammar and punctuation errors out of his paper. When I intentionally gave him general answers so he could take care of his specific errors himself, he grew impatient and panicked, especially when he saw that the writing center was getting busier and busier and that I was less able to give him my undivided attention. When I would try to help him with one problem, he would listen to only half of my suggestion before jumping on to the next area of concern.

After attempting to help several students like Darren and listening to the other tutors talking about their frustrating encounters with them, I realized these students had several characteristics in common beyond their overdependency. First, these students tended to be ones coming back to school after a long absence and seemed to be unaware of the kind of writing skills (using clear organization, standard English, and critical thinking) their instructors were looking for. Second, these students feared they would fail in their efforts at returning to school, and third, as a result of that fear, these students were powerfully motivated to do well. These characteristics, produced students who might cling desperately to a person or people who could help them succeed. Before recommending what writing center directors should pass on to their tutors to help these students, I would like to draw attention to a recent discussion in writing center theory that will put my analysis of overdependency in perspective.

The current issue in writing center theory doesn't seem to be whether clients should be independent or dependent but how dependent they should be. In a recent *Writing Lab Newsletter* article, Dave Healy points out the harmful effects of the clinic/hospital metaphors on definitions of writing centers' purpose. He notes that even though writing center theory has abolished those metaphors, the fact that writing centers see their purpose as making clients independent supports the ideology behind the clinic metaphors. Clients who need the writing center are "ill" and require its services; clients who are "well" do not need the center and are independent of it (1–2). Healy goes on to say that, in the past, even writing center theorists such as Mary Croft and Irene Clark have emphasized the need for writing center clients' independence (2) and that this myth of independency counteracts the reality that writers need other writers for feedback on writing. He says:

> *Few teachers of composition would argue with the claim that academic success depends upon a certain resourcefulness or the ability to work independently. But getting feedback on one's writing does not constitute a state of*

deprivation that the developing writer will eventually outgrow.... [T]o suggest that a place where talk about writing occurs is not a place for the linguistically independent reflects an impoverished understanding about the nature of writing and writers (3).

Healy obviously believes that there should not be such a concept as a totally independent writer because that concept flies in the face of theories supported by Andrea Lunsford, Peter Elbow, Ira Shor, Lisa Ede, Kenneth Bruffee, and others who promote the importance of other writers at some point in the writing process. What Healy only touches on, however, is what to do about finding a balance between dependency and independency. He says:

Writers who find in the writing center a haven may need to be challenged to become more self-directed and proactive. The challenge for the writing center is not, however, to work itself out of a job, but rather to redefine the jobs that need to be done; not to wean writers from the center, but instead to provide nourishment for writers at various stages of development; not to cure people of their writing illnesses, but to infect them with the bug to collaborate (3).

Healy's three recommendations—redefining jobs that the writing center should do, providing nourishment for writers, infecting clients with the bug to collaborate—suggest ways of finding balance between independency and dependency. Using these suggestions, I will list possible "plans of action" writing center directors can promote to tutors dealing with difficult clients who are unable to find that balance themselves.

REDEFINING JOBS

Most writing center directors would agree that it is not the writing center's job to hold clients' hands throughout the entire writing process, guiding them and giving them specific answers to their questions so that the tutors end up doing clients' work for them. Since this philosophy is acceptable, the focus then moves to *how* do we as writing center directors practically redefine jobs that the writing center does? One important way is by concentrating on receiving more information from students instead of giving it. James Upton in "Beyond Correctness: Context Based Response from the Writing Center" presents a way for clients to give themselves and tutors information on the writing assignment through a Writing Assignment Worksheet (page 323. This Worksheet "is designed to help students better understand each specific assignment and the writing process and improve their critical thinking skills by having them think about, write about, and talk about the specific assignment and content BEFORE they actual [sic] write the paper" (13).

Although Upton stresses using the Worksheet before writing. it can also be used for revising/rethinking a paper.

Tutors can be instructed about the benefits of using the Worksheet (or a modification of it) to gain information from the students about specific assignments; then, tutors should present the Worksheet to students seeking help, going over the Worksheet with them so that there won't be confusion about how to complete it. Tutors should later read over the completed Worksheet to obtain as much information as possible about the students' assignments before helping them. It will not be necessary for *all* students to complete the Worksheet because not all students will be working on major writing assignments: however, those students working on papers should be required to complete the Worksheet before receiving tutorial assistance. By implementing tools such as the Worksheet in their writing centers, writing center directors can redefine the jobs of the writing center to focus more on gaining information instead of mostly giving it.

PROVIDING NOURISHMENT FOR WRITERS

Healy's suggestion to provide nourishment for writers at various stages of development (3) can be implemented with this type of overly dependent client through the help of the Writing Assignment Worksheets by helping these clients learn to become more self-sufficient; however, once tutors gain the information from the worksheets, they also need to verbally nourish and interact with clients through verifying and encouraging. First, tutors need to be instructed in the process of verification, making sure the answers the client puts down on the worksheet are accurate ones. Sometimes, difficult clients may rush through the sheet in order to receive tutorial assistance faster because they are unwilling to do work on their own, and other clients may have misunderstood some of the information prompts on the sheet and need to discuss the questions with a tutor (for example, some clients may not understand the term *audience* or may be having trouble deciding who the audience should be). Depending on the Worksheet questions writing centers choose to implement, they should also design a list of some verifying questions tutors can ask clients about the Worksheets if necessary.

Tutors can provide nourishment for these writers also by encouraging them. Oftentimes, one reason why these clients are so dependent is that they are insecure about their writing and their ability to write. Offering encouragement such as, "It looks like you understand the assignment" or "You have identified your audience well" helps these clients realize they can accomplish writing tasks on their own.

Another way to nourish writers who have reached the editing stage in the writing process is teaching them to become more self-sufficient by editing their own papers. Sometimes, these difficult clients may demand help only for editing concerns like grammar and punctuation. Because some instructors at Midlands Technical College deduct large numbers of points off students' papers for grammar errors (some fail a paper if it contains one comma splice or fragment), we see clients in the writing center who want tutors to point out their every error and tell them how to correct it. I have had clients ask me to proofread their papers several times to make sure they have corrected all the errors. If tutors comply with these clients' demands, the writing center appears to be a proofreading service and fix-it shop; plus, clients become increasingly dependent on the writing center for skills they should be able to replicate on their own.

There are ways, however, to avoid falling into such traps. Edward Vavra recommends a way for students to edit their own papers using their own writing. Vavra states that "traditional" methods of improving grammar such as studying definitions or completing exercises do not work because they tend to focus on one error at a time: subject/verb disagreement, vague pronoun reference, etc. According to Vavra, when the students look at their own papers, they're not sure which errors to look for since there probably will be a variety of them in their papers. Vavra says, "[the] students' problem is often not in *correcting* the error, but in *recognizing* it" (6).

The sequential grammar system that Vavra recommends begins with students' being able to identify prepositional phrases by putting parentheses around them. Once that step is completed, the students label subjects, verbs, and simple complements. Vavra says:

> With prepositional phrases visually set off in parentheses, students are forced to find the syntactic, and not just semantic, subject of the verb. I have watched many students underline the subjects and verbs in their own writing, and I have seen many of them correcting errors in agreement as they did so, even though they were not told to correct errors; others automatically added previously omitted '-ed' inflexions (9).

Instead of tutors' saying, "You have a subject/verb agreement error here," the errors are never identified as errors; the students, once they have identified parts of their sentences, recognize what needs to be changed on their own. "This system teaches students what is considered right, not what is wrong," Vavra emphasizes (10).

The next step is identifying subordinate clauses, a process that should eliminate fragments, run-ons, and comma splices. Finally, students identify gerunds and therefore eliminate dangling and misplaced modifiers. Vavra says that some students may need a review of punctuation rules so that they won't have comma splices simply because they do not know they need a semi-colon between two sentences instead of a comma. Overall, though, students take control of editing their texts (once they know how the sequential, syntactic tutorial operates), and they work with their own writing, focusing on corrections that need to be made in their writing individually. In addition, Vavra says:

> [T]hese four steps are not only sequential, but also cumulative: *whenever a student starts working with a new text, he begins with prepositional phrases and takes the steps in order. The tutor can decide how quickly a student should pass from one step to the next as well as how many of the steps the student needs to do. There is, for example, no pressing reason to do step four if the student has no trouble with dandling modifiers* (11).

Vavra also mentions that the format of the syntactic tutorial can also be applied to stylistics by identifying main ideas and varying sentence structure by changing forms of words (13).

Implementing this kind of system for clients who have reached the editing stage in the writing process spans Healy's recommendations both for redefining jobs and providing nourishment for writers by having tutors strongly resist the proofreading role and help writers become more self-sufficient. Although clients may resent taking the time to label parts of their sentences, they will soon be able to perform the process more quickly, and they will be able to correct their own errors in papers as well as in essay tests and in-class writing assignments which students cannot bring to the writing center. In addition, since most writing centers probably do not promote proofreading students' papers and identifying every error, tutors will no longer have to deal with the frustration of looking at a paper with numerous types of errors and not knowing where to begin. By using handouts outlining Vavra's procedures and by having tutors briefly discuss the system with clients, writing center directors can almost completely redefine the writing-center-as-proof reader mentality (still prevalent among students and faculty who are unaware of writing center/composition theory) to the writing center as facilitator of self-help and learning strategies.

One point to emphasize is that this syntactic tutorial *should not* be used as a substitution for revision. This system should be implemented much later in the writing process when clients have already addressed organization, coherence, audience, etc. The syntactic tutorial (as Vavra presents it) should be used for editing concerns.

FOSTERING COLLABORATION

By saying tutors can help nourish dependent clients, I am not implying that the tutor is all-knowing and is bestowing encouraging comments from a superior position in order to manipulate the client into believing (perhaps mistakenly) that he/she possesses the ability to be a successful writer. True nourishment comes in part as a result of collaboration, collaboration that is neither overly critical nor insincerely flattering. Because there may not be other students in the writing center working on the same assignment, the tutor becomes a collaborator.

In order to assist in facilitating the collaboration process. Upton presents a "Reader Evaluation Sheet" (on page 324), which the tutor can use to respond to the client's writing. (The Sheet is designed to be used when evaluating a completed paper; however, the Sheet can be modified to assist with prewriting as well.) Upton, who says this Sheet is a written model taken from Bill Lyons' "Praise-Question-Polish" model of responding to writing, recommends that the reader read the student's whole paper first before responding. He also says that the comments should be "as specific and positive as possible" (21). Writing center directors need to guide tutors on how best to utilize these sheets; tutors could practice using them on sample student papers or on their own writing. Tutors can also practice using samples of students' papers at various stages of revision in order to learn how the Sheet can provide different feedback on those stages. As clients revise, some parts of the paper may become more effective, and other parts that have been added may need clarification. All sections of the sheet may not be appropriate when evaluating every draft; for example, tutors probably won't focus too heavily on section six of the Sheet if the client has brought in only a rough draft.

In addition, Upton lists some other benefits to using the Sheet for collaboration:

a. The sheet provides a more permanent response to student works, and many students keep the Sheet as a reference as they work to improve their writing.
b. Students can be asked to complete a Sheet about their own specific work or body or [sic] works to help develop their own self-assessment skills.
c. The student can complete the sections of the Sheet in his/her own words during a conference with the [tutor] (21–22).

Upton stresses that this sheet does not take the place of actual writing processes, and it does not eliminate the need for oral interaction (22); rather, it is a tool to assist in collaboration. By emphasizing the need for collaboration for clients at all stages of writing development, writing center directors can truly banish the ideology that independent writers don't need the writing center. At the same time, directors can help discourage overdependency by having clients and tutors use worksheets when collaborating.

Writing Assignment Worksheet
(Adapted from Upton)

This sheet is a suggested guide to help you with your major writing assignments. Write or think the "answers" in *your* own words.

Name: _____

Subject: _____

Paper due date: _____

Assignment: (a) Formal assignment (what the teacher/textbook says):
              (b) Assignment in *my* words:
                   (Double-check my understanding of the assignment with
                   the teacher.)

Audience (To whom am I writing this?):
Intention (What do I want to accomplish in this paper?):
Length required:
Evaluative criteria (How will my paper be graded?):
Special notes or instructions about the paper:
Background information needed?
What kind(s) of sources?
Where can I work on this paper?
When can I work on this paper?
Possible pre-writing activities:

        (A) Class activities:
        (B) Own acitivities:

Can I work with others on this paper?
With whom?
When?
After pre-writing activities and thinking, what are the major ideas I want to
    share in this paper?
Writing self-diagnosis/improvement (What writing skills do I want to work on
    in this paper?):

There is no panacea for overly dependent writers. There are ways for difficult clients to abuse the systems Upton and Vavra present by demanding constant tutorial assistance. One process that may be necessary is to compose a list of your writing center's philosophies and operating procedures (including points such as "Writing center tutors are here to help you learn, not to do your work for you" and "The writing center will not function as a proofreading or editing service by identifying every error and correcting it)

Reader Evaluation Sheet
(adapted from Upton)

Author's name: _____   Title of paper: _____
Audience for paper: _____   Intention/purpose: _____
Draft number: _____
Evaluation criteria (How will paper be graded?): _____
Reader's Name: _____   Date: _____

   I. Describe the structure of my paper. How do the beginning and ending work?

  II. What parts of my paper do you like? What parts are most effective?

 III. What parts do you *see* most? What is the *one* best part of my paper?

 IV. What questions do you have about my paper? What parts are not clear?

  V. What suggestions do you have to improve my revision of this paper?

 VI. Please circle the items which detract from the readability of my paper:

mechanics	word choice	transitions
grammar	sentence variety	spelling
usage	vivid/precise wording	

VII. Thank you for reading and responding to my paper. Please make any additional comments about my paper and my ideas on the back of this sheet. I hope to discuss my paper with you before I begin my next draft.

---

to give to students before they receive assistance. You may even want to go so far as to have clients sign the paper as an indication that they understand the terms by which the writing center operates; then, if an overly dependent client becomes difficult, the tutor could point out the list, indicating that the writing center can assist him/her in many ways but that it is the tutors'/ writing center director's responsibility to make sure writing center services are not abused.

By following Healy's recommendations to redefine writing center jobs, provide nourishment for writers, and infect clients with the collaboration bug through implementing the worksheets and programs discussed here, writing center directors and tutors can begin to help overly dependent clients like Darren. In addition, clients will begin to sense what writers are: not people who must gain information from tutors in order to become self-sufficient writers in the future, but collaborators willing to give information to tutors as well as receive it, take the time to learn from and change their own writing, and accept feedback on their writing during the various stages of development. Clients will then leave the writing center with the sense that their efforts and feedback from others both make a difference in their writing instead of leaving with the idea that the writing center exists to do their writing for them.

WORKS CITED

Healy, Dave. "Countering the Myth of (In)dependence: Developing Lifelong Clients." *The Writing Lab Newsletter* 18.9 (1994): 1–3.

Upton, James. "Beyond Correctness: Context Based Response from the Writing Center." Guides for Teachers, 1987. ERIC ED 290 158.

Vavra, Edward. "The Sequential, Syntactic, Remedial Tutorial." Erie, Pennsylvania: Writing Centers Association East Central Conference, 1985. ERIC ED 263 594.

An Ongoing Tutor-Training Program

Evelyn Posey

Although tutors are usually excellent students, they seldom have previous tutoring experience. For this reason, tutor training is an important aspect of any writing center program. A general training program—which includes two to three hours of orientation focusing on procedures, tutoring roles, responsibilities, and policies—is usually required of all new tutors. During their first semester of employment. additional training in study skills, communications, critical thinking skills, and interpersonal skills may also be required. In addition to this general training, tutors also need specific training in the tutoring of writing. Most tutors learned to write using the product method—a formal, grammatical approach with instruction beginning at the sentence level, moving to the paragraph, and finally culminating with the entire essay.

The challenge for the writing center coordinator is to convince tutors that the writing process itself is a powerful means of discovery and learning and that the emphasis should be on this process. Tutors must realize that intervention at all stages is more beneficial than reading only the finished product and that evaluation should be based on the student's success in communication with an audience. The purpose of this article, then, is to describe three ways to involve writing center tutors in daily, ongoing training—training that is not added to their already heavy work and class schedule but is incorporated into their daily tutoring job. These three methods encourage tutors to develop writing center resources, to use a process-oriented worksheet while tutoring, and to participate in a writers' workshop.

DEVELOPMENT AND ADMINISTRATION

Recent management theory, as described by Peters and Waterman (13), indicates that "productivity through people," with every worker a respected

Posey, Evelyn. "An Ongoing Tutor-Training Program." *Writing Center Journal* 6.2 (1986): 29–35. Reprinted by permission of *The Writing Center Journal*.

source of ideas, not only improves quality and production, but serves as excellent training. If tutors are encouraged to become involved in the development and administration of the writing center, they learn to be better writing tutors. Thus the first method of training involves the participation of tutors in writing center development and administration. This participation includes encouraging tutors to write resource materials, teach workshops, plan promotion, and administer parts of the program.

Tutoring students has top priority in a writing center, but there are times when tutors are not busy (rainy days, the first few days of the semester, the day of the Homecoming Parade). Tutors can be asked to use this available time to work on some aspect of administration. For example, at the beginning of each semester, I post a list of projects that need attention and encourage tutors to add other projects to the list. Tutors are then asked to volunteer to work on one of these projects when they are not busy tutoring. The list includes projects in four categories: writing resource materials, preparing and teaching workshops, promoting tutoring services, and performing clerical duties. Experienced tutors usually volunteer for writing and workshop projects while new tutors prefer promotion and clerical projects, possibly because these do not demand as much expertise.

During the past two semesters tutors who volunteered for writing projects updated our "Handbook for Writing Room Tutors," a manual that explains the goals and procedures of our program. Two Computer Science majors worked on CAI (Computer Assisted Instruction), transferring usage drills to the computer and writing simple programs that provide feedback to the student on correct responses and that allow the student to try again on incorrect responses. Four tutors prepared and taught workshops in spelling, vocabulary, grammar, and research papers. These tutors planned and organized notebooks of instructional and evaluation materials for the workshops. After going over their plans with the coordinator, they taught the workshops and then spent the remainder of the semester reworking, refining, and adding to workshop materials in preparation for next semester. Four new tutors volunteered to sit in on the preparation and teaching of the workshops so that they will be trained to instruct them in future semesters.

Because new tutors are often not confident enough to write resource materials or to present workshops during their first semester, they often volunteer for promotion projects. These tutors are responsible for distributing fliers and writing promotional spots for radio. television, and the campus newspaper. Another important promotional project is making classroom visits. For example, one semester two tutors organized tutor visits to approximately 150 sections of freshman composition and linguistics. They notified the instructor of our visit, assigned a tutor to make the visit to the class, and finally confirmed that the tutor actually went to the class.

New tutors also often volunteer for clerical duties. Clerical jobs include updating files with new handouts, updating library materials by sending for complimentary copies, and keeping student records current.

No matter what the project, writing center tutors learn about the center and its resources and services by working to improve them. Of course, it is important to highlight the accomplishments of the tutors, so the coordinator should spend a portion of each staff meeting acknowledging tutors who successfully complete their projects.

Although there are some drawbacks—such as overzealous tutors who want constant attention paid to their projects, disappointment in some project results, and a few projects that are not completed—the benefits to the tutors far outweigh the disadvantages. Many times, too, tutors are extremely capable and will think of innovative ideas and ways of doing things. Therefore, both the coordinator and tutors benefit from their involvement.

REFERRAL/RESPONSE WORKSHEET

The second way of providing ongoing, daily training is to ask tutors to use a writing-process worksheet while tutoring. Much has been written in the past fifteen years about reaching writing as a process, particularly since the publication of Britton's *The Development of Writing Abilities* (11–18) in 1978. Therefore, at the beginning of each semester, I discuss writing as process to the tutors and ask them to role play a tutoring situation using their knowledge of this process. But after this initial session, tutors often forget the details of using the writing process if they are not reminded. To train tutors to use their knowledge of the writing process when tutoring, I designed a referral/response worksheet. The referral/response worksheet acts as a daily training guide for the writing center tutors. It reminds them of the writing process, it allows them to communicate with the instructor, and it provides a heuristic by which the students can complete a writing assignment.

The worksheet includes a checklist to be used by the referring teacher and the responding tutor. When the instructor checks a particular item, the tutor knows specifically how to focus the tutorial. After the session, the tutor checks the appropriate items and indicates how much time was spent on the session.

Tutors like the worksheet because it protects them when a student comes into the writing center thirty minutes before a paper is due to ask for help with an assignment. The tutor does the best job possible with the time allowed, but when the student receives a low grade on the paper, the student's reaction often is "I don't know what happened; I went to tutoring. I guess those writing center tutors don't know what they're doing." The referral/response worksheet lets the student and instructor know just what instruction was given and how much time was spent.

Referral/Response Worksheet

Name of Student _____   Date _____

Course _____

Referring Instructor _____   Responding Tutor _____

Please assist this student in: Tutored in:

PREWRITING

_____   selecting a topic   _____

_____   generating ideas   _____

_____   determining audience   _____

_____   understanding purpose   _____

_____   tone   _____

_____   other (please indicate)   _____

COMPOSING

_____   thesis paragraph development   _____

_____   paragraph development   _____

_____   supporting detail   _____

_____   introduction/conclusion   _____

_____   other (please indicate)   _____

REVISION

_____   organization   _____

_____   clarity/unity   _____

_____   sentence structure/variety   _____

_____   additional supporting detail   _____

_____   word choice   _____

_____   transitions   _____

_____   other (please indicate)   _____

COPYEDITING

_____   spelling   _____

_____   punctuation   _____

_____   grammer/mechanics (specify)   _____

Tutor Comments: Time tutored:

The tutors are asked to use the worksheet as a guide each time they tutor a writing assignment. The tutor might begin by asking "What is your topic?" "What ideas do you have about it?" "Who is the audience?" When the tutor feels that the student has completed the prewriting stage, they move on to composing. The tutor may ask, "What is your thesis?" "Will you read your paper aloud so that we can hear how you've supported your thesis?" Finally, when all rhetorical considerations have been addressed, the tutor reviews the spelling, punctuation, and usage errors with the student.

WRITERS' WORKSHOP

The third method of training is to involve tutors in a writer's workshop. Writing center tutors are usually good writers, with a desire for more recognition of their abilities. If we encourage them to write, to share their writing, and to publish, we not only help them with their writing, but we also have an opportunity to "shape" their tutoring. In a workshop in which their own work is edited and critiqued, they also see how it feels to be the tutee and realize that it can be a painful experience.

The idea for using editing response groups is not new. Elbow in *Writing With Power* devotes much of his discussion of revision to them. Judy also has many good suggestions for using editing response groups in *An Introduction to the Teaching of Writing*. However, in addition to participating in the workshop, we encourage our tutors to publish. Thus we have organized a weekly Writers' Workshop for writing center tutors to which they are encouraged to bring anything that they are writing, including essays, research papers, short stories, and poetry. Only those tutors who are writing and willing to share with the group may attend. The coordinator also shares personal writing projects to assure the tutors that we all struggle with the process. Judy suggests "that there is a 'transfer' from learning how to help another person with a paper and the long-range goal of helping students learn to revise their own work" (96). There is also a "transfer" when tutors learn to revise their own work and then begin to help another student with a paper.

In the writers' workshop we insure that tutors practice good response techniques. Groups are limited to five or six members, with each member required to bring some type of draft. One person in the group reads a draft aloud while the others listen. After finishing, the author may want to explain the purpose of the paper and ask if it has been achieved. Does the paper work for the audience for whom it is intended? The group may then comment on organization, tone, supporting detail, or other areas requiring major revision.

If the major concerns are taken care of, the author may request criterion-based feedback. In other words, are there any awkward sentences, incorrect word choices, misspelled words, or usage errors? The discussion must include supportive suggestions for revision, and tutors are encouraged to be tactful in giving suggestions. When members of the workshop finish revising their work, we encourage them to publish. We have collected information on all campus publications and have purchased books that list professional and commercial sources for all types of writing.

The Writers' Workshop is excellent training for tutors. They are less likely to be critical or dictating with students who come for tutoring because they know the feeling of having someone listen to and criticize their own writing. They practice non-directive responses in the workshop and are therefore more likely to use this approach when tutoring.

The only drawback to the workshop is that not all tutors participate. Those who are in creative writing classes seem to be the most regular participants, with those writing essays or research papers less likely to attend. Also, some tutors say they are not required to do any writing in their classes. It would be ideal if all tutors wrote every semester and were willing to share their writing in the workshop.

CONCLUSION

These suggestions for daily, ongoing training by no means exhaust the possibilities for achieving well-trained writing tutors. But some form of continuous training in tutoring and writing is essential as a supplement to the usual orientation sessions and handbooks that are typical of most tutor-training programs.

WORKS CITED

Britton, James, et al. *The Development of Writing Abilities* (11–18). London: Macmillan Education (distributed by NCTE. Urbana, Ill.), 1978.

Elbow, Peter. *Writing With Power: Techniques for Mastering the Writing Process.* Oxford: Oxford P. 1981.

Judy, Stephen and Susan Judy. *An Introduction to the Teaching of Writing.* New York: John Wiley, 1976.

Peters, Thomas and Robert Waterman, Jr. *In Search of Excellence: Lessons from America's Best-Run Companies.* New York: Harper & Row, 1982.

5

WELCOMING DIVERSITY: MULTIPLE CULTURES IN THE WRITING CENTER

Writing center culture is forged by thoughtful, hardworking directors and tu-tors who constantly negotiate their positions between student and institution. The culture is shaped by what happens inside the center and how the center interacts with its academic community. Carino's article in the first section on the history of writing describes the changes of centers over time, including their growth spurt coinciding with open admissions. As more writing centers open in schools with diverse demographics and missions, writing center cul-ture becomes more varied and complex. Writing centers have moved beyond the stereotyped grammar fix-it shop and developed outreach, writing across the curriculum programs, electronic resources, and a body of scholarship. In spite of these changes, writing centers remain what Marilyn M. Cooper calls a "border space," positioned between students and the institution. Cooper claims we must take advantage of the position by adopting a cultural studies agenda. She questions assumption in Jeff Books's article on minimalist tutor-ing in the fourth section and claims that tutors, as members of the border space, are poised to be "radical intellectuals" who can collaborate with stu-dents to help empower them to be "agents of their writing."

Another transformation takes place in the third article in this section. The second article is a case study of a Native American student, Fannie, and her tutor, Morgan, written by Annie DiPardo. Fannie negotiates the aca-demic world and its language while maintaining her reservation roots and native tongue. Whereas DiPardo explores the cultural and language issues Fannie faced, Judith K. Powers focuses more on language difficulties in her article on tutoring ESL writers. In it, she problematizes traditional tutoring methods, such as using an ear to edit. Instead, she argues that tutors must collaborate with ESL writers to understand their backgrounds so we can help them more effectively with writing in English.

Diversity in the writing center includes minorities and second-language students, but an often unnoticed visitor is the learning disabled student. Julie Neff's article provides a thorough description of learning disabilities, misconceptions about them, and how the writing center can meet learning disabled students' needs by working with them to access information they already possess.

Adopting a cultural studies agenda and serving diverse populations are not the only considerations when establishing or developing a writing center. As Judith Kilborn writes, writing centers should both recruit minority and international students to be tutors and train tutors to be culturally and linguistically sensitive. And writing centers should not forget to assess their work to measure their level of success and find areas in which to improve.

Cooper's essay shows writing center potential for educational reform. But that reform cannot take place without an understanding of diversity issues raised by DiPardo, Powers, Neff, and Kilborn. A writing center should be a "safe space" for students to collaborate and learn, and that setting can be a model for the entire university and community.

Really Useful Knowledge: A Cultural Studies Agenda for Writing Centers*

Marilyn M. Cooper

People—not just my students—often tell me that as a writing teacher, I am "different" (if they're being polite) or "crazy" or "bizarre" (if they're being frank). I believe students should be intellectually challenged in their writing classes, that they need to be engaged in a struggle over complex ideas that matter to them. I give them hard books to read, I ask them hard questions, I ask them to make up their own assignments. I believe that college students are completely capable of reading hard books and writing in interesting ways. I also know that they often don't believe that, and that they have faced a variety of obstacles that have taught them that they are "bad" or "non-standard" or (what is sometimes worse) "good" writers. Changing their attitude toward writing and their understanding of what it means to write well is a long and difficult task, not to be achieved in one or two classes or by a single teacher. So as a writing teacher I see writing centers as essential places where students can go to continue the conversations about ideas begun in class and in electronic conferences, to find people they can complain to, to work out solutions to the problems they face in their writing, to find a friend and a colleague and an advocate—all of those things I cannot really be for them. But because I have also worked with the writing center research group at MTU and am now directing dissertations by a number of graduate students who are doing research in the writing center, I also see writing centers as a site of a great deal of exciting research, a site where we can really

Cooper, Marilyn M. "Really Useful Knowledge: A Cultural Studies Agenda for Writing Centers." *The Writing Center Journal* 14.2 (1994): 97–111. Reprinted by permission of *The Writing Center Journal*.

*This essay was delivered as the keynote address at the Pacific Coast Writing Centers Association Conference at California State University, Chico, in October 1993. I would like to thank Judith Rodby, who organized the conference, for giving me the occasion to think more systematically about writing center work, and Diana George, Nancy Grimm, Kate Latterell, and Cindy Selfe who read an early draft of this essay on very short notice and who generously shared with me their ideas and experiences.

begin to see what goes on with students' writing and what keeps them from writing.

The question I have already begun to answer—what is the function of writing centers? or, as it is alternatively framed, what is the role of the writing center tutor or coach or consultant in teaching writing?—is, I would venture to say, the central concern of recent discussions of writing centers. In fact, the ongoing discussion over what to call writing center tutors is a good demonstration of the centrality of this concern. I want to align myself with certain answers to this question: that writing centers are in a good position to serve as a site of critique of the institutionalized structure of writing instruction in college, and that, as a consequence of this, the role of the tutor should be to create useful knowledge about writing in college and to empower students as writers who also understand what writing involves and who act as agents in their writing—these two goals being closely intertwined. Since I know that writing centers vary a lot from site to site, I should say at the outset that I am thinking primarily about writing centers that are staffed by undergraduate students and that allow students to work over a period of time with a single tutor, although I believe that all types of writing centers and all kinds of tutors can have the function and role I describe. I should also say that my ideas about these questions have been most heavily influenced by Nancy Grimm, who directs the writing center at Michigan Tech and who has written very directly about a critical role for writing centers. Nancy says, "Writing centers are places where students struggle to connect their public and private lives, and where they learn that success in the academy depends on uncovering and understanding tacit differences in value systems and expectations" (5). In this struggle, students and their tutors come to know a lot about the real situation of college writing.

What I want to do here is to develop a rationale for thinking of writing centers as having the essential function of critiquing institutions and creating knowledge about writing, a rationale that will make clear the politics of such a belief and that will connect the goal of inquiry with the daily practice of writing center tutors. This rationale also will have clear implications for what tutors should know and how they should be trained. But I'd like to start by suggesting why it is useful to think of writing centers in this way by looking closely at some advice on tutoring offered by Jeff Brooks in his article on minimalist tutoring that came out in 1991 in the *Writing Lab Newsletter*.

I chose Brooks' article because it has been widely admired and because it enunciates very clearly some oft-heard advice for tutors. I also like a great deal of what he suggests, particularly his emphasis on tutors' responsiveness to students and on students as active writers. He argues that tutors should not be in the business of "fixing" student papers but rather should focus on students as writers, offering them strategies and support and encouraging them to fix their own papers; he says, "The student, not the tutor, should 'own' the paper and take full responsibility for it. The tutor should take on a secondary role, serving mainly to keep the student focused on his own writing" (2). He goes on to suggest how this principle can be implemented, pointing out that "The primary value of the writing center tutor to the student is as a living human body who is willing to sit patiently and help the student spend time with her paper" (2). He offers a list of "ways we can put theory into practice" (3) and concludes, "If, at the end of the session, a paper is improved, it should be because the student did all the work" (4).

Perhaps because I am "outside" the writing center culture, I did also find a couple of things odd in Brooks' suggestions. For one thing, almost all of his specific suggestions involve tactics designed to distance tutors from students' papers in order to "establish the student as sole owner of the paper and [the tutor] as merely an interested outsider" (4). I worry about the notion of students' owning papers, and this worry connects with the other thing I find odd in Brooks' suggestions: the focus on improving individual student papers. Brooks repeatedly asserts that in writing center sessions tutors are not to focus on papers but instead on students and on their writing. But students are still expected to focus on their papers, and thus their individual papers remain the focus of writing center sessions.

Now, of course, in some ways this is not odd: students overwhelmingly show up at writing centers to get help with particular papers and particular assignments, and it would be incredibly perverse for writing center tutors simply to refuse to respond to this very real need. At the same time, it is not obvious to me—even though classroom teachers often believe this—that helping students fix papers is or should be the central purpose of writing centers, and I expect many of you agree with me on this. But I also think that it is this assumption that writing center sessions must focus on improving individual papers that leads to the trap Brooks describes, the trap of tutors serving as editors of student papers, and that leads to his emphasizing negative tactics that help tutors to refuse that role.

When writing center sessions remain resolutely focused on how a student can fix a paper, it is difficult for tutors to focus instead on what students know and need to know about writing. In such sessions, tutors can find little to do other than directly fix papers, indirectly show students how to fix papers, or simply abdicate all responsibility for mistakes in papers. Though Brooks asserts that "we forget that students write to learn, not to make perfect papers," he remains fixated on the notion of perfection in student texts: "student writing…has no real goal beyond getting it on the page," he says, and, "Most students simply do not have the skill, experience, or talent to write the perfect paper" (3). Given these assumptions, it is not at all surprising that, as Brooks says, "writing papers is a dull and unrewarding activity for most students" (2). Nor do I think that, in this situation, simply insisting that students take responsibility for their papers and treat them as valuable will either change their attitude toward writing in college or help them learn much about writing.

In order to make my point, I've emphasized how Brooks' suggestions lead to a focus on fixing student papers. But clearly, other things besides editing for effectiveness and correctness go on in the kind of writing center sessions he is talking about. Tutors help students learn processes of writing by helping them figure out what an assignment asks them to do or by helping them brainstorm in response to assignments. By asking students, "What do you mean by this?" tutors help students learn that readers often need more information or explanation in order to understand what writers had in mind. By asking students, "What's your reason for putting Q before N?" and similar questions, tutors help students learn to think about the decisions they make in writing as reasonable rather than simply a matter of following rules. By asking students to read final drafts aloud in order to find mistakes, tutors help students learn that they can correct many of their own mistakes. As long as students understand that it is what they are learning about writing in these activities that is important, not that their papers are being improved, these are useful things to do.

This, of course, is the position advocated by Stephen North in the axiom which has become a writing center mantra: "Our job is to produce better writers, not better writing." North explains,

> *Any given project—a class assignment, a law school application, an ency-clopedia entry, a dissertation proposal—is for the writer the prime, often the exclusive concern. That particular text, its success or failure, is what brings them to talk to us in the first place. In the center, though, we look beyond or through that particular project, that particular text, and see it as an occasion for addressing our primary concern, the process by which it is produced. (438)*

In other words, tutors can use the situation of students writing particular papers to focus on what students know and need to know about college writing. Brooks certainly has activities like this in mind when he suggests that tutors have better things to do with their time than to edit student papers, when he says that "we sit down with imperfect papers, but our job is to improve their writers" (2). But North's formulation of this position also makes clear how the goals of students and tutors can conflict: students come for help in making their document perfect (for very good reasons, like getting into law school, getting their dissertation proposal approved, passing the course and getting their degree) and are confronted with tutors who have their own primary concern, a concern with the process of writing. In this situation, I think that tutors must not only make clear what their concern in tutoring sessions is but also explain why they think this concern should be primary for students as well, and they must negotiate a common goal in their sessions, one that does not simply ignore the students' concerns. If tutors are not up front about their concerns, they risk losing track of them as they strive to help students or frustrating and confusing students with their uncooperativeness—both of these reactions seem inevitable in the kind of minimalist tutoring Brooks describes.

At the same time, in spite of the problems I see in Brooks' suggestions for minimalist tutoring, I think he is reaching for a purpose for writing centers beyond that enunciated by North. Brooks wants students to get more from writing center sessions than just instruction in how to write well. In his insistence that "we need to make the student the primary agent in the writing center session" (2) and that "ideally the student should be the only active agent in improving the paper" (4), I hear the desire to empower students as agents that has characterized many recent calls for reforms in writing pedagogy. It is a desire I heartily endorse, but also one that has turned out to be decidedly difficult to enact. One of the difficulties in implementing this goal arises, as Lester Faigley has pointed out, from the strong rationalist and expressivist traditions in composition studies that encourage us to see agency in writing as Brooks does in his article, in terms of owning or taking responsibility for a text. These are the same traditions Andrea Lunsford sees operating to produce the notions of the writing center as a storehouse of positivistic knowledge or as a garret where individual students get in touch with their genius.

As Lunsford points out, both traditions "tend to view knowledge as individually derived" (4), and, as Faigley points out, both traditions deny "the role of language in constructing selves" (128). For both rationalists and expressivists, knowledge and writing are dependent on a preexisting coherent and rational self. Given this assumption, agency in writing becomes a matter of subduing the text to the self by achieving personal control over it, either by creating in it a rational and coherent point of view on the topic addressed, a point of view that is dependent on the rational and coherent self of the writer, or by expressing one's personal vision or true self in it—often referred to as achieving an authentic voice. Unfortunately, as the modern world taught us that selves (or, as we learned to call them, subject positions) are constantly in the process of construction and that one of the activities that contributes most to the construction of subject positions is language use (including writing), we came to understand that writers cannot and do not achieve agency in writing by subduing language to their selves but rather by using language to construct subject positions. Agency in writing depends not on owning or taking responsibility for a text but on understanding how to construct subject positions in texts. From Brooks' point of view, it is ironic, then, that what this comes down to is that tutors can best help students become agents of their own writing by helping them understand how and the extent to which they are *not* owners of their texts and *not* responsible for the shape of their texts, by helping them understand, in short, how various institutional forces impinge on how and what they write and how they can negotiate a place for their own goals and needs when faced with these forces.

Students know that they don't own their texts only too well, and tutors know it too, but the overwhelming discourse in textbooks, classroom advice, training materials for teachers and tutors, and in much of the scholarship and research in composition studies on the importance of individual control in producing writing works to obscure this fact and to keep both students and tutors from realizing what they know. In her *Writing Center Journal* article, Nancy Welch observes,

> *my work in the writing center at a large public university has also introduced me to students who arrive at the center already aware, sometimes painfully so, that their meanings are contested and that their words are populated with competing, contradictory voices.... Even alone, these students write with and against a cacophony of voices, collaborating not with another person but with the Otherness of their words. (4)*

Students and tutors who are outside mainstream culture are usually more aware of the way language coerces them, but all students and tutors know how institutions coerce them in writing classes. They know that students in writing classes are offered and can exercise little or no control over such things as the topic or genre of their papers, the argument structure or organization of their papers, the length of their papers, and the style or register of language in their papers. Students know that in order to get a good grade they must carefully follow assignments that specify these things, and tutors are advised explicitly not to criticize or in any way try to subvert teachers' assignments. Students and tutors respond—quite rationally—by trying to make the papers match as perfectly as possible the specifications of assignments while at the same time—quite irrationally—trying to believe that in doing this students are asserting ownership over their texts and learning to write. Meg Woolbright says, "In thinking one thing and saying another, the tutor is subverting the conflict she feels" (23); she is not being honest, and thus she subverts her chances of establishing egalitarian conversations with her students and alienates both herself and them (28–9).

But if tutors need to help students—and themselves—realize that what they know about institutional constraints is true and important, they also need to help students understand that if they are to achieve agency in writing, they must learn how to challenge these constraints productively in the service of their own goals and needs. Agency in writing is not a matter of simply taking up the subject positions offered by assignments but of actively constructing subject positions that negotiate between institutional demands and individual needs. In his discussion of what cultural studies offers to teachers of writing, John Trimbur explains that "one of the central tasks that [cultural studies] sets for radical intellectuals is to point out the relatively autonomous areas of public and private life where human agency can mediate between the material conditions of the dominant order and the lived experience and aspirations of the popular masses" (9). Because writing assignments, no matter how tightly specified, require the active participation of human agents, they offer relatively autonomous spaces in which the institutional constraints on writing imposed by the dominant order can be made to respond to the lived experience and aspirations of students.

If tutors want to help students develop agency in writing, they need to cast themselves as radical intellectuals who help students find and negotiate these spaces. Such tutors cannot, as Stephen North advises them to do, simply help students operate within the existing context without trying to change it. And, yes, I *am* thinking about undergraduate tutors, whose cogent critiques of assignments often leak out in writing center sessions even when they don't make them explicit. Furthermore, in helping students become agents of their own writing, tutors also become agents of change in writing pedagogy, helping teachers create better assignments, letting teachers know what students are having trouble with. As intellectuals, tutors contribute both to the endeavor of helping students learn about writing and to the endeavor of creating useful knowledge about writing. Speaking of what tutors can learn and how they can affect writing pedagogy, Nancy Grimm says,

> *Our excursions into students' heads, like our excursions into films and novels, change the way we see and the way we act and the way we think and the way we teach. Our promise to support the teachers' position completely prevents us from sharing these altered perspectives that can in turn change the rhetorical context of teaching. In a writing center, one discovers how smart students are and how arbitrary and limiting linguistic conventions and educational hierarchies can be. (6)*

And, I want to argue, it is in a writing center that one discovers how the goal of empowering students as agents of their writing can actually be achieved, for writing center tutors, by virtue of their constant contact with institutional constraints *and* with students' lived experiences, are best positioned to serve as what Trimbur calls radical intellectuals, or what Gramsci calls organic intellectuals.

In order for you to better understand why I believe that the goal of empowering students can best be achieved in a writing center and why tutors are more likely to be organic intellectuals than are classroom teachers of writing, I now want to explain the rationale that underlies my argument. To do so, I will draw on some theories that are connected with work in cultural studies and especially on the ideas of a theorist who has arguably had the most influence on cultural studies, Antonio Gramsci. Gramsci's work has also heavily influenced Paulo Freire, and recently we have begun to see some direct influences of Gramsci in composition studies. As a member of the Communist Party in Italy, Gramsci was arrested by Mussolini in 1924. In his trial, the prosecutor claimed, "We must stop this brain working for twenty years!" But, during the eight years he spent in prison, Gramsci wrote 2,848 pages in thirty-two notebooks, working out his theories of how social groups gain legitimacy and power, how political change comes about, and, most importantly for us as writing teachers, what role intellectuals and education play in this process.

Gramsci argues that the function of education in a democratic society is to produce intellectuals, for "democracy, by definition, cannot mean merely that an unskilled worker can become skilled. It must mean that every citizen can 'govern' and that society places him, even if only abstractly, in a general condition to achieve this" (40). According to Gramsci, everyone is on some level and potentially an intellectual:

> each man…carries on some form of intellectual activity, that is, he is a "philosopher," an artist, a man of taste, he participates in a particular conception of the world, has a conscious line of moral conduct, and therefore contributes to sustain a conception of the world or to modify it, that is, to bring into being new modes of thought. (9)

Thus, intellectuals are produced not by "introducing from scratch a scientific form of thought into everyone's individual life, but [by] renovating and making 'critical' an already existing activity" (330–31). According to Gramsci, intellectuals become intellectuals not by virtue of any inherent qualifications but by virtue of their efforts to elaborate critically and systematically the philosophy of their social group.

When a social group becomes well established and dominant, its intellectuals often come to see what they do as valuable in and of itself and see themselves as somehow specially qualified for intellectual activities; they lose sight of how their activities function primarily to further the goals of their particular social group. These intellectuals are what Gramsci calls traditional intellectuals, intellectuals who because of their tenure as the intellectuals of a successful and powerful social group come to see themselves as "autonomous and independent of the dominant social group" (7). A second characteristic of traditional intellectuals is that they are the apologists for a dominant group whose vision is failing, whose ideas are no longer productive in a changing society. In his recent article on Gramsci in *Pre/Text*, Victor Villanueva offers E. D. Hirsch as a good example of an American traditional intellectual, an apologist for the status quo whose recommendations for instilling cultural literacy in all students, though well intentioned, are neither disinterested nor progressive, but rather serve the interests of an established but increasingly discredited elite.

Traditional intellectuals are no longer agents of change in a society for these two reasons: they have lost contact with the purposes and goals of the group whose philosophy they represent, and they serve, although often unknowingly, the status quo. Organic intellectuals, in contrast, are those intellectuals who understand that their function as intellectuals derives from their involvement in the work and the purposes of their social group. Furthermore, they are the intellectuals of an emergent social group, one which is not yet dominant but whose vision is more directly responsive to the current historical conditions of the society than that of the dominant group, whose vision developed out of past historical conditions. Organic intellectuals exemplify the basic marxist postulate of the unity of theory and practice. Gramsci calls them "the whalebone in the corset," "*elites*...of a new type which arise directly out of the masses, but remain in contact with them" (340).

Organic intellectuals are agents of change because they develop through their fusion of theory and practice and through critique of the common sense of their group the philosophy of an emergent social group. Both contact with everyday practice and critique are important in this process. Contact with everyday practice ensures that the philosophy of the group more accurately represents the real historical situation; critique of the commonsense knowledge of the group frees it from the influence of the views and beliefs of the dominant social group, who have achieved power in large part because of their success in persuading all groups in a society that their world view is true and useful. Organic intellectuals must work to achieve critical understanding of the current situation of a society; they must sort through the various arguments and perspectives that are represented in the common sense of their group in order to produce what Richard Johnson has called really useful knowledge, knowledge that arises out of everyday practice and that is purified of contradictory beliefs left over from the world view of the dominant group. In Johnson's terms, critique is always an ongoing process that resists closure and is antithetical to the procedures of academic codification and disciplinarity, for critique offers "procedures by which other traditions are approached both for what they may yield and for what they inhibit" (38). Ongoing critique ensures that organic-intellectuals do not turn into traditional intellectuals, that really useful knowledge is not turned into disciplinary knowledge, that knowledge is continually produced in the contact of theory and practice. Really useful knowledge, Johnson argues, demands that the priority always be "to become more 'popular' rather than more academic" (40).

To return now from the realms of theory to the situation of students writing in college, I want to argue that composition studies and its scholars and researchers and classroom teachers function for the most part as traditional intellectuals of the dominant social group, intellectuals who have lost sight of how their beliefs and practices are dependent on the world view of the white middle class of America and whose everyday experience is quite separate from and foreign to the life experiences of most students in college writing classes. Some scholars and teachers, it is true, struggle to remain in contact with the everyday experience of students in writing classes and struggle to define their problems and practices on the basis of this contact, but neither scholars nor classroom teachers of writing are favorably positioned to succeed in this effort. Whether scholars or teachers, whether regular faculty, part-time teachers, or graduate students, their position in the writing classroom is guaranteed by the institutional structures of the dominant social group: they are responsible to standards developed by this group in service to its purposes; they are subject to education and training that has developed within the perspective of the dominant group; they are in daily contact with the discourse of other traditional intellectuals; and, finally, they are usually expected to separate theory from practice. In the case of faculty and graduate students they are admonished that their own work should have priority over teaching, and, in the case of part-time teachers, they are subjected to work loads that preclude efforts at reflection and critique and theory building. It is thus not surprising that it is difficult for classroom writing teachers to empower students as agents of their own writing, for the main prerequisite of such an endeavor is, as Freire has long pointed out, having some idea of what students' purposes and experiences are.

In contrast, tutors in writing centers who are in close contact with students and their everyday writing concerns, who reflect on their practices as tutors, and who study and critique theories of writing and language in light of their practice are better positioned to be organic intellectuals, who, along with their students, develop really useful knowledge of writing practices and of ways of teaching writing that help students achieve agency. Because writing centers are marginalized in relation to the central institutional structures of writing pedagogy and because writing center tutors are not generally expected to perform the function of intellectuals, the pressure on them to promulgate beliefs and practices that serve the purposes of the dominant group is less organized and less direct, although it is certainly not absent. North details some of the informal attempts of faculty to bring writing center practice into line with the authorized knowledge about writing, and his widely followed stricture that tutors are to support the classroom teacher's position completely is clear evidence of how writing centers do not escape domination. Yet one of the benefits of being excluded from the dominant group is that in this position one has less to protect and less to lose. Undergraduate students who serve as tutors have little investment in disciplinary beliefs and practices, and they are thus less responsive to its standards and expectations than they are to the needs and experiences of their peers. And, even for classroom teachers and graduate students, the continuous contact with the needs and experiences of writing students moves tutors to critique, to observe both what the traditional practices of writing instruction yield and what they inhibit.

I could continue to argue in support of my contention that tutors should and can serve as agents of change who empower students and who produce really useful knowledge, but I suspect that I can win your agreement better in another way. I want to conclude by recounting examples of how this is already happening in writing centers across the country. Following are five examples of practices of tutors and writing center administrators that seem to me to exemplify how writing centers can serve as a site of critique and how tutors can function as organic intellectuals.

1. Alice Gillam draws on Bakhtin to suggest a dialogic approach to tutoring that encourages students to negotiate between the demands of an assignment and their own interests in writing. She asks "whether the univocal conventional wisdom about reading ought to organize [a particular student's] interpretation of her [reading] experience or whether [the student's] experiences ought to reorganize or complicate conventional wisdom" (6), and she suggests that

> *opening or dialogizing this text through the play of oppositions might enable Mary to see ways of satisfying her teacher's demand for focus without sacrificing [her own] richness of voice and detail.... Rather than stripping her "story" to the bone in order to impose a focus, perhaps Mary needs to flesh out the contradictions embedded in the text and puzzle over the off-key shifts in voice as a way of discovering focus.... In short, a Bakhtinian perspective might have allowed [Mary's tutor] to help Mary see the dissonances in voice and narrative as opportunities to dialogize and clarify meaning rather than as the enemies of focus, as forces to be subdued and "normalized." (7)*

2. Lucy Chang demonstrates how through conversation with a Chinese student she "came to understand the cultural reasoning" that dictated the shape of the student's paper, which she describes as "a chaotic dance of ten letter words" (17). She found out that

> *First, in China a scholar's intellectual power is measured by the number of Chinese characters he or she knows, not by how coherently words are arranged as this particular assignment demanded. Second, the words she knew in English translated into something else, a distant relative of her initial thought. She believed that with one English word she could express everything she was feeling as she could with one Chinese character. Third, she believed that good writing was the kind that is found in textbooks,*

language that is condensed and lacking in emotion. The confusion and con-
flict began here. Last, her deficiency in English grammar was a huge inse-
curity. As a result, she took no responsibility for her writing, as a means of
protecting herself from the shame of her grammatical mistakes. (17–18)

Chang concludes, "From this collective understanding, I believe that I was better equipped to facilitate her writing process" (18). Chang's experience contrasts strikingly with the experience of the tutor described by Anne Di-Pardo, whose ignorance of her Native American student's culture and experiences with writing frustrated all her persistent and well-intentioned efforts to help the student succeed.

3. Kate Latterell, in exploring the actual practices of student-centered tutoring, discovers that, for the two tutors she interviewed,

being student-centered…does not seem to mean being passive, for they both
stressed the importance of developing personal relationships with students
as being a big factor…. Suzanne…suggests that "the more effective teach-
ing that I've seen happens in places like this…where there's personal inter-
action and personal factors that are helping out." And Dave seems to
suggest the same thing, saying, "I really believe very strongly in the pow-
erful influences of individual and personal relationships" in making learn-
ing meaningful. (10)

Dave also refers to the importance of active engagement between tutor and student when he tells Kate that his idea of what tutoring involves has changed "'from believing that this is totally undirected stuff to thinking that his role is to provide a focus for the session by 'keying in on' what the student needs to talk about" (9).

4. Drawing on Julia Kristeva's notion of exile as the creation of a space in which writers can question received knowledge and social norms and in the process transform them, Nancy Welch elaborates a style of tutoring that enables both tutors and students to achieve critical distance. She recounts her work with Margie, who is engaged in writing about her experience of sexual harassment for a panel discussion during the university's annual Women's Week. Welch notes how, early in the process, she has "already constructed a template of what [Margie] should eventually write for her Women's Week panel" and is "disturbed by the gap between that 'Ideal Text' (to borrow Knoblauch and Brannon's term) and the actual text [Margie] reads to" her and how, when she resists "the pressure of perfection," Margie "displaces that template text I had formed and encourages me to listen to her emerging text instead" (9–10). At the end of a prolonged series of sessions, when Margie is about to write a draft of the actual presentation, Welch offers her only one suggestion, that she remind herself to describe what hap-

pened to her. Welch recounts Margie's reaction: "Margie grins. 'Sure, I get it,' she replies. 'I still tend to avoid that. Yeah. The monster needs a description. *I* can do that. *I* know what the monster looks like'" (16).

5. Tom Fox describes the tutor training program at Chico in which tutors are asked "to reflect critically on how social and educational inequalities affect writing and learning" and how he explores with tutors "how the institution around us is shot through with actual hierarchies and habits of hierarchies and how we more easily fall into these habits than into a truly democratic writing center, no matter whether the tables are round or square" (21). His tutors read theory—"Paulo Freire on how all education is political, Dale Spender, Richard Ohmann, Geneva Smitherman-Donaldson, and John Ogbu on how gender, class, and race affect language use, and…Mike Rose on how institutional history and politics shape our conceptions of writing, especially remedial writing" (22–23)—and they reflect on their own practices and educational histories. Fox concludes,

> When tutors reflect on and define their own role in a multi-cultural writing center and explore the relationship between a progressive writing center and a conservative university, they gain a sense of control over the interpretation of their experience. This control can lead to action both within and without the writing center. (23)

In these practices I see the beginnings of a vision of a writing center as a site of inquiry and critique, where tutors not only are helping students learn how to improve their writing but also are developing better practices of teaching writing and really useful knowledge about the experiences of students writing in college and in our society. Rather than "always focusing on the paper at hand" (Brooks 2), tutors build personal relationships with their students and come to understand how their students' lives and experiences shape their writing practices. Rather than insisting that students are the only ones responsible for their texts, tutors help students understand how their words and their texts are inhabited by multiple and often alien voices that they must learn to deal with. Rather than "supporting the teacher's position completely" (North 441), tutors help students negotiate a place within the confines of writing assignments for interests and abilities that arise out of their experiences. Rather than lamenting the inability of students to produce perfect papers, tutors celebrate students' ability to develop new "templates" for texts. Rather than learning to sit across from the student and not write on their papers, tutors learn to critique the social and institutional setting of writing pedagogy and to reflect on their practices in light of theories of writing and language.

I think we can push this vision further. I would like, for example, to see writing center sessions sometimes focus on the critical reading of the syllabuses and assignments that students are given to work with so that tutors could help students see what subject positions are being offered to them in these texts and what spaces are left open in which they can construct different subject positions. Classroom teachers occasionally try to get their students to engage in such critical readings, but the teachers' investment in the subjectivities they have imagined for their students fairly regularly defeats their efforts. In critical reading sessions in writing centers, tutors could also help students figure out why their teachers' ideas of what they need to learn sometimes conflict with what they think they need to learn and how recognizing these conflicts can lead to change as well as to accommodation.

I would also like to see tutor training seminars begin to blend with research groups, so that faculty, writing center administrators, and/or graduate students work together with undergraduate tutors and with the students who come to writing centers to develop systematic inquiries into the nature of writing in college and the value of different methods of teaching writing. I know that this is happening in some writing centers, and I think that in such research we can begin to bridge the chasm that often separates writing center workers from classroom teachers and theorists of writing. Writing centers are and can be at the heart of our joint inquiry into the functions of literacy in our society. We need to make better use of these "border" spaces within our institutions, spaces where the lines of power blur and the demands of discipline and evaluation weaken in ways that allow us to create together better ways of writing and of teaching writing.

WORKS CITED

Brooks, Jeff. "Minimalist Tutoring: Making the Student Do All the Work." *Writing Lab Newsletter* 15.6 (1991): 1–4.

DiPardo, Anne. "Whispers of Coming and Going': Lessons from Fannie." *The Writing Center Journal* 12.2 (Spring 1992): 125–44.

Faigley, Lester. *Fragments of Rationality: Postmodernity and the Subject of Composition.* Pittsburgh: U of Pittsburgh P, 1992.

Gillam, Alice M. "Writing Center Ecology: A Bakhtinian Perspective." *The Writing Center Journal* 12.2 (Spring/Summer 1991): 3–11.

Gramsci, Antonio. *Selections from the Prison Notebooks.* Ed. and tr. Quintin Hoare and Geoffrey Nowell Smith. New York: International, 1971.

Grimm, Nancy. "Contesting 'The Idea of a Writing Center': The Politics of Writing Center Research." *Writing Lab Newsletter* 17.1 (September 1992): 5–6.

Johnson, Richard. "What Is Cultural Studies Anyway?" *Social Text* 16 (1986/87): 38–80.

Latterell, Kate. "Revising Our Roles: Writing Center Coaches Talk about their Roles." Paper delivered at the Midwest Writing Center Association, St. Louis, Missouri. 1 Oct. 1993.

Lunsford, Andrea. "Collaboration, Control, and the Idea of a Writing Center." *The Writing Center Journal* 12.1 (Fall 1991): 3–10.

North, Stephen M. "The Idea of a Writing Center." *College English* 46 (1984): 433–46.

Okawa, Gail Y., Thomas Fox, Lucy J. Y. Chang, Shana R. Windsor, Frank Bella Chavez, Jr., and LaGuan Hayes. "Multi-cultural Voices: Peer Tutoring and Critical Reflection in the Writing Center." *The Writing Center Journal* 12.1 (Fall 1991): 11–33.

Trimbur, John. "Cultural Studies and Teaching Writing." *Focuses* 1 (1988): 5–18.

Villanueva, Victor, Jr. "Hegemony: From an Organically Grown Intellectual." *PrelText* 13 (1992): 18–34.

Welch, Nancy. "From Silence to Noise: The Writing Center as Critical Exile." *The Writing Center Journal* 14.1 (Fall 1993): 3–15.

Woolbright, Meg. "The Politics of Tutoring: Feminism within the Patriarchy." *The Writing Center Journal* 13.1 (Fall 1992): 16–30.

"Whispers of Coming and Going": Lessons from Fannie

Anne DiPardo

> *As a man with cut hair, he did not identify the rhythm of three strands, the whispers of coming and going, of twisting and tying and blending, of catching and of letting go, of braiding.*
> —MICHAEL DORRIS, A YELLOW RAFT IN BLUE WATER

We all negotiate among multiple identities, moving between public and private selves, living in a present shadowed by the past, encountering periods in which time and circumstance converge to realign or even restructure our images of who we are. As increasing numbers of non-Anglo students pass through the doors of our writing centers, such knowledge of our own shape-shifting can help us begin—if *only* begin—to understand the social and linguistic challenges which inform their struggles with writing. When moved to talk about the complexities of their new situation, they so often describe a more radically chameleonic process, of living in non-contiguous worlds, of navigating between competing identities, competing loyalties. "It's like I have two cultures in me," one such student remarked to me recently, "but I can't choose." Choice becomes a moot point as boundaries blur, as formerly distinct selves become organically enmeshed, indistinguishable threads in a dynamic whole (Bakhtin 275; Cintron 24; Fischer 196).

Often placed on the front lines of efforts to provide respectful, insightful attention to these students' diverse struggles with academic discourse, writing tutors likewise occupy multiple roles, remaining learners even while

DiPardo, Ann. "'Whispers of Coming and Going': Lessons from Fannie." *The Writing Center Journal* 12.2 (1992): 125–44. Reprinted by permission of *The Writing Center Journal*.

emerging as teachers, perennially searching for a suitable social stance (Hawkins)—a stance existing somewhere along a continuum of detached toughness and warm empathy, and, which like all things ideal, can only be approximated, never definitively located. Even the strictly linguistic dimension of their task is rendered problematic by the continuing paucity of research on the writing of nonmainstream students (see Valdés; "Identifying Priorities"; "Language Issues")—a knowledge gap which likewise complicates our own efforts to provide effective tutor training and support. Over a decade has passed since Mina Shaughnessy eloquently advised basic writing teachers to become students of their students, to consider what Glynda Hull and Mike Rose ("Rethinking," "Wooden Shack") have more recently called the "logic and history" of literacy events that seem at first glance inscrutable and strange. In this age of burgeoning diversity, we're still trying to meet that challenge, still struggling to encourage our tutors to appreciate its rich contours, to discover its hidden rigors, to wrestle with its endless vicissitudes.

This story is drawn from a semester-long study of a basic writing tutorial program at a west-coast university—a study which attempted to locate these tutor-led small groups within the larger contexts of a writing program and campus struggling to meet the instructional needs of non-Anglo students (see DiPardo, "Passport"). It is about one tutor and one student, both ethnic minorities at this overwhelmingly white, middle-class campus, both caught up in elusive dreams and uncertain beginnings. I tell their story not because it is either unusual or typical, but because it seems so richly revealing of the larger themes I noted again and again during my months of data collection—as unresolved tensions tugged continually at a fabric of institutional good intentions, and as tutors and students struggled, with ostensible good will and inexorable frustration, to make vital connections. I tell this story because I believe it has implications for all of us trying to be worthy students of our students, to make sense of our own responses to diversity, and to offer effective support to beginning educators entrusted to our mentorship.

"IT, LIKE, RUINS YOUR MIND": FANNIE'S EDUCATIONAL HISTORY

Fannie was Navajo, and her dream was to one day teach in the reservation boarding schools she'd once so despised, to offer some of the intellectual, emotional, and linguistic support so sorely lacking in her own educational history. As a kindergartner, she had been sent to a school so far from her home that she could only visit family on weekends. Navajo was the only language spoken in her house, but at school all the teachers were Anglo, and only English was allowed. Fannie recalled that students had been punished for speaking their native language—adding with a wry smile that they'd spoken Navajo anyway, when the teachers weren't around. The elementary school curriculum had emphasized domestic skills—cooking, sewing, and, especially, personal hygiene. "Boarding school taught me to be a housemaid," Fannie observed in one of her essays, "I was hardly taught how to read and write." All her literacy instruction had been in English, and she'd never become literate in Navajo. Raised in a culture that valued peer collaboration (cf. Philips 391–93), Fannie had long ago grasped that Anglo classrooms were places where teachers assume center stage, where students are expected to perform individually: "No," her grade-school teachers had said when Fannie turned to classmates for help, "I want to hear *only* from *you.*"

Estranged from her family and deeply unhappy, during fifth grade Fannie had stayed for a time with an aunt and attended a nearby public school. The experience there was much better, she recalled, but there soon followed a series of personal and educational disruptions as she moved among various relatives' homes and repeatedly switched schools. By the time she began high school, Fannie was wondering if the many friends and family members who'd dropped out had perhaps made the wiser choice. By her sophomore year, her grades had sunk "from A's and B's to D's and F's," and she was "hanging out with the wrong crowd." By mid-year, the school wrote her parents a letter indicating that she had stopped coming to class. When her family drove up to get her, it was generally assumed that Fannie's educational career was over.

Against all odds, Fannie finished high school after all. At her maternal grandmother's insistence, arrangements were made for Fannie to live with an aunt who had moved to a faraway west-coast town where the educational system was said to be much stronger. Her aunt's community was almost entirely Anglo, however, and Fannie was initially self-conscious about her English: "I had an accent really bad," she recalled, "I just couldn't communicate." But gradually, although homesick and sorely underprepared, she found that she was holding her own. Eventually, lured by the efforts of affirmative action recruiters, she took the unexpected step of enrolling in the nearby university. "I never thought I would ever graduate from high school," Fannie wrote in one of her essays, adding proudly that "I'm now on my second semester in college as a freshman." Her grandmother had died before witnessing either event, but Fannie spoke often of how pleased she would have been.[1]

Fannie was one of a handful of Native Americans on the campus, and the only Navajo. As a second-semester first-year student, she was still struggling to find her way both academically and socially, still working to overcome the scars of her troubled educational history. As she explained after listening to an audiotape of a tutorial session, chief among these was a lingering reluctance to speak up in English, particularly in group settings:

Fannie: When, when, I'm talking.... I'm shy. Because I always think I always say something not right, with my English, you know, (Pauses, then speaks very softly.) It's hard, though. Like with my friends, I do that too. Because I'll be quiet—they'll say, "Fannie, you're quiet." Or if I meet someone, I, I don't do it, let them do it, I let that person do the talking.

A. D.: Do you wish you were more talkative?

Fannie: I wish! Well I am, when I go home. But when I come here, you know, I always think, English is my second language and I don't know that much, you know.

A. D.: So back home you're not a shy person?

Fannie: (laughing uproariously) No! (continues laughing).

I had a chance to glimpse Fannie's more audacious side later that semester, when she served as a campus tour guide to a group of students visiting from a distant Navajo high school. She was uncharacteristically feisty and vocal that week, a change strikingly evident on the tutorial audiotapes. Indeed, when I played back one of that week's sessions in a final interview, Fannie didn't recognize her own voice: "Who's that talking?" she asked at first. But even as she recalled her temporary elation, she described as well her gradual sense of loss:

Sometimes I just feel so happy when someone's here, you know, I feel happy? I just get that way. And then (pauses, begins to speak very softly), and then it just wears off. And then they're leaving—I think, oh, they're leaving, you know.

While Fannie described their week together as "a great experience," she was disturbed to find that even among themselves, the Navajo students were speaking English: "That bothered me a lot," she admitted, surmising that "they're like embarrassed...to speak Navajo, because back home, speaking Navajo fluently all the time, that's like lower class." "If you don't know the language," Fannie wrote in one of her essays, "then you don't know who you are...It's your identity...the language is very important." In striking contrast to these students who refused to learn the tribal language, Fannie's grandparents had never learned to speak English: "They were really into their culture, and tradition, and all of that," she explained, "but now we're not that way anymore, hardly, and it's like we're losing it, you know." Fannie hoped to attend a program at Navajo Community College where she could learn to read and write her native language, knowledge she could then pass on to her own students.

Fannie pointed to the high drop-out rate among young Navajos as the primary reason for her people's poverty, and spoke often of the need to encourage students to finish high school and go on to college. And yet, worried as she was about the growing loss of native language and tradition, Fannie also expressed concerns about the Anglicizing effects of schooling. Education is essential, she explained, but young Navajos must also understand its dangers:

> *I mean like, sometimes if you get really educated, we don't really want that. Because then, it like ruins your mind, and you use it, to like betray your people, too…That's what's happening a lot now.*

By her own example, Fannie hoped to one day show her students that it is possible to be both bilingual and bicultural, that one can benefit from exposure to mainstream ways without surrendering one's own identity:

> *If you know the white culture over here, and then you know your own culture, you can make a good living with that…when I go home, you know, I know Navajo, and I know English too. They say you can get a good job with that.*

Back home, Fannie's extended family was watching her progress with warm pride, happily anticipating the day when she would return to the reservation to teach. When Fannie went back for a visit over spring break, she was surprised to find that they'd already built her a house: "They sure give me a lot of attention, that's for sure," she remarked with a smile. Many hadn't seen Fannie for some time, and they were struck by the change:

> *Everybody still, kind of picture me, still, um, the girl from the past. The one who quit school—and they didn't think of me going to college at all. And they were surprised, they were really surprised. And they were like proud of me too…'cause none of their family is going to college.*

One delighted aunt, however, was the mother of a son who was also attending a west-coast college:

> She says, "I'm so happy! I can't wait to tell him, that you're going to college too! You stick in there, Fannie, now don't goof!" I'm like, "I'll try not to!"

"I ALWAYS WRITE BAD ESSAYS": FANNIE'S STRUGGLES WITH WRITING

On the first day of class, Fannie's basic writing teacher handed out a questionnaire that probed students' perceptions of their strengths and weaknesses as writers. In response to the question, "What do you think is good about your writing?" Fannie wrote, "I still don't know what is good about my writing"; in response to "What do you think is bad about your writing?" she responded, "Everything."

Fannie acknowledged that her early literacy education had been neither respectful of her heritage nor sensitive to the kinds of challenges she would face in the educational mainstream. She explained in an interview that her first instruction in essay writing had come at the eleventh hour, during her senior year of high school: "I never got the technique, I guess, of writing good essays," she explained, "I always write bad essays." While she named her "sentence structure, grammar, and punctuation" as significant weaknesses, she also added that "I have a lot to say, but I can't put it on paper...it's like I can't find the vocabulary." Fannie described this enduring block in an in-class essay she wrote during the first week of class:

> From my experience in writing essays were not the greatest. There were times my mind would be blank on thinking what I should write about.
>
> In high school, I learned how to write an essay during my senior year. I learned a lot from my teacher but there was still something missing about my essays. I knew I was still having problems with my essay organization.
>
> Now, I'm attending a university and having the same problems in writing essays. The university put me in basic writing, which is for students who did not pass the placement test. Of course, I did not pass it. Taking basic writing has helped me a lot on writing essays. There were times I had problems on what to write about.
>
> There was one essay I had problems in writing because I could not express my feelings on a paper. My topic was on Mixed Emotions. I knew how I felt in my mind but I could not find the words or expressing my emotions.
>
> Writing essays from my mind on to the paper is difficult for me. From this experience, I need to learn to write what I think on to a paper and expand my essays.

"Yes," her instructor wrote at the bottom of the page, "even within this essay—which is good—you need to provide specific detail, not just general statements." But what did Fannie's teacher find "good" about this essay—or was this opening praise only intended to soften the criticism that followed? Fannie had noted in an interview that she panicked when asked to produce something within 45 minutes: "I just write anything," she'd observed, "but your mind goes blank, too." Still, while this assignment may not have been the most appropriate way to assess the ability of a student like Fannie, both she and her instructor felt it reflected her essential weakness—that is, an inability to develop her ideas in adequate detail.

At the end of the semester, her basic writing teacher confided that Fannie had just barely passed the course, and would no doubt face a considerable struggle in first-year composition. Although Fannie also worried about the next semester's challenge, she felt that her basic writing course had provided valuable opportunities. "I improved a lot," she said in a final interview, "I think I did—I know I did. 'Cause now I can know what I'm trying to say, and in an afternoon, get down to that topic." One of her later essays, entitled "Home," bears witness to Fannie's assertion:

> *The day is starting out a good day. The air smells fresh as if it just rained. The sky is full with clouds, forming to rain. From the triangle mountain, the land has such a great view. Below I see hills overlapping and I see six houses few feet from each other. One of them I live in. I can also see other houses miles apart.*
>
> *It is so peaceful and beautiful. I can hear birds perching and dogs barking echos from long distance. I can not tell from which direction. Towards north I see eight horses grazing and towards east I hear sheep crying for their young ones. There are so many things going on at the same time.*
>
> *It is beginning to get dark and breezy. It is about to rain. Small drops of rain are falling. It feels good, relieving the heat. The rain is increasing and thundering at the same time. Now I am soaked, I have the chills. The clouds is moving on and clearing the sky. It is close to late afternoon. The sun is shining and drying me off. The view of the land is more beautiful and looks greener. Like a refreshment.*
>
> *Across from the mountain I am sitting is a mountain but then a plateau that stretches with no ending. From the side looks like a mountain but it is a long plateau. There are stores and more houses on top of the plateau.*
>
> *My clothes are now dry and it is getting late. I hear my sister and my brother calling me that dinner is ready. It was a beautiful day. I miss home.*

"Good description." her instructor wrote on this essay, "I can really 'see' this scene." But meanwhile, she remained concerned about Fannie's lack of sophistication: "Try to use longer, more complex sentences," she added, "avoid short, choppy ones." Overwhelmed by the demands of composing and lacking strategies for working on this perceived weakness, Fannie took little away from such feedback aside from the impression that her writing remained inadequate.

Although Fannie was making important strides, she needed lots of patient, insightful support if she were to overcome her lack of experience with writing and formidable block. Only beginning to feel a bit more confident in writing about personal experience, she anticipated a struggle with the expository assignments that awaited her:

> She's having us write from our experience. It'll be different if it's like in English 101, you know how the teacher tells you to write like this and that, and I find that one very hard, cause I see my other friends' papers and it's hard. I don't know if I can handle that class.

Fannie was trying to forge a sense of connection to class assignments—she wrote, for instance, about her Native American heritage, her dream of becoming a teacher, and about how her cultural background had shaped her concern for the environment. But meanwhile, as her instructor assessed Fannie's progress in an end-of-term evaluation, the focus returned to lingering weaknesses: "needs to expand ideas w/examples/description/explanation," the comments read, not specifying how or why or to whom. Somehow, Fannie had to fill in the gaps in her teacher's advice—and for the more individualized support she so sorely needed, she looked to the tutorials.

"ARE YOU LEARNIN' ANYTHING FROM ME?": THE TUTORIALS

Morgan, Fannie's African American tutor, would soon be student teaching in a local high school, and she approached her work with basic writers as a trial run, a valuable opportunity to practice the various instructional strategies she'd heard about in workshops and seminars. Having grown up in the predominantly Anglo, middle-class community that surrounded the campus, Morgan met the criticisms of more politically involved ethnic students with dogged insistence: "I'm first and foremost a member of the *human* race," she often said, going on to describe her firm determination to work with students of all ethnicities, to help them see that success in the mainstream need not be regarded as cultural betrayal. During the term that I followed her—her second semester of tutoring and the first time she'd worked with non-Anglo students—this enthusiasm would be sorely tested, this ambition tempered by encounters with unforseen obstacles.

Morgan's work with Fannie was a case in point. Although she had initially welcomed the challenge of drawing Fannie out, of helping this shy young woman overcome her apparent lack of self-confidence, by semester's end Morgan's initial compassion had been nearly overwhelmed by a sense of frustration. In an end-of-term interview, she confessed that one impression remained uppermost: "I just remember her sitting there," Morgan recalled, "and talking to her, and it's like, 'well I don't know'...I don't know'...Fannie just has so many doubts, and she's such a hesitant person, she's so withdrawn, and mellow, and quiet.... A lot of times, she'd just say, 'well I don't know what I'm supposed to write.... Well I don't like this, I don't like my writing.'"

Although Fannie seldom had much to say, her words were often rich in untapped meaning. Early in the term, for instance, when Morgan asked why she was in college, Fannie searched unsuccessfully for words that would convey her strong but somewhat conflicted feelings:

Fannie: Well...(long pause)...it's hard...

Morgan: You wanna teach like, preschool? Well, as a person who wants to teach, what do you want outta your students?

Fannie: To get around in America you have to have education...(unclear).

Morgan: And what about if a student chose not to be educated—would that be ok?

Fannie: If that's what he wants...

At this point Morgan gave up and turned to the next student, missing the vital subtext—how Fannie's goal of becoming a teacher was enmeshed in her strong sense of connection to her people, how her belief that one needs an education "to get around" in the mainstream was tempered by insight into why some choose a different path. To understand Fannie's stance towards schooling. Morgan needed to grasp that she felt both this commitment *and* this ambivalence; but as was so often the case, Fannie's meager hints went unheeded.

A few weeks into the semester, Morgan labored one morning to move Fannie past her apparent block on a descriptive essay. Fannie said only that she was going to try to describe her grandmother, and Morgan began by asking a series of questions—about her grandmother's voice, her presence, her laugh, whatever came to Fannie's mind. Her questions greeted by long silences, Morgan admitted her gathering frustration: "Are you learnin' anything from me?" she asked. Morgan's voice sounded cordial and even a bit playful, but she was clearly concerned that Fannie didn't seem to be meeting her halfway. In the weeks that followed, Morgan would repeatedly adjust her approach, continually searching for a way to break through, "to spark something," as she often put it.

The first change—to a tougher, more demanding stance—was clearly signalled as the group brainstormed ideas for their next essays. Instead of waiting for Fannie to jump into the discussion, Morgan called upon her: "Ok, your turn in the hot seat," she announced. When Fannie noted that her essay would be about her home in Arizona, Morgan demanded to know "why it would be of possible interest to us." The ensuing exchange shed little light on the subject:

Fannie: Because it's my home!

Morgan: That's not good enough…that's telling me nothing.

Fannie: I was raised there.

Morgan: What's so special about it?

Fannie: (exasperated sigh) I don't know what's so special about it…

Morgan: So why do you want to write about it, then?

Morgan's final question still unanswered, she eventually gave up and moved to another student. Again, a wealth of valuable information remained tacit; Morgan wouldn't learn for several weeks that Fannie had grown up on a reservation, and she'd understood nothing at all about her profound bond with this other world.

Two months into the semester, Morgan had an opportunity to attend the Conference on College Composition and Communication (CCCC), and it was there that some of her early training crystallized into a more definite plan of action, her early doubts subsumed by a new sense of authoritative expertise. Morgan thought a great deal about her work with Fannie as she attended numerous sessions on peer tutoring and a half-day workshop on collaborative learning. She returned to campus infused with a clear sense of direction: the solution, Morgan had concluded, was to assume an even more low-profile approach, speaking only to ask open-ended questions or to paraphrase Fannie's statements, steadfastly avoiding the temptation to fill silences with her own ideas and asides. As she anticipated her next encounter with Fannie, she couldn't wait to try out this more emphatic version of what had been called—in conference sessions and her earlier training—a "collaborative" or "non-directive" stance.

Still struggling to produce an already past-due essay on "values," Fannie arrived at their first post-CCCC tutorial hour with only preliminary ideas, and nothing in writing. Remembering the advice of Conference participants, Morgan began by trying to nudge her towards a focus, repeatedly denying that she knew more than Fannie about how to approach the piece:

Morgan: What would you say your basic theme is? And sometimes if you keep that in mind, then you can always, you know, keep that as a focus for what you're writing. And the reason I say that is 'cause when you say, "well living happily wasn't...."

Fannie: (pause)...Well, America was a beautiful country, well, but it isn't beautiful anymore.

Morgan: Um hm. Not as beautiful.

Fannie: So I should just say, America was a beautiful country?

Morgan: Yeah. But I dunno—what do you think your overall theme is, that you're saying?

Fannie: (long pause).... I'm really, I'm just talking about America.

Morgan: America? So America as...?

Fannie: (pause)...Um...(pause)

Morgan: Land of free, uh, land of natural resources? As, um, a place where there's a conflict, I mean, there, if you can narrow that, "America." What is it specifically, and think about what you've written, in the rest. Know what I mean?

Fannie: (pause)...The riches of America, or the country? I don't know...

Morgan: I think you do. I'm not saying there's any right answer, but I, I'm— for me, the reason I'm saying this, is I see this emerging as, you know, (pause) where you're really having a hard time with dealing with the exploitation that you see, of America, you know, you think that. And you're using two groups to really illustrate, specifically, how two different attitudes toward, um the richness and beauty of America, two different, um, ways people have to approach this land. Does that, does this make any sense? Or am I just putting words in your mouth? I don't want to do that. I mean that's what I see emerge in your paper. But I could be way off base.

Fannie: I think I know what you're trying to say. And I can kind of relate it at times to what I'm trying to say.

Morgan: You know, I mean, this is like the theme I'm picking up...(pause) I think you know, you've got some real, you know, environmental issues here. I think you're a closet environmentalist here. Which are real true, know what I mean. (pause) And when you talk about pollution, and waste, and, um, those types of things. So I mean, if you're looking at a theme of your paper, what could you pick out, of something of your underlying theme.

Fannie: (pause)...The resources, I guess?

Morgan: Well I mean, I don't want you to say, I want you to say, don't say "I guess," is that what you're talkin' about?

Fannie: Yeah.

Morgan: "Yeah?" I mean, it's your paper.

Fannie: I know, I want to talk about the land...

Morgan: Ok. So you want to talk about the land, and the beauty of the land...

Fannie: Um hm.

Morgan: ...and then, um, and then also your topic for your, um, to spark your paper...what values, and morals, right? That's where you based off to write about America, and the land, you know. Maybe you can write some of these things down, as we're talking, as focussing things, you know. So you want to talk about the land, and then it's like, what do you want to say about the land?

What *did* Fannie "want to say about the land"? Whatever it was, one begins to wonder if it was perhaps lost in her tutor's inadvertent appropriation of these meanings—this despite Morgan's ostensible effort to simply elicit and reflect Fannie's thoughts. While Fannie may well have been struggling to articulate meanings which eluded clear expression in English, as Morgan worked to move her towards greater specificity, it became apparent that she was assuming the paper would express commonplace environmental concerns:

Fannie: I'll say, the country was, um, (pause), more like, I can't say perfect, I mean was, the tree was green, you know, I mean, um, it was clean. (long pause) I can't find the words for it.

Morgan: In a natural state? Um, un-, polluted, um, untouched, um, let me think, tryin' to get a...

Fannie: I mean everybody, I mean the Indians too, they didn't wear that (pointing to Morgan's clothes), they only wore buffalo clothing, you know for clothing, they didn't wear like...these, you know, cotton, and all that, they were so...

Morgan: Naturalistic.

Fannie: Yeah. "Naturalistic," I don't know if I'm gonna use that word...I wanna say, I wanna give a picture of the way the land was, before, you know what I'm, what I'm tryin' to say?

The Navajos' connection to the land is legendary—spiritual nexus, many would maintain, that goes far beyond mainstream notions of what it means to be concerned about the environment. However, later in this session, Morgan observed that Fannie was writing about concerns that worry lots of people—citing recent publicity about the greenhouse effect, the hole in the ozone layer, and the growing interest in recycling. She then brought the session to a close by paraphrasing what she saw as the meat of the discussion and asking, "Is that something that you were tryin' to say, too?" Fannie replied, "Probably. I mean, I can't find the words for it, but you're finding the words for me." Morgan's rejoinder had been, "I'm just sparkin', I'm just sparkin' what you already have there, what you're sayin'. I mean I'm tryin' to tell you what I hear you sayin'."

Morgan laughed as, in an end-of-term interview, she listened again to Fannie's final comment: "I didn't *want* to find the words for her," she mused; "I wanted to show her how she could find 'em for herself." Still, she admitted, the directive impulse had been hard to resist: "I wanted to just give her ideas," Morgan observed, adding that although Fannie had some good things to say, "I wanted her to be able to articulate her ideas on a little higher level." Although it was obvious to Morgan that the ideas in Fannie's paper were of "deep-seated emotional concern," she also saw her as stuck in arid generalities: "I don't know, it's just such a beautiful country," Morgan echoed as she reviewed the audiotape. While Morgan emphasized that she "didn't wanna write the paper for her," she allowed that "it's difficult—it's really hard to want to take the bull by the horns and say, 'don't you see it this way?'" On the one hand, Morgan noted that she'd often asked Fannie what she was getting out of a session, "'cause sometimes I'll think I'm getting through and I'm explaining something really good, and then they won't catch it"; on the other hand, Morgan emphasized again and again that she didn't want to "give away" her own thoughts.

Although Morgan often did an almost heroic job of waiting out Fannie's lingering silences and deflecting appeals to her authority, she never really surrendered control; somehow, the message always came across that Morgan knew more than Fannie about the ideas at hand, and that if she would, she could simply turn over pre-packaged understandings. While her frustration was certainly understandable, I often had the sense that Morgan was insufficiently curious about Fannie's thoughts—insufficiently curious about how Fannie's understandings might have differed from her own, about how they had been shaped by Fannie's background and cultural orientation, or about what she stood to learn from them.

When asked about Fannie's block, a weary Morgan wrote if off to her cultural background:

> *You know, I would have to say it's cultural; I'd have to say it's her you know, Native American background and growing up on a reservation... maybe...she's more sensitive to male-female roles, and the female role being quiet.*

On a number of occasions Morgan had speculated that Navajo women are taught to be subservient, a perception that contrasted rather strikingly with Fannie's assertion that she wasn't at all shy or quiet back home.[2] Hoping to challenge Morgan's accustomed view of Fannie as bashful and retiring, in a final interview I played back one of their sessions from the week that a group of Navajo students were visiting the campus. Fannie was uncharacteristically vocal and even aggressive that morning, talking in a loud voice, repeatedly seizing and holding the floor:

Fannie: You know what my essay's on? Different environments. Um, I'm talking, I'm not gonna talk about my relationship between my brothers, it's so boring, so I'm just gonna talk about both being raised, like my youngest brother being raised on the reservation, and the other being raised over here, and they both have very different, um, um, (Morgan starts to say something, but Fannie cuts her off and continues) characteristics or somethin' like that. You know, like their personalities, you know.

Morgan: Um. That's good. (Morgan starts to say something more, but Fannie keeps going.)

Fannie: It's funny, I'm cutting, I was totally mean to my brother here. (Morgan laughs.) Because, I called, I said that he's a wimp, you know, and my brother, my little brother's being raised on the reservation, is like, is like taught to be a man, he's brave and all that.

Luis: (a student in the group) That's being a man?!

Fannie: And…

Luis: That's not being a man, I don't find.

Fannie: (her voice raised) I'm sorry—but that's how I wrote, Ok?! That's your opinion, I mean, and it's…

Luis: I think a man is sensitive, caring, and lov-

Fannie: (cutting him off) No, no…

Luis: …and able to express his feelings. I don't think that if you can go kill someone, that makes you a man.

Fannie: I mean…

Luis: That's just my opinion (gets up and walks away for a moment).

Fannie: (watching Luis wander off) Dickhead.

Morgan listened with a widening smile to the rest of this session, obviously pleased with Fannie's sometimes combative manner and unflagging insistence that attention be directed back to her. "Ha! Fannie's *so* much more forceful," Morgan exclaimed, "and just more in control of what she wants, and what she needs." When asked what she thought might have accounted for this temporary change, Morgan sidestepped the influence of the visiting students:

> *I would love to think I made her feel safe that way. And that I really um, showed her that she had, you know, by my interactions with her, that she really had every right to be strong-willed and forceful and have her opinions and you know, say what she felt that she needed to say, and that she didn't have to be quiet, you know. People always tell me that I influence people that way. You know? (laughs). "You've been hangin' around with Morgan too much!"*

Hungry for feedback that she'd influenced Fannie in a positive way, Morgan grasped this possible evidence with obvious pleasure. Fannie was not a student who offered many positive signals, and it was perhaps essential to Morgan's professional self-esteem that she find them wherever she could. In this credit-taking there was, however, a larger irony: if only she'd been encouraged to push a little farther in her own thinking, perhaps she would have found herself assisting more often in such moments of blossoming.

CONCLUSION: STUDENTS AS TEACHERS, TEACHERS AS STUDENTS

When Morgan returned from the CCCC with a vision of "collaboration" that cast it as a set of techniques rather than a new way to think about teaching and learning, the insights of panelists and workshop leaders devolved into a fossilized creed, a shield against more fundamental concerns. Morgan had somehow missed the importance of continually adjusting her approach in the light of the understandings students make available, of allowing their feedback to shape her reflections upon her own role. At semester's end, she still didn't know that Fannie was a non-native speaker of English; she didn't know the dimensions of Fannie's inexperience with academic writing, nor did she know the reasons behind Fannie's formidable block.

Even as Morgan labored to promote "collaborative" moments—making an ostensible effort to "talk less," to "sit back more," to enact an instructional mode that would seem more culturally appropriate—Fannie remembered a life-time of classroom misadventure, and hung back, reluctant. Morgan needed to know something about this history, but she also needed to understand that much else was fluid and alive, that a revised sense of self was emerging from the dynamic interaction of Fannie's past and present. Emboldened by a few treasured days in the company of fellow Navajos, Fannie had momentarily stepped into a new stance, one that departed markedly from her accustomed behavior on reservation and campus alike; but if her confidence recalled an earlier self, her playful combativeness was, as Fannie observed in listening to the tape, a new and still-strange manifestation of something also oddly familiar, something left over from long ago.

Rather than frequent urgings to "talk less," perhaps what Morgan most needed was advice to *listen more*—for the clues students like Fannie would provide, for those moments when she might best shed her teacherly persona and become once again a learner. More than specific instructional strategies, Morgan needed the conceptual grounding that would allow her to understand that authentically collaborative learning is predicated upon fine-grained insight into individual students—of the nature of their Vygotskian "zones of proximal development," and, by association, of the sorts of instructional "scaffolding" most appropriate to their changing needs (Bruner; Langer and Applebee). So, too, did Morgan need to be encouraged toward the yet-elusive understanding that such learning is never unilateral, inevitably entailing a reciprocal influence, reciprocal advances in understanding (Dyson). As she struggled to come to terms with her own ethnic ambivalence, to defend herself against a vociferous chorus proclaiming her "not black enough," Morgan had reason to take heart in Fannie's dramatic and rather trying process of transition. Had she thought to ask, Morgan would no doubt have been fascinated by Fannie's descriptions of this other cultural and linguistic context, with its very different perspectives on education in particular and the world in general (John; Locust). Most of all, perhaps, she would have been interested to know that Fannie was learning to inhabit both arenas, and in so doing, enacting a negotiation of admirable complexity—a negotiation different in degree, perhaps, but certainly not in kind, from Morgan's own.

Having tutored only one semester previously, Morgan was understandably eager to abandon her lingering doubts about her effectiveness, eager for a surefooted sense that she was providing something worthwhile. Her idealism and good intentions were everywhere apparent—in her lengthy meditations on her work, in her eager enthusiasm at the CCCC, in her persistent efforts to try out new approaches, and in the reassurance she extended to me when I confessed that I'd be writing some fairly negative things about her vexed attempts to reach Fannie. Morgan had been offered relatively little by way of preparation and support: beyond a sprinkling of workshops and an occasional alliance with more experienced tutors, she was left largely on her own—alone with the substantial challenges and opportunities that students like Fannie presented, alone to deal with her frustration and occasional feelings of failure as best she could. Like all beginning educators, Morgan needed abundant support, instruction, and modeling if she were to learn to reflect critically upon her work, to question her assumptions about students like Fannie, to allow herself, even at this fledgling stage in her career, to become a reflective and therefore vulnerable practitioner. That is not to suggest that Morgan should have pried into hidden corners of Fannie's past, insisting that she reveal information about her background before she felt ready to do so; only that Morgan be respectfully curious, ever attentive to whatever clues Fannie might have been willing to offer, ever poised to revise old understandings in the light of fresh evidence.

Those of us who work with linguistic minority students—and that's fast becoming us all—must appreciate the evolving dimensions of our task, realizing that we have to reach further than ever if we're to do our jobs well. Regardless of our crowded schedules and shrinking budgets, we must also think realistically about the sorts of guidance new tutors and teachers need if they are to confront these rigors effectively, guiding them towards practical strategies informed by understandings from theory and research, and offering compelling reminders of the need to monitor one's ethnocentric biases and faulty assumptions. Most of all, we must serve as models of reflective practice—perennially inquisitive and self-critical, even as we find occasion both to bless and curse the discovery that becoming students of students means becoming students of ourselves as well.

NOTES

1. "Fannie" was the actual name of this student's maternal grandmother. We decided to use it as her pseudonym to honor this lasting influence.

2. Morgan's assumption is also contradicted by published accounts of life among the Navajo, which from early on have emphasized the prestige and power of female members of the tribe. Gladys Reichard, an anthropologist who lived among the Navajos in the 1920s, reported that "the Navajo woman enjoys great economic and social prestige as the head of the house and clan and as the manager of economic affairs, and she is not excluded from religious ritual or from attaining political honors" (55). Navajo women often own substantial property, and children retain the surname of the matrilineal clan; the status accorded women is further reflected in the depictions of female deities in Navajo myths (Terrell 57; 255).

ACKNOWLEDGMENTS

Special thanks to Sarah Warshauer Freedman for encouragement and sage advice throughout this project. Thanks also to Don McQuade, Guadalupe Valdés, and the members of my fall 1991 writing research class at The University of Iowa.

This work was supported by a grant from the NCTE Research Foundation.

WORKS CITED

Applebee, Arthur, and Judith Langer. "Reading and Writing Instruction: Toward a Theory of Teaching and Learning." *Review of Research in Education*. Vol. 13. Ed. E. Z. Rothkopf. Washington, DC: American Educational Research Association, 1986.

Bakhtin, Mikhail Mikhailovich. *The Dialogic Imagination: Four Essays by M. M. Bakhtin.* Ed. Michael Holquist, trans. Caryl Emerson and Michael Holquist. Austin: U of Texas P, 1981.

Bruner, Jerome. "The Role of Dialogue in Language Acquisition." *The Child's Conception of Language.* Ed. A. Sinclair. New York: Springer-Verlag, 1978.

Cintron, Ralph. "Reading and Writing Graffitti: A Reading," *The Quarterly Newsletter of the Laboratory of Comparative Human Cognition* 13 (1991): 21–24.

DiPardo, Anne. "Acquiring 'A Kind of Passport': The Teaching and Learning of Academic Discourse in Basic Writing Tutorials." Diss. UC Berkeley, 1991.

———. *'A Kind of Passport': A Basic Writing Adjunct Program and the Challenge of Student Diversity.* Urbana: NCTE, [1993.]

Dorris, Michael. *A Yellow Raft in Blue Water.* New York: Holt, 1987.

Dyson, Anne. "Weaving Possibilities: Rethinking Metaphors for Early Literacy Development." *The Reading Teacher* 44 (1990): 202–13.

Fischer, Michael. "Ethnicity and the Postmodern Arts of Memory." *Writing Culture: The Poetics and Politics of Ethnography.* Ed. J. Clifford and G. E. Marcus. Berkeley: U of California P, 1986.

Hawkins, Thom. "Intimacy and Audience: The Relationship Between Revision and the Social Dimension of Peer Tutoring." *College English* 42 (1980): 64–68.

Hull, Glynda, and Mike Rose. "Rethinking Remediation: Toward a Social-Cognitive Understanding of Problematic Reading and Writing." *Written Communication* 6 (1989): 139–54.

———. "This Wooden Shack: The Logic of an Unconventional Reading." *College Composition and Communication* 41 (1990): 287–98.

John, Vera P. "Styles of Learning—Styles of Teaching: Reflections on the Education of Navajo Children." *Functions of Language in the Classroom.* Ed. Courtney B. Cazden and Vera P. John. 1972. Prospect Heights: Waveland, 1985.

Locust, Carol. "Wounding the Spirit: Discrimination and Traditional American Indian Belief Systems," *Harvard Educational Review* 58 (1988): 315–30.

Philips, Susan U. "Participant Structures and Communicative Competence: Warm Springs Children in Community and Classroom." *Functions of Language in the Classroom.* Ed. Courtney B. Cazden and Vera P. John. 1972. Prospect Heights: Waveland, 1985.

Rethinking Writing Center Conferencing Strategies for the ESL Writer

Judith K. Powers

Judith Powers states that collaborative approaches that tutors use to good effect with native writers often fail when applied to ESL writers, who bring to the writing center different cultural values, needs, rhetorical strategies, and attitudes toward the tutor-student relationship. For example, the minimalist technique of having students read their papers aloud so that they can "hear" when diction or organizational problems arise does not appear to work for ESL writers. As a consequence, tutors may have to intervene more directly in ESL writers' texts, acting less as collaborators than as "informants." Powers makes a strong case for what she calls the need for an "attitude adjustment" on the part of writing center tutors when it comes to assisting ESL writers; tutors will find her article, which first appeared in 1993 in The Writing Center Journal, *especially helpful in making such an adjustment.*

The University of Wyoming Writing Center has recently experienced a dramatic increase in ESL conferencing, brought about mainly by the establishment of a writing across the curriculum program on campus and by changes in the way we teach first-year composition courses for international students. In responding to the almost three-fold increase in numbers of ESL conferences over the past two years, our writing center faculty has begun to question whether traditional collaborative strategies are appropriate and effective for second-language writers.

Probably more than anything else, the past two years' influx of ESL writers has pointed up two significant—and interrelated—concerns to writing center faculty. The first is how firm our assumptions are about our job and the "right" way to accomplish it. The second is how little training we as a faculty have in the principles and techniques of effective ESL conferencing. On both counts, we probably do not differ greatly from writing center faculties across the country. This paper presents the problems we encountered in conferencing with ESL writers and discusses the processes that evolved as we sought solutions.[1]

Powers, Judith K. "Rethinking Writing Center Conferencing Strategies for the ESL Writer." *The Writing Center Journal* 13.2 (1993): 39–47. Reprinted by permission of *The Writing Center Journal*.

TRADITIONAL CONFERENCING STRATEGIES AND THE ESL WRITER

Since our writing center faculty was largely untrained in teaching ESL writing and unaware of the many differences in acquiring first- and second-language writing skills, the increase in numbers of ESL conferences proved a mixed blessing, We were delighted, on the one hand, to be reaching a greater number of second-language writers on campus; on the other hand, we sometimes felt frustrated when these conferences did not work the way we expected. Unfortunately, many of the collaborative techniques that had been so successful with native-speaking writers appeared to fail (or work differently) when applied to ESL conferences.

When ESL writers came into the writing center, we tended to approach those conferences just as we would conferences with native-speaking writers, determining what assistance the writers needed through a series of questions about process and problems, purpose and audience. In both cases, our intention in adopting this strategy was to establish a Socratic rather than a didactic context, one which we hoped would allow us to lead writers to the solution of their own problems. Occasionally, conferences might involve the direct exchange of information (e.g., when numbers should be spelled out). More typically, though, we intended to lead writers to discover good solutions rather than answers, solutions that were theirs, not the tutor's. Unfortunately, this process, which has generally served native-speaking writers well (Harris, Leahy) and is justifiably a source of pride for those who can make it work, was often ineffective for our second-language writers, especially those confronting college-level writing in English for the first time.

Perhaps the major reason for this failure is the difference in what the two groups of writers bring to the writing center conference. Most native-speaking writers, for better or for worse, have come to us with comparatively broad and predictable experiences of writing and writing instruction in English. When they have problems with some concept or technique, it is therefore relatively easy for writing center faculty to intuit the source of their difficulty and adjust our questioning to help them discover new, more workable principles. A writer, for example, who is trying to force two points (or four points) into three paragraphs is likely to have been drilled in the five-paragraph essay format and can be guided fairly easily to discover that not all ideas break down into three parts. ESL writers, however, seldom come to the writing center conference with any substantial background in writing and writing instruction in English. Attempts, therefore, to play off such experience in devising collaborative strategies are likely to fail.

Furthermore, ESL writers typically come to the writing center conference with first-language rhetorics different from the rhetoric of academic English with which they are struggling (Grabe and Kaplan; Leki). Since what these writers already know about writing is based in those first-language rhetorics, it is likely that attempts to use common collaborative strategies will backfire and lead them away from, not toward, the solutions they seek. Consider, for example, the common and fairly simple problem of helping a writer understand that a *conclusion* should contain no new, unsupported ideas. While it is fairly easy to impress a native-speaking writer with the logic of this rule (because the term conclusion itself implies it), the rule is not at all logical to writers from cultures where effective conclusions do, in fact, include new ideas. In this, as in other conferencing situations, those attempting to assist second-language writers may be hampered not only by the writers' limited backgrounds in the rhetoric of written English but also by their learned patterns as educated writers of their own languages. As another example, bringing ESL writers to see the logic of placing important material at the beginnings of English paragraphs may, at times, involve overriding their long-time cultural assumptions that such material should appear at the end. Because collaborative techniques depend so heavily on shared basic assumptions or patterns, conferences that attempt merely to take the techniques we use with native-speaking writers and apply them to ESL writers may fail to assist the writers we intend to help.

The sense of audience that ESL writers bring to the writing center has also affected the success of our typical conferencing strategy. Experienced writing center faculty can lead native-speaking writers to a fuller awareness of certain writing principles through questions about their audience—what the members of their audience already know about a subject, what purpose a reader might have for reading their piece of writing, what kind of people make up their audience and what qualities will impress that group. Using this Socratic technique, in fact, helps us avoid the didactic role of identifying correct and incorrect approaches. However, second-language writers, already handicapped by an unfamiliar rhetoric, are likely to be writing to an unfamiliar audience as well. Part of what they need from us is knowledge of what that unknown audience will expect, need, and find convincing. Thus, ESL writers are asking us to become audiences for their work in a broader way than native speakers are; they view us as cultural informants about American academic expectations.

Predictably, as a result of these differences in the educational, rhetorical, and cultural contexts of ESL writers, our faculty found themselves increasingly in the role of informant rather than collaborator. We were becoming more direct, more didactic in our approach, teaching writing to ESL writers essentially as an academic subject.

UNDERSTANDING THE NEED FOR INTERVENTION

In this shifted role lay the crux of the difficulty we increasingly experienced with ESL conferencing. Because our whole writing center philosophy—our

Socratic, nondirective approach—was (and is) geared away from the notion that we are teachers of an academic subject, it was not easy for us to see ourselves as cultural/rhetorical informants with valuable information to impart. One unfortunate result of this situation was that writing center faculty tended to define conferences where ESL writers got what they needed from us (i.e., direct help) as failures rather than successes.

This problem occurred in ESL conferences involving all aspects of writing. Writing center instructors found themselves, for example, telling writers what their audiences would expect rather than asking the writers to decide, answering questions about the sufficiency of the evidence provided in a particular context rather than leaving that decision to the writer, or showing writers how to say something rather than asking them what they wanted to say. When such exchanges occurred, we found it difficult to view them from the standpoint of the ESL writer for whom the conference might have been a success; rather, we measured them against our nondirective philosophy which we appeared to have betrayed.

The distance between the needs of the ESL writer and the assumptions of the system has perhaps been most apparent in conferences where ESL writers have come to us for help with editing and proofing. Like many writing centers, the University of Wyoming Writing Center handles the perennial problem of students wanting drafts edited with a policy statement: We will teach writers editing and proofing strategies but will not edit or proof for them. This distinction serves us reasonably well when dealing with native-speaking writers. It is less successful, however, in setting workable parameters for ESL conferences, partly because our ESL conferees have difficulty understanding the line it draws, but mostly because the techniques we use to teach editing/proofing strategies to native-speaking writers seldom work for ESL writers. These techniques, which largely involve reading aloud and learning to use the ear to edit, presume that the writer hears the language correctly and is more familiar and comfortable with the oral than the written word. Native-speaking writers reading aloud can typically locate problem passages, which we can then discuss with them, suggesting principles upon which they can base editing decisions. In this scenario, we hope, writers learn to raise and answer their own questions.

Neither reading aloud nor editing by ear appears to work for the majority of ESL writers we see, however. Few beginning second-language writers "hear" the language "correctly," and many are more familiar with written than with spoken English. Since they have no inner editor prompting them to stop and raise questions, we are likely to adjust our technique to their needs and discover we are locating errors for ESL writers in a way that looks very much like editing. When we find ourselves backed into this situation, we immediately begin to raise questions about our appropriation of writers' texts, an anathema in writing center methodology not only for practical reasons inherent in working with classroom assignment but also because our aim is to demystify writing for conferees and increase their self-reliance and self-confidence. While the intervention that ESL writers appear to require of us in working with editing problems does not differ greatly from the intervention involved when we assist those same writers with rhetorical structure and audience, it strikes us more forcibly because it is familiar and easy to perceive. In fact, it looks very much like the "bad" kind of help native speakers sometimes want when they bring papers in to be "corrected."

The mixed feelings that the ESL editing issue engendered were not a new problem for the writing center. Throughout our history, we had faced and handled requests for assistance in editing ESL texts, responding to them more or less on a case-by-case basis, with varying levels of confidence in our decisions. Almost every semester, for example, the demand for editorial assistance with ESL theses and dissertations reaches the point at which writing center faculty begin to complain in frustration about ESL writers expecting them to correct and rewrite texts. Each year, the staff has vowed to establish a clearer policy that will prevent abuses of the system, discussed the subject vigorously, realized that doing so would limit the open-door policy we value so much, and consequently let the subject slide.

The primary difference between our past ESL conferencing experiences and our experiences of the last two years was our awareness of an emerging pattern in ESL conferencing that called into question some of our fundamental assumptions about what we do. Increased numbers of second-language conferences, as well as conferences involving a larger variety of writing tasks, highlighted difficulties in applying our traditional conferencing strategies to all aspects of second-language writing, not just editing. What had once appeared scattered instances of ineffectiveness in our typical approach became symptomatic of a broader inability to meet the needs of ESL writers with the same basic methods we use to assist native speakers. This realization led us to question whether our past reluctance to confront directly the issues involved in ESL conferencing was really the benign neglect we had assumed it to be or whether we were unintentionally undermining the principles we meant to protect and distancing ourselves from the needs of a large group of writers.

ADAPTING CONFERENCING STRATEGIES
TO ASSIST ESL WRITERS

Once genuinely convinced that traditional collaborative strategies often do not work with ESL writers, our faculty realized that the key to more effective ESL conferencing was an attitude adjustment on our part. We had to accept that ESL writers bring different contexts to conferences than native speakers do, that they are, therefore, likely to need different kinds of assistance from us, and that successful assistance to ESL writers may involve more intervention in their writing processes than we consider appropriate with native-speaking writers.

For those of us whose experience has demonstrated the virtues of non-directive conferencing techniques, simple acceptance of the need to adopt more directive strategies was not always an easy first step. Part of the difficulty in taking this step stemmed from the fact that the differences between native-speaking and second-language writers are sometimes masked by a deceiving familiarity in what they say and do. When native-speaking writers come into the writing center expecting us to tell them what is the *answer* to a problem or the right way to express an idea, we may see them—often quite rightly—as either "timid" writers who need their self-confidence boosted, teacher-dependent writers who want an authority to appropriate their writing, or "lazy" writers who want someone else to do their work. In any of these cases, we see our job as getting the writer to assume responsibility for the writing ESL writers who come to us expecting answers to questions about where their thesis statements should appear, how many developmental paragraphs they must have, how much and what kind of support a point requires, or how an idea should be phrased too often appear to fall into one of these categories: they appear to be insecure, to be abdicating responsibility for their texts for one of the above reasons.

Although the questions that ESL writers ask us are deceivingly similar to the questions native speakers sometimes raise, the contexts of the questions make them substantially different. What we discovered is that failure to recognize the essential difference in these seemingly similar questions severely undercuts our ability to assist second-language writers in acquiring the academic writing skills they need. If we assumed such writers were shy or dependent writers who merely needed encouragement to take charge of their texts, and if we adopted our usual collaborative approach to bring about that recognition of ownership, we were unlikely to achieve our accustomed results because we were applying an attitude solution to an information problem. If we assumed the worst—that the writers were lazy and were trying to get us to take over the writing—we might be travelling even further toward the wrong solution, based on the wrong evidence. We were, in fact, unlikely to provide useful help to ESL writers until we saw the questions they raised about basic form and usage not as evasions of responsibility but as the real questions of writers struggling with an unfamiliar culture, audience, and rhetoric.

To extend the benefits of conferencing and collaborative learning to ESL writers, writing center faculty must understand what these writers need from us and how their needs differ from those of native-speaking writers. The principal difference in the two conferencing situations appears to be the increased emphasis on our role as informant (rather than collaborator) in the second-language conference. Because we know little about ESL writers' rhetorics, backgrounds, and cultures, and because they know little about their current academic discourse community and the rhetoric of academic English, we can assist them only by becoming more direct in our approach, by teaching them writing as an academic subject. Doing so may, in fact, involve teaching them directly what their writing should look like by supplying them with formats for presenting written responses to various academic assignments and informing them of what their audiences will expect in terms of presentation, evidence, shape, etc.

CONCLUSION

Although collaborative learning is not a familiar process to most of the international students we see in the writing center, and some of the Socratic techniques we have developed as a result of this theory do not serve the ESL population particularly well, collaborative writing and conference teaching do work for these writers in some important ways. As with native-speaking writers, the process of verbalizing an idea often helps ESL writers discover a direction, and the act of sketching a structure (even with the help of a faculty member) clarifies the principles of that construct in a way merely reading about it cannot. ESL writers who describe their conferencing experiences mention a new awareness of audience, a clarification of the principles of organization, and the discovery of new vocabulary and sentence structures as benefits. In fact, just by acquiring a vocabulary to discuss their writing in English, second-language writers make a first step toward understanding and self-sufficiency.

But these benefits of collaboration accrue to ESL writers through *successful* writing center conferences. We can assist ESL writers to become more capable writers of English only if we understand what they bring to the writing center conference and allow that perspective to determine our conferencing strategies. Structuring successful ESL conferences probably requires that we reexamine our approach as outsiders might, making a real attempt to discard the rhetoric and patterns of thought that are so familiar to us as to seem inevitable. We might, for example, better assist our second-language writers by analyzing academic assignments from an outside perspective to see exactly what is expected in American academic prose, gathering information about audience expectations that recognize our culturally based assumptions, and learning to ask questions in conferences that will allow ESL writers to understand more about idea generation and presentation of evidence. Conferences based on this information and approach might appear different, on the surface, from conferences we conduct with native-speaking writers, but they bring us closer to accomplishing our writing center's goal of providing meaningful help to all campus writers with all kinds of writing questions.

When writing center faculty, with the best of intentions, apply collaborative techniques devised for native-speaking writers to ESL writers, the possibility of cultural miscommunication and failed conferences is inherent in the methodology itself. Since its inception, our writing center has struggled in concern and frustration over a frequent inability to make ESL conferences both successful for the participants and consistent with our conferencing philosophy. In retrospect, it appears that much of this struggle basically involved attempts to determine which of the conference participants was responsible for conferences that failed to meet one or both of these criteria. Sometimes we concluded that the writer was at fault for refusing to accept responsibility for the text and thereby undermining the collaborative process. More frequently, we blamed ourselves for failing to apply our conferencing principles and techniques appropriately or allowing ourselves to be drawn into directive conferencing by an unusually clever or forceful writer. Our experience of the past two years has convinced us that we will increase the effectiveness of ESL conferencing only when we understand, accept, and respond to the differences between the needs of ESL and native-speaking writers. Attempts to reform or reshape the participants in the conference are unlikely to prove effectual; we must reexamine and revise the method itself.

NOTE

1. Our ESL population (currently 465 students) is almost exclusively international students who have studied English in their own countries before coming to the United States. The largest group of students come from China, India, Malaysia, Norway, and Taiwan; they have achieved a minimum TOEFL score of 525 and have been admitted to the university.

WORKS CITED

Grabe, William, and Robert B. Kaplan. "Writing in a Second Language: Contrastive Rhetoric" *Richness in Writing: Empowering ESL Students.* Ed. Donna Johnson and Duane Roen. New York. Longman, 1989.

Harris, Muriel. "What's Up and What's In: Trends and Traditions in Writing Centers. *The Writing Center Journal* 11 (1990): 15–25.

Leahy Richard. "What the College Writing Center Is—and Isn't." *College Teaching* 38 (1990): 43–48.

Leki, Ilona. "Twenty-five Years of Contrastive Rhetoric: Text Analysis and Writing Pedagogies." *TESOL Quarterly* 25 (1991): 123–43.

Learning Disabilities
and the Writing Center

Julie Neff

Since September 1984, when Stephen North's now famous article, "The Idea of a Writing Center" appeared in *College English*, a picture of the writing conference has developed: the writer and the writing advisor sit side by side, the writer holding the pencil, the writing advisor asking probing questions about the development of the topic; or the student types text into a computer as the writing advisor fires questions designed to help the student think through the writing problem; or, in a revising session, the advisor points to a word or phrase that seems to be "wrong" for this particular paragraph as the student jots notes so she can later correct the text. In these conferences, the writing advisor tells the student to check punctuation and spelling and gives the student a handout to help with the process. After all, the writing center is not a "fix-it" shop for student papers; it is a place for writer to meet reader in order to receive a thoughtful response.

Behind these pictures of writing center conferences lie some basic assumptions: students can improve their ability to invent, organize, draft, revise, and edit based on the responses of a thoughtful reader. Even though the conference is in many ways collaborative, most of the responsibility for composing and transcribing is placed on the student writer. Recent theory and pedagogy in rhetoric and composition support these pictures of the collaborative writing conference, e.g., Bruffee, Harris, Ede, and Lunsford.

But one group of students does not and cannot fit into this pedagogical picture: students with learning disabilities. Though their particular disabilities vary, these students need a different, more specific kind of collaboration than the average student who walks through the doors of the writing center.

WHAT IS A LEARNING DISABILITY?

Although there is still some disagreement about the precise definition, learning disabilities are generally a varied group of disorders that are intrinsic to the individual.

The Learning Disabilities Act of 1968, which has only changed in small ways since it was drafted, defines a learning disability as "a disorder in one or more of the basic psychological processes involved in understanding or in using spoken or written languages." Individuals with learning disabilities are likely to experience trouble with "listening, thinking, talking, reading, writing, spelling, or arithmetic." Learning problems that are primarily due to a physical condition, like visual or hearing impairment, retardation, emotional dysfunction, or a disadvantaged situation, are not considered to result from learning disabilities. While these other problems sometimes accompany a learning disability, they are not the cause or the result of the disability. Nor are learning disabilities the result of social or economic conditions. People who have learning disabilities are born with them, or they have acquired them through a severe illness or accident, and the disability will continue to affect them over their lifetimes. Although many people overcome their learning disabilities, they do so by learning coping strategies and alternate routes for solving problems. People with learning disabilities cannot be "cured." However, with help, those with learning disabilities can learn to use their strengths to compensate for their weaknesses.

A learning disability is the result of a malfunction in the system in one or more areas. We cannot look into the brain and see the malfunction, but we can see the results in a student's performance on a discrete task. The Woodcock-Johnson Test of Cognitive Ability, one of the most widely used tests for measuring learning disabilities, uncovers discrepancies between capacity and performance. Although the requirements differ from state to state, two standard deviations between potential and performance on the Woodcock-Johnson test (or similar tests such as the WAIS-R, TOWL, or WRAT) suggest that a student is learning disabled, as does an extreme scatter of subtest scores.

Some learning disabilities are truly debilitating in that the individual is unable to cope with or overcome the problems. However, many people with learning disabilities are able to function at the highest levels in one area while having difficulty in another. In fact, many people who are learning disabled in one area are gifted in another. Dyslexic and slow to read, Albert Einstein was learning disabled, as was Thomas Edison (Lovitt 1989, 5). Although these are two of the most well-known cases, they are not exceptional ones. According to specialists at a learning disabilities clinic, Another Door to Learning, one successful businessman claimed his learning disability has contributed to his success because it allowed him to view problems from a different perspective. Often learning-disabled students who come to college score in the above-average range of standard IQ tests and have finely honed skills for compensating for and adapting to their particular disability.

WHAT DO WE KNOW ABOUT THE BRAIN?

While no one yet knows the precise causes of a learning disability, the materials drafted by the National Joint Committee on Learning Disabilities presume that the disability, which manifests itself in problems with the acquisition and use of listening, speaking, reading, writing, reasoning, mathematical or spatial skills, grows out of some sort of brain dysfunction.

Although researchers know much more now than they did a decade ago, the debate over just how the brain works continues. Some scientists believe that the brain is bicameral, with the left side responsible for language and reason, and the right side responsible for nonverbal, intuitive activities—the mystical if you will (Berglund 1985, 1). Others believe that the bicameral model oversimplifies the workings of the brain and is more misleading than it is useful.[1]

Richard Berglund (1985) explains that in the last several years a new "wet model" of the brain has emerged, one that is based on the theory that the brain runs on hormones. The idea that the brain is a gland run by hormones has resulted in a new, burgeoning field of medicine known as neuroendocrinology which gives credence to the idea that the learning disability has a physiological basis.

Meantime, over the past decade, cognitive psychology has moved away from the Platonic idea that human rationality grows out of pure intelligence. Instead, researchers are seeing the brain as "a knowledge medium," a storehouse for great quantities of knowledge about the world. This view of the brain represents a paradigm shift from the Platonic view, which asserts that only by reasoning with formal rules we can come to general understanding: if worldly knowledge is more important than pure reason, we have a model of human rationality that relies on information in the brain and vast associative connections that allow the human mind to turn a fragment of information into a considerable amount of knowledge. Human cognition consists not of pure reason but is instead composed of the information stored in the brain and the brain's ability to connect those pieces of information. Worldly knowledge, according to Jeremy Campbell (1989), has become far more important than pure logic.

HOW DOES THIS THEORY HELP US UNDERSTAND A LEARNING DISABILITY?

The idea of the brain as a knowledge machine, and as an organ run by hormones, can help us understand a learning disability. The brain processes enormous amounts of information. The brains of learning-disabled persons have these same properties; but often learning-disabled persons have trouble accessing and retrieving the information, and occasionally gathering and storing it. This is not because they are unintelligent but because of a physiological problem. Judy Schwartz, author of the book *Another Door to Learning,* says that individuals not only have to have basic information, they have to know they have it. The substance and assumptions are inside the learning-disabled person's brain, but he or she may not know the information is there. To access what is known, he or she must consciously learn how to tap the information through self-cuing or other methods. In these circumstances, the writing center can be helpful.

MISCONCEPTIONS ABOUT LEARNING DISABILITIES

Although brain theory and research support the idea that a learning disability has a physiological basis, many people, including educators, continue to have a number of misconceptions about people with learning disabilities. Some see the learning-disabled students as "special education" students who are now being mainstreamed. Some see them as manipulative individuals looking for an excuse for bad spelling and punctuation. Some see "learning disability" as a euphemism for "retarded." Others claim that learning disabilities do not actually exist.[2]

Since a learning disability has a physiological basis and is not due to low intelligence, social situations, or economic conditions, a learning disability is not unlike other kinds of disabilities that have a physiological basis. Renee must use a wheelchair because she was born with an imperfect spine. This defect, not caused by low intelligence, social situation, or economic factors, is a physiological problem that Renee overcomes by taking a slightly different route to accomplish her goals. Renee can reach the second floor, but she won't use the stairs; she'll use the elevator. Similarly, the learning-disabled student can master the material; but she may need to write the exam on a computer, and she may also need extra time to access the information she has.

A CASE STUDY

Although learning disabilities vary widely, it may be easier to understand how a learning disability affects an individual by looking at a specific student with a specific disability. When Barb was in middle school, her mother asked her to take a roast from the refrigerator and put it in the oven at 350 degrees so it would be ready when she got home from work. The roast was in the baking dish, seasoned, and covered with plastic wrap. At the appropriate time, Barb did exactly as asked. The roast was done perfectly when her mother came home, but it was coated with melted plastic.

Why hadn't Barb removed the plastic? She had taken cooking in school and often baked cakes and cookies at home. Even though she has 20/20 vision, Barb couldn't comprehend the plastic. Because the plastic exists in space, Barb's spatial problems kept her from seeing it until her mother tied it to language by saying, "This roast is covered with melted plastic." Barb replied, "I'm sorry. I didn't notice it."

Barb has a disability that affects her ability to access and create reliable images and thus to understand things spatially. She understands and gains access to her world and spatial relationships by building and shaping images with language, which in turn gives her access to the images.

Barb needed written or oral directions to remove the plastic. As soon as she had words, Barb could grasp the situation and accomplish the task. According to Carol Stockdale of Another Door to Learning, the image was recorded, but Barb only had access to it through language. Barb often said, "Well, I know that," but, in fact, she did not know it consciously until she had the language to refine the image.

In middle school, Barb was placed in an English class that taught grammar as a discrete subject: two weeks for literature, two weeks for grammar. Barb's spoken English was excellent; her speech included sophisticated syntax and vocabulary, and she was most successful with the reading and discussion of the literature. But the spatial quality of the grammar drills confounded Barb. Because she failed to grasp the spatial task of retrieving the mechanics of written English, spatial labels like "adverb" meant nothing to her. While she could use an adverb correctly in spoken and written English, she could not "see" the term "adverb" any more than she could see the plastic wrap.

When Barb started high school, her classes were content rich; they stressed worldly knowledge. Although she continued to have difficulty with math and chemistry, she found that her writing and especially the mechanics improved as she took courses in history, literature, and art and music history. In these courses, she was learning the language that would allow her to store and retrieve the information. The more information she had the better she became at making connections, and these connections were as apparent in the classroom as in the kitchen.

Because Barb was coping well with her reading and writing in her high school classes, she did not anticipate that "driving class" would be a problem. But as Barb sat behind the wheel of the family sedan to have a practice session with her mother, her mother realized that learning to drive, a spatial task, would be much more difficult than learning art history.

Barb edged the car toward the pavement from the gravel shoulder of the road. "Turn the car a little to the left, Barb, and as you pick up speed, ease onto the pavement," her mother said patiently. Barb eased the car onto the grey cement at about 20 mph. But soon she was back on the gravel, and then a minute later she had drifted to the left side of the road. Many novice drivers drift, but Barb remained unaware of both the drift and resulting position. "Barb, you're driving on the wrong side of the road! Do you realize what could have happened?!" Barb's mother exclaimed.

"I'm sorry," Barb replied calmly; "I didn't notice." And indeed she did not notice, even though she saw. Barb had not yet used language which "uncovered" the images before her eyes to build and access the images that would allow her to drive safely.

Though she had never thought much about it before, Barb's mother realized that driving is in many ways a spatial task. According to Jeremy Campbell's theories, Barb's brain was capable of storing and connecting great amounts of information; her learning disability kept her from accessing it.

Carol Stockdale, a learning-disabilities specialist who had worked with Barb, suggested several strategies for conquering the problem. Barb walked around the car, touching it and measuring it against herself to see how big it was, all the time having a conversation with herself that translated the spatial into verbal dimensions. She went back to the country road near her home to look at the lines that marked the road and to touch the road and the gravel on the shoulder of the road and to say, "These are the lines that mark the lane, and these are the rocks that mark the side where I do not want to drive." As she found her way to all of her usual spots—the store, the school, the hardware store—she developed an internal conversation: "Turn right at the Exxon sign; turn left at the blue house on the corner."

NAVIGATING THROUGH SPACE

And so Barb learned to use verbal clues to navigate through space. Understanding how to learn to drive gave Barb insight into conquering all kinds of spatial problems. Although she continued to have difficulty with mathematics and foreign language in high school, her ability to write academic papers about topics in her language-based academic courses—history, literature, and art history—continued to improve.

When Barb went to college, she needed help with kinds of structures that were new to her, and she needed specific models to understand the shapes of analytical papers particular to certain courses. She also needed these models translated into language. For Barb, looking at something was not seeing it, at least not until she had shaped and refined the image with language.

More and more confident of her ability to know the world through language, Barb was increasingly comfortable with difficult ideas, for instance, in her college philosophy class: "Plato uses serval [sic] arguments to prove the existence of the forms: the first argument occurs in the Meno when Socrates shows that learning is merely a recollection of previous knowledge of forms by questioning a slave boy about the Pythagorean theorem." Despite the misplaced letter in the word "several," and the misplaced final phrase, the sentence involves sophisticated content communicated in an equally sophisticated sentence structure. This sentence is not the work of a basic writer or a person unable to deal with the intellectual challenges of higher education. Still, because of her difficulty accessing spatial information, Barb needed help with organization, mechanics, and new kinds of writing tasks.[3]

THE ROLE OF THE WRITING CENTER

Although learning-disabled students come to the writing center with a variety of special needs, they have one thing in common: they need more specific help than other students.

Often writing center directors do not know what kind of a learning disability the student has, but because the spatial systems and language systems overlap and act reciprocally, students who are dyslexic and students who are spatially impaired may demonstrate many of the same problems with spelling, grammar, development, and organizations Therefore, they will need similar kinds of assistance.

By changing the picture of the writing conference, the writing center director can ensure that learning-disabled students, no matter what the disability, are being appropriately accommodated. The writing advisors still need to be collaborators, but they also may need to help the students retrieve information and shape an image of the product. They may be called upon to demonstrate organization or to model a thesis sentence when the students cannot imagine what one might look like. The advisors may have to help the students call up detail in ways that would be inappropriate for the average learner. They may need to help with the physical production of texts. And they may need to help with correcting mechanics when the papers are in their final stages.

Paradoxically, and at the same time, the writing advisor must help the students be independent through self-cuing; creating a dependent atmosphere does not foster the students' ability to cope, does not develop the students' self-esteem, and does not help the students become better writers. The writing advisor must treat learning disabled persons as the intelligent, resourceful persons they are. Conferences without respect and understanding are seldom successful.

PREWRITING

Many of the discovery techniques commonly used in the composition class and in the writing center may not be productive for students with learning disabilities because, though these students may have the information, they may have no way to access it. The picture of the eager student freewriting to discover ideas needs to be amended when one works with learning-disabled students. Freewriting is almost impossible for most because they do not know, and can't imagine, what to write. Students with language retrieval problems may not be able to call up any words at all to put on the paper. This holds true for students with either spatial impairments or language difficulties.

For learning-disabled students, freewriting leads from one generalization to another or from one specific to another. Because they do not see the relationship between the specific and the general, without intervention they are locked in a non-productive cycle, unable to succeed unless it is by accident. And if they do succeed by accident, they do not understand their success. According to Carol Stockdale at Another Door to Learning, many learning disabled students have no way of intentionally creating order.

Freewriting is also frustrating for persons who are learning disabled because it requires them to write without knowing where they are going. Just as Barb had trouble understanding the road, other learning-disabled students need to know where they are going so they will know when they get there. Unable to recognize what is relevant and what is not, they find the freewriting an exercise in futility, while other students may find it a way to create knowledge.

In the writing center, directed conversation can take the place of freewriting. Because these students have trouble accessing what they know, they are unlikely to realize they know great amounts of information. Here, the writing advisor plays an important role. Nowhere else on most campuses can writers find an individual who will ask the leading questions that can unlock trapped information.

In some cases, the writing advisor may need to ask students like Barb specific, seemingly obvious questions to help them unlock the ideas in their minds and then take notes for them as they generate ideas for their papers. In essence the writing advisor is helping them see the plastic wrap.

Here is an example of a writing conference that respects the student's intelligence and at the same time helps him gain access to what he knows, and helps him find an organizational pattern for it.

Writing Advisor: Hi David, how are you? Have a seat.

David: Not good. I have another paper to write for my Intro to Fiction class.

Writing Advisor: Hmmm, you did well on your last paper, didn't you?

David: Yes, but this time I don't have anything to write about.

Writing Advisor: Now just think back to that first paper. As I recall, you didn't have a topic for that one either the first time we talked.

David: I guess you're right, but this time I really don't know what to write about.

The writing advisor knows that David has a learning disability. Understanding the brain as Jeremy Campbell explains it, as the great storehouse of knowledge, she suspects that David knows a great deal about the potential topic; she knows she will need to help David gain access to the tremendous information he does have.

Writing Advisor: What is the assignment?

David: To write a 3–4 page paper about *The Great Gatsby.*

Writing Advisor: David, I know you're worried about this paper, but I also know from the last paper we talked about how smart you are and how much you actually know. So let's just chat for a few minutes about the book without worrying about the paper.

The writing advisor turns her chair toward David and takes off her glasses. She realizes that despite David's high scores on standard I.Q. tests and good study habits many of his teachers have considered him "slow," careless, or lazy. She wants to be sure she treats him as the intelligent person he is. She begins with the obvious questions that will help him focus on the book and what he knows.

Writing Advisor: Who wrote *The Great Gatsby?*

David: F. Scott Fitzgerald. He was married to Zelda. And he also wrote Tender Is the Night. Some people think he stole his stories from Zelda's journals. Don't you think that's right?

Writing Advisor: I do think it's "right." I did know she had a big influence on him....

David: I mean he was drunk a lot and Zelda was the one who was writing all this stuff about their life. It's not fair.

Writing Advisor: I agree. This whole idea of fairness…was there anything in Gatsby that wasn't fair?

David: Yes, I don't think Tom was fair in the way he treated Daisy. He had an affair and he lied to her. Gatsby wasn't all that good either. He made his money illegally.

Writing Advisor: Do you think that was fair?

David: I guess not, at least not for the people he took advantage of.

Writing Advisor: I wonder if a word like "honesty" or "integrity" might help get at what we're talking about.

David: "Integrity," that's it.

When the writing advisor saw David lean forward, his eyes bright, she knew it was time to write something down. She took out a piece of paper and a pencil, wrote "integrity" in the middle of the page and showed it to David. She continues to take notes so that David can work at connecting the information without worrying about the physical production of text.

Writing Advisor: Tell me who has it and who doesn't.

David: Tom doesn't and Gatsby doesn't.
[The writing advisor wrote "Tom" on the left side of the page and "Gatsby" under it and connected each word to "integrity" with a line.]

Writing Advisor: Tell me why you don't think they have integrity.

David recounted example after example and the tutor noted each one under the appropriate name. As he talked, David included other characters and decided whether each had integrity or not and gave appropriate examples. In each case the tutor noted the information David produced and drew lines around similar information.

Writing Advisor: This is going to be a wonderful paper. Can you see the development taking shape? Look at the connections you've made.

David: Yes, but I'm not sure how to start the introduction.

Writing Advisor: Well, what kinds of things will your reader need to know in order to follow you through the paper?

By the time David had listed the kinds of things that he would include in the introduction, almost an hour had passed. The writing advisor wanted to conclude the session on a reassuring note, and she wanted David to know that he could teach himself to self-cue.

Writing Advisor: David, you know so much about your topic, and you have really good ideas. All I did was ask you questions. Eventually you'll be able to ask yourself those same questions. But now, why don't you do some writing, and then we'll have another appointment, if you like, to look at transitions, mechanics, and those sorts of things. It's fun seeing the connections in your mind unfold.

David: I think I can write a draft now. Will you be able to help me with spelling later in the week?

Writing Advisor: Sure, I'll see you when the draft is done, and we'll look at all kinds of things.

Because the act of calling up the words and getting them onto paper is so difficult for some learning-disabled students, the student may be unable to concentrate on the ideas and instead only focuses on the production of text. The writing advisor may need to do the typing or the drafting so the student is free to concentrate on answering the fairly specific, sometimes leading, questions proposed by the writing advisor. The writing advisor will know when to do the typing by asking the student, "Would you like me to record so you can work on generating the words?"

ORGANIZATION

Even after generating a page or two of material, students may still not be able to distinguish the important information from the supporting detail. Again writing advisors should understand that they must help the student over or around the problem. The advisors will probably say what they think is the most important element; once they say it, the students may be able to agree or disagree even though they cannot invent or articulate the idea on their own. The writing advisors might draw a map of the ideas and support for the student, or color-code the information to help with organization. The writing advisors should always be doing and saying at the same time. With learning-disabled students, just pointing seldom helps.

The writing advisor might need to model a thesis sentence for the student, asking simple questions like "What is your paper about?" "Rice," the student replies. "What about rice?" Students are often delighted and surprised when they come up with the single statement that will set the paper spinning.

The advisor may need to be just as explicit about the paper's development: "What is your first point going to be?" As the student responds, the advisor takes down the information, and then asks, "And what is your second point?" "And your third?" Showing students how to create an overview of the information and then teaching them how to categorize information will help the students manage the spatial qualities of organization.

Simply using a model like the five-paragraph essay to teach organization is unlikely to produce successful writing. Since structure grows out of content, the students may be successful one time with a five-paragraph essay, but when they try to apply the formula the next time, the formula may not work. They may be further hindered by being unable to let go of the formula or image.

A student like Barb may not be able to see paragraph breaks until the writing advisor says, "Notice how long this paragraph is," while at the same time pointing to the too-long paragraph. She may even need to say, "This is a paragraph." But the instant the advisor points it out, Barb will say, "Well, I know that." And after saying so, she does indeed know it.

PROOFREADING AND EDITING

Frank Smith (1982) makes the distinction between composition and transcription, between the composing of thought and the mechanics of getting the language down on paper according to certain conventions. Spelling and punctuation need to be done with the students so that they feel part of the process; most importantly, the editing must be specific and hands-on and must involve detailed explanations of what the advisor is doing. The writing advisor cannot expect the students to make the changes based on a rule or principle. The explanation must be specific, and it may need to be written as well as said: "Look at the beginning of this sentence. You have five words before your subject. How about a comma?" Students may agree that something is so, but they may be unable to hold the thought in their minds or recall it later.

Encouraging students to be independent through the use of a spell checker and grammar checker is essential, but the writing advisor may need to sit at the computer with students explaining how it works and its limitations. Telling students to put text through a spell check is seldom enough. The advisor may need to read the paper aloud to the students so they can catch errors: a final proofreading by the writing advisor is also appropriate for the learning-disabled students because these students may not be able to see the mistakes until they are pointed out to them.

Wheelchair-bound students can get to the third floor, but they may not be able to take the stairs. Their only routes are the elevator or the ramp. It's not that students with a learning disability can't get it, it's that they can't get it the same way the normal learner can.

OTHER KINDS OF ORGANIZATION
THAT AFFECT WRITING

Learning-disabled students sometimes have as much trouble coping with the organization of the writing and research time as they do with the organization of the text. Writing advisors can help by showing the students how to use a study planning sheet that contains small but regular accomplishments, and which will lead to the accomplishments of a larger task. It is not enough to tell students to do it; the writing advisors need to demonstrate the strategy, especially the first time. They should also ask the students to refer to the list on a regular basis; the markers of accomplishment need to be tangible.

SOCIAL INTERACTION

Many, but not all, learning-disabled students have trouble in social situations. A visit to the writing center may be one of these social situations. The student's behavior may be inappropriate: he interrupts another conversation, she stands too close or talks too much. Many people with learning disabilities are unable to "read" the nonverbal behavior of others. So even if the writing advisor frowns or looks away, the inappropriate behavior continues. Being explicit but positive will help the individual change this behavior: "Marty, please stop talking; I have something important to tell you." "Glad to see you, Sara. I'll sit here; you sit across from me; that will be a comfortable distance. I'll be ready to talk to you in a minute."

Despite the need for specific instructions and clear questions, the writing advisor must remain positive and encouraging. Often teachers and others misunderstand learning disabilities and accuse students of being lazy or dumb. As a result, college students with learning disabilities often have low self-esteem and may be defensive or uncertain of their own academic ability. Writing advisors can make a major contribution to a learning-disabled student's success if they are positive, encouraging, and specific about the writing, the revision, and the writing process.

Working with these students in the writing center is sometimes difficult because it means modifying or changing the usual guidelines, and it may mean more and longer appointments, for instance, appointments that last an hour instead of a half hour, and a writing advisor may need to proofread. Writing centers may need to change the rules and policies that govern these sessions and change the training that staff receive. But the students have a right to services, and writing centers have a responsibility to help learning-disabled students succeed.[5] Writing centers have always been places that help students reach their full potential, and this philosophy should extend to students with learning disabilities.

Most learning-disabled students need more support and help rather than less. And writing centers can provide that assistance. For these students, writing center professionals need a new picture of the writing conference that includes the writing advisor's becoming more directly involved in the process and the product. With adequate help and support, students with a learning disability can produce better papers, and they can also become better writers.

NOTES

1. At the October 1991 meeting of the International Conference on Leaning Disabilities, the debate over the left brain-right brain model continued in the conference sessions. The debate is interesting in that writing center professionals often use the model to explain parts of the composing process.

2. The same law that defines a learning disability guarantees the rights of the learning-disabled person. It is just as illegal to discriminate against a learning-disabled person as it is to discriminate against a person of an ethnic minority or a person with a physical disability. Recently a professor at the University of California Berkeley refused to accommodate a student's request for untimed tests. The student filed suit, and the faculty member was required to pay monetary damages to the student. Faculty members and institutions can be held accountable for blatant discrimination (Heyward).

3. Barb's is not an unusual case. As the diagnosis of learning disabilities has improved, students can be helped sooner and can be taught compensatory strategies that lead to success in high school as well as in college. In 1978 when statistics on learning disabilities were first kept, 2.6 percent of all freshmen reported having a disability. In 1988, it was 6 percent. In ten years of record keeping, the number had more than doubled. Still, many experts in the field believe that 6 percent is much too low and the number of learning disabled students is actually between 10 and 20 percent. Many cases have gone undetected.

4. Because problems with spelling and mechanics are the easiest to recognize and fix, many educators have believed that these are the only problems that learning-disabled students have with writing. But a University of Connecticut study showed that 51 percent of the students had trouble with organization compared to 24 percent who had trouble with proofreading (McGuire, Hall, Litt).

5. In 1993, the American Disabilities Act (ADA), which makes discrimination against a learning-disabled person illegal, became law.

REFERENCES

Bergland, Richard. 1985. *Fabric of Mind*. New York: Penguin.

Brinkerhoff, Loring. 1991. "Critical Issues in LD College Programming for Students with Learning Disabilities." International Conference on Learning Disabilities. Minneapolis, MN: October 11.

Campbell, Jeremy. 1989. *The Improbable Machine*. New York: Simon & Schuster.

Hammill, Donald D., James E. Leigh, Gaye McNutt, and Stephen C. Larsen. 1981. "A New Definition of Learning Disabilities." *Learning Disability Quarterly* 4.4, 336–42.

Heyward, Lawton & Associates, ed. 1992. *Association on Handicapped Student Service Programs in Postsecondary Education Disability Accommodation Digest* 1.2, 6.

Heyward, Salome. 1991. "Provision of Academic Accommodations." *Postsecondary LD Network News* 12, 7.

Levy, Nancy R., and Michael S. Rosenberg. 1990. "Strategies for Improving the Written Expression of Students with Learning Disabilities." *LD Forum* 16.1, 23–26.

Lipp, Janice. 1991. "Turning Problems into Opportunities." *Another Door to Learning Newsletter*, 1–3.

Longo, Judith. 1988. "The Learning Disabled: Challenge to Postsecondary Institutions." *Journal of Developmental Education* 11.3, 10–12.

Lovitt, Thomas. 1989. *Introduction to Learning Disabilities*. Needham Heights, MA: Allyn and Bacon.

McGuire, Joan. 1991. "Access and Eligibility." International Conference on Learning Disabilities. Minneapolis, MN: October 11.

McGuire, Joan, Debora Hall, and A. Vivienne Litt. 1991. "A Field-Based Study of the Direct Service Needs of College Students with Learning Disabilities." *Journal of College Student Development* 32, 101–108.

National Clearinghouse on Postsecondary Education for Individuals with Handicaps 8.2 (1989), 4.

Philosophy take-home exam. Smith College, 1991.

"The Rehabilitation Act of 1971." 1977, May 4. *Federal Register*, 93–112.

Schwarz, Judy. 1991. Personal interview. October 13.

Schwenn, John. 1991. "Stereotyped Football Players: Poor Students or Undiagnosed Learning Disabilities?" International Conference on Learning Disabilities. Minneapolis, MN: October 12.

Smith, Frank. 1982. *Writing and the Writers*. Hillsdale, NJ: Lawrence Eribaum Associates.

Stockdale, Carol. 1991. Personal interview. October 13.

U.S. Congress. 1969. *Children with Specific Learning Disabilities Act of 1969*. Washington, D.C.: U.S. Government Printing Office.

Woodcock, Richard, and M. Bonner Johnson. 1989. *Woodcock-Johnson Tests of Achievement*. Allen, TX: Teaching Resources.

Cultural Diversity in the Writing Center: Defining Ourselves and Our Challenges

Judith Kilborn

Reports from campuses nationwide describe both cultural diversity initiatives and backlash from students and faculty. According to Donna Gorrell, "Students not protected and favored by new legislation and policies, the reports go, are reacting with racism, sexism, and other forms of hatred toward those groups who are so favored" (1). This "new intolerance" is not limited to campuses which have seen national exposure in both print and film journalism. Actually, we are all affected in some way by the dynamics of the controversy and by the backgrounds out of which we come. Barbara Ehrenreich argues in an essay responding to multiculturalism's critics that all of us are victims of monoculturalism, a "narrow and parochial" education "that [has] left us ill-equipped to navigate a society that truly is multicultural and is becoming more so every day" (84). If we are indeed all victims of a narrow, parochial education that has left us ill-equipped to deal with a multicultural society, and if many of us are in fact white tutors and administrators in writing centers in predominantly white institutions, how can we effectively prepare ourselves to respond to the challenging—and, at times, murky—political climate in which cultural diversity immerses us? The issues are complicated, and the answers are not simple.

If we are to survive and thrive as the population in the United States becomes more diverse, we in writing centers must adapt our services to the changing clientele. We must be proactive in defining models of multicultural centers unless we want others to define what we are and what we might become. Moreover, writing center personnel must meet the challenges and move toward diversity by formally and informally collaborating with faculty and administrators of color as they plan and implement services for minority students.

Writing center personnel wishing to make their centers truly culturally diverse face six challenges:

1. Defining what we see as multicultural
2. Working with administrators and faculty on campus who can lend support to our endeavors and enable us to institutionalize changes, and—perhaps most importantly—working with personnel within our institutions who have been hired to work with minority and international students
3. Recruiting and retaining a multicultural writing center clientele
4. Recruiting, training, and retaining minority and international tutors
5. Training our tutors to become more sensitive to students with cultures, languages, and dialects different from their own
6. Assessing writing center services.

Each of these challenges is significant, complicated, and worthy of ongoing dialogue.

DEFINING WHAT WE SEE AS MULTICULTURAL

The definition of what we see as multicultural will underlie all of our endeavors. In Minnesota, the terms "multicultural" and "cultural diversity" are defined by both the legislature and the state university system as targeting African American, Hispanic, and Native American minorities. For the purposes of academic initiatives, funding, recruitment, and retention, these minorities are favored. Thus, for the state and state university system, specific minorities equal diversity. However, when considering cultural diversity for the purposes of university curriculum and academic programs, the university itself includes non-mainstream American cultures as well as foreign cultures; thus, diversity includes such foreign cultures as African and Asian as well as American minorities such as Asian American, Native American, African American, and Hispanic. This is also true when focusing on the quality of academic, campus, and community life for the purposes of addressing racism and ethnocentrism or developing specialized support services; the university includes in its definition of cultural diversity students and faculty who are refugees, who are visiting from other countries, or who are naturalized citizens. Thus, Pacific Islanders, Indians, Africans, and Middle-Easterners, for example, are included along with American minorities. In other words, for my university, minority plus non-western equals diversity.

Although I report to the university and state university system administrators using their specific definitions of cultural diversity, I think of multiculturalism in the writing center in a very different way. For me, cultural diversity includes minority, non-western, and western—Caucasian as well as African American, Hispanic, and Native American; rural as well as urban; southern as well as northern; non-traditional as well as traditional, and so on. In other words, my definition is inclusive rather than exclusive.

WORKING WITH THOSE WHO CAN HELP INSTITUTIONALIZE CHANGE

For those of us working in predominantly white institutions, an overriding concern is support. In a very real sense, we cannot change the complexion of our staffs or clientele without the assistance of administrators and faculty who can lend support to our endeavors and enable us to institutionalize changes, and—perhaps most importantly—personnel within our institutions who have been hired to work with minority and international students: minority and international student recruiters, advisors, and those who work in minority and international support services such as cultural or academic centers. Ideally, networking with people in these positions should lead naturally to recruitment of minority and international tutors and to minority and international student use of center services.

In reality, however, this networking is frequently undercut by two distinctly different views of what the nature of support services should be—especially when it comes to minority students. On one hand are those who believe that minority students are best served by mainstreaming them into the general population to prepare them to interact with the diverse population they will meet in the work place. For example, in "10 Principles for Good Institution Practice in Removing Race/Ethnicity as a Factor in College Completion," Alfredo de los Santos, Jr. and Richard C. Richardson, Jr. argue that "Good practice...moves away from providing minority support, primarily through peripheral special programs, toward the integration of minority programs with those for majority students" (45). De los Santos and Richardson believe such services address barriers minority students face to both academic achievement and social integration. On the other hand are those who believe that minority students are best served by services designed and run by minorities for minorities; they feel that such services provide a sense of community and cultural pride.

Although the answer probably lies somewhere between these two camps, the presence of these two drastically different perspectives may seriously undercut the ability of writing centers to develop and implement cultural diversity initiatives which will truly change the complexion of writing centers and have long term impact. In some places, in fact, tutorial services for minority students are available in two places: in the writing center and in some sort of minority tutoring center. Such is the case at St. Cloud State. Although tutorial services for the general student population and ESL students are housed in the writing center, a separate Minority Academic Support Center provides minority students with tutors in all subjects, including writing.

In the past, students tutoring in this program received no formal training: they were given no strategies that would enable them to empower students to do their own work and had no means of avoiding the proofreading trap. It should be noted that Minority Academic Support Center administrators were working under two false assumptions. First, they believed that since the tutors they had hired were good students and good writers, they needed no training to be good tutors. They also believed that since their tutors were minority students, they were already culturally sensitive and required no additional background or training to deal with students having backgrounds different from their own. Addressing these concerns required that I meet with the Dean of Fine Arts and Humanities, the academic vice president, and the director and assistant directors of the Minority Academic Support Center and gain their support in working out a resolution. Centers implementing cultural diversity initiatives will find such administrative support essential.

As a result of administrative input, two collaborative projects emerged: minority students worked with writing center tutors in producing the minority newsletter, and the writing center began publication of an annual multicultural magazine, called *Kaleidoscope*, which is a collection of students' poetry, short stories, essays, artwork, and photography. The writing center also co-hosted with Minority Student Programs a reading at the minority cultural house of the award winning writing from the magazine. This event not only enabled voices which are frequently marginalized to be heard, but co-sponsorship of this event demonstrated that Minority Student Programs has publicly acknowledged support of this magazine. In addition, the magazine has validated the excellence of work produced by ethnic minorities, has educated the university community about minority and international experience in an intimate, non-threatening way, and has included minority students in the writing center community so they are not resistant to receiving tutorial assistance.

Our experience convinces us that administrative support of writing center cultural diversity initiatives—including the support of administrators of minority academic support services as well as those administrators to whom they report—is critical to the success of these initiatives. In addition. administrators of minority academic services must be encouraged to contribute to the development of these initiatives so that they feel ownership over the programs.

Such ownership and collaboration has also been encouraged at St. Cloud State through the writing center's involvement in the summer Advanced Placement Program (APP), an early entry program for minority, international, and refugee students. According to de los Santos and Richardson, such bridge programs, which always include tutoring as an integral component, "help make the learning environment less formidable during periods when students are most vulnerable to academic failure" (46).

As a result of this program, coordination and cooperation with those hired to work with minority students has begun to work more smoothly. An additional strength of the writing center's involvement with this program is that minority students work in the center during their first quarter in the university. Positive instructional experience early in their college career has convinced many of these students to use center services throughout their university schooling. Hence, the center's work with students in the APP has assisted in recruiting and retaining a multicultural writing center clientele.

RECRUITING AND RETAINING A MULTICULTURAL WRITING CENTER CLIENTELE

Minority and international students, who already feel labeled by virtue of their race, language, or cultural background, are unlikely to attend services which stamp them with yet another label. That is why it is essential that these students, in particular, do not see our centers as remedial. Therefore, at St. Cloud State, part of recruiting minority and international clientele involves simply emphasizing what we tell all students: that we work with all students, freshmen through graduate school, from departments across campus, on any aspect of the writing process. The distribution of *Kaleidoscope* has also helped: it has shown that we support and encourage creativity and appreciate a multitude of voices and backgrounds. Students wandering in to pick up a copy of the magazine have rarely made that their only visit to the center.

The writing center will soon begin outreach to minority student groups on campus by offering to present workshops on writing resumes, job application letters, and essays for graduate and law school applications. We hope that emphasizing writing that is not for freshman composition will completely undercut any myths students may have about who we are and what we do.

Much of our success so far, though, has resulted from informal communication. I and members of my staff have attended such events as the Chinese New Year; poetry readings during African American Awareness Week; banquets, potlucks, and pow wows; and panel discussions, teleconferences, and speakers on such topics as racism and racial violence, global awareness, the "Making of *Dances with Wolves*," and the Persian Gulf War. Our steady presence and active interest in such activities shows that we are serious about what we are doing and that we are not just paying lip service to cultural diversity to fill quotas. Our presence at such events also enables us to meet and get to know students and faculty on campus with backgrounds different from our own. In addition, we have made connections by asking on-campus speakers on cultural diversity topics to submit articles to our writing center newsletter, which is distributed to all faculty and administrators on campus.

One of the most important aspects of recruiting and retaining a multicultural clientele, however, has to do with whether or not minority students are comfortable working in the center. We can create a comfortable environment for minority students through careful tutor training and ongoing assessment of our services, which will be discussed later. However, no matter how careful our training and assessment, minority students will be uncomfortable if our staffs do not themselves reflect diversity. Recruitment, training, and retention of minority and international student tutors, then, is essential.

RECRUITING, TRAINING MINORITY AND INTERNATIONAL TUTORS

Many of the strategies we have used to recruit and retain minority writing center clientele have also improved our ability to attract minority tutors. For example, our involvement in the Advanced Placement Program, our production of *Kaleidoscope*, and our assistance in the production of the minority student newsletter have helped us to recruit minority tutors and desk workers. However, we have used additional informal and formal recruitment strategies. On-going, informal discussions with the ESL director. for example, have enabled us to recruit international graduate students.

Nevertheless, we have found that professional development opportunities are the key to recruiting both minority and international tutors. We have, in informal discussions with prospective tutors, and teachers and administrators who might recommend them, stressed the opportunities available to tutors. Professional development possibilities include, of course, experience in working one-to-one. In addition, however, we offer the opportunity to help in supervising and training other tutors through such activities as presentations at staff meetings and in the practicum class as well as formal observation and mentoring of other tutors. We also encourage minority tutors to become involved in the judging of *Kaleidoscope* submissions and in the production and editing of the magazine. Moreover, we encourage minority tutors to write articles and to serve as editors of *Writing Consultants' Ink,* the writing center's newsletter. Finally, we encourage them to present papers and workshops at regional conferences. These professional development opportunities—and the warmth and acceptance of other center personnel—have helped us to retain both minority and international tutors.

We have also been able to retain these tutors by offering them the option to become involved in cultural diversity activities, in problem-solving, in planning, and in researching; by listening to them and supporting them when they receive negative reactions from students simply because of their race, language, or cultural backgrounds; and by simply being there when they feel tom between their obligations as students and the many requests they get from various units on campus to help out by being their "resident minority person." On a homogeneous campus such as ours, demands on minority students to serve as spokespeople for their race or ethnic group are strong. It is important to remember that minority students should have the option not to speak: they may, in fact consider their ideas, opinions, or background too private; they may be disinterested in culture or race relations or in educating others about these topics; or they may simply be—like other students—busy and involved in their own education. If we wish to retain minority students as tutors, we must respect them as individuals; although we should provide opportunities for professional development, as we do for all tutors. the focus of this professional development should be the student's choice, not ours.

The writing center plans this year to promote professional development opportunities available to tutors and to extend our recruitment of minority and international tutors by meeting with minority faculty and student special interest groups. We have also developed a brochure as a recruitment tool for our writing center practicum, which is used to screen and train tutors. This brochure will be distributed to all minority and international students with GPAs of 3 or better (on a 4-point scale) who have completed the freshman composition sequence.

TRAINING TUTORS TO BE MORE CULTURALLY AND LINGUISTICALLY SENSITIVE

Clearly, all of our attempts to recruit and retain minority and international tutors and writing center clientele will be in vain if our tutors are not linguistically and culturally sensitive. I am reminded, for example, of a tutoring session three years ago when an African American woman was working with two tutors taking the graduate-level writing center practicum. Although the African American's teacher had not objected to dialogue using black dialect and "ghetto humor" in her essay, the tutors in training clearly did; ignoring the teacher's suggestion that the student work on development, these tutors instead kept trying to get her to take the black dialect and humor out of her paper. In addition to stepping in to resolve the situation, I have added several things to tutor training to prevent such tutor responses.

First, I use books in the tutoring practicums which raise pertinent topics. Meyer and Smith's *The Practical Tutor,* for example, has a chapter on dialect and second language interference, and Muriel Harris' *Teaching One-to-One:*

The Writing Conference covers rhetorical patterns Kaplan has identified in the writing of other cultures. Finally, sections of Lustig and Koester's *Intercultural Competence: Interpersonal Communication Across Cultures* introduce theories relevant to intercultural communication: Stewart's taxonomy of cultural patterns (including activity, orientation, social relations orientation, self-orientation, and world orientation); Hall's high- and low-context patterns (covering use of covert and overt messages, importance of ingroups and out-groups, and orientation to time); and Hofstede's cultural patterns (relating to power distance, individualism/collectivism, and their effects). Lustig and Koester's book also provides in-depth discussions of verbal and nonverbal cultural communication and potential obstacles to intercultural communication, including ethnocentrism, stereotyping, prejudice, and racism. Readings in books such as these provide tutors with background knowledge of subjects relating to cross-cultural tutoring. These readings also highlight issues—both overt and covert—which affect intercultural communication and sensitize tutors to the complexity and multiple dimensions of tutoring in a culturally diverse writing center. Discussions of such readings are inevitably lively. They also sometimes surface behaviors and attitudes that are unwelcome in writing centers; these can be addressed immediately in the practicum classroom, and potential tutors who are deemed uneducable can be eliminated from the list of those who will be hired to tutor long-term in the writing center.

Second, I require that practicum tutors write a paper about the discourse or speech communities of which they are a part. This paper requires that they analyze their own experience: specifically that tutors reflect upon the various dialects and rhetorical patterns they use when interacting with different groups they belong to (whether formal or informal groups) and share their insights with their peers. Students learn from this assignment how much they adapt the language, content, and organization of their writing and speaking to their audience; how much their use of language determines whether or not they gain "membership" in a group; and how flexible they already are in addressing the demands of various speech communities. Such assignments also encourage potential tutors to appreciate the similarities and the differences between discourse communities.

Third, the ESL director makes presentations in the practicums and staff meetings about contrastive rhetoric and other topics pertinent to tutoring ESL students. We have practiced identifying the rhetorical patterns of different cultures, talked about strategies for encouraging international students to adapt to the direct American organizational plan, and considered the emotional responses that frequently accompany such a shift. In addition, we have talked about tutorial strategies for addressing sentence-level errors. Finally, we have reviewed how ESL teachers comment on student papers and have coordinated classroom and tutorial instruction.

Fourth, we work in small groups problem-solving possible tutor responses to cultural conflict scenarios which have taken place in the center. I also provide on-going training in cultural diversity by asking minority and international faculty to speak at staff meetings, to educate tutors about issues facing students, and to raise concerns pertinent to tutoring a multicultural clientele. Additionally, I have used videotapes on culture shock and on ivory tower racism on St. Cloud's campus to facilitate discussion about minority and international students' experiences in the university. Finally, we are currently in the process of developing a videotape which shows segments of three tutorials: one between an African American tutor and a white student, one between an Hispanic student and a white tutor, and one between an Asian student and a white tutor. The goal of this videotape is to show subtle examples of racial/ethic stereotypes at work in the writing center and to illustrate how they undercut the success of the tutorials. This videotape will be used in practicums and staff meetings as a vehicle for small group discussion.

ASSESSING WRITING CENTER SERVICES

Assessment is the key, and it should begin with establishing yearly goals. For us at St. Cloud State, yearly goals have included planning specific multicultural activities we will complete, as well as targeting the number of minority and international tutors we hope to recruit and the number of tutoring and workshop hours we hope to reach for specific populations. Setting these goals, and then keeping careful records to show how well we have met them, helps us to reflect upon what we have achieved and what we have yet to do.

Evaluations are also a central part of this assessment. First of all, we have added a cultural sensitivity question to our student evaluations which we distribute at the end of each quarter. Specifically, we ask students, "Was your tutor sensitive to your individual needs, including academic, racial, and cultural background?" In addition, we have developed specialized evaluations which we send to teachers of minority and international students, asking them to comment on students' progress in the specific aspects of writing covered in tutorial instruction. Finally, we have interviewed a random sample of minority students to find out whether or not students have taken advantage of center services and why, what they like about the services, what they feel could be improved, and what their impressions of the center's comfort level for minority students are. This survey has informed us that many minority students are simply unaware of our services; we now know that we need to advertise our services more widely in media that will reach this potential clientele. We plan to survey minority students on a regular basis to track our progress and to monitor our services in an on-going way.

By thinking carefully about how we define cultural diversity; by working with administrators and faculty on campus who can support our endeavors and enable us to institutionalize changes; by recruiting and retaining minority and international tutors and clientele; by training our tutors to become more sensitive to students with cultures, languages, and dialects different from their own; and by assessing our services, we can develop writing centers which are truly multicultural. We need to define ourselves as centers of diversity and embrace the challenges that diversity brings.

WORKS CITED

de los Santos, Alfredo and Richard C. Richardson, Jr. "10 Principles for Good Institution Practice in Removing Race/Ethnicity as a Factor in College Completion." *Educational Record* Summer/Fall, 1989: 43–47.

Ehrenreich, Barbara. "Teach Diversity—with a Smile." *Time* 8 April 1991: 84.

Gorrell, Donna. "The Rhetoric of Cultural Diversity." *Minnesota English Journal* 12.1 (1991): 1–10.

Harris, Muriel. *Teaching One-to-One: The Writing Conference* Urbana, IL: National Council of Teachers of English, 1988.

Lustig, Myron W. and Jolene Koester. *Intercultural Competence: Interpersonal Communication Across Cultures*. New York: Harper Collins, 1993.

Meyer, Emily and Louise Smith. *The Practical Tutor*. New York: Oxford UP, 1990.

6

WRITING CENTERS AND WRITING ACROSS THE CURRICULUM: A SYMBIOTIC RELATIONSHIP?

In 1988, Ray Wallace published an article examining the role of writing centers in writing across the curriculum (WAC) programs and concluded that the writing center can be an integral part of WAC work. Obviously, two programs that advocate writing on campus would work well together, particularly since one focuses primarily on students and the other on faculty and programs. Mission statements of the two are similar, and writing center administrators are often WAC directors as well. Some schools have one program and not the other. Depending on how individual institutions are organized and philosophically influenced, writing centers and WAC programs manifest differently, and current discussions within the writing center and WAC community surround generalist and discipline-based writing centers and WAC programs.

This section begins with the aforementioned Wallace article, which, within the context of his own program, combines the optimism of writing center potential with discipline-specific tutors to serve more students and writing center and WAC missions. His program involves extensive interaction between faculty and tutors drawn from many disciplines, similar to the University of Massachusetts at Boston program described by Louise Z. Smith in her article that follows Wallace's. Both programs draw tutors from across the university, but the UMass/Boston writing center, based in the English department, decentralized by moving from the physical space that traditional writing centers hold into classrooms with faculty. UMass/Boston paired tutors with every first-year composition course and, when faculty requested, other classes across campus.

Mark Waldo's article follows Smith's with a different approach to writing centers and WAC. Waldo's work at the University of Nevada, Reno, effectively eliminated the division between programs and moved both outside the English department. He argues that a successful WAC program should be housed in an "independent" writing center with a tenured or tenureable director, skilled tutors, and ambitious WAC consultancy. Muriel Harris soberly responds to Waldo in her article about the De Facto WAC Center/Writing Center. Unlike Waldo's assertive plan to place WAC within a writing center, Harris methodically describe Purdue's writing lab, having a WAC program essentially thrust upon it, and the lab's ability to handle the task.

As faculty assume that WAC and writing centers are one entity, and as writing center and WAC personnel team to meet institutional challenges, Michael Pemberton asks administrators to rethink the WAC/writing center connection. He questions the compatibility of the prevalent generalist tutoring approach used in writing centers and the current emphasis on writing in the disciplines. And based upon his examination, he believes compatibility can be achieved in the future with thoughtful approaches to both programs.

The future is the focus of the final essay of the section, written by Christina Murphy and Joe Law. In it they look at the future of writing centers and WAC programs through a futurist lens that moves both programs into an electronic space that transcends traditional university bounds. Because of their vision, they argue that WAC and writing center scholars must become involved in "macro-debates that will engage a broader audience from many areas in the social and educational spectrum."

The scholarship here defines a relationship between writing centers and WAC programs, but the nature of that relationship is varied. The Wallace and Pemberton articles are optimistic, yet contradictory, when considering discipline-based WAC and generalist tutoring. Waldo, Smith, and Harris describe successful programs that operate from dramatically different positions, and Murphy and Law show us what the future may look like and what directors should do to help shape it. Read together, they show the partnership possibilities for different types of programs in different institutions.

The Writing Center's Role in the Writing Across the Curriculum Program: Theory and Practice

Ray Wallace

Over the last quarter of a century, university professors and administrators have discovered an alarming trend on our campuses: many graduating seniors prove deficient in writing skills. As a result, many universities recently have developed proficiency, or "exit," exams in an attempt to stop the flow of writing-deficient graduates. However, this procedure used alone is akin to throwing water on a smoldering ruin; while much smoke and confusion occur, there is no change in the final state of the once-great building. It became increasingly clear that one semester of English composition is not sufficient to turn writing deficiencies into writing proficiencies. As a result, many universities have implemented writing-across-the-curriculum programs.

Like other universities throughout the country, our institution implemented a writing-across-the-curriculum program last year. This article describes how we coordinated this program through the writing center and discusses the solutions we developed to counter the strain of an added program to our center's already overburdened mission.

After approximately two years of heated intra- and inter-disciplinary argument, it was agreed that all general education courses in our university had to develop the students' writing, and/or quantitative skills. It was then that the writing center faculty was asked to help ease the problems involved in the introduction of writing skills across the curriculum. With this added program, the writing center was now home for three highly diversified, but equally important programs:

1. One-to-one and small-group tutoring in writing for all English classes.
2. Computer-assisted remedial instruction in grammar and usage.
3. Specialized tutoring, in writing for the writing-across-the-curriculum program.

Wallace, Ray. "The Writing Center's Role in the Writing Across the Curriculum Program: Theory and Practice." *The Writing Center Journal* 8.2 (1988): 43–48. Reprinted by permission of *The Writing Center Journal.*

Freisinger and Burkland (1982) list five components by which writing-across-the-curriculum programs can be implemented and improved in the writing center. These components include the following guidelines:

1. The discipline professor can and should refer students with writing problems to the writing center; this referral can be voluntary or a course requirement.

2. The writing center tutor must understand what the discipline professor expects as an end-product from the student being tutored.

3. The writing center tutor and the discipline professor must communicate with each other. The tutor must document how each student was tutored, what tutoring methods were used, the effectiveness of these methods, and the student's response to these methods. In turn, the professor must document how these methods helped, or did not help, when the student was finally evaluated.

4. The discipline professor should provide examples of effective papers, style sheets, documentation formats, and copies of each assignment question. These documents should be filed in the writing center.

5. The discipline professor should take an active interest in the administration of the writing center. (176–177)

Theorists disagree about who should tutor writing-across-the-curriculum students in the writing center. Arfken (1982) and Steward and Croft (1982) point to the almost exclusive use of English majors as the most effective tutoring personnel. Scanlon (1986), however, comments that selecting "tutors from several disciplines...can substantially strengthen the services of the writing center" (40). Scanlon's argument that "the discourse in each discipline also has its own features [so] an interdisciplinary writing center needs to be staffed by tutors who are familiar with these different features" (38) helped us decide that we could use non-English majors as tutors.

MAKING THE WRITING CENTER WORK IN PRACTICE

Before any philosophical and/or structural chances could be made, the writing center faculty and the discipline professors had to define what they considered effective writing. Therefore, a two-day writing, workshop was held in the center, and, as people gradually got to know each other's views on writing, effective and ineffective writing, samples from many disciplines were discussed. From this intensive, but relaxed, workshop, both writing center faculty and discipline professors were able to agree that

1. There should be *at least* one out-of-class writing assignment of not less than 1000 words in each course.

2. The professor should set an appropriate deadline so each student could have *at least* one tutoring session in the writing center on each paper. Assignment deadlines therefore were approximately two weeks.

3. The professor should devote *at least* one class lecture to a discussion of rhetorical considerations, the writing process, documentation, and the benefits of visiting the writing center.

4. The professor should provide a copy of the assignment question to the tutor.

The writing center faculty turned to the discipline professors to nominate their most responsible majors as possible tutors. These professors developed their own criteria for the selection of tutors for the writing across the curriculum program. These criteria included the following:

- A declared major in the discipline to be tutored
- A cumulative grade-point average between 2.5 and 4.0
- Junior standing
- Two letters of recommendation from discipline professors

Even with these somewhat restrictive criteria, cross-disciplinary tutors were readily available. Such availability was due to an effective recruiting strategy used by the discipline professors. When these students were told that such tutoring experience would enhance their resumes, help them gain admittance to graduate school, or make them more marketable in terms of their interpersonal and administrative skills, the discipline professors were able to nominate so many fine student writers that the writing center faculty could then select those with the greatest potential.

Both the writing center faculty and the discipline professors viewed the training of these new tutors as a very important task if writing-across-the-curriculum were to succeed at the institution. The center's faculty had already been holding tutor-training sessions for the general tutors (all English majors) who were assigned to tutor the writing classes in English. However, the faculty and the other discipline professors felt that the inclusion of the new writing-across-the-curriculum tutors in the general tutor-training sessions would be counterproductive in terms of time and goals. Therefore, these new tutors had to attend their own weekly two-hour special training workshops. The workshops were held for a total of twelve weeks. In the first hour of each workshop, selected members of the writing center faculty discussed various aspects of the composing process and tutoring techniques. In the second hour of each workshop, the discipline professors met in small groups with their discipline's tutors to explain future assignments, tutoring problems, course materials, and pertinent goals. The following is a brief outline of the twelve-week tutor-training course:

Week #1:   Introduction of the center faculty, the discipline professors, and the course content and goals. A brief discussion of the writing center layout and the ethics of tutoring.

Week #2:   Beginning to Tutor: The initial meeting, roles, models, and expectations. A discussion on how to evaluate writing, and how to develop a tutee profile.

Week #3:   The Writing Process: More intensive discussion of prewriting, writing, and rewriting tutoring techniques.

Week #4:   Discipline-Specific Writing Assignments: Small-group discussions of discipline-specific organizational/rhetorical writing patterns and individual tutoring techniques.

Week #5:   Role-Playing: How to work with the student who just wants the assignment proofread.

Week #6:   Tutoring/Counseling: How to motivate the student and an overview of counseling approaches.

Week #7:   Discipline-Specific Documentation Styles: Small-group discussions of discipline-specific styles, formats, and requirements.

Week #8:   Role-Playing: Tutoring the ESL learner. A discussion of the tutoring methods used to help these students with idioms, prepositions, tenses, count and non-count nouns, articles, and other common ESL problems.

Week #9:   Tutoring Mechanics: Grammar, punctuation and spelling. Guidelines on how to avoid proofreading for the tutee.

Week #10:   Role-Playing: Dealing with the paper which is too technical for its intended audience. Discussion of levels of formality, audience awareness, and other audience considerations.

Week #11:   Revision: How to tutor students to rethink and to reorganize their papers.

Week #12:   Evaluation: Both tutor and discipline professor evaluate each other.

MERGING THEORY AND PRACTICE

As the writing center became a place where professors and tutors could exchange ideas and techniques that proved effective, theory and practice merged. Although some professors were at first rather hesitant about submitting their documentation style sheets, they soon realized that they needed to update their style sheets for their own research. So, with tutors chastised into keeping better tutoring records and discipline professors persuaded that it was in their best interests to update their own writing standards, the center had accumulated over forty different examples of discipline-specific writing. By the end of the semester, these included lab reports, program documentation reports, abstracts, summaries, analyses, and mechanism descriptions. These examples, combined with individual documentation style sheets and extensive reports of which techniques worked and which did not, proved invaluable in training the next group of writing-across-the-curriculum tutors.

CONCLUSION

The writing center, both in theory and practice, can play an important role in the implementation of writing across the curriculum at any institution. Our institution's attempt to use the writing center worked well. While administration of the center remained securely anchored to the English discipline, other disciplines took an active interest in what was happening in the center. A completely new team of tutors was selected and trained. New insight into other disciplines' evaluation of writing was gained, and a new corpus of materials and tutoring handouts was developed.

In this situation, the writing center's role is to provide additional instruction for a group of discipline professors interested in improving their students' writing skills. The center is, and should always be, only a support service; writing-across-the-curriculum advocates should never expect writing and content to be separated in terms of instruction. As writing center personnel, we owe it to these new colleagues to provide the most effective support. If these professors demonstrate the important goals that effective written communication can achieve, then the writing center must be there to support these goals, to add to the instruction of students' writing skills, and to help these future biologists, geographers, economists, and educators reach these goals.

WORKS CITED

Arfken, D. "A Peer-Tutor Staff, Four Crucial Aspects." *Tutoring Writing*. Ed. Muriel Harris. Glenview: Scott, Foresman, 1982. 111–22.

Freisinger, Diana, and Jill Burkland. "Talking About Writing: The Role of the Writing Lab." *Language Connections: Writing and Reading Across the Curriculum*. Eds. Toby Fulwiler and Art Young. Urbana: NCTE. 1982. 167–79.

Scanlon, Leone. "Recruiting and Training Tutors for Cross Disciplinary Writing Programs." *The Writing Center Journal* 6.2 (1986): 1–8.

Steward, Joyce, and Mary Croft. *The Writing Laboratory*. Glenview: Scott, Foresman, 1982.

Independence and Collaboration: Why We Should Decentralize Writing Centers

Louise Z. Smith

Two strong movements in composition pedagogy, writing centers and writing-across-the-curriculum, often work at cross purposes. Intellectual and political movements often seem to require an early phase of separatism, of gathering their self-definitions into a fist. Witness the black separatism of the late '60's and feminist separatism of the early '70's. But once having said, "This is who we are and how we're different from them. Here are our authorities, our philosophies, and our methods as distinct from theirs," those movements outgrow their fierce need for separatism. The fist begins to open, to relax its grip on authority, and to welcome collaboration with other, sometimes quite variously dextrous and differently motivated, hands.

Writing centers as loci of specialized authority played a role in achieving recognition of composition as a discipline; now writing-across-the-curriculum programs share that authority among many different kinds of collaborators. Unfortunately, institutional structures tend to resist this historical process. The resulting problems—turf wars, conflicts between centralized and distributed authority, contradictions between uniform and diverse pedagogies, and issues of exploitation—now make some writing center directors wonder if writing centers have outlived their usefulness (Kail, Trimbur).

Writing centers conflict with writing-across-the-curriculum in matters of authority and pedagogy. On the one hand, writing centers are centripetal. They invite the faculty who assign, comment upon, and grade student writing to "send us your writing problems." Supervisors of goldfish-bowl writing centers and peer-tutoring programs feel pressured to adopt a uniform "best" pedagogy, knowing that whichever pedagogy they adopt must inevitably of-

Smith, Louise Z. "Independence and Collaboration: Why We Should Decentralize Writing Centers." *Writing Center Journal* 7.1 (1986): 3–10. Reprinted by permission of *The Writing Center Journal*.

fend some part of the faculty. They also fear intruding in the traditional authoritarian syntax of teaching, "teacher teaches student" (Kail 596, 598). Communication between the faculty and the writing center staff becomes cumbersome at best, depending upon faculty referral forms and tutor report forms (Harris, *Tutoring Writing* 259–94). Writing center supervisors are "on duty" to help "peer" tutors solve problems as they arise (Bruffee 144). But because these supervisors are seldom, if ever, the same teachers who actually designed the assignment, they cannot possibly know the contexts of assigned readings and class discussions in which the various writing assignments are supposed to be prepared. The result is an inevitable tension between the authority of teachers and that of writing center supervisors. Another source of tension is that so-called peer tutors are by definition NOT—nor can they usefully pretend to be—the referred students' peers in writing skill, experience, or confidence, Despite these tensions of authority, once "problems" become the writing center's turf, faculty may all-too-willingly refer students with problems to the writing center, thus freeing themselves to get on with content.

On the other hand, writing-across-the-curriculum is centrifugal. Since writing is a mode of investigating content and forming concepts in many disciplines, the responsibility and authority for writing instruction are shared among many departments. Since teaching writing is everybody's business, turf rivalries are minimized. However, unless writing-across-the-curriculum faculty have regular opportunities to articulate and modify their composition philosophies and pedagogies, the potentially fruitful variety may turn into wearying confusion (Schor, Fulwiler).

These centripetal/centrifugal tuggings also raise questions of exploitation among professors, writing center staff, and students. Writing-across-the-curriculum faculty may feel overwhelmed or imposed upon by the demanding new task of learning how to teach writing—not just assigning and perhaps editing it—as a integrated part of their courses without sacrificing "content." Writing center tutors may see themselves as the EMT's of academe, exhausted by ministering to sprained syntax, rhetorical contusions, and broken logic. Trimbur describes them as exploited by low pay and low esteem, resentful of serving systems and pedagogies they neither design nor control, delegated the "drudgery" of working with "basket cases" (34–35).

Students may also feel punished—sent by professors to stay after school in the writing center—and thus estranged. Instead of operating on a walk-in basis, the best writing centers now wisely urge tutor-student partners to meet throughout a semester. While continuity offers them better results and greater personal satisfaction, even such partners work at an intellectual and social distance from the professors who assigned the writing. Student writers—wondering whether to consult their history professors, writing professors, or writing center tutors—may simply consult no one. Those most in need of help are least likely to find it.

The Queens College model (Held and Rosenberg) solves some of these problems. In basic and regular writing courses, it pairs volunteer faculty-mentors with highly qualified undergraduate team-teachers (who receive four credits for four class-hours and one seminar-hour weekly). These partners "choreograph" their steps for each class and take turns writing paper comments, grading, and holding conferences. Faculty, some initially fearful of relinquishing classroom authority, discover that division of labor offsets "loss." Moreover, because "Equal partners demonstrate communication as a *negotiated way* rather than *the right way*," students' writing becomes more genuine and lively. Within these collaborations, "Independence must be maintained for the true decentralization to take effect" (819).

Another solution may be found in administratively decentralizing writing centers and in resisting pressures to assume a uniform composition pedagogy. The decentralized tutoring program in the College of Arts and Sciences of the University of Massachusetts at Boston offers an example. The program gathers together faculty and tutors, writing assignments and student essays from many departments. It then transmits these collaborators' experiences and disseminates contemporary theory and research in composition. By both gathering and distributing, the decentralized tutoring program nurtures communal discourse on composition.

UMass/Boston's tutoring program fosters independence and collaboration by coordinating its work with many parts of the college-wide writing program. The Office of Academic Support and Advising (which *inter alia* teaches study skills courses and an intensive review course for the college-wide Writing Proficiency Examination required for junior-standing) refers students who request extra help with writing—whether for English or other courses—to the English Department's tutoring program. Is this just trading Tweedledum for Tweedledee? No, because the English tutoring program itself is decentralized:

- it recruits undergraduate and graduate tutors from ALL departments, not just from the English Department;
- it offers to pair tutors with faculty-mentors *throughout the college-wide core curriculum* (a writing-across-the-curriculum program of introductory freshman and sophomore courses);
- it assigns a tutor to every section of Freshman English; since each tutor works with two or three faculty-mentors each semester, *no single pedagogy* prevails;
- faculty from the English Department, the Office of Academic Support and Advising, and the English as a Second Language program share in teaching the required Seminar for Tutors, assuring a *variety of perspectives* on the teaching of writing, including the following:

    the special nature of tutorial dialogue; psychological aspects of reading and writing processes;

alternative strategies for generating, shaping, and revising ideas;

ways of addressing sentence-level problems;

identifying "patterns of error" and understanding them as the hypotheses being tested by second-dialect and second-language learners;

helping writers read and write about literary and "non-literary" texts;

- Tutors, writing faculty, and Core Curriculum faculty (as well as guests from other schools, colleges, and universities in the Boston area) are invited to present and attend Composition Colloquia on current theory, research, and pedagogy.

This multi-centered structure preserves the independence of each of its components—the Office of Academic Support and Advising, the English Department faculty, the ESL Program, the Core Curriculum.

The UMass/Boston model differs from the Queens College model in representing—through its Seminar for Tutors and its flexible system of faculty-tutor partnerships—several cross-sections of composition pedagogy. The decentralized tutoring program gathers and disseminates the theories and practices embodied in three cross-sections of writing instruction in the College: the tutors' experiences as writers, the theories considered in the tutors' Seminar and applied to real UMass/Boston student papers, and the variety of pedagogical styles and philosophies each tutor shares with several faculty. Let's look at these cross-sections one at a time.

Decentralization begins with the process of selecting tutors. In consultation with a member of the Office of Academic Support's professional staff, an English professor directs the tutoring program. Together they select the tutors and teach the seminar. Graduate and undergraduate tutors are chosen from all majors through one procedure: faculty recommendation, writing samples, and an hour-long interview focusing on how they might apply their own composing processes to helping inexperienced writers gain independence. The tutors' own writing experiences—the kinds of reading and writing assignments, as well as the pedagogies and standards, actually used in the College—constitute one kind of cross-section.

The required Seminar for Tutors (English 475, three credits) makes no attempt to espouse "*The* right way" to teach writing. Tutors apply readings in current theory and research (e.g. Berthoff, Horton, Murray, Perl, Flower and Hayes, Hirsch, Zamel and Bartholomae) to real UM/B student papers (usually bearing comments and grades) contributed anonymously by students and faculty in English and Core Courses. Tutors keep notebooks analyzing and evaluating selected tutoring sessions. In addition, they present demonstration lessons and complete research projects that enable them to read about problems they have encountered in practice. Besides seminar credit, tutors also earn an hourly rate paid through the Office of Academic

Support (or through Work-Study for those eligible) for an average of ten hours per week of actual tutoring. Most tutors continue working for several semesters after completing the seminar. Some specialize in ESL tutoring, for which another seminar is given. The old hands are welcomed back to the seminar to share their insights with the new tutors. The Seminar thus constitutes another cross-section of writing instruction.

Unlike the Queens College program, which pairs tutors with faculty volunteers, the UMass/Boston program assigns a tutor to every section of freshman English (and to Core courses in English and other departments at faculty request, a small but growing means of collaboration). Each tutor works with several partners and pedagogies, the "choreography" reflecting each professor's preferences. Once the partners have agreed upon the extent and nature of their collaborations, tutors explain their roles to the students in their sections. With their partners' help, they teach in class (if only briefly) in order to establish themselves as approachable and knowledgeable people (since disembodied telephone numbers or even walk-on roles practically guarantee that the students most in need of help will remain too shy or too hostile to seek it).

Even tutors working mostly through after-class referrals keep regularly in touch with each professor, in order to understand the priorities and the assignments of the course. Tutors keep professors abreast of the work each student has undertaken and seek guidance for future tutorials. Conferences—not bales of paper-work—provide tutors with immediate guidance, vitally augmenting the necessarily more general instruction provided in the Seminar. Through these various collaborations, the techniques of which can be discussed objectively in the Seminar, the tutors learn that there are many effective ways to accomplish good writing instruction. As the Seminar gathers all these tutorial experience in, a third cross-section is formed. This flexible pairing brings two further benefits. First, it encourages more professors to collaborate. Over the years, more and more professors have volunteered as mentors, sharing classes and/or arranging tutorial conferences. If a professor requests a tutor without quite knowing how to collaborate, the tutor (primed by the seminar) suggests ways of sharing in-class workshops. If a professor prefers a more limited collaboration, the tutor can arrange to meet with referred individuals outside of class. Rarely, some professors prefer not to work with tutors. Then their students may request tutorial help through the Office of Academic Support, and tutors simply work independently.

The successes of such tutorials often encourage professors to invite the tutors little-by-little into their classrooms. Flexibility thus minimizes the threat of "relinquishing" authority and helps professors see tutors as helpful apprentices. Second, the dialogue entailed in flexible collaboration helps faculty to articulate and modify their ways of teaching writing. Once tutors earn trust, faculty-mentors often reexamine with them some of their favorite practices and try out other ideas the tutors bring from the Seminar. Thus distributing what it has gathered in (i.e. the three cross-sections constituted by tutor selection, the theories and sample papers used in the Seminar, and the flexible collaborations), the tutoring program functions as a tactful "change agent" throughout the college-wide writing program.

The flexibility of tutors' roles is safeguarded from exploitation. Tutors do not take over class meetings for absent professors unless very intensive collaborations have already been established (and even then only in emergencies). For obvious reasons, tutors brought in from the cold could do little more than babysit. Nor do they merely observe classes or play "straight men," dependable respondents in two-way "discussions" that reduce students to spectators. They generally do not select readings or design assignments (though they can spot ambiguities). They do not grade quizzes and papers. Whatever paper comments tutors write are in addition to—never instead of—professors' comments. Thus tutors are not exploited by being delegated the onerous or labor-intensive tasks. They enter the program not just to get "a job," but to explore themselves as writers and to practice imagining and removing the barriers to someone else's understanding. As apprentices rewarded by credit, pay, and less tangible but more valuable opportunities, most tutors stay with the program, often combining tutoring with other attractive choices in research, in honors programs, and in college publications. Several have even prolonged their degree programs for an extra semester—just so they could keep on tutoring! Instead of feeling exploited, they know that as they give, they gain.

Still another means of gathering and disseminating current theory, research, and pedagogy both within and beyond the College is the annual series of Composition Colloquia, an outgrowth of the tutors' Seminar. Recent colloquia have included panel discussions; one panel featured pairs of collaborators describing their various modes of "choreography," while another brought together professors in the Departments of History, Sociology, and Chemistry to characterize the discourse of their respective disciplines.

Other colloquia have featured individual presentations by professors in the English Department; for instance, Ann Berthoff analyzed relationships between reading and writing, Taylor Stoehr described connections between personal and academic writing, and Gillian Gane and Maine Willey demonstrated ways to teach composition with various word processors.

Sometimes a colloquium becomes a workshop applying current research; for instance, participants applied an analysis of teachers' paper comments (Sommers) to comments they had written on three sample papers. Recent guest presentations included a descriptive explanation of the University of Pittsburgh's Basic Reading and Writing program (Salvatori) and Professor Nancy Martin's sharing of writing notebooks from her work with James Britton in the London Schools. Professor Rosemary Deen, with Marie Ponsot co-author of *Beat Not the Poor Desk* (Boynton/Cook, 1982) put us to work writing our own fables so that we could experience, in her words, "the power of writing a whole structure" that we were already able to write and consequently "couldn't do wrong." A small but growing number of guests from other writing programs in the Boston area contribute their responses to those of our own faculty and tutors, thus expanding the opportunity to create more widespread collaborations.

If writing centers have outlived their usefulness, as Kail and Trimbur suggest, it is because issues of authority, "correct" pedagogy, and exploitation have begun to obstruct sharing of the valuable, practical knowledge writing centers have helped acquire over the years. The idea of a "center" has gotten in the way. Interestingly, the features recently attributed to "ideal writing center(s)" depend upon only one kind of centralization—neither administrative nor pedagogical, but ideological "commitment to change" (Harris "Theory"). New models for integrating writing centers with writing-across-the-curriculum are beginning to appear (Haviland). Instead of discarding writing centers, we should find ways of decentralizing them so they can use their knowledge more effectively. Perhaps we can borrow Saussure's model as a metaphor for independence and collaboration: while each professor and tutor retains his or her own theoretical and pedagogical *parole*, together their conversation—facilitated by decentralization—constitutes a vital *langue*, and on-going negotiated communication about ways of communicating.

WORKS CITED

Bruffee, Kenneth A. "Staffing and Operating Peer-Tutoring Writing Centers." *Basic Writing*. Eds. Lawrence N. Kasden and Daniel R. Hoeber. Urbana: NCTE, 1980. 141–149.

Fulwiler, Toby. "How Well Does Writing Across the Curriculum Work?" *College English* 46 (1984): 113–125.

Harris, Muriel. "Theory and Reality: The Ideal Writing Center(s)." *The Writing Center Journal* 5–6 (1985): 4–9.

———. *Tutoring Writing: A Sourcebook for Writing Labs*. Glenview: Scott, Foresman, 1982.

Haviland, Carol Peterson. "Writing Centers and Writing-Across-The-Curriculum: An Important Connection." *The Writing Center Journal* 5–6 (1985): 25–30.

Held, George, and Warren Rosenberg. "Student-Faculty Collaboration in Teaching College Writing." *College English* 45 (1983): 817–23.

Kail, Harvey. "Collaborative Learning in Context: The Problem with Peer Tutoring." *College English* 45 (1983): 657-666.

Schor, Sandra. "Preparing Volunteers from Disciplines of Currently Diminished Student Interest to Teach Basic Writing." *Ade Bulletin* 76 (1983): 46–48.

Sommers, Nancy. "Responding to Student Writing." *College Composition and Communication* 33 (1982): 148–156.

Trimbur, John. "Students or Staff: Thoughts on the Use of Peer Tutors in Writing Centers." *Writing Program Administration* 7 (1983): 33–38.

The Last Best Place for Writing Across the Curriculum: The Writing Center

Mark L. Waldo

In a recent issue of *College English*, two writers advance opposing viewpoints concerning where to "house" writing across the curriculum programs. Catherine Blair, described as teaching writing "both in and out of English departments," works in the cross-curricular program at Bucknell. She argues that WAC programs "should be designed, administered, and taught equally by all departments. True writing across the curriculum should be based on dialogue among all the departments, and, in this dialogue, the English department should be only one of the voices" (383). Louise Smith directs Freshman English and the Writing Tutors program at the University of Massachusetts. Unlike Blair, she believes that cross-curricular programs should be located in English departments, "secular and process oriented," housing "WAC by keeping open-house, initiating and sustaining dialogue throughout the curriculum" (391). Each of these writers offers substantive reasons for her position, reasons I want to explore in some detail; however, each ignores what I believe to be the most logical home for writing across the curriculum—the writing center.

Stephen North hints at this role for writing centers in his important *College English* piece, "The Idea of a Writing Center," where he observes: "[Centers] have played central roles in the creation of writing across the curriculum programs" (445). He buries this comment, however, midway in a paragraph with the topic sentence "writing centers have begun to expand their institutional roles." For North, WAC in the writing center seems no more or less important than establishing "resource libraries for writing teachers" or "opening a 'Grammar Hotline' or 'Grammaphone'." But that was 1984, and North did not intend to show writing centers as potential homes for WAC; instead, he wanted to ask colleagues for some respect and understanding, to dispel confusion about what writing center personnel do. At that time, it was important to define a good center's characteristics and to counter the persistent impression of centers as skills labs or grammar garages.

Waldo, Mark L. "The Last Best Place for Writing Across the Curriculum: The Writing Center." *WPA: Writing Program Administration* 16.3 (1993): 15–26. Reprinted by permission of the publisher from *WPA: Writing Program Administration* 16.3 (1993): 15–26.

This perhaps remains an important task, given the observations of Valerie Balester in "Revising the 'Statement': On the Work of Writing Centers," included in "Symposium: The Professional Standards Committee 'Progress Report':"

> *Writing center staff are not seen as professionals, not even among compositionists. Consequently, we are not receiving support in terms of budgets, staffing, salaries, release time, recognition of our scholarship and teaching—in any of the considerations due academic faculty or programs. We are the third-class citizenry in English departments, and nothing is being done to rectify our situation. Rather than describing our place in the profession as a "niche," we might describe it as a "ghetto," mindful of the word's connotations of poverty, isolation, and low prestige. (166)*

Lamentably, I believe Balester is mostly right about these attitudes toward writing centers. So many of the nation's hundreds of centers and labs still focus on remediation, testing, and worksheets. So many are subsets of English departments, composition programs, and basic writing classes. So many are directed by untenured and untenurable faculty. Because of these features, too many may be characterized as "ghettos," their residents as "third-class citizenry." Far from writing across the curriculum, these places may barely touch writing at all or may touch it only at the sentence level; it is not the skills lab or "fix-it" shop that I assert would be a good home for the cross-curricular program.

It is instead a new breed of writing center, characterized by several qualities that require serious institutional commitment: 1) independence from any department; 2) a tenured or tenurable director; 3) highly skilled tutors, themselves teachers and students from various departments; and 4) an ambitious writing-across-the-curriculum consultancy, steeped in the literature on critical thinking, assignment making and writing to learn. Given these qualities, why are writing centers the best "home" for a cross-curricular program?

There are three reasons, primarily. First, centers provide a definable space for expertise, with identifiable goals and services, which the campus will need to initiate and sustain WAC. Second, through their varying services for faculty, they encourage the dialogue between diverse rhetorical communities. Finally, they offer a rhetorically neutral ground on which to carry out the program, perhaps the only such ground on the academic side of campus. Michel Foucault defines the term "discourse" as "the group of statements that belong to a single system of formation"; thus, he "shall be able to speak of clinical discourse, economic discourse, the discourse of natural history, psychiatric discourse" (107–08). He makes a convincing case that one of the primary goals of education is appropriation of a discourse, "with the knowledge and powers it carries with it" (227). Because writing centers aren't disciplines, with "a single system of formation," they do not have the rhetorical agenda common to one discourse community; they can thus resist imposing what they value about writing on other departments. Rather than imposing values, they are well-positioned to help students succeed in any discourse endeavor or community.

In short, housing WAC in writing centers unites the best characteristics in the reasoning of Blair and Smith and rejects their less convincing arguments. Blair argues persuasively for removing WAC from English:

> *Entrusting the writing program to the English department is based on the belief that the English department has a special relationship to language and is, therefore, the department that knows the most about writing—in fact, the department that* owns *writing. But what the basic theory behind writing across the curriculum tells us is that the English department owns only its particular brand of writing that carries its particular context. Each discipline has its own relationship to language; the English department context is not a privileged one. There is no way to decide the primacy of a particular context because no discipline is better than any other. (Blair 384, her emphasis)*

An irresistible logic exists in the proposition that each discipline has its own relationship to language, which should be shown through use of writing assignments in a variety of classes. Blair's position on English, that it "owns only its particular brand of writing that carries its particular context," seems largely accurate to me. Writing in English courses is very often different from writing in other disciplines—with its own purposes, audiences, patterns, and values. While not less than other contexts, it is not a "privileged" context either.

I want to observe, however, that Blair's position would find rough footing in English, which is becoming increasingly nervous about giving up ownership of composition. Think of the university-wide dependence that the department loses when a broad range of faculty use writing successfully in their classes. In a worst case scenario, think of the credit hours and full time equivalences lost if the number of composition classes lessens significantly because of WAC. Blair's remarks about the theory behind writing across the curriculum do little to lessen anxiety, not only about where English fits but the composition program itself. She states plainly that "the English department should have no special role in writing across the curriculum—no unique role and no exclusive classes to teach—not even freshman composition." Thus, she lumps composition with English as owning "only its particular brand of writing that carries its particular context."

Cross-curricular programs, however, were not conceived to curtail the power of English departments or composition programs. Quite the contrary. They were designed to broaden responsibility for teaching writing and to generate a larger environment for active learning. They were meant to help, not hurt, English departments, which cannot successfully bear sole responsibility for writing competence on any campus and which cannot be expected to know, let alone to teach, writing in disciplines outside their own. Blair replaces English department control with interdisciplinary dialogue: "Dialogue among equals is the way to make and maintain true writing across the curriculum by ensuring that all linguistic communities are heard from" (386). On an intellectual level, most academics would agree, including those in English, but at some fundamental level, perhaps the level of survival, Blair's proposition becomes threatening: "[The dialogic approach] could irritate the English department and make others on the faculty feel rudderless without English department control" (388). "Could irritate English departments" is probably politic understatement on her part.

Nonetheless, Blair's proposal and Bucknell University's practice of decentering the cross-curricular writing program is very appealing, primarily because the purposes for writing land in the hands of the various disciplines. It seems to me sound policy, for example, for faculty in the economics department to help their students develop writing competence, rather than complain that English is failing to do its job. A broad, shared responsibility for writing further lessens chances for "ghettoizing" composition, sometimes the consequence of designating one or two classes within a department as "writing" classes. Such writing-intensive programs make more possible the dumping of writing on junior faculty and more likely the view of writing as isolated punishment. David Russell writes,

> *Writing-intensives, sometimes supported by a remedial lab, are perhaps the most common curricular model for WAC. But writing-intensive courses… concentrate responsibility for initiating students into the discourse community in a few professors or TAs, while freeing most faculty resources for activities which the community views as more important than initiating new members. As Brown's WAC director Tori Haring-Smith points out, when a few courses are labeled writing-intensive, students object when other courses require writing. (65)*

In principle, at least, the dialogic approach supports a widely shared responsibility for using writing assignments in classes, thus contradicting the writing-intensive model. As Blair remarks, the majority of faculty at Bucknell volunteer "to teach writing courses."

Blair's proposal, therefore, has many attractive features. One of its most positive qualities, however, is also potentially one of its most negative: Being housed everywhere, writing across the curriculum runs the risk of being housed nowhere. There seems to me a danger that such dispersion might lead to diffused focus and confused purpose. Under the dialogic model, do individual teachers turn to the "writing committee" for help with assignment design? With techniques for grading papers? Who initiates the dialogue between disciplines? Because of the prevalent tendency at colleges and universities to resist change, sometimes sorely disappointing WAC enthusiasts, I wonder who sustains that dialogue? Is it the part-time director or the consultants? Where are the consultants housed? If more than 50% of the faculty use writing in courses, students must be looking for a great deal of help. Do students line up at faculty doors, drafts in hand, ready to conference? Do they go to the English department?

Blair does not set out in her article to answer these questions, yet I believe that they call for answers because each question suggests the need to house writing across the curriculum somewhere. Each question suggests that a purely dialogic, cross-curricular program may be impractical and "probably does not exist" (Blair 388). Is the English department, then, the last best place for WAC? Smith offers two reasons favoring English. The first is "our expertise in the study of the construction and reception of texts." Second, she suggests that since we are the experts, we will want to house WAC "so that we can invite—and keep on inviting—the historians and sociologists, the chemists and biologists to join with us in dialogue" (392). I do not deny the expertise in composition theory and pedagogy that often exists in English departments, which use that expert knowledge to develop composition programs and train teachers; their faculty should have much to share in the cross-curricular dialogue.

I note, however, the sense of control that English has in a relationship like the one described by Smith. She argues that English faculty, at least the non-hermetic members, understand and care about the writing process more than other faculty do: "To the extent that they have informed themselves in composition theory, English faculty are more likely to [apply similar assumptions and questions to both professionals' and students' processes of composing] than are faculty in other departments who, however well-intentioned, may see composition theory and pedagogy as even more peripheral to their professional interests than do the English department's most 'hermetic' members" (392–393). Smith is probably right about the deeper concern for process, but she displays an ironically elitist attitude here. Composition theory and pedagogy, clearly important to her, *are* peripheral to the professional interests of most faculty in the disciplines. Does this mean that these faculty cannot use writing to very positive effect in their classes? Absolutely not. If they use writing to advance the critical consciousness of their students, they put it to very good use indeed. The English department may attempt to make "English teachers" out of their colleagues, but doing so is unnecessary to the success of WAC and may even work to its detriment.

Smith attacks the two notions that she assumes keep English from its cross-curricular calling: 1) its "supposed devotion to the traditional canon" and 2) the claim that "literary texts are metaphorical and non-literary texts are literal." As she asserts, English departments can show other departments how their writing is "contextualized—though not constrained—by the knowledge of canonical and non-canonical 'intertexts'.... English faculty can share with other departments' experts in textual theory their mutual insights on how to carry textual studies over into pedagogy" (392–93). Finally, English faculty can share their "relatively expert knowledge of such matters as reader-response theory, error analysis, writing-to-learn, and collaborative composition pedagogies" (394).

There is refreshing optimism in the idea that our expertise will make colleagues eager to converse with us, and there is good-natured generosity in "knowing we're equally interested in their expertise" (391). As positive in tone as her reasoning is, however, Smith does not show why writing across the curriculum belongs in the English department but why English faculty may be consulted, along with other faculty, about features of the program. Offering invitations is not sufficient reason for housing WAC because any discipline with a rhetoric, and every discipline has a rhetoric, can offer such invitations with the same confining consequences. Imposing our expertise on others may have stunting effects on the growth of WAC. For example, I'm not sure that a faculty member in engineering could ever see as important the fact that his or her discourse is contextualized by "intertext." This sounds like more of the same from English departments (although I've never heard anyone in my department speak or write like this). Besides, which departments outside of English and perhaps philosophy have "experts in textual theory"? Which departments could afford to have such experts?

Even the observations perhaps most compelling to content faculty—our expertise in reader response, error analysis, writing-to-learn, collaboration—have a curiously insular sound here. "English faculty," Smith writes, "can show colleagues that errors provide windows into writers' minds as they acquire new modes of discourse." Maybe they can, but why would they want to? Making error a focal point of the cross-curricular program, I believe, would be a serious mistake. On the one hand, some content teachers avoid writing assignments in class because they fear that they cannot correct the errors; on the other hand, some focus almost exclusively on the errors. In either case, the student loses.

I realize that Smith says repeatedly, "our colleagues have a lot to show us, too." English departments, she tells us, can resist ownership of writing, can avoid colonization of other departments, can initiate and sustain the dialogue; but her argument shows us something different—an agenda that places English in control. More exactly, her position implies an imposed linguistic control by making the English department's relationship to language a privileged one. I find her argument theoretically less attractive than Blair's because it contradicts Blair's most important premise: "There is no way to decide the primacy of a particular context because no discipline is better than any other." Smith's proposal suggests, even openly states, a preferable context: English.

The positions of Blair and Smith are essentially incompatible despite Smith's apology to the contrary. Blair's program encourages the view that all academic rhetorics are equal, that students will learn the language of a major by writing in that major, and that faculty should carry on dialogue about writing. Blair would share responsibility for using writing among all the disciplines. The problem posed by her argument is a practical one: If writing across the curriculum is wholly dialogic, where do faculty and students turn for help? Even as Smith urges equality and dialogue, her proposal argues the need for expertise—a place where faculty and students can turn for help—but she blankets the cross-curricular program with English department values, making English primarily responsible for teaching writing. The problem posed by her argument is philosophic: If we believe that disciplines have different discourses and values for discourse, each equal, what gives English primacy?

Writing centers bridge the gap between these two positions—Blair's homelessness and Smith's cloister. Potentially, centers are in the best position to offer the expert services that the WAC program needs while preserving the rhetorical integrity of the disciplines. They focus not on what separates disciplines but on what they share as a common goal: to increase a student's ability to analyze and synthesize material, see opposing points of view, make arguments, solve problems, and develop hypotheses, given the parameters of the assigned paper. This focus may itself be a rhetoric. If so, however, it is a rhetoric that we at least claim to share across disciplines.

As homes for WAC, writing centers combine two features vital to the campus: consulting for faculty and tutoring for students. The degree of success depends largely on the academic status of the program's leaders, particularly its director, who must be tenure track. Remarking not on writing centers but on WAC programs generally, Fulwiler and Young point out as one of the "enemies of writing across the curriculum" the temporary and transient status of many of its leaders and administrators:

> *Often when programs are successful after several years upper administrators find themselves having to turn over the key people who have made their programs successful and who have gained immeasurable experience in doing so. This unstable leadership and lack of community commitment inevitably lead to the decline of once successful programs. (288)*

Their comments, like Balester's about writing center personnel, demonstrate an essential point—that lack of tenure leads to lack of respect and stability.

Increasingly, writing center directors may be tenured outside of English, as a recent job advertisement indicates: "Director of the University Writing Center.... Qualifications: PhD (discipline open), significant training and experience in writing across the curriculum theory and instruction.... The Director will hold rank [associate or full professor] in an academic department, but will report directly to the Office of the Vice Chancellor for Academic Affairs" (*The Chronicle of Higher Education,* January 22, 1992, B51). At once, this advertisement seems to recognize how valuable writing centers can be and to imply the need not to emphasize one rhetoric over another; it also understands 1) that directors must be tenure track and 2) they may come from outside English. I believe that the qualifications for university writing center directors will ordinarily place them in English departments, which may also help lessen the angst the department feels as it loses control of writing; but directors need not necessarily come from English. Regardless of their home department, they must be aware of and open to the varying rhetorical communities on campus.

The writing center's consultants will reinforce this openness by focusing on such areas as assignment design, evaluative techniques, and writing to learn, all within the context volunteered by instructors. Consultants will ask a faculty member questions, not give directives, and carry on conversations, not deliver lectures. Aware that different writing assignments encourage different types of learning (Applebee and Langer 130–131), consultants will ask questions that reveal what faculty want to accomplish with writing assignments and what they most value in grading. They will help faculty clarify goals, contexts, and audiences, given the class in which an assignment is used, and sponsor "norming" sessions, turning goals into criteria. Although such features as writing from the self, personal voice, "energetic,"free" and "non formulaic" writing, "powerful imagery," implied theses, and "contextualized intertext" would not be rejected, this consultancy would not insist on them. I realize how controversial this viewpoint may sound; however, as English teachers, and I am one, we must accept that values for writing exist other than our own. WAC consultants must learn the values held by instructors and help them design and grade assignments out of those values.

The writing center's tutoring program will complement the consultancy by developing appropriate questions and collaborative strategies for drawing students to make improvements on their papers. Why is tutoring essential? Hillocks presents convincing evidence that teacher assessment and intervention during the process of writing a paper has a significant effect for good on the final product, far better than teachers' written comments on final drafts (Chapter 9). Thus, tutoring intervention during the process also helps improve writing. My own experimental research supports this conclusion (13–19). Students write better across the curriculum if they receive good tutoring. Blair's dialogic model probably does produce much student writing, but I object to the model's homelessness mainly because it offers little indication where students turn for help.

Students might turn to their professors. Many times I have heard the argument that professors must be willing to conference with students about writing. "It's part of their job," people say. I would agree with this position if the academy were perfect. But professors will resist using writing, especially in large classes, if they perceive conferencing as an overwhelming consequence. Further, few professors outside of composition will collect, write comments on, and return student drafts before the paper is due. They don't have time. Therefore, offering the university a strong tutoring program, one to which faculty and students can turn with confidence, is crucial to the success of WAC.

This confidence comes from having a tutoring staff experienced and versatile enough to work with students from any class at any level. On the surface, this may seem so commonsensical it doesn't bear comment, but the depth of experience and versatility I'm talking about actually contradicts typical approaches in writing centers. That is, any center housing writing across the curriculum should be staffed primarily with professional tutors, whose minimal qualifications include BA degrees from various disciplines, broad experience with academic writing, and prior teaching or tutoring experience. A comprehensive writing center will include tutors who have these qualifications, but often this group is a small minority, the majority being undergraduate student tutors.

Of course, undergraduates can be good tutors; they might be even more comfortable with question-asking and collaboration than some teacher/tutors who tend toward the prescriptive in tutoring. Problems arise, however, from the student tutor's lack of experience with upper-division and graduate student writing, problems that become more glaring as tutoring sessions with this population increase. Other difficulties stem from having too many student tutors from one department (English). Students choose a discipline, consciously or not, in large part because they are attracted to its rhetoric. Just becoming immersed in the language themselves, they are likely to adopt the rhetorical values of their teachers. Since these values are not necessarily shared across the curriculum, effort should be made to counter them or any other pervasive influence from one discourse community. The best way to counter this influence is to employ a highly experienced, eclectic staff and fewer students.

Perhaps more practical, however, is to focus tutor training and philosophy on the values shared between disciplines. Training should show tutors how to advance conceptual thinking by creating an atmosphere in which students re-see their papers with regard to the assignment and their response to it. What types of questions will help students to achieve the goals set by an assignment and to write to the audience? In view of the assignment, how can tutors help with a paper's organization and coherence; its details, tone, and syntax; its references? I recognize that not all assignments will include goals or audiences. Some may be as open-ended as "write on a topic of interest to you," making tutoring (and grading) a trying task. Even so, the tutor's responsibility is not to determine the instructor's values or assert his or her own. In this situation, the tutor needs to understand the student's interpretation of the assignment and then work with him or her on purpose, context, and audience for the paper.

As a home for consulting and tutoring, the writing center must be its own program, not a subset of English or any other department. Independence, desirable in itself, is critical in this case because of the varying disciplines with which the center will work. Physics, for example, usually has a purpose different than composition for using writing and measuring its effectiveness. In a composition course, students learn to write by writing, whereas, in a physics course, they learn to solve problems and pass those solutions on by writing. Physics would probably not presume to impose its goal or community on English; why then should English presume to impose its goal or community on physics? The writing center must be versatile enough in practice to handle these differences and broad enough in theory to bridge them.

The center needs a theoretical frame independent of discipline for its practice, a frame that gives tutoring, workshop, and consulting activities research legitimacy. Fulwiler and Young conclude that most institutions base their WAC programs "on a common core of language theorists, most often including some mix of James Britton, Don Murray, Janet Emig, and Peter Elbow" (2). I'm sure that Fulwiler and Young mean this as quite a positive feature of WAC, and my own teaching and research incline me toward this mix, but it is hardly neutral. Each of these educators draws from an organic rhetorical tradition; together they have heavily influenced the natural-process approach to teaching writing while challenging mechanic perspectives. Their struggle has taken place primarily within English and, more particularly, within the field of composition. Out of that struggle, a process rhetoric has developed.

While the deeper principles of organicism are no doubt applicable across the curriculum, these educators' interpretation of those principles is more specialized and more directly applicable to a type of writing class within an English department. Their theory implies a format for the class, along the lines of the "natural process" approach George Hillocks describes (119) and types of writing assignments (most likely some progression from personal to public). As each of these teachers points out in his or her own work, even within English this approach has had vocal opponents.

Whatever the rightness or wrongness of the paradigm, then, basing WAC programs on this core of language theorists would not pass the Blair neutrality test; to do so lodges WAC in English. It makes more sense to me to go to a less discipline-controlled theoretical base, evolved from the developmental research of Piaget, Vygotsky, and Bruner, the psychology of Carl Rogers and Abraham Maslow, the linguistics of Noam Chomsky, William Perry's findings on critical thinking in college-aged students, and research into writing and thinking done by George Hillocks, Arthur Applebee and Judith Langer, to name a few. Just one of many possible theoretical frames, this one has an important advantage. It is bound, not by what one discipline values about writing, but by insights into human development and learning, especially with regard to language and thinking.

When the type of writing center I've been describing houses WAC, the number of classes using writing across campus will increase substantially. This increase results in part from the expertise offered to students and faculty through the center's programs; more abstractly, however, it grows out of the center's rhetorically neutral focus on the relationship between writing and learning. Foucault shows how a professional's authority for speaking derives from the appropriation of a discipline's discourse (227). The academy places much value on this appropriation for students. The disciplines themselves insist on it. Little wonder, then, at the friction one discipline generates by attempting to impose its values for discourse on another discipline. Little wonder, too, why writing centers have an advantage in housing WAC. They can build on what we share about language and thinking even as they help students gain the authority to succeed in their discourse community.

WORKS CITED

Balester, Valerie. "Revising the 'Statement': On the Work of Writing Centers." *College Composition and Communication* 43 (1992): 154–175.

Blair, Catherine Pastore. "Only One of the Voices: Dialogic Writing Across the Curriculum." *College English* 50 (1988): 383–389.

Foucault, Michel. *The Archeology of Knowledge and the Discourse on Language.* New York: Pantheon, 1972.

Fulwiler, Toby, and Art Young. *Programs That Work: Models and Methods for Writing Across the Curriculum.* Portsmouth, NH: Boynton/Cook, 1990.

Hillocks, George Jr. *Research on Written Composition.* Urbana: National Conference on Research in English, 1986.

Langer, Judith A., and Arthur N. Applebee. *How Writing Shapes Thinking: A Study of Teaching and Learning.* NCTE, 1987.

North, Stephen. "The Idea of a Writing Center." *College English* 46 (1984): 433–446.

Russell, David R. "Writing Across the Curriculum in Historical Perspective: Toward a Social Interpretation." *College English* 52 (1990): 52–73.

Smith, Louise Z. "Why English Departments Should 'House' Writing Across the Curriculum." *College English* 50 (1988): 390–395.

Waldo, Mark. "More Than 'First Aid': A Report on the Effectiveness of Writing Center Intervention in the Writing Process." *Issues in College Learning Centers* 5 (1988): 13–21.

A Writing Center without a WAC Program: The De Facto WAC Center/Writing Center

Muriel Harris

Reflecting on the twenty-fifth anniversary of Writing Across the Curriculum (celebrated in 1995), Barbara Walvoord takes a long look at WAC's past in order to assess where it should be heading (1996, 58–79). She looks back at WAC as an academic movement and concludes that, among other steps to be taken for the health of WAC's future, WAC Programs need to connect to Writing Centers. She writes as if WAC and Writing Centers, at least in some institutions, have gone their separate ways despite overlapping and reinforcing interests. Among the many configurations and varieties of WAC/Writing Center connections, she notes the absence of a consistent linkage. While many WAC Programs have connected in productive ways with the campus Writing Center, it is true that some WAC specialists have not perceived there to be lines of connections—a phenomenon I observed first hand a few years ago. When a nationally recognized WAC specialist came to my campus, it was clear from this person's remarks and responses to questions in public forums that the person seemed well meaning but clueless as to what Writing Centers do beyond some vague sense that they repair remedial writers in some way.

But the perspective of some WAC specialists that Writing Centers have little or no apparent connection to WAC is neither a universally nor even a widely held one. In the descriptions of various programs in Toby Fulwiler and Art Young's collection, *Programs That Work: Models and Methods for Writing Across the Curriculum,* there are a variety of models for ways Writing Centers and WAC Programs can and do work together. At some institutions WAC Programs and Writing Centers coordinate their efforts; in other cases the administration of both is delegated to the same person. Mark Waldo, in "The Last Best Place for Writing Across the Curriculum: The Writing Center," argues for a somewhat different configuration—situating WAC within the Writing Center. In yet other cases, there are WAC Program directors who recognize the need for a Writing Center when there is none and work actively to bring one into existence. For example, Pat McQueeney, in "Proposing a Writing Center: Experts, Advice," details the rationale in her proposal for a Writing Center on her campus and notes that their WAC Program needs the support service that the faculty want for the writing in their courses.

Yet another variation on this theme of connections between Writing Centers and WAC Programs is the Writing Center on a campus where there is no officially sanctioned or institutionalized WAC Program. Such is the case on my campus, Purdue University—a large land grant, research-oriented university where to varying degrees, faculty with varying goals and varying awareness of what writing can do to enhance learning assign writing in their courses. For reasons discussed below, our Writing Lab has become a de facto WAC Writing Center, that is, a Writing Center where there is no WAC Program but where we meet with all students working on writing who seek our tutorial help, where we recognize a need to respond to faculty interest in using writing in their courses, and where—we hope—we try to nurture an interest in developing more formalized WAC Programs on our campus. From my perspective, as we attempt to work with faculty who interact with our Writing Lab and to meet with their students in tutorials, I can see how mutually advantageous a WAC/Writing Center relationship might be, and I offer the example of our Writing Lab, a de facto WAC center, as a case study in what a Writing Center situated in a context like ours can and cannot do.

Such Writing Centers can, if resources permit, take on some faculty development as well as the tutorial support for students writing in various courses. But, in addition, a closer look at what a Writing Center with no institutionally supported WAC Program cannot achieve is also a rationale for why WAC Programs are needed on a campus committed to strong integration of writing into all disciplines. For those who forecast the end of institutionalized WAC, a clearer sense of what a Writing Center cannot achieve alone is a strong argument for maintaining a WAC Program where there is the commitment to its goals. Even if the WAC Program is situated in the Writing Center, as Waldo argues for, it has to be an institutionally supported WAC Program, not a bottom-up attempt by the Writing Center to launch a WAC-like program of its own.

While Walvoord and McQueeney argue for the WAC/Writing Center connection from the perspective of WAC directors, I thus add—from a vantage point inside a Writing Center—my argument for such a linkage. Without a WAC Program, our Writing Lab can achieve certain goals but is limited in its ability to bring about the self-sustaining changes a WAC Program seeks, Looking at what we can and cannot do in our Writing Lab is also another argument for Walvoord's insight into how reinforcing a WAC/Writing Center relationship can be. When there is careful, thoughtful integration and mutual working out of goals and responsibilities, each can complement and strengthen the other's work. But without institutionally provided resources and institutional sanction for WAC, a Writing Center has limits beyond which it cannot go in working with students Writing Across the Curriculum and the teachers assigning that writing. This case study will attempt to flesh out the particulars of that statement and to provide a clearer sense of what a Writing Center can contribute to WAC programs as well as what it cannot reasonably be expected to accomplish and what might be unrealistic to incorporate into the Writing Center's mission statement or future goals. As Stephen North cautioned, in his reconsideration of the idea of a Writing Center, a Writing Center's mission should match its resources and should not "be seen as taking upon its shoulders the whole institution's (real or imagined) sins of illiteracy" (1994, 17). But, matching its efforts to its resources, a Writing Center can work to develop campus-wide awareness of how writing can enhance learning and how it can be used to help students become proficient in the disciplinary thinking and writing they will need when they enter those fields.

GUIDELINES AND GOALS FOR WAC PROGRAMS

When using the term WAC both in this essay or in my own thinking and planning for our Writing Lab, I have found it useful to keep in mind the defining features of WAC as a movement. Otherwise, a Writing Center without a WAC Program can fall into limited—and limiting—perceptions of Writing Across the Curriculum, thinking of it merely as any writing done in any course with the WAC Writing Center being any center which offers a few faculty workshops and tutorial assistance with writing in any course. Writing Across the Curriculum as the particular movement Walvoord was examining in her article—the movement that has spawned national conferences, books, articles, an electronic listserv, and the book in which this essay appears—has broader, more substantive defining features. WAC, as Susan McLeod has written so eloquently, is a transformative program in that it seeks to change the way teachers and students use writing in the curriculum (1992, 3). Beyond using writing as a way to measure or evaluate mastery of a subject and beyond grading writing as a means of improving Grammatical proficiency, WAC promotes writing as a tool for learning and as a way to write and think in discipline-specific ways. McLeod adds that WAC also encourages writing to learn and learning to write in all disciplines (1992, 5). Her description of what a WAC Program needs in terms of combining top-down and bottom-up support also impinges on what a Writing Center can and cannot do without a program that can be called a Writing Across the Curriculum program:

> *A WAC Program needs strong administrative support, but it also has to be a bottom-up phenomenon, usually starting with a few committed faculty members and growing as others see how successful these faculty have been.*

Profound curricular and pedagogical change can come about as a result of a WAC Program, but such change will not take place unless it comes from the faculty themselves. And change takes time. Successful WAC Programs start slowly, phasing in various components over a period of years as a consensus develops that the program is useful. (1992, 6)

The emphasis on faculty here reinforces both Toby Fulwiler's description of WAC as "teacher centered" (3) and Walvoord's cautionary comment that because WAC is intended to change teaching, WAC Programs need to work with teachers directly, usually through workshops or linked courses or team teaching. The choice to focus on teachers was a deliberate one made by early WAC proponents, Walvoord notes, and faculty development is therefore a key ingredient in a WAC Program. But extended faculty development can exist only where there is institutional support, and that support can take a number of forms such as encouraging attendance at retreats, workshops, or seminars with inducements such as release time or extra funding, providing writing fellows or teaching assistants, limiting class size, offering course reduction, or finding some means of lessening the load in other ways to compensate for the increased work that WAC requires. There also has to be some institutional recognition that such work is valuable, and if this is in the form of being incorporated into the review process, the reward is particularly strong.

Without some form of compensation and without some means of bringing teachers together for faculty development so that they become aware of what they want to do and how they might achieve the new goals they set for themselves, a WAC Program can falter. There are other factors that must be present as well. As Jody Swilky notes, in her discussion of faculty resistance, there is a falling off of faculty interest when there is no follow through after a workshop. A workshop or intensive training can bring great expectations and can fire teachers up to plunge in, in new and challenging ways. But then, with no follow up and the onset of reality (which is never quite what the workshop might lead the newly inspired to expect), interest wanes. Teachers retreat, fall back to old patterns, and drop out. Swilky thus concludes that the short seminar approach for faculty training has serious limitations in producing strong follow through. And, as already mentioned, Pat McQueeney argues for an additional component in WAC, a strong support system such as a Writing Center, for without that faculty resist taking on WAC work by themselves.

RATIONALE FOR A DE FACTO WAC WRITING CENTER

If a Writing Center exists in an institution where there is no WAC Program to focus its full attention on instituting WAC goals, why then might a Writing Center attempt to be a de facto WAC Writing Center? As a Writing Center director in this context, I have to thread my way through a number of complex considerations in deciding how we will expend our limited resources. How do I respond when a faculty member across campus assigns all seventy-five students in her class to see a Writing Lab tutor before handing in their papers, and about two-thirds of them come in the morning the paper is due? If the other third of the students from that class schedule appointments beforehand and cause us to turn away other students as they fill up the appointment book—particularly the students in our writing courses in the English Department who constitute the largest group of users—what is my response, given the fact that the English Department funds us and that the University has no history of funding for services crossing school lines? How should I respond to phone calls or visits from faculty who want to know about adding more writing to their classes? And how much time should I invest in responding to such a request, given the fact that I can not provide the kinds of extended workshops and seminars we know are needed?

If we offer brief workshops on various writing topics and class visits to publicize our Writing Lab, what do we do if there are so many responses that we seriously have to decrease our available time for tutoring? Do we agree to do workshops anywhere on campus or only in composition courses? If an instructor in another field is truly interested in using the Writing Lab in the most appropriate manner he can, including an offer to come to our staff meeting to coordinate with us, do I encourage his interest? What if eight or fourteen more faculty do the same? (That might seem like a large number to some, but on a campus with over a thousand faculty and perhaps another thousand graduate teaching assistants, fourteen requests would be a tiny fraction of the University's instructional staff.) If one of the purposes of our OWL (Online Writing Lab) is to provide a campus resource on using the Internet for writing research papers, should we be offering classroom workshops for instructors in other disciplines interested in seeing how this all works and how OWL can be coordinated into their classes? These and other questions come up regularly in our Writing Lab, and because we have always made our services available to any writer in the University, drawing boundaries is neither easy nor obvious. How do I determine what are appropriate Writing Center responsibilities (in a large institution with administrative oversight dispersed in various ways, our responsibilities are not clearly defined), which requests, fall within our perceived mission and goals, and when do we have to admit that without more extensive resources and programs, we are only offering Band-Aid WAC help? Writing Center theory and practice is drenched in discussions of how to avoid Band-Aid writing help to students, but de facto WAC Writing Centers also need to think about how to avoid Band-Aid WAC help.

However, there are a number of reasons that argue for taking on some of the work of assisting writers from all disciplines even if the center can not do it all or do it in a way that will be substantive or lead to self-sustaining change—and even if we agree (as I do) that Michael Pemberton raises valid considerations for rethinking the Writing Center/WAC connection. One of the theoretical justifications for tutorial work is the Writing Center claim that all writers benefit from tutorial collaboration, especially as they move on to more complex writing challenges (Harris, "Collaboration" 1992 and "Talking in the Middle" 1995), and we have a commitment in our Writing Lab to enact that principle, to keep our doors open to all writers. Since Writing Centers are student-centered, it would also be difficult for us (unless mandated to do otherwise) not to respond to students who come in asking for help.

Moreover, we have a commitment to providing tutorials that are as effective as we can make them. If there are obstacles that are likely to diminish the possibility that we are assisting writers, we have to improve those conditions if possible. One of the major impediments to helping a writer is a writing assignment so poorly designed that it can only provoke bad writing. A tutorial that focuses on helping the student become a better writer as she writes a paper in response to such an ill-conceived assignment is a study in frustration and, too often, defeat. Some years ago, several Writing Center colleagues and I offered a session at the Conference on College Composition and Communication dealing with how to cope in the Writing Center with what we called "Assignments from Hell" (AFH's, as they are familiarly known in our Writing Lab). The flood of attendees at that session, with people cramming and shoving to get in, attested to the high frequency as well as high level of frustration Writing Center specialists experience with this problem. Writing Center tutors need to deal, somehow, with students trying to write papers in response to AFH'S, and there is little we can do when the assignment is from the darkest depths of Hell, even more horrible than we might have otherwise imagined. In my early years as a Writing Lab Director, I was complaining to a colleague about the problem of students trying to cope with poorly written assignments, and in his astute Southern manner, he answered with a proverb, "You don't want to waste your energy swatting mosquitoes when you really need to drain the pond."

The source of the AFH problem, of course, is the teacher, not the student, and to start draining the pond, we need to find ways to help teachers master the complex art of designing effective writing assignments. That can range from calling the instructor and gently attempting one-to-one consultation to holding faculty workshops, and some of the responses we have come up with in our Writing Lab are discussed below. But the point here is that if Writing Centers want to help students in truly effective ways, we have to dip a toe (or, more likely, both feet) into faculty development. And that assistance is needed across the curriculum of an institution, especially in large institutions when there are students coming to the center from all corners of the campus where faculty may even be award-winning teachers and cutting-edge researchers but have never stopped to think about the elements of an effective writing assignment in their field.

Another compelling reason for a Writing Center to engage in some WAC work when there is no WAC Program has to do with the public image of the center. A Writing Center on a campus with no WAC Program becomes the lightening rod for faculty questions about using writing in their classes or faculty complaints or faculty interest in helping particular students. And a Writing Center, if it is working well, draws students who have heard from other students how valuable their tutoring experience was. Part of the success of a Writing Center is the campus-wide perception of it as being responsive to user needs, and by users, I mean faculty and students. Writing Centers that draw tight boundaries around what they can and cannot do, that carefully limit their services and conserve resources, that train tutors to confine their assistance only to what is possible or required of them are soon known to be just that—not responsive. Campus perceptions are important to the health of a Writing Center, particularly one that relies on voluntary attendance, and it does not bode well for a center to be perceived as being less than helpful. Moreover, a non-responsive center is not true to basic Writing Center principles of being nurturing and supportive. A number of different strands of Writing Center theory and pedagogy (e.g., feminist theorizing on nurturing practices that promote learning; borderlands or contact zone theorizing, that promotes the center as the place for different cultures to meet; literacy theorizing that looks at the role of a center to provide a space for different literacies, etc.) reinforce the view of the Writing Center as being positioned to help students, regardless of the source of the writing assignment or problem.

Moreover, if a Writing Center advertises on its publicity materials, as many do, that it welcomes all students, it should do just that—welcome all students. An added bonus in a Writing Center open to all students is the sense of accomplishment tutors feel when helping students with complex writing tasks in various disciplines. The collaborative effort is truly collaborative when it is particularly apparent in the tutorial that while the tutor brings rhetorical knowledge to the conversation, the student brings disciplinary knowledge. This is a powerful enactment of tutorial theories of collaboration. From another theoretical perspective, Writing Centers have always welcomed challenges for new ways to work with writing. Some see this as a reason for the health of the Writing Center concept, that Writing Centers are flexible enough to move forward easily. While curricular changes happen slowly, Writing Centers can respond quickly and energetically to changing climates for writing instruction. Writing Center practice can thus move forward by experimenting and trying out and seeking new ways to help writers and to assist with new forms and genres of writing that students in various disciplines are engaging in. This has led some Writing Center enthusiasts to view Writing Centers as being on the cutting edge of current practice, and certainly there is a freedom to explore opportunities and challenges. One example of this is the rapid growth of online writing labs—known by the acronym OWL—that have become resources for faculty and students, and our OWL, as discussed below, has certainly developed into a campus-wide resource on writing.

Finally, from the perspective of administrative concerns, there is yet another rationale for being a de facto Writing Center. A Writing Center that to some degree relies on demonstrating its effectiveness through statistics showing high (or steadily increasing) usage will find that opening its doors to all students is one more bit of insurance that the center will be used. Initiating contact with faculty, holding faculty workshops, or responding to faculty contacts for help make faculty more aware of the center and more likely to refer their students to the center. And when a Writing Center builds a strong constituency among the faculty across campus, the center builds a strong base of support that helps it grow and prosper. Given these broader reasons for a Writing Center to engage in WAC efforts, I turn now to our Writing Lab—who we are in terms of our institutional setting, what we do to fill the gap in WAC efforts, and finally what we cannot do to fully implement the goals of a successful WAC Program.

THE INSTITUTIONAL SETTING FOR OUR DE FACTO WRITING CENTER

Purdue University is a huge institution—with 35,000 students on my campus—that has a strong centralized administration overseeing ten academic schools, all of which are decentralized to the extent that they control their own curricula and core requirements. Some of these schools, such as Pharmacy and the ten schools of engineering within Engineering, have nationally mandated emphases on communication skills as part of accreditation requirements (see Eric Hobson and Neal Learner's "Writing Centers/WAC in Pharmacy Education: A Changing Prescription" in this book for a closer look at one School of Pharmacy's institutionalized WAC Program). Of the engineering schools, some more than others are also responding to pressures from the world that hires their graduates to improve their students' communication skills. The responses vary, but the most common model has been to hire a writing specialist who works closely with the report writing in a course, usually an upper-level one. This is the case in several of the engineering schools (the School of Chemical and Mechanical Engineering, the School of Mechanical Engineering, and the School of Civil Engineering).

In a somewhat different arrangement, the School of Management has a small staff of writing professionals to teach writing courses and offer writing support for Management students. Some of the students from these and the other schools on campus come to the Writing Lab, either because of faculty or staff referral (or a friend's recommendation), and some come in with papers after having acquired the habit of working with a tutor in their composition courses. In addition, graduate students also appear in our Writing Lab with drafts of course papers, dissertation proposals, and other writing projects. Although the other land-grant institution in our state—Indiana University—has a university-wide WAC Program, Purdue's structure is such that curricular requirements are handled within each school, and it is not likely that this will change in the foreseeable future. If WAC enters the curriculum here, it is more likely that it will be at the school level and not campus-wide.

Within the School of Liberal Arts, a recent and very extensive core curriculum revision effort resulted in a recommendation for instituting a WAC Program, but the lack of funding has kept that from becoming a reality. The English Department, with a large writing program (first-year composition, advanced composition, business writing, technical writing, creative writing, etc.), still provides most of the writing instruction on campus and enrolls in its upper-level writing courses students from various majors, some of whom are required to take the courses as part of their majors in their schools. Thus, the Writing Lab, housed in and funded by the English Department, has attempted to meet the need for writing support for both the faculty and students in writing courses as well as provide campus-wide writing assistance. But we exist on the usual tight English Department budget and perennially cope with the usual maximum strain on our resources.

Our Lab's largest constituency are the students in both first-year and upper-level writing courses, though, as noted, many of these students are fulfilling writing requirements in their own schools. We also work with under-graduates and graduate students writing papers in a variety of courses across campus, though our statistics show that 40 percent of these students are enrolled in the School of Liberal Arts. That is, when we exclude the students in our first year writing courses, 40 percent of the remaining students are Liberal Arts majors, though all other schools in the University are represented in this group. By this I mean that when we exclude all students in first-year writing classes from the statistical survey of usage, the remaining group includes students writing in courses in all schools in the University, a further demonstration that we do serve the entire University. In the majority of cases across campus, where faculty are incorporating writing into content courses, they are left to their own devices to structure assignments and to figure out how to respond appropriately to that writing. The faculty have diverse perceptions of how writing can be used and how it can be evaluated, and they vary greatly in the degree to which they are willing to make contact with writing resource people and places to assist them.

In this setting, the English Department houses the Writing Lab which I, as a tenured faculty member, direct. We have two staffs of tutors funded by the department: one staff is composed of graduate students who work with all students who seek tutorial help (except for students in our developmental writing program) and another staff of undergraduate peer tutors who are integrated into the developmental writing program, attending one class a week and tutoring every student in that program every week in the Writing Lab. An additional staff of peer tutors is funded by other sources in the University to assist with resumes and job applications. We also have a support staff consisting of a professional person who acts as secretary and general assistant, a receptionist, and work-study students who provide clerical and reception assistance. Although I report usage statistics, our services have grown so complex that no single number adequately represents our work. We work with about 6,000 students a year in tutorials or workshops or brief phone consultations, we give out hundreds and hundreds of handouts on writing skills to students and instructors who come in to ask for materials, and our OWL recorded about 1,500,000 hits (excluding graphics) last year, over 40,000 of which were initiated on campus. This vast usage, coupled with numerous awards from Internet companies (the usual handouts from four-star ratings companies so that the site will then post their award and thereby promote traffic for that company), is the kind of "good news" news that universities like to promote about themselves. In the flurry of articles in university publications that mention the success of our OWL, the description of its services is a highly effective means of getting the word out to faculty around campus that OWL is a resource for them too.

OUR WRITING LAB'S WAC EFFORTS

The major expenditure of our resources is for tutoring and working with all students who come to the Writing Lab. However, because WAC is a teacher-centered movement, this discussion of our de facto WAC efforts focuses primarily on the assistance we offer instructors in terms of faculty development and faculty support (though, of course, faculty support does encompass offering one-to-one assistance to their students when they assign writing). Faculty consultations occur most often in response to instructors who contact me with a question or complaint or whom I contact after they have begun to refer students to the Writing Lab. If the assignment that brought some students in is an AFH, I try to initiate a conversation with the instructor that can offer some help with revising the assignment. And there are other opportunities for connecting faculty across campus. If I notice a sudden surge of papers from a particular course in economics or political science, I can contact the teacher to establish lines of communication. Sometimes, that line is merely a thin thread, but other times, it can turn into a productive relationship. Some consultations are initiated by faculty who have called to ask for help in writing essay exam questions or who want some feedback on an assignment they are about to hand out or who want some information about how they can use the Lab for their students. If possible, I try to invite more interaction than a single phone call or meeting provokes, and in some cases, that has worked. In other cases, teachers look upon that one interaction either as sufficient or as the extent of the time they can devote to the topic.

Phone conversations and personal consultations are, seemingly, reactive responses, but they can also be the result of proactive efforts: sending out publicity notices, offering my services to departments when I meet administrators from that department, and reminding teachers whom I meet that the Writing Lab is a resource for them as well as their students. A more structured proactive approach is to offer my services for campus workshops on popular topics such as using writing in the classroom or evaluating papers. Faculty workshops are effective in that participants are there because of some interest in the topic, and useful contacts are made in those workshops. In addition to the few who are attracted to the workshop for the sole purpose of complaining about how badly students write these days, I meet teachers who begin to think about using the Writing Lab and about how they should assign and respond to writing. Even a brief introduction in a workshop or a short phone conversation can also be the opening to explain why our Writing Lab is not a grammar fix-it shop and why we do not proofread papers. If possible, by moving the conversation in appropriate directions, I can promote the notion of writing as a tool for learning. By being known on campus as a person willing to help with writing, I have been invited to departments to talk with instructional staff who are grading writing assignments, and I have been asked to talk to majors in various fields about the importance of writing in their future careers. Another result of all these efforts, I hope, is simply to keep the topic of using writing on the academic table.

Our most focused large-scale WAC effort is our OWL (Online Writing Lab; http://owl.english.purdue.edu). A number of forces have spurred the growth of our Writing Lab's OWL, and one of them has been a challenge to serve the campus—both faculty and students—in ways we are not normally able to do. Online, we are providing a WAC-like service, one that expands on a familiar service in most Writing Centers—offering print materials on writing skills from our cabinets of instructional handouts developed originally to accompany tutorial talk. It also, as Irene Clark discusses in her chapter in this book on the role the Web plays in the Writing Center, expands the space for working with writing to include a virtual space as well as a physical one. Our OWL, originally an e-mail service that is now primarily (in terms of usage) a Web site, includes among its resources a large number of handouts on writing. We have offered these materials to all faculty on campus who are invited to download and use them in their classes or refer their students to the materials which are available in any campus computer tab or anywhere they can access the

Web or e-mail. Making materials on writing available to students and faculty is easily done online, and the Internet is a perfect means for our Writing Lab and any other Writing Center to make those materials available to any teacher for any course anywhere in the world. Thus, we have heard (informally) that our OWL is listed as the "writing assistance" on Web course pages beyond Purdue in fields as diverse as anthropology, medicine, engineering, and geology, as well as in institutions all over the world.

Across campus, we have had numerous requests for workshops on using OWL as a resource. In addition to providing online materials on writing (including assistance with citing electronic sources), OWL was set up to help writers search the Internet for information. At present that includes a collection of Internet search engines, and under development will be online materials on using search engines effectively and evaluating sources. Thus, we offer various services because of OWL, and our workshops around campus are usually tailored to the specific teacher's need to help that class use the Internet when writing papers and to the teacher's additional need to think about how to incorporate use of the Internet in his or her curriculum.

In this way, our OWL is a resource both for students and faculty, but working from the perspective that WAC is a faculty movement, our OWL also assists faculty development. One section of our OWL is labeled as "Teacher Resources," and here we have useful links on teaching writing as well as links to WAC pages at other institutions. This provides our faculty with the means to read about WAC Programs as well as to read WAC papers and online versions of WAC newsletters (such as the excellent one at Boise State University). Some institutions with WAC Programs have flourishing and rich Web sites where their faculty can find resources on using writing in their disciplines, and our OWL becomes the conduit for our faculty to have access to those same materials. We hope that by developing that part of our OWL site further, we can be more proactive in offering easily accessed information about using writing effectively.

In addition, to assist faculty who want to know more about how to grade English as a Second Language (ESL) papers, we are developing the ESL resources for teachers, including materials on responding to ESL writing. We hope that teachers in all fields will visit that section of our OWL to gather ideas for how to evaluate papers written by ESL students, and we also hope that it will deter some teachers from reacting too harshly to minor surface errors in ESL writing. If we meet up with such problems when the ESL student comes to the Writing Lab desperate for proofreading help (because of unrealistic teacher comments about the need to fix the errors in the paper), we can suggest to the teacher that he or she consider the suggestions offered on OWL for how to respond to ESL papers. Again, the purpose is both to help instructors and also to improve tutorials by having students come in for appropriate kinds of tutorial help.

LIMITATIONS TO OUR WRITING LAB'S WAC EFFORTS

While we provide faculty support and some faculty development, there are limitations to what our Writing Lab can hope to accomplish on a campus with no WAC Program. In Toby Fulwiler and Art Young's *Programs That Work* and other discussions of WAC, there are a number of recurrent themes in descriptions of successful WAC Programs, factors that are of crucial importance in creating the sustained transformative change that McLeod defines as necessary for WAC integration in the curriculum. The retreats and workshops that start off an instructor's introduction to WAC are intended to immerse teachers, to bring them together in collaborative ways, to create what Mary Jane Dickerson, Toby Fulwiler, and Henry Steffens describe as "engaged faculty" (1990, 46). In their WAC Program at the University of Vermont: "Instructors go away from our two-day workshops full of good feelings, enthusiasm about teaching, a renewed interest in their own writing, and, of course, with some ideas about the ways to implement more writing into the courses they teach. Perhaps even more important, however, is the sense of community they discover at the workshops" (46).

Joyce Neff Magnotto and Barbara R. Stout describe the "spirit of collegiality [that] develops" (33) in extended workshops, and they detail some of the ground that must be covered, introducing faculty to the complexities of writing processes, to "re-examin[ing] pedagogies in light of WAC values" (32), to various kinds of writing beyond the traditional forms they knew as students and so on. Without the opportunity to engage in such extended dialogues with faculty or to provide contexts for the kinds of enriching collegial interaction and collaboration described by Magnotto and Stout, we cannot expect that our short workshops will provide the stimuli needed for substantive change. Moreover, without the means to encourage or provide extended individual consultations and follow up, we have to realize that our efforts will fall prey to various problems. As Judy Gill notes, such assistance is needed because when reality sets in, "instructors don't see the improvement they had hoped for, they are frustrated and their earlier anxieties and skepticism may return" (1996, 168). An inference that Swilky draws from her analysis of teacher resistance to using writing is that "to assist teachers who are serious about changing their pedagogy, we need to collaborate with instructors as they revise their courses" (1992, 58). Clearly, sustained interaction cannot be provided by a Writing Center without resources provided for such work.

But even if our Writing Lab were to apportion our resources so that we could somehow set up more workshops or use some of our time to offer more faculty consultation, there has to be some incentive for faculty to plunge in to course revision and to take on the labor-intensive work of interacting with more student writing. Some faculty are, of course, motivated by a genuine desire to be good teachers, but even they are not likely to be able to sustain that interest in an institution that does not reward them for the effort in some way, either through course support (e.g., offering release time or providing graduate student or writing fellow assistance) or recognition at review time. Worse yet, when the institution has made no overt commitment to WAC and when it encourages by rewarding research efforts, some faculty members may find themselves quietly warned by mentors not to devote so much effort to teaching because they will, finally, be reviewed for promotion and tenure (and salary raises) on the basis of research. Without institutional support in terms of rewards for the teacher, the most well-meaning teacher will eventually figure out that all this work may be personally and intellectually rewarding but is not a strong career move. In these days of tight job markets for academics, faculty catch on fairly quickly. At my university where research is encouraged and valued, how could I reasonably expect faculty to come to extended workshops or to devote the necessary time to those consultations that we would offer if we could when we can not provide the kinds of stamps of approval they need to survive in their jobs? As Malcolm Kiniry, Ellen Strenski, and Mike Rose note, in their description of the University of California, Los Angeles' cross-curricular writing program ("UCLA"), "[r]esearch universities…are just not structured to reward scholars for spending time assigning and responding to student writing" (1990, 30). Even in successful WAC Programs, there are what Dickerson, Fulwiler, and Steffens describe as mixed messages:

> *All the forces in the university, from department to college and university level, conspire to make research and publication more important than teaching. No matter what we say or do, our program [University of Vermont's Faculty Writing Project] asks instructors to think and do more about their teaching than the university rewards them for. And though we promote the workshops in part by suggesting that faculty will learn how to assign and assess student writing more effectively and efficiently, etc., thoughtful teaching does take more time-time away from something else. (1990, 59)*

But given all this, for a Writing Center that is a de facto WAC Writing Center, there should be some recognition that there is merit in assisting with small changes even when there may be no likelihood of large-scale ones. Without a WAC Program for extended and extensive faculty development, a scaling down of expectations is necessary in order to acknowledge that merit. Part of that scaling down is to recognize what happens in our Writing Centers in other contexts. That is, when Judy Gill reminds us that in Writing Centers, we are not likely to see many of the students again and have learned to live with "not seeing the fruits of our labors" (1996, 175), it is no great stretch to expand this to de facto WAC Writing Center efforts as well. We should remember that we can contribute in ways that we may not see and that there is a lot more fruit out there than we are likely to be aware of. But to complete the picture, I need to switch to a water metaphor. Some days in the Writing Lab as I watch students come and go, I worry that we are trying to empty the ocean with a teaspoon. I had a similar sense when reading the comments on an end-of-the-semester evaluation from a faculty member across campus, several of whose students had come to the Writing Lab: "Thanks for your assistance, but Tim's paper still had a few grammatical errors that slipped through your net." But in that same pile of teacher evaluations was one from another faculty member with whom I had talked after he initially sent two of his "miscreants" (his term) to the Lab (both had some grammatical errors in their papers): "Matthew is beginning to write critically and thoughtfully now. I am not sure about Loni but she did have a tighter grip on her conclusions in that last paper. Thanks for your efforts—and for that reprint on using micro-themes." In that pile there were no evaluations from any of the biology instructors with whom I had met, the instructors in quiz sections who graded papers for a large lecture course. The faculty member who directed that course had contacted me about her interest in adding writing to the course. She and I talked and later agreed to a follow-up meeting with a graduate student Writing Lab staff member interested in working with faculty across the curriculum. After he met with her, she called to ask if I would talk with her staff since they would be the ones interacting with the student writing. I had difficulty determining what the agenda for my visit to the staff meeting would be, but when I arrived, the faculty member enthusiastically informed me that she had allotted ten minutes for my part of her staff meeting and asked if I could introduce the Writing Lab and its services, talk about writing and its importance in a biology course, and suggest to these quiz section instructors how to work with writing in their quiz sections. She assumed that I could adequately cover all that in ten minutes. In a de facto WAC Writing Center, you win some and you lose some, and it is never quite clear which is which.

WORKS CITED

Dickerson, Mary Jane, Toby Fulwiler, and Henry Steffens. "The University of Vermont." In *Programs That Work: Models and Methods for Writing Across the Curriculum,* Toby Fulwiler and Art Young eds. Portsmouth, NH: Boynton/Cook, 1990. 45–63.

Fulwiler, Toby, and Art Young, eds. *Programs That Work: Models and Methods for Writing Across the Curriculum.* Portsmouth, NH: Boynton/Cook, 1990.

Gill, Judy. "Another Look at WAC and the Writing Center." *Writing Center Journal* 16.2 (1996): 164–178.

Harris, Muriel. "Collaboration Is Not Collaboration Is Not Collaboration: Writing Center Tutorials vs. Peer-response Groups." *College Composition and Communication* 43 (1992): 369–383,

———. "Talking in the Middle: Why Writers Need Writing Tutors." *College English* 57 (1995): 27–42.

Kiniry, Malcolm, Ellen Strenski, and Mike Rose. "UCLA." In *Programs That Work: Models and Methods for Writing Across the Curriculum*, Toby Fulwiler and Art Young eds. Portsmouth, NH: Boynton/Cook Heinemann, 1990. 29–43.

McLeod, Susan H. and Margot Soven, eds. *Writing Across the Curriculum: A Guide to Developing Programs*. Newbury Park, CA: Sage, 1992.

McQueeney, Pat. "Proposing a Writing Center: Experts' Advice." *Writing Lab Newsletter*, forthcoming.

North, Stephen. "Revisiting 'The Idea of a Writing Center.'" *Writing Center Journal* 15.1 (1994): 7–19.

Pemberton, Michael A. "Rethinking the WAC/Writing Center Connection." *Writing Center Journal* 15.2 (1995): 116–133.

Swilky, Jody. "Reconsidering Faculty Resistance to Writing Reform." *WPA: Writing Program Administration* 16.1–2 (1992): 50–60.

Waldo, Mark L. "The Last Best Place for Writing Across the Curriculum: The Writing Center." *WPA/Writing Program Administration* 16.3 (1993): 15–26.

Walvoord, Barbara E. "The Future of WAC." *College English* 58 (1996): 58–79.

Rethinking the WAC/Writing Center Connection

Michael A. Pemberton

At first glance, it might be difficult to find two writing programs that seem to work together more harmoniously than Writing Across the Curriculum and writing centers. WAC engenders more writing in more classes, and writing centers help students to improve their writing skills and produce, presumably, better papers. Administratively, the two programs are often seen as complementary if not conjoined. If more writing is going to be demanded of more students in more classes, then those students will need additional support services as they work to complete their assignments. And though there may, in some cases, be the money and motivation necessary to create intradepartmental tutorial services for the benefit of students within each major, most often the responsibility for writing assistance either falls on (or is specifically delegated to) the campus writing center.

This approach may appear to have significant merit and may, in fact, be looked on with a good deal of satisfaction by interested parties on all sides. Administrators will likely be pleased because they won't have to create a brand-new support system for WAC; at most institutions, writing centers have generally been in place longer than WAC programs, and in some cases, writing centers may actually have been starting points for early writing across the curriculum efforts (Griffin 400). Faculty will generally be pleased because they have the somewhat illusory impression that writing centers will reduce the additional workload imposed by an increased number of writing assignments. And writing center directors will generally be pleased because their integral role in helping to implement and sustain WAC programs provides the center with more students coming in; an increased sense of budgetary and political security; and, in some cases, additional funding

Pemberton, Michael A. "Rethinking the WAC/Writing Center Connection." *The Writing Center Journal* 15.2 (1995): 116–33. Reprinted by permission of *The Writing Center Journal*.

for tutors, supplies, and equipment. Difficulties are generally downplayed, and much of what is written about the relationship between WAC and writing centers concerns itself with descriptions of specific programs and the ways in which instructional articulation is played out. Dinitz and Howe, for example, describe the "evolving partnership" between WAC and writing centers at their respective institutions, suggesting that some of the weaknesses in each institution's models can be fruitfully addressed through the use of "group critiques"(49–50). Ray Wallace, in a similar fashion, details the tutor-training program at the University of Tennessee, Knoxville, stressing the important links that need to be forged between the writing center and the disciplinary faculty; and Carino, et al. and Walker echo this point of view. The popular and, perhaps, conveniently pragmatic impression seems to be that writing centers have, in some senses, *always* been writing-across-the-curriculum centers. They have always opened their doors to students working on writing projects for any classes that those students happen to be enrolled in, and they have always had to engage students on a wide variety of topics that vary on a daily, sometimes hourly, basis.

I would like to question, however, whether this arranged marriage between WAC and writing centers, enacted at a growing number of institutions across the country, demonstrates true love and a natural compatibility or merely a disturbing kind of administrative expediency. There are compelling reasons, I think, to reconsider the nature of the relationship between these two programs, particularly when WAC is construed as WID or Writing In the Disciplines.[1]

Though WAC and writing centers have clear pedagogical similarities in their joint focus on text production and writing-as-learning, their underlying epistemologies and resulting assumptions about what qualify as significant rhetorical and textual features remain strikingly different. Much of the current scholarship about WAC programs, for example, focuses on the diverse rhetorics which students are expected to master during their college careers. Drawing from the work of rhetorical and social theorists such as Burke, Foucault, Vygotsky, and Bakhtin, many composition scholars (Bartholomae, Bruffee, and McCarthy, among others) have situated WAC programs in the paradigm of polyvocalism, reflecting the diverse nature of specialized conversations in the "content-area" disciplines and rejecting the notion that a general-purpose "academic discourse" exists. WAC pedagogies often tend, therefore, to address the needs of multiple discourse communities, situated knowledge, and complex, socially-constructed conventions of language by treating each discipline as if it were a separate entity with its own set of practices to be explored.

Writing centers, on the other hand, seem grounded in an opposing set of assumptions, including the widely held tenet of practitioner lore that many aspects of text production (such as tone, awareness of audience, coherence, use of specific detail to support arguments, grammar, etc.) are "generic" in nature and, for the most part, extend across disciplinary boundaries. Tutors who work in writing centers are usually not trained as experts in the rhetoric of a particular discipline (other than their own), and they are expected to work with student writing in a wide variety of disciplines, many of which they may know very little about. Their ability to provide writing assistance to students working in specialized discourse communities often depends upon their ability to draw from their own experiences as writers and readers in a discipline, to work with the aspects of text production they interpret as "common" to virtually all academic texts, and then to apply these common principles to new and possibly unfamiliar academic subjects or genres. In this regard, then, writing center practice operates as if an "academic discourse" does indeed exist, a discourse that can be explained and utilized successfully in student conferences no matter which interpretive community a particular student might be addressing in a given paper. (See, for example, Clark 11–12.)

The epistemologies that inform each of these instructional programs are oppositional but not necessarily in direct conflict. The existence of situationally-embedded, discipline-specific features in academic texts may not, in itself, preclude the possibility that some "transdisciplinary" textual or rhetorical features also exist, features that might be addressed successfully by tutors in a writing center. The need to support generalizations with specific evidence, for example, may display some subtle variations depending upon the discipline and audience addressed in particular texts, but the fact that there must be *some* relationship between generalizations made and evidence offered in support is a feature common to virtually all academic writing. Other "generic" concerns such as sentence- and paragraph-level coherence are also potential subjects for tutorial conferences, and some higher-level rhetorical features which may be shaped only partially by disciplinary conventions—organization, evidence, logical development, tone, introductions, conclusions, etc.—can, perhaps, be discussed a contextually or as "general rules" that must be adapted to specific texts, audiences, or purposes.

Though this *pedagogy of the generic* may be a useful and effective approach for some students, assignments, and contexts (particularly first-year composition courses), I am concerned that it may do a disservice to students who are writing in a multidisciplinary WAC program, particularly because—as I indicated above—the central purpose of writing across the curriculum is to familiarize and train students to become fluent in exactly those discipline-specific rhetorical features that a "generic" writing center pedagogy is geared to overlook. Let me make clear that I do not wish to dismiss the generic pedagogy out of hand; I can envision a number of circumstances—particularly in the case of first-year composition students—when this particular approach and set of tutorial practices might be especially useful and appropriate. But in the context of a writing center that wishes to address the needs of students writing in a WAC program, this approach is insufficient.

My concern over this issue is exacerbated by what I see as compelling evidence that a number of WAC programs often fail to live up to their own foundational principles and slip carelessly into writing pedagogies that provide students, particularly undergraduates, few opportunities to rehearse disciplinary modes of inquiry or forms of discourse. The reasons for these institutional failures are many, but two of the most significant—*conscious myopia* and the *myth of disciplinarity*—may be especially pervasive and worthy of review. As I will show, these failures may actually make it easier for writing centers to work within WAC programs, and they certainly provide some justification for the generic tutorial approach described above. But they paint, I think, an incomplete and somewhat jaundiced picture of how WAC programs and writing centers might work together productively. The differing goals and epistemological perspectives advanced by WAC programs and writing centers will complicate any sort of pedagogical interrelationship we might wish to propose between them. We are obligated, therefore, to consider very carefully what social and instructional role the writing center and its tutorial staff should assume in conferences with WAC students. These considerations will be the focus of the latter portion of this paper.[2]

CONSCIOUS MYOPIA

One disturbing yet all-too-common way that WAC and writing centers can work together is through a kind of *conscious myopia*, by simply choosing to ignore any problems, pretending they don't exist, or rationalizing them away. For most people, especially the instructors and students who are enmeshed in WAC programs and institutional requirements, this may be the easiest thing to do. Though WAC faculty training programs often work hard to stress the important role faculty play in constructing assignments and guiding students through the conventions of a new discipline, these lessons may be conveniently forgotten after the training is over, especially if they were never fully believed in the first place or if the practicalities of implementing WAC pedagogy appear too complex or burdensome in retrospect (Fulwiler, "How Well" 114–120; Mayher, et al. 89). Instructors, students, and tutors may wish to believe that there really is such a thing as Writing with a capital "W" that either transcends or can be attended to separately from content issues that are the sole province of the content-area faculty. WAC instructors may require more writing from their students and use writing as a learning tool in their classes, but in spite of assurances from writing specialists that the instructors themselves are the best persons to comment on student writing within a discipline, they may continue to feel a good deal of anxiety about their ability to do so in a useful or helpful way. Reports from faculty workshops tend to bear this out (Kinneavy 15; Knoblauch and Brannon; Mallonee and Breihan).

Many successful, publishing academic professionals do not think of themselves as writers and, consequently, doubt their own ability to comment on and respond effectively to student writing. They are also uneasy about spending time on "writing" in their classrooms when there is so much other "material" to be covered in their courses, so the writing center becomes an important resource by default. The refrain is a familiar one: "I don't have time to teach English in my class; that's your job" (Russell 297; Raimes).

And the people who work in writing centers may be perfectly happy to accept this construction of their identity. It does, after all, *give* them an identity as well as a sense of authority and expertise—precious commodities for tutors in otherwise low-paying and low-status jobs. In order to maintain this sense of expertise, tutors may consciously resist the social-constructionist theory that undergirds WAC programs. The social-constructionist paradigm argues, in part, for the distribution of writing expertise within and among the disciplines, locating the sires of textual authority in many diverse fields and interpretive communities. As a result, it also deconstructs and decentralizes the traditionally-accepted, institutionally-constituted authority of the writing center, the writing teacher, and others who claim to know something about "writing" as a subject in itself. Writing center tutors, in this distributed model, are almost never allowed to be authorities or insiders; they are perpetually outside the conversation (not unlike the students they are trying to help), and they will never even be extended an invitation to enter the Burkean parlor. In the face of this disempowering construction of writing center reality, it would be small wonder if the people who work there chose to embrace an alternative construction.

THE MYTH OF DISCIPLINARITY

A second and perhaps more insidious way that WAC programs and writing centers can work together depends on what I call the *myth of disciplinarity* in undergraduate education. As I have indicated above, WAC is grounded, in part, on social-constructionist tenets about knowledge construction, social practices, and education. One of the most important of these tenets is that since different disciplines comprise different discourse communities with different sets of discursive practices, it should be the responsibility of instructors to acquaint students with those practices and associated modes of inquiry. Certainly, this is the case that Art Young makes when he says that

> writing is a social activity; it takes place in a social context. If we want students to be effective communicators, to be successful engineers and historians, then we cannot separate form from content, writing from knowledge, action from context. We should not teach writing generically, in a vacuum,

as if it were a skill unconnected to purpose or context. Student writers need to join a community of learners engaged in generating knowledge and solving problems, to join, even as novices, disciplinary conversations and public-policy discussions. WAC programs, therefore, began to stress the role...of social context in learning to write and writing to learn. (60–61)

As admirable as these principles might be in theory, in practice the idealistic vision of WAC they present may be just that—an idealistic vision. The truth of the matter may be that on the one hand, undergraduate WAC courses, no matter how well-intentioned, do not and will not offer students the opportunity to participate in disciplinary conversations, and on the other hand, undergraduates are, for the most part, unprepared and unable to do so even if the opportunity were allowed them.

As a general rule, the locus of much undergraduate (and pre-undergraduate) instruction remains rooted in the Freirian "banking model." Instructors and textbooks are regarded as repositories of content information which is disseminated to students, and the students are expected to absorb this information and, on command, to replay—some would say regurgitate—it. (Applebee; Nelson; Sherrard; Geisler) This model, of course, ignores the social, cultural, and interpretive forces which shape the knowledge structures that are embraced by a discipline, just as it overlooks the value of collaborative learning as an instructional methodology. Nevertheless, for WAC instructors in the content-area disciplines who are particularly concerned with the issue of "coverage," the banking model is a powerful and persuasive one (Russell 295–7; Waldo 23; Mayer, et al. 87). And in keeping with this model, many of the writing assignments that students are asked to complete, even in WAC courses, may not ask students to do more than parrot information gleaned from sources or to "analyze" this information in anything other than a superficial way. My own experience working in writing centers with students from WAC courses indicates that students are often given assignments that allow them to write, for the most part, in pre-disciplinary forms that use the traditional modes of discourse—comparison and contrast, classification, definition, description, etc.—to report or analyze information in generic ways rather than to master the rhetorical conventions of a particular field. A survey of academic writing tasks conducted by Bridgeman and Carlson in 1984 suggests that this practice may, indeed, be widespread. In this study, the researchers investigated "the kinds of writing skills that might be expected of students at entry level, or in early training in their academic fields." Of the ten possible "expected writing skills" to choose from in this survey, seven of the ten were variations on description, comparison and contrast, or summary (255). As David Bartholomae laments, "[m]uch of the written work students do is test-taking, report or summary, work that places them outside the working discourse of the academic community, where they are expected to admire and report on what we do, rather than inside that discourse, where they can do its work and participate in a common enterprise" (144). Though this approach may do a disservice to students and, as Bartholomae claims, be "a failure of teachers and curriculum designers who, even if they speak of writing as a mode of learning, all too often represent writing as a 'tool' to be used by an (hopefully) educated mind" (144), it nevertheless alleviates the problem of discipline-specific rhetorics for tutors in writing centers. Tutors can be trained in the generic modes of discourse, in the structure of argument, in the form of the "standard" research paper, or in the shape of the "typical" lab report, and apply them with some confidence to student papers in political science, biology, chemistry, or sociology. Since undergraduates will not be asked to participate in specialized discourse, tutors need not worry about their own unfamiliarity with it.

Further, there is some evidence that the representations students build about specialized discourses in the early stages of their undergraduate education are relatively naive and that these naive representations impact heavily on the students' own writing (Fulwiler, et al. 61; Walvoord and McCarthy; Hare and Fitzsimmons; Geisler). Beginning writers, as Pat Bizzell has noted, are often "unaware that there is such a thing as a discourse community with conventions to be mastered" (230), and as a consequence, students' written texts do little more than duplicate the informational structure of the texts they will be examined on. "Students know intuitively that to do more [than this sort of duplication] would jeopardize their mastery of content knowledge they will be required to demonstrate on tests" (Geisler 42–43). Since undergraduate students are not likely to recognize a rhetorical dimension to knowledge construction in the discipline they are writing for, they are not likely to reproduce that dimension in their own work other than trying to incorporate what they see as the "jargon" of the field. (See, for instance, Schwartz; McCarthy.) If this assessment of students' cognitive representations for specialized discourse is correct, then the disciplinarity problem raised by WAC is once again greatly diminished for writing centers. Since students are not likely to write using discipline-specific discourse conventions, tutors will not have to worry about addressing them. And since instructors will not overtly expect their students to write like experts who are fully conversant with the "commonplaces" of the field (to use Bartholomae's term), tutors need not worry—for the most part— about such deficiencies in student texts.

THE QUESTION OF RESPONSIBILITY

Now, as I said before, these two perspectives on the WAC/writing center relationship are unsettling, partly because they depend upon certain kinds of instructional failure in WAC programs and partly because they depict writing centers as institutions that are willing to embrace these failures and avoid confronting complex, discipline-specific rhetorical issues that would undoubtedly problematize writing conferences. But is the passive role adopted by some writing centers under these circumstances necessarily a bad thing? Is it really the responsibility of a writing center staff to introduce and address matters of disciplinary discourse when WAC courses and their modes-based writing assignments fail to do so? To my mind, the answer is a yes, but a tentative and qualified one. Some research, for example, indicates that even though instructors in the disciplines may give assignments that enable students to fall back on conventional, generic strategies for academic papers learned in high school, those instructors nevertheless may evaluate the papers on the basis of how well they conform to discipline-specific rhetorical standards. (See Faigley and Hansen; Walvoord and McCarthy.) This being the case, then it may very well be the responsibility of writing center tutors to attend to such standards.

The need to attend to matters of disciplinary discourse is even more pronounced when writing centers must support WAC programs which are enacted successfully, when dedicated progressive instructors work diligently to make their students "insiders" rather than "outsiders," and when students are both enthusiastic and active learners in a new and unfamiliar discipline. But this returns me to my original questions: If WAC is working as it *should*, theoretically, then how do we resolve the opposition between its epistemological assumptions about texts, discourse, and writing and those which inform the operations of writing center practice? If we accept the fact that writing center tutors will never be able to master all the discursive practices of all the disciplines which students are writing in under the auspices of a fully-realized WAC program, then what exactly should the tutors' role be in these writing conferences?[3] What benefits can the writing center and its tutors provide in conferences that would not be more fully realized in meetings with professors or other experts in the field? These questions strike at the heart of what we do in writing centers, and I cannot help but approach them with a certain degree of trepidation. They resist simple answers and all-purpose solutions. I would, however, like to suggest two perspectives—the *environmental* and the *cognitive*—that can provide at least partial and provisionary answers.

ENVIRONMENTAL: THE ROLE
OF THE WRITING CENTER

Much has been said and written about the nature of the power and authority relationships which are enacted in tutorial conferences. Though it is sometimes tempting to talk about the writing center conference as if it were completely egalitarian, a site where students and tutors can interact as peers or co-authors, this representation is clearly naive. Characterizations of the writing center as a "rhetorically neutral ground" where tutors "do not have the rhetorical agenda common to one discourse community…[and] can thus resist imposing what they value about writing on other departments" (Waldo 18–19) overlook the dynamics of power inherent in any tutoring session. Many power relationships, instantiated along a multitude of dimensions, come into play in all tutorial conferences. Some of these dimensions are economic, some gendered, some cultural, some institutional, and some situational. As John Trimbur and others have remarked, the very term "peer tutor" is itself a contradiction in terms. Students come to the writing center for assistance, and tutors are presumably there—authorized by some sort of institutional power structure—to provide it. Tutors, in the very act of giving suggestions, offering advice, or asking pointed questions, are *de facto* imposing what they value about writing on students and, by implication, on other departments. Nevertheless, the authority granted tutors by their institutional status *as* tutors may be counterbalanced by other dimensions of authority that lean more heavily toward the students. The students, for example, own and control the texts they choose to discuss. They are also likely to know more about the papers' subject matter and discipline-specific conventions than the tutors and therefore be able to speak more knowledgeably about what material is relevant and what is not. The ideal tutorial conference, then, is characterized by *parity*, a balance of power, rather than egalitarianism, where power relationships are either absent or dismissible.

The tutor's very ignorance of discipline-specific subject matter and rhetorical conventions, then, can be seen as an equalizing force in writing center conferences (Hubbuch). Tutors can ask what rhetorical conventions exist for a particular discipline, and students can articulate and explain them, checking at the same time to see that these conventions are being followed in their own texts. The tutor's authority and the student's authority can strike a balance which allows the opportunity for questions and advice (on the tutor's part) and considered judgment (on the student's part). This balance of power is facilitated by the tutor's unique status as an *interested, disinterested other*—someone who attends to and focuses on the students' papers in the context of the tutorial session but who has no real stake in the papers' success or failure. This is quite different from the relationship which is likely to hold between students and instructors, where such a balance of power can rarely be achieved. When conferring with instructors about their papers, students can no longer claim the same authority over the subject matter since the instructor will probably have a greater level of expertise, and they can no longer claim the same control over their texts since the instructor's power to evaluate and grade the final product will exert a tremendous pressure on how rigorously the student will feel compelled to follow the advice given. The student-teacher conferences transcribed and analyzed by Sperling, for example, reveal conspicuous differences in how the instructor, "Mr. Peterson," worked with three students, but they also show the alacrity with which these students were willing to follow the teacher's lead in making revisions to their drafts (136–154; see also Marsella, et al. 182–3). What can be concluded from these observations, perhaps, is that although writing center tutors may not be the *best* people to comment on papers produced for courses in WAC programs (in terms of their subject-area knowledge and familiarity with discipline-specific conventions), they may very well be the one quasi-authoritative source that students feel most *comfortable* with, and this, I think, places them and the writing center in an important and worthwhile position.

COGNITIVE: THE ROLE OF THE TUTOR

Cognitive perspectives on the study of writing and conferencing practices also suggest important ways in which WAC and writing centers can work together productively. When writers try to think about or "generate" material that they can use in their writing, they begin by searching their long- and short-term memories, looking for information that can provide them with new ideas, appropriate plans for their writing tasks, or relevant information that can be included in their texts. As writers' search their memories, they do so in ways that are both recursive and associational (Hayes and Flower; Flower and Hayes, "Cognitive Process"; Scardamalia and Bereiter). That is, each piece of information they retrieve from their memories becomes, in turn, the basis of a new probe they can use to look for more information. A student writing a paper on the Clinton health plan, for example, might first recall that one of its critical features has to do with catastrophic health coverage for all Americans. This recalled memory ("catastrophic health coverage") is linked, associationally, to the first probe ("the Clinton health plan"), and may, in turn, become the basis for a further memory search. Catastrophic health coverage may bring to mind topics such as medical costs, the insurance industry, or grandma's last stay in the hospital. Each of these may, in turn, lead to further memory searches and further associational chains. The recursive nature of this operation—called "spreading activation"— makes it a powerful search strategy, since it may be modified as needed or redirected to more productive types of search as the goals of the textual plan are themselves met, unfulfilled, or modified.

But this search strategy, in and of itself, may be insufficient to generate the information necessary for successful disciplinary writing. The type and quality of information retrieved from memory are dependent upon the type and quality of the probes which are used to search it, but more fundamentally, these memory probes are dependent upon the nature of the task representation which students construct to guide the search process. Students who do not have functional and productive representations of their writing tasks or textual goals will have difficulty generating ideas or evaluating specific memories for appropriateness. One of the features which distinguishes "novice" from "expert" writers in Flower and Hayes' cognitive model of writing process behaviors is the richness of the task representations which those writers construct for their developing texts. Rich task representations generally take into account factors as audience, rhetorical goals, and alternative views, while less-rich representations are often "writer-based" and egocentric—seemingly unaware of the textual and rhetorical needs of an audience other than themselves. For novice writers whose potential task representations are entirely dependent upon the limited range of textual options and constructions of audience which may available to them in their own memories, the struggle to become "expert" writers may be a long and tortuous one. Not only will the types of probes they construct to search their memories be limited by their own cognitive processes and perspectives, but the means by which they learn and assimilate new rhetorical strategies will usually be implicit and diffuse, slowly internalized from detectable patterns of reading, writing, and talking behaviors in a discourse community, rather than explicit and focused, derived via an interactive engagement with writing tasks and supportive collaborators.

One important contribution which tutors in writing centers can provide for WAC programs, or more pointedly, for students writing papers in WAC programs, then, is to support and enrich students' cognitive processes by offering them new perspectives for thinking about their tasks (Harris, "Writing Center and Tutoring" 167). When writers confront new writing tasks, they often draw on familiar representations and strategies that have proven useful in the past, hoping that they will prove equally productive in the present. These cognitive constructs may be the result of their previous writing experiences, the social and cultural forces that shape their cognition, or their sense of the rhetorical and discursive conventions they are crying to satisfy. Often these familiar strategies work well for writers; other times—such as when the representations of the writing task are poor or misdirected—they can trap writers in blind alleys.

Writing center conferences can provide opportunities for writers to break out of these representational dead-ends. Each comment, each question, each suggestion or observation made by a writing center tutor can enable student writers to engage their topics in new ways, ways that would not likely occur *sui generis*. Each new probe from a tutor can help writers to break out of conditioned patterns they find themselves immersed in, offering the possibility, on the one hand, of a solution to a perplexing writing problem or, on the other hand, of a dramatic new insight. In this way, a writing tutor's unfamiliarity with discourse conventions can be seen as one of his or her greatest strengths. Not only can the tutors provide access to new pathways and search strategies, but they can also help students to attain what Arthur Koestler has referred to as "bisociative thought"—the ability to discover previously-undetected connections between the knowledge structures of two different fields.

The experience of a tutor in my own writing center can help to illustrate this phenomenon particularly well, I think. As she explains it,

> *I was working with a civil engineering student, Rashid, on a paper about housing construction practices in Saudi Arabia, his native country. Rashid had written the paper in conjunction with a survey he planned to conduct when he returned home, a survey which asked questions about personal preferences in architectural style like, "Do you prefer open or enclosed spaces?" and "Do you prefer natural or artificial lighting?" As we worked through the paper and the survey questions, I had to ask Rashid several times to explain some of the construction and architecture terms, since I don't really know much about the field myself And I also had to ask him to clarify exactly what his point was in the paper. He didn't seem really sure about it either, probably because there were so many questions on so many different topics in the survey that the paper had a lot of trouble pulling them all together. As we kept going through it, I noticed that a lot of the questions had to do with gender issues—"Do you think women should be seen in public?" "What rooms in the house should be for women's use?"—and the like. I thought this was really interesting, given my interest in women's issues, so I started asking him questions about it, and the more we talked, the more he began to see that gender could be a focus for his paper, and he really started to pull it together.*

CONCLUDING REMARKS

Ultimately, I think, this is the kind of thinking that WAC—and a college education in general—strive for, and it seems clear that writing centers can play an important role in helping to forge these new, revealing, and insightful connections in student writing. Questions about discourse communities, discursive practices, and discipline-specific conventions will continue to be the subjects of debate in writing centers and in WAC programs (as well they should), but they need not be seen as reasons for despair. Under less-than-perfect circumstances, when WAC programs stray from the principles of writing-in-the-disciplines or writing-to-learn, then writing centers can—if they wish—take a proactive role with students, encouraging them to confront issues of disciplinary through pointed questions about audience, tone, style, and format.[4] Under more ideal circumstances, when WAC programs are working hard to immerse students in a particular discipline's modes of inquiry and rhetorical tropes, then writing centers should feel confident that their institutional position (the *environmental* role) and their pedagogical practices (the *cognitive* role) can supply significant, concrete benefits to students even though their tutors may not share the content knowledge of the students they work with.

In sum though WAC programs and writing centers may work well together when there are administrative, institutional, or pedagogical failures involved in their operations, they function together best and most productively when the instructional mission of each is enacted fully, when the epistemological differences between the two programs are seen not as points of contention but as alternative positions of strength.

NOTES

1. For the purposes of this paper, I wish to focus on the difficulties that emerge from WAC programs that are construed as WID, or Writing In the Disciplines, rather than as WTL, or Writing to Learn. Though related in some aspects of their pedagogy, the two WAC approaches have distinctly different goals and generally employ writing for quite different purposes. WAC as Writing to Learn encourages the use of writing as a tool to help students learn subject matter and, often, to make personal connections to their own experience and interests. It employs personal journals, short in-class writing activities, and writing-process teaching strategies to facilitate learning, and since much of the writing students produce as a consequence is relatively short, personal, and ungraded, writing center tutors see relatively little of it. A WID program, on the other hand, though it may use some Writing-to-Learn activities as a part of classroom process, has *professionalization* as its focus, a desire to teach students what it means to write, talk, and think as members of a particular discipline. The writing projects students undertake in these courses may be collaborative, but they are also, presumably, longer, more complex, more centered in the activities of a discipline than those in WTL courses, and writing center tutors are more likely to encounter and engage with the results. When I refer to WAC in this paper, then, I wish to make it clear that I am referring explicitly to the practice of Writing In the Disciplines.

2. I should emphasize once again at this point that the commentary and critique I am advancing are directed specifically at the problems which arise from the epistemological differences between WID classes, with a primary focus on disciplinary discourse and discipline-specific modes of inquiry, and writing centers. It is not my intention to argue that the WID model is or should be adopted by all undergraduate courses, and neither is it my intention to suggest that conscious myopia or the myth of disciplinarity are endemic—or even applicable—to the majority of classes in an undergraduate curriculum. Nevertheless, I would maintain that whenever tutors are asked to work on papers in subject areas that are unfamiliar to them, they will confront difficulties similar to those they would face with WID papers (which would be even more deeply immersed in the language, tropes, and modes of inquiry in the field).

3. I realize, of course, that no tutorial conference will ever be completely generic or limited only to those aspects of writing that can be abstracted from all

texts. Each tutor will have a wide range of knowledge that intersects many subject areas to a greater or lesser degree. In this respect, no tutor is likely to be completely ignorant about the topic or field of a given paper. However, to the degree that he or she is unfamiliar with the discipline, generic strategies will undoubtedly play a more prominent role in conferences.

4. Richard Leahy offers a strongly proactive model in his article, "Writing Centers and Writing-for-Learning." He, too, notes that many WAC programs run the risk of "losing sight of writing across the curriculum as a whole," noting that many WAC courses and faculty slip quickly into purely transactional writing assignments that deny students the opportunity to make personal connections with their subject matter. He argues that writing centers can take up the slack, as it were, by actively promoting—among both students and faculty—the value of more expressive writing assignments.

WORKS CITED

Applebee, Arthur N. *Writing in the Secondary School: English and the Content Areas.* Urbana, IL: NCTE, 1981.

Bartholomae, David. "Inventing the University." *When a Writer Can't Write.* Ed. Mike Rose. New York: Guilford Press, 1985. 134–165.

Bizzell, Patricia. "Cognition, Convention, and Certainty: What We Need to Know about Writing." *Pre/Text* 3.3 (1982): 213–243.

Bridgeman, Brend, and Sybil B. Carlson. "Survey of Academic Writing Tasks." *Written Communication* 1.2 (1984): 247–280.

Bruffee, Kenneth A. "Collaborative Learning and the 'Conversation of Mankind.'" *College English* 46.7 (1984): 635–652.

Carino, Peter, Lori Floy, and Marcia Lightle. "Empowering a Writing Center: The Faculty Meets the Tutors." *Writing Lab Newsletter* 16.2 (October 1991): 1–5.

Clark, Irene L. Writing in the Center. *Teaching in an Writing Center Setting.* 2nd ed. Dubuque: Kendall/Hunt, 1992.

Dinitz, Susan, and Diane Howe. "Writing Centers and Writing-Across-the-Curriculum: An Evolving Partnership?" *Writing Center Journal* 10.1 (1989): 45–51.

Faigley, Lester, and Kristine Hansen. "Learning to Write in the Social Sciences." *College Composition and Communication* 36.2 (1985): 140–149.

Flower, Linda, and John R. Hayes. "The Cognition of Discovery: Defining a Rhetorical Problem." *College Composition and Communication* 31.1 (1980): 21–32.

——. "A Cognitive Process Theory of Writing." *College Composition and Communication* 32.4 (1981): 365–387.

Fulwiler, Toby. "How Well Does Writing Across the Curriculum Work?" *College English* 46.2 (1984): 113–125.

Fulwiler, Toby, Michael E. Gorman, and Margaret E. Gorman. "Changing Faculty Attitudes Toward Writing." *Writing Across the Disciplines: Research Into Practice.* Ed. Art Young and Toby Fulwiler. Portsmouth: Boynton/Cook, 1986. 53–67.

Geisler, Cheryl. "Literacy and Expertise." *Language and Learning Across the Disciplines* 1.1 (1994): 35–57.

Griffin, C. W. "Programs for Writing Across the Curriculum: A Report." *College Composition and Communication* 36.4 (1985): 398–403.

Hare, Victoria Chou, and D. A. Fitzsimmons. "The Influence of Interpretive Communities on Use of Content and Procedural Knowledge in a Writing Task." *Written Communication* 8.3 (1991): 348–378.

Harris, Muriel. *Teaching One-to-One. The Writing Conference.* Urbana, IL: NCTE, 1986.

———. "The Writing Center and Tutoring in WAC Programs." *Writing Across the Curriculum: A Guide to Developing Programs.* Ed. Susan H. McLeod and Margot Soven. Newbury Park: Sage, 1992. 154–174.

Hayes, John R. and Linda S. Flower. "Identifying the Organization of Writing Processes." *Cognitive Processes in Writing.* Ed. L. W. Gregg and E. R. Steinberg. Hillsdale, NJ: Erlbaum, 1980. 3–30.

Hubbuch, Susan M. "A Tutor Needs to Know the Subject Matter to Help a Student With a Paper: ___Agree ___Disagree ___Not Sure." *The Writing Center Journal* 8.2 (1988): 23–30.

Kinneavy, James L. "Writing Across the Curriculum." *Profession 83.* New York: MLA, 1983. 13–20.

Koestler, Arthur. *The Act of Creation.* New York: Macmillan, 1964.

Knoblauch, C. H., and Lil Brannon. "Writing as Learning Through the Curriculum." *College English* 45.5 (1983): 465–474.

Leahy, Richard. "Writing Centers and Writing-for-Learning." *Writing Center Journal* 10.1 (1989): 31–37.

Mallonee, Barbara C., and J. R. Briehan. "Responding to Students' Drafts: Interdisciplinary Consensus." *College Composition and Communication* 36.2 (1985): 213–231.

Marsella, Joy, Thomas L. Hilgers, and Clemence McLaren. "How Students Handle Writing Assignments: A Study of Eighteen Responses in Six Disciplines." *Writing, Teaching, and Learning in the Disciplines.* Ed. Anne Herrington and Charles Moran. New York: MLA, 1992. 174–188.

Mayher, John S., Nancy B. Lester, and Gordon Pradl. *Learning to Write Writing to Learn.* Portsmouth: Boynton/Cook, 1983.

McCarthy, Lucille Parkinson. "A Stranger in Strange Lands: A College Student Writing Across the Curriculum." *Research in the Teaching of English* 21.3 (1987): 233–265.

Nelson, Jennie. "This Was an Easy Assignment: Examining How Students Interpret Academic Writing Tasks." *Research in the Teaching of English* 24 (1990): 362–393.

Raimes, Ann. "Writing and Learning Across the Curriculum: The Experience of a Faculty Seminar." *College English* 41.7 (1980): 797–801.

Russell, David R. *Writing in the Academic Disciplines, 1870–1990: A Curricular History.* Carbondale: Southern Illinois UP, 1991.

Scardamalia, Marlene, and Carl Bereiter. "Knowledge Telling and Knowledge Transforming in Written Composition." *Advances in Applied Psycholinguistics: Vol. 2. Reading, Writing, and Language Learning.* Ed. S. Rosenberg. Cambridge: Cambridge UP, 1987. 142–175.

Schwartz, Mimi. "Response to Writing: A College-wide Perspective." *College English* 46.1 (1984): 55–62.

Sherrard, Carol. "Summary Writing: A Topographical Study." *Written Communication* 3 (1986): 324–343.

Sperling, Melanie. "Dialogues of Deliberation: Conversation in the Teacher-Student Writing Conference." *Written Communication* 8.2 (1991): 131–162.

Trimbur, John. "Peer Tutoring: A Contradiction in Terms?" *The Writing Center Journal* 7.2 (1987): 21–28.

Waldo, Mark. "The Last Best Place for WAC: The Writing Center." *Writing Program Administration* 16.3 (1993): 15–26.

Walker, Carolyn. "Communications with the Faculty: Vital Links for the Success of Writing Centers." *Writing Lab Newsletter* 16.3 (November 1991): 11–16.

Wallace, Ray. "The Writing Center's Role in the Writing Across the Curriculum Program: Theory and Practice." *The Writing Center Journal* 8.2 (Spring/Summer 1988): 43–48.

Walvoord, Barbara E., and Lucille P. McCarthy. *Thinking and Writing in College: A Naturalistic Study of Students in Four Disciplines.* Urbana, IL: NCTE, 1990.

Young, Art. "The Wonder of Writing Across the Curriculum." *Language and Learning Across the Disciplines* 1.1 (1994): 58–71.

Writing Centers and WAC Programs as Infostructures: Relocating Practice within Futurist Theories of Social Change

Christina Murphy

Joe Law

Ellen Fremman always enjoys the surge of activity that comes with the beginning of a new school term, and academic year 2008–2009 promises to be especially busy. At the moment Fremman, a team leader with Campus Writing Programs (CWP), is consulting with Keith Johnson. Johnson is new to the faculty at Western Valley State University, where fall classes will begin in two weeks. While he was completing his doctorate at a much larger, research-oriented institution, his teaching experience was limited to grading exams for a large lecture section each semester and twice taking over his major professor's graduate seminar when she was away for a conference. Part of Johnson's teaching assignment for this fall is a section of Economics 200, a writing-intensive course in the general education sequence required of all students. He will have fifty students from all majors, and each will be expected to produce at least 2,000 words of writing, some of it revised in light of his response to it.

Working together in a synchronous chat mode, Johnson and Fremman are going over the drafts of a syllabus and writing assignments he has previously e-mailed to her. At their first meeting, Fremman had guided him through Western Valley State University's Institutional Research online profile of the students enrolled in his class and had shown him EC 200 assignments from WVSU and from similar courses at the other schools in the Campus Writing Programs' Online Archive. At the moment they are discussing ways to connect his writing assigments more explicitly to the instructional goals of the class and to accommodate the various learning styles identified in the student profiles. Before their meeting is over, they will have established an agenda for the training sessions that will be held for the WVSU Writing Center consultants who will be working with Johnson's students on campus. By the time classes begin, Johnson's syllabus and assignments will be posted on the CWP Web page, where they will be available to the students in his class, consultants in the Writing Center, the rest of the campus community, and the other schools served by CWP. Because Johnson's materials for his writing-intensive courses will be archived indefinitely, they will also provide one means for the department to assess Johnson's progress as a teacher.

Fremman's next online appointment is with Anna Collier, who teaches chemistry at Middletown Community College. Fremman wants to enlist Collier for an interactive video conference at which Collier would demonstrate the project she worked out with CWP last year, online lab books with video simulations of several experiments. This conference will be joined by another CWP associate, Pat Lopardo, who will discuss upgrading the graphics in the program and increasing its speed, While that meeting is going on, other members of the CWP team may be working on any number of projects at the twenty schools where they have contracts: pairing instructors teaching their first writing-intensive courses with mentors in the same discipline, facilitating online alliances between businesses and technical writing classes, training local campus Writing Center consultants to work with specific classes and assignments, troubleshooting network problems, documenting changes in instructional practice and institutional culture, and designing assessment instruments to measure the effectiveness of those changes. Providing these customized services requires specialists in a number of fields, sometimes freelancers who are contracted for individual projects. More often, the core group of people employed by CWP work together on different aspects of a number of assignments, assuming more or less responsibility in the group according to their expertise. Though CWP has a central office with workstations and conference rooms available, many of the staff work from their homes, staying in constant contact electronically but seldom seeing each other.

For academicians used to the centrality of the classroom—and of the academy itself—in education, this scenario might seem an unlikely futuristic projection. Yet many aspects of this scenario are already in place, and three dominant trends indicate that Ellen Fremman's methods are more likely to be the future of educational delivery systems in writing instruction than will the traditional academic classroom buttressed by independent local Writing Centers and Writing Across the Curriculum Programs. Those three trends are technology, demographics, and the available funding sources for education. Because the history of education proves undeniably that social trends shape the educational process, it is crucial that writing program professionals understand how these trends will redefine educational systems in the twenty-first century. As social systems theorist Don Tapscott (1996) indicates, these trends offer both "promise and peril." The most important role for educators will be to configure these trends toward significant social and educational goals.

In the October 3, 1997, issue of *The Chronicle of Higher Education,* Jeffrey R. Young's "Rethinking the Role of the Professor in an Age of High-tech Tools" raises the question of how radically technology will change the roles of faculty members. Young states that "new technologies could take over many of the instructional duties that now define professors' jobs" and offers some striking possibilities:

- Courses could be designed in distant cities by teams of top faculty members and technology experts who could craft lessons that might mix online materials and face-to-face meetings with on-site instructors.
- Individual professors' lectures could be replaced by multimedia Web sites that could include video clips of famous scholars in the field.
- Tests could be selected from national test databases, or administered by outside organizations—eliminating even grading from the professor's portfolio. (A26)

As a result of the "unbundling" of their many duties, "professors could spend more time leading discussions that take place in classrooms and in online chat areas" (A26). "None of those ideas are science fiction," Young emphasizes. "Experiments in each of the areas are already under way, and seem certain to succeed eventually in one form or another" (A26).

For writing program professionals, it is vital to comprehend the immediacy and dramatic momentum of the technological change in educational settings that Young describes. Prior to the emergence of this technology, Writing Centers and Writing Across the Curriculum Programs, for example, had changed very little from their original concepts. Both Writing Centers and WAC Programs emphasized one-to-one contact or small group dynamics, both programs were relatively easy to situate within an institution in terms of the academic personnel shaping the program and the audience for whom the programs were intended, and the focus of both programs was consistently narrow in serving specific populations of students and faculty on a given campus. A person associated with early manifestations of such programs—such as the Writing Lab at the University of Iowa in the 1930s (Kelly 1980) or the university-wide Prose Improvement Committee at the University of California at Berkeley in the late 1940s (Russell 1992, 28)— would have had little difficulty taking over one of these programs in the late 1980s since so little had changed in the knowledge structures and day-to-day operations of either program. Even more significantly, hardly anything had changed in the paradigms that defined both programs because the controlling philosophies of education had not changed throughout most of the twentieth century.

The wide-scale introduction of new technology in the early 1990s, especially the development of multimedia applications and the extensive use of the Internet, generated the need to rethink many traditional components of education. This need to rethink philosophies and practices, Don Tapscott and Art Caston claim, is the central fact of contemporary society's transition into the twenty-first century. In *Paradigm Shift: The New Promise of Information Technology* (1993), they point out that social institutions responsive to this paradigm shift will survive; those that have "severe difficulties embracing the change" or that remain "constrained by traditional approaches" are in danger of elimination through irrelevance (xi). We find the concerns of Tapscott and Caston of particular importance to education because, as Michael D. McMaster claims in *The Intelligence Advantage: Organizing for Complexity,* "politics, business, and education have managed to remain far behind in their integration of new thinking" (1996, x). Peter Drucker makes this point even more trenchantly: "Every few hundred years throughout Western history, a sharp transformation has occurred. In a matter of decades, society altogether rearranges itself, its world views, its basic values, its social and political structures, its arts, its key institutions. Fifty years later, a new world exists. And the people born into that world cannot even imagine the world in which their grandparents lived and into which their own parents were born" (qtd. in McMaster 1996, xv).

We would like to argue that the "new world" educational institutions are entering will have particular relevance for the shape of writing programs in the twenty-first century. Writing Centers, WAC Programs, and their offshoots in centers for academic excellence are the primary means through which students and faculty are introduced to technology in educational settings. Therefore, writing program professionals must be aware of major trends currently influencing electronic technologies as educational delivery systems. Like many social theorists, McMaster sees in the contemporary era a major paradigm shift in the transformation from machine-based to information-based economies and social realities. Describing this transformation as the move from the Industrial Age to the Age of Information or the Age of Knowledge, he claims that "to make the shift in thinking, we need the willingness to unlearn the old and the courage to grapple with the new and unfamiliar" (xviii). Tapscott describes this change in similar terms. In *The Digital Economy: Promise and Peril in the Age of Networked Intelligence,* he defines twelve themes as central to the new "digital economy" of the Information Age: knowledge, digitization, virtualization, motecularization, integration/internetworking, disintermediation, convergence, innovation, prosumption, immediacy, globalization, and discordance (1996, 43–72). We find that all twelve themes are relevant to the future of writing programs and to the influence writing programs will have upon educational practices in the twenty-first century.

With the theme of Knowledge, Tapscott claims that the "knowledge content" of products is increasing and will continue to be a central component of future products. Copy machines that can pinpoint the source of their dysfunction and can phone a central repair station to schedule repairs are but one instance of the ways in which machines will assume many of the functions previously carried out by humans. In writing programs, the theme of Knowledge will play an important role in the ways in which multimedia technology interacts with users by assuming many of the lower-level "cognitive" functions and by serving as "instructors" in some aspects of the learning process. That writing program professionals should be aware of this trend and participate in structuring the "knowledge content" of educational technology seems fundamental to the success—indeed, to the very survival—of writing programs in increasingly technological settings. At an even more fundamental level, learners who come to Writing Centers or who participate in WAC classes will come from a world in which the "knowledge content" of machines will be a given, and the cognitive processes of these learners already will have been shaped by this type of technological interaction. Thus, it is essential that writing program professionals understand the new ways in which learners will process, interpret, and apply knowledge via their continued interactions with technology in nearly all aspects of their lives.

Tapscott uses the term digitization to describe the movement from the physical transportation of information to the conversion of information into bits that are conveyed electronically at the speed of light. The advantages are not only speed but also capabilities to compress vast amounts of information and to merge many forms of information into multimedia documents. Digitization makes e-mail possible, in contrast to the earlier transportation of mail via physical delivery systems of trucks, planes, post offices, and mail carriers. While e-mail has speeded up the delivery process, it has also radically changed the way in which people can collaborate by eliminating all spatial and temporal restrictions and making collaboration immediate and global. That digitization will continue to be a component of how people will communicate and collaborate is a given of the Knowledge Age, and Writing Centers and WAC Programs must be aware that students will learn and communicate through virtual texts in the next century. The knowledge of how to teach students to create virtual texts, as well as to teach students via virtual texts, will be an essential component of Writing Center and WAC instruction.

Once information has been digitized, virtualization is possible. Tapscott uses the example of how numerous options are created when physical shelf space in a grocery store is transformed into virtual shelf space in a computer. Certainly, we already see similar virtualization when writing programs no longer need to be housed in physical spaces on campuses but can become, instead, virtual centers for interaction and instruction. Online Writing Centers (OWLS) are but one small application of virtualization to writing instruction, but they presage future trends in the movement away from the concept of a "center" or location toward a virtual "center" of global access.

Tapscott describes molecularization in this fashion: "The old corporation is being disaggregated, replaced by dynamic molecules and clusters of individuals and entities that form the basis of economic activity. The organization does not necessarily disappear, but it is transformed. 'Mass' becomes 'molecular' in all aspects of economic and social life" (51). In the transition from mass to molecular economic activity, the roles of consumer and producer can be merged—a development that digitization and other aspects of virtualization make possible. Tapscott illustrates with the manufacture of blue jeans. Previously, manufacturers would generate large runs of jeans for a mass market of "unindividualized" individuals. In the Knowledge Age, one consumer with technological access can customize the fit of the jeans, the color, the fabric, and so forth and can order one "molecularized" pair of jeans designed expressly for that one consumer. In time, the concept of "mass marketing" will be replaced by "molecularized marketing" as consumers play an increasingly active individual role in the creation, marketing, and production of merchandise that fits their own particular tastes and needs.

In the world of writing programs, as in the business world, molecularization will be the future of educational technology and instruction. The old industrial concept of "mass" instruction that has dominated classrooms and large lecture halls will be replaced by educational methods in which the individual is an active and interactive creator in the instructional process. While Writing Centers have tended to emphasize one-to-one instruction (as articulated, for example, by North 1984 or Harris 1986), the learning structure of the tutoring session still tends to follow broad principles or conceptual designs determined by the tutor. With molecularization, an increased emphasis upon individual learning will enhance one-to-one instruction in that the learner will have more control in conceptualizing, shaping, and assessing the tutoring process. The learner will be able to design tutoring sessions and approaches geared to his or her own highly individualized needs, whereas, currently, this responsibility rests largely with the tutor.

Likewise, molecularization will require that WAC professionals respond more dynamically and more extensively to the course design and pedagogical needs of individual faculty members. Workshops designed to emphasize commonalities among disciplines or among faculty members with similar pedagogical and assessment concerns will most likely yield to a more individualized approach drawn from an "archive" of knowledge that is "molecularized" for each instructor. Similarly, each instructor will also expect from WAC professionals the ability to participate in the "molecularization" of his or her own pedagogical needs and objectives—much as the consumer used Virtualization to create the physical product that best suits that consumer's immediate needs and objectives. High among the instructor's needs, more-over, will be accommodating the varying needs of the students who consti-tute each class. The customer "market of one" in business will become the instructor "market of one" for each pedagogical requirement associated with the instructor's educational objectives.

Integration/internetworking are central components of many Writing Centers and WAC Programs through the use of the Internet. What the future will offer will be the extension of Integration/internetworking beyond indi-vidual campuses to broader, perhaps centralized, national databases—much in the fashion that Young suggests in *The Chronicle of Higher Education* (1997). At present the integration of Writing Center and WAC information is often conducted informally through conferences, meetings, and limited discussions on listservs and other online discussion groups. Internetworking is similarly informal. Though some groups have tried to establish clearing houses for In-ternet resources, individual writing program professionals continue to set up independent Web sites that may be linked to only a few others or none at all, and that often needlessly produce similar versions of existing materials. Ex-tending integration/internetworking so that the knowledge base is broadened and made more accessible will be a central challenge for Writing Center and WAC professionals. It will also be an important component of how new pro-fessionals are introduced to the field and trained for future roles.

Integration/internetworking enhances the movement toward molecular-ization, convergence, innovation, prosumption, and immediacy. In a molecu-larized learning environment, the older roles of instructor (producer) and learner (consumer) are collapsed via Prosumption into one role in which the learner creates the instructor and the instructional means by which to learn. Like Tapscott's purchaser/producer of customized blue jeans, learners become involved in the actual production process of their knowledge; in this case, though, the product has greater consequences in that "human collaboration on the Net becomes a part of the international repository of knowledge" (Tapscott 70). In addition, presumption and integration/internetworking demonstrate Tapscott's theme of convergence; in an educational setting, computing, com-munications, and content merge into something new that cannot be defined exclusively as either process or product. Immediacy is the most important as-pect of learning and instruction via the Internet in that all learning becomes real-time learning that is constantly updated. Compare the process to the pub-lication of data in print media. By the time a book or journal article is being printed, the information it contains often is outdated or could be enhanced by the inclusion of new information. With the Internet, the updating and imme-diacy of information can be made real for learners in a matter of seconds so that knowledge is current, dynamic, fluid, and interactive. The implications of this process invite—and necessitate—innovation in instructional methods and technology. Ultimately, globalization will be the largest outcome of the twelve themes Tapscott describes in that the global network will become the backbone of educational instruction with immediate access to increasingly broader bases of knowledge as well as to interaction in wider ranges of discourse communities supporting, sustaining, evaluating, and disseminating that knowledge. Again, these are important aspects of how future writing program professionals will be trained and will carry out their roles via electronic technologies.

Disintermediation involves the elimination of intermediaries in economic activity—in essence, the classic elimination of the middleman. Travel agents represent to Tapscott one group that faces imminent disintermediation through the introduction of online booking of airline tickets. Once a consumer has access to all flight and fare information and can book his or her tickets via the Internet, as is now possible, the travel agent no longer has a meaningful function and can be disintermediated from the process. We would like to argue that disintermediation is one of the key likelihoods facing writing programs. We can easily envision a scenario in which writing programs within the academy are disintermediated by the business and professional communities—a prospect we can also easily envision for many other aspects of educational systems. Nor are we alone in forecasting the possibility. Jeanne Simpson makes a similar argument in "Slippery Sylvans Sliding Sleekly into the Writing Center—Or Preparing for Professional Competition" (1996). In fact, her scenario is not a projection but an emerging educational reality. For example, a headline in the September 19, 1997, issue of *The Chronicle of Higher Education* announces, "Tutoring Companies Take Over Remedial Teaching at Some Colleges." In that story, Ben Gose states, "Remedial education is becoming big business. Kaplan [Education Centers] and another company, Sylvan Learning Systems, are designing, overseeing, and in some cases actually teaching remedial courses at a handful of colleges" (1997, A44). While, at present, the focus of Kaplan and Sylvan is upon remedial programs, it is not difficult to imagine the same approach applied to freshman composition, advanced writing courses, writing courses across the disciplines, the tutoring practices of Writing Centers, and the instruction of faculty members on the use of writing as a pedagogical tool.

Threats of disintermediation—together with the unfamiliarity of much of the technology and the bewildering speed of its development—lead to Tapscott's final theme: discordance. As he says, because of these developments, "unprecedented social issues are beginning to arise, potentially causing massive trauma and conflict" (66). Tapscott singles out traditional education as particularly vulnerable, noting its failure to meet the needs of the economy and predicting that learning will be provided increasingly by the private sector (67). Because learning can take place outside schools and because technology can take over many of the functions of teachers within schools, Tapscott sees teachers facing "a Catch-22 situation—become irrelevant by resisting change or possibly become irrelevant by leading it" (67).

If disintermediation alarms teachers, it is understandably attractive to academic administrators. Simply put, purchasing, maintaining, and updating computer, network, and software systems is expensive, and the cost can be disproportionate to other educational priorities and needs. Thus, it is not surprising that businesses offer attractive replacements or allies in this process of providing educational technology. Businesses generally have more capital to invest in technology and to keep systems current than do most public school systems, community colleges, colleges, and universities. This most important fact is an outgrowth of the two connected major trends that, in conjunction with technology, are currently shaping educational system—demographics and available funding sources for education.

Demographics play an important role in education through their influence upon funding patterns. In America, the fastest growing segment of the population is individuals over the age of eighty-five. One consequence of this pattern is that a large proportion of the tax burden for education falls to people of retirement age and beyond. Often these individuals have paid taxes to support the schooling of one or two generations and, upon reaching retirement, no longer have the means for or interest in providing further funding for still another generation of students. The tight educational funding in Florida, Arizona, California, and Texas—states with large retirement populations and a high percentage of senior citizens—suggests the coming national trend in educational funding. Whereas education used to be state supported, it is now state assisted and may soon be merely state located. In a related vein, the public's trust in education is down as increased spending on education through the 1950s to the 1980s has not resulted in higher testing scores or in a better educated work force. In fact, scores have declined, and business and professional communities regularly question the quality of the education those entering the work force have received. As a consequence, educational funding generally can no longer depend upon the traditional nexus between the populace and the schools but must look instead to other sources for additional revenues. Ironically, as the need for educational technology increases to prepare each generation for the work force and social systems they will encounter, educational systems are increasingly unable to bear the cost.

In tight budget times, in which each expenditure for education must be examined carefully, it makes perfect sense that the high cost of technology would come under the greatest scrutiny. Thus, we see disintermediation for writing programs and other aspects of education as a strong possibility for the next century. That is why writing program professionals must be aware of this trend in order to shape the trend rather than be shaped by it. If social changes driven by economics and demographics lead to the "outsourcing" of writing programs, writing program professionals should help design the alliances education will create with the business and professional communities. Otherwise, we are only a few steps away from the disintermediation of many educational functions that will be taken over by businesses. Businesses, for example, can design Writing Centers of their own to train employees for the specific writing tasks and software systems they will encounter. Businesses have greater resources to set up and to maintain state-of-the-art Writing Centers than do many state universities struggling to survive with greatly reduced tax revenues. WAC Programs will not be immune to possible disintermediation by businesses in that corporations, knowing what types of training in writing and critical thinking skills their employees will need, can easily set up institutes for teachers and students that will do much of the work of WAC workshops and conferences, perhaps doing so with greater skill and efficiency because of their precisely developed emphasis.

Some academicians might view the scenarios of disintermediation we have described as alarming, but we see heartening possibilities if four important attitudes are embraced. First, we must be aware that the training for future writing program professionals will change and must change and that those of us currently at work in this field must have significant input into the training of our future Ellen Fremmans. The training of writing program professionals has gone through only two cycles in this century. In the earliest days, those drawn to this work generally were trained in traditional literature programs and found the way into Writing Centers or WAC Programs by chance more often than by design. In the second cycle, starting in the mid-1970s when universities began to offer Ph.D.s in rhetoric and composition, writing program professionals could study rhetorical theory and the application of cognitive psychology and composition theory to tutoring practices in the Writing Center and writing pedagogy in WAC Programs. In the next century, a third cycle will begin as people like Ellen Fremman come to writing program administration through different paths than a Ph.D. in English. Such people will receive training in literacy issues and rhetorical theory as part of their studies in educational technology. In fact, many may receive multiple majors in computer science, neurolinguistics, cognitive psychology, business administration, systems theory, and so forth. Their degrees may represent true interdisciplinarity in assimilating, from many disciplines, the training and perspectives necessary for carrying out the complex demands of teaching writing and critical thinking via electronic literacy. We must give careful consideration to the types of courses, internships, and learning environments that will constitute this new preparation, and we must be active participants in designing new programs and philosophies.

Second, we must begin to direct attention away from the recurring micro-debates that have characterized Writing Center and WAC scholarship and onto the macro-debates that will engage a broader audience from many areas in the social and educational spectrum. Debates on whether Writing Centers are extensions of classroom pedagogy or exist in opposition to the classroom as the central learning structure in education will be meaningless when the concepts of "Writing Center" and "classroom" will themselves be redefined in the next century. We must move toward broader discussions of literacy in a technological age and ground our discussions in the social changes we are encountering now.

Third, we must look at what is actually happening in education and in systems theory in our social institutions and reduce the fear zone surrounding dynamic change so that we can be active participants in the process. We can no longer afford to idealize what used to be or to cling to the past because it is familiar. Instead, we must have a willingness to turn loose of the familiar in order to examine what constitutes value and quality within the new paradigm and the new realities it will create. As James C. Wetherbe argues, we must find the "points of leverage" through which we can have an effect on society and the broadest aspects of the educational process (1995, 12). Although it is uncertain what forms education will take in the next century, it is certain that education will always continue within social systems. Therefore, we must look to those systems so that we can assume roles of leadership in education. While we must be attuned to change, we must also seek continuities from which we can construct new roles and practices.

Fourth, we must be willing to learn from our students. They deal with and live in this emerging world, and their sensibilities will help orient us to the new landscape, the cognitive, affective, and behavioral backgrounds against which perspective and vision will develop. Their views of "text," for example, will necessarily differ from ours, and theirs is the view that will emerge as the leading one. For example, definitions of who "owns" the text are becoming increasingly problematic in the Internet era, and the eventual resolution of those issues will have important ramifications for tutoring and tutor training. From students familiar with the new ways of working with electronic texts, we need to learn to reconceptualize collaboration, for contemporary technologies are opening innovative possibilities that far exceed our current paperbound practices. In fact, we need to be prepared to reconceptualize far more fundamental concerns about writing itself. Jay Bolter, a professor at Georgia Tech who studies the impact of technology upon language change, is concerned about the difficulties that will arise in teaching writing as computers become increasingly adept at transcribing speech. What will happen to the familiar conventional boundaries between speech and writing when we dictate everything? "The English community is totally unprepared for this," he says bluntly (qtd. in Hamilton and Rhodes 1997, 15). Such a statement constitutes a mandate for writing program professionals to find ways to take action now.

Learning is an action concept. It is not simply having a new idea or insight; instead, learning involves taking effective action (Argyris 1993). Certainly, there are compelling opportunities for us to act upon what we learn from the emerging digital economy, as two recent developments indicate. Since the fall of 1995, a design team commissioned by the Western Governors' Association has been at work on plans for a virtual university that will serve that entire region. The "Goals and Visions" statement for that university explicitly says that it is being developed in response to the constraints of "limited resources and the inflexibility and high costs of traditional educational practices and by outdated institutional and public policies." The new virtual university is committed to "shifting the focus of education to the actual competence of students and away from 'seat time' or other measures of instructional activity." Instead, instructional activity should be "focusing on needs of students and employers rather than instructional providers." That means, among other things, providing "flexible and responsive" delivery of instruction that is not "constrained by the fixed schedules and sequential structure typical of current educational delivery." In fact, this virtual university is identified as a "non-teaching" entity, one "not providing instruction directly, but drawing upon needed capacity whenever it exists, both in colleges and universities, and in the private sector and among individual experts as well" ("Western Governors" 1997). Similar to the Western Governors University plan is the Southern Regional Electronic Campus, an enterprise being organized by the Southern Regional Educational Board, a consortium of schools from a fifteen-state region. Drawing on existing resources at a dozen schools, the new electronic campus is scheduled to "open" in January 1998 (Blumenstyk 1997).

There is much to be gained by working in tandem with new enterprises like these. For many years, Writing Center and WAC practitioners have rightly opposed the standardized mass instruction created by traditional corporate structures. However, the digital economy provides the technical capability to create genuinely individualized instruction, and ventures like Western Governors University and the Southern Regional Electronic Campus demonstrate that society values and seeks innovation that responds to its needs. Because Writing Centers and WAC Programs have a consistent history of developing pedagogical strategies to meet the needs of the students and faculty with whom we work, we may be better positioned than more traditional forms of instruction to adapt to new conditions. Writing programs need to learn from businesses that have succeeded in the new digital economy, like those described by Richard J. Mahoney, former CEO of Monsanto. In "'Reinventing' the University," he notes that corporations learned to form alliances with other companies "to share expertise, cut costs, reduce risk, and increase profits." These partnerships "enabled companies to combine disparate skills and share the ultimate rewards" (1997, B5). As a source of funding and technological resources, private industry may well have much to offer educators; in turn, writing program professionals can offer their knowledge of learning theory, interpersonal skills, collaborative practices, rhetorical theory, cognitive theory, and assessment. This exchange will benefit all involved, particularly students, whose education would then be integrated into the world in which they are actually living. Mahoney's conclusions are just as relevant for writing programs as for corporations: "Redesign need not mean 'gulag' living standards or sacrificing programs that enrich the university experience for students and faculty members. But a university's failure to redesign itself may, by default, make straitened standards a reality" (B5).

While disintermediation seems a threat to what we know now, it may be an invitation for us to transform ourselves as we embrace and actually shape change. In discussing the "empowering nature" of the digital revolution, Nicholas Negroponte, Professor of Media Technology at Massachusetts Institute of Technology, writes, "The harmonizing effect of being digital is already apparent as previously partitioned disciplines and enterprises find themselves collaborating, not competing.... The access, the mobility, and the ability to effect change are what will make the future so different from the present" (1995, 230–31). If there is peril in the Digital Economy, there is promise as well.

WORKS CITED

Argyris, Chris. *Knowledge for Action: A Guide to Overcoming Barriers to Organizational Change.* San Francisco: Jossey-Bass, 1993.

Blumenstyk. Goldie. "Southern States Make Plans for Distance-education Program." *The Chronicle of Higher Education* (16 Oct. 1977): n. pag. Online. Internet. 17 Oct. 1997. Available at: http://chronicle.com/che-data/internet.dir/itdata/1997/10/t971016.htm.

Gose, Ben. "Tutoring Companies Take Over Remedial Teaching at Some Colleges." *The Chronicle of Higher Education* (19 Sept. 1997): A44–A45.

Hamilton, Kendall H., and Steve Rhodes. "So I'm Like, 'Who Needs This Grammar Stuff?'" *Newsweek* (20 Oct. 1997): 15.

Harris, Muriel. *Teaching One-to-One: The Writing Conference.* Urbana, IL: NCTE, 1986.

Kelly, Lou. "One-on-One, Iowa City Style: Fifty Years of Individualized Writing Instruction." *The Writing Center Journal* 1.1 (1980): 4–19.

Mahoney, Richard J. " 'Reinventing' the University: Object Lessons from Big Business." *The Chronicle of Higher Education* (17 Oct. 1997): B4–B5.

McMaster, Michael D. *The Intelligence Advantage: Organizing for Complexity.* Boston: Butterworth-Heinemann, 1996.

Negroponte, Nicholas. *Being Digital.* New York: Random-Vintage. 1995.

North, Stephen M. "The Idea of a Writing Center." *College English* 46 (1984): 433–446.

Russell, David R. "American Origins of the Writing Across the Curriculum Movement." *Writing, Teaching and Learning Across the Curriculum,* eds. Anne Herrington and Charles Moran. New York: MLA, 1992. 22–42.

Simpson, Jeanne. "Slippery Sylvans Sliding Sleekly into the Writing Center—Or Preparing for Professional Competition." *The Writing Lab Newsletter* 21.1 (1996): 1–4.

Tapscott, Don. *The Digital Economy: Promise and Peril in the Age of Networked Intelligence.* New York: McGraw-Hill, 1996.

———, and Art Caston. *Paradigm Shift: The New Promise of Information Technology.* New York: McGraw-Hill, 1993.

"Western Governors University: Goals and Visions." WGU Home Page. Online. Internet. (17 Oct. 1997). Available at: http://www.westgov.org/smart/vu/vuvision.7html.

Wetherbe, James C. "Principles of Cycle Time Reduction: You Can Have Your Cake and Eat It Too." *Cycle Time Research* 1.1 (1995): 1–24.

Young, Jeffrey R. "Rethinking the Role of the Professor in an Age of High-tech Tools." *The Chronicle of Higher Education* (3 Oct. 1997): A26–A28.

7

BEYOND THE PHYSICAL SPACE: TECHNOLOGY IN THE WRITING CENTER

Technology is coming to your writing center if it isn't already there. This section provides some guideposts for understanding and controlling the use of technology in writing centers. Advances in technology allow writing centers to assist students in new and interesting ways, yet administrators must take care to consider theoretical and pragmatic concerns when designing writing center services.

Eric Hobson's Introduction to *Wiring the Writing Center*, "Straddling the Virtual Fence," opens this section by exploring possibilities for technology in writing centers and the theoretical underpinnings of those options. His cautious approach to the issue offers a thoughtful beginning to this discussion. Following Hobson's survey of technology issues, Peter Carino offers an informative history of computers in writing centers, beginning in the late 1970s. The trends and changes Carino describes broadens the context with which readers can consider Hobson's cautionary discussion.

Narrowing the issue of technology and writing centers, Muriel Harris and Michael Pemberton's essay systematically describes many options for the virtual writing center, or the Online Writing Lab (OWL), from automated file retrieval to synchronous chat systems to computer programmer considerations for those learning about the technological options of online services. And, they include brief discussions about remembering institutional missions and writing center goals. Dave Healy's essay moves from Harris and Pemberton's initial discussion into a more thorough examination of writing center theory and its relationship with technology, providing questions and insight for consideration when instituting an OWL or improving services that Harris and Pemberton describe. David Coogan outlines a practical example of OWL work by detailing his writing center's early experience with online tutoring and discovering first-hand much of what Harris and Pemberton, Carino, and Hobson discuss.

Closing the section, Irene Clark raises issues of information literacy by exploring what her writing center at the University of Southern California offers students by examining theoretical issues surrounding information literacy support in writing centers. Together, these essays show the possibilities for technology in the writing center. The Carino, Healy, and Cooper and Selfe essays provide a history with theoretical understanding that will enable readers to make more informed decisions about instituting changes that Harris and Pemberton and Coogan detail. Finally, Hobson's essay advocates a cautious, thoughtful advance that will provide the best services to our students.

Straddling the Virtual Fence

Eric H. Hobson

The merging of computers and communication technology has created a new educational frontier, albeit a virtual one. Faced with seemingly endless possibilities for incorporating computers and electronic communication technology into the classroom and other learning environments, many literacy educators are attempting to stake their claim to some of the territory up for grabs on the internet, World Wide Web (WWW), and other emerging and yet-to-be-realized electronic environments. In a scenario akin to the land rushes of the nineteenth century, educators have climbed on to whatever available mode of conveyance (PC, Mac, UNIX, etc.) and have attempted to keep up with the hoard of other users who, metaphorically, are heading west into this virtual landscape. Yet, like their historical predecessors, many educators moving online do so with little chance of achieving their idealized visions of success and limitless bounty for their students and themselves: they use obsolete or inadequate technology; have little-to-no guidance; aren't prepared to deal with hostile neighbors and other predators; haven't planned beyond the initial trip.

As with most new developments, approval for the universal use of computer technology in the teaching of writing has not been unanimous. Many educators, particularly those in the humanities, distrust claims made to support a mass adoption of computer assisted instruction. Most teachers of writing respond to the presence of technology and teaching in one of four ways: rail against its dehumanizing potential; ignore it and hope that it won't affect them too much; explore its uses and implications tentatively; and a small percentage embrace it enthusiastically. Regardless of our individual reactions to the presence of computer and electronically mediated technology in the writing center, one must acknowledge, as does Diana George (1995, 333), that

> the technology is here. We cannot ignore it. Furthermore, we already know that computer technology—the communication revolution—is more powerful than skills-and-drills workbooks on a screen. What we don't quite yet

Hobson, Eric H. "Straddling the Virtual Fence." *Wiring the Writing Center.* Ed. Eric H. Hobson. Logan: Utah State University Press, 1998, ix–xxvi. Permission given by Utah State University Press.

know, I am convinced, is how this 'New World' really will reconfigure our teaching and our tutoring.

Among writing teachers, writing center personnel often have been at the vanguard of the move to online instructional applications, developing a range of variations on tutorial and consulting services that translate to the unique conditions of electronic/computer-mediated communication. As Murphy, Law, and Sherwood's *Writing Centers: An Annotated Bibliography* (1996), and Sherwood's update of that information demonstrates, discussions of educational technology's role, particularly of computers and computer-mediated communications, in working with writers in the writing center setting has been an ongoing and, at times, contentious topic in the composition studies and the writing center communities. The writing center community's discussion of this issue is recorded most consistently within the pages of *The Writing Lab Newsletter*, and more recently in the archives for the email discussion group, Wcenter. This process of program development and critical assessment has been highlighted most prominently in special issues of *The Writing Center Journal* 8.1 (1987) and *Computers and Composition* 12 (1995) which focused on the role(s) of computers within the writing center setting. Writing in the special issue of *Computers and Composition*, David Healy (1995 "From Place") raises the following questions about wired writing centers:

What is the ontological status of a virtual writing center, and what kind of relationship will clients develop with it? How will it be perceived by the rest of the academy? What possibilities and what threats are opened up by going online? (191)

"These are the kinds of questions," Healy continues, "that writing centers must confront in the age of information technology.... Online writing centers represent a window of opportunity. Our challenge is to be reflective and self-critical while the opportunities before us are still flush" (191–92).

While advocating that writing center professionals make use of and take full advantage of the current and emerging potentials for online writing center applications, there is also the need for an equally critical and careful examination of what is to be gained and lost from moving in the direction of more wired writing center work. Given the relative newness of these applications, however, we would be remiss to advocate that the community dive into this type of activity without an awareness of the dangers (real and imagined) and shortcomings that can and do exist. As Dickie Selfe admonished the writing center community in his engagingly titled *Computers and Composition* article, "Surfing the Tsunami: Electronic Environments in the Writing Center,"

Voices of dissent from workers and students in writing centers are or should be an essential element of the planning process if computers and composition specialists and writing center workers want to mediate—at least locally—the massive and often blind "will to technologize" in this culture. (312)

And, as Bruce Pegg demonstrates (1998), the increased numbers of writing centers that offer or are planning to offer online services suggests an abiding interest in the subject of computer-mediated applications for the wired writing center. That interest often crashes against the harsh realities of these writing center professionals' lives—often tenuous professional status; heavy teaching and administrative loads; heavy service expectations; etc.— in such a way as to make the immediate implementation of many of the online services described in the following pages improbable or of secondary importance to more pressing or more pragmatic issues. One common issue that limits the use of online writing center services is that most of the people currently directing writing centers and training the tutors who work in these centers usually have neither the time nor the expertise to explore all the available options and to create online tutorial services. Beyond this limitation, they often lack convenient or adequate access to the required technology and the computer skills needed to undertake the construction and maintenance of these services. Additionally, there are few print resources available on the topic of computer-mediated writing center activity. Articles appear in *The Writing Center Journal* and *Writing Lab Newsletter* on this topic, but rarely in a coordinated, connect manner. Ironically, the best articles and guides appear in electronic forums, such as *Kairos*, a medium still unavailable or unknown to many writing center directors. This lack of access is especially acute for writing center directors and staff in community colleges and secondary schools where computers are neither always widely accessible nor Internet access a given. Regardless of the allure of electronic media, paper documents such as this book remain a primary source for disseminating information among members of this academic community.

PAUSING TO ASK

It is not too far off the mark to say that an increasingly large percent of my professional time and self-definition is mediated and largely determined by the myriad available forms of electronic communication. I benefit directly as a writer, teacher, and member of the writing center community from my colleagues' (those whose work this book reflects directly and those it echoes) efforts to theorize, tinker with, implement, proselytize, and praise the potential applications emerging for electronically mediated forms of writing assistance and professional development based in the writing center. As these technologies expand, develop, and become easily accessible, I anticipate that this linking of personal/professional identity to technology will only continue. Yet, trained in the humanistic and post-enlightenment-bleeding-into-postmodern tradition of skepticism and critique, I tend to step back and ask probing questions—even about things and systems to which I am growing increasingly dependent and indebted.

I have little doubt that computers—and other electronic communication technologies presently available or currently in planning, testing, or initial distribution phases—will continue to play a pronounced role in the work that literacy educators undertake. Who determines what that role will be and the shape(s) it will take, however, is not a given. As Dickie Selfe states, the wave of change is coming—about that there is no doubt. Therefore, as teachers charged with helping students develop needed literacy abilities, we must start to determine how we will interact with this change. Between the alternative of standing defiantly in front of the tidal wave of technological change or of harnessing its momentum to the needs of writing centers and their clients, Selfe opts for the latter for himself and likewise recommends that choice to the writing center community. I concur. Here is a real need for writing center personnel who theorize and implement online and other technological, writing center instructional services and learning environment to explore the implications of these actions, to stop and to check the community's sometimes unbridled enthusiasm.

Peter Carino's reference (1998) to Neil Postman's critique of technology's shaping influence on culture (1998) is particularly apropos given this book's overall careful (re)assessment of computer-mediated communications technology in the writing center. In both Postman's work and in Carino's use of this material is the warning that technology does not "pause to ask" about its impact on culture. This guardedness, shared by all of this book's contributors, is an important critical stance—more so than a comfortable "proceed with caution" stance based on timidity—because it allows these authors the space they need to carefully, insightfully, and precisely assess the results of their actions to date. Keeping with this collection's overriding agenda—pausing to ask—in setting the stage for the material that follows, I want to make a number of observations about the (sometimes ironic; always revealing) way in which the writing center community has wired itself.

Specifically, a number of issues that my colleagues raise and/or reveal about technologically-rich writing center programs warrant careful scrutiny. As we grow increasingly aware, there are implications (positive and negative) to each decision that writing center personnel make about the role(s) that technology will/should play in their particular context. As such, the writing center community's members must carefully (re)assess their desires to join the electronic/virtual wagon train, even as they continue their initial online forays. Critical reflection will help us all decide how and to what extent we will move the types of educational encounters and philosophies held dear by the writing center community at large into the admittedly unknown (a simultaneously terrifying and exciting situation) territory/ies inhabited and made possible by wired writing centers.

WHAT IS THE WRITING CENTER (COMMUNITY) TO (BE)COME?

My understanding of writing processes and literacy/ies is shaped in ways I do/do not easily recognize by my increasing reliance on the personal computer as my primary writing tool and on such electronic communication systems as email and the World Wide Web as both conduits for professional communication and collaboration and as mediums for classroom instruction. At the same time, my fundamental self-definition(s) as a writer and a writing teacher is most definitely *not* yet wedded inextricably to technology in terms of my thinking about, creating, and maintaining the interpersonal relationships found in traditional writing center instructional dyads—teacher/student, tutor/client, mentor/mentee—or in small-group, collaborative settings. This apparently paradoxical personal/professional reality is one that I think I share with writing center colleagues of my generation—first and second generation writing center practitioners.

Cynthia Selfe (1995) acknowledges "the complex knot of issues generated by technology use in writing centers" (309). While she pays attention to a wide range of issues, she focuses particular attention on the give-and-take reality that accompanies any new literacy technology (pencil, printing press, computer, MUD/MOO, etc.), what she describes as

> the potential for increased communication, community building, information access, and literacy education that technology offers students and teachers, but also of the many dangers that technology poses for the academic ecosystem of writing centers, humanities and English departments, and universities—the ways in which technology, many [sic] affect coach-student relationships; the nature of the teaching and learning that goes on in these richly textured spaces; the goals and the missions of writing centers, and the status of these places within educational communities; the lives and Outlooks of coaches, staff, and students who labor within writing centers. (309)

As Selfe tells its, in the midst of our enthusiasm for and implementation of the various ideas, applications, dreams, and desires that inhabit the concept of the wired writing center, there is a pressing need to stop and consider what are the results—immediate and potential—of our online forays. What are the potential reconfigurations of writing centers and of the writing center community that result from its rush to go online, to explore virtual configurations?

The Collaborative Dream Realized?

Although it is too soon to gauge the longevity of these claims, there is no hiding from the fact that the literature about technology and writing—both for the discipline of composition studies and the writing center community—rests on the assumption that technology allows those teachers charged with improving students' writing abilities to do their jobs much more efficiently. Within the closer confines of the literature on online writing centers, including material presented here, there exists a palpable enthusiasm for online writing activity, an almost utopian vision of what the computer-mediated writing environment can help us to achieve. As it has to a large extent in composition circles, so too is it becoming commonplace to encounter many of the following types of claims about the benefits of computers in the writing center: computers in the tutorial setting allow for more equitable and convenient access to center resources and services (Gardner 1998; Kinkead 1988); computers and computer networks encourage collaboration among writers (Farrell 1987, 1989, Jordan-Henley and Maid 1995 "MOOving"); computers decanter authority and enhance tutor training (Chappell 1995, Johanek and Rickly 1995); virtual tutoring represents the future (Coogan 1995, Crump, Jordan-Henley and Maid 1995 "Tutoring," 1995 "MOOving," Kinkead 1988). The consensus of these proponents of a tight integration of computer-mediated tutoring activities is that the computer and writing activities facilitated by computer networks realize the social constructivist ideology and pedagogy advocated by the writing center community within the past decade. Particularly, computers can help to establish community among tutors and encourage collaboration among writers in ways that help to create writing environments and collaborative relationships that are more natural than the artificial ones found in the typical classroom (Crump 1994, Chappell 1995, Jordan-Henley and Maid 1995 "MOOving").

A Technology Defined Caste-Based Community?

In the midst of our enthusiasm for emerging technological applications, and in the midst of our eagerness to tell everyone else about the uses to which we put these applications, the writing center community must recognize the potential for it to unwittingly develop and enact a hierarchy—a class structure—based solely on the extent to which centers do/do not embrace or foreground technology in their day-to-day operations. Much of the community's strength and vitality results directly from its willing acceptance of its members' diverse missions and practices, a recognition of each writing center's situatedness as a primary agent in determining its priorities and procedures. To lose this tolerance to a yardstick based upon websites, online tutoring, and other technological applications would be devastating. Yet, despite our well-meaning assurances to the negative, the potential for doing so is real.

At each conference sponsored by the National Writing Centers Association, as well as at writing center sessions at NCTE and CCCC, the sessions about computer applications in the writing center fill to overflowing and generate tremendous amounts of highly animated and optimistic discussion.

As much as I enjoy these sessions, I am bothered by the looks of consternation on many colleagues' faces, looks that suggest they feel somehow out of the loop, or less viable than their techophile colleagues. In our rush to show what we can do and have done with computers within the context of a particular writing center, it is easy to forget a number of very powerful realities:

Not every center has access to the many resources needed to replicate these efforts;

Not every center's clientele have access to the technology needed to make such projects expedient;

Not every center can determine its future and fate to the extent needed to follow suit;

Not every center's mission or philosophical foundation is commensurate with the assumptions contained in many online writing center projects.

To forget these fundamental differences while we celebrate the technologically innovative achievements of others is to celebrate uncritically. The composite result of that type of spotlighting (and, simultaneously, shunting aside) sends powerfully norming messages about what the community values, about what constitutes full community membership and recognition, and about what types of activity the community validates. This type of community definition, replete with ex/inclusions, is a reality to which we must pay careful attention as we explore technology's role in the writing center and as we continue to discuss the results and the implications of these activities.

A Computer Lab for Writing?

As writing centers develop online resources that increasingly reflect, mimic, replicate, or provide prototypes for many of the online resources found in computer assisted composition classrooms (or, vice versa), and as writing centers encourage more writers to interact with other writers virtually rather than within the close confines of the face-to-face (f2f) tutorial, at what point is the allocation of the current monetary and physical resources no longer easily justified? "What is the value added by the physical writing center?" might become a question that we are forced to respond to should our OWLs and other electronic services attract the focused attention of budget-conscious administrators. The answers we supply must be ones we have thought through with care because they will be directed most often to administrators who understand the powerful sway that technology-linked educational programs hold over the public through a deeply rooted cultural assumption that technology holds the answers to problems, particularly such vexing problems as found in literacy education. To reiterate Wallace's point (1998), if the writing center begins to duplicate (even if only in appearance) the computerized composition classroom and its virtual resources for writers, including online materials and conferencing capabilities, what has the writing center become? What will be its fate? At what point in its expansion into online applications, asks Wallace, does a writing center cease to be a writing center and become a computerized writing classroom? While this is not a popular question, and certainly is not a question answered by this article, it is quite possibly the most important question facing the writing center community as it wrestles with the task of if and how it is possible to take the writing center online with its services and guiding philosophies and value systems intact.

An Obsolete Service?

I raise these questions neither to sound alarmist nor to draw a line in the sand and tell my colleagues that they cross it at their own peril. Issuing ultimatums and yelling "fire" are not effective rhetorical options because they ignore the many pressures that combine within the complicated calculus of most writing center practitioners' program development and maintenance process. I know how hard it is to make time to step back from the pressing needs of the program and assess its present status and needs. In my day-to-day, frenetic existence as a teacher and writing center educator, for instance, it is quite easy for me to react to other writing center's highly visible technology adaptations and to think, "I'd better get a web page up and running that looks as good as Utopia U's," or, "I need to get online tutoring started." What is more difficult, however, is to find/make the time needed to think ahead, to play out the possible scripts that represent my and my program's potential futures its a result of these online enactments. When I make the time to do so, however, one possible future I see finds the writing center and my work within it rendered at worst obsolete and/or redundant, or fundamentally redefined. What I have yet to determine in these scenarios is whether that potential for obsolescence is due to evolution or replacement of the services and attitudes that have defined the writing center and its community. As Peter Carino remarked during the later stages of writing this book, "We could end up complicitous in our own obsolescence if we jump on the bandwagon without asking where it is headed."

DO WIRED WRITING CENTERS SUPPORT TECHNO-CURRENT TRADITIONAL RHETORIC?

As a quick review of the writing center community's literature over the past decade reveals, the community has expended a great deal of energy in the attempt to distance its existence, mission, and pedagogical practices from the "undesirable" taint of serving the conservative ideology imbedded in positivist approaches to writing (Ede 1989, Hobson 1992, Lundsford 1991, Murphy 1991). This desire occupies the philosophical (although, probably not the political) heart of the "writing lab vs. writing center" debate. Writing center proponents found their rallying cries of "individualized instruction," "process," "collaborative learning," "peer feedback," "audience and community accommodation," in a frequently idiosyncratic mix of expressivist and social constructivist thought and practice (Hobson 1992, 1994, Carino 1995 "Theorizing"). The upshot of this concerted and deeply-felt activity was to link the term "writing lab" with pedagogy derided as bereft of validity: worksheets dedicated to grammar and mechanics; repetitive drill exercises for developing and demonstrating mastery of the language; and formulaic writing tasks which reflect conservative culture's value of form and convention over developing writers' critical thinking and communicative flexibility. In opposition to the label "writing lab," "writing center" has come to represent innovative, process-based and contextually- located pedagogy focusing on the student and her need to negotiate her position within many discourse communities (Wallace 1991).

While this overstated history travels well-covered ground, I do so to highlight the following, a situation I find distressing and entertainingly ironic: in their first forays online, many writing centers are creating themselves in the form of their antithesis, that nemesis writing lab. Put bluntly, many OWL's consist primarily of the contents of old filing cabinets and handbooks—worksheets, drill activities, guides to form—pulled out of the mothballs, dusted off, and digitized. In addition to a reliance on these types of materials, by allowing—even encouraging—writers to make use of these online resources, many of these writers write in isolation, simultaneously re-inscribing tenets found in current traditional rhetoric's insistence on originality of ideas (collaboration is a form of cheating) and expressivist rhetoric's Romantic portrayal of the individual as the locus of a personal truth (Berlin 1987, Hobson 1992). While I do not ascribe pernicious motives to my colleagues who have developed these sites—I firmly believe in their good intentions, as I hope they concede my good will and humor as I critique these sites—the explosion of filing-cabinet-like online information available at an increasingly large number of writing center websites, programs that espouse a commitment to seeing writing as complex social phenomenon in their tutoring and tutor training, raises several other points worth reflecting on.

WHAT CAN('T) AN OWL DO THAT A WRITING CENTER CAN('T)?

OWLs, as entities that exist within the physical and virtual space of a computer system, offer writing centers highly efficient and expeditious means to store large amounts of information in incredibly small areas (a hard drive; a 3.5" disk). Stored in the semi-public domain of LANS, Gopher files, and webpages, this is information that writers can access on their own and at their convenience. With this bulk digitized and stored in personal computers and other computer configurations, physical space once devoted to filing cabinets full of print materials and other records can become available tutorial space; staff can also be relieved from the repetitious and tedious clerical task of digging out these materials.

The argument that an OWL offers increased access to many traditionally underserved client populations is quite compelling. It makes sense that Internet access, for instance, does make it possible for many of the less-frequently served client groups that Gardner (1998) mentions to use writing center materials and services at their convenience. Convenience is an important issue for students who commute, who juggle work/family/school obligations, whose access and mobility are hindered by physical disabilities, who are enrolled in distance education programs, who take courses at night or on weekend schedules, and, perhaps, who are exceedingly shy (Kinkead 1988). Does convenience, however, necessarily translate to a quality of service equal to that found in the physical writing center? The jury is still out on this issue. This question is both essential and complex.

Helping novice writers develop the ability and confidence needed to practice the demanding activities of critical thinking, audience analysis and accommodation, idea invention and development, implementation of conventions within specific, discourse communities is a subtle task. Michael Spooner (1994 "A Dialogue"), Jeffrey Baker (1994), and Katherine Grubbs (1994) each raise important questions about how effective online tutorials are for working with less-mature writers, particularly given the medium's lack of paralinguistic cues from which both the tutor and client glean continuous information about the conversation's movement and success. Can an OWL, in its most common current configuration as repository of forms and handouts, accomplish results that are in the writer's best interests and that are consistent with the philosophical and pedagogical principles the writing center community has fought dramatically to make the centerpiece of the community's practice and self-definition?

While I think it is possible to do so, it isn't easy. And ease is the overriding factor behind the fact that the majority of OWL resources look suspiciously like skill driven, current traditional "writing labs." Formatting static webpages isn't that demanding an activity, once one learns basic HTML commands; their upkeep, however, can be incredibly time consuming, a process that a colleague recently referred to as "a sinkhole into which I seem to have cast all of my and my tutors' spare time trying to develop, debug, and maintain." If getting an OWL to the stage where most currently are is a demanding process, creating OWLS that are consistent with the best of the writing center community's social constructivist–influenced theory and practice takes an incredible commitment of time, resources, energy, and continuing/continuous education on the part of everyone involved—planners, administrators, tutors, clients. Most writing center programs do not currently have the resources or the expertise to undertake this more pedagogically defensible version of the wired writing center. Time is a commodity in short supply without the exponentially increasing demands created by the addition of sophisticated online services.

On a much more pragmatic level, I ask, why is it that we feel compelled to pull all this stuff out of the closet anyway? Didn't we work very hard to relegate positivist-based pedagogy to the very margins of writing center activity (Carino 1995 "Theorizing," Ede 1989, Hobson 1992, 1994, Lundsford 1991, Murphy 1991)? If we think that writers can benefit from such electronic handouts and forms, why not let the textbook publishers take on the task—one it seems they already do well, based on the incessant flow of handbooks and workbooks on floppy disks and CD-ROMs flowing across my desk? Is the time it takes to develop (or to digitize) these materials worth the investment and the associated risk of appearing to condone their uncritical use? Frankly, we can tell writers, and other stakeholders who may have an investment (ideological, financial, dependency) in these types of materials, where they can be found—like the U. of Michigan OWL, we can always provide links to such websites—without having to create them ourselves, and in the process of doing so implicitly give our stamp of approval to them and to the pedagogy and ideology to which they adhere. Might we do so for reasons other than pedagogical, driven instead by politics, opportunities for expansion and self-aggrandizement?

WHERE SHOULD WE FOCUS OUR ENERGY?

As each chapter in this collection demonstrates, writing center professionals are being called upon to do more and more, often with the same or fewer resources and with increased expectations. In addition to their roles developing, implementing, and overseeing important support services for all writers within their community, they increasingly wear any number of hats: technology coordinator and chief computer fixer, email and web guru, faculty developer and curriculum coordinator. Nowhere is this situation made more clear than in Ellen Mohr's (1998) detailed history of all of the computer-related courses she has taken in the past few years and extent to which the presence of computers in her writing center has reconfigured both her time and her role in the center. She has moved from being continually engaged in tutoring and tutor training to having less time to be part of these central writing center activities. Now she spends a majority of her time working with such computer-related issues as learning and teaching software packages; ironically, however, her evaluation process still assumes that she is responsible for those tutorial-related activities on which she once focused her activity.

In "Computer Centers and Writing Centers: An Argument for Ballast," an article that responds to the types of situations Mohr describes, Nancy Grimm (1995) points to the costs of trying to accomplish everything and to be everything to everyone when she writes that "writing center professionals need time to focus on issues unique to their location" (324). Using her situation as writing center director at Michigan Technological University as an illustrative example upon which to investigate the costs associated with developing the knowledge and skills base needed to plan and oversee expansion of the writing center into virtual space(s), she writes,

> *If I had to develop expertise in hardware and software, for example, I would not have been able to engage our staff in the program of critical reflection that is leading to some interesting literacy research; nor would I have had time to carry the idea of peer tutoring to other departments on our campus. (324)*

As Ellen Mohr candidly states, "I quickly discovered that I had better things to do with my time." As more writing center directors and their staffs push beyond the first phase of using online resources to advertise general information about the writing center and to make handouts available, Mohr's sentiment may become quite common.

WHEN ARE SOME THINGS PATENTLY ABSURD?

I marvel at the ingenuity and commitment that writing center colleagues bring to their efforts to explore the potential uses to which they can put new technology to work in the writing center. At points, however, we need to acknowledge that, in spite of our best intentions, the results of some of our online efforts approach the sublimely ridiculous, particularly when students take the products of our idealized intentions and use them to achieve their decidedly idiosyncratic ends. My favorite example of this technologically-mediated irony comes from a colleague's writing center, and is, I think, a story that has the potential to become writing center legend:

> *In the hour or so before a regularly scheduled writing center staff meeting, the writing center director observes staff as they worked with clients, particularly the one staff member engaged in a synchronous online tutorial—something that the director had wondered if clients would opt to use, given the need to learn to use the needed chat program. Looking over the tutor's*

shoulder, the director talked to the tutor about the tutorial, its process, ease and difficulties, as well as the tutor's sense of how the client was responding to the advice given and to the online tutorial itself. The tutor mentioned that the process was slow and that she really wished she could talk (f2f) with the client in order to push the discussion to a needed level of depth about the project. Sensing the tutor's need to return to the tutorial, the director moved on.

Two students were using the center's computers in the adjacent room: one printing a paper; one "talking" online. Glancing at the screen, the director realized with a jolt that the student was talking to the tutor sitting fewer than twenty feet away, a situation the tutor was not aware of. The student had opted for the online tutorial because, "I wanted to be able to leave anytime without feeling guilty. And, I thought I could just get my questions answered and not have to talk about all that other stuff the tutors always want you to talk about, like who I'm writing to and why I need more info."

RESEARCHING AND ASSESSING THE "WIRED" WRITING CENTER

As demonstrated throughout this collection, there exist any number of exciting next steps for members of this community to explore within the concept of the wired writing center—video conferencing, distance learning, virtual conferencing spaces, etc. One area that has not received the detailed discussion it should, however, is that of needed types of research related to the technological innovations that writing centers have or are considering implementing. A host of questions about online tutoring, for instance, need to be investigated: What types of writers benefit the most from online tutoring? Are gains in writing development consistent between (f2f) and virtual f2f conferences? What are the dynamics of online talk in comparison to (f2f) conversation? The lack of detailed discussion about how to begin to methodically research and assess our online activity has many sources, including the following:

We are caught up in the rush to get our programs online.
   We are just beginning to zero in on the types of questions we can and should ask.
   We are not generally familiar with or conversant about research methodologies that might apply to this area of writing center practice, and we are generally suspicious about the results of such study.

Stuart Blythe (1998) provides a primer for those members of the writing community who wish to build into their forays into electronic communications, for example, the types of careful and audience-aware planning steps and research necessary to more successfully tailor online services to the needs of actual, not hypothetical, users—users who often come to our services with radically different agendas and needs than we might wish for them or even imagine. Usability research is essential, at some level, to help us create and to justify technology-based writing center innovations. Additionally, while it is not always easy, a point Stuart reiterates, the benefits of doing this type of work are many and can lead us to begin to carry out other types of needed investigation.

Raising the issue of needed research is almost routine call-to-action for the writing center community, one put before the community, it seems, every few years (Neuleib 1984, North 1984 "Writing Center," Severino 1994). As such, I replicate and reiterate comments and charges others have made while raising research issues that I consider promising, enlightening, warranted— even, admittedly, fun—that present themselves as a direct result of the community's exploration of the uses to which it can put technology. Implicit in the following research agenda are the makings of any number of tutor research projects, master's theses, doctoral dissertations, and grant proposals.

1. Who Uses Our OWL? How?

Although I know that initial data keeping is underway in many places, there are currently no published analyses of the user/audience demographics of any OWL, or of how these users interact with the site and the available information and services. While this may not be the easiest data to collect, it seems essential for a number of reasons: to inform specific, concerned stakeholders about the OWL's activity, either to justify maintenance or expansion of budgeted time and monies; to identify the writing support needs of this population of writers, particularly if these needs differ from those identified among users of the physical writing center; to analyze if the current configurations of the service encourage a critical use of the service(s) and increasingly mature approaches to the writing process and the issues that surround it.

Several relatively simple data collection strategies offer a start in this research project, particularly "hit counters" and questionnaires. Because most OWLs are web based, using HTML coding, it is easy to embed a "hit counter" to track the number of times the site is accessed. And most websites do so. Yet, to get a more accurate picture of how the site is used, these tallying devices need to be part of every page in the site. Considered individually and together, the numbers provide a rough composite of the site's high- and low-demand areas, findings that may correlate to user's perceptions of most/least usefulness. A fascinating project would be to see the extent to which these perceptions do/do not coincide with the findings of composition research into composing processes of novice and experienced writers.

The down side of this strategy, however, is the realization that the data collected are highly unreliable, as these counters do not discern between new users and users who, in moving within a site, return to a specific page several times on the way to other pages. Yet, for an initial, low-risk research project, this activity could yield tentative information on which to begin to test the validity of many assumptions that undergird the site's mission and structure.

Questionnaires offer another line of research into OWL users, their experiences, and motivations. Because of the manner in which OWL users access these sites, it seems entirely possible—most likely with the assistance of outside technical expertise—to trace many users to their home email accounts where a questionnaire can be sent. Additionally, it is easy to build a questionnaire into the site itself. In both cases, response depends on the user—they become a self-selecting group, and, thus, their responses cannot be taken as normative—a problem encountered whenever one attempts to research a population using questionnaire instruments. Yet, for the purposes of developing research questions on which to build research projects designed to garner more reliable results, this approach is a good starting place. Additionally, the gathered responses are often illuminating.

As to the question of how do writers use online services, Barbara Monroe (1998) has provided a groundbreaking analysis of online tutorial interaction. She provides a model for many writing center scholars who have the requisite background in linguistics and discourse analysis to replicate her study both to corroborate the patterns she found and to expand on them. There is much to be learned about issues of access, power relations, gender differences and user profiles, online conversational patterns, tutorial dynamics in the absence of physical and contextual paralinguistic cues from this type of analysis of the online tutorial. And, by extension, there is much to be learned about the physical (f2f) tutorial interaction from these studies as well. By comparing what we know about (f2f) tutorials with what we can learn about virtual (f2f) tutorials, we may begin to find answers to a pressing pedagogical question, one with important implications for writing center administration and planning: What client groups benefit the most from online tutoring in terms of their growth as writers?

2. What defines a successful online tutorial? What does one look like?

David Coogan (1998) and Barbara Moore provide a jump start to a fruitful and needed area of writing center research by recording and analyzing the online tutorial and by raising a number of important questions about its relation to the type of face-to-face (f2f) interaction found in the physical writing center tutorial. This inquiry must continue if we are to answer a number of critical questions about virtual tutoring, of which the following are representative examples:

Does/can the online tutorial work effectively and efficiently with higher-order composing concerns?

What does the lack of paralinguistic cues in the virtual tutorial do to the tutorial in terms of how the interlocutors interact and how they define their roles, the conversation strategies employed, the way(s) in which turn-taking and collaboration is signaled, how emphasis and empathy is presented, read, and maintained?

What are the cues tutors use to assess their client's level of engagement and commitment to the tutorial?

Do pacing differences between synchronous and asynchronous online tutorials affect the type and quality of the tutorial interaction and the participants' attitudes?

3. What are the costs of going online?

A refrain common to conference sessions devoted to computer applications in the writing center addresses the unexpected costs of getting and maintaining both computers themselves and online services. Yet, the discussion rarely gets specific: how much did it cost to do X at Y? Admittedly, the dollar costs of computer equipment is hardly static; however, there is a need for members of the community to make a public accounting of the costs incurred in wiring their centers. Other programs need a conceptual ballpark in which to play as they plan and budget their technologically mediated writing center activities.

Beyond presenting in specific dollar amount the costs of creating and maintaining such services as those described in this book, we need people to undertake a more detailed, broader perspective cost analysis. There are costs incurred in attempting any innovation in the writing center and, most of these costs are not immediately translatable into specific dollar figures. For places to start this line of inquiry, consider the following questions: how much is the director's time worth to plan for and to oversee the implementation and upkeep of an OWL? How will this time be replaced in order to ensure continued coverage of the director's preexisting duties? How much is the tutorial staff's time worth while they are trained to tutor in a virtual writing center? What are the costs in terms of replacement time for staff and equipment designated to these new endeavors? What is the impact of such innovation on the center's materials, fixed costs, and services budget? What are the costs in terms of the center's productivity, mission, and staff morale?

4. How should we theorize and/or modify the writing center's mission to reflect technology's influence?

At the same time that writing center practitioners are faced with the question of what to do with the available technology at their disposal, a number of converging factors suggest the necessity to reexamine the writing center's traditional mission in order to determine if it should be modified. Linked to the technological explosion in education is the rapidly expanding and highly competitive distance-education market. Most colleges, many private companies, and even some secondary institutions are beginning to offer credit-bearing coursework via the Internet and the WWW. In the face of these developments, the writing center needs to think carefully about its mission and its duty to students and to its home institution (often competing duties). This (re)assessment will require us to review the theories and practices on which we define our current mission, and may require us to retheorize the center in terms of its mission and configuration; we should also entertain the possibility that the writing center as we have known it has served its purpose and is now facing its demise or absorption into other service providers.

In this line of thought, Selfe and Hilligoss (1994) provide a possible starting point for intrepid members of the writing center community in their attempts to theorize and critique the wired writing center and its role within literacy education. They write,

> As teachers and researchers, we need to study literacy, with computers as an important feature of the setting and the means, a feature that changes literate practices and our understanding of them but neither wholly sustains nor destroys any given literacy....If we have wrongly identified text with literate knowledge, the next fallacy may be "computer knowledge," in which the computer—even a certain kind of computer— becomes the new picture of literate orientation. This is a real possibility. (339)

While these issues are broad and daunting, they are ones that the writing center community must address in order to assure its intellectual and ethical high standards. They may also help to ensure its continued existence in the current or revised form.

WORKS CITED

Baker, Jeffrey S. 1994. An Ethical Question About Online Tutoring in the Writing Lab. *Writing Lab Newsletter* 18.5: 6–7

Berlin, James. 1987. *Rhetoric and Reality: Writing Instruction in American Colleges, 1900–1985*. Carbondale: South Illinois UP.

Blythe, Stuart. 1998. Wiring a Usable Center: Usability Research and Writing Center Practice. Hobson 103–18.

Carino, Peter. 1998. Computers in the Writing Center: A Cautionary History. Hobson. 171–196.

———. 1995. Theorizing the Writing Center: An Uneasy Task. Dialogue: A *Journal for Writing Specialists* 2.1: 23–37.

Chappell, Virginia A. 1995. Theorizing in Practice: Tutor Training 'Lie, from the VAX Lab.' *Computers and Composition* 12: 227–36.

Coogan, David. 1998. Email "Tutoring as Collaborative Writing. Hobson. 25–43.

———. 1995. Email Tutoring: A New Way to Do New Work. *Computers and Composition* 12: 171–181.

Crump, Eric. 1994. A Dialogue on OWLing in the Writing Lab: Some Thoughts on Michael Spooner's Thoughts. *Writing Lab Newsletter* 18.6: 6–8.

Ede, Lisa. 1989. Writing as a Social Process: A Theoretical Foundation for Writing Centers. *The Writing Center Journal* 9.2: 3–13.

Farrell, Pamela B. ed. 1989. *The High School Writing Center: Establishing and Maintaining One.* Urbana: NCTE.

———. 1989. Computers Interact with Writers and Tutors. Farrell. 107–10.

———. 1987. Writer, Peer Tutor, and Computer: A Unique Relationship. *The Writing Center Journal* 8.1: 29–34.

Gardner, Clinton. 1998. Have You Visited Your Online Writing Center Today?: Learning, Writing, and Teaching Online at a Community College. Hobson. 75–85.

George, Diana. 1995. Wonder of It All: Computers, Writing Centers, and the New World. *Computers and Composition* 12: 331–34.

Grimm, Nancy. 1995. Computer Centers and Writing Centers: An Argument for Ballast. *Computers and Composition* 12: 171–81.

Grubbs, Katherine. 1994. Some Questions About the Politics of Online Tutoring in Electronic Writing Centers. *Writing Lab Newsletter* 19.2: 7, 12.

Healy, Dave. 1995. In the Temple of the Familiar: The Writing Center as Church. Stay, Murphy and Hobson. 12–25.

Hobson, Eric. ed. 1998. *Wiring the Writing Center.* Logan, UT: Utah State UP.

———. 1994. Writing Center Theory Often Counters Its Theory. So What? Mullin and Wallace. 1–10.

———. 1992. Maintaining Our Balance: Walking the Tightrope of Competing Epistemologies. *The Writing Center Journal* 13.1: 65–75.

Johanek, Cindy and Rebecca Rickly. 1995. Online Tutor Training: Synchronous Conferencing in a Professional Community. *Computers and Composition* 12: 237–46.

Jordan–Henley, Jennifer and Barry Maid. 1995. Tutoring in Cyberspace: Student Impact and College/University Collaboration. *Computers and Composition* 12: 211–218.

———. 1995. MOOving Along the Information Superhighway: Writing Centers in Cyberspace. *Writing Lab Newsletter* 19.5: 1–6.

Kinkead, Joyce. 1988. The Electronic Writing Tutor. *Writing Lab Newsletter* 12.4: 4–5.

Lundsford, Andrea. 1991. Collaboration, Control, and the Idea of a Writing Center. *The Writing Center Journal* 12.1: 3–10.

Mohr, Ellen. 1998. The Community College Mission and the Electronic Writing Center. Hobson. 151–162.

Mullin, Joan A. and Ray Wallace. eds. 1994. *Intersections: Theory–Practice in the Writing Center.* Urbana: NCTE.

Murphy, Christina, Joe Law, and Steve Sherwood. 1996. *Writing Centers: An Annotated Bibliography.* Westport: Greenwood.

———. 1991. *Writing Centers in Context: Responding to Current Educational Theory.* Wallace and Simpson. 276–288.

Neuleib, Janice. 1984. Research in the Writing Center: What to Do and Where to Go to Become Research Oriented. *Writing Lab Newsletter* 9.4: 10–13.

North, Stephen. 1984. Writing Center Research: Testing Our Assumptions. *Writing Centers: Theory and Administration.* Olson. 24–35.

Olson, Gary A. ed. 1984. *Writing Centers: Theory and Administration.* Urbana: NCTE.

Pegg, Bruce. 1998. UnfURLed: 20 Writing Center Sites to Visit on the Information Highway. Hobson. 197–215.

———. 19 February 1998. Writing Centers Online. *National Writing Centers Association, an NCTE Assembly.* 21 October 1997. <http://departments.colgate.edu/diw/NWCAOWLS.html>.

Self, Cynthia. 1995. Three Voices on Literacy, Technology, and Humanistic Perspective. *Computers and Composition* 12: 309–10.

———, and Susan Hilligoss. eds. 1994. *Literacy and Computers.* New York: MLA.

Selfe, Dickie. 1995. Surfing the Tsunami: Electronic Environments in the Writing Center. *Computers and Composition* 12: 311–22.

Severino, Carol. 1994. The Writing Center as Site for Cross–Language Research. *The Writing Center Journal* 15.1: 51–61.

Spooner, Michael. 1994. A Dialogue on OWLing in the Writing Lab: Some Thoughts About Online Writing Labs. *Writing Lab Newsletter* 18.6: 6–8.

Wallace, Ray. 1998. Random Memories of the Virtual Writing Center: The Modes–to–Nodes Problem. Hobson. 163–170.

———. 1991. Sharing the Benefits and the Expense of Expansion: Developing a Cross–Curricular Cash Flow for a Cross–Curricular Writing Center. Wallace and Simpson. 82–101.

Wallace, Ray and Jeanne Simpson. eds. 1991. *Writing Centers: New Directions.* New York: Garland.

Computers in the Writing Center

A CAUTIONARY HISTORY

Peter Carino

In recent years historical inquiry has found a niche in writing center scholarship. Most of this history has addressed macro issues—such as the professionalization of writing centers (Riley 1994), global notions of center theory or practice (several in *Landmark Essays* 1995), the development of writing center organizations (Kinkead 1995), the nature of early centers (Carino 1995 "Early"), and models for historicizing the center (Healy "Temple," Carino 1996). Micro issues such as tutor training, one-to-one techniques, or computers in writing centers have received less attention as the scholarship has first tried to trace a broader historical arc. Yet these smaller matters certainly underpin macro-histories. Computers in particular present a challenge for center historians because from the early workbook-on-screen programs such as the Comp-Lab modules, to the cumbersome heuristics of early CAI programs such as WANDAH, to todays OWLs, MOOs, and MUDs, computer applications in writing centers have been so varied that it is difficult to draw historical generalizations.

Further complicating this project are the entanglements of center history with larger institutional contexts. While centers can usually reach at least uneasy consensus on matters such as tutor-training, attitudes toward students, and the like, computer use in the center is more closely tied to local funding, technological expertise, and politics—matters further outside the control of directors and tutors than, say, one-to-one pedagogy. For example, at one university a center, without asking, receives twenty networked computers because the administration must spend a large technological grant or state allocation. The center then must craft a pedagogy to include the technology, though lacking the expertise to do so. On a campus less flush the center may have to make do with hand-me-down hardware despite its expertise. These are extremes, but various scenarios in between have governed the acquisition and implementation of technology in writing centers. While many have

Carino, Peter. "Computers in the Writing Center: A Cautionary History." *Wiring the Writing Center*. Ed. Eric H. Hobson. Logan: Utah State University Press, 1998. 171–196. Permission given by Utah State University Press.

often risen to the occasion, the technology has at least partly determined the direction of many more.

And technology can be a determining force in more ways than one. As Neil Postman (1992, 8–9) writes, "technology imperiously commandeers our most important terminology. It redefines 'freedom,' 'truth,' 'intelligence,' 'fact,' 'wisdom,' 'memory,' 'history'—all the words we live by. And it does not pause to tell us. And we do not pause to ask." While Postman speaks here of the larger culture, the same effect obtains in technological applications in writing centers, as computers have contributed to defining center pedagogy and the notion of the center itself. Indeed, at many institutions in the 1980s, newly-created computer classrooms were designated as "writing labs," appropriating a term that had been long filled by face-to-face (f2f) centers. In the grip of such forces, centers have not always "paus[ed] to ask," happily implementing technology to satisfy larger campus entities such as a writing program or central administration. This response is somewhat understandable given the romance of technology—its promises of efficiency and ease, its promises of status in terms of funding and a recognized place on the cutting edge, whether on campus or in the profession. Other times, centers have "paused to ask," indeed have paused to scream with Luddite recalcitrance, taking the humanist high ground to fend off perceived threats of obsolescence.

This tension between technological endorsement and technological resistance marks writing center discourse on computers since the early 1980s, providing several sets of polarities from which a historical view of computers in the writing center might be drawn, a historical view that, like many other histories, reveals only conflict as its thesis. Though this thesis may seem obvious, unpacking it allows for investigation of several less obvious issues regarding centers and computers. Thus, it is within conflict that I want to situate this history of computers in writing centers.

Viewing the techno-history of centers as conflict necessarily excludes other possible constructions, such as ameliorative notions of progress—and there has been progress—or Marxist critiques of economics, politics, and technological determination. Though these structures, like others, could easily drive this history, foregrounding progress would ignore some of its costs and capitulate to the global capitalism which computers help support, while a Marxist perspective would engender too easy a chic radicalism that condemns the system in which center professionals willingly participate and from which they benefit. Likewise, I could place pedagogy at the center of this history, tracing and demonstrating the ways in which centers have struggled, usually creatively, to implement technology to help student writers. Though not centered, issues of progress, economics, politics, and pedagogy will necessarily arise in various combinations as polarities or intersections from the broader thesis of conflict.

This is not to say that centering conflict renders a master narrative delivering The Truth, and certainly I recognize my own situatedness as a writing center director conflicted by technology. That is, I am not among the more zealous who imagine computers can enable centers to do everything on campus but take over the athletic program, nor as I oversee a beginning OWL in my own center am I a romantic technophobe, though I like to proceed more slowly than some, as the cautionary title and tone of this history indicate. From this position, I choose conflict as the organizing principle of this brief history, for I believe it allows the largest number of voices to speak. I am not saying these voices, a sample of roughly fifteen years of scholarship on writing centers and computers, will not be inflicted by my own; nevertheless, I believe that, set in conflict, they can provide a richer sense of computers in the writing center than other histories I might construct. But before turning to writing centers, it is necessary to outline briefly the broader context of computers and composition against and within which center history unfolds, for composition history demonstrates some of the same technological conflicts centers encounter while simultaneously standing as another point of opposition and commiseration against which to trace the writing center's individual history.

COMPUTERS AND COMPOSITION

Computers and the Teaching of Writing in American Higher Education, 1979–1994: A History, by Gail Hawisher, Paul Le Blanc, Charles Moran, and Cynthia Selfe (1996) provides a detailed history of computers in composition, and, as I hope will be evident, adumbrates some of the same issues relevant to writing centers. This work contextualizes a sixteen-year pedagogical history in the technological developments that made electronic writing instruction possible: early experiments on mainframe computers, the personal computer, LANS, hypertext, WANs, e-mail, the pentium chip, and computer mediated communication systems such as real-time chat, MOOs, and MUDs. Situated in these technologies, computers and writing instruction are historically examined, perhaps a little too incrementally but nevertheless effectively, in five periods beginning from 1979 through 1982 and in three-year segments through 1994:

1. *1979–1982: The Profession's Early Experience with Modern Technology.* Here Hawisher et. al. identify a struggle between current-traditional and process pedagogy, with grammar-drill programs and style checkers existing side by side with such early CAI developments in process software as Hugh Burns's Topoi, Selfe's and Billie Wahlstrom's Wordsworth, William Wresch's Writer's Helper, and Lisa Gerrard's SEEN, among others. The key development technologically in these years is the availability of the micro-computer (as op-

posed to main frame instructional systems such as Brigham Young's TICCIT and the University of Illinois's PLATO) which made it possible to view the computer not only as a data processor "but as a writing instrument." (46)

2. 1983–1985: Growth and Enthusiasm. In these years, computers and composition professionals grew in number and visibility with a special interest group at CCCC (dubbed "the fifth C") in 1983 and the Assembly for Computers in English (ACE) recognized by NCTE in 1985. Additionally, journals (most notably *Computers and Composition*) and newsletters were founded, the first Computers and Writing conference was established, instructor developed CAI software began to be distributed commercially, and NCTE published *Computers in the English Classroom: A Primer for Teachers* (1983) and an edited collection of essays, *The Computer in Composition Instruction: A Writer's Tool* (1984). Pedagogically, as new and easy word-processing software began to appear, word processing, with its composing and revision potential, began to challenge CAI for dominance in classrooms. Technologically, the first LANs began to appear in classrooms, and the first hypertext program for microcomputers was released.

3. 1986–1988: Research, Theory, and Professionalism. As the chapter title indicates, these years are celebrated as a time of further growth, with increased visibility within composition (9% of the sessions at the 1987 CCCC), the growth of professional organizations and journals, the increasing publication of books on computers and writing, and the dovetailing of LAN technology and early e-mail use with post-process collaborative learning and constructionist pedagogics. At the same time, research anxieties began to appear over the fact that most studies failed to discover important differences between students writing on and off line" (147).

4. 1989–1991: Coming of Age—The Rise of Cross Disciplinary Perspectives. This chapter might just as well have been called "growing pains," for while the authors report rapid advances in hypertext, LAN, and WAN technologies, they also report the lagging behind of classroom practices due to a lack of knowledge and/or funding. There is, nevertheless, a "coming of age," as scholars in the field began to politicize and theorize their work on computers and writing, in keeping with the shift from the individual writer of process pedagogy to the politicizing and contextualizing of all acts of composing in social pedagogics. In doing so, scholars and teachers began to confront the unsettling possibility that, imbricated in the larger culture, "electronic writing classes...supported only a limited potential for change." (201)

5. 1992–1994: Looking Forward. While the authors here speculate on technological developments in computer mediated communication (CMC), next generation processors, multimedia, and the internet, among others, they also lament the beginnings of a fragmentation in the field and the increasing division between privileged researchers and the underclass of graduate and adjunct teachers who actually teach beginning writers. In terms of pedagogy they speculate on how computers fit in with compositions increased interest in the cultural politics of literacy, which has sometimes fostered feminist and cultural studies analyses that question the notion that new computer technologies provide "the egalitarian social spaces promised in the research literature." (250)

This snapshot of Hawisher et al.'s history is necessarily reductive and can in no way do justice to the book's depth and texture. While the incremental organization of the book may seem lockstep (and my summary definitely does), the authors are also aware of the synchrony of history, recognizing that some of the grammar drilling and style checking programs they locate in current-traditional beginnings persist today or that the macro history they construct in narrating a sixteen-year period may at times recur in a local setting in a compressed time frame. At whatever point in time, Hawisher and her colleagues also discuss numerous issues affecting those involved in using computers to teach writing and in researching this practice: among others, community formation, struggles for respect in English departments, battles to have computer work valued in tenure and promotion decisions, fights with administrators for funding, attempts to educate colleagues, the commitment to improving student writing, fear and enthusiasm toward technology, and feelings of marginalization both on campus and in the profession. Such issues writing center professionals-know all too well, yet despite these shared concerns, Hawisher et.al. barely mention writing centers. "Writing Laboratories" are listed only once in the index, and they discuss labs only in the context of conference teaching, erroneously reporting them as facing the prospect of being transformed into computer classrooms:

> *The writing rooms described by Garrison and Murray, and the conference-centered or tutorial based pedagogy, whose literature was assembled by Muriel Harris in* Tutoring Writing. A Sourcebook for Writing Labs, *foregrounded the student writer's writing and the teacher/editor's intervention. With the advent of the microcomputer in the 1980s, the already established writing labs and writing workshops became computer-writing labs and classrooms, with teacher editors conferring, one-to-one, with student writers. (29)*

While some blurring of boundaries likely occurred as many computer classrooms were designated as "writing labs" I think the thousands of peer tutors working f2f during the years discussed would be surprised to learn that they had been replaced by teacher/editors working on computers. Thus though Hawisher, LeBlanc, Moran, and Selfe offer a finely detailed and historigraphically sophisticated document on the entrance and continued presence of computers in composition, though they provide a socio-techno-cultural context for thinking about writing instruction and computers, it is necessary to look elsewhere to attempt to document the impact of computers on writing centers, a task to which I will now turn.

It would be tempting to adopt the same chronological sequence for writing centers that Hawisher and her colleagues construct for composition, but though much of their chronology applies to writing centers, the trajectory of center history differs as centers likely began implementing the technology after composition programs (an assumption based on the scholarship as well as on institutional funding hierarchies). Furthermore, as a different pedagogical space, centers had as many different as similar problems and successes. Because of these differences and due to limitations of space, I will create a somewhat different chronology, but though proceeding chronologically I will attempt to address the recurring issues that demonstrate that history is also synchronic.

FEARS AND HOPES: THE EARLY YEARS, 1982–1986

It is difficult to pinpoint the first public expression, either in print or at a conference, about computers in writing centers. In the first four years (1979–82) that Hawisher et. al. designate for historical treatment, no articles in the *Writing Lab Newsletter* discuss computer tutorials. Similarly in the first book on centers, Muriel Harris's 1982 collection of essays *Tutoring Writing*, only one article treats computers: Don Norton's and Kristine Hansen's "The Potential for Computer-Assisted Instruction in Writing Labs." As its title indicates, the piece is optimistically speculative, but it evidences many of the same tensions that will continue to define the writing center community's future discourse on computers. On the one hand, Norton and Hansen conclude that "CAI may yet make it possible that across the nation learning will occur more effectively at computer terminals than in more traditional settings" (161). On the other, the authors lament the costs of terminals and fees to plug into the instructional programs of the TICCIT and PLATO mainframes, the difficulty of creating software (a concern shared in composition circles), and the limitations of computers at that time to teach more than discrete skills.

Since it seems likely that microcomputers and word processing, both then commercially available, would have been big news in those days, the lack of articles in *The Writing Lab Newsletter* before 1982 and the limited coverage of the Norton and Hansen piece suggest that centers had not yet received the technology in significant proportion. But a spurt of discourse on computers in writing centers only a year later bears out the cliche that technology moves fast. The *1984 Writing Lab Directory* (compiled in 1983) lists 88 of 184 centers as having at least one computer, and center professionals began to make their voices heard, with three articles directly treating computers and two discussing them within broader topics in the *Proceedings of the Writing Center Association Fifth Annual Conference* (1983) and at least one paper delivered at the First Midwest Writing Centers Association Conference the same year.

These six articles outline the same conflict between CAI and word processing application found in composition circles. Evidently early CAI programs for prewriting, such as Hugh Burns's Topoi or Lisa Gerrard's WANDAH, had not reached writing centers, for to writing centers at this time CAI usually meant current-traditional grammar drills or at most style checkers. Countering these were word processing programs, hailed as a powerful tool for process writing. At the Writing Centers Association (now ECWCA) Conference, Mary Croft extolled the use of word processing to "diminish the concern over the physical act of writing and the worry over neatness and correctness" arguing that computers allow for "thorough revision not merely surface revision" and "encourage students to be both abandoned experimenters and disciplined self editors" (58–59). Croft denounces a CCCC presentation she saw the previous year on a CAI program used to flag grammatical errors, claiming it turned the computer into "just a big, expensive red pencil" (59). She also cautions against grammar software, saying "I haven't seen any I really believe our students can't live without" (60). Like Croft, Beatrice Johnson, in the same proceedings, celebrates the potential of word processing: "From free writing through final proof reading, writers find the Apple an efficient tool" (105). Finally, Janice Neuleib in an article on center research challenges directors to forego "merely putting on a computer exercises that do not work in books" and to implement instead the "valuable tool" of word processing (215–216).

In contrast, at the same conference, two articles promote grammar instruction via CAI. Frances Key, of Ball State, arguing the benefits of multimedia autotutorial programs, claims that flagging surface errors on computer forces the student into "precision in thinking" (137)—though never really explaining how. He also values the privacy of autotutorials, computer assisted and otherwise. Don Payne, of Iowa State, offers "a comprehensive sequence of lessons dealing with spelling, proofreading, vocabulary, and error" (239), though concluding his piece with hopes for developing prewriting heuristic programs. Payne's accommodation of the technology is clearly the most current-traditional of the six. But while endorsing his pedagogy, he also apologizes for it, opening the essay with a discussion of an "administrative arrangement [that] means we have a narrower focus than many writing centers, that we concern ourselves more with mechanics than with general compositional skills" (239).

Considering the range of positions here, one wonders how these presenters may have reacted to one another had they attended one another's sessions. On the one hand, this diversity testifies to the writing center community's tendency (still healthily in place) to tolerate a variety of opinion. Indeed, well before this conference center professionals were implementing instruction beyond grammar and identifying themselves with the by then entrenched process pedagogies, yet Payne's and Key's papers were welcome. On the other hand, while demonstrating the community's capacity for accommodation, these articles also, and more importantly, indicate its situatedness in the same pedagogical debates going on in computers and composition and in larger cultural debates regarding technology, Recall the plight of Don Payne at Iowa State. In an institution with a large engineering program, his lab was technologically rich in terms of the software development resources he reports coming out of the university's Computation Center. These riches, however, result in graduate students in computer science assigned to program for his writing center. Though working with the programmers, he has difficulty maintaining control: "For instructors accustomed to more autonomy in developing instructional materials, this mixture of managerial and consultative roles may convince them that indeed they are the ones being integrated into some other system" (242). Payne's lament echoes the early caveats by scholars in computers and composition that teachers, not programmers, must control software development (Hawisher et. al., see also Wresch). In larger cultural terms, Payne warns that though the title of his essay speaks of integrating computers in the center, "one of the first things you discover when you begin working with CAI is that in many ways you are fitting into another discipline, not just incorporating technology" (241). Here Payne echoes Neil Postman's contention that when a new technology enters a culture, the result is more than additive; that is, what results is not the old culture with something new added but a new culture.

The anxieties of these early discussions are laid bare by Dennis Moore in a paper presented at the 1983 Midwest Writing Centers Association Conference with the provocative title, "What Should Computers Do in the Writing Center?" To this question, Moore flatly answers that we don't yet know and then forcefully derides what he sees as the techno-evangelism of the voices in the 1983 issue of *College Composition and Communication* dedicated to computers. For instance, when Collette Daiute (in an article deemed "seminal" in the editor's note to the issue) claims that the cursor "reminds the writer that the program is waiting to receive more input, which encourages the writer to say more and to consider whether what is written makes sense," Moore rightly asks how a mere blinking light can accomplish all that for a beginning writer. In addition, in response to Richard Lanham's early style-checking program, Homer, Moore notes, as many others have, that style checkers merely count words and flag particular grammatical and stylistic elements (-tion words, to be verbs etc.) without any regard for context or rhetorical purpose: "There seems little point in telling a basic writing student that she has written 205 words in 17 sentences with an average of 12.05 words per sentence—a typical Homer item" (8). To be fair to Lanham, he himself recognized the program's limitations in print. Nevertheless, Moore's near jeremiad asks the writing center community "to take a critical attitude toward educational computing: to learn all you can about it and to keep asking questions" (2).

It would be easy to dismiss Moore as a Luddite or to argue that the conflicts I cite are more pedagogical than technological in that they pit grammar-drill-on-screen against word processing, current-traditionalism versus notions of process writing at the time. However, one wonders how the technology affected the persistence and implementation of both pedagogics. Take, for example, the Comp-Lab modules, a self-paced workbook series with audiotapes that had enjoyed some popularity in writing centers before computers (see Epes 1979; Epes, Kirkpatrick, and Southwell 1983; Baker and Whealler). One would think that contemporary with Maxine Hairston's process clarion, "The Winds of Change: Thomas Kuhn and the Revolution in the Teaching of Writing" (1982), such materials would die a rapid death, but two years later Comp-Lab's software version was featured in an essay by Michael Southwell in Willam Wresch's NCTE collection, *The Computer in Composition Instruction: A Writer's Tool* (1984). Southwell touts computerized autotutorials as transferring "responsibility for learning to the learner" (93), a nice alliterative phrase but one that collides with the collaborative pedagogy and tutor talk being championed in the same year by such revered writing center scholars as Steven North and Kenneth Bruffee. Nevertheless, despite its current-traditional moorings, Southwell's article enjoyed status alongside numerous others by some of the most notable scholars, then and now, in computers and composition, most of whom, in contrast, were looking to adapt process pedagogy electronically. Granted that Comp-Lab may have been one of the better autotutorials of its time, I do not think it cynical to say that had it not gone electronic, it would have withered on the shelves of most writing centers by 1984 and would never have seen print in an NCTE publication, least of all in one hailed as "a breakthrough" (Hawisher et al. 84).

As in composition studies, computers continued to engage writing center scholars following the earliest work. This it not to say there is a large body of work following the initial pieces, but certainly interest was growing. Jim Bell (1989) reports that between 1984 and 1988 *The Writing Lab Newsletter* published thirteen articles and nine software reviews, making computers the second most popular topic, and essays continued regularly in regional conference proceedings. While these essays express some of the same tension as the early work, they begin to take on a less conflicted tone, demonstrating more confidence and resulting in a genre I will call "the success story." Essays in this genre begin by raising concerns about technology, usually to ease humanist anxieties and then move to an ameliorative narrative of successful pedagogical implementation. For example, Richard Marshall's "Word Processing and More: The Joys and Chores of a Writing Lab Computer" (1985) rehashes all the problems of implementing computers—technological fear, software needs, possibilities of losing documents, maintaining the equipment—but concludes confidently with several solutions and a plea: "Please Santa, send us a few more computers" (181). In a similar "success story," Robert Royar (1986) discredits studies that were claiming word-processing does not change the revision habits of inexperienced writers, arguing that instruction in revision and the right software will do the trick. Charles E. Beck and John A. Stibrany (1985) corroborate Royar's claim in a study of graduate students at the Air Force Institute of Technology.

It would be redundant to recount the many essays in the "success story" genre. Suffice it to say that they tend to illustrate what Stuart Blythe (1997) has called "a logistical view" of technology: the assumption that technologies are neutral tools whose benefit or bane depends on those implementing them. This view, Blythe argues, ignores the possibility that technology transforms culture, an argument that had long been advanced by noted technological critics such as Postman, Joseph Weizenbaum, and Hubert Dreyfus. Postman's position has already been cited, but Weizenbaum (1976), an early developer of artificial intelligence (AI),[1] warns that technology transforms the very way we think of ourselves in our surroundings. He notes that AI, for example, tends to cast computers in human metaphors (witness also the cute anthropomorphic names often assigned to composition programs: Wandah, Homer, Wordsworth, or more specific to writing centers, OWL). Weizenbaum argues that this attitude reciprocally causes us to think of humans as machines, in terms of a Cartesian rationality long considered limited in philosophical tradition. Weizenbaum's positions are bolstered by Dreyfus in his seminal challenge to AI, *What Computers Can't Do* (1971, 1979) and his revised edition, *What Computers Still Can't Do* (1992).

It would be unfair to charge early center professionals working in computers with technological naivete in confidently ignoring such questions in their "success stories" (in fact some of their trepidations show they were not ignoring them completely), for they were using computers to help students write and to solidify the institutional place of their centers. Given institutional constraints, the lack of time to reflect on technology, and the need to create more effective pedagogies, it is not surprising that success stories, as a genre, continue in subsequent years side by side with more restless discourse.

NEW TECHNOLOGIES, NEW PEDAGOGIES, NEW QUESTIONS: 1987–1991

As LAN and hypertext applications began to make their way on to campus, the number of articles in the *Writing Lab Newsletter*, as well as in conference proceedings of the time, indicates a continual but not significantly increasing stream of commentary. The notable exception is the special issue of *The Writing Center Journal* entitled "Computers, Computers, Computers," and its appearance governs my choice of 1987 as the point of demarcation for a new historical segment. Closing this period, Jeanne Simpson's and Ray Wallace's 1991 collection of essays, *The Writing Center: New Directions*, despite its forward looking title, contains only one article on computers, and after its dedicated issue *The Journal* surprisingly published only one more article in these years (in the 1991 Tenth Anniversary Issue) and not another until 1997. This lack of a marked increase in publication on computers in writing centers may be attributable to the increase of LAN and hypertext technology. Not only was this technology likely beyond the budget of most centers, LANs also lent themselves more readily to creating user groups in classrooms than to tutoring one to one. Thus it is not surprising that many articles on computers and writing centers (see, for example, Berta 1990 or Brown 1990) duplicated the logistical success stories previously discussed, concentrating on microcomputer applications for various purposes, usually with the typical anxieties of previous years ameliorated by claims of student success and without much technological or cultural reflection.

The special issue of *WCJ*, however, demonstrates that center professionals, though still seeking instructional applications, were returning to the critical perspectives prevalent in the initial work but glossed over in the success stories. Fred Kemp's lead article, "Getting Smart with Computers: Computer-Aided Heuristics for Student Writers," challenges binary thinking that would see computers as threat or panacea, arguing that "computers can do marvelous things for us in our classrooms and learning labs, but only if we are imaginative enough to forsake the anthropomorphic prejudices of robotry and develop truly innovative instruction based upon characteristically computer abdities" (9). With this stance, Kemp aligns himself with artificial intelligence researchers such as Weizenbaum to argue that the difference between human intelligence and artificial intelligence is "so vast, especially in terms of Natural Language Processing, the similarities are theoretical, not practical" (9). Though observing the benefits of computers, Kemp advises writing center professionals to "to employ a very sophisticated, and possibly new, understanding of the writing process" (9).

Kemp's admonition parallels what Hawisher and her colleagues trace in the composition community at large: that by the mid- to late eighties, more social and politicized notions of context were beginning to create a post-process, culturally-interpellated, constructivist model of composing that questioned the simplicity of the student-centered, often stage-model notions of the process movement. That post-process models rendered composing far more complex an activity than CAI programs then could represent or address begins to surface in Jeanne Luchte's bibliographic essay on process software available in 1987. Luchte organizes her essay in terms of pre-writing, organizing, drafting, revision, and editing—the steps of the process model—and then evaluates the degree to which computers might facilitate each step. Yet as she concludes her essay she is not fully confident in this model: "Though I am delineating the five processes to examine how using the computer can help teach them, I should stress that the most viable computer applications will be those that address the process integratively and cohesively" (18). With this statement Luchte recognizes that composing is recursive—one of the earliest arguments challenging step-models of process—and implies that CAI software had yet to account for recursiveness. Luchte's reservations emerge more prominently in the issue's paired reviews, by David Partenheimer and Bill Emmett, of WANDAH, which by this time combined CAI features and word processing and was entering the commercial market as HBJ Writer. Partenheimer essentially trashes WANDAH, arguing that its heuristic, editing, and revision features are intrusive and cumbersome and (echoing Kemp) that the program encompasses only a fraction of the skills involved in effective writing" (53). Even Emmett, taking the pro position, lukewarmly contends that WANDAH/HBJ Writer gives beginners "one more tool" but concedes that the program soon "will be outdated" (58).

While neither Kemp, Luchte, Partenheimer, nor Emmett directly allude to social notions of writing, they implicitly and explicitly doubt that the software fits what was known about composing. This stance separates them from early objectors to computers and writing, who couched their fears more in terms of traditionally humanist objections to machinery. Conversely, these later commentators base their objections on informed experience with the technology. Situated thus, they repeat not only the disappointments of composition studies (Hawisher et al. chapters five and six) but also those of AI researchers, who were beginning to realize the difficulties, if not impossibility, of programming computers to account for all the social subtleties encoded in language and the "consensus knowledge" humans employ in making decisions in complex acts such as writing (Dreyfus 1992, xvi). Faced with this problem, the U.S. Department of Defense had discontinued funding for all AI research except neural-network modelling by the late 1980s, and the Japanese government had discontinued funding AI research altogether.

Because post-process pedagogies such as social construction, feminism, and cultural studies rhetoric deflated some of the early promise of computers, writing center scholars sometimes turned from pure pedagogy to begin investigating ways in which computers affected social situations related to composing. The beginnings of this line of inquiry are illustrated in Pamela Farrell's "Writer, Peer Tutor, and the Computer: A Unique Relationship" in the special *WCJ* issue. Farrell reiterates the same pedagogical claims for the computer as writing tool as earlier advocates had, but adds that the computer promotes collaboration among students of "varying social, educational, and ethnic backgrounds" (29). This happens, according to Farrell, because tutors and tutees, often hampered by social difference (which would be quite powerful in Farrell's high-school setting), direct themselves toward the computer, an interest they share, and away from the writing deficiencies of the tutee or the social positions of either party. Farrell's essay, given the complexities of social difference that subsequent scholarship has revealed, is, in retrospect, a bit too much the happy tale, the success story. However, in 1987 her introduction of the social element into discourse on computers in the writing center implies that she was starting to reflect upon the technology in ways brand its obvious application as a tool for teaching process writing.

This focus on social dynamics also occupies Maurice Scharton two years later in his 'The Third Person: The Role of Computers in the Writing Center" (1989). Scharton presents four case studies that demonstrate how various aspects of computer writing helped four different students with four different writing processes. One student learned to ask for help (no small accomplishment); another discovered possibilities of macrostructural changes, working with a tutor who encouraged her to play with the block-and-move function like a video game; a third overcame his obsession with grammatical correctness; and a fourth realized that document design and appearance are often part of the social contract between author and audience. In each case, students surmounted their problems because the computer, Scharton implies, defused some of their previously inhibiting behaviors. Like Farrell, but with less obvious enthusiasm, Scharton argues that "the computer supplies a social basis for that relationship [tutor-tutee] because it represents a Common interest and a new language with which to discuss that interest" (40). While one might argue that Farrell and Scharton barely scratch the surface of social theories of composing, their work signals an increasing awareness of new questions and a more sophisticated stance toward technology.

In addition to concerns grounded in newly developing social pedagogies, writing center scholars, though not in large numbers, were beginning to examine uses of technologies other than word processing and CAI—but again not without conflict. Joyce Kinkead's "The Electronic Writing Tutor" (1988), in *The Writing Lab Newsletter*, is likely the first work that considers email tutoring. Kinkead endorses email as a means of reaching commuting students off-campus or students in distance education courses. Simultaneously she raises issues that show an awareness of the social complexities of writing and the politics of institutional culture. On the former, she argues that though email "combats the problems of time and distance," it does not equal the "value of dialogue in a f2f conference" and is no "replacement for the immediate questioning and discussion of tutorials" (5). Kinkead not only demonstrates an allegiance to the collaborative dialogue underpinned by social theories of composing but also warns against administrators who, lacking theoretical sophistication, might view email tutoring as a more efficient and cheaper method of delivering tutorials. A pioneering anachronism,

Kinkead's essay, in its concern with distance learning and electronic tutoring, foreshadows themes and conflicts that become increasingly important for writing centers of the 1990s.

Irene Clark's "The Writing Center and the Research Paper: Computers and Collaboration" (1991) is another work that turns its attention to the possible effects of then new technologies. In possibly the first writing center article to discuss hypertext applications, Clark describes "Project Jefferson," a program in which students working with tutors access a pre-programmed bank of texts online to research and write a documented essay. She stresses the collaborative nature of the tutor's role in helping to find, evaluate, and use information, citing, like Farrell and Scharton, the computer as a social intermediary. Though sometimes representing research writing in the "steps" of early process pedagogy, Clark recognizes that tutors must explore with students "different models of the research process" rather than a right way (212). What is significant here in terms of future applications is Clark's emphasis on "evaluating the quality and relevance of the articles" accessed to discern "the relative merit of one source over another" (213), a function that will become crucial with the availability of unregulated internet sources of information such as news groups, listservs, and, of course, the world wide web. Clark expands on this concern in a 1993 essay (to be discussed below) on teaching "information literacy," but her position is already outlined in this 1991 piece.

Before turning to the years both Kinkead's and Clark's work implicitly predicts, I would like to close this section by examining Janice Neuleib's and Maurice Scharton's essay, "Tutors and Computers, An Easy Alliance" (1990). Published in the prestigious tenth-anniversary issue of *The Writing Center Journal* issue, looking back on the eighties and forward to the nineties, describing a center with a variety of state-of-the-art hardware and software, and demarcating the year with which I end this period, this essay expresses numerous hopes and reveals numerous anxieties as centers were moving from one decade to the next and from a pedagogy largely dependent on free-standing microcomputers to more widespread network applications.

In many senses, Neuleib's and Scharton's essay reads as if they do not want to utter an unkind word about computers, and perhaps in the tenth-anniversary issue of *WCJ*, they don't, preferring rather to argue that the writing center community had confidently and effectively accommodated technology. And to a degree they show it had, if their center represents others. Indeed, they touch on nearly all relevant issues of the 1980s: the aggressiveness needed to secure funding, the efficacy of word processing in the face of the limits of CAI, the effect of computers on the social aspects of writing, the use of computers as a public relations device, the need for directors to educate themselves in new hardware and software, the differences in resources among institutions. However, though Scharton's and Neuleib's is an informed and savy essay, beneath its varnished seamlessness lurk several tensions worth noting. To begin, the essay is at times disconcertingly enthusiastic, as these outcroppings attest:

> *The six years [since the introduction of computers in the center] have reflected the national revolution in computer use.* (49)
>
> *Tutors' assumption that everyone writes or ought to write on computers suggests to us that a revolution in our tutors' thinking has indeed occurred.* (52)
>
> *[Writing] becomes more like singing. In the computer world, we can all have a voice like Pavarotti's. In comparison, with text produced on a color monitor, print on paper is a pale and lifeless imitation of writing.* (54)
>
> *We explain to our visitors [administrators and "a steady stream of dignitaries" (56)] that the computers are there to close the personal distance between writer and tutor. So far electricity has warmed our tutoring atmosphere; we hope to keep it that way.* (56).

This enthusiasm masks several unreconciled conflicts. Neuleib and Scharton speak of modelling writing behaviors by refusing to write themselves, "short of grocery lists and postcards," without a computer and take pride in the fact that several of their tutors feel the same way. "Thus a powerful force," they claim, "is operating in the tutoring situation to socialize writers to the new medium of transmission of knowledge" (53). They compare those who resist this "powerful force" to poor readers remembered from their childhoods: "The few who still do not like to use the machine are all too sadly familiar as the non-readers who struggled and eventually fell by the wayside unable to understand the symbols that would give them access to the world of text. We can still see their faces" (55).

To some degree, this subtle coercion and open condescension can be attributed to the satisfaction Neuleib and Scharton must have deservedly felt in securing equipment and implementing technological pedagogy. But one wonders that if all were so electronically well at their center, why three-quarters of their tutors, in answer to a survey, preferred discussing papers with tutees in hard copy, that "pale and lifeless imitation of writing" Neuleib and Scharton chalk this preference up to the tutors' desire to resist the temptation, promoted by the malleability of text on screen, to appropriate the tutees' texts and revise for them, a writing center taboo. But rather than leave it at that, they further support their tutors' resistance, saying it accords with their "strong feeling, voiced in conversation with our new president, that the computer has as much potential for impairing as for improving communication" (55). However, earlier in the essay they report making this argument to quell the new president's desire for grammar drill software, not to validate hard text revision. On the plus side, they also note that they want students to "consider text, as a human not a mechanical issue" (55)—good point and one I believe they believe—but curiously they never return to how computers might impair communication, or how the computer interfered with one-to-one revision, a fundamental element of center pedagogy, choosing rather to pile on excuses for the tutors's preference for hard copy.

Despite the essay's glossy veneer, the conflicts show through like scratches too deep to be sanded smooth and in hindsight (always 20–20 I know) raise the possibility that the community had not fully understood the implications of the technology with the same success as it had implemented it. These shortcomings can be largely attributed to the authors deserved pride in their lab's successes and the essay's occasion. The tenth-anniversary issue of *The Writing Center Journal* would not have been a likely venue to address the fear Hawisher et al. cite in the composition community that "electronic writing classes...supported only a limited potential for change" at a time when almost 80% of the centers in the 1991–92 *National Directory of Writing Centers* reported using computers. This fear and new expectations, however, would continue to be contested in the 1990s as new technologies began to enter the writing center on a wider scale.

OWLS, LANS, MOOS AND WEBS: 1992–PRESENT

I choose 1992 as the opening of this last period in this history because it marks the year WCENTER, the writing center listserv, began and the establishment of Eric Crump's regular column, "Voices from the Net," which recounts selected WCENTER discussions in *The Writing Lab Newsletter*. I will not examine WCENTER, for it could be the subject of another essay, nor is it a direct delivery system for tutoring students. Rather I see it as the symbolic entrance of computer mediated communication (CPC) into the community on an increasingly wider scale. In addition, I would argue that the success of WCENTER positively contributed to the community's confidence in implementing new technology, serving as both an example of technological potential and a source for hashing out new technological issues.

While most center scholars began to assess new technologies and new concerns, others once again demonstrated the synchronicity of history with some articles focussing on concerns of the previous decade (see, for example, Vasile and Ghizzone 1992 and Simons 1995). I will not treat work that goes over old ground but only that which confronts and attempts to negotiate the potential conflicts and possible changes wrought by new technologies. Much of this work appears in 1995 in the special number of *Computers and Composition* dedicated to writing centers. Needless to say the articles here often touch upon conflicts previously discussed: funding, the relationship of pedagogical and technological expertise, social issues in writing, and the like, but these issues are raised in relation to the implementation of new online systems. And although some of the authors, like their predecessors, ensnare themselves in their own enthusiasm, the majority speak in a more even-handed tone and demonstrate a critical sophistication sometimes missing in earlier work. Yet even the more sophisticated pieces are not always able to resolve the problems they raise—not because these authors are obtuse but because the problems are complex and in flux.

Muriel Harris's and Michael Pemberton's "Online Writing Labs (OWLs): A Taxonomy of Options and Issues" surveys various technological applications available, from online storehouses of handouts accessible from a home page to synchronous chat systems. They also advise directors to consider local contexts in implementing anything, noting that computerized centers vary greatly depending on their purposes, funding, and available technological expertise. Although Harris's and Pemberton's essay is primarily informational, their concerns surface to show the power (positive and negative) of the technology to transform center pedagogy and the way we think about it. Most obviously, in response to synchronous chat tutorials, Harris and Pemberton warn of "the losses in this faceless disembodied world as the lack of the personal contact may seem to dehumanize a setting that writing centers have traditionally viewed as personal and warm" (156). However, recouping this loss, they pose the possibility that chat systems create "a world where gender, ethnicity, and race are not immediately evident" and where the shy might be more inclined to speak. There may be some truth to this claim, but it had been challenged in earlier work in the wider field of computers and composition. For example, in a study of discourse on Megabyte University, a listserv on writing and computers, Cynthia Selfe and Paul Meyer in 1991 found online talk to be dominated by "men and higher status members of the academic community (read tutors for writing center chat) and to be much more adversarial than the egalitarian space initially imagined (qtd. in Hawisher et al 209).

Though hashing out the ups and downs of synchronous chat, Harris and Pemberton sound surprisingly neutral in their treatment of automatic file retrieval, by which clients access handouts stored on a website. Often these handouts offer the same type of grammatical instruction and information centers have distributed from file cabinets for years. This use of the technology evokes the storehouse metaphor of the writing center constructed by Andrea Lunsford in 1989 to denounce current-traditional center practice based on correctness and grammar drill. Much previous and subsequent center scholarship joined Lunsford in using this metaphor to repudiate the practice it represents. But Harris and Pemberton remain silent on the issue. To be fair, their essay, as its title professes, is more an informational taxonomy than a polemic. Furthermore, I believe Lunsford's metaphors gained an undeserved currency.[2] After all, people use handbooks for reference, and placing a corollary online can only provide good will for a center. Rather I raise this question to demonstrate how the technology can reshape our views of a pedagogy. Other than convenience, there is no evidence that handouts accessed online are any better than handouts pulled from a file cabinet. File cabinet or computer, each is a storehouse, a point I doubt Harris and Pemberton would contest. Yet redecorated by technology, the storehouse, generally regarded as a disreputable image of the writing center, is now redeemable, which may be good or bad, depending on the way we feel about storehouses. But however we feel, we need to recognize the pressures technology exerts on our feelings.

Ultimately, Harris's and Pemberton's work provides a useful compendium of the possibilities of technology, and though I would like to hear more from them about the issue of storehouse centers, essentially they avoid the seductions of technology that sometimes plague others. Also in the same issue, David Coogan's "Email Tutoring, A New Way to Do Old Work," though enthusiastic about the method, demonstrates that center scholars, in many cases, have become more guarded, more reflective. Though Coogan finally endorses email as an alternative, he recognizes many of the problems Kinkead had pointed out back in 1988, admits that he is not unreservedly "ready to recommend email to writing centers" (179), and concludes modestly that "Email gives [tutors and tutees] a chance to write and a chance to explore the meaning of writing" (180), a claim one could just as easily make for live tutoring. This same caution is evident in the article by Cindy Johanek and Rebecca Rickly, who in describing a survey of responses to a series of synchronous LAN interchanges among tutor trainees, temper their overall enthusiasm, pointing out that this application is "not intended to replace f2f discussion" and that "Negative responses should be attended to to help implement (the practice) more productively not only for the majority but for all tutors" (245).

In contrast, Virginia Chappell's discussion of a similar tutor-training effort, using asynchronous email discussions she calls "Party Line," illustrates that the unqualified "success story" is not a dead genre. Chappell does show, through quotations from her students' dialogues, the wonderful potentials of the medium as students collaboratively make knowledge about their tutorial experiences. However, with her assertion that "Email discussions allow students to write about, read, and respond to a broader spectrum of experience than do private journals, with all the vividness inherent in an electronic medium" (231), she lapses into the blinding assumption that the electronic way is always the better way. First, it is suspect to suppose that students will feel free to say the same thing (though they might say different things) in a group discussion, online or otherwise, that they would say in a "private journal." (Not surprisingly, privacy is often a casualty of electronic enthusiasm) Furthermore, Chappell's claims about "the vividness inherent in an electronic medium" recall McLuhan's cautions to a world where "the medium is the message." To be fair, Chappell demonstrates significant learning going in the "Party Line" group, but her essay lacks the temperance of Johanek and Rickly.

This temperance, as well as an innovative use of the technology, also informs Jennifer Jordan-Henley's and Barry Maid's "Tutoring in Cyberspace: Student Impact and College/University Collaboration," but their concomitant enthusiasm shows how technology can take us unawares. Maid and Jordan-Henley present an impressive method of sychronously connecting graduate-student tutors at Maid's four-year institution with tutees at Jordan-Henley's community college via MOO technology. The result is cyberspace tutorials as the miles between Arkansas and Tennessee disappear through the fiber-optic looking glass. Negotiating the difference between f2f and online tutoring, Maid and Jordan-Henley weigh the advantages and disadvantages of both—like Harris and Pemberton, the negative loss of personal cues in f2f tutorials but the positive loss of social pressure—and caution that "Solid writing center theory applies in cyberspace as it does in the traditional center" (212). All in all, this is impressive stuff, and Maid and Jordan-Henley are to be commended for their imaginative application of one of the newest technologies.

However, their essay contains a rather disturbing subtext. On the surface, it is evident that Maid and Jordan-Henley proceed carefully, but a closer look at their rhetoric indicates that center scholars, in their enthusiasm, are not always fully aware of the transformations technology can bring about without their knowing it. First, Maid and Jordan-Henley too easily fall into casting the non-electronic writing center as the "traditional center," a term used throughout. Were America a culture that valued tradition, this would be one thing, but in a nation cultishly dedicated to "the new," the f2f writing center—which has long celebrated itself as a space for anything but traditional pedagogy—is subordinated in a binary hierarchy with cybertutoring as the privileged term. Second, Maid and Jordan-Henley confess that they were "disappointed" (215) with students resistant to the technology. While their disappointment is understandable given their efforts, less understandable is their subsequent reference to these students as "dropouts" (215), a stigmatizing term associated with academic failure and reminiscent of Neuleib's and Scharton's casting of the less technologically enthusiastic as "slow readers." One wonders how the "dropouts" fared when Maid had to assign them grades in the tutor-training seminar in which this work was done, or how Jordan-Henley assessed the work of those who did not warm to the cyber tutors. While certainly introducing students to new and enabling technologies can be valuable, demeaning those who prefer other means of work violates the democratic principles "traditional" centers have long cherished. I doubt Maid and Jordan-Henley chose these terms—"traditional" and "dropout"—consciously, but that is exactly the point: technology can think in us if we are not careful. Thus one begins to worry when they conclude their essay with an enthusiastic flourish, suggesting the obsolescence of live centers: "Perhaps cybertutor Joel English was overstating the case when he said, 'I believe that virtual reality will continue to revolutionize writing instruction and education as a whole' but then again, perhaps he was not" (218).

Indeed "perhaps he was not" if we can believe Dawn Rodrigues's and Kathleen Kiefer's 1993 essay in *Writing Centers in Context*. This book, as many writing center professionals know, contains descriptions of model writing centers at various types of institutions, from Harvard to community colleges. Rodrigues and Kiefer, of Colorado State, start out describing a marginalized center moved all over campus, lacking peer tutors, and dedicated to basic writing courses. Though this center makes some strides, the primary thrust of the essay (given a privileged space as the last in the book) details plans for CSU's Electronic Writing Center, a facility dedicated to a WAC initiative, to exist parallel with the old center. The new center will include cross-disciplinary efforts for developing software for writing in the disciplines, a large capacity for online tutoring, and access to electronic handouts as well as to the internet. Though this electronic center was largely in the planning stages at the time of the essay, one wonders how long the old center lasted, given its checkered history and the institutional commitment to the new one. In fact, a cluster diagram of the new center's place on campus accentuates its centrality with several campus entities, including the old center, as satellites. I am not questioning the wisdom or the efficacy of such a center at Colorado State. On a campus emphasizing "the sciences and engineering" (216), it is likely appropriate to its context. My fear rather is that such a center will become the benchmark for judging others and the desired norm in contexts where it may not be as appropriate. This possibility becomes evident when Rodrigues and Kiefer disclose that "some cynics began to suspect that the university as a whole valued computers over personal instruction" (216). This is a valid concern, but once again *ad hominem* is deployed to contain the more technologically cautious.

Computers will not go away, and we would be fools to want them to, but we would also be fools to ignore the wisdom Dave Healy shows when he writes, "Online writing centers represent a window of opportunity. Our challenge is to be reflective and self-critical while the opportunities before us are still fresh" (192). Healy's "From Place to Space: Perceptual and Administrative Issues in the Online Writing Center" (1995), as its title suggests, approaches technology in terms of its effects on the autonomy of the center as place, as opposed to (cyber)space, and on human relations such as the director's relationship to tutors as employees. On this latter point, Healy wonders how tutors might feel knowing every response they make to a client could be monitored electronically by the director. He also worries about the possible loss of "work-place community" and the knowledge transfer that occurs when tutors hear other tutors at work. Drawing on Geoffrey Chase's claim that "the ways in which our centers are designed—physically and socially—imply an ideology" (qtd. in Healy 19 1). Healy poses several questions directors would be wise to heed: "What is the ontological status of a virtual writing center, and what kind of relationship will clients develop with it? How will it be perceived by the rest of the academy? What possibilities and what threats are opened up by going online?" (191).

Like Healy, Stuart Blythe in his "Networked Computers + Writing Centers = ?" recommends caution, as he calls for a critical theory of computers in the center. Blythe reiterates several of the questions raised by Healy and also points out how center scholars have either looked at technology through "instrumental theories" that view it as a neutral tool or "substantive theories" that view it as a strong determining cultural factor. He finds both views inadequate, the first because it is naive (my term, not his); the second, because it leads people to believe they lack power to manipulate the technology. Both theories, for Blythe, "place technology beyond the need or ability of human beings to intervene" (102). Blythe recommends that center professionals begin to ask questions, to intervene, to attempt to come up with theory that enables us to proceed "without feeling that we are trapped into a choice between accepting whatever comes our way or remaining adamantly anti-technological" (102). Rather than this "take-it-or-leave-it" view, Blythe calls for theory that "prompts us to consider how we have implemented current technologies and who has been involved in that process" (105). Despite their cautions, neither Blythe nor Healy can be called a Luddite. Both recognize several possible benefits of computers. Furthermore, Healy, a few years back, managed a listserv for peer tutors, and Blythe coordinated Purdue's OWL and wrote a dissertation on technologies in writing centers. But for each, enthusiasm is balanced with a measured thoughtfulness too often missing in writing center discourse on computers.

Content to move more rapidly is Cynthia Haynes-Burton in her "Intellectual (Proper)ty in Writing Centers: Retro Texts and Positive Plagiarism" (1995). Masterfully written in a frenetic style possibly meant to mimic in print the rapidity of hypertext, Haynes-Burton's essay moves with the speed of a Pentium II chip to challenge accepted definitions and prohibitions of plagiarism—long a thorny issue for writing centers. She metaphorically constructs current prohibitions as "a fortress" protecting capitalist principles of private property and implicating writing centers in a "punitive system that brings students in line with a particular morality and a dominant economy" (88–9). Arguments about plagiarism have regularly entered writing center discourse with the emergence of social-constructionist pedagogy. Haynes-Burton adds to this debate by contending, as others have, that free access to electronic knowledge on the net (or "Infobahn" as she prefers to call it) challenges "our current system of accountability, academic scholarship" (89). She locates a model for an alternative to academic scholarship in postmodern art forms that pastiche together, allude to, and parody traditional artworks, as well as in the work of "Designers Republic," a design firm that appropriates and reshapes recognizable corporate logos to say something new. To the question of how these efforts might play out in writing—that is, what form "positive plagiarism may take" as an alternative to current forms of scholarship, she turns to the *MONDO 2,000 Users Guide to the New Edge*, suggesting that "a hypertext user can create a whole basket of links and 'publish' this as a kind of sampler, anthology, or work of criticism" (92).

There are some problems here. First, Haynes-Burton bases much of her justification for these alternative texts on contemporary challenges to the idea of authorship. In literary theory, these challenges certainly have been valuable in debunking naive notions of individual genius and have shown how culture contributes to textual production, yet theory has yet to account for why particular individuals in a culture—James Joyce or Toni Morrison, for example—become the ones who construct exceptional texts from their situatedness while others do not. In composition and writing center theory, critiques of individual authorship have been inscribed (and reified) in pejorative representations of expressionist rhetoric and "garret" centers, against which to portray the culturally situated writer of social construction. These representations of the individual author, however, have often relied on overstatement, constructing her as an isolated figure, when even a cursory historical glance indicates such an autonomous view of authorship never existed. Even formalist critics recognized that historically known authors often enjoyed cross-fertilizing relationships. We know that Melville talked to Hawthorne, that Emerson brought Whitman "to a boil." that the Bronte sisters read their works to one another, that Pound helped Eliot revise "The Wasteland," and that authoritative texts of Shakespeare's plays are difficult to establish because the plays were often revised by stage managers and even actors. One could catalogue more of these great moments in peer tutoring. In short, neither literary critics of earlier times nor expressionist theorists in composition have ever thought of individual authors as enjoying the degree of autonomy that Haynes-Burton and others posit to deconstruct. As for authors of scholarly works, though their names may be on a title page, their "collaborators" are recognized in the text and bibliography. And it is not for nothing that we call these references "citations," a word which not only signifies honorific recognition of others but which also shares Latin roots with *city* and *citizen*, evoking community rather than individualism. Second, Haynes-Burton's comparison of "positive plagiarism" to postmodern art and avantgarde design ignores the fact that the works appropriated in such pieces are so well known that they are self-citing or they could not elicit their intended effect. And finally Haynes-Burton does not recognize (at least not overtly) that the kind of writing she proposes would require a high-degree of literacy to discern the value of one text from another, something many student writers lack. Certainly every hot dog stand on Haynes-Burton's Infobahn does not serve the same grade of meat.

Though I have been rough on Haynes-Burton's essay, it is not one to dismiss, for it enters into new textual spaces that beckon writing centers to blaze some trails. Haynes-Burton attempts such trailblazing, boldly going where no one has gone before, but rather than scrap what she calls an "outdated notion of scholarship that is at odds with the digiototalitarian state in which we now live" (86), I think writing centers would do better to reject anything we can call "totalitarian," digio- or otherwise, and listen to Blythe to interrogate the substantive view of technology in which Haynes-Burton essay eagerly participates. Irene Clark's "Information Literacy in the Writing Center" (1995) tenders a pedagogy for this effort. Clark defines information literacy as "the ability to access, retrieve, evaluate, and integrate information from a variety of electronically generated resources" (203). She goes on to describe a program in which writing center tutors work with novice writers to produce research papers from electronic and print sources. I give Clark's essay the final word in this discussion of new developments in the 1990s, for I believe it offers exactly the kind of advice writing centers need as they move into the next century. In short, Clark knows that anyone can operate a computer but only the literate can use it, and her emphasis on evaluating rather than merely accessing information makes her pedagogy the sort of driver's ed. course students will need to navigate future textual spaces, cyber or otherwise.

CONCLUSIONS AND FUTURES

If we have not already noticed, distance education is one of the hottest topics in administrative and legislative forums. It is cheap, it serves a broad clientele, and it can be tailored to individual student needs. Indeed it may not be long before universities begin pooling resources to offer courses by distance that could count toward degrees in any of the allied institutions. Such an arrangement is already in the works with the newly formed Western Governors University, whose campus, it is projected, will be totally in cyberspace. We in writing centers will need to be versed in technology if we are to be part of these efforts. At the same time we will need to assert what we know about live pedagogy to prevent the mere placing of services online simply because they can be, rather than because they should be.

As the world wide web expands with digital speed, chances are that it will continue to replicate our culture with cyber shopping malls, infotainment, virtual spaces for socializing, and the like, more than it will provide scholarly information. Yes, libraries are and will continue to be on the web, but libraries are on campuses and street corners too, competing, usually unsuccessfully, with designer boutiques, movie theaters, Super Walmarts, sports bars, video arcades, strip clubs, and amusement parks to shape the

American consciousness. I suspect the proportions differ and will differ little, if at all, on the internet. Just as students have to learn to negotiate material culture, they will need to do the same in cyber culture.

This is not to say technology will not generate change, but as it does and as we develop pedagogy to respond, we should remember with Joseph Weizenbaum that "rejection of direct experience was to become one of the principal characteristics of modern science" (25). Granted direct experience is not always welcome living in a house, a product of many technologies, is as sensible as it is comfortable. Likewise accessing a writing center tutor via computer to avoid walking across a dark campus at night is an intelligent decision. Nevertheless, we should maintain, as Michael Spooner does, that "flesh and blood is richer stuff than fiber optics" (8). If OWLS are going to carry us into flight rather than eat us like rodents, if MOOs are going to produce more milk than dung, if we are going to cruise the information superhighway without becoming roadkill, we will need to remain vigilant against the intoxication of our enthusiasm.

NOTES

1. Weizenbaum, an MIT computer scientist, created one of the first interactive programs, ELIZA. ELIZA mimicked Rogerian therapy, asking such questions as "How do you feel?" and then after the user responded. "Why do you feel that way?" Weizenbaum wrote the program as an experiment and initially was amused that people would engage with it but was horrified when professional therapists thought it could be effective in real therapy.

2. My position here is corroborated by Angela Petit in a 1997 article in *The Writing Center Journal*. Petit argues that such metaphoric definitions often divide writing centers into "rigid ideological categories" turning them into 'purified spaces" (a term borrowed from Min-zhan Liu) that do not account for the fluidity of diverse student needs.

WORKS CITED

Baker, Tracy and Susan Wheallar. 1982. The Comp-Lab Exercises: Use and Effectiveness with Basic Writers in the Writing Lab. *Proceedings: Writing Centers Associations Fourth Annual Conference*. Columbus: Ohio Dominican College. 9–18.

Beck, Charles E. and John A Stibrany. 1985. User Perceptions of Improved Writing Quality through Extended Use of Word Processors. Le Van. 223–34.

Bell, Jim. 1989. What Are We Talking About?: A Content Analysis of *The Writing Lab Newsletter*, April 1985 to October 1988. *Writing Lab Newsletter* 13.7: 1–5.

Berta, Renee. 1990. Computer Modification for Disabled Students. *Writing Lab Newsletter* 14.9: 67.

Blythe, Stuart. 1997. Networked Computers + Writing Centers = ? Thinking About Networked Computers in Writing Center Practice. *The Writing Center Journal* 17: 89–110.

Brown, Alan. 1990. Coping with Computers in the Writing Center. *Writing Lab Newsletter* 15.4: 13–15.

Carino, Peter. 1996. Open Admissions and the Construction of Writing Center History: A Tale of Three Models. *The Writing Center Journal* 17.1: 30–48.

———. 1995. Early Writing Centers: Toward a History. *The Writing Center Journal* 15: 103–15.

Chappell, Virginia A. 1995. Theorizing in Practice: Tutor Training 'Lie, from the VAX Lab.' *Computers and Composition* 12: 227–36.

Clark, Irene. 1991. The Writing Center and the Research Paper: Computers and Collaboration. Wallace and Simpson. 205–15.

———. 1995. Information Literacy and the Writing Center. *Computers and Composition* 12: 203–09.

Coogan, David. 1995. Email Tutoring:. A New Way to Do New Work. *Computers and Composition* 12:171–181.

Croft, Mary. 1983. Theresa Joins the Staff. A Microcomputer in the Writing Lab. Harris and Baker. 58–62.

Dryfus, Hubert L. 1992. *What Computers Still Can't Do: A Critique of Artificial Reason.* Cambridge, MS: NET.

Epes, Mary and Carolyn Kirkpatrick. 1979. The Autotutorial Lab at the CCCC. *Writing Lab Newsletter* 3.8: 1.

Farrell, Pamela B. 1987. Writer, Peer Tutor, and Computer: A Unique Relationship. *The Writing Center Journal* 8.1: 29–34.

Hairston, Maxine. 1982. The Winds of Change: Thomas Kuhn and the Revolution in the Teaching of Writing. *College Composition and Communication* 33.1: 76–88.

Harris, Muriel. ed. 1983. *Tutoring Writing: A Sourcebook for Writing Labs.* Glenview, IL: Scott, Foresman.

———. and Tracy Baker. eds. 1983. *New Directions, New Connections: Proceedings of the Writing Center Association Fifth Annual Conference.* West Lafayette, IN: Purdue University.

———. and Michael Pemberton. 1995. Online Writing Labs (OWLs): A Taxonomy of Options and Issues. *Computers and Composition* 12: 145–59.

Hawisher, Gail E., Paul Le Blanc, Charles Moran, and Cynthia L. Selfe. 1996. *Computers and the Teaching of Writing in American Higher Education, 1979-1994.* Norwood, NJ: Ablex.

Haynes-Burton, Cynthia. Intellectual (Proper)ty in Writing Centers: Retro Texts and Positive Plagiarism. Stay, Murphy and Hobson. 84–93.

Healy, Dave. 1995. In the Temple of the Familiar: The Writing Center as Church. Stay, Murphy and Hobson. 12–25.

Johanek, Cindy and Rebecca Rickly. 1995. Online Tutor Training: Synchronous Conferencing in a Professional Community. *Computers and Composition* 12: 237–46.

Jordan-Henley, Jennifer and Barry Maid. 1995. Tutoring in Cyberspace: Student Impact and College/University Collaboration. *Computers and Composition* 12: 211–218.

Kemp, Fred. 1987. Getting Smart with Computers: Computer-Aided Heuristics for Student Writers. *The Writing Center Journal* 8.1: 3–10.

Key, Francis. 1983. Technology and the Writing Center: A Humane Approach. Harris and Baker. 133–37.

Kinkead, Joyce. 1996. The National Writing Center Association as Mooring: A Personal History of the First Decade. *The Writing Center Journal* 16.2: 131–143.

———, and Jeannette G. Harris. Ed. 1993. *Writing Centers in Context*. 216–26.

———. 1988. The Electronic Writing Tutor. *Writing Lab Newsletter* 12.4:4–5.

Kirkpatrick, Carolyn. and Michael G. Southwell. 1979. The Comp-Lab Project: An Experimental Basic Writing Course. *Journal of Basic Writing* 2: 19–37.

LeVan, Sally. ed. 1985. *Writing Centers Coping with Crisis: Proceedings of the Writing Centers Association: East Central, Seventh Annual Conference*. Erie, PA: Gannon University.

Luchte, Jeanne. 1987. Computer Programs in the Writing Center: A Bibliographic Essay. *The Writing Center Journal* 8.1: 11–20.

Marshall, Richard. 1985. Word Processing and More: the Joys and Chores of a Writing Lab Computer. LeVan. 166–8.

Moore, Dennis. 1983. What Should Computers Do in the Writing Center? Paper presented at the 1983 Midwest Writing Centers Conference, Iowa City. ERIC 208 553.

Neuleib, Janice. 1984. Research in the Writing Center: What to Do and Where to Go to Become Research Oriented. *Writing Lab Newsletter* 9.4: 10–13.

———, and Maurice Scharton. 1990. Tutors and Computers, and Easy Alliance. *The Writing Center Journal* 11.1: 49–58.

Norton, Don and Kristine Hanson. 1982. The Potential of Computer-Assisted Instruction. *In Tutoring Writing: A Sourcebook for Writing Labs*. Harris. 153–62.

Partenheimer, David and Bill Emmett. 1987. Two Perspectives on Wandah/HBJ Writer. *The Writing Center Journal* 8.1: 49–58.

Payne, Don. 1983. Integrating Computer Instruction into a Writing Center. Harris and Baker. 239–49.

Postman, Neil. 1992. *Technopoly: The Surrender of Culture to Technology* New York: Knopf

Riley, Terrance. 1994. The Unpromising Future of Writing Centers. *The Writing Center Journal* 15.4: 20–34.

Rodrigues, Dawn and Kathleen Kiefer. 1993. Moving Toward an Electronic Writing Center at Colorado State University. Kinkead and Harris. 216–26.

Royar, Robert. 1986. Developing Word Processing Software for Composition. *Words Reaching Out to Worlds: Proceedings of the Writing Centers Association: East Central, Eighth Annual Conference*. Highland Heights, KY: Northern Kentucky University. 85–96.

Scharton, Maurice, 1995. The Third Person: The Role of the Computer in Writing Centers. *Computers and Composition* 7.1: 37–48.

Simons, Susan. 1995. CAI: Instruction and Change in the Writing Center. *Writing Lab Newsletter* 20.1: 11, 16.

Southwell, Michael G. 1984. The Comp-Lab Writing Modules: Computer-Assisted Grammar Instruction. Wresch. 91–104.

Spooner, Michael. 1994. A Dialogue on OWLing in the Writing Lab: Some Thoughts About Online Writing Labs. *Writing Lab Newsletter* 18.6: 6–8.

Stay, Byron, Christina Murphy and Eric Hobson. eds. 1995. *Writing Center Perspectives*. Emmittsburg, MD: NWCA.

Vasile, Kathy and Nick Ghizzone. 1992. Computer-Integrated Tutoring. *Writing Lab Newsletter* 16.9–10: 17–19.

Wallace, Ray and Jeanne Simpson. eds. 1991. *Writing Centers: New Directions.* New York: Garland.

Weizenbaum, Joseph. 1976. *Computer Power and Human Reason: From Judgement to Calculation.* San Francisco: W.H. Freeman.

Wresch. William. ed. 1984. *The Computer in Composition Instruction: A Writer's Tool.* Urbana: NCTE.

Online Writing Labs (OWLs):
A Taxonomy of Options and Issues

Muriel Harris

Michael Pemberton

As increasing numbers of writing centers consider instituting Online Writing Labs (OWLS) as adjuncts to existing tutorial services, careful planning decisions must be made about the nature, purpose, and feasibility of online offerings. In this article, we offer an overview and schema for understanding some of the most frequently used network technologies available for OWLs—e-mail, Gopher, Worldwide Web (WWW), newsgroups, synchronous chat systems, and automated file retrieval (AFR) systems. We also consider ways in which writing centers' choices among these technologies are impacted by such factors as user access, network security, computer illiteracy, institutional missions, writing center goals, computing center priorities, and computer programmers' attitudes. Successful OWLS, we believe, are those which navigate institutional and technological constraints while still managing to enhance the services provided writers and to uphold pedagogical goals.

Harris, Muriel, and Michael Pemberton. "Online Writing Labs (OWLS): A Taxonomy of Options and Issues." *Computers and Composition* 12 (1995): 145–59. Reprinted with permission from Elsevier Science.

Although the names of the co-authors of this essay are, by default, listed alphabetically, they would prefer some alternative, nonhierarchical means of characterizing the equal contributions made to this collaboratively written article.

Correspondence and requests for reprints should be sent to Muriel Harris, Department of English, Purdue University, West Lafayette, IN 47907-1356. e-mail: harrism@mace.cc.purdue.edu. or to Michael Pemberton, Department of English, University of Illinois, Urbana-Champaign, IL 61801. e-mail: <michaelp@uxl.cso.uiuc.edu>.

> cyberspace writing centers   online writing centers
> Online Writing Lab (OWL)   tutoring online   computers in writing centers
> Internet resources in writing centers   electronic writing services

Writing centers using computers are not a new phenomenon, but extending tutorial services by going online is, and the term Online Writing Lab (OWL) has gained popularity as a name for such projects. As writing centers move into this new online environment, there is great potential, but planning and shaping of effective, user-friendly OWLs takes considerable thought and energy. Attempting only to replicate familiar face-to-face tutorial settings in an electronic, text-oriented environment can lead to frustration and to defeat as OWL planners find themselves unable to simulate all characteristics of effective tutorials. Instead, it is important to recognize that OWLs can have a number of very different configurations—configurations that take advantage of the strengths of online environments and that work with, not against, both local conditions and writing center theory. For those colleagues interested in the shapes of OWLs that have already taken wing and for those exploring options, considering configurations, and/or weighing issues, we offer a model that outlines some choices and relates them to degrees of interaction and time-displacement, as well as to institutional and writing center concerns. We hope that by doing so, we will offer useful considerations for configuring OWLS. In addition, we hope others will see OWLs as yet another service offered by writing centers, which enhances and expands present work, but not as a service displacing what we find so valuable and effective in writing center tutorials.

A MODEL FOR OWL INTERACTIONS

The particular combination of software and/or systems for an OWL will be determined partly by computer facilities available on campus and partly by types of writing services to be offered online. If a campus doesn't provide access to newsgroups or to a Gopher system, for example, or if most students don't know how to use these services, then a writing center will probably want to choose other venues for providing online assistance. By the same token, some centers might choose only to provide access to standardized handouts—on comma usage, resume formats, and subject-verb agreement, for example—whereas others may wish to create *virtual writing spaces*, chatting online with students about drafts that both students and tutors view simultaneously onscreen or offering writers easy gateways to Internet resources. All these potential offerings have strengths and weaknesses, opportunities and limitations. Some types of access are better for providing specific information; other types are preferable because they offer more complex or flexible ways to interact with writers.

As one means of understanding and interrelating some important factors in the technology/pedagogy dynamic for writing centers, we offer Figure 1 which will be used to discuss our consideration of the opportunities for online assistance. This model of contact points and intersections, like all models, is clearly reductive and does not encompass all possible technologies or site-specific variations in programming or hardware. For example, restrictions on e-mail at one institution may prevent a writing center from using it in the same way and for the same purposes as a center at another campus. Nevertheless, this model illustrates some critical relationships that exist between technological capacity and pedagogical opportunity when putting a writing center online. Generally speaking, these interactions can be grouped into four categories according to their relative *degree of interaction* and the *displacement in time.* The time dimension can range from immediate interaction or reaction to delayed response between the service and the writer. The interaction dimension, on the other hand, ranges from automated reaction to personal interaction. On one side of this dimension, for example, are Gophers and Worldwide Webs (WWWs) and automated file retrieval systems. These reactive, decontextualized systems provide standardized responses to simple inquires without need for variation. At the other end of the interaction dimension are synchronous chat systems, newsgroups, and e-mail, which allow students to ask tutors text-specific questions about particular problems and rhetorical features. These interactive, contextualized systems permit a high degree of variation in possible inquiries and in possible responses.

These two kinds of computerized interactions and points of contact differ according to whether individual queries and responses are handled immediately or over a period of time. Gopher, WWW, and interactive chat

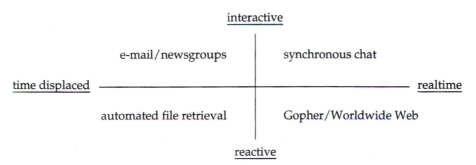

FIGURE 1:   A Model of Computer Interations.

systems, for example, are structured for immediate, online interactions. Users ask questions or give directions while sitting at computer terminals, and they receive immediate responses that they can then respond to. Newsgroups, e-mail, and automated file retrieval systems, on the other hand, do not allow direct, immediate, person-to-person or person-to-resource contact in the same way. Conversations are indirect, mediated by an intervening virtual space, and usually require a time delay between the moment in which the inquiry is made and the moment when a response is returned. Under some circumstances, these conditions may be sufficient for writers needs and preferable for a writing center's daily operations.

Interestingly enough, we decided to collaborate on this article, in part, because though we each opted to institute online writing assistance at our respective campuses—Purdue University and the University of Illinois—at about the same time, we either chose or were forced to use completely different avenues for providing that assistance. In Purdue's first configuration of its OWL (now incorporated into a much larger complex of options), students could use either an automated file-retrieval system or an e-mail dropbox. At Illinois, students can use either a dedicated newsgroup or a branch of the campus Gopher system. Purdue's OWL has developed and grown since its inception, partly in response to problems we perceived and partly because we started to explore new options and services. Dave Taylor, the system designer at Purdue, has written WORDS (Writers' On-line Reference Desk Services), a software program for local use that serves as a writer's desk tool—a set of references for writers linked to the campus network—and Purdue now has a Gopher site and a WWW page, with both serving several purposes. Neither Illinois nor Purdue has, as yet, established an online chat system. Our reasons for selecting—or not selecting—these systems as extensions of our writing centers should become clear as we describe each system.

AUTOMATED FILE RETRIEVAL

Automated file retrieval (AFR) systems vary in their mechanics and in the means by which files can be requested, but they generally require two things: (a) a user-owned e-mail account from which requests can be sent and to which files can be returned, and (b) a formal command structure that will tell the writing center's computer program what to do with requests it receives. Purdue's OWL provides an example of how such a system can be structured. We offer it here as representative. The Purdue AFR is located at an e-mail Internet address <owl@sage.cc.purdue.edu> that also supports the Writing Lab's interactive e-mail OWL (which also responds to user messages either sent directly or through WORDS). When an e-mail message is received, the OWL system first scans the Subject: header for information. If the keywords "owl-request" appear, the message is handled by AFR; if any additional or other words appear in this line, the text of the message is saved in the writing center's e-mail box for handling by a tutor. Once the OWL system has determined that a user wishes to use AFR, it checks the message's first line to find out, more specifically, what sort of request is being made. Typically, AFRs have three possible commands: to request a help file with information about using the system, to request a list of files available for downloading, or to request a specific file (by its unique filename). At Purdue, these commands are, respectively, "Send Help," "Send Index," and "Send <<filenumber>>." Everything in the message beyond these few keywords is ignored, and after the request has been responded to, virtually all traces of its existence are purged from the system.[1] The University of Richmond's writing center has a similar configuration in that it has some online interactive exercises and quick reference sheets for rules of punctuation, style, and mechanics, plus advice sheets on prewriting, writing, and revising (Essid, 1994; Hickey, 1994). These are available in the University of Richmond's public labs as well as in the writing center. The University of Texas at Austin's writing center is also building an online set of resources for writers, in addition to other services.

AFRs are *reactive, time-displaced* systems. Users send e-mail requests to a computer system that will—assuming the requests have been phrased correctly—respond in predictable, invariant ways. After sending their requests, users must wait varying lengths of time for the system to respond. Depending on the volume of user traffic and on the system capacity at a given institution, delay between request and response can be anywhere from several seconds to several minutes. When the response (either a list of files or a particular text file) is finally received, users can read and/or manipulate it with their mail-reader programs. (At Purdue, for example, faculty across campus are advised that they can download and modify handouts according to individual needs.) Purdue's AFR presently offers over 100 handouts on grammar and mechanics, on writing concerns such as nonsexist language and conciseness, on resume writing, and on citation format. These files, as will be described later, can also be made available through a Gopher or WWW.

A FURTHER CONSIDERATION: USER ACCESS

Which users should be allowed to avail themselves of materials being offered? Operating as they do through Internet e-mail exchanges, AFRs are

---

[1]We say "virtually" here, because numerical and qualitative information about the nature of the request is tallied for later evaluation and assessment purposes.

generally available to anyone with an e-mail account that can send messages to a host computer. The Purdue AFR, for example, has received thousands of file requests from all over the world: from school districts in British Columbia, from technical writing groups at NASA and government offices, new writing centers starting their own collections with these handouts, from universities in Europe and Asia, companies on several continents, and from individual users all over the globe who surf the Internet. Unlimited access may or may not be a problem, depending on the server's capacity, on institutional financing, and on writing centers' instructional missions, (an issue we explore in the following discussion). Simply put, the bigger the computer system, the more users can be accommodated; the less restrictive an institution's mission and funding, the wider an audience it can rationalize supporting. If a system is not overloaded and if the campus looks upon international access as both a kind of "outreach" and as inexpensive publicity, then an increase in the number of users will be seen as a benefit rather than a liability.[2] On the other hand, if the computer system is being asked to respond to more user requests than it can handle, if the institution feels it has responsibilities to its own students and no others, or if computer budgets are pinched to the point that international e-mail messages are discouraged (remember, e-mail may be cheap, but it's definitely not free), then a writing center may think seriously about restricting access to local users.

GOPHERS AND WORLDWIDE WEB PAGES

Gopher is an international network of servers and databases that can be accessed by a common system of commands from nearly every other Gopher server in the world. One of Gopher's most powerful features, in fact, is the ease with which users can access servers anywhere in "Gopherspace"—in Finland, in Japan, or at the other end of the state. By keying the command "gopher" at the system prompt, users can enter the Gopher system and explore its many nooks and crannies. Gopher, a menu-driven system, usually requires that its users know only how to operate the arrow keys on their keyboards and to hit the "RETURN" key when they wish to make a choice. Gopher servers at educational institutions typically offer information about the institution and its community, as well as information of scholarly interest. They also offer gateways to thousands of other Gopher servers and their resources. With just a few keystrokes, working their way through a series of

---

[2]Responses to a user survey sent out by Purdue's OWL bordered on the lyrical, heaping praise from users in many states and several continents on its services and usefulness.

menu choices and selecting options like "Other Gopher servers in the USA" or "All the Gopher servers in the world," users can find themselves connected to Gopher servers in distant countries, all ripe for investigation as rich sources of information.

The main Gopher server at the University of Illinois is typical of such systems and can be accessed in one of two ways. The slower but more user-friendly way is for users to log into their campus Gopher system and by moving through a series of hierarchically-arranged menus reach the University of Illinois server. At Illinois, this entails selecting "Other Gopher servers in the USA," then "Gopher servers in Illinois," and finally "University of Illinois at Urbana-Champaign." A quicker but less user-friendly way to connect is to key in the command <gopher -p gopher.uiuc.edu 70> at the system prompt. Once connected, users can choose item "#9 Libraries and Reference Information" to get a menu that includes: "#6 Writers' Workshop On-line Handbook" where the University of Illinois' version of an OWL can be found. The *On-line Handbook* contains a highly structured and organized database of information about bibliography formats—MLA, APA, and Old-MLA (notes and bibliography). It will be expanded to include information about punctuation, mechanics, and basic grammar. The Purdue University Writing Lab Gopher can be accessed directly by keying the command <<gopher owl. trc.purdue.edu>> at the user's main prompt. Once there, users find a topical guide to writing skills handouts and can "Read," "Save," and/or "Print" files. To build a national pool of writing center online resources, the Purdue Gopher also lists other writing centers and their writing resources. The Gopher also enables users to immediately connect to these. Also, for users who want to get to the Internet to find information in a variety of disciplines, the Purdue Writing Lab Gopher provides a gateway to link to particularly rich sites of information we've located. The intent here is to assist students gathering information in preparation for writing research papers—to become their easy gateway out—a particularly important service for novices learning to surf the Internet.

Gopher systems are *reactive, real-time* systems. They offer uniform, standardized responses to inquires and commands given online by users. Users remain connected to the Gopher system/server at all times: they gradually navigate their way into and out of file locations that are of interest. Files that users locate can easily be saved, printed and/or read off-line. Gopher's real attraction is the opportunity for users to browse through a succession of files, to move up and down through menu trees, to pick and choose what they want to read before moving on. For this reason, files at Illinois are brief, specific, and compact. The *Writers' Workshop On-line Handbook* at Illinois contains over 100 distinct files of bibliographic information, but each file's average length is only between one and two computer screens of text. The files can each be located easily and read quickly, and, then, users can move elsewhere if they wish. By comparison, a file in the Purdue OWL usually contains a more complete discussion of a specific topic. Thus, the MLA file includes all material offered on MLA bibliographic information. As with AFRs, system capacity and extra-institutional access may become a problem at some campuses and with some servers. However, because Gopher was conceived as an international network, long-distance access is generally considered to be a part of normal operating practice and is usually provided for. In addition, Gopher file structures can easily be transferred among servers, so users frequently "move up" to a server with greater capacity.

Gophers also permit a writing center to offer a panoply of services. At the University of Delaware, the university Gopher includes their writing center handouts and some general information about the center (Penna, 1994). Kennesaw State College's writing center plans are for an online information center on the college Gopher that will provide various information services (Barrier, 1994). Because Gophers permit writers to roam the Internet's vast resources and because students will also need to know how to download files, how to use e-mail, and so on, the Purdue Writing Lab is developing hypertext tutorials aimed at assisting students with these processes. However, because hypertext tutorials are not accessible on Gophers and because of the growing popularity of the WWW (which permits hypertext links) as a different and more visually compelling way to connect to the vast pool of Internet resources, Purdue has constructed a WWW page, on which hypertext programs will be available. Also available through its Web are writing center handouts (visually formatted in more readable ways), direct links to other online writing centers and their services, and immediate links to an even more vast universe of materials than are available through Gophers. Student novices will eventually learn how to search the Web on their own, but initially, with a click of a mouse, they can start with the Purdue Writing Lab's home page, and link from the lab page, for example, to the Library of Congress's page or to Carnegie Mellon's page where they can browse through the *Encyclopedia Britannica*.[3]

E-MAIL DROPBOXES AND NEWSGROUPS

In some respects, e-mail dropboxes are the easiest type of OWL to envision because they are simply an extension of the kind of e-mail messaging many of us engage in every day. Students send papers and/or writing-related questions to OWL e-mail addresses: the writing center's tutor (or tutors) responsible for monitoring the e-mail box read and respond to inquiries in a

---

[3]Those with software viewers such as Mosaic or Netscape that provide access to the WWW can connect to the Purdue Writing Lab's Web page at <http://owl.trc.purdue.edu/>.

timely fashion. Some OWLs invite students to send papers and questions about writing. At the University of Minnesota, online consulting is available both for texts that are sent in and for questions. Whole papers can be sent via POPMAIL (for the Macintosh) or MINUET (for DOS). Students who don't have access to either of these software programs copy their papers into an e-mail message (Healy, 1994). The writing center at SUNY-Albany invites students to send papers via their VAX e-mail (Coogan, 1994). At the City College of New York, David Tillyer (1994) reported that his writing center's e-mail service invites papers, but funding and software problems have kept that OWL from flying. Other writing centers offering e-mail service are listed at the Purdue Gopher and WWW sites.

E-mail dropboxes and newsgroups are *interactive, time-displaced* systems. Users send questions to an electronic site and wait for a response. Delays from several minutes to several hours (or even days) are possible, depending on question complexity, frequency of tutor logins, transmission delays, and other interfacing factors. For the most part, questions that users ask of writing center tutors on these systems are text-based, context-driven, and situationally embedded. Because they often address issues of language use, stylistics, organization, and tone within the context of a specific paper or rhetorical situation, the questions do not lend themselves to standardized responses and prepackaged handouts. Tutors must engage each writing problem individually, with all of the corresponding demands on their time and effort. Sometimes this includes questions from the tutor asking for clarification, expanding the time required to respond to even the simplest problems. E-mail dropboxes may seem to invite quick questions in the same manner that Grammar Hotlines do, but Purdue's experience indicates that the questions sent via e-mail are—for the most part—vastly different. Phoned-in questions tend to be focused on brief, sentence-level concerns or format issues that can be answered by checking a handbook. E-mailed questions, because they are presented as text messages, tend to be larger and more complex, asking about audience concerns, writing strategies, and so on. The e-mail environment also permits long, complex explanations from the sender, such as in a two-page question to Purdue's OWL about hyphen use, sent by a Dutch engineer working in a Bell laboratory in Belgium. As the writer explained, his first language permits word combining in ways that English does not, so he began by asking for a general orientation to hyphenation in English. He went on to explain that, as an engineer, his need for clarity leads him to misuse hyphenation rules in English as he understands them, and he finally wound up asking for a rationale for breaking rules in the name of clarity. Such messages are very different from Grammar Hotline calls.

Newsgroups may be less familiar to students and more awkward to use than dropboxes, but their intent and operation are essentially the same. Students can post questions to newsgroups using specialized software (such as READNEWS or NONEWS); tutors monitor these newsgroup postings at regular intervals, replying to questions soon after they appear. One important difference between these two posting systems exists, however: messages posted to a newsgroup are accessible to the general public. Users other than "official" tutors may choose to monitor newsgroups and may, in fact, choose to respond to student questions posted there. Unauthorized response may or may not be seen as a problem, depending in part on the quality of advice and/or information provided by "rogue" tutors and, in part, on the degree to which writing centers wish to open themselves to this kind of opportunistic collaboration. Ideally, on one hand, newsgroups moderated by campus writing centers could provide a forum for multiple student and tutor voices, creative brainstorming, and mutual support—not unlike activities that take place on newsgroups many of us participate in as professionals. On the other hand, students hoping for quick responses to simple questions from people working in the writing center may be annoyed, overwhelmed, or intimidated by a flurry of responses from people they never expected or cared to hear from. The On-line Writers' Corner set up by Eric Crump (1993) at the University of Missouri at Columbia has not drawn much interest, perhaps for these reasons. The campus newsgroup at the University of Illinois has drawn, for the most part, an underwhelming response. Fewer than a handful of questions have been posted on <<uiuc.org.writers>> all year, and not due to a lack of publicity. Why so few questions? Two more reasons: network security and computer literacy.

FURTHER CONSIDERATIONS: NETWORK SECURITY AND COMPUTER LITERACY

Network Security

Without question, security issues must be taken into consideration when establishing an OWL, but writing center directors will be frustrated to discover that as important as account security might be to them, it is far, far more important to the people in charge of the campus computing network. Computer-using communities are replete with stories of account abuse by students, ranging from the exchange of copyrighted software (referred to by software pirates as "warez") to trojan programs that steal other users' passwords, to e-mail pyramid schemes. In the eyes of computer specialists, nearly every user with access to a university's mainframe computer is a potential abuser; they consider it their special duty—often with good reason—to protect the majority of users from the abuses of a few. The sad result of this difference in priorities often can be restrictions on the types of services that writing centers can offer through their institution's computing system. Convenience and ease of use are sacrificed on the altar of security, or, as the computer experts and Trekkers might put it, "The needs of the many outweigh the needs of the few."

Such is the case at Illinois. An initial proposal for an e-mail dropbox system was swiftly quashed by a university systems manager. "People have e-mail accounts; places don't," was the tersely worded ruling. The reason given for this inflexible and seemingly arbitrary policy was network security. At most institutions, e-mail is only one of many computer services (Gopher, anonymous ftp, telnet, IRC, etc.) available to users who have computer accounts, and there is no such thing as e-mail without such an account. Access to one entails access to all. The only way to ensure that users act responsibly is to have some way to trace violations back to them. Unfortunately, for e-mail dropboxes to be workable in a writing center setting, they must generally be accessible by more than one tutor; no single tutor would want to be responsible for monitoring all incoming mail 12–16 hours a day, five days or more a week. But because multi-user accounts will not allow network administrators to track abuses to a single user, some institutions may prohibit such accounts, whereas other institutions may only permit accounts as long as they are the responsibility of a writing center director, who closely monitors access to the account. However, some institutions have overcome this obstacle, as is evident in the growing list of writing centers which respond to e-mail questions on the Purdue Gopher and WWW page.

Computer Illiteracy

Computer illiteracy among students, particularly humanities students, at our respective institutions has also proven to be a major obstacle to the successful implementation of OWLS. Most students simply do not use university computing systems. Our experiences with OWLs and informal surveys of students bear this out. One of us, for example, asked an upper-division English class of juniors and seniors how many class members had used the campus computing system—for e-mail, newsgroups, class assignments, etc. Only 3 students of 34 raised their hands. Those few students who do use university computers tend to use them for e-mail alone and, then, usually only to correspond with friends and classmates. Fewer students know what newsgroups are, and fewer than that read them with any regularity. At both Purdue and Illinois, the campus computing centers do not offer courses or training sessions for students interested in learning about newsgroups. Small wonder that so few messages were posted on the Illinois writing center newsgroup over the course of a year. The WORDS program at Purdue was developed in part to answer the problem of students' lack of familiarity with e-mail.

SYNCHRONOUS CHAT SYSTEMS

Another computerized support service that a writing center might offer is a synchronous chat system, which offers students the possibility of connecting online directly with a tutor and engaging in an extended, typewritten conversation about a text, an issue, or a rhetorical problem. Synchronous chat systems are *interactive, realtime* systems. Depending on the sophistication of the technology involved, students and tutors can converse electronically, view a draft onscreen, and/or share files and references with one another as they collaborate. Again, depending on the sophistication of the technology available, it is foreseeable that several students and/or tutors could link simultaneously, all working on the same document in different ways. The writing problems and situations addressed in these conversations are as unpredictable, complex, and varied as any writing problems are likely to be. Students and other users ask questions, get responses or new questions, and then respond. Both user(s) and respondent(s) are online simultaneously, directly connected, and reacting to one another in realtime. True conversational interactions are played out onscreen, though with occasionally tortured slowness as both participants must take the time to write—rather than speak—their observations and commentary.

Interactions fostered by this system are time- and tutor-intensive. Tutors must "listen" to what students are saying about their papers, consider these comments, and respond in much the same way as they would in a traditional conference. Students must do the same.

Wilkie Leith (1993), director of the writing center at George Mason University, posted the following message to the WCENTER electronic bulletin board:

> *One of the methods we're "testing" (meaning we have yet to find real time to proceed) is the PHONE component of VAX. By setting appointment times, having students send drafts through e-mail, downloading and then using the PHONE to have an interactive conversation about the text. This process is clumsy, hard to adjust to, and can be annoying, but—for students (writers) who feel more comfortable on computers or cannot be on campus, this process can produce some interesting results. The tutor and writer can "converse" IN WRITING about the draft.*

Dave Coogan (1993a), at SUNY-Albany, has had a few tutorials over VAX PHONE and compared it to his e-mail interactions:

> *I found the experience much closer to the f2f (face-to-face) tutorial—I could hear the silences, get a good sense of the pacing, and a better sense of who the person I had been tutoring via e-mail actually was. It also felt more exposed: I could no longer craft my "image" or my rhetoric of the tutor. This, most of all, reminded me of the back-and-forth style of f2f interaction where thinking on your feet is everything! I have hope for VAX Phone, but...I think it's a little too obscure for the average student. And the idea*

of making virtual appointments—while tempting—may be counter-intuitive to the rhythms of the VAX, user room access, etc.

Certainly, there are advantages to this sort of interaction. To begin with, to use the system, students must do the one thing we work hardest to get them to do: write. They must not only reflect upon their texts and respond to our questions; they must do so by composing, by putting their thoughts and ideas into written form. Don't we often consider this act alone to be the mark of a successful conference? In this respect, then, the conversations facilitated by synchronous chat systems achieve success from the moment a student question is first transmitted.

Another benefit of chat systems is the ease with which students can save transcripts of online conversations to a file and later review them when they are revising the papers they discussed. No longer would we need to worry about how much students remembered from their conferences. The entire conference would be laid out before them. In fact, a more pressing concern would be whether students would have too much of the conference available to them and might be tempted to appropriate tutors' words as their own (Baker, 1994; Spooner, 1994).

A particularly promising direction for synchronous chat systems is that of meeting students in a MOO, defined by Jennifer Jordan-Henley as "a computer space designed for people to log on and converse while building a textual environment" (Jordan-Henley, 1994). The Virtual Writing Center built by Jordan-Henley and Barry Maid allowed students at Jordan-Henley's college in Tennessee to receive online tutorial help from Maid's graduate students in Arkansas. The result, concluded Jordan-Henley and Maid (1995), is that along with enthusiasm for this new environment, there was significantly more interest in revision on the students' part. Describing another MOO environment, the On-line Writery at the University of Missouri. Eric Crump (1994a) detailed for us one experience of working online with a student. After some initial e-mailing back and forth with a tutor.

> [T]he student then showed up at DaedalusMOO and talked with the tutor about the tutor's comments. Later, the student posted via e-mail a revised version of the introduction. He and I met at the MOO. I had his various drafts in one window, and a realtime discussion going with him in another. We referred to his texts and talked about ways to improve organization and phrasing. When necessary, I cut bits from the text and pasted them into the discussion. He was keeping a log of the discussion, so when I asked him to explain, at one point, what he meant by a particular phrase, he was able to capture his new explanation (which was a whole lot clearer to me), and paste it right into the developing text.... We were both more literally engaged in the revision process. There was no gap

between discussion and implementation. We weren't talking about writing. We were doing it.

THE INSTITUTIONAL MISSION

With the varieties of electronic configurations in mind, we turn now to local issues that also factor into shaping an OWL, and one of the most important of such issues, as we have mentioned, is the mission of the institution in which a writing center resides. The degree to which an institution will support a writing center's online initiative depends on whether an OWL complements the institution's stated missions. For example, when an institution values its forward motion in the use of technology, a writing center's OWL is likely to be viewed as valuable in being yet another bit of visible evidence that the school is at the cutting edge of computer use. Research institutions may also regard OWLs as a marvelously rich source of research data, for these projects can be studied in a variety of disciplines, from very divergent perspectives. Of merit also is the public visibility that some institutions may gain when their writing center's work becomes valuable to the local community or to Internet users everywhere. Where community outreach is important, the institution will value an online service that is also available to the local community and to area high schools. Or this kind of outreach may be seen as a good recruiting tool for the institution. In such cases, OWLs need to be accessible from the Internet so outside users can enter the system through e-mail, a Gopher, or the WWW. But as we have mentioned, this also means that OWLs are open to use from anywhere in the world.

If an institution does not want to expend its limited resources outside the campus, then an OWL should be aimed at—and only accessible to—the institution's students and faculty. Another institutional consideration is the degree to which it promotes accessibility to university services for all students. Physically disabled students, students with learning disabilities, hearing-impaired students, part-time students, students with jobs that leave them little free time during the hours of the writing center's operation, and commuting students are likely to find an OWL far more convenient than attempting to journey to the writing center. On a large university campus, an OWL offers accessibility to students who have no time to trek across long distances or who rarely visit that part of the campus where the writing center is located.

WRITING CENTER GOALS

Perhaps the largest set of options facing writing center directors are those that will shape OWLs' configuration within the context of a writing center's

goals. For example, directors must decide to what degree OWLs will dominate a center's work. This is a question of what constitutes augmenting
present services and when an OWL seems to take over and consume too
much of a center's resources—and a director's energies. Centers also need a
clear sense of what their present student population is and who OWL users
will be. If centers view OWLs as outreach to new populations, then options
exist to explore in locating those populations, in considering how they can
be served and what they need. At institutions with large populations of commuting students, a service that offers opportunities to interact with tutors at
their convenience may be the most useful emphasis—if those communicating students have online access (as some do in their work environments). At
Purdue, another target population are writers (especially novice Internet
browsers) who profit from tapping into Internet resources for papers they
are writing in various disciplines. Another major focus of Purdue's energies
at present is on developing online hypertext tutorials aimed at giving these
students strategies for searching the Internet and helping them learn how to
download what they find. This expands a writing center's goals so it also
becomes a resource center for writers, providing opportunities to learn new
tools for writing that may not be taught in courses. Yet a different goal for
an OWL, provided at Dakota State University, is a set of services intended
both as a faculty resource and as a student tutorial environment (Ericsson,
1993).

People who configure or plan OWLs must also weigh other options and
make decisions as to which aspects of writing center theory and pedagogy
are to be retained and which cannot be replicated exactly. In other words,
there has to be some degree of acceptance of (and a sense of challenge in
inquiring into) new tutorial environments. Dialogue online can be interactive, but if tutors and students engage in nonsynchronic talk situations (not
in a "chat" option), they may not experience the immediate back-and-forth
clarification that is so productive in face-to-face tutoring sessions. All dialogue in online configurations will be text driven, eliminating the subtle
voice and body cues that indicate to students that control is turned over to
them (as in the "minimalist tutoring" strategies discussed by Brooks, 1991).
Onscreen text will also have fewer clues to composing processes (those
scratched out options, arrows, inserts, and other drafting techniques evident
in the hard copy that some students bring to the center) and to possible
learning disabilities that become evident in the disparity between the students' conversations and written products. Although tutors, thus, have to
learn to rely on other clues as to who writers are, meeting onscreen will also
mean meeting in a world where gender, ethnicity, and race are not immediately evident except through lexical and social cues. Voices normally shy
may be stronger and clearer, and stereotypes are less likely to impact the tutorial. But there are losses as well in this faceless disembodied world as the

lack of the personal contact may, seem to dehumanize a setting that writing centers have traditionally viewed as personal and warm.

THE COMPUTING CENTER

The degree to which computing centers are wiling to assist in development of OWLs can vary greatly. It may be a matter of personalities of various administrators, of local politics, of available resources, or of computing center priorities. Personnel may be very receptive to new challenges and new uses of computers for the humanities, or they may have very different agendas. In those cases where knocking on their doors is met with massive silence, indifference, or hostility, trying to get the attention of computer-center personnel can be a highly frustrating—and inordinately time-consuming—experience. No matter how eloquently—or often—the argument is made, some administrators set their priorities for scientific use, or they may be less than enthusiastic about yet another student service that will strain their resources even more. Eric Crump (1994b) recommended that when we are trying to win friends in the computing center, we think of ways we can help the computing center. For example, as Crump suggested, if the computing center is less than enthusiastic about teaching students how to use e-mail, we can offer to hold such training sessions in the writing center, thereby gaining the computing center's gratitude for one less responsibility they have to worry about. In cases where student knowledge of online interaction is minimal and where a writing center is determined to offer online services, software such as Purdue's WORDS may have to be developed to smooth the way.

Because computing centers vary in the degree to which they want to or are able to assist student computer use, this is a major factor in setting up OWLS. Do students have easy access to computing labs? Does the computing center (or some course) provide training or short courses? Is good documentation available? Do all students get accounts? How aggressive is the computing center in assisting students in becoming computer literate? University policy may dictate some of these concerns, but in those cases where there is not a university-wide mandate (or resources) for computer literacy, the computing center may by its assistance, by its inability, by its indifference, or by its capacity for stonewalling control the degree to which students will use OWLS.

THE COMPUTER PROGRAMMER

Yet another major consideration is the skill level, creativity, and philosophical orientations of the people who actually set up OWLS. Some programmers who delight in the complexities of their creations also see merit in user-friendly systems: others simply delight in the complexities. No matter how much coordination there is between the writing center staff who are planning their online environment, at some point plans turn into reality through program designers' abilities, ingenuity, and general approach to creating software. Complications can develop, systems can be created that seem infested with glitches and bugs, and environments can be friendly or not. Or ingenious solutions and clever additions may be introduced by imaginative program designers, whereas others less imaginative may settle for more limited or unnecessarily complicated ways to do things. Moreover, from the perspective of the writing center, there may be preferences—for example, keeping records—that can be easily dismissed by program designers who do not see the importance of building systems in which they have to work around such preferences or who have to worry about how to incorporate them in the software. It becomes important to find programmers who will attempt to understand a writing center's goals, methods, and philosophy as well.

STUDENT COMPUTER LITERACY

As mentioned earlier, a critical factor in setting up an OWL is the computer literacy of student users. By and large, the experiences of those who have fledgling OWLs aloft seem to indicate that while e-mail is a viable option for connecting to students who want to send questions and/or drafts of papers, electronic mail is not something at which most undergraduates are adept. Because it is likely that students become more familiar with uses of computers beyond word processing as they progress through college, writing centers that serve mainly first-year students may find this population least likely to find e-mail a convenient process. Groups who might benefit from an e-mail connection are commuter students sufficiently affluent to have home modems, physically handicapped students who have specialized (and networked) computer equipment available to them elsewhere on campus, students who use networked computers in areas of a large campus remote from the writing center, and students at satellite locations off-campus or in residence halls with networked computers.

WRITING CENTER TUTORS

Another factor that shapes the particular configuration of an OWL is the writing center staff, their attitudes toward online interaction, and their level of enthusiasm. Tutors who see this new opportunity for a somewhat different and potentially exciting means of communication with students will look upon the inconveniences and system breakdowns, the training period, and the struggle to find an "online voice" as opportunities to grow in new directions and to meet students in a new environment. Other tutors, themselves not adept at e-mailing, who haven't made it part of their lives, or who are suspicious about this cyberspace universe, will proceed with more grumbling, hesitancy, and uneasiness about giving up the face-to-face interaction they value and thrive on, a situation already noticed by Jordan-Henley and Maid in their MOO project (1995). As Paula Gillespie (1994) has noted, directors must work with their staffs, not against them, and directors have to see tutor preparation as part of building successful OWLS. This may mean moving slowly until tutors are ready to take on online interaction. It also means training tutors in a number of ways. If OWLS are going to provide a space to respond to papers, then hardcopy oriented tutors may need practice responding to large chunks of text onscreen rather than printing out a paper to read it. As Dave Coogan (1993b), at SUNY-Albany reported, they've successfully begun to read the test onscreen:

> We have the option of printing a student's paper before commenting but rarely use it.... more often we let ourselves get sucked into the screen-scrolling through the text and either holding comments to the end or commenting along the way in separate mail messages. It works, but it is hard to get used to: it's a lot to hold in your head at one time!

Tutors will also need help learning how to respond in ways that overcome the inherent tendency of onscreen text to appear authoritative. Although a question or comment thrown into a tutorial conversation can be left hanging with the intonation indicating the tentativeness of the comment, onscreen text suggests delivered answers. Moving the online interaction away from mere question/answer to a true discussion takes practice as tutors find strategies and a vocabulary for OWL-ing with students. Of concern, also, is the question of the permanence of the tutors' response. In a face-to-face tutorial, tutors' words may become part of writers' thought processes and, ultimately, may appear on the page, filtered through writers' consciousness. But onscreen responses can be used more directly, copied into students' papers, thus raising ethical questions of where online collaboration ends and plagiarism begins, a concern already discussed in *Writing Lab Newsletter* articles (Baker, 1994; Spooner, 1994). Online interaction is also problematic in that it has the potential—if not approached thoughtfully—to move tutoring away from collaboration and to take on the characteristics of the more familiar response in the margins of a paper.

CONCLUSION

As we have tried to demonstrate here, OWLS can meet a variety of needs just as they cannot handle others. OWLS can also take a variety of shapes, and they can create new challenges, extend our reach, and make us ask finally what our rationales are for going online. Do we want to explore new environments in which to meet with writers? Or have writers meet with tutors at other institutions? Do we want to move into—and help our students move into—a future which will certainly include writing, researching, and working on the Internet? Do we want to reach new groups of students who don't have easy access to the center? Given the changing demographics in higher education as increasing numbers of students have part-time status, Dickie Selfe (1994) warned us of the importance of considering their needs in new ways:

These students often work full time, they have families, they are returning to school to retrain, and as a result they are often unable to commute to schools during the hours that many writing centers are available. As much as WCs need to protect and develop their face-to-face interactive skills, they must also recognize that this very strength is a significant burden to a growing number of students.

If such considerations are uppermost in the planning of OWLS and if these students have off-campus access to online computers, then providing tutorial interaction online will be a major component in a service that assists this population. Whatever shapes our OWLS take, they promise to lead us into interesting new directions. Fortunately, writing centers are familiar with exploring new paths, even as we wonder where they will lead us.

REFERENCES

Baker, J. (1994). An ethical question about on-line tutoring in the writing lab, *Writing Lab Newsletter, 18* (5), 6–7.

Barrier, B. (1994, April). The on-line writing and reference center. Poster presented at the National Writing Centers Association Conference. New Orleans, LA.

Brooks, J. (1991). Minimalist tutoring: Making the student do all the work. *Writing Lab Newsletter, 15* (6), 1–4.

Coogan, D. (1993a, December 15). On-line—why not use PHONE? In *WCENTER* [Online]. Available: <listserv@unicorn.acs.ttu.edu.>.

Coogan, D. (1993b, December 14). On-Line Writing Lab. In *WCENTER* [Online]. Available: <listserv@unicorn.acs.ttu.edu.>.

Coogan, D. (1994, May 20). (e-mail to Muriel Harris). Question (a brief one). [Internet]. <harrism@mace.cc.purdue.edu.>.

Crump, E. (1993, December 10). What's up with your wiole? *WIOLE-L.* <listserv@MIZZOUI.missouri.edu.>.

Crump, E. (1994a, November 4). On-line wc. In *WCENTER* [Online]. Available: <listserv@unicorn.acs.ttu.edu.>.

Crump, E. (1994b, March). Politics: Conflicts between humanists and technologies and how tensions affect the development of on-line writing environments. Paper presented at Conference on College Composition and Communication. Nash-ville, TN.

Ericsson, P. (1993, November 2). The OWL in flight. In *WIOLE-L* [Online]. Available: <listserv@MIZZOU1.missouri.edu.>.

Essid, Joe. (1994, May 20). (e-mail to Muriel Harris). A question. [Internet]. <harrism@mace.cc.purdue.edu.>.

Gillespie, P. (1994). Tutors' roles in developing an OWL. Paper presented at the meet-ing of East Central Writing Centers Association Conference. Toledo, OH.

Healy, D. (1994, May 20). (e-mail to Muriel Harris). Our OWL. [Internet]. <harrism@mace.cc.purdue.edu.>.

Hickey, D. (1994, May 20). (e-mail to Muriel Harris). A question. [Internet]. <harrism@mace.cc.purdue.edu.>.

Jordan-Henley, J. (1994, November 7). Trends. In *WCENTER* [Online]. Available: <listserv@unicorn.acs.ttu.edu.>.

Jordan-Henley, J. & Maid, B. (1995). MOOving along the information superhighway: Writing centers in cyberspace. *Writing Lab Newsletter,* 19 (5), 1–4.

Leith, W. (1993, December 14). On-line—why not use PHONE? In *WCENTER* [Online]. Available: <listserv@unicorn.acs.ttu.edu.>.

Penna, C. (1994, May 16). (e-mail to Muriel Harris). Writing Centers & Gophers. [Internet]. <harrism@mace.cc.purdue.edu.>.

Selfe, D. (1994, January 24). Some stats. In *WIOLE-L* [Online]. Available: <listserv@MIZZOU1.missouri.edu.>.

Spooner, M. (1994). A dialogue on OWLing in the writing lab: Some thoughts about on-line writing labs. *Writing Lab Newsletter,* 18 (6), 6–8.

From Place to Space: Perceptual and Administrative Issues in the Online Writing Center

Dave Healy

Online conferencing, including both synchronous and asynchronous exchanges, started in the composition classroom and moved to the writing center. Writing centers, no longer limited to face-to-face encounters, have begun exploring the potential of electronic conferencing. So far, most discussions of online conferencing have focused on how conference dynamics are affected by the computer. This article explores other implications of online writing centers, specifically the effects of electronically decentralizing the center and how such a move might affect tutors and writing center directors. For directors, asynchronous conferencing promises to simplify scheduling but complicate supervision, while its potential effects on workplace ethos are more difficult to predict. The potential for information technology to preserve conference talk is explored, as are some of its darker implications, such as threats of Big Brother and panopticism. The author concludes that a writing center's autonomy within the institution is potentially both enhanced and threatened by introducing online conferencing.

asynchronous	informational technology	scheduling	autonomy
	online conferencing	supervision	decentralization
	panopticism	work place ethos	

Healy, Dave. "From Place to Space: Perceptual Administrative Issues in the Online Writing Center." *Computers and Composition* 12 (1995): 183–93. Reprinted with permission from Elsevier Science.

Correspondence and requests for reprints should be sent to Dave Healy. University of Minnesota, General College, 140 Appleby Hall, 128 Pleasant St. SE, Minneapolis, MN 55455-0434. e-mail <healy001@maroon.tc.umn.edu>.

As the online composition classroom has become more common on college and university campuses, student writers have become increasingly comfortable not only composing and revising but also sending, receiving, and responding to text electronically. Through file servers, LANs, electronic mail, MUDs, MOOs, MUSHes, Internet Relay Chat, and the like, writers have access to both asynchronous and synchronous interaction with other readers and writers. As writers have expanded their horizons and their repertoires, writing centers have looked for ways to meet the needs of a new kind of client—one no longer limited by the constraints of face-to-face conferencing. As writing centers have begun to offer online consultation, questions have arisen about the strengths and weaknesses of the new medium. Thus far, these questions have focused mainly on how the writer-reader interaction is affected by the intervening computer (Coogan, 1994: Grubbs, 1994: Harris, 1994).

But online conferencing has implications that extend beyond the dynamics of the tutorial itself, including issues that get at the heart of what a writing center is. One such issue that has long engaged the attention of writing center theorists is the matter of place. Historically, though they have gone by different names (Carino, 1992), writing centers have been physical locations: Writing center clients go to a particular place. Where that place should be, what it should look like, whether it should be a single or multiple locations—these are questions that writing center personnel have debated at length.

DECENTRALIZING THE WRITING CENTER

Geoffrey Chase (1985) has argued for decentralizing the writing center by moving it into other places, such as dormitories and academic departments. For Chase, a large, centralized center reinforces writing as an individual, product-oriented, extrinsically motivated behavior. Small, decentralized centers, on the other hand, promote the social dimension of writing as well as "being connected to the central experience of students" (p. 3) by contextualizing writing within the environments where students live (residence halls) and do the bulk of their academic work (departments). Louise Smith (1986) argued that writing centers should be decentralized to offset tutors' isolation from the "contexts of assigned readings and class discussions in which the various writing assignments are supposed to be prepared" (p. 4). At Smith's institution, undergraduate and graduate tutors are paired with faculty mentors in the writing-across-the-curriculum program.

More recent commentators amplify Chase's and Smith's call for decentralization. Adams (1991) has attempted to serve the Writing Across the Curriculum (WAC) program at her large university by establishing "satellite centers" in separate locations, for example, the journalism department and the law school. Animated by Bruffee's (1984) notion of communities of knowledgeable peers. Adams sees her satellite centers as "not just new versions of our first center, but different facilities for serving different population (p. 76). For Devenish (1993), "decentering" the writing center is bound up with a mission of outreach: "If we re-figure writing centers as places to go out *from* and not merely places students are sent or come *into,* we offer ourselves a sustaining metaphor for a much more proactive role" (p. 4). Like Chase's small-is-beautiful, decentralized center, Devenish's writing-center-without-walls places tutors in residence halls beyond the center's normal hours and also facilitates WAC efforts by inserting tutors "within and beyond the curriculum" (p. 4).

Online writing centers may be seen as another example of this movement toward decentralization because online clients are no longer bound to a single location. The virtual writing center is, however, fundamentally different from one in the residence hall or law school. Chase, Smith, Devenish, and Adams recommend moving from "our" turf to our clients' turf. Clearly, movement to residence halls and academic departments is significant and has the potential to affect the attitudes that both consultant and client bring to the writing conference, but the result is still place-bound talk about writing. Online conferencing moves from place to space. What are the consequences of *this* kind of move?

Writing Center Vs. Curriculum-Based Tutoring

One result might be to render further autonomous what Kail and Trimbur (1987) called the "semiautonomous" space of writing centers. They argue that a writing-center-based, peer-tutoring model is superior to a curriculum-based one because the former, by locating itself "at a remove from the normal delivery system of curriculum and instruction" is better able to precipitate a "crisis of authority" in a traditional hierarchical approach to teaching and learning: a curriculum-based model is more closely tied to and implicated in that hierarchy (p. 9).

Interestingly, the decentralization called for by these commentators tends to be presented as a move toward curriculum-based tutoring. Adams' (1991) satellite tutors corresponded regularly with teachers. "creating the important triangle of tutor/teacher/student which the writing fellows program provides at the main center" (p. 79). Devenish's (1993) writing-center-without-walls called for "designated tutors" who work with a particular professor, attend class, lead discussions, present workshops, and direct small groups. Smith (1986) described the tutor's role in similar terms (even going so far as to call the tutor a teacher's "apprentice") and observes that successful tutor–professor collaborations "often encourage professors to invite the tutors little-by-little into their classrooms" (p. 8). And Chase (1985) saw his decentralized center as an important part of the larger curriculum: "The writing center in our program is an extension of what goes on in the classroom, not an addition for a segment of our students" (p. 4).

By blurring the line between the writing center and the classroom, these theorists relocate the center—not just physically, but pedagogically and institutionally. They move the writing center away from the student-centered role it occupies in the vision of perhaps its most famous apologist, North (1984): "In short, we are not here to serve, supplement, back up, complement, reinforce, or otherwise be defined by any external curriculum" (p. 440). In response to the teacher's question, "How can I make use of the writing center?" North says. "[T]eachers, as teachers, do not need and cannot use a writing center; only writers need it, only writers can use it" (p. 440).

For Kail and Trimbur (1987), too, a movement toward curriculum-based tutoring would threaten writing centers' autonomy. That autonomy, they realize, is limited because "[p]eer tutoring programs based on collaborative learning [i.e., the writing center model] are, of course, located inside the institutions of higher education" (p. 9). A virtual writing center would at one level still share this locational status vis-à-vis the institution, but its "location" might be less obvious to clients than that of its place-bound counterpart. Online conferencing makes the "Your place or mine?" question obsolete. In so doing, it may fundamentally alter the way that both clients and consultants perceive their relationship to the institution because the meeting place is no longer physically tied to the institution at all. Most writing center personnel feel that their biggest hurdle is getting clients inside the door. What if there is no door? Might otherwise reluctant clients for whom either inertia or embarrassment is a barrier to visiting the writing center be more likely to seek online consultants with whom they can correspond more conveniently and anonymously from their classroom or computer lab or dorm room? And might the conversations that take place online be less directly implicated in institutional hierarchy because the institution is less obviously present in those conversations?

ADMINISTRATIVE ISSUES IN THE ONLINE WRITING CENTER

I have suggested that a virtual writing center may be perceived differently by clients than the traditional, place-bound center. But what about writing center employees—tutors and their supervisors? How will their work lives be affected by movement from place to space? In the place-bound center, employees typically work set hours in a set location. In an online writing center offering asynchronous conferencing, however, consultants would not necessarily have to do their work in any particular place or at any particular time. What implications does this revised definition of the work place have for the supervisory efforts of writing center directors?

Although it is possible to conceive of a virtual writing center existing entirely in cyberspace, it seems unlikely that online conferencing would ever replace face-to-face consultation in a given writing center. Even advocates for decentering the place-bound center (e.g., Devenish, 1993) generally try to make it clear they are not advocating that existing centers be replaced but, rather, that services be supplemented. Similarly, discussions of online writing centers (such as those of Coogan and of Harris and Pemberton in this issue) do not predict the demise of face-to-face conferencing; instead, online conferencing is seen as an alternative that may supplement, but will not supplant, that which centers have traditionally offered. What seems likely to emerge, then, are writing centers that offer both face-to-face and online consulting. What might this amalgam look like, and how might a reconstituted center affect writing center directors?

Scheduling, Supervision, and Ethos

The addition of electronic conferencing to a traditional writing center has implications for several important administrative functions, including scheduling, supervision, and maintaining a positive work place ethos. Scheduling is the bane of most writing center directors' existence, especially those whose centers are staffed by students, whether undergraduates or graduates. Because students have their own academic work to schedule, staffing the writing center to meet client demand can be an ongoing challenge. For the beleaguered supervisor, faced with the certainty of peak demand between 10 a.m. and noon and the realization that most of their staff will be in class during those hours, the prospect of some walk-in traffic being replaced by online clients is welcome because asynchronous conferencing need not be "scheduled." Furthermore, asynchronous conferencing can help regularize not only the peaks but also the valleys of the drop-in center. One challenge for directors of drop-in centers is what to have employees do during down time. Insisting that they confine themselves to center-related business invites make-work scenarios, although allowing them to do their own studying while waiting for business runs the risk that they will come to view clients as an interruption of their own academic work. Responding to clients' e-mail messages provides a constructive alternative for slack times in the center.

But although increasing online business promises to lessen some scheduling hassles, it could make other supervisory tasks more complicated. As I've noted, asynchronous conferencing, though it could be done during regular working hours, by definition is not limited to those conditions. Consider this scenario: Arie sends an e-mail message to the writing center and attaches the text of the paper she's working on. Talia responds with several observations and questions. Arie's next post is sent to the writing center, but it now begins "Dear Talia." Another tutor notices this post and directs Talia's attention to it. However, Talia is just going off duty. Later that day, while working on her own paper in a campus computer lab. Talia remembers Arie's post and decides to respond, knowing she is not scheduled to be at work again for two days. Should Talia be paid for the time she spends in the computer lab responding to Arie? How can she document how much time she spent on this task?

To be sure, this scenario is not unique to asynchronous tutoring. A similar situation could have emerged from a face-to-face conference in the writing center and a chance meeting later in the library. The dilemma faced by a tutor in such an encounter is familiar to many other professionals, for example, the doctor who encounters a patient in the grocery store, or the lawyer whose client happens to be at the same party. When is one off duty, and how does one handle requests for services outside of the office? Where do "billable hours" begin? What is different about asynchronous conferencing, though, is that it need not be limited to happenstance. Talia could build it into her day—but on her own terms. And unless a writing center director could argue that the online consulting Talia does from the center during office hours is demonstrably better than what she provides from a remote site, it seems somewhat arbitrary and capricious to limit her consulting to the 15 hours a week when she is scheduled to be physically present in the center. But if Talia can do her job, or at least part of her job, from any networked computer—on campus or off campus—how will her supervisor know when she is working?

This is a question managers increasingly face in the business world as more and more employees do at least part of their work at home. A recent survey by Link Resources, a New York-based technology research group, found that such employees number 7.6 million, up 15% from a year ago (Van. 1994, p. 1B). This trend clearly results from technological developments, but it has just as much to do with changing attitudes on the part of managers, according to Joel Goldhar, professor of technology management at the Illinois Institute of Technology:

> The big thing is the change in view among managers that a wider range of people can be trusted to manage their own work. It's not so much that telephones and computers make it possible for people to work at home as this changing view by management. (Van, p. 2B)

Oversight of employees, then, is one aspect of writing center administration that could be affected by introducing electronic conferencing into a hitherto place-bound center. But employees stand in relation not only to their supervisor but also to each other, and working relationships among peers have much to do with the ethos clients experience in the center. How might the introduction of online conferencing affect collegiality and work-place ethos?

Most tutoring positions require formal training that typically includes readings in composition and writing center theory, role-playing, etc. Much of a tutor's how-to knowledge, however, is acquired by observing experienced tutors in action and by engaging in informal conversation with colleagues. Online consulting constitutes both a threat to and an opportunity for work-place community.

Unlike face-to-face talk, computer-mediated communication does not get overheard. In the traditional writing center, consultants have ample opportunity to watch their colleagues in action without making themselves obvious. One-to-one conferences are the hallmark of the writing center, but those conferences, because of the social space in which they typically occur, have many windows. The result is an atmosphere that invites informal, often unintentional role modeling on the part of experienced tutors. The online conference, on the other hand, is closed to casual observation. Any exchange of information or sharing of strategies among asynchronous online consultants has to be done deliberately.

Zuboff (1988) explored effects of computerization on work-place ethos in factories, banks, and offices. Of the different types of workers Zuboff studied, clerks seem to have the most in common with writing center tutors because of the importance of office dynamics on the definition and execution of their jobs. As Zuboff noted.

> *[O]ffice functions have always had a "soft" character. They have been sufficiently unspecified so that clerks, in collaboration with their supervisors, must take on a certain amount of coordinative and communicative responsibility if the work is to be accomplished in a way that can be held accountable to generally recognized criteria of orderliness and rationality. (pp. 136–137)*

This "coordinative and communicative responsibility" goes beyond simple mastery of functional tasks and traditionally has depended on an environment that fosters interpersonal communication. Such communication might appear to the casual observer to be incidental to the task at hand but is, in fact, a source of the practitioner knowledge that individuals depend on to do their work.

> *The knowledge traditionally associated with clerical work is not limited to the substantive knowledge of the methods by which a task should be executed. Such substantive understanding has been embedded in a much wider, richer, more detailed, and largely unspecified interpersonal reality. It is through "informal" contact with peers and supervisors that appropriate courses of action generally are determined. Office work is chatty, but that chattiness is more than a social perquisite of the job. It is the ether that transmits collaborative impulses, as people help each other form judgments and make choices about the work at hand. (Zuboff, 1988, p. 136)*

THE WRITING CENTER
AND INFORMATION TECHNOLOGY

The online writing center threatens to dissipate this ether or to change its composition by reducing the amount of overhearable talk that occurs in the center. But if electronic conferencing potentially reduces the informal observation and unrehearsed modeling that goes on in the writing center, it compensates by preserving that which is always being lost, namely the very talk on which the traditional writing center depends. For the fact is that although some writing center talk may be overheard and appropriated, most is not. From one perspective, talk is the center's ether; from another, talk is always dissipating into the ether, from whence it can never be reliably retrieved. In the traditional writing center, most of what actually transpires during a conference is not preserved, nor is it usually open to inspection—barring such extraordinary interventions as audio or video taping. Only partial, reconstructed, mediated accounts of writing center tutorials typically survive the actual event, usually in the form of brief synopses written by tutors. An online conference, however, can be preserved in its entirety—subject to analysis by colleagues or a supervisor, available for record keeping, for training, for employee evaluation.

As a complete and permanent record, the online conference transcript eliminates a problem often faced by tutors in a drop-in center. How to maintain continuity and avoid duplication of efforts when more than one consultant works with the same client. With online conferences, there is no question about what was covered in a previous session. Also, as a tool for tutor training or evaluation, online transcripts supplement audio and video tapes as a way to capture a conference and subject it to others' analysis. The online conference thus becomes part of what Zuboff (1988) called "information technology," which not only accomplishes a particular function but also

> *reflects back on its activities and on the system of activities to which it is related. Information technology not only products action but also produces a voice that symbolically renders events, objects, and processes so that they become visible, knowable, and shareable in a new way. (p. 9)*

So although some voices have been stilled in the online writing center, others have been added. The one-to-one conference, once only partially accessible to nonparticipants, becomes part of a larger conversation. But what kind of conversation is that likely to be?

PANOPTICONISM

Actually, to call these voices a "conversation" is perhaps presumptuous, for that term implies a certain degree of reciprocity and mutuality—qualities that may or may not fit the assumptions and perceptions of either tutors or directors in an online writing center. When describing the prospects of online conferences in the writing center, it might be just as appropriate to invoke the specter of Big Brother. That, in fact, is the spirit that animates many recent descriptions of computers in the classroom, although the most popular referent is not Orwell, but Jeremy Bentham and his "Panopticon," as described and interpreted by Foucault (1977; e.g., Bowers, 1988; Hawisher & Selfe, 1991; Provenzo, 1992; Zuboff, 1988).

The Panopticon, or Inspection House, as conceived by Bentham and eventually built by his brother Samuel, was a 12-sided polygon that would house prisoners with a central observation tower. Through a combination of strategically placed windows and mirrors, inmates are always visible to guards, though the prisoners cannot see each other or their observers. As Foucault (1977) noted the Panopticon was a radical departure from the dungeon, that in effect makes prisoners invisible; instead, the Panopticon traps them in constant visibility. The effect is that individuals come to believe they are being observed constantly—whether they actually are or not.

> *Hence the major effect of the Panopticon: to induce on the inmate a state of conscious and permanent visibility that assures the automatic functioning of power. So to arrange things that the surveillance is permanent in its effects, even if it is discontinuous in its actions: that the perfection of power should tend to render its actual exercise unnecessary. (p. 201)*

The beauty of the Panopticon, from a narrow administrative perspective, is its ability to create self-regulating behavior.

> *He who is subjected to a field of visibility, and who knows it, assumes responsibility for the constraints of power; he makes them play spontaneously upon himself; he inscribes in himself the power relation in which he simultaneously plays both roles: he becomes the principle of his own subjection. (Foucault, 1977, p. 202)*

This effect is, of course, the same as that of Big Brother's "telescreen," that could never be turned off—that recorded every movement and whisper.

> *There was of course no way of knowing whether you were being watched at any given moment. How often, or on what system, the Thought Police plugged in on any individual wire was guesswork. It was even conceivable that they watched everybody all of the time. But at any rate they could plug in your wire whenever they wanted to. You had to live—did live from habit that became instinct—in the assumption that every sound you made was overheard, and, except in darkness, every movement scrutinized. (Orwell, 1949, pp. 6–7)*

The implicit identification that these references suggest between supervisors and prison wardens or Thought Police is no doubt troubling for most writing center directors. No one wants to be identified with Big Brother, least of all academics who live and move and have their being in an environment that jealously protects academic freedom and constantly questions the distribution of power in its ranks. It should be just as disturbing, though, to contemplate the prospect of self-regulating behavior among tutors aware that every response they make to a client's writing can be monitored. Although most directors want employees who don't require constant supervision, they also want tutors who feel free to take risks, to try new strategies, to act on their own intuitive hunches. Panoptic principles threaten these qualities and behaviors.

In one of the corporations studied by Zuboff (1988), management developed a computer conferencing system designed to improve the efficiency of communication within the organization. Initially, employees greeted the new medium enthusiastically and participation grew rapidly. Eventually, though, they came to see their participation in the network through a darker lens as management reasserted its need to monitor and control exchanges on the network. Employees responded by limiting themselves to

> *perfunctory messages and routine electronic mail. The textualization of sociality accomplished in the service of learning and innovation had opened the firm to a rich new array of possibilities for the organization of communicative behavior. Gradually, that text was subverted by managers' need to impose their own conception of appropriate work behavior. (p. 363)*

Closer to home, writing center tutors on a computer network recently displayed a similar response to what they perceived as the incursions of management into their electronic space. In the Fall of 1993, one thread on the popular list WCENTER,[1] that is dominated by writing center directors, had to do with whether tutors' contributions were appropriate and welcome. Though participants uniformly asserted that they valued everyone's participation and that tutors should feel free to contribute to discussions on WCENTER, some tutors' comments indicated that they did not feel entirely comfortable doing so. In response to this perceived reluctance. I ventured the suggestion that perhaps tutors should have their own list. Though this idea met with mixed reactions. I sensed enough support to prompt me to create a new list, called WRITINGC.[2]

Participation on this list grew slowly. By April, 1994, WRITINGC had 57 subscribers, about two thirds of whom were tutors, the rest being writing

---

[1]To subscribe to WCENTER, send e-mail to <listproc@unicorn.acs.ttu.edu.> Leave the subject line blank, and in the first line of the note type <set wcenter mail ack>.

[2]WRITINGC has changed sites and is now WRIT-C. To subscribe. send e-mail to <listserv@vml.spcs.umn.edu>. Leave the subject line blank, and in the first line of the note type: <subscribe writ-c Your Name>.

center directors. Contributions were sporadic, but several interesting threads did develop. One of these concerned an incident at a list member's writing center involving a tutor who reported to work drunk. A spirited discussion ensued about workplace ethics and the rights and responsibilities of employees, as well as a good deal of fairly irreverent commentary about the advantages of drinking on the job. Just when this thread had begun to unravel, its instigator made a most disquieting revelation: The whole incident was a hoax; it had never occurred. Reaction was forceful and polarized. Some respondents said they felt betrayed, whereas others asserted that the discussion had been valuable even if it had been based on a fictitious incident.

At this point, a list member who was a writing center director posted a response to the drunken tutor thread, the general tone of which was perceived by at least one tutor as fairly patronizing. This tutor posted a rather pointed response that began "Dear Dad." "Dad" replied, expressing dismay that his remarks had been misconstrued as well as anger that he had been addressed so sarcastically. The effect of this exchange on the retest of the list was chilling. Participation dwindled almost immediately, and by the end of the school year the list was dormant.

Incidents such as this one are a reminder of how complex issues of power and authority can become, and how computers rarely remain a neutral presence in those incidents. The non-neutrality of technology in education is Bowers' (1988) thesis, and his greatest concern is for the long-term, internalized effects that technology may have by intensifying a cultural mindset that normalizes surveillance, monitoring, and data collection. What frightens Bowers, and should frighten us, is that accepting such a system could become automatic and unconscious, seen as "essential to the development of the socially responsible citizen," and thus viewed as "a normal, even necessary, aspect of adult life" (p. 19).

AUTONOMY AND PROFESSIONALISM

As I have argued elsewhere (Healy, 1993), to help foster self-direction and initiative in their clients, writing centers need to preserve their semi-autonomous space. And as I have suggested in this article, adding online conferencing to the traditional writing center can be a way of maintaining and even increasing the center's autonomy in the academy. But if institutional autonomy can be enhanced in the virtual writing center, individual autonomy may be threatened. That threat ultimately affects not only individual employees, but the larger enterprise of which they are a part. For as Aronowitz (1992) reminded us, professionalism and autonomy have always been linked, and professionalization is an indication of an occupation's relative status.

The cornerstone of the ideology of professionalism is the belief that some professionals in various categories of labor possess skills or knowledge that entitle them to considerable autonomy in the performance of their work. Thus there is a contrast between the capacity to make independent decisions based upon specialized knowledge and the close supervision of most labor...presumably because [those] jobs require little or no training. (p. 122)

To the extent, then, that computers in the writing center threaten autonomy, they threaten professionalism and hence the writing center's status in the academy. Information technology, it turns out, like any technology, always has unintended and unanticipated effects. For the writing center, those effects may fundamentally alter how the center is perceived both by clients and employees. Chase (1985) has said that

the way in which our centers are designed—physically and socially—imply an ideology or set of attitudes of which we may not be aware. Students do not develop a relationship only with a tutor but with a whole writing center. (p. 2)

Chase is talking about the traditional place-bound writing center, but his observation is relevant for enthusiasts of the online center as well. What is the ontological status of a virtual writing center, and what kind of relationship will clients develop with it? How will it be perceived by the rest of the academy? What possibilities and what threats are opened up by going online?

These are the kinds of questions that writing centers must confront in the age of information technology. But though the questions are inevitably theoretical and speculative, they must not, as Zuboff (1988) reminded us, be entertained only in the abstract.

The choices for the future cannot be deduced from electronic data or from abstract measures or organizational functioning. They are embedded in the living detail of daily life at work as ordinary people confront the dilemmas raised by the transformational qualities of new information technology. (p. 12)

Our research, says Zuboff, should focus on the "texture of human experience—what people say, feel, and do—in dealing with the technological changes that imbue their immediate environment" (p. 12). The enemy of such research, she goes on to say,

is what philosophers call "the natural attitude," our capacity to live daily life in a way that takes for granted the objects and activities that surround us. Even when we encounter new objects in our environment, our tendency is to experience them in terms of categories and qualities with which we are already familiar. (p. 13)

In her research on the effects of information technology on the work lives of ordinary people. Zuboff looked for a "'window of opportunity" during which people who were working with the technology for the first time were ripe with questions and insights regarding the distinct qualities of their experience" (p. 13). Once that window had closed, people "would find ways to accommodate their understanding to the altered conditions of work, making it more difficult to extract fresh insights from beneath a new crust of familiarity" (p. 13). Online writing centers represent a window of opportunity. Our challenge is to be reflective and self-critical while the opportunities before us are still fresh.

REFERENCES

Adams, K. H. (1991). Satellite writing centers: A successful model for writing across the curriculum. In R. Wallace & J. Simpson (Eds.), *The writing center: New directions* (pp. 73–81). New York: Garland.

Aronowitz, S. (1992). Looking out: The impact of computers on the lives of professionals. In C. Tuman (Ed.), *Literacy online: The promise (and peril) of reading and writing with computers* (pp. 119–137). Pittsburgh, PA: University of Pittsburgh Press.

Bowers, C. A. (1998). *The cultural dimensions of educational computing: Understanding the non-neutrality of technology.* New York: Teachers College Press.

Bruffee, K. A. (1984). Peer tutoring and the "conversation of mankind." In G. Olson (Ed.), *Writing centers: Theory and administration* (pp. 3–15). Urbana, IL: National Council of Teachers of English.

Carino, P. (1992). What do we talk about when we talk about our metaphors: A cultural critique of clinic, lab, and center. *The Writing Center Journal, 13*(1), 31–42.

Chase, G. (1985, April). Small is beautiful: A plan for the decentralized writing center. *Writing Lab Newsletter 9*(8), pp. 1–4.

Coogan, D. (1994, September). Towards a rhetoric of on-line tutoring. *Writing Lab Newsletter 19*(1), pp. 3–5.

Devenish, A. (1993, September). Decentering the writing center. *Writing Lab Newsletter, 18*(1), pp. 4–7.

Foucault, M. (1977). *Discipline and punish: The birth of the prison* (A. Sheridan, Trans.). New York: Pantheon. (Original work published 1975)

Grubbs, K. (1994, October). Some questions about the politics of on-line tutoring in electronic writing centers. *Writing Lab Newsletter 19*(2), pp. 7–12.

Harris, M. (1994). *Trade-offs: What is gained and what is lost when writers and tutors interact via machines?* Paper presented at the Conference on College Composition and Communication, Nashville, TN.

Hawisher, G. E., and C. L. Selfe. (1991). The rhetoric of technology and the electronic writing class. *College Composition and Communication, 42*, 55–65.

Healy, D. (1993). A defense of dualism: The writing center and the classroom. *The Writing Center Journal, 14*(1), 16–29.

Kail, H., and J. Trimbur, (1987). The politics of peer tutoring. *WPA: Writing Program Administration, 11*(1–2), 5–12.

North, S. M. (1984). The idea of a writing center. *College English, 46,* 433–446.

Orwell, G. (1949). *1984.* New York: Harcourt Brace Jovanovich.

Provenzo, E. F., Jr. (1992). The electronic panopticon: Censorship, control, and indoctrination in a post-typographic culture. In C. Tuman (Ed.), *Literacy online: The promise (and peril) of reading and writing with computers* (pp. 167–188). Pittsburgh, PA: University of Pittsburgh Press.

Smith, L. Z. (1986). Independence and collaboration: Why we should decentralize writing centers. *The Writing Center Journal, 7*(1), 3–10.

Van, J. (1994, May 16). Technology may imperil office work. *St. Paul Pioneer Press,* pp. 18–28.

Zuboff, S. (1988). *In the age of the smart machine: The future of work and power.* New York: Basic.

Towards a Rhetoric of On-Line Tutoring

David Coogan

In the spring of 1993 I got this great idea: why not turn a writing tutorial into an actual *writing* tutorial? So often writing center tutorials have nothing to do with the act of writing. Students read aloud, make conversation, do some editing or planning, but rarely compose or communicate in writing. And there is no guilt here: As Stephen North reminds us in "Training Tutors To Talk About Writing," the student's "text is essentially a medium" for conversation (439), a starting point, a place to *begin* the session, not end it. But what would happen to that conversation if I took away the paper, took away speech, and took away physical presence? What would happen to the idea of a writing tutorial if we decided to make the act of writing the main event?

To test this idea, I added to conduct writing tutorials over electronic mail. I wanted to see how such interaction would work. My plan went like this: students would send me their texts and questions over e-mail during posted hours and I would respond right away. The motive was to exchange lots of e-mail—say, over the course of an hour. In a sense, I wanted to replicate the conditions of face-to-face tutoring: two people conversing about a text. What I learned, however (surprise, surprise), was that e-mail could not—and probably should not—replicate the conditions of face-to-face tutorials. Virtual appointments were hard to keep, and hardly anyone actually made contact with me during the posted hours (Sunday—Tuesday, 7:00 p.m.—12:00 a.m.).

It was just as well. The advantage of e-mail, I soon found out, was that you didn't *need* an appointment. You didn't even need regular hours for drop-in sessions. I began to advertise quick turn-around instead of appointments: "Send your text whenever you want. Get a response within six hours!" This became the drop-everything-and-tutor method. Instead of sitting in front of the monitor "doing time" waiting for someone to send me some e-mail, I'd log on every other hour: when there was e-mail, there was a session.

From these new working conditions, I began to figure out a methodology of e-mail tutoring. The main difference underlying all the issues I discuss below is that e-mail changes our sense of time, and in so doing, it

Coogan, David. "Towards a Rhetoric of On-Line Tutoring." *Writing Lab Newsletter* 19.1 (1994): 3–5. Reprinted with permission. All Rights and Title reserved unless permission is granted by Purdue University. Material will not be reproduced in any form without express written permission.

changes the power dynamics of tutoring. After all, a face-to-face tutorial takes place in real time. It is bound by beginning, middle, and end. A session must have a point. And we often feel cheated if there is no point. (We're not comfortable with "dead air.") We even have to train ourselves to recognize different kinds of silence so that it doesn't *feel* like dead air. But e-mail tutorials have nothing but dead air. They are mute, silent—like any text. Often they take place over a few days. They are open-ended, sprawling, not bound by the hour or the actual writing center. E-mail tutorials could happen anywhere, anytime. However, access to the writing center doesn't necessarily get easier. In fact, it may get harder. Many students don't know how to do e-mail, let alone upload files. (And it goes without saying that many students don't have PCs and modems in their rooms.) These sessions are also solitary. They take place at the scene of writing. Wherever the student and tutor may be—in a crowded user room or a room of one's own off campus—the student and tutor extend themselves into a social space, but only in their minds, only in writing. The tutor's job is to create a textual scene of learning. In this scene, the tutor and the student have time—perhaps too much time—to revise their thoughts and *construct* the tutorial. They become aware—even self conscious—of their emerging rhetorical identity: "tutor" and "student" become characters in a story, elements of an instructional "plot." Phatic cues no longer set the scene. All we have is text.

As we know from the writing center, presence is everything. A student wears his paper like clothing, often asking right away, "how does this look to you? Is it ok?" The paper doesn't communicate by itself—the person communicates. But an electronic text *announces itself* as communication. It arrives in the mail without the benefit of speech to support its content, defend its appearance, or in other ways indicate who (or what) is inside. Thus in a face-to-face meeting, the student and tutor talk "over" a paper. The paper connects them. They see the same text. And the paper creates tension: who touches it? reads from it? marks it? The underlying question soon becomes, what will be DONE to the paper? As a methodology, then, the f2f tutorial is grounded by paper, and The Paper can limit tutor-student interaction.

In his experiment with an asynchronous, e-mail based writing class, Ted Jennings concludes the following:

> The crucial difference between the paper-bound and paperless environment lies in how a writer's texts are perceived. In the electronic medium they are harder to "own," harder to possess and defend, than are tangible pseudo-permanent sheaves of paper. Sharing an electronic text does not imply giving it away, and telling writers what you remember about their texts is not like defacing their intellectual property. (47)

The catch-all theory is that the paper-bound environment creates vertical relationships while the paperless environment creates horizontal relationships, precisely because the student's "property" (in the paperless environment) is disembodied, less clearly marked. When students send me their electronic texts and we correspond, I'm asking them—implicitly or explicitly—to re-envision their writing: to use writing to improve their writing. I'm not asking them to focus on line five of paragraph six. The pedagogical idea is to encourage them to write by telling them how their words affected me while I read them; give them what Peter Elbow calls in *Writing Without Teachers*, a "movie of my mind"—a rendering of their text. In turn, the student stretches out to "me," the *idea* of a tutor, and in the process stretches her own thinking, her own writing. The net result is a bunch of e-mail stretched out on a clothes line.

Of course, movies of the mind are nothing new. Perhaps the only innovation here is that e-mail leaves a tangible trace—a transcript of the interaction. Pedagogically, we could even say that *nothing* has changed. The spirit of tutoring—intervention in the composing process—remains intact along with the political issues defining that intervention. But the actual tutorial becomes something different. Classroom teachers who teach in a networked environment describe a similar change. Thomas Barker and Fred Kemp say that "using the computer as a communication medium 'purifies' informal exchanges in interesting and pedagogically advantageous ways" (21). They praise computer conferencing for its ability to cut to the chase, to foster a "pure," informal dialogue at the level of *ideas* instead of *personality*. Without the "distracting" elements of personality, computer-mediated discourse establishes a more egalitarian atmosphere. No one has to compete for the floor.

But without the classroom context, which Barker and Kemp rely on, how might on-line tutors gauge learning, or even communication, as discourse-specific? More to the point: as a cyborg tutor, am I an integral part of the writer's world or a ghost in the machine? Does my discourse construct a tutorial setting? Or does my discourse become something else? The fuel for somebody else's fire....

E-mail tutoring, so it seems, puts us smack dab in the middle of the postmodern condition—the critique of presence in discourse. We hold onto this idea of "personality" in order to make tutoring work. But as Barker and Kemp show us, computer-mediated discourse reduces the guiding logic of personality. This makes it fascinating, but also confusing. I like the idea of intuiting a writer "in" the text. (I like to imagine I'm helping a real person.) But what I intuit ("who" I imagine) has nothing to do with the writer, per se. As Roland Barthes says, "I must seek out this reader (must 'cruise' him) without knowing where he is. A site of bliss is then created. It is not the reader's 'person' that is necessary to me, it is this site; the possibility of a dialectics of desire" (4).

This, of course, is tricky turf and I'm no postmodern theorist. In fact I'd rather keep this essay practical. But I bring up Roland Barthes to raise the specter of textual indeterminacy—our best laid plans to create a scene of learning slipping down a chain of signifiers. My instinct is to fight this. Let me put it to you this way. In face-to-face tutorials, half the job is reading the person, paying attention to silences, tone of voice, body language, and so on. On-line there is no difference between reading a person and reading a text. The threat seems to be that we could lose the tutorial by forgetting about these imaginary students we are helping. Another threat is more practical: e-mail tutoring lavishes a lot of time on the student's text—it takes a while to read and respond—and there is no guarantee that anything will happen. The student might not respond. (A challenge for the 21st century: how can we shape our e-mail instruction to elicit response and create a scene of learning?)

Michael Marx's study of e-mail exchanges between students in two composition courses at different colleges, explores the rhetoric of anonymous instruction. Students had to read essays by writers they had never met and write "critique letters." much like on-line tutors write feedback and questions to writers they have never met. The students' reactions to this experiment were complex. On the one hand, Marx indicates anonymous feedback was easy:

> *At the end of the semester one Skidmore student summarized her experience of writing for the network: 'When writing to someone in class, I can talk to them if they do not understand a point. When writing to Babson [College], I found that I was concentrating on giving a complete critique. I also found new freedom because I did not have to worry about the Babson student getting upset with me.' (31)*

But on the other hand, e-mail critiques were demanding—more focused and intense. Another student comments, "I wanted to make sure that I made useful suggestions because they couldn't get in touch with me; so my critique needed to be self explanatory" (34). Marx concludes that e-mail "creates a distance between student critics and student authors which, ironically, brings students closer together in analyzing and discussing written texts" (36). The pressure to communicate fights the pressure of ambiguity.

But even that's not enough. As Andrew Feenberg summarizes, "communicating on-line involves a minor but real personal risk, and a response—any response—is generally interpreted as a success while silence means failure" (24). If Feenberg is right, and I think he is, then the goal of an on-line tutorial must never be to fix meaning on the "page" but to engage meaning in a dialectic. We need ambiguity. We need open texts. Ironically, ambiguity works *for* us and *against* us. In a different context, Stephen North describes this dialectic between readers as acts of "textual good faith." Specifically, he describes his written correspondence with David Bartholomae, and more generally, the impulse to find 'common sense' in composition studies, as "negotiating (establishing, maintaining) good faith agreements about the conditions that will make it possible for us to communicate. Or, to put it another way, negotiating (establishing, maintaining) good faith agreements about which of the conditions that make communication impossible we will set aside so that we can communicate" ("Personal Writing" 117). When e-mail tutorials work, so it seems, they work by engaging this dialectic. They work when we somehow negotiate a scene of learning.

One graduate student sends me a long philosophy paper and asks if his main idea is coming across. He wants to send the paper out for publication. I read the text, comment extensively in six separate messages (snapshots of my mind), and we correspond for about a week. The ideas percolate. A relationship forms. Eventually we meet in the writing center to talk about the paperbound issues: sentence level stuff, the actual length of the manuscript, bibliography, and so on. We are both encouraged and amazed at the novelty of this arrangement. Where else in the university can two people correspond about a work-in-progress? As a partner to the face-to-face tutorial, or even a solo act, e-mail could help us sustain long-term instructional relationships, much like Internet discussion groups such as WCenter or MBU help us sustain our own professional relationships.

This of course represents the ideal. I *dream a network nation where we all exchange our texts*. But there is no network nation, at least not the kind I imagine. The technology, itself, is not the problem. The Internet is certainly growing. The Conference on College Composition and Communication will be on-line in 1995. But who in the university values the lateral exchange of texts, the "pure" exchange of ideas unfastened from the classroom? Let me be specific here. For students to even *use* the online tutorial service at SUNY-Albany, they need to know how to use a word processor, save an ASCII (text-only) file, upload it to the VAX mainframe, and send it to the virtual writing center as an e-mail message. That's asking a lot—especially on a campus where most computer labs are NOT linked to the mainframe, and posters for the service have to compete with commercial advertisements for proofreading services. Advertisements on the mainframe, though successful, tend to lure students more interested in computing than in writing (an unfortunate division of talent). The vast majority of paperwriters (students in the humanities and social sciences) don't know about the e-mail tutorial service. How could they?

I guess what I'm concluding is that the idea of e-mail tutoring cannot change these institutional politics. I can dream a network nation if I want. But the reality is something else. Again, this is not a technical problem. We just don't know what we want technology to do. The university and the larger society still value paper, intellectual property, and authorship (all deregulated on the net), and the writing center—for good reason—still values face-to-face interaction over a text. But while we continue to work face-to-face, new technologies such as e-mail will continue to grow. If we don't decide what to do with them, somebody else will. As the writing center moves into the 21st century, I'd urge us to grab the bull by the horns: we should have a say. That's our responsibility. This essay is just one attempt to imagine the future. But what the on-line tutorial will *actually* become is something we are just beginning to understand.

WORKS CITED

Barker, Thomas, and Fred Kemp. "Network Theory: A Postmodern Pedagogy for the Writing Classroom." In *Computers and Community*. Ed. Carolyn Handa. Portsmouth, NH: Boynton/Cook, 1990. 1–27.

Barthes, Roland. *The Pleasure of the Text*. New York: Hill and Wang, 1973.

Elbow, Peter. *Writing Without Teachers*. New York: Oxford UP, 1973.

Feenberg, Andrew. "The Written World: On the Theory and Practice of Computer Conferencing." *Mindweave*. Ed. Robin Mason and Anthony Kaye. New York: Pergamon Press, 1989. 22–39.

Jennings, Edward M. "Paperless Writing Revisited." *Computers and the Humanities*. 24 (1990): 43–48.

Marx, Michael Steven. "Distant Writers, Distant Critics, and Close Readings." *Computers and Composition*. 8.1 (1991): 23–39.

North, Stephen. "Training Tutors to Talk About Writing." *College Composition and Communication* 33 (1982): 434–441.

———. "Personal Writing, Professional Ethos, and the Voice of Common Sense." *PRE/TEXT* 11.1–2 (1990): 105–119.

Information Literacy
and the Writing Center

Irene L. Clark

Defining "information literacy" as the "ability to access, retrieve, evaluate, and integrate information from a variety of electronically generated resources," this article examines the rationale for making information literacy a writing center goal and suggests several possibilities for implementation. It points out that the current process students engage in when they conduct research presumes linearity and solitude, rather than process, recursiveness and collaboration and suggests that writing centers should become more directly involved in helping students develop more effective research process. The article also stresses the role that information literacy will ultimately play in determining life quality and economic independence and the political implications that familiarity with technological resources will have for students.

information literacy   information retrieval   process knowledge   research
technology   topic knowledge   writing centers

Flexibility and adaptability are fundamental to the idea of a writing center. Both literally and ideologically, writing centers are places that leave their doors open, places that cultivate the exchange of ideas, places that are receptive to experiment and expansion. This spirit of openness and inquiry makes writing centers a natural site for helping students acquire information

Clark, Irene L. "Information Literacy and the Writing Center" *Computers and Composition* 12 (1995): 203–09. Reprinted with permission from Elsevier Science.

literacy—that is, the ability to access, retrieve, evaluate, and integrate information from a variety of electronically generated resources. However, writing centers will not become such sites unless those of us who work in them designate information literacy a writing center priority. This article will examine the rationale for making information literacy a writing center goal and suggest several possibilities for implementation.

WRITING CENTERS, RESEARCH PAPERS, AND INFORMATION LITERACY

Writing center pedagogy has long acknowledged the importance of both process and collaboration—that is, a typical writing center model consists of a student and a tutor working together to develop text that, ideally, will help the student acquire a more effective writing process and ultimately make him or her a more successful writer. However, despite their advocacy of process and collaboration, writing centers rarely apply either of these approaches to the related process students engage in when they undertake research; in fact, when students are assigned papers involving research, they tend to spend a fair amount of time working alone—often wandering ineffectually around the library or aimlessly surfing the Web, looking for anything that seems remotely related to their topic. Writing centers become involved in student research papers usually either fairly early or fairly late in the process—students may consult with a tutor before they begin research, when they have no idea what topic to write about. Or else, they may come in after they have presumably completed their research, usually with a text they want revised or corrected. The steps in between, the decisions students make about what sort of information they might need, the strategies they use to locate and evaluate that information, and the methods they use to integrate that information and reshape the text—these are the steps the writing center usually doesn't see.

Process, recursiveness, collaboration—these are the monuments of our profession—yet the research process as presented to students (in spite of note cards and in spite of computers) still presumes both linearity and solitude. When students are assigned research papers, well-meaning teachers and librarians often segment the process into sequential steps that give students the impression that what they have to do is take accurate notes, assemble information into some coherent whole, properly acknowledge and document sources, and manage to avoid plagiarism. In fact, the approach to the research paper that is still favored is remarkably similar to the steps outlined by James M. Chalfant in 1930, in the first edition of the *English Journal*—that is, choose a subject and narrow it, compile a bibliography, take notes, write an outline, and, finally, compose the theme. This model presupposes that once students have chosen a topic, the next step is simply to locate appropriate outside materials and then organize them.

This model's problem is that it not only assumes a dauntingly neat sequence and an unrealistically manageable linearity but, more importantly, it overlooks the significant role additional information plays in thesis formation, in modifying an approach to a topic, or even in changing it altogether. Moreover, the model is further restricted in that it doesn't take into account students' limited understanding of what is involved in working with outside information—that is, students

- are unaware of when they need information from outside sources;
- have not developed effective search strategies for locating appropriate information;
- don't know how to evaluate information once they locate it;
- are unfamiliar with techniques for integrating information smoothly into their own texts once they have decided that they wish to use it.

These skills are all encompassed in the information literacy concept and if a writing center is going to incorporate this concept into its pedagogy and to help students develop an effective research process, then a center needs to prioritize the following pedagogical goals:

- Enable students to perceive when additional information is needed to fulfill a writing task;
- Teach students critical-thinking skills, including strategies for examining a broad range of resources and for evaluating their credibility, appropriateness, and relevance to a given writing task;
- Provide opportunities for students to synthesize and incorporate information within a text;
- Enable students to access and retrieve information from a variety of sources, both print and electronic.

POLITICAL IMPLICATIONS
OF INFORMATION LITERACY

Why should the writing center become involved in helping students acquire information literacy? One important reason is that in an increasingly information-oriented age, those who can access and work with information will have a significant advantage over those who cannot. According to the American Library Association Presidential Committee on Information Literacy (1989), acquisition of information literacy is crucial not simply because of its traditional role of enabling students to locate information for college research papers but, more significantly, because it will ultimately become a primary determiner of life quality and economic independence. The committee report makes the case that because

> *information is expanding at an unprecedented rate and [because], enormously rapid strides are being made in the technology for storing, organizing, and accessing the ever growing tidal wave of information...how our country deals with the realities of the Information Age will have enormous impact on our democratic way of life and on our nation's ability to compete internationally. (p. 1)*

The report further suggests information literacy is "needed to guarantee the survival of democratic institutions. All men are created equal but voters with information resources are in a position to make more intelligent decisions than citizens who are information illiterates" (p. 5).

To live a satisfying life in an information oriented society requires not only the ability to work with existing technology, but also the power to determine the form and shape of technology as it evolves in the new century. In an essay published in 1994, Haas and Neuwirth critique several misconceptions concerning the relation of literacy to technology; two are relevant in this context. The first is that literacy exists independently of technology and is, therefore, unaffected by it—that is, technology is viewed merely as a tool making reading and writing more efficient but has no impact on the nature of literacy. This assumption presumes that the

> *essential processes of reading and writing are universal and unchanging: writers and readers simply exchange their pens and books for word processors, replace their face-to-face conversations with computer conferences, and continue to produce texts and construct meanings in the ways they always have." (p. 329)*

The second misconception is the notion that "computers are not our job," which distances the composition field from technology by presuming a division of labor and produces a vast gulf between those who create literacy oriented technology and those who use and teach it. Composition scholars and teachers that adhere to this view tend to "see themselves as users, but not as shapers of technology" (p. 327). Both assumptions, are flawed and dangerous, Haas and Neuwirth maintain—flawed, because they do not recognize the dynamic interaction between literacy and technology, dangerous because they condone a passivity that usually results in powerlessness.

Those of us in writing centers, who have long been concerned with literacy, must recognize that technology impacts literacy as much as literacy impacts technology and that we must become involved with technology so that we can contribute to its creation and determine how it is utilized. Although tools are not always used as they were intended, "those who fund, design, and build computer tools exert a powerful control over what kind of activities those tools facilitate" (Haas & Neuwirth, p. 329). Writing centers must, therefore, make information literacy an important goal to facilitate "interaction between those who know about literacy and those who know about computers," to facilitate an interaction that should occur not "after the artifact but during its shaping" (p. 329).

TOPIC KNOWLEDGE AND THE WRITING PROCESS

An additional rationale for writing centers to focus on information literacy is based on the important role that topic knowledge plays in the writing process. Stein (1986) maintained that topic knowledge is "probably the most essential knowledge for the production of discourse" (p. 247). Most of us agree that writers must have adequate knowledge about a topic before they can successfully write about it. Nevertheless, many compositionists (including some of us in writing centers) tend to underplay the role topic knowledge plays in determining a piece of writing's quality, thereby reducing writing acquisition to learning what Landis (1993) referred to in her essay as "patterns and processes, steps and strategies" (p. 107). Such a view erroneously assumes students already have all the information they need in order to write—composing simply becomes a matter of arrangement and style.

All of us who teach composition and/or work with students in writing centers, however, know that first-year college students are

> Generally inexperienced writers writing on topics about which they are not already knowledgeable. That is, their writing process takes place alongside an 'acquisition of knowledge' process—a parallel that occurs not only in freshman composition but in other college courses and in 'real life' writing tasks as well. (Landis, p. 108)

Accessing information is a key component of this acquisition-of-knowledge process, but information without context and coherence does not result in knowledge; it remains an overload of undigested facts. Naisbitt (1983), in his popular book *Megatrends: Ten New Directions Transforming Our Lives* prophetically bemoaned this phenomenon, stating that the world is "wallowing in detail, drowning in information, but is starved for knowledge" (p. 24). Part of the research process involves learning to transform information into knowledge. It is a process component that warrants greater attention from writing centers.

Examining the role knowledge plays in the writing process Glaser (1984), a cognitive psychologist, pointed out that a process pedagogy that does not include the "role of knowledge" is predicated on an artificial separation between knowledge and skills. Glaser maintained that acquired knowledge is organized and stored in "knowledge structures" that function not only as storehouses of information but also as interpretive "triggers." Knowledge structures serve not only as places where knowledge is kept but as influences on how new information is interpreted and categorized. Given the importance of building knowledge structures, Glaser recommended that skills not be taught in isolation, as "subsequent add-one to what we have learned," but rather, skills should be "developed in the process of acquiring knowledge" (p. 93). Writing from a librarian's perspective, Schmersahl (1987) similarly maintained that we treat "research as part of the recursive generative process of writing and so encourage students to see that doing research, whether in the library, the laboratory, or the "real world, is also a recursive process of discovery" (p. 232).

IMPLEMENTING INFORMATION LITERACY IN THE WRITING CENTER

Prioritizing information literacy as a writing center goal suggests a need for at least a few computers located within or near the writing center so tutors can help students to acquire a workable research, as well as a writing, process. At the University of Southern California, for example, the writing center has priority to an adjacent classroom size computer lab, which enables students and tutors to explore the world of the Internet and conduct searches as they would in a library. Within our writing center's comfortable environment and under the tutor's guidance. students access the university library catalog, various databases, and a myriad of additional informational resources via multiple search engines, the World Wide Web, and hundreds of news groups. The writing center has, thus, assumed an important role in helping first-year students learn to work with electronic resources, by scheduling whole-class workshops and small-group sessions as well as incorporating search strategies into tutor-student conferences held directly at the keyboard. Moreover, our writing center's computer room has become a place for tutors to congregate when not on duty—helping one another when the inevitable glitch occurs and learning to navigate various information resources, expertise they can pass along to students.

Until on-line access became an integral feature of the Writing Center, students whose papers needed additional information would be advised to return to the library and conduct searches on their own. Frequently, however, because they had not developed effective search strategies, their second or even third search attempts would yield very little additional information, resulting in considerable frustration. All of us have heard students complain that "the library didn't have any information on my topic," a misperception that more often reflects students' inability to search effectively for what they need and their corresponding reluctance to seek help from librarians that it does any real shortage of materials in the library.

With access to information resources within the writing center, however, writing center tutors can work with students directly at the screen, demonstrating how search terms can be manipulated to narrow and expand a search and helping them to understand that different search words may yield very different possibilities and choices even if their definitions are almost identical. One student, for example, was searching for information on various attitudes toward the Information Superhighway. However, when he entered the terms *Information Superhighway Attitudes*, he found that there were only 42 occurrences in 5 records, a number he felt was insufficient for his purposes. Realizing that this student needed help in finding materials before he could plan or write his paper, the tutor suggested that they work together in the computer lab, where they entered the terms *Information Superhighway*. These terms yielded an overwhelming 2179 occurrences in 480 records, this time far too many to browse. Trying another term, they entered *Information Technology*, and found that there were even more references to these terms than to *Information Superhighway*—21,887 occurrences in 5,625 records. Finally, they were able to conduct a manageable search using the terms *Information Technology Attitudes*, which yielded 529 occurrences in 85 records. The tutor and the student then browsed these possibilities to obtain a topic overview and to compile a list of additional descriptors for further explanation. This was a facet of the research process that writing center tutors could not have addressed without on-site electronic resources.

Accessibility to electronically generated information resources means that the acquisition of information literacy can more easily be integrated into writing center pedagogy. As soon as a new information tool is added to the university system, everyone in the writing center can become immediately aware of it and can then pass that awareness on to their students. And because the writing center fosters a collaborative environment and tolerates a higher noise level than do most libraries, both students and tutors are able to ask one another questions freely and help each other learn, keeping abreast of the technology as it develops and changes.

Of course, I also recognize there are many writing centers that do not have nor are likely to get computers that provide this type of information access. Nevertheless, whatever hardware may or may not exist within the writing center itself, information literacy can be prioritized as a concept that encourages both students and tutors to seek additional perspectives through electronic resources and transcend parameters set by a particular student text. A writing center that has made information literacy its goal can forge strong links with the library and with librarians, so that all tutors become comfortable using available technology and other resources that their students might need to conduct research. When information literacy becomes a writing center priority, tutors can arrange to spend time with students at the library, collaborating with them during the search process, rather than before or after, showing them how information discovery can lead to further discovery and even to the reformulation of a topic. Both tutors and students can also develop confidence in their ability to work with technology, using it to make connections between their own experiences and the information they discover, not simply accepting what they find, passively and uncritically.

Information literacy as a concept means helping students become critical readers who can assess the quality, reliability, and appropriateness of the resources they have discovered, to become readers who question, to become readers who do not accept everything that is either printed or published electronically. In a writing center, students can collaborate with tutors in information evaluation, learning to ask basic questions about the sources available to them, questions such as, How do you know that? What evidence do you have for that? Who says so? and How can we find out?

The information literacy concept also means a changed perspective on a writer's role in relation to community: an awareness that all text is increasingly becoming intertext. Hawisher (1992), citing work of Langston and Batson, noted that "teaching and learning writing in the virtual age might have more to do with bringing together multiple perspectives and creating new understandings, rather than in producing something that is thought to be original" (p. 89). Such insight can enable students to become a part of the academic conversation instead of remaining outside of it. When students understand that outside information is not separate from the self, they will be less likely to lose their own voices in the research papers they write, less likely, to use Sommers' words, to disappear "behind the weight and permanence of their borrowed words, moving their pens, mouthing the words of others, allowing sources to speak through them unquestioned, unexamined" (p. 425). How many of us have waded through the voiceless hodgepodge of information many students mistake for a research paper, papers that do little more than paste pieces of information together without using information to solve real problems or to explore real questions to which the writer wants a real answer.

The fact that we are living in an information age does not mean either students or tutors will automatically know how to work with information, and just because information is available in a university library does not mean students will benefit from it. As Paul Saffo (1989) said in *Personal Computing:*

Technology does not drive change per se. Instead, it merely creates new options and opportunities for change. It is our collective response to tech-

nologies that drives change. We can exploit innovations any way we collectively see fit. We can even choose not to adopt a technology at all just as the Japanese once eliminated firearms from their culture for the three centuries following the mid-1500's. (p. 269).

Or, as Richard Lanham (1990) phrases it,

It is becoming increasingly clear that technology will interact with literacy instruction in our democracy in ways not so deterministic as early thinkers predicted. We will have to decide how technology can be orchestrated into socially responsible patterns of use. (p. xv)

Writing centers cannot afford to ignore the potential of the technology that is becoming so significant a part of daily life in the 21st century. Those of us who teach and tutor writing have never conceived ourselves as isolated from what is happening in the university community or as removed from the world around it. To meet our students needs, both at the university and in the life situations they will encounter afterwards, writing centers need to branch out—through online connections, through modems, or, if necessary, simply by walking with their students over to the library. Whatever implementation is chosen, writing centers in the information age have the responsibility of teaching students to navigate the rapidly changing world of new information sources.

REFERENCES

American Library Association Presidential Committee on Information Literacy. (1989). Washington, DC.

Glaser, R. (1984). Education and thinking: The role of knowledge. *American Psychologist 39*, 9–104.

Haas. C. and C. M. Neuwirth (1994). Writing the technology that writes us: Research on literacy and the shape of technology in C. L. Selfe & S. Hilligoss (Eds.), *Literacy and computers: the complications of reaching and learning with technology* (pp. 310–335). New York: Modern Language Association.

Hawisher, G. (1992). Electronic meetings of the minds: Research, electronic conferences, and composition studies. In G. E. Hawisher & P. LeBlanc (Eds.). *Re-imagining computers and composition: Teaching and research in the virtual age* (pp. 81–101). Portsmouth. NH: Boynton/Cook.

Landis, K. (1993). The knowledge of composition. *Ilha do desterro, 29*. 107–118.

Lanham, R. (1990). Foreword. In C. Handa (Ed.). *Computers and community: Teaching composition in the twenty-first century* (pp. xiii–xv). Portsmouth, NH: Boynton/Cook.

Niasbitt, J. (1983). *Megatrends: Ten new directions transforming our lives.* New York: Warner.

Saffo. P (1989). The main event is yet to come. *Personal Computing.* 13(4). 269–270.

Schmersahl, C. B. (1987). Teaching library research: Process, not product. *Journal of Teaching Writing* 6(2), 23 1–239.

Sommers, N. (1993). I stand here writing. *College English* 55(4), 420 428.

Stein, N. L. (1986). Knowledge and process in the acquisition of writing skills. In E. Z. Rolhkopf (Ed.). *Review of research in education.* (Vol. 14, pp. 244–249.). Washington, DC: American Educational Research Association.

INDEX